American Lives and Times

A LIVING HISTORY FROM NEWSPAPERS OF THE DAY

THE REVOLUTIONARY WAR

From LEXINGTON & CONCORD *to* VALLEY FORGE.

edited by
Gerald Reilly

The Raleigh Press, Publisher

Copyright © 2019 by Gerald Reilly

All rights reserved. No part of this publication may be reproduced, distributed, or transmitted in any form or by any means, including photocopying, recording, or other electronic or mechanical methods, without the prior written permission of the publisher.

Cover: *The Grand Union flag of the thirteen United Colonies indicates the colonists' loyalty to Great Britain but their insistence on liberty. This flag was first flown at Prospect Hill, overlooking Boston, on January 2, 1776, as is reported in an article on page* 134.

For permission requests, please contact the publisher.

The Raleigh Press
Cataumet, Massachusetts

publisher@theraleighpress.com

ISBN: 978-0-9892753-7-8

Printed in U.S.A.

SELECTED HEADLINES

January 30, 1775	THE BLACK LIST	12
February 10, 1775	ARREST THE REBELS	14
February 28, 1775	LOYALIST LIBERTY SUBVERTED	16
April 15, 1775	GENERALS SAIL FOR AMERICA	20
April 20, 1775	BATTLES AT LEXINGTON & CONCORD	22
April 28, 1775	PAUL REVERE MISSING	26
May 17, 1775	AMERICANS TAKE FORT TICONDEROGA	41
June 14, 1775	COL. WASHINGTON TO COMMAND TROOPS	49
June 17, 1775	BATTLE AT BUNKER'S HILL	50
June 25, 1775	THE GREATEST SCENE.	54
July 3, 1775	WASHINGTON ARRIVES AT CAMP	57
July 6, 1775	CAUSES & NECESSITY OF ARMING	58
July 18, 1775	CONGRESS FORMALIZES MILITIAS	66
August 23, 1775	PROCLAMATION OF REBELLION	84
August 23, 1775	JOHN HANCOCK MARRIES	87
August 31, 1775	LIBERTY TREE CUT DOWN	87
September 28, 1775	COL. ARNOLD 20 DAYS FROM CANADA	95
September 25, 1775	ETHAN ALLEN CAPTURED	100
October 28, 1775	KING TO INCREASE FORCES	106
November 1, 1775	ETHAN ALLEN'S MISFORTUNE	108
November 3, 1775	St. JOHN'S SURRENDERS	109
November 15, 1775	COL. ARNOLD ARRIVES AT QUEBEC	118
December 4, 1775	4000 DEAD AT HALIFAX	124

SELECTED HEADLINES

January 1, 1776	NORFOLK BURNT BY BRITISH	132
January 2, 1776	UNION FLAG ON PROSPECT HILL	134
January 6, 1776	GENERAL MONTGOMERY DEAD	133
January 6, 1776	GENERAL ARNOLD WOUNDED	135
January 24, 1776	AMERICAN DEFEAT AT QUEBEC	140
February 4, 1776	QUEBEC UNDER SIEGE	143
February 6, 1776	THE FIRST AMERICAN FLEET	146
February 19, 1776	COMMON SENSE	151
February 29, 1776	WIDOW MOORE'S CREEK	154
March 6, 1776	THE SIEGE OF BOSTON	157
March 14, 1776	BRITISH EVACUATING BOSTON	159
March 23, 1776	CONGRESS AUTHORIZES PRIVATEERS	168
April 4, 1776	DR. FRANKLIN TO QUEBEC	171
April 12, 1776	NORTH CAROLINA FOR INDEPENDENCY	175
April 15, 1776	WASHINGTON AT NEW YORK	177
May 15, 1776	VIRGINIA URGES INDEPENDENCE	184
May 20, 1776	10,000 BRITISH AT NEW YORK	187
June 11, 1776	A WARNING TO NEW YORK	195
June 13, 1776	BRITISH ABANDON BOSTON HARBOUR	197
June 24, 1776	PLOT TO KILL GEN. WASHINGTON	200
June 29, 1776	FURIOUS BATTLE AT FORT SULLIVAN	201
July 1, 1776	THE MOST IMPORTANT EVENT	204
July 4, 1776	INDEPENDENCE DECLARED	204

SELECTED HEADLINES

July 4, 1776	BRITISH FLEET AT NEW YORK	206
August 15, 1776	HESSIAN FORCES ARRIVE	217
August 21, 1776	THE BATTLE OF LONG ISLAND	221
August 31, 1776	SUDDEN RETREAT IN SECRECY	225
September 21, 1776	NEW YORK IN FLAMES	231
October 11, 1776	DEFEAT ON LAKE CHAMPLAIN	234
October 18, 1776	THE WIFE IS A SPY	237
October 28, 1776	THE BALL IS OPENED.	239
October 31, 1776	THE SPEECH OF GEORGE III	242
November 16, 1776	THE REDUCTION OF MOUNT WASHINGTON	246
November 27, 1776	FORT LEE EVACUATED	246
December 8, 1776	CONGRESS MOVES TO BALTIMORE	250
December 14, 1776	ENEMY POSSESS NEWPORT	252
December 27, 1776	WASHINGTON CROSSES THE DELAWARE	255
December 31, 1776	GREAT VICTORY AT TRENTON	256
January 7, 1777	AMERICANS TAKE PRINCETON	258
January 25, 1777	SKIRMISHES IN THE JERSEYS	266
February 3, 1777	BRITISH MURDER OUR WOUNDED	268
February 15, 1777	20£ FOR EVERY SCALP	272
March 18, 1777	FRENCH FLEET AT CHARLESTOWN	276
April 27, 1777	BRITISH BURN DANBURY	280
June 5, 1777	WASHINGTON MOVES HEAD QUARTERS	284
June 26, 1777	BURGOYNE IN CANADA	291

SELECTED HEADLINES

June 26, 1777	A SCALPING ACCIDENT	292
June 28, 1777	BRITISH AT CROWN POINT	293
July 4, 1777	THE LADIES OF AMELIA COUNTY	294
July 4, 1777	THE 4TH OF JULY	294
July 7, 1777	RETREAT FROM TICONDEROGA	297
July 26, 1777	A YOUNG WOMAN MASSACRED	302
August 1, 1777	WASHINGTON AT PHILADELPHIA	306
August 15, 1777	GENERAL ARNOLD ON HIS MARCH	308
August 18, 1777	BATTLE OF BENNINGTON	310
August 26, 1777	ENEMY LAND AT HEAD OF ELK	313
September 1, 1777	REWARDS FOR SCALPS STOPPED	315
September 2, 1777	BATTLE OF STATEN ISLAND	317
September 11, 1777	BATTLE AT THE BRANDYWINE	319
September 20, 1777	BURGOYNE WOUNDED AT STILLWATER	323
October 2, 1777	AMERICANS ATTACK AT GERMANTOWN	325
October 9, 1777	BATTLE OF FORT MONTGOMERY	327
October 10, 1777	THE BATTLE OF SARATOGA	328
October 15, 1777	BURGOYNE'S CAPITULATION	330
November 15, 1777	ENEMY EVACUATE TICONDEROGA	337
November 23, 1777	LOSS OF FORTS MIFFLIN AND MERCER	338
December 1, 1777	PHILADELPHIA LAID WASTE	341
December 10, 1777	BATTLE OF WHITE MARSH	342
December 14, 1777	BLOOD IN THEIR FOOTSTEPS	346

COME rouse up my lads, and join in this great cause,
In defence of your liberty, your property, and laws!
'Tis to honour we call you, stand up for your right,
and ne'er let our foes say we are put to the flight.

The Scotch politicians have laid a deep scheme,
By invading America to bring Charlie in;
And if the Scotch mist's not remov'd from the Throne,
The Crown's not worth wearing, the kingdom's undone.

The Placemen and Commoners have taken a bribe
To betray their own country, and the empire beside;
And though the colonies stand condemned by some,
There are no rebels here, but are traitors at home.

The arbitrary Minister he acts as he please,
He wounds our constitution, and breaks through our laws;
His troops they are landed, his ships they are moor'd,
But boys all stand together, they will fall by the sword.

The great magna charta is wounded severe;
By accounts from the Doctors, 'tis almost past cure.
Let's defend it with the sword, or die with the braves,
For we had better die in freedom than live and be slaves.

They tax us contrary to reason and right,
Expecting that we are not able to fight;
But to draw their troops home I do think would be best,
For Providence always defends the opprest.

The valiant Bostonians have entered the field,
And declare they will fall before they will yield:
A noble example! In them we'll confide,
We'll march to their town, and stand or fall by their side.

An Union though the colonies will ever remain,
and ministerial taxation will be but in vain;
For we are all resolved to DIE or be FREE:
So they may repeal the acts, for repeal'd they must be.

Recreated from The Virginia Gazette, July 29, 1775.

INTRODUCTION

American Lives and Times, The Revolutionary War, from Lexington & Concord to Valley Forge, is an anthology of selected articles and advertisements from contemporary newspapers, arranged chronologically, that tells the story of the American Revolution from April, 1775 to December, 1777.

The colonists demanded liberty from Great Britain, not independence. However, increasing British military and commercial measures to subdue the Americans, and the publication of Thomas Paine's pamphlet "Common Sense", changed the argument to one of total separation from England.

This anthology follows the story of the people, places and battles of American history as that history was being made. It begins with an article from the April 19, 1775, edition of the Pennsylvania Gazette.

The battles at Lexington and Concord had just begun, however, this day's news concerned a meeting of merchants and tradesmen that was held in London, on January 23, 1775, who presented a petition to Parliament lamenting the unhappy state of commercial affairs with America.

News travelled slow. In the colonies it moved by an express rider on horseback, and, it would be days, or even weeks, before events occurring in one colony would be reported elsewhere. From abroad it came by ship, and it could be as long as three months for letters and papers to reach America.

Articles are arranged to follow the sequence of events as nearly as possible. However, since news of a particular event may not have appeared in print for weeks, or even months after the event, the actual date an article was printed may not be relevant to its placement in the book.

Facts could be incomplete or change over time. We have included the news as it was reported, subsequent articles often update or correct information as events proceed.

Also, some locations or places may be referred to by different names. Fort Stanwix, near what is today Rome, NY, is one example that warrants mention. It was built by the British during the French and Indian War; when the Americans took over the fort in July, 1776, it was renamed Fort Schuyler. Articles in the book may refer to it by either name.

WILLIAMSBURG, *August* 18, 1775.

THE subscriber begs leave to acquaint the ladies and gentlemen, that on Friday next, at Mr. Blovet Pasteur's, in this city, she intends opening a DANCING SCHOOL, and hopes to be favoured with the instruction of their daughters in that genteel accomplishment. As she is resolved to spare no pains with her scholars, she does not doubt of being able to give entire satisfaction. Her days for teaching are Fridays and Saturdays, every week; and her price is 20s. at entrance, and 4l. a year.

SARAH HALLAM.

ANY young, healthy, and strong man, not under 5 feet 7 inches high, that is free and willing to enlist as a MATROSS in my company of artillery, will please to repair to my quarters in Williamsburg, where he will be kindly received, have 3l. advance money paid to him, besides new clothes, and 2s. per day, for one, two, or more years, if not sooner discharged.

God save the Congress.

DOHICKY ARUNDEL.

TO BE SOLD,
A HEALTHY NEGROE WOMAN, suitable only for the Country. Enquire of the PRINTERS.

LONDON.

To the Honourable the COMMONS *of* GREAT BRITAIN, *in* PARLIAMENT *assembled.*

The humble PETITION *of the Merchants, Traders and others, of the City of* LONDON, *concerned in the Commerce* of North America, *January* 23, 1775.

THAT your Petitioners are all essentially interested in the Trade to North America, either as Exporters and Importers, or as vendors of British and Foreign Goods for Exportation to that Country.

That your petitioners have exported, or sold for Exportation, to the British Colonies in North America, very large Quantities of the Manufactures of Great Britain and Ireland; and in particular the Staple Articles of Woollen, Iron and Linen, also those of Cotton, Silk, Leather, Pewter, Tin, Copper, Brass, with almost every British Manufacture. Also large Quantities of Foreign Linens, and other articles imported into these Kingdoms, from Flanders, Holland, Germany, the East Countries, Portugal, Spain and Italy, which are generally received from those Countries, in Return for British Manufactures.

That your Petitioners have likewise exported, or sold for Exportation, great Quantities of the various Species of Goods imported into this Kingdom from the East Indies, Part of which receive additional Manufacture in Great Britain.

That your Petitioners receive Returns from North America to this Kingdom directly, Pig and Bar Iron, Timber, Staves, Naval Stores, Tobacco, Rice, Indigo, Deer and other skins, Beaver and Furs, Train Oil, Whale Bone, Bees Wax, Pot and Pearl Ashes, Drugs and Dying Woods, with some Bullion; and also Wheat, Flour, Indian Corn, and Salted Provisions, when (on Account of Scarcity in Great Britain) those Articles are permitted to be imported.

That your Petitioners receive Returns circuitously, from Ireland (for Flax Seed, &c. exported from North America) by Bills of Exchange on the Merchants of this City, trading to Ireland, for the Proceeds of Linens imported into these Kingdoms. From the West Indies (in Return for Provisions, Lumber and Cattle, exported from North America, for the Use and Support of the West India Islands) by Bills of Exchange on the West India Merchants, for the proceeds of Sugar, Molasses, Rum, Cotton, Coffee, or other Produce imported from those Islands into these Kingdoms. From Italy, Spain, Portugal, France, Flanders, Germany, Holland, and the East Countries, by Bills of Exchange or Bullion, in Return for the Wheat, Flour, Rice, Indian Corn, Fish and Lumber, exported from the British Colonies in North America for the Use of those Countries.

That your Petitioners have great Reason to believe, from the best information they can obtain, that on the Balance of this extensive Commerce, there is now due from the Colonies in North America, to this City only, Two Millions Sterling, and upwards.

That by the direct Commerce with the Colonies, and circuitous Trade thereon depending, some Thousands of ships and Vessels are employed, and many Thousands of Seamen are bred and maintained; thereby increasing the Naval Strength of Great Britain.

That in the year 1765, there was a great Stagnation of the Commerce between Great Britain and her Colonies, in Consequence of an Act of Parliament, entitled "An Act for granting and applying certain Stamp Duties, and other Duties in the British Colonies and Plantations in America, &c." by which the Merchants trading to North America, and with the Artificers employed in the various Manufactures consumed in those Countries, were subjected to many Hardships.

That in the following Year, the said Act was repealed, under an express Declaration of the Legislature, that, "the Continuance of the said Act would be attended with many Inconveniences, and might be productive of Consequences greatly detrimental to the Commercial Interests of these Kingdoms;" upon which Repeal, the Trade to the British Colonies immediately resumed its former flourishing State.

That in the Year 1767, an Act passed entitled "An Act for granting certain Duties in the British Colonies and Plantations in America, &c." which imposed certain Duties to be paid in America on Tea, Glass, Red and White Lead, Painters Colours, Paper, Pasteboard, Mill-board and Scale-board, when the Commerce with the Colonies was again interrupted.

That in the Year 1770 such Parts of the said Act as imposed Duties on the Glass, Red and White lead, Painters Colours, Paper, Paste-board, Mill-board and Scale-board, were repealed, when the Trade to America soon revived, except in the Article of Tea, on which a Duty was continued to be demanded on its Importation into America, whereby that Branch of our Commerce was nearly lost.

That in the Year 1773, an Act passed entitled "An Act to allow a Drawback of the Duties of Customs on the Exportation of Tea to his Majesty's Colonies or Plantations in America, and to impower the Commissioners of the Treasury to grant Licenses to the East India Company, to export Tea, Duty-free, &c."

By the Operation of these and other Laws, the Minds of his Majesty's subjects in the British Colonies have been greatly disquieted, and total Stop is now put to the Export trade with the greatest and most important Part of North America, the Public Revenue is threatened with large and fatal Diminution, your Petitioners with grievous Distress, and Thousands of Industrious Artificers and Manufacturers with utter Ruin. Under these alarming Circumstances, your Petitioners, that the Representatives of the People, newly delegated to the most important of all Trusts, will take the whole of these weighty Matters into their most serious Consideration.

Best FLORENCE OIL, in Chests,
AND A FEW HUNDRED WEIGHT OF
ENGLISH CHEESE,
TO BE SOLD BY
SAMUEL YOUNG,
A few Doors below the DRAWBRIDGE.

And your Petitioners humbly pray this Honourable House, that they will enter into a full and immediate Examination of that System of commercial Policy, which was formerly adopted and uniformly maintained, to the Happiness and Advantage of both Countries. And will apply such healing Remedies, as can alone restore and establish the Commerce between Great Britain and her Colonies, on a permanent Foundation.

And your Petitioners also humbly pray, that they may be heard by themselves or Agents, in Support of this Petition.

Published by the Authority of the Committee,
THOMAS LANE, Chairman.

Recreated from The Pennsylvania Gazette, April 19, 1775.

Extract of a Letter from an honest Member of Parliament in LONDON, *dated January 28.*

"I admire the resolutions of your Congress, with the whole of their proceedings, as the greatest productions of human virtue and wisdom.

"The present parliament is, if possible, more at the disposal of the Minister than the last, and measures the most hostile to America are determined on. We shall in a few days come to some flaming resolutions in the House of Commons. More regiments are to be sent, and sloops of war are to block up all your harbours. They talk of you as an easy conquest, depending much on the advantage of regulars, and want of courage in Americans. I hope they will be deceived, for besides that my love of universal liberty would make me interest myself in favour of all those who assert their natural rights, I am convinced the moment America is enslaved, Great Britain must cease to be a free country."

Extract of a Letter from LONDON, *February 6.*

"New England is singled out as the peculiar object of ministerial wrath, and if, by relaxing somewhat with respect to the other colonies, the Ministry think they can shake the present union, I should suppose the attempt probable, though not the success."

Recreated from The Pennsylvania Gazette, April 26, 1775.

THE BLACK LIST.

The following letter, dated January 30, 1775, came by the Earl of Dunmore, Captain Lawrence, *just arrived from* London.

"From unquestionable authority I learn, that about a fortnight ago, dispatches were sent from hence by a sloop of war to Gen. Gage, containing among other things, a royal proclamation declaring the inhabitants of Massachusetts Bay, and some others in the different colonies, actual rebels; with a blank commission to try and execute such of them as he can get hold of; with this is sent a list of names to be inserted in the commission, as he may judge expedient. I do not know them all, but Messrs. Samuel Adams, John Adams, Robert Treat Payne, and John Hancock, of Massachusetts Bay; John Dickenson, of Philadelphia; Peyton Randolph, of Virginia; and Henry Middleton of South Carolina, are particularly named with many others.

"This black list the General will, no doubt, keep to himself and unfold it gradually, as he finds it convenient. Four regiments from Ireland, one of them light dragoons, are under sailing orders for Boston, with several capital ships of war, from hence, and six cutters to obstruct the American trade, and prevent all European goods from going there, particularly arms and ammunition, which makes it expedient, without a moment's delay, to be provided with such things as you may want.

"Last Friday night, the 27th instant, in a Privy Council, the American measures were all settled by the Ministry; part of them is, to pass an act of Parliament, inflicting pains and penalties on particular persons, and provinces in America, to countenance the infamous Proclamation and commission already sent to General Gage; also it is determined to take away the charters of Rhode Island and Connecticut. I have not been able to learn the whole; though in general I am informed, it is denouncing utter destruction to American liberty. Depend upon all this to be fact."

Recreated from The Virginia Gazette, April 29, 1775.

HOUSE OF LORDS.

Americans in Rebellion.

February 2, 1775.

A MOST interesting debate on American affairs was this day agitated in the house of peers; it originated from a motion by Lord Chatham, who brought in a bill, which in the noble Lord's opinion would have an happy tendency in reconciling the present subsisting differences between Great Britain and America.

The two leading propositions of this bill were, the one of a declaratory, the other of a conciliating nature.

As a fundamental basis of negociation, the sovereignty of Great Britain over the American colonies was primarily insisted on. That being admitted, the propositions of a conciliating kind were,

"That an American congress should be established, as by the consent of Great Britain might constitute it, in every sense of the word a legal meeting.

"That the delegates chosen to represent the several provinces in this congress should be invested with full and efficient powers to treat with Great Britain in behalf of America.

"That the conciliating propositions offered on the part of Great Britain, through these delegates to America, should be a total exemption from parliamentary taxation, on the condition that the colonies contributed a certain annual subsidy by way of a free gift, which was to be set apart as an accumulating fund, and appropriated solely to the purpose of paying off the national debt."

With respect to the Americans, Lord Chatham continued, "that they were the best subjects in the King's dominions; that by repeated ill usage they had been exasperated even to madness; their petitions were rejected; their agents refused a hearing; their merchants had been treated with a contemptuous insolence unknown in polished governments, and thus, driven to desperation, worked up by an enthusiastic zeal for religion on the one hand, and liberty on the other, it was not surprising they had been provoked to commit actions, and pass resolves, which, if not strictly justifiable in the abstract, were yet, with relation to circumstance, entitled to every degree of favourable mitigation."

His lordship concluded by observing, "that he would by no means undertake to say, the Americans were not now in, what administration might call, rebellion; but, even admitting them to be in this state, it proceeded not from political turpitude, but an heroism of soul, a love of liberty, for which our fathers were famed; and it was this principle which rendered these thoughts obnoxious to a ministry, whose souls were of too dastardly a cast to feel the force of political virtue."

HOUSE OF COMMONS.

THE KING INCREASES HIS FORCES.

February 9, 1775.

Lord North acquainted the house that he had a message from his majesty, which he read in his place, and is as follows:

G.R.

"His majesty has determined, in consequence of the address of both houses of parliament, to take the most speedy and effectual measures for supporting the just rights of his crown and the two houses of parliament; think it proper to acquaint this house, that additions to his forces by sea and land will be necessary for that purpose, and does not doubt but his faithful commons, on whose zeal and affection he entirely relies, will enable him to make such an augmentation to his forces, as the present occasion shall be thought proper."

Ordered, that his majesty's said message be referred to the consideration of the committee of supply.

Recreated from The Maryland Gazette, April 20, 1775.

FORTY SHILLINGS REWARD.

FOR apprehending RALPH, a *Virginia* born Negro Man, about 23 Years old, 5 Feet 8 or 10 Inches high, well made, and of a yellowish Complexion; had on, when he went away (the Beginning of *Sept.* last) a blue Fearnought Waistcoat, white Cotton Breeches, Canvas Shirt, and coarse Felt Hat. He took other Clothes with him, and perhaps may change his Dress. He is an artful Negro, and will endeavour to pass for a free Man. Whoever delivers him to Mr. *George Turner*, at *Moss's Neck*, in *Caroline* County, or to the Subscriber in *King & Queen*, shall have the above Reward, and reasonable travelling Expenses allowed.
RICHARD CORBIN, Jun.
LANEVILLE, *April* 20, 1775.

TAKEN up, at *Swan's Point* Ferry, some Time in *February* last, a large MOSES BUILT BOAT, about 14 Feet Keel, 6 Feet Beam, with a Ring and Ringbolt to her Stern, and a Painter 4 Feet long.
APRIL 5, 1775. JOHN HARTWELL COCKE.

TAKEN up, at *Tucker's* Mills, near *Norfolk*, a CLINCH WORK BOAT, 12 Feet Keel, the upper Streak painted red, the next Streak of a Chocolate Colour, and from that to the Water Line painted white. Posted, and appraised to 40s. Also taken up, a PETTIAUGER about 20 Feet long, sharp at both Ends, made of Poplar. Posted, and appraised to 7s. 6d.
GOODRICH BOUSH.

FOR SALE,
A NEW Brig, burthen about 115 Tons now on the Stocks, and ready for launching. Her upper Timbers are altogether of Black Walnut, Cedar, Locust, and Mulberry. The Terms of Sale will be made known to any person inclining to purchase, by applying to the Steward at *Stratford*, the Seat of the late Hon. Philip Ludwell Lee, Esq; in *Westmoreland* County.

TO BE SOLD
To the highest Bidder, at BLANDFORD, on MONDAY the first of MAY next, for ready Money, Tobacco, or Merchants Notes payable the ensuing Meeting,
TWENTY FIVE LIKELY NEGROES,
Consisting of Men, Women, Boys, and Girls
CHARLES

Recreated from The Virginia Gazette, April 22, 1775.

ARREST THE REBELS.

Extract of a Letter from LONDON *Feb.* 10.

"I have waited in great hopes I could find something to write to encourage you, but to my great grief, worse and worse! It is impossible to describe the alarming situation of our affairs. While the debate was in Parliament, I still had some small hopes; but this morning at 2 o'clock the death warrant was passed, and the colonies declared rebels.

"The petitions and all attempts have failed. The great Lords Cambden, Chatham, Richmond, and all the 32 Lords, could not prevent the fatal [illegible] from taking place. An address to the King has passed both houses, to give the King power to call you rebels, and to proceed against you on the late acts, and direct to put them in force against the Congress, and to support the King against the Colonies, with their lives and fortunes. Nothing on earth can equal the consternation of all who have heard of it, and in their usual way now begin to see, when too late, the bad effects of their silence.

"Orders have now gone out to take up Mr. Hancock, Adams, Williams, Otis, and six of the head men in Boston. I have a copy of the proceedings before me. My heart aches for Mr. Hancock. Send off expresses immediately that they intend to seize his estate, and have his fine house for General _____. They have ordered five commanding officers, General Howe, General Burgoine, General Clinton, General M'Kay, General Drogheda;—from Ireland, for the dragoons, or horse. A troop of light horse is now actually embarking, and will land before this comes to hand. You will see by the news-papers, and I know it to be so. I saw the Generals, and know of sending 1500 chests of arms, part of which are for New York, and to be distributed among such of the inhabitants who are willing to take up arms against you.

"A proclamation is to be given out that it is mostly the four governments of New England; but depend upon it, all the colonies are to be treated in the same manner.

"General Burgoine says, that he will not let New York know his intentions, but dance and sing with the ladies, and coax the inhabitants to submit, by giving money and provisions to those who will fight for the King, against the country—put your militia in good order—call the Delegates together, who will all be safe at Philadelphia—act wisely, and if possible save Old England.—Thirty-two Lords and Dukes, the richest and best men in the kingdom, are your friends, and of the opinion that America must save England."

Recreated from The Hartford Courant, May 1, 1775.

PIGG DRINKS TEA.

At PITTSYLVANIA *courthouse, on Feb.* 22, 1775.

A COMPLAINT being made to this committee, that a certain John Pigg had violated the association, by drinking, and making use of in his family, the detestable *East India* TEA, and also that he, the said Pigg, had taken uncommon pains in order to defeat the intention of the said association, by exclaiming much against the measures adopted by the General Congress; upon which the said Pigg was summoned to appear before the said committee to answer the said charge, which he absolutely refused to do, declaring to the person who gave him notice to attend, that his intention was to do as he pleased, and that he should not pay any regard to the summons of the committee. Whereupon it is the opinion of this committee, that the said Pigg ought to be looked upon as a traitor to his country, and inimical to American liberty. And it is recommended to all people to break off all intercourse and connexion with the said Pigg, until such time as he reinstates himself in the good will and affection of all the good people of this county.

Ordered, that the clerk of this committee do transmit the above proceedings in Williamsburg, and beg they will publish the same in their papers.

WILLIAM P. MARTIN, Clerk.

Recreated from Purdie's Virginia Gazette, July 7, 1775.

ENGLAND'S PLAN.

SUBDUE THE COLONIES.

Extract of a letter from LONDON, *February* 24th, 1775.

"Part of the troops now ordered for embarkation here and Ireland, are to rendezvous at New York, to make it a place of arms, securing the defection of that province, from the general alliance in the cause of freedom, and everything that is dear to man; and to prevent the communication between Virginia, Maryland, and the other southern colonies with New England, where Gen. Gage with such assistance as he may get from New York, is to subdue those colonies first, and then all of America; in which if he succeeds, New York is to be a garrison town, and place of arms, with assistance of Quebec to rule with a rod of iron all the SLAVES of America.

"Without the concurrence of New York, this scheme can never be carried into execution, of which every gentleman and man of knowledge in this kingdom is fully convinced; therefore on your virtue, in a great measure it depends, whether America shall be free, or be reduced to the most abject and oppressive servitude; worse than that of Egyptian bondage, in which you must inevitably be involved, if you lend your aid to enslave your brethren in the other colonies.

"I have to inform you, that the bill for preventing the four colonies and provinces of New England from fishing, getting provisions from any other colonies, or carrying on any commerce whatever to any part of the world, except Great Britain, Ireland or the British West Indies, will finally pass the House of Commons to-morrow, and is to take place the first of next July.

"You may also depend that in a few days another bill will be brought in, to prohibit any of the other colonies from carrying on any trade whatever with each other, or to any other part of the world except to Great Britain, Ireland or the British Indies, which will probably take place in July also; and let this be publicly known."

Recreated from The Hartford Courant, April 24, 1775.

AMERICAN ARMY IS READY.

Extract of a letter from SALEM, *Feb.* 24.

"We have at last fixed our standard here, under which all the persons who have joined the American army, have been sworn in the most solemn manner imaginable. We are now above 3000 strong, all completely accoutered, and in readiness for any thing that may offer, and disposed into companies in true military order. Two hundred tents are going to be pitched at Charles Passage, where another body of the same strength, will encamp in a short time.

"The ensuing summer will certainly determine our fate and that of Great Britain, as far as it concerns America. General Gage is very solicitous to cultivate a correspondence with our Officers, but they are too cautious of him; nothing therefore but common civilities pass, and that as seldom as possible. God bless you, I cannot write more, time here is too precious to lose a moment in idle compliments.   Adieu."

HARD DUTY AT BOSTON.

A letter received last week from an Officer at Boston to a gentleman in Limerick, informs, that instances of treason multiply there every hour, and matters are ripening for a civil war. They are anxious for the determination of Parliament, and it is thought full time by General Gage to enforce coercive measures. The troops are sickly, being denied straw and other necessaries, they are daily insulted and injured without the power of redress. Every necessary preparation is making to take the field in the spring; only 128 men have deserted, but the use of New England rum, and the open weather, threatens to carry off a much greater number.

Recreated from Finns Leinster Journal, Ireland, May 3, 1775.

Extract of a Letter from London, Feb. 28.

"We learn this afternoon, with some surprise, that the Assembly of New York have revolted against the proceedings of Congress; an event which I fear bodes no good to your cause."

Recreated from The Pennsylvania Gazette, April 26, 1775.

PETITION FOR NANTUCKET.

London, *February* 28, 1775.

A petition was presented from a deputation of the Quakers in behalf of their brethren inhabitants of the island of Nantucket, against some clauses in the bill now pending for restraining the fisheries of the New Englanders.

Capt. Seth Johnson, a native of the island of Nantucket, was called to prove "that the said island contained between five and six thousand inhabitants, nine tenths of whom were Quakers; that the island did not produce more than would maintain twenty families, and that they received their provisions from North Carolina, Virginia, Pennsylvania, New Jersey, New York and Connecticut; that 140 vessels belonged to that port, 132 of which were employed in the whale industry, and that 128 of them belonged to quakers; that they had no other employment in the island, and that the total number of vessels employed in the whale fishery, belonging to New England, was 309 sail, from about 50 to 150 tons, that they went out on the whale fishery all seasons of the year, and made two or three trips when they found fish on the coast, but had lately extended their fishery to Falkland Island, and were sometimes twelve months on the voyage to advantage; that he had known ships from England come on their coast, in search of whales, but were always unsuccessful in catching them, though the Nantucket men at the same time succeeded well, so much is experience necessary to that business; that they receive all their manufactures from London, as well for the fishery as for their consumption, and send all their oil to Great Britain, except a trifling quantity to the continent for their consumption; that, in his opinion, if the whale fishery was prohibited, the inhabitants, from their principles, would patiently suffer as long as they could subsist, in hopes that so grievous a law could not continue; but as there was seldom above three months provision in the island, they must be obliged to emigrate to the southward, as they would on no account go to live under the military government of Halifax."

Recreated from The Maryland Gazette, May 11, 1775.

LOYALIST LIBERTY SUBVERTED.

Extract of a Letter from a Merchant at Newport, Rhode Island, *to* London, *Feb.* 28, 1775.

"You may want to hear something of the state of affairs in America; then believe me when I tell you, at present you had better remain in England, this country now being reduced from the happiest on earth, taking all its circumstances together, to a wretched condition; a total suspension of trade is likely to take place, and, in fact, has in a great measure commenced; this, with the neighbouring provinces of Massachusetts and Connecticut, are absolutely arming, and making preparations to take the field against the King's troops this spring; provided any attempts should be made to enforce the acts made relative to the province of the Massachusetts Bay, and, what the consequences will be, God only knows.

"In the contest for liberty and privileges, with which we first set out, we have absolutely subverted the very grounds of all true liberty, for a person who does not fall in with the tempers and disposition of the majority, is *ipso facto* denied the liberty of free speech, and dares not declare his sentiments without being subject to the grossest insults; and the revenge, rancour, and malice against such persons is so inveterate, that some have been treated in such a manner that it is shocking to relate, and what the infernals themselves would have been ashamed of— And all this in a Christian country, where the most despotic tyranny has taken place.

"A man's person is not safe, and property is sported with, in the most unheard of manner; ships laden with goods from England are forced, without unloading, to return back by the populace, who have taken the reins of government into their hands, and rule with uncontrolled power; such is our state at present, and when we are to be relieved from it no conjecture can be made."

Kilkenny.—Last Tuesday Patrick Flood and Mathias Nowlan, were whipped thro' the town of Carlow, pursuant to their sentence.

Recreated from Finns Leinster Journal, Ireland, May 3, 1775.

BRITISH TROOPS RELUCTANT.

Extract from a Letter from CORK, *March* 1.

"Most of the troops destined for America are arrived here. Both Officers and men never went upon an expedition with greater reluctance than on the present intended one. I shudder at the consequences of being obliged to fight against our fellow subjects.

"This morning upwards of 1200 drums were sent down the river, to be carried to the Downs, in order to be put on board the transports bound to America."

Extract of a Letter from London, *March* 2.

"Providence seems to have placed me here, in order to give you the earliest intelligence of the most interesting affairs relative to the colonies. To my great astonishment, I have now before me, an act for blocking up the other colonies, and another, called the Black Act, to prevent the fisheries. The whole nation seems to be deeply affected at such an enormous crime, which is supposed to done at the request of the K__ and his creatures. God forbid that you should be intimidated at this iniquitous law, which is calculated to ruin what was a mutual benefit to you and us. This must convince you what you are to expect, if you submit to the most shocking set of men that England can produce. You see their humanity. Rouse up the with a just indignation, and exercise your militia, watch your Governor and Council."

Recreated from The Hartford Courant, April 24, 1775.

LONDON.

March 1. Orders are sent to Portsmouth for the men of war designed to sail to Boston, to be ready at Spithead by the 12th instant, by which time three Generals will be ready to embark with their troops.

March 7. Yesterday a paper, called the Crisis, and a Pamphlet with the same title, containing Thoughts on American Affairs, were burnt by the Common Hangman, at Westminster-hall-gate, pursuant to an unanimous order of the House of Lords and Commons.

As soon as the condemned papers were burnt, a man threw into the fire the "Address of both Houses of Parliament to his Majesty, declaring the Bostonians in actual rebellion."

And this day, at twelve o'clock, the Sheriffs attended at the Royal Exchange for the same purpose; but as soon as the fire was lighted, it was put out, and dead dogs and cats thrown at the officers; a fire was then made at Cornhill, and the executioner did his duty.

Recreated from The Pennsylvania Gazette, April 26, 1775.

MONKEY TRICKS.

Extract of a genuine letter from a Clergyman at BOSTON *to his friend, a gentleman of character near* SOHO-SQUARE, *dated March* 4.

"Unhappy, infatuated people! None, sure, were ever so industrious to accomplish their own destruction as the Americans. Every resolution they take is big with mischief, and, though formed for the subversion of Government, actually strengthens it, and recoils upon the contrivers. Let me prove this to you in one instance, and a few words.

"In compliance with the wise direction of the Congress, the inhabitants of most of the Governments have abandoned their respective employments, to play their monkey tricks with fire arms and warlike instruments, which they call learning the military exercise; the consequence of this is, uncultivated land, empty shops, and starving wives and children.

"These measures, therefore, pursued but two or three months longer, famine must eat them up, without giving his Majesty's troops the trouble of hanging or shooting a single person. I admire the conduct of General Gage—Wisdom, courage, and humanity are centered in him. You need not express so much concern, for I think I may venture to affirm that there will be no bloody battles, to endanger the life of your son, and that in a few weeks the principals of these insidious people will be imploring his Majesty's pardon."

Recreated from Finns Leinster Journal, Ireland, May 3, 1775.

TARRED AND FEATHERED.

CHARLESTOWN, SOUTH CAROLINA, *March* 7.—From Savannah, in Georgia, the Collector of the Customs there, having seized some molasses and foreign sugars, on the 15th day of last month, about a quarter of a mile from the said town, put the same under the care of a waiter, and two seamen from on board his Majesty's schooner St. John. About 11 o'clock the ensuing night, a large number of people, disguised and armed, went to the Wharf, tarred and feathered the waiter, threw the two seamen into the river, and carried off the sugar and molasses. One of the seamen, was seen in the water begging for mercy, and, as he has not since been heard of, there is great reason to believe that not being permitted to come out of the river, he there perished, and was drowned.

His Excellency Sir James Wright, Governor of Georgia, has issued a proclamation, offering a reward of fifty pounds for the discovery of any one or more of the offenders, to be paid on their conviction; and if any of the persons concerned, except those who actually tarred and feathered the waiter, or forced the seaman, now missing, into the river, on their informing his Excellency, are offered his Majesty's pardon, and to be permitted as King's evidence.

Recreated from The Virginia Gazette, April 22, 1775.

A FRENCH THREAT?

March 8. A number of persons are now employed in Ireland, in making carriages for the artillery of that kingdom, which will be ready for any service in a short time. There are many conjectures in consequence of these extraordinary preparations; some say Lord Harcourt has lately had certain intelligence, that the French intend making a descent upon Ireland, when the troops destined for America are embarked; and, indeed there is something very natural in such a suspicion, for these perfidious people can never have a better opportunity to execute such a design, than when the nation is in almost a defenceless state.

Recreated from The Pennsylvania Gazette, April 26, 1775.

HOUSE OF COMMONS.

RESTRAINING TRADE.

LONDON, *March* 9.—This day the expectations of all men, both within doors and without, were wound up to the highest pitch, it being whispered for some days past, by those who pretend to be in the secret, that the Minister intended to propose a bill that would at once charm his friends, confound his enemies, and please the people on both sides of the Atlantic. After the benches had been all crowded, a silence of some minutes ensued, and up rose the Minister, not to open his grand conciliatory plan, but to extend the powers of his New England restraining bill to all other principal provinces on the American continent.

He said, that as the colonies were come to an agreement to carry on no trade whatever with Great Britain, Ireland, or the West Indies, he was clearly of opinion that it became indispensably necessary to restrain their commerce, and prevent them from trading with any other country. He therefore made the following motion:—That the Chairman be directed to move the House, that leave be given to bring in a bill to restrain trade and commerce of the colonies of New Jersey, Pennsylvania, Maryland, Virginia, and South Carolina,* to Great Britain, Ireland, and the British islands in the West Indies, under certain conditions and limitations.

After a short debate, the bill was ordered in.

[*It appears that the province of NEW YORK, whose assembly hath resolved not to abide by the resolutions of the CONGRESS, is not included in this restraining bill.]

WILLIAMSBURG, *April* 15, 1775.

THE Subscriber has on Hand a neat Assortment of GOLD and SILVER WORK, which he will sell cheap for ready Money.——He makes all Kinds of JEWELLERS WORK, particularly MOURNING RINGS, in the newest Fashions, and sets MINIATURE PICTURES in Gold and Silver. JAMES CRAIG.

N. B. All Kinds of CLOCKS and WATCHES cleaned and repaired.

Recreated from The Virginia Gazette, April 29, 1775.

IN PROVINCIAL CONGRESS.

CONCORD, *March* 24, 1775.

WHEREAS it is indispensably necessary for the safety of a free people, and the preservation of their liberties, that they at all times keep themselves in a state of actual defence against every invasion or depredation; and this country being still threatened by a powerful army posted in its capital, with a professed design of executing certain acts of the British Parliament, calculated to destroy our invaluable rights and liberties, and the government of this colony as by charter and law established therein:

Therefore resolved, that the measures that have heretofore been recommended by this and the former Provincial Congress, for the purpose of putting this colony into a complete state of defence, be still most vigorously pursued by the several towns, as well as individual inhabitants; and that any relaxation would be attended with the utmost danger to the liberties of this colony and of all *America*, especially as by the latest advices from Great Britain we have undoubted reasons for jealousy that our implacable enemies are unremitting in their endeavours, by fraud and artifice, as well as by open force, to subjugate this people; which is an additional motive to the inhabitants of this colony to persevere in the line of conduct recommended by the Congress; and be ready to oppose with firmness and resolution, at the utmost hazard, every attempt for that purpose.

Signed by the order of the Provincial Congress,
      JOHN HANCOCK, President.

FOR SALE,
A SET of very fine BLACK COLTS, and another of BAYS, all of the best breeds, and from 3 to 4 years old, with long tails, and just broke; also a set of young BAY HORSES, that are large and strong, and go very well. Inquire of the Printer.

Recreated from Purdie's Virginia Gazette, April 21, 1775.

IN PROVINCIAL CONGRESS.

CONCORD, *April* 3, 1775.

WHEREAS several members of this Congress are now absent by leave of the congress, and as the important intelligence received by their last vessels from Great Britain renders it necessary that every member attend his duty.

Resolved, That the absent members be directed forthwith to attend in this place so that the wisdom of the province may be collected.   *By order,*
      JOHN HANCOCK, president.

A few days ago, his excellency governor Gage, upon the road to Roxbury, came up with a minute officer exercising a company of about 60 men under arms, and commanded them immediately to disperse, they all obeyed, and instantly went to the right about, but Grayton, their captain has been since broke by the congress at Concord, for obeying the governor's orders.

Recreated from The Maryland Gazette, April 20, 1775.

A DISGRACE TO HUMAN NATURE.

LONDON, *April* 3.

The seamen in the river are so afraid of an impress for the American service, that none of them sleep on board their vessels at night.

If the Americans continue unanimous, and proceed as they have begun, the whole force of this island against them, is no more than a drop in the ocean. It must strike every man with horror, when he reflected but a moment on the subject of the dispute; nothing but the prerogative of one man, manifestly managed by a Stuart and his junto, a set of low, despicable wretches, whose existence is a disgrace to human nature.

Government proposes that in future all Governors of Boston shall be the Commanders in Chief in America, for the time being, by which means both the civil and military system will be under one and the same arbitrary power.

Recreated from The Hartford Courant, July 3, 1775.

GENERALS SAIL FOR AMERICA.

LONDON, *April* 4.— From Petersburg we have just received advice, that the Empress has given orders for 30,000 of her choicest troops to be in readiness to take the field at a moment's notice. A circumstance which has occasioned various conjectures.

April 7.—The Cabinet Council has lately taken a new turn more adverse to America than before. It is in the great outline, that General Gage should be re-inforced to 15,000, and that he should have positive orders, on the meeting of the Congress, to march to Philadelphia, and arrest the whole assembly, and send them prisoners to England. This is to bring the dispute to a speedy decision.

The wharfs and quays about the Custom House are loaded with all kinds of merchandise (marked Army) which are going in the transports to Boston. One house ships 20,000l. in this manner, and it is said to be done on a very advantageous footing, as the price of all European goods are much advanced in America.

• • • •

April 11.—The plan of the ministry operations projected against the Americans, is said to be thus: General Gage is to continue chief in command, the head quarters to be at Boston, detached parties of 2000 men each, commanded respectively by the Generals Clinton, Howe, and Burgoyne are to be sent to Virginia, and such of the provinces as are deemed the most refractory.

• • • •

April 15.—The generals Burgoyne, Howe, and Clinton, sailed yesterday for America.

It was last year reported, that Sir Jeffery Amherst had said, that with 5000 English regulars he would engage to march from one end to the other of the continent of North America. This being spoken of publicly in a Coffee House in North America, Col. Washington who was present, declared, that with 1000 Virginians he would engage to stop Sir Jeffery's march.

It is the fashion at St. James's to despise the Americans, to call them cowards, poltroons, &c. and the resolution seems to be taken to put their courage to the proof. The very able, spirited, and prudent conduct of this gallant officer when he covered and preserved the remains of the English army after one of their defeats last war in North America, has endeared him to every brave man, and stamped him with the name of being a most able officer.

HER MAJESTY'S NEW PALACE.

HOUSE of COMMONS.
Lord North delivered by his Majesty's command the following message to the House:

"His Majesty, desirous, that a better and more suitable accommodation should be made for the residence of the Queen, in case she should survive him, and being willing that the palace in which his Majesty now resides, called the Queen's House may be settled for that purpose, recommends it to his faithful Commons, to take the same into consideration, and to make provision for settling the said palace upon her Majesty; and for appropriating Somerset House to such uses as shall be found most beneficial to the public."

Recreated from The Pennsylvania Packet, June 12, 1775.

PARIS, France, *April* 11.

ORDERS have been issued to all parts of this kingdom, prohibiting all commerce with the British colonies; and advertising those who shall attempt it, that it will be at their own hazard.

Recreated from The Hartford Courant, July 3, 1775.

NEW YORK, *April* 13.

A gentleman in Boston, writes to his friend in this city, that their provincial congress have voted 10,000 men to be immediately raised for the summer campaign, the expense of which was to be defrayed by an emission of £30,000 of paper currency.

Recreated from The Maryland Gazette, April 20, 1775.

AMERICAN POLTROONS.

LONDON, *April* 15, 1775.

ON the landing of the general officers who have sailed for America, a proclamation will be published throughout the provinces, inviting the Americans to deliver up their arms by a certain stipulated day, and that such of the Colonists as are afterwards proved to carry arms shall be deemed rebels, and be punished accordingly. *Quere*, if the Americans are such arrant poltroons as Lord Sandwich would make us believe, what necessity is there to deprive them of arms they have not the courage to make use of?

Recreated from The Pennsylvania Gazette, June 21, 1775.

MINUTE MEN TAKE TORIES.

BOSTON, *April* 17.—A letter from Taunton, dated last Friday, mentions "that on the Monday before, parties of Minute Men, &c. from every town in that county, with arms and ammunition, met at Freetown early that morning, in order to take Col. Gilbert, but he had fled on board the men of war at Newport; they then divided into parties, and took 29 Tories, who had signed inlistments and received arms in the Colonel's company, to join the King's troops; they also took 35 muskets, a case of bottles of powder, and a basket of bullets, all of which they brought to Taunton the same afternoon, where the prisoners were separately examined, 18 of whom made such humble acknowledgements of their past bad conduct, and solemn promises to behave better for future, they were dismissed; but the other 11 being obstinate and insulting, a party was ordered to carry them to Simsbury Mines; but they were sufficiently humble before they had got 14 miles on their way thither; upon which they were brought back the next day, and after signing proper articles to behave better for the future, were escorted to Freetown.—There was upwards of 2000 men embodied there last Monday."

CITY and LIBERTIES of PHILADELPHIA.

COMMITTEE CHAMBER, *April* 17, 1775.

WHEREAS it is now under consideration of the committee, to suspend all trade and commerce with such colonies as have not acceded to the association of the Continental Congress, the committee have therefore thought it proper to apprize their fellow citizens of this matter, that they govern themselves accordingly, and avoid entering into any engagement with respect to such colonies, from which they may be subjected to great inconveniences thereafter.

By order of the Committee,
JONATHAN B. SMITH, Sec'ry.

Recreated from The Virginia Gazette, April 29, 1775.

HORRORS OF CIVIL WAR.

April 17. (Monday)—Capt. Collins brings Advice, That the Act for restraining the Trade and blocking up all the Ports of New England, had passed the House of Commons. That Lord Chatham with a Number of his patriotic Friends, finding their Efforts for saving the Nation from Tyranny and the Horrors of a Civil War ineffectual, arose from their Seats & abruptly left the House of Lords, giving as a reason for their Conduct, that they would have no further Concerns in a Legislature who were involving the Nation in Blood and Slaughter.

A Pair of handsome Bay HORSES, Young, and well broke to a Carriage, TO BE SOLD, Enquire of *Benjamin Davids*, at the George-Tavern.

Entertainment for Man and Horse, By ANTHONY FORTUNE, At the HORSE & GROOM in Shippen-street, The second House from the Corner of Third-street, near the NEW-MARKET. N. B. Convenient Grass Lots for Horses committed to his Care.

Recreated from The Pennsylvania Gazette, April 26, 1775.

BATTLES at LEXINGTON & CONCORD.

A Letter from BOSTON, *Dated April* 20, 1775.

"Yesterday produced a scene the most shocking New England ever beheld. Last Saturday P.M. orders were sent to the several regiments quartered here not to let their grenadiers or light infantry do any duty till further orders; upon which the inhabitants conjectured some secret expedition was on foot, and being on the look-out, they observed three bodies on the move between ten and eleven o'clock on Tuesday night, observing a perfect silence in their march, towards the point opposite Phipps's farm where boats were in waiting, that conveyed them over; the men appointed to alarm the country on such occasions, got over by stealth as early as the troops, and took their different routes.

"The first advice we had was about eight o'clock in the morning, when it was reported, that the troops had fired upon, and killed five men in Lexington, previous to which an officer came express to his Excellency Governor Gage, when between eight and nine o'clock a brigade marched out, under the command of Earl Piercy, consisting of the marines, the Welsh Fuzileers, the 4th regiment, 47th and 38th, and two field pieces. About 12 o'clock it was given out by the General's Aide de Camp, that no person was killed, and that not a single gun had been fired, which report was variously believed; but between one and two certain advices came, that eight were killed outright, and fourteen wounded, of the inhabitants of Lexington, who had about forty men drawn out early in the morning, near the Meeting-house Bridge; the party of light infantry and grenadiers, to the number of about 800, came up to them, and ordered them to disperse; the commander of them replied that they were only innocently amusing themselves with exercise; that they had not any ammunition with them, and therefore should not molest or disturb them. Which answer not satisfying, the troops fired upon and killed 3 or 4; the others took to their heels, and the troops continued to fire, a few took refuge in the Meetinghouse, when the soldiers shoved up the windows, and pointed their guns in and killed three; thus much is the best I can learn of the fatal day.

"You must naturally suppose that such a piece of cruelty would rouse the country, allowing the report to be true. The troops continued on their march to Concord, entered the town, and refreshed themselves in the meeting and town-house. In the latter place, they found some ammunition and stores belonging to the country, which finding they could not bring away, by reason the country people had occupied all the posts around them, they therefore set fire to the house, which the people extinguished, they set fire a second time, which brought on a general engagement at about 11 o'clock. The troops took two pieces of cannon from the countrymen, but their number increasing, they soon regained them, and the troops were obliged to retreat towards town. About noon they were joined by the other brigade under Earl Piercy, when another very warm engagement came on at Lexington, which the troops could not stand, therefore were obliged to continue their retreat, which they did with bravery becoming British soldiers—but the country was in a manner desperate—not regarding their cannon in the least, and followed on till seven in the evening, by which time they got into Charlestown, when they left off the pursuit, lest they might injure the inhabitants.

"I stood upon the hill in the town, and saw the engagement very plain, which was very bloody for 7 hours. It is conjectured that one half the soldiers at least are killed. The last brigade was sent over in the ferry in the evening, to secure their retreat, where they are this morning entrenching themselves upon Bunker's Hill, till they could get a safe retreat to this town. It is impossible to learn any particulars, as the communication between town and country is at present broke off.

"They were till 10 last night bringing over their wounded, several of which are since dead, two Officers in particular. When I reflect and consider that the fight was between those, whose parents but a few generations ago were brothers, I shudder at the thought—and there is no knowing when our calamities will end."

Recreated from The Pennsylvania Gazette, May 3, 1775.

A COMPLETE VICTORY.

Another Account of the Battles from BOSTON, *April* 19, 1775.

I HAVE taken up my pen to inform you, that last night, about eleven o'clock, 1000 of the best troops in a very secret manner embarked on board a number of boats at the bottom of the Common, and went up Cambridge river, and landed. (In the mean time they stopped every person going over the Neck or any ferry; however we soon found a way to get some men to alarm the country.) From thence they marched to Lexington, where they saw a number of men exercising; they ordered them to disperse, and immediately fired upon them, killed eight men on the spot, and then marched to Concord. This alarmed the country, so that it seemed as if men came down from the clouds. The news coming to town the General sent out another thousand men, with a large train of artillery. In the mean time those troops at Concord had set fire to the Court-house there.

We then had our men collected, so that an engagement immediately ensued, and the King's troops retreated very fast, and our men kept up at their heels, loading and firing till they got to Charlestown, where our men thought it not prudent to come any further, fearing the ships of war would be ordered to fire on Boston and Charlestown.

They have gained a complete victory, and, by the best information I can get, most of the officers and soldiers are cut off. There were two waggons, one loaded with powder and ball, the other with provisions, guarded by seventeen men and an officer, going to the army, when six of our men way-laid them, shot two, wounded two, took the officer prisoner (the others took to the woods) and brought off the waggons.

The engagement began about twelve o'clock, and continued till seven, in the mean time they retreated 20 miles. We have now at least ten thousand men round this town. It has been a most distressing day with us, but I pray God we may never have reason to be called to such another.

Recreated from The Pennsylvania Gazette, May 3, 1775.

WILLIAMSBURG.—*This morning arrived an express from the Northward, with the following:*

To all friends of American liberty, be it known, that this morning, before break of day, a brigade consisting of about 1000 or 1200 men landed at Phipp's Farm, at Cambridge, and marched to Lexington, where they found a company of our militia in arms, upon whom they fired without any provocation, and killed six men, and wounded four others. By an express from Boston we find another brigade are now upon their march from Boston, supposed to be about 1000. The bearer, Trail Brissel, is charged to alarm the country quite to Connecticut; and all persons are desired to furnish him with fresh horses, as they may be needed. I have spoken with several, who have seen the dead and wounded. Pray let the Delegates from this colony to Connecticut see this; they know Col. Foster, one of the Delegates.   J. PALMER.

I am this moment informed by an express from Woodstock, taken from the mouth of the express, then two o'clock, afternoon, that the contest between the first brigade that marched to Concord, was still continuing this morning at the town of Lexington, to which said brigade had retreated, that another brigade had, said to be the second brigade in the letter of this morning, landed with a quantity of artillery, at the place where the first did. The provincials were determined to prevent the two brigades from joining their strength if possible, and remain in great need of succour.   E.B. WILLIAMS.

Recreated from The Virginia Gazette, April 29, 1775.

KILKENNY, [Ireland] *April* 22.—Yesterday the 1st division of the 44th regiment of foot marched out of the town for Cork, and this morning was followed by the second division, in order to embark for Boston.

This day the first division of the 40th regiment will march in here from Dublin, and the second division on Monday next, on their way to Cork, to embark for Boston. The above are a part of the second embarkation for America, consisting of four regiments.

Recreated from The Maryland Gazette, June 22, 1775.

SMALL POX AT BOSTON.

LONDON, *April 21, 1775.—Extract of a Letter from Boston, by the last mail.*

"The small pox prevails here, and has been spread by the practice of inoculation. On the first breaking out of this disease, General Gage issued a proclamation, forbidding inoculation under pain of the highest displeasure; nevertheless many of the officers who have wives and children here caused them to be inoculated; and what is worse, a putrid malignant fever has broke out, both amongst the soldiers and inhabitants; and of many others who have died, General Gage's own private Secretary was taken off by this contagion; the soldiers have been buried with military honours.

"As to the malcontents in these provinces, I think they will not come down to attack us here, but next summer, in case we should march forty or fifty miles from hence, it is not only mine, but the general opinion of our friends, that they will meet us, and that there will be much bloodshed before we are done."

April 25. Messengers are continually passing and re-passing from this kingdom to Ireland; but the business has not yet transpired.

About six o'clock yesterday morning an express arrived at Buckingham House, from General Gage, at Boston.

IRELAND.

CORK, *April* 27. We hear that eight of the transports expected from England are put into Plymouth, to bring from thence, two regiments, to replace those going to Boston.

Yesterday and this day the 44th regiment of foot arrived in this city, in order to embark for America.

LIMERICK, *April* 27. This morning the first division of the 45th regiment marched hence for Cork, and tomorrow will be followed by the remainder, in order to embark for America.

WATERFORD, *April* 29. Yesterday twenty-three vessels sailed from Passage for Newfoundland.

12,000 MEN EMBODIED.

The advice which administration has received from America, and which they have not thought proper to communicate, is, in substance, that the Militia of Massachusetts and Connecticut are actually embodied, have prepared magazines, and are assembled, to the number of twelve thousand effective men. Salem was the headquarters when these advices came away; but a considerable body were on their march to Boston. So, that there is not a doubt, and Ministers themselves expect it, that the next news will bring an account of an action.

PLANS FOR BRITISH GENERALS.

We hear the disposition of the General Officers who are gone on the American expedition, is to be as follows: General Gage to remain at Boston with a reinforcement in the same situation as at present; whilst Generals Burgoyne, Clinton, and Howe, are to march with a large army thro' the principal provinces, offering an indemnity to all those who renounce the tenets of the Congress, but acting on the offensive to all those who do not. The peremptory resolution will, it is thought, very shortly decide the fate of America.

The authenticity of the following paragraph a correspondent assures us may be depended on:—

"Capt. Brown and another officer of the 52d regiment at Boston being sent to make a survey of the roads about the country, very narrowly escaped being tarred and feathered at Marlborough. They were entertained by a Mr. Barnes, and tho' in disguise, were discovered by a drummer, who had formerly deserted from the same regiment.—The consequence was, the people assembled in great numbers and surrounded the house; the two officers got to Boston, but Mr. Barnes' house was almost tore to pieces, and his family dreadfully alarmed. Since that (for the smallest circumstances gives them the alarm) the back country have rose, and drove in here for shelter a great number of people well affected to Government."

Recreated from Finns Leinster Journal, Ireland, May 3, 1775.

DUNMORE SEIZES MAGAZINE.

WILLIAMSBURG, *April* 21.

This morning, between 3 and 4 o'clock, all the gunpowder in the magazine, to the amount, as we hear, of about 20 barrels, was carried off in his Excellency the Governor's waggon; escorted by a detachment of marines from the armed schooner Magdalen, now lying at Burwell's ferry, and lodged on board that vessel. The whole city was alarmed, and much exasperated, and many got themselves in readiness to repair to the castle, to demand from the Governor a restoration of what they so justly supposed was deposited in this magazine for the country's defence. However, in a decent and respectful manner, the Common Hall assembled, who, after deliberating some time, waited upon his Excellency with the following address, which was presented by the Hon. Peyton Randolph, Esq., Recorder of this city:

To his Excellency the Right Honourable John Earl of Dunmore:

My Lord, We his Majesty's dutiful and loyal subjects, the mayor, recorder, alderman, and common council, of the city of Williamsburg in common hall assembled humbly beg leave to represent to your Excellency, that the inhabitants of this city were this morning exceedingly alarmed, by a report that a large quantity of gunpowder was, in the preceding night, while they were sleeping in their beds, removed from the public magazine in this city, and conveyed under an escort of marines on board of his Majesty's armed vessels lying at a ferry on James river.

We beg leave to represent to your Excellency, that as this magazine was erected at the public expense of this colony, and appropriated to the safe keeping of such ammunition as should be there lodged from time to time for the protection and security of the country, by arming thereout such of the militia as might be necessary in case of invasion and insurrections, they humbly conceive it to be the only proper repository to be resorted to in times of imminent danger.

We farther beg leave to inform your Excellency, that from various reports, at present prevailing in different parts of the country, we have too much reason to believe that some wicked and designing persons have instilled the most diabolical notions into the minds of our slaves, and that therefore the utmost attention to our internal security is become the more necessary.

The circumstances of this city, my lord, we consider as peculiar and critical. The inhabitants, from the situation of the magazine, in the middle of their city, have for a long tract of time been exposed to all those dangers which have happened in many countries by explosions and other accidents. They have from time to time, thought it incumbent on them to guard the magazine. For their security, they have for some time past judged it necessary to keep strong patrols on foot in their present circumstances, then, to have the chief and necessary means of their defence removed, cannot but be extremely alarming.

Considering ourselves as guardians of the city, we therefore humbly desire to be informed by your Excellency, upon what motives, and for what particular purpose the powder has been carried off in such a manner, and we earnestly entreat your Excellency to order it to be immediately returned to the magazine.

LIES, LIES, LIES.

His Excellency returned this verbal answer:

THAT, hearing of an insurrection in a neighbouring county, he had removed the powder from the magazine where he did not think it secure, to a place where it would be in perfect security, and that upon his word and honour, whenever it was wanted on any insurrection, it should be delivered in half an hour. That he had removed it in the night time to prevent any alarm and that Capt. Collins had his express commands for the part he had acted. He was surprised to hear the people were under arms on this occasion, and that he should not think it prudent to put powder into their hands in such a situation.

Recreated from Purdie's Virginia Gazette, April 21, 1775.

PAUL REVERE MISSING.

HANCOCK AND ADAMS ESCAPE.

By an Express arrived last Friday evening, we have the following:

Dear Sir, Hartford, *April 23, 1775.*

"These are to inform you, that we have undoubted intelligence of hostilities being begun at Boston by the regular troops, the truth of which we are assured divers ways, and especially of Mr. Adams the post; the particulars of which, as nigh as I can recollect are as follows: General Gage, last Tuesday night, draughted out about 1000 or 1200 of his best troops in a secret manner, which he embarked on board transports, and carried and landed at Cambridge that night, and early Wednesday morning by day break they marched to Lexington, where a number of inhabitants were exercising before breakfast as usual, about 30 in number, upon whom the regulars fired without the least provocation about 15 minutes, without a single shot from our men, who retreated as fast as possible, in which fire they killed 6 of our men, and wounded several, from hence they proceeded to Concord, on the road thither, they fired at, and killed a man on horseback; went to the house where Mr. Hancock lodged, who with Samuel Adams, luckily got out of their way by secret and speedy intelligence from Paul Revere, who is now missing, and nothing heard of him since; when they searched the house for Mr. Hancock, and Adams, and not finding them there, killed the woman of the house and all the children, and set fire to the house; from thence they proceeded on their way to Concord, firing at, and killing hogs, geese, cattle and every thing that came their way, and burning houses.

"When they came to Concord, they took possession of the court-house, they destroyed 100 barrels of flour, and a number of pork, spiked one cannon and broke in pieces another belonging to the provincials, after which they marched back to Boston.

"But before they marched far, they were met by 300 provincials, who received two fires from the regulars before they returned it. On the second fire from the provincials they had increased to 5 or 600 when the troops took to their heels and ran helter skelter, they running, and our men pursuing and killing them, till they came to a place called Bunker's Hill in Charlestown. General Gage knowing they were attacked, sent out a reinforcement of about 900 men with waggons of provisions, which reinforcement was boldly attacked by a less number of provincials, on which a brisk skirmish ensued, in which our men had so much the better of them, as to take their waggons of provisions; and kill the commander of the waggons; Capt. Hogshie made eight prisoners, ten more clubbed their firelocks and came over to us; many were killed on both sides; the remainder of their reinforcement proceeded and joined the main body of troops, then they all retreated together till they came to said Bunker's Hill, where they encamped, it being night, and the firing ceasing.

"The country being instantly alarmed, the provincials poured into this place in great numbers; when Adams came away, he says there were 30 or 40,000 of our men under arms, and more coming fast. The provincials had surrounded the troops, and were throwing up entrenchments to hinder their retreat. The north-east is under the protection of a ship of war, which lies within a mile of them from that end; they are animated with the prospects of glory or death. The troops are much the reverse, carry pale countenances, &c. There is supposed to be about 150 of the troops killed, amongst whom they say is Lord Piercy and General Haldiman; the truth of which we are not sure of; Mr. Adams says he does not doubt it; of our men 30 or 40, they think probably more. This colony is all alarmed, every town is preparing for a march; many companies have already marched, bag and baggage.

"Stop—This moment an express is arrived, the troops encamped, Thursday night got into Boston, under the guns of the ships."

Recreated from The Pennsylvania Packet, May 1, 1775.

BOSTON BESIEGED.

Extract of a Letter from a resident at BOSTON, *dated April 23 and 24.*

"We have been closely besieged, and no provisions brought to market for several days, which has reduced us to an allowance. Lieutenant Knight was the only officer killed in the engagement; 14 officers wounded, two of whom dangerously, 62 privates killed and missing, and 105 wounded (part of every regiment, except that at the castle) exclusive of the marines, who suffered more than any regiment.

"The Governor and Gentlemen of Boston have agreed to open the town, on condition of the inhabitants delivering up their arms to the Selectmen. The Governor engages to protect the lives and property of such as choose to stay; those who choose to quit the town, to go where they please, and the boats of the fleet to assist in conveying such persons with their effects, as choose to go to any part of the harbour.—The town was besieged by 20,000 men who it was expected would attack the fortifications.

"The wounded officers and soldiers were treated with great humanity by the inhabitants of Charlestown, on their return."

Recreated from The Pennsylvania Gazette, May 3, 1775.

WILLIAMSBURG, *April* 22.— Last Wednesday the freeholders of Williamsburg unanimously elected Peyton Randolph, Esq., to represent them in Convention for one year, from the first day of May next.

They have also unanimously resolved to continue their contributions to the Bostonians; upon which a subscription was immediately opened.

• • • •

We learn from Pittsylvania that there is now living in that county one Mrs. Smith, in the 109th year of her age, formerly of James City county. She lately danced at a wedding, and sung a song of thirteen verses distinctly, which she learnt at nine years old. She mounts a horse with great agility, goes to mill, fords a river 200 yards broad, and labours for subsistence.

Recreated from The Virginia Gazette, April 22, 1775.

PHILADELPHIA.

AFFIDAVITS *and* DEPOSITIONS *relative to the commencement of the late hostilities in the province of Massachusetts Bay, together with an* ADDRESS *from the Provisional Convention of said province, to the inhabitants of Great Britain, transmitted to the* CONGRESS *now sitting in this city, and published by their order.*

CHARLES THOMPSON, Secretary.

DISPERSE YOU REBELS!

LEXINGTON, *April* 23, 1775.

I Thomas Fessenden, of lawful age, testify and declare, that being in a pasture near the meeting house at said Lexington, on Wednesday last, at about a half an hour before sunrise, I saw a number of regular troops pass speedily by said meeting house, on their way towards a company of militia of said Lexington, who were assembled to the number of about 100 in a company, at the distance of 18 or 20 rods from said meeting house, I saw three officers on horseback advance to the front of said regulars, when one of them being within six rods of said militia, cried out "disperse you rebels immediately;" on which he brandished his sword over his head three times, meanwhile the second officer, who was about two rods behind him, fired a pistol pointed at said militia, and the regulars kept huzzaing till he had finished brandishing his sword, and when he had thus finished brandishing his sword he pointed it down towards said militia, and immediately on which the said regulars fired a volley at the militia, and then I ran off as fast as I could, while they continued firing till I got out of their reach: I further testify that as soon as ever the officer cried "disperse you rebels", the said company of militia dispersed every way as fast as they could, and while they were dispersing the regulars kept firing at them incessantly, and further saith not.

Thomas Fessenden.

Recreated from The Pennsylvania Gazette, May 17, 1775.

Lincoln, April 23, 1775.

I John Bateman, belonging to the 52d regiment, commanded by Col. Jones, on Wednesday morning, on the 19th of April instant, was in the party marching to Concord, being at Lexington, in the County of Middlesex, being nigh the meeting house in said Lexington, there was a small party of men gathered together in that place, when our said troops marched by, and I testify and declare, that I heard the word of command given to the troops to fire, and some of the said troops did fire, and I saw one of said small party lay dead on the ground, nigh said meeting house; and I testify that I never heard any of the inhabitants so much as fire one gun on said troops.

John Bateman.

• • • •

Lexington, April 25, 1775.

We Solomon Brown, Jonathan Loring, and Elija Sanderson; all of lawful age, and of Lexington, in the county of Middlesex, and colony of the Massachusetts Bay in New England, do testify and declare, that on the evening of the 18th of April instant, being on the road between Concord and Lexington, and all of us mounted on horses, we were about ten of the clock, suddenly surprised by nine persons, whom we took to be regular officers, who rode up to us mounted and armed, each having a pistol in his hand, and after putting pistols to our breasts, and seizing the bridles of our horses, they swore that if we stirred another step, we should be all dead men, upon which we surrendered ourselves; they detained us until two o'clock the next morning, in which time they searched and greatly abused us, having first enquired about the Magazine at Concord, whether any guards were posted there, and whether the bridges were up, and said four or five regiments of the Regulars would be in possession of the stores soon; they then brought us back to Lexington, cut the horses bridles and girths, turned them loose, and then left us.

Solomon Brown, Jonathan Loring and Elija Sanderson.

Lexington, 25th of April, 1775.

Simon Winship, of Lexington, in the county of Middlesex, and province of Massachusetts Bay, New England, being of lawful age, testifieth and saith, that on the 19th of April instant, about four o'clock in the morning, as he was passing the public road in said Lexington, peaceably and unarmed, about two miles and a half distant from the meeting house in said Lexington, he was met by a body of the King's regular troops, and being stopped by some officers of said troops, was commanded to dismount; upon asking why he must dismount, he was obliged by force to quit his horse, and ordered to march in the midst of the body, and being examined whether he had been out warning the minute men, he answered no, but had been out, and was then returning to his father's. Said Winship further testifies, that he marched with said troops until he came within about half a quarter of a mile of said meeting house, where an officer commanded the troops to halt, and then to prime and load; this being done, the said troops marched on till they came within a few rods of Captain Parker's company, who were partly collected on the place of parade; when said Winship observed an officer at the head of said troops flourishing his sword, and with a loud voice giving the word fire, fire, which was instantly followed by a discharge of arms from said regular troops; and said Winship is positive and in the most solemn manner declares, that there was no discharge of arms on either side till the word fire was given by said officer above.

Simon Winship.

• • • •

Lexington, April 23, 1775.

We, Joseph Butler and Ephraim Melvin, do testify and declare, that when the regular troops fired upon our people at the North Bridge in Concord, as related in the foregoing descriptions, they shot one, and we believe two, of our people, before we fired a single gun at them.

Joseph Baker, Ephraim Melvin.

Lexington, April 23, 1775.

We John Hoar, John Whitehead, Abraham Garfield, Benjamin Munroe, Isaac Parks, William Hosmer, John Adams, Gregory Stone, all of Lincoln, in the county of Middlesex, Massachusetts Bay, all of lawful age, do testify and say that on Wednesday last, we were assembled at Concord, in the morning of said day, in consequence of information received, that a brigade of regular troops were on their march to the said town of Concord, who had killed six men at the town of Lexington; about an hour afterwards we saw them approaching, to the number, as we apprehended, of about 1200, on which we retreated to a hill about 80 rods back, and the said troops then took possession of the hill where we were first posted; presently after this we saw the troops moving towards the North-bridge, about one mile from the said Concord meeting house, we then immediately went before them and passed the bridge just before a party of them, to the number of about 200, arrived; they there left about one half of their 200 at the bridge, and proceeded with the rest towards Colonel Barrett's, about two miles from the said bridge; we then seeing several fires in the town, thought the houses in Concord were in danger, and marched towards the said bridge, and the troops who were stationed there, observing our approach, marched back over the bridge, and then took up some of the planks; we then hastened our march towards the bridge, and when we had got near the bridge they fired on our men, first three guns, one after the other, and then a considerable number more; and then, and not before (having orders from our commanding officers not to fire till we were fired upon) we fired upon the regulars, and they retreated. On their retreat through the town of Lexington to Charlestown, they ravaged and destroyed private property, and burnt three houses, one barn and one shop.

Signed by each of the above Deponents as true and accurate.

• • • •

Medford, April 25, 1775.

I Edward Thornton Gould, of his Majesty's own regiment of foot, being of lawful age, do testify and declare, that on the evening of the 18th instant, under the orders of General Gage, I embarked with the light infantry and grenadiers of the line, commanded by Col. Smith, and landed on the marshes of Cambridge, from whence we proceeded to Lexington; on our arrival at that place we saw a body of provincial troops armed, to the number of about 60 or 70 men; on our approach they dispersed, and soon after firing began, but which party fired first I cannot exactly say, as our troops rushed on, shouting, huzzaing, previous to the firing, which was continued by our troops so long as any of the provincials were to be seen. From thence we marched to Concord; on a hill, near the entrance of the town, we saw another body of provincials assembled, the light infantry companies were ordered up the hill to disperse them, on our approach they retreated towards Concord. The grenadiers continued on the road under the hill towards the town; six companies of light infantry were ordered down to take possession of the bridge which the provincials retreated over; the company I commanded was one, three companies of the above detachment went forward about two miles, in the mean time the provincial troops returned to the number of about 300 or 400, we drew up on the Concord side of the bridge, the provincials came down upon us, upon which we engaged, and gave the first fire: This was the first engagement after the one at Lexington, a continued firing from both parties lasted thro' the whole day; I myself was wounded at the attack of the bridge, and am now treated with the greatest humanity, and taken all possible care of by the provincials at Medford.

Edward Thornton Gould, Lieut. King's own Regt.

[All the foregoing depositions are sworn to before Justices of the Peace, and duly attested by Notaries Public.]

Recreated from The Pennsylvania Gazette, May 17, 1775.

In Provincial Congress.

To the Inhabitants of GREAT BRITAIN.

WATER-TOWN, *April* 26, 1775.

FRIENDS AND FELLOW SUBJECTS,

HOSTILITIES are at length commenced in this colony by the Troops under the Command of Gen. Gage, and it being of the greatest importance, that an early true and authentic account of this inhuman proceeding should be known to you, the Congress of this Colony have transmitted the same, and, from want of a Session of the Honourable Continental Congress, think it proper to address you on the alarming occasion.

By the clearest depositions relative to this transaction it will appear, that on the night preceding the nineteenth of April instant, a body of the King's Troops, under command of Colonel Smith, was secretly landed at Cambridge, with an apparent design to take or destroy the military and other stores provided for the defence of this Colony, and deposited at Concord—that some inhabitants of the Colony on the night aforesaid, whilst travelling peaceably on the road between Boston and Concord, were seized, and greatly abused by armed men, who appeared to be officers of General Gage's army—that the town of Lexington by these means was alarmed, and a company of the inhabitants mustered on the occasion—that the regular troops on their way to Concord marched into the said town of Lexington, and the said Company on their approach began to disperse—that, notwithstanding this, the Regulars rushed on with great violence, and first began Hostilities by firing on said Lexington company, whereby they killed eight and wounded several others—that the Regulars continued their fire until those of said company, who were neither killed nor wounded, had made their escape—that Col. Smith, with a detachment, then marched to Concord, where a number of Provincials were again fired on by the troops, two of them killed and several wounded, before the Provincials fired on them—and that these hostile measures of the troops produced an engagement that lasted thro' the day; in which many of the provincials and more of the regular troops were killed and wounded.

To give a particular account of the ravages of the troops, as they retreated from Concord to Charlestown, would be very difficult, if not impracticable; let it suffice to say, that a great number of the houses on the road were plundered, and rendered unfit for use; several were burnt; women in child-bed were driven, by the soldiery, naked into the streets; old men peaceably in their houses were shot dead; and such scenes exhibited as would disgrace the annals of the most uncivilized nation.

These, brethren, are marks of Ministerial vengeance against this Colony, for refusing with her sister colonies a submission to slavery; but they have not yet detached us from our royal Sovereign. We profess to be his loyal and dutiful subjects, and so hardly dealt with as we have been, are still ready with our lives and fortunes to defend his person, family, crown and dignity. Nevertheless, to the persecution and tyranny of his cruel Ministry we will not tamely submit—appealing to Heaven for the justice of our cause, we determine to die or be free.

We cannot think that the Honour, Wisdom and Valour of BRITONS will suffer them to be longer inactive spectators of measures, in which they themselves are so deeply interested—Measures pursued in opposition to the solemn protests of many noble Lords, and expressed sense of conspicuous Commoners, whose knowledge and virtue have long characterized them as some of the greatest men in the nation—Measures executing contrary to the interest, petitions, and resolves of many large, respectable and opulent counties, cities and boroughs in Great Britain—Measures highly incompatible with justice, but still pursued with a specious pretence of easing the nation of its burdens—Measures which, if successful, must end in the ruin and slavery of Britain as well as the persecuted American Colonies.

We sincerely hope, that the Great Sovereign of the Universe, who hath so often appeared for the English Nation, will support you in every rational and manly exertion with these colonies, for saving it from ruin, and that in a constitutional connection with the Mother Country, we shall soon be altogether a free and happy people.

Per Order,
JOSEPH WARREN, *President, Pro. Tem.*

At a meeting of the Committee for the county of Chester, at the borough of Chester, May 15, 1775, ANTHONY WAYNE, *Esq., in the Chair, the following Resolves were made, viz.*

WHEREAS the British Parliament, instead of hearing our just complaints, are showing the least regard to the dutiful and loyal petition of the late Continental Congress in behalf of America, have proceeded to fresh acts of tyranny and oppression, which, added to an address of both Lords and Commons to his Majesty, declaring the inhabitants of the province of Massachusetts-Bay to be in a state of open rebellion, and several of the other Colonies encouragers of the same, have induced the soldiery under the command of General Gage, at Boston, to commence a civil war, by wantonly firing upon and murdering a number of the inhabitants of that province. And whereas the said address militates equally against all the inhabitants of the other Colonies, who have the virtue to refuse obedience to laws and measures destructive to the best rights and liberties of America, which, if suffered to take effect, must inevitably reduce these Colonies to a state of abject slavery, from which, in all probability, no human efforts would ever be able to rescue them; and although we will not yield to any of our fellow subjects, in point of duty and loyalty to our most gracious Sovereign, yet we cannot be so far negligent of our own happiness, as totally to neglect providing for our common safety.

Therefore Resolved unanimously, 1st. That it is the indispensable duty of all freemen of this county, immediately to form, and enter into Associations, for the purpose of learning the military art. And that they provide themselves with proper arms and ammunition to be ready in case of emergency to defend our liberty, property and lives, against all attempts to deprive us of them. And we solemnly engage to promote such Associations to the utmost of our power.

2d. *Resolved, nem. con.* That no powder be expended in this county, except on emergent occasions, and the store and shop-keepers are requested not to dispose of any, except to some one or more of this Committee, who are ordered to purchase the same.

3d. *Resolved, nem. con.* That this Committee, confiding in the wisdom and virtue of the Continental Congress, now sitting in Philadelphia, will adopt, and use their utmost endeavours to carry into execution, all such measures as the said Congress shall recommend, for the preservation of American liberty.

4th. It is earnestly recommended to every subscriber in this county for the relief of the poor of Boston, that they immediately pay the same, as it is much wanted for the purposes intended.

5th. *Resolved, nem. con.* That each member of this Committee will give his attendance at the borough of Chester on the 31st of this instant, at 10 o'clock, A.M. in order to consult the Justices, Grand Jury, and Board of Commissioners and Assessors, on ways and means to procure a proper quantity of arms and ammunition, for the use of this county.

The Committee then adjourned to the time and place above mentioned.

By order of the Committee,
FRANCIS JOHNSTON, Secretary.

TO BE SOLD,
THE TIME of a SERVANT GIRL, about 14 Years of Age, who has 3¼ Years to serve. Enquire of the PRINTERS.   I:W.

Recreated from The Pennsylvania Gazette, May 17, 1775.

LATEST FROM BOSTON.

40,000 UNDER ARMS.

April 24, 1775.

By the latest accounts from Boston we learn, that last Tuesday night the Grenadiers and Light Companies belonging to the several regiments in the Town of Boston were ferryed in long-boats from the bottom of the common over to Phipps's farm in Cambridge; they arrived at Lexington early the next morning, when they gave a specimen of their savage designs, by firing several times on a number of innocent men who were collected at that place, and among whom were the Selectmen of the town.

Six men were killed on the spot and a number wounded. From thence, being about 12 hundred in number, they marched with speed to Concord, killing some on the road, firing some houses, and making considerable destruction until they arrived at Concord, where they designed to have destroyed the ammunition and provisions; and carried off some field pieces; but as about 300 of our men had collected under arms at that place, their intentions were frustrated in that respect; however, they immediately fired on the militia, and the fire was as briskly returned by our MEN, who attacked and pursued them on their retreat to Charlestown where they had a large reinforcement under the command of Lord Piercy, with two pieces of artillery, and whence under cover of their shipping they retired to Boston.

Large numbers were continually flocking in from all parts of the country, and by Friday morning between 30 and 40 thousand were assembled under arms. Our men took some of their waggons and stores, 20 prisoners, and killed upwards of 200 Regulars, among whom are General Haldiman, Major Hodgson, and some other Officers, and one Murray, son to Col. Murray, a mandamus counsellor, who piloted the troops out of Boston. Lord Piercy it is supposed was among the slain. The loss on our side was not so considerable, not more then 32 or 33 are killed, and but very few wounded.

This engagement occasions a universal muster of the troops in Connecticut; great numbers of whom, completely equipped with arms, ammunition and provisions, are gone to the relief of their distressed brethren. The major part of the members of the Provisional Congress had convened at Concord last Friday and the rest of the members were expected soon to be there.

Recreated from The Hartford Courant, April 24, 1775.

Extract of a Letter from NEW YORK, *April* 24.

"I do not doubt but the interesting News from Boston must give every good and virtuous Man much Concern, that, from present Appearances, a Reconciliation between us and Great Britain is at a farther Distance than we of late had rational Grounds to hope, surely this Proceeding on the Part of General Gage, is not the Olive Branch held up by the Government.

"Yesterday this Whole City was in a State of Alarm, every Face appeared animated with Resentment, soon after the News arrived by Express, many Citizens went to two Transports loaded with Bread, Flour, &c. for the Troops, and they were speedily unloaded."

Recreated from The Pennsylvania Gazette, April 26, 1775.

A Letter from HARTFORD, *April* 26, 1775.

"I send this by express to inform you, that by advice this instant received, General Gage has ordered all the vessels that may be found on the coast of New England, to be immediately secured for the King's use, pray communicate this intelligence that all concerned may take the necessary precaution."

THREE DOLLARS Reward. WAS LOST, on Wednesday, the 19th of April laſt, on the road leading from John Pennock's mill, to David Harlin's ſaw-mill, A RED MOROCCO POCKET-BOOK, or Surgeon's Pouch of Inſtruments, covered with a caſe of blue ſilk damaſk. Whoever has found ſaid Inſtruments, and will bring them to the ſubſcriber, living in New-London townſhip, Cheſter county, ſhall have the above reward, and reaſonable charges, paid by FRANCIS ALLISON, junior.

Recreated from The Pennsylvania Gazette, May 3, 1775.

In Provincial Congress.

Watertown, *April* 30, 1775.

WHEREAS, an agreement hath been made, between General Gage, and the inhabitants of the town of Boston, for the removal of the persons and effects of such of the inhabitants of the town of Boston, as may be so disposed, excepting their fire-arms and ammunition, into the country.

Resolved, That any of the inhabitants of this colony, who may incline to go into the town of Boston with their effects, fire-arms and ammunition excepted, have toleration for that purpose; and that they may be protected from any injury and insult whatsoever, in their removal to Boston, and that this resolve be immediately published.

P.S. Officers are appointed for the giving of permits for the above purposes; one at the sign of the sun at Charlestown, and another at the house of Mr. John Greaton, jun. at Roxbury.

JOSEPH WARREN, President, Pro. tem.

Recreated from The Hartford Courant, May 8, 1775.

Boston Citizens Disarmed.

A Letter from Boston, *dated April* 30.

"The communication between this town and the country is entirely stopped up, not a soul permitted to go in or out without a pass. This day the Governor has disarmed all the inhabitants, after giving them his word and honour that the soldiers should not molest nor plunder them.

"Cambridge is the head quarters of the provincials, and they are commanded by General ____. They are entrenching themselves at Roxbury, and erecting batteries to play on our lines."

• • • •

The men of war at Rhode Island have taken two sloops bound from thence for Providence, with flour, belonging to Mr. Brown, of Newport; and the owner was taken on board one of the King's ships.

Recreated from The Pennsylvania Gazette, May 3, 1775.

Exports Suspended.

Committee Chamber, New York, *1st May,* 1775.

WHEREAS it appears by the public papers, that all exportations from Philadelphia to Quebec, Nova Scotia, Georgia, and Newfoundland, or any part of the Fishing Coasts, or Fishing Islands, is suspended; and that it be accordingly recommended to every merchant, immediately to suspend all exportations to those places, until the Continental Congress shall give further orders therein.

Resolved, That the above measure be recommended by the Committee, to the merchants and inhabitants of this city and county, and that henceforth, no provisions, or other necessaries be sent from this port to the army, or navy at Boston, until the Continental Congress shall give further orders therein.

Ordered, That the above be made public.

ISAAC LOW, Chairman.

Recreated from The Pennsylvania Packet, May 22, 1775.

Annapolis, *May* 1.

In Provincial Convention.

Resolved Unanimously, that all exportation from this province to Quebec, Nova Scotia, Georgia, and Newfoundland, or any part of the fishing coasts or fishing islands, and to the town of Boston, ought immediately to be suspended, until the Continental Congress shall give further directions therein.

For SALE at *Tappahannock,*

AN exceeding likely young negro man, who is a very good house servant, understands taking care of horses, and is a tolerable good cook. If the purchaser is not perfectly satisfied with him after a month's trial, he may return him if in health.

(tf.) ARCHIBALD M'CALL.

Recreated from Purdie's Virginia Gazette, May 12, 1775.

EVERYTHING TO LOSE. NOTHING TO GAIN.

LONDON, *May* 1. While the Jacobites under the term of Ministers, were carrying through the House of Commons, in February last, the Declaration of War against our fellow subjects the Whigs in America, in the form of an Address to his Majesty, orders were sent to General Gage, to secure some of the leading men in Boston.

When the Address had gone through all its formalities, positive orders were sent to General Gage, signed by a certain _____, to take up particular persons in Boston, and hang them up by a decree of a Council of War, as Rebels. By a private dispatch from the General, received a few days ago at St. James's, he acknowledges the receipt of the first orders, and declares, that so far from his being able to take up the persons mentioned, he looks upon himself only as a prisoner at large in Boston; and that, if he was to attempt execution of such orders, it is more than probable he should never write another letter. This intelligence has thrown the blustering Lord North and his Tory crew into wonderful confusion.

May 2. By the last accounts from America, there is too much reason to fear we shall hear of some bloody action by the next. The Ministry themselves with the utmost unconcern, say, they expect it. But should so fatal event happen, an event that would, in all probability, tear the whole American continent forever from the British Crown, the ministry, if there be any sense of honour or justice remaining in the nation, or if the people have any just notions of their own interest, safety and well being, will have sufficient cause not to be so much unconcerned.

By the most authentic letters and narratives from America, we are told, that the Colonies are preparing to resist force by force. What shall we get if the King's army conquer? Absolutely nothing. What shall we lose if the royal army is beaten? Every thing! What a wretched politician must be he who puts every thing to the hazzard where nothing can be gained?

Recreated from The Hartford Courant, July 3, 1775.

60,000 MEN AT BOSTON.

NEW YORK, *May* 1.—We hear there are letters in this town from Connecticut, which say, that the number of men lately assembled at Boston, including those from Connecticut and Rhode Island, amounted to 60,000; that they mostly returned to their respective homes, leaving an army of about 15,000 to watch General Gage's motions.

MILITIA LIKE BEARS.

PHILADELPHIA, *May 3*.—Sunday last Captain Anthony arrived here in a short passage from Rhode Island, by whom we learn, that General Gage had dispatched a frigate to England a few hours after the defeat of his troops. That the British Officers and Soldiers have done ample justice to the bravery and conduct of the Massachusetts Militia—they say that no troops ever behaved with more resolution. A soldier who had been in action, being congratulated by a fellow soldier on his safe return to Boston, declared, "that the Militia had fought like bears, and that he would as soon attempt to storm hell, as to fight against them a second time."

Recreated from The Pennsylvania Gazette, May 3, 1775.

Extract of a Letter from an American Gentleman at Paris, dated May 2, 1775, to his Friend in Philadelphia.

"I find the French are extremely attentive to our American politics, and to a man strongly in favour of us. Whether mostly from an ill-will to Britain, or friendship to the Colonies, may be a matter of doubt; but they profess it to be on a principal of humanity, and a regard to the natural rights of mankind. They say that the Americans will either be revered or detested by all Europe, according to their conduct at the approaching crisis; they will have no middle character; for in proportion as their virtue and perseverance will render them a glorious, their tame submission will make them a despicable people."

Recreated from The Pennsylvania Gazette, July 5, 1775.

ARMED MEN GAIN REDRESS.

Lady Dunmore Flees.

WILLIAMSBURG, May 5.

LATE on Wednesday night, Col. Carter Braxton arrived in town with a number of armed people, all men of property, led by Patrick Henry, Esq., on their march for this city, from the counties of Hanover, New Kent, and King William. The intent of their coming, we are well assured, is the general alarm spread over the country by the removal of the gunpowder from the publick magazine, and to secure the treasury from a like catastrophe; as also to seize upon the person of his Majesty's Receiver General (then in this city) till either the gunpowder was restored, or a sum of money paid down to its value.

Next morning Col. Braxton returned, with the Hon. Richard Corbin's bill of exchange for 320l. sterling; and, at the same time, the inhabitants of this city engaging themselves to guard the publick treasury, the Gentlemen dispersed yesterday afternoon, and returned to their respective homes, perfectly satisfied with the success of their expedition. They had proceeded as far as Doncastle's, about 15 miles from town, where they were encamped to a number of 150 men and upwards, all well accoutred, and had a very martial appearance.

As soon as his Excellency the Governor received intelligence of the above armed force coming down, he despatched a messenger to the Fowey man of war, now lying before York town, and by 10 o'clock yesterday morning a detachment of 40 sailors and marines belonging to that ship, under the command of Capt. Stretch, arrived at the palace; they did not march through the main street, but were led through the Governor's park.

The town of York, we are well informed, was threatened with a cannonade from his Majesty's ship Fowey, by her commander, if the inhabitants presumed to molest the troops in their landing, or on their march to this city. They are now at the palace; how long they will stay is uncertain.

This morning a warrant was issued to search certain houses, for arms, suspected to have been taken out of the magazine in this city, a considerable number being missing; but the officer, we hear, has not been able to find any.

The Right Honourable the COUNTESS of DUNMORE, with all the Governor's family, are now on board the Fowey man of war.

THREE months ago I purchased, from the executors of *Littlebury Hardiman*, a negro woman named RACHEL, formerly Mr. *Hardiman*'s cook, since which I have not seen her. I am informed she has a husband at one of Col. *Carter*'s quarters on *James* river, through whose benevolence I imagine she is now harboured. Whoever brings her to me, at *Drummond's Neck*, near *Cowles's* ferry, shall receive 30s. or 20s. if conveyed to *Charles City* prison. I am determined not to dispose of her, and will sue any person who entertains her.
  6   JOHN AYLETT.

THOSE Gentlemen who may be inclined to consign any tobacco to *William Lee*, Esq; merchant in *London*, are respectfully acquainted, that a good *British* built ship will be in *York* river, in a very short time, to take in tobacco to his address, when the Gentlemen shippers will be waited on by the Captain in person.   (2)

WILLIAMSBURG, *April* 28, 1775.
I INTEND to leave the colony immediately.   JOHN KATHER.

Recreated from Purdie's Virginia Gazette, May 5, 1775.

THE KING'S SPEECH.

[*By the ship Barclay,* Capt. Cox, *arrived at* Philadelphia, *from* Liverpool.]

His MAJESTY's most gracious SPEECH from the Throne, on Friday the 6th May, 1775.

My Lords and Gentlemen,

I Cannot in Justice to you, forbear to express my entire satisfaction in your conduct during the course of this important session. You have maintained, with a firm and steady resolution, the rights of my crown and the authority of Parliament; which I will ever consider as inseparable. You have protected and promoted the commercial Interests of my Kingdom; and you have at the same time, given convincing proofs of your readiness (as far as the constitution will allow you) to gratify the wishes, and remove the apprehensions of my subjects in America; and I am persuaded, that the most salutary effects must, in the end, result from measures formed and conducted on such principles.

The late mark of your affectionate attachment to me, and to the Queen, and the zeal and unanimity which accompanied it, demand my particular thanks.

I have the satisfaction to acquaint you, that as well from the general disposition of other powers, as from the solemn assurances which I have received, I have great reason to expect the continuance of peace. Nothing on my part, consistent with the maintenance of the honour and interest of my kingdoms, shall be wanting to secure the public tranquility.

Gentlemen of the House,

It gives me much concern, that the unhappy disturbances in some of my colonies, have obligated me to propose to you an augmentation of my army, and have prevented me from compleating the intended reduction of the establishment of my naval forces.

I cannot sufficiently thank you for the cheerfulness and public spirit with which you have granted the supplies for the several services of the current year.

My Lords and Gentlemen,

I have nothing to desire of you, but to use your best endeavours to preserve and to cultivate, in your several counties, the same regard for the public order, and the same discernment of their truest interests, which have in these times distinguished the character of my faithful and beloved people, and the continuance of which cannot fail to render them happy at home and respected abroad.

Recreated from The Hartford Courant, July 24, 1775.

DR. FRANKLIN HIGHLY PLEASED.

Extract of a letter from Philadelphia *to a gentleman at* New York, *May 6, 1775.*

"Yesterday evening Dr. Franklin arrived here from London in six weeks, which he left the 20th of March, which has given great joy to this town. He says we have no favours to expect from the Ministry, nothing but submission will satisfy them, they expect little or no opposition will be made to their troops, those that are now coming are for New York, where it is expected they will be received with cordiality.

"As near as we can learn there are about four thousand troops coming in this fleet, the men of war and transports are in a great measure loaded with dry goods, to supply New York, and the country round it.

"Dr. Franklin is highly pleased to find us arming and preparing for the worst events, he thinks nothing else can save us from the most abject slavery and destruction, at the same time he encourages us to believe a spirited opposition will be the means of our salvation. The Ministry are alarmed at every opposition, and lifted up again at every thing which appears the least in their favour, every letter and every paper from hence are read by them."

••••

We hear Dr. Franklin has been by the unanimous vote of the Assembly of Pennsylvania, and approbation of the people, added to the number of delegates to attend the Continental Congress.

Recreated from The Hartford Courant, May 15, 1775.

By his Excellency the Right Hon. JOHN *Earl of* DUNMORE, *his Majesty's Lieutenant and Governor General of the Colony and Dominion of* VIRGINIA:

A PROCLAMATION.

WHEREAS I have been informed, from undoubted Authority, that a certain Patrick Henry, of the County of Hanover, and a Number of deluded followers, have taken up Arms, chosen their Officers, and styling themselves an Independent Company, have marched out of their County, encamped, and put themselves in a Posture of War, and have written and despatched Letters to divers Parts of the Country, exciting the People to join in their outrageous and rebellious Practices, to the great Terror of all his Majesty's faithful Subjects, and in open Defiance of Law and Government; and have committed other Acts of Violence, particularly in extorting from his Majesty's Receiver General the Sum of 330l. under Pretence of replacing the Powder I thought proper to order from the Magazine; whence it undeniably appears, that there is no longer the least Security for the Life or Property of any Man: WHEREFORE I have thought proper, with the Advice of his Majesty's Council, and in his Majesty's Name, to issue this my Proclamation, strictly charging all Persons, upon their Allegiance, not to aid, abet, or give Countenance to, the said Patrick Henry, or any other Persons concerned in such unwarrantable Combinations; but, on the Contrary, to oppose them and their Designs by every Means; which Designs must, otherwise, inevitably involve the whole County in the most direful Calamity, as they will call for the Vengeance of offended Majesty and the insulted Law, to be exerted here, to vindicate the constitutional Authority of Government.

GIVEN under my Hand, and the seal of the Colony, at WILLIAMSBURG, *this 6th Day of May,* 1775, *and in the 15th Year of his Majesty's Reign.* DUNMORE.

GOD SAVE THE KING.

Recreated from The Virginia Gazette, May 13, 1775.

CANNON ON HORSEBACK.

LONDON, *May* 9.—Upwards of 1000 pieces of cannon, of a new construction, so light as to be carried by a man on horseback, and which carry balls from four to seven pounds weight, and 10,000 stands of arms, were shipped from the Tower in the course of the last week, for the use of the troops in America.

Fifty tons of ordnance stores is ordered to be got ready with all expedition to be shipped for the use of his Majesty's forces at Boston.

Orders are given for the men of war destined for the Newfoundland station, to be considerably augmented to carry into execution an act of this session, to prevent any vessel from some of the North American provinces fishing on that coast, &c.

May 12.—They write from Guernsey, that three French men of war, with upwards of 30 sail of vessels under convoy, passed by that island on the 4th instant, about eight o'clock in the evening, and that they were not all out of sight the next morning at day-break.

Recreated from The Pennsylvania Gazette, July 5, 1775.

PROVIDENCE, *May* 8.

Mr. John Brown, of this Place, Merchant, whom we mentioned in our last to have been taken in a Packet Boat, and sent to Boston has been released by the Admiral and General, and returned here on Wednesday Night.

Recreated from The Hartford Courant, May 15, 1775.

SENECAS SUPPORT AMERICANS.

WORCESTER, *May* 10.—We hear that the Senecas, one of the Six nations of Indians, are determined to support the Americans against the arbitrary exactions of the British Parliament, and, if desired, will lend their help in this day of general distress, expecting if the Colonies are subjected, they shall also fall a sacrifice to the relentless fury of Great Britain.

Recreated from The Pennsylvania Packet, May 29, 1775.

HANCOCK'S HOUSE PILLAGED.

NO MORE YANKEE DOODLE.

WORCESTER, *May* 10.—The Tories of Boston seem in general, as desirous of quitting that capital as the Whigs, many have embarked in a ship, Capt. Callahan master, for London, some have gone to Halifax, and others, among whom are a number of Addressers to the late Gov. Hutchinson, chose rather to put confidence in the people, and are retiring into the country.

It is confidently asserted, that several houses in Boston belonging to persons who had moved out of that distressed town, have been plundered of effects left therein, by the soldiery. The Hon. John Hancock, Esqr's. house, we hear was entered by a number of soldiers, who began to pillage and break down the fences; but upon complaint being made to Gen. Gage, he ordered the fences to be repaired, and Earl Piercy to take possession of the house.

All accounts agree that five or six hundred marines, to reinforce the King's troops, arrived at Boston on Saturday last from Nova Scotia.

Our army have begun an entrenchment at Cambridge.

General Gage is making Boston as secure from an attack as he possibly can. However, it is thought by some that the bulwarks are not so strong as to be impregnable.

When the second brigade marched out of Boston to reinforce the first, nothing was played by the fifes and drums but *Yankee Doodle*, which had become their favourite tune ever since that *notable exploit*, which did such honour to the troops of *Britain's King*, of tarring and feathering a poor country man in Boston, and parading with him through the principal streets, under arms with their bayonets fixed. Upon their return to Boston, one asked his brother officer how he liked the tune now, "*D__n them*", returned he, *"they made us dance it till we were tired."* Since which *Yankee Doodle* sounds less sweet to their ears.

There were not above 400 at most, of our people who pursued and engaged the murdering troops of Briton's King, from Concord to Charlestown.

The Commanding officer at Cambridge has given leave to regulars who were taken prisoners, either to go to Boston and join their respective regiments, or have liberty to work in the country for those who would employ them. In consequence of which those who were confined in this town, fifteen in number, heartily requested to be employed by the people, not choosing to return to their regiments to fight against their American brethren, tho' some of them expressed willingness to spill their blood in defence of their King *in a righteous cause*. They all set out yesterday for different towns.

• • • •

One Mansfield, a breeches-maker, in Boston, who went out with the troops in the late engagement, was in the skirmish fired at by the regulars through mistake, they taking him to be one of our men. The ball entered his neck and came out of his mouth. *Wretches like him often meet their joyful reward.*

Recreated from The Hartford Courant, May 15, 1775.

BRITISH ANXIETY HEIGHTENS.

Extract of a Letter from LONDON, *dated May* 10.

"Before you receive this, you will probably have determined the fate of both parts of the British empire in that venerable Assembly the Continental Congress. We have no fears for you, but the infatuation of the Ministry here gives us as much to apprehend as ever. It is still the full persuasion of all the Courtiers (and I almost think of the greatest part of the nation) that notwithstanding all your seeming firmness and hostile preparations, you will submit to any thing rather than contend with us. A very short time will now determine that matter; for there is no appearance of any relaxation here. We wait for the great event with the most anxious and distressing impatience."

Recreated from The Pennsylvania Gazette, July 5, 1775.

DELEGATES AT NEW YORK.

NEW YORK, *May* 11.—On Saturday last arrived from the eastward, on their way to Philadelphia, to attend the continental congress, the Hon. John Hancock, and Thomas Cushing, Esqrs.; Samuel Adams and Robert Treat Paine, Esqrs.; Delegates for the Province of Massachusetts Bay; and the Hon. Eliphabet Dyer & Roger Sherman, Esqrs.; and Silas Deane, Esq.; Delegates for the colony of Connecticut. They were met a few miles out of town by a great number of the principal gentlemen of this place, in carriages and on horseback, and escorted into the city by near a thousand men under arms, the roads were lined with greater numbers of people than were ever known on any occasion before. Their arrival was announced by the ringing of bells, and other demonstrations of joy. They had double centries placed at the doors of their lodging.

The General Assembly of the Colony of Rhode Island have resolved to raise immediately Fifteen Hundred effective Men, for the Preservation of the Liberties of America.

Recreated from The Hartford Courant, May 15, 1775.

LADY DUNMORE RETURNS HOME.

WILLIAMSBURG, *May* 12.

THIS day, about two o'clock, the Right Hon. the Countess Dunmore, with the rest of the Governor's family, who have for some time past been on board the Fowey man of war, arrived at the palace in this city, to the great joy of the inhabitants, and, we have no doubt, of the whole country, who have the most unfeigned regard for her Ladyship, and wish her long to live amongst them.

HALIFAX, *April* 27, 1775.

I INTEND to leave the colony with all convenient speed.

GEORGE YUILLE.

Recreated from Purdie's Virginia Gazette, May 12, 1775.

DELEGATES ARRIVING AT CONGRESS.

PHILADELPHIA, *May* 10.—On Friday evening arrived here Captain Osborne, from London, in whom came passenger the worthy Dr. BENJAMIN FRANKLIN, Agent for the Massachusetts government and this province. Saturday last John Sullivan, and John Langdon, Esqrs., Delegates for New Hampshire arrived here.

Monday evening the brig Charlestown Packet, Captain Barton, arrived here from South Carolina, with whom passengers the Hon. Henry Middleton, Christopher Gadsden, John Rutledge, Esqrs., Delegates for that province. Thomas Lynch, Esq., the other Delegate, sailed the day before in a schooner.

Yesterday arrived the Hon. Peyton Randolph, Esq., George Washington, Patrick Henry, Richard Henry Lee, Edmund Pendleton, Benjamin Harrison, and Richard Bland, Esquires, Delegates for Virginia. Richard Caswell, and Joseph Hewes, Esquires, Delegates for North Carolina. Samuel Chace, Thomas Johnson, and John Hall, Esquires, Delegates, for Maryland. Also Caesar Rodney, and George Reidy, Esquires, Delegates for the Counties of New Castle, Kent and Sussex, on Delaware.

And this Day the Hon. John Hancock, and Thomas Cushing, Esquires, Samuel Adams, John Adams, and Robert Treat Paine, Esquires, Delegates for the Province of Massachusetts Bay; and the Hon. Eliphalet Dyer, Robert Sherman, and Silas Deane, Esquires, Delegates for the Colony of Connecticut, are expected in town from New York.

Recreated from The Pennsylvania Gazette, May 10, 1775.

A GENTLEMAN, who ſerved as Officer all laſt War in the King of Pruſſia's Army, offers his Service to the Province of Pennſylvania. The Men that will be entruſted to his Care, he obliges himſelf to teach, in a very ſhort time, the moſt uſeful and neceſſary Manœuvres, eſpecially quick Firing, even without a Rammer, for which purpoſe he knows how to prepare ſuitable Cartridges, beſides the Art of advancing and retiring properly, and laſtly how to avoid all Confuſion in an Engagement. Enquire of the PRINTERS hereof.

Recreated from The Pennsylvania Gazette, May 31, 1775.

FORTY DOLLARS REWARD.

RUN away from the subscriber, on the 19th instant, at night, two servant men, viz. THOMAS SPEARS, a joiner, born in *Bristol*, about 20 years of age, five feet six and a half inches high, slender made, has light gray or bluish eyes, a little pock marked, freckled, sandy coloured hair cut pretty short, his voice is coarse and somewhat drauling; he took with him a coat, waistcoat, and breeches, of light brown duffil, with black horn buttons, another light coloured cloth waistcoat, old leather breeches, check and osnabrug shirts, a pair of new milled yarn stockings, a pair of old ribbed do. new osnabrug trousers, and felt hat, not much the worse for wear.------WILLIAM WEBSTER, a brick-maker, born in *Scotland*, and talks pretty broad, about five feet six inches high, well made, rather turned of 30, with light brown hair, and a roundish face; he had on an olive coloured coat, pretty much worn, with black horn buttons, duffil waistcoat and breeches, the same as *Spears*'s, osnabrug trousers, and check and osnabrug shirts. They went off in a small yawl, with turpentine sides and bottom, the inside painted with a mixture of tar and red lead. Masters of vessels are cautioned against receiving of them, and the above reward is offered to any person who will deliver them at my dwelling-house in this county, or twenty dollars for each, from

(2) GEORGE WASHINGTON.

FAIRFAX county, *April* 23, 1775.

Recreated from Purdie's Virginia Gazette, May 12, 1775.

COL. ARNOLD COMMANDS PROVINCIALS.

NEW YORK, *May* 15, 1775.

We hear the important Passes of Crown Point and Ticonderoga, are taken Possession of by a Number of Provincials from Connecticut, in order to prevent the Canadians and Indians from making Incursions into the New England Provinces; but by a Letter from Hartford, on the 7th Instant, we hear Governor Carleton had dispatched a Number of Regulars from Canada, and reinforced those garrisons; however, Col. Arnold who commanded the Provincial Party, was determined to proceed at all Events, as he expected a Reinforcement on his March.

The Martial Spirit diffused through this Province at this Juncture is almost beyond Conception; many new Companies have been already raised in this City, and several more are in Contemplation, most of them are in very neat Uniforms; much of their Time is spent in perfecting themselves in the Manual Exercise, and several of them are already so compleat as to vie with the best Veterans.

Recreated from The Pennsylvania Gazette, May 17, 1775.

BRITISH EMBARKATION STOPPED.

NEWPORT, (RHODE-ISLAND) *May* 15.—A gentleman, who left Roxbury, near Boston, on Wednesday last, says, that just before he came away, two letters were received there from England, by a vessel in a short passage to Salem, one was dated the third, the other the 9th of April; both of which gave an account, that most of the troops, which had been several times ordered to embark, were, on account of the great disturbances among the people finally stopped.

Yesterday a sloop arrived here from Boston, with about 80 of the inhabitants of that barbarously distressed town.

It is said the Governor of Canada, has wrote General Gage, he can get officers there, to act against New England, but no privates, the people in general declaring they will not fight against the Colonies.

AMERICANS TAKE TICONDEROGA

CROWN POINT ALSO FALLS.

PHILADELPHIA, *May* 24, 1775.—On Wednesday evening, the 17th instant, arrived here, John Brown, Esq., from Ticonderoga, express to the General Congress, from whom we learn, that on the beginning of this instant, a company of about fifty men, from Connecticut, and the western part of Massachusetts, joined upwards of one hundred from Bennignton, *in New York government*, and the adjacent towns, proceeded to the eastern side of Lake Champlain, and on the night before the 11th current, crossed the Lake with 85 men (not being able to obtain craft to transport the rest) and about day-break invested the fort, whose gate, contrary to expectation, they found shut, but the wicker open, through which, with the Indian war whoop, all that could, entered one by one, others scaling the wall on both sides of the gate, and instantly secured and disarmed the centries, and pressed into the parade, where they formed the hollow square; but immediately quitting that order, they rushed into the several barracks on three sides of the fort, and seized on the garrison, consisting of two officers, and upwards of forty privates, whom they brought out, disarmed, put under guard, and have since sent prisoners to Hartford, in Connecticut. All this was performed in about ten minutes, without the loss of life, or a drop of blood on our side, and but very little on that of the King's troops.

In the fort were found about thirty barrels of flour, a few barrels of pork, seventy odd chests of leaden ball, computed at three hundred tons, about ten barrels of powder in poor condition, near two hundred pieces of ordnance of all sizes, from eighteen pounders downwards, at Ticonderoga and Crown-point, which last place, being held only by a corporal and eight men, falls of course into our hands.

By this sudden expedition, planned by some principal persons in the four neighbouring colonies, that important pass is now in the hands of the Americans, where we trust the *wisdom* of the Grand Continental Congress, will take effectual measures to secure it, as it may be depended on that the administration means to form an army in Canada, composed of British regulars, French and Indians, to attack the colonies on that side.

Mr. Brown brought intercepted letters from Lieut. Malcolm Fraser, to his friends in New England, from which appear, that Gen. Carleton has almost unlimited powers, civil and military, and has issued orders for raising a Canadian regiment, in which Mr. Fraser observes, the officers find difficulty, as the common people are by no means fond of the service.

BRITISH FOOL INDIANS.

Mr. Brown also related, that two regular officers of the 26th regiment, now in Canada, applied to two Indians, one a head warrior of the Caughanawaga tribe, to go out with them on a hunt, to the south and east of the rivers St. Lawrence and Sorrel, and pressing the Indians farther and farther on said course, they at length arrived at Cohass, where the Indians say they were stopped and interrogated by the inhabitants, to whom they pretended they were only on a hunt, which the inhabitants (as the Indians told Mr. Brown) replied must be false, as no hunters used silver (bright) barrelled guns.

However, the Cohass people dismissed them all; and when they returned into the woods, the Indian warrior insisted on knowing what their real intention was, and they told him, that it was to reconnoiter the woods, to find a passage for an army to march to the assistance of the King's friends in Boston. The Indian asked, where they would get the army? They answered in Canada, and that the Indians in the upper castles would join them.

The Chief, on this, expressed resentment, that he, being one of the headmen of the Caughanawaga tribe, had not been consulted in the affair. But Mr. Brown presumes the aversion of this honest fellow and his friends to their schemes, was the reason of their being kept from the knowledge.

Recreated from The Pennsylvania Gazette, May 24, 1775.

In Congress.

Resolved Unanimously, May 17, 1775.

That all exportations to Quebec, Nova Scotia, the Island of St. John's, and to East and West Florida, immediately cease; and that no provisions of any kind, or other necessarys, be furnished to the British Fisheries on the American Coasts, until it be otherwise determined by the Congress.

A true copy from the minutes.
CHARLES THOMPSON, Secretary.

GENERALS ARRIVE AT BOSTON.

NEW YORK, *May* 22.—By Capt. Lawrence from Boston, we are informed, that the Cerberus sloop of war, with the Generals Howe, Clinton, and Burgoyne, are arrived there.

Recreated from The Pennsylvania Packet, May 29, 1775.

CONNECTICUT VOLUNTEERS.

HARTFORD, *May* 22.—We hear that the six regiments of volunteers, ordered to be raised by the General Assembly of this colony, for the defence of the same, are all filled, and only wait for marching orders. The greatest part of those destined for Boston are now on their march for the head quarters at Cambridge. The company from Farmington, under the command of Capt. Noadiah Hooker, passed through this town for that place on Thursday last; and on Saturday a company from Middletown, commanded by Major Meigs, and Col. Samuel Wylly's company, of this place, are ordered to march on Thursday next. May God preserve them, and make them VICTORIOUS!

NEWPORT, *May* 22.—An express arrived here this morning from Providence, with advice, that a party of soldiers from Boston had landed at Weymouth, and burnt the town down, and were ravaging the country when the express came away. Troops from all parts of the country were going to oppose them. The particulars are not yet come to hand.

TROOPS TAKE SLOOP.

NEW YORK, *May* 29.—Saturday morning last, an express arrived here from Ticonderoga, in 8 days. By him we learn that Major Arnold dispatched Mr. Oswell, and 35 men, in a schooner and some battoes, to take possession of a sloop that lay at St. John's; at the same time Capt. Ethan Allen set out with 80 men to facilitate the undertaking, and stopped on the way for a reinforcement of 20 more; but Mr. Oswell pursued his scheme, and took possession of the vessel that lay at St. John's, with all the battoes, and made 14 soldiers and 6 seamen prisoners of war, before Capt. Allen came up; but the latter, contrary to advice, proceeded to St. John's, where he unluckily fell in with 250 Regulars that were dispatched to the succor of Crown Point and Ticonderoga, and after exchanging a few shots, made a good retreat, with the loss of 3 men only.

TRANSPORTS FROM IRELAND.

Extract of a Letter from NEW YORK, *May* 23.

"A few hours ago a person arrived here from Boston, who brings an account, that several Transports with a few Troops are arrived there from Ireland. He likewise mentions, that the people in Ireland would let no more Transports take in any provisions, and the troops of horse which were coming out had entirely declined to come—the former occasioning a small skirmish, those troops which were already embarked on board the vessels were obliged to disembark, in order to defend themselves and quell the people, in which fray seven officers were killed."

HANCOCK APPOINTED PRESIDENT.

May 31. On Wednesday last, the Hon. Peyton Randolph, Esq., set off for Virginia, in order to attend in his place, as Speaker of the Honourable House of Burgesses of that Colony, called by proclamation to meet at Williamsburg, on Thursday the first of June next; and the Hon. John Hancock, Esq., was appointed President of the Congress in his room.

Recreated from The Pennsylvania Gazette, May 31, 1775.

CUSTOM-HOUSE, PHILADELPHIA.

INWARD ENTRIES.

Brig Charlotte, J. Fryers, Rhode-Island.
Sloop America, P. Allen, Salem, N. E.
Brig Jenny, W. Workman, South-Carolina.
Brig Minerva, E. Wigglesworth, Surinam.
Sloop Mary, M. Siddon, Tortola.
Brig Speedwell, S. G. Frith, Grenadoes.
Brig Hannah, D. Coates, St. Lucia.
Brig Addition, T. Candell, Barcelona.
Snow Jane, T. Whitlock, Ditto.
Sch. Elizabeth, J. Watt, Jamaica.
Brig Sally, T. Nelson, Ditto.
Ship America, J. M'Kay, Londonderry.
Brig Sea Nymph, W. Moore, South-Carolina.

OUTWARDS.

Sloop Sally, J. Alberson, New-York.
Brig Polly, J. Robinson, Cork.
Brig Two Friends, R. Inkson, St. Vincents.
Brig Unity, P. Flynn, St. Kitts.
Ship Nancy and Sukey, J. Robinson, Falmouth.
Sch. Mary, J. Allen, Jamaica.
Brig Addition, T. Candell, Lisbon.
Brig George, W. Simpson, Ditto.

CLEARED.

Sloop Prudence, H. Norris, Georgia.
Sloop Dispatch, B. Minos, New-Providence.
Sch. Rebecca, J. Holden, Virginia.
Sloop James, A. Gibbons, North-Carolina.
Sch. Betsey and Nancy, J. Poulton, Georgia.
Sloop Molly, B. Partridge, Portsmouth, N. E.
Brig John, J. Ashmead, Barbados.
Sch. Lloyd, J. Smith, South-Carolina.
Sloop Betsey, V. Wightman, Rhode-Island.
Brig Success, G. May, Cork.
Sch. Jenny, R. Benison, Jamaica.
Brig Chance, J. Craig, Grenadoes.
Sloop Discovery, B. Quithell, North-Carolina.
Ship Molly, T. Randall, Newfoundland.
Brig Betsy, T. Bernard, Jamaica.
Ship Jane, J. Mathie, Bristol.
Sch. Molly, G. Robotham, Cadiz.
Brig Betsy and Nancy, P. Flynn, St. Kitts.

Recreated from The Pennsylvania Packet, May 29, 1775.

LETTER FROM ETHAN ALLEN.

A correspondent has sent an exact copy of a letter addressed to the merchants of MONTREAL *by* ETHAN ALLEN, *who commanded the provincials at the taking of* CROWN POINT *and* TICONDEROGA, *and who penetrated into* QUEBEC *as far as* ST. JOHN'S; *the authenticity of which may be depended on.*

Gentlemen,   *May* 18, 1775.

I have the pleasure to acquaint you that Lake George and Champlain, with the fortresses, artillery, &c. particularly the armed sloop of George the Third, with all water carriages of these lakes, are now in possession of these colonies. I expect the English merchants, as well as all virtuous disposed gentlemen, will be in the interest of the colonies. The advanced guard of the army is now at St. John's, and desire immediately to have a personal intercourse with you. Your immediate assistance as to provisions, ammunition, and spirituous liquors is wanted, and forthwith expected, not as a donation; for I am impowered by the colonies to purchase the same, and desire you would forthwith and without further notice, prepare for the use of the army those articles to the amount of 500l. and deliver the same to me at St. John's, or at least a part of it instantaneously, as the soldiers press on faster than provisions. I need not inform you that my directions from the colonies are not to contend with, or any way injure or molest the Canadians or Indians; but on the other hand treat them with the greatest friendship and kindness. You will be pleased to communicate the same with them, and some of you immediately visit me at this place, while others are active in delivering the provisions.

I write in haste; and am, Gentlemen,
      Your obedient and humble servant,
            ETHAN ALLEN.

To Mr. James Morrison, and the Merchants that are friendly to the cause of liberty in MONTREAL.

Recreated from The Hartford Courant, October 16, 1775.

BATTLE AT CHELSEA.

On Saturday, May 27th, a party of the American army at Cambridge, to the number of between 200 and 300 men, had orders to drive off the live stock from Hog and Noddle's Island, which lie near Chelsea and Winnesimmet, on the N.E. side of Boston harbour. From Chelsea to Hog Island, at low water, it is but knee high, and from that to Noddle's Island about the same. The stock on the former belonging to Mr. Oliver Wendell, at Boston, and Mr. Jonathan Jackson, at Newberry Port; that on Noddle's Island was owned by Mr. Williams, of Boston, who hires the island.

About 11 o'clock, A.M. between 20 and 30 men went from Chelsea to Hog Island, and from thence to Noddle's Island, to drive off the stock which was there, but were interrupted by a schooner and a sloop, dispatched from the fleet in Boston harbour, and 40 marines, who had been stationed on the island to protect the live stock.

However, they sent off 2 fine English stallions, 2 colts, and 2 cows, killed 15 horses, 2 colts, and 3 cows, burnt a large barn full of salt hay, and an old farm house. By this time they were fired on from the schooner and sloop, and a large number of marines, in boats, sent from the several men of war, upon which they retreated to a ditch on the marsh, and kept themselves undiscovered till they had the opportunity to fire on the marines, when they shot down two dead, and wounded two more, one of whom died soon after. They then retreated to Hog Island, where they were joined by the remainder of their party from Chelsea, and drove off all the stock thereon, viz:. between 300 and 400 sheep and lambs, some cows, horses, &c. During this there were firings between the provincials, and the schooner, sloop, boats, and marines on the other island.

Having cleared Hog Island, the provincials drew up on Chelsea Neck, and sent for a reinforcement of 800 men, and two pieces of cannon (4 pounders) which arrived about 9 o'clock in the evening; soon after which general Putnam went down and hailed the schooner, and told the people that, if they would submit, they should have good quarters, which the schooner returned with 2 cannon shot; this was immediately answered with 2 cannon from the provincials. Upon this a very heavy fire ensued from both sides, which lasted till eleven o'clock at night, when the fire from the schooner ceased, the fire from the shore being so hot that her people were obliged to quit her, and take to the boats, a great number of which had been sent from the ships to their assistance, and also a large reinforcement of marines sent to Noddle's Island, with two 12 pounders.

The schooner being thus left, drove ashore, where about break of day, the provincials carried some hay under her stern, and set her on fire, the sloop keeping up a small fire on them; at which time a heavy cannonading was begun at Noddle's Island hill, with the 12 pounders upon the provincials; also general Putnam kept a heavy fire on the sloop, which disabled her much, and killed many of her men, so that she was obliged to be towed off by the boats, when the firing ceased, excepting a few shot which were exchanged between the party at Chelsea, and the marines on Noddle's Island.

Thus ended this long action, without the loss of one provincial, and only four wounded, one of whom was wounded by the bursting of his own gun, and another only lost his little finger. The loss of the enemy amounted to 20 killed, and 50 wounded. The provincials took out of the schooner 4 double fortified 4 pounders, 12 swivels, chief of her rigging and sails, many clothes, some money, &c.

IN PROVINCIAL CONGRESS, AT NEW YORK, *May* 31.

RESOLVED, that it be recommended to the inhabitants of this colony in general immediately to furnish themselves with necessary arms and ammunition, to use all diligence to perfect themselves in the military art, and, if necessary, to form, themselves into companies for that purpose, until the further orders of this congress.

A true copy from the minutes,
ROBERT BENSON, Secretary.

Recreated from Rind's Virginia Gazette, June 22, 1775.

PHILADELPHIA.

IN CONGRESS, *Monday, May 29, 1775.*
On motion resolved,

That no provisions or necessaries of any kind be exported to the island of Nantucket, except from the colony of Massachusetts Bay; the convention of which colony is desired to take measures for effectually providing the said island, upon their application to purchase the same, with as much provision as shall be necessary for its internal use and no more.

The congress deeming it of great importance to North America, that the British fishery should not be furnished with provisions from this continent, through Nantucket, earnestly recommended a vigilant execution of this resolve to all committees.

A true copy from the minutes,
CHARLES THOMPSON, Secretary.

IN CONGRESS, *June 2, 1775.*
Upon motion resolved,

That no bill of exchange, draught, or order of any officer in the British army or navy, their agents or contractors, be received or negotiated, or any money supplied to them by any person in America. That no provisions or necessaries of any kind be furnished to or for the use of the British army or navy in the colony of Massachusetts Bay—and that no vessel employed in transporting British troops to America, or from one part of North America to another, or warlike stores or provisions for said troops, be freighted or furnished with provisions or necessaries, until further orders from this congress.

A true copy from the minutes,
CHARLES THOMPSON, Secretary.

WANTED IMMEDIATELY,
A Journeyman PRINTER,
Who is willing to work at Cafe or Prefs---by the Printer hereof.

Recreated from The Hartford Courant, June 12, 1775.

"TAKE EVERY PROVISION VESSEL."

PORTSMOUTH, NEW HAMPSHIRE, *June 3.*

LAST Tuesday about 30 or 40 men from on board the Scarborough man of war, now in this harbour, came on shore at Fort William and Mary, and have torn down a great part of the breastwork of said fort, and did other damage.

The day before this attempt, the Scarborough took two provision vessels, loaded with corn, pork, flour, rye, &c. coming in from Long Island; which were for the relief of this place; as the inhabitants are in great want of provisions; and notwithstanding the most prudent application of the principal gentlemen of this town, the captain refused to release them.

Upon this unwarrantable transaction, the inhabitants of this and neighbouring towns, were greatly alarmed; and the next morning between 500 and 600 men in arms, went to the battery called Jerry's point, and brought off eight cannon, 24 and 32 pounders, being the whole that were there; weighing 4800lb. each, and brought them up to this town.

While they were taking the above cannon, the Canceaux, with a tender, set sail with the two provision vessels for Boston. The next day the town was full of men from the country in arms.

This uncommon exertion of arbitrary power, immediately alarmed the inhabitants, and the committee of safety met, a memorial was by their approbation presented to the governor and council, who took every prudent method in their power to pacify the people, and to obtain a release of the captures.

His Excellency repaired on board the Scarborough, and informed the captain that the provisions were the property of some of the inhabitants, who had before contracted for the same, but the only answer he could obtain was "that admiral Graves, and the general had forwarded orders to take every provision vessel that should be met with, on every station, and to send them forthwith to Boston for the supply of the army and navy."

Recreated from The Maryland Gazette, June 22, 1775.

OUR LIVES AND FORTUNES.

CHARLES-TOWN ASSOCIATION,

Unanimously agreed to in Provincial Congress of SOUTH-CAROLINA, *on Saturday the 3d of June,* 1775.

THE actual Commencement of Hostilities against this Continent, by the British troops, in the bloody scene on the 19th of April last, near Boston—the increase of arbitrary impositions from a wicked and despotic Ministry, and the dread of instigated insurrections in the Colonies, are causes sufficient to drive an offended people to the use of arms: We therefore, the subscribers, inhabitants of South Carolina, holding ourselves bound by that most sacred of all obligations, the duty of good citizens towards an injured country, and thoroughly convinced that under our present distressed circumstances, we shall be justified before God and Man, in resisting force by force, DO UNITE ourselves, under every tie of religion and honour, and associate, as a band in her defence, against every Foe:—Hereby solemnly engaging, that, whenever our Continental or Provincial Councils shall decree it necessary, we shall go forth, and be ready to sacrifice our lives and fortunes to secure her freedom and safety.

This obligation to continue in full force until a reconciliation shall take place between Great Britain and America, upon Constitutional Principles; an event which we most ardently desire. And we will hold all those persons inimicable to the Liberty of the Colonies, who shall refuse to subscribe to this Association.

Subscribed by every Member present, on the 4th *day of June,* 1775.

Certified by HENRY LAURENS, President.

TO BE SOLD, A STRONG healthy NEGROE MAN, 21 Years of Age, this Country born, who has been bred to Farming, and understands it well in all its Branches. Enquire of JOHN SWIFT, of Bensalem Township, in Bucks County.

Recreated from The Pennsylvania Gazette, July 5, 1775.

OLD MAN'S COMPANY.

PHILADELPHIA, *June* 7.—The spirit of opposition to the arbitrary and tyrannical acts of the Ministry and Parliament of Great Britain, hath diffused itself so universally throughout this province, that the people, even to its most extended frontiers, are indefatigable in training themselves to military discipline. The aged, as well as the young, daily march out under the banners of liberty, and discover a determined resolution to maintain her cause even until death.

In the town of Reading, there had been some time past three companies formed and very forward in their exercise; since, however, we are well informed a fourth company has associated under the name of the Old Man's Company. It consists of about 80 Gentlemen of the age of 40 and upwards. Many of them have been in the military service in Germany.

The person who, at their first assembling, led them to the field, is 97 years of age, has been 40 years in the regulars service, and in seventeen pitched battles; and the drummer is 84. In lieu of the cockade, they wear in their hats a black crepe, as expressive of their sorrow for the mournful events which have occasioned them, at their late time of life, to take arms against our brethren, in order to preserve their liberty which they left their native country to enjoy.

A correspondent, who lately saw them perform their exercise for several hours, says, he discovered such a sober firmness in their countenances, and such vigour and address in handling their arms and performing their evolutions, as filled him with the highest respect and esteem for this truly venerable band.

Recreated from The Hartford Courant, July 3, 1775.

All Sorts of Military Articles, Such as Cartouch-boxes, Morocco and other Sword-belts, Scabbards, Pistol Holsters, Rangers Pouches, &c. All made on the best Construction, by WOLERE MING, In MARKET-STREET, about 10 Doors above the GOAL, Where the Military Gentlemen, from Town or Country, may be supplied on the most reasonable Terms, and on the shortest Notice.

Recreated from The Pennsylvania Gazette, May 31, 1775.

PRISONERS EXCHANGED.

CAMBRIDGE, *June* 8.—Tuesday last being the Day agreed on for the Exchange of Prisoners, between 12 and 1 o'clock, Dr. Warren and Brigadier General Putnam, in a Phaeton, together with Major Dunbar, and Lieut. Hamilton of the 64th on horseback; Lieut. Potter of the Marines, in a Chaise; John Hilton of the 47th, Alexander Campbell of the 5th; John Tyne, Samuel Marcy, Thomas Perry, and Thomas Sharp of the Marines, wounded Men, in two Carts; the whole escorted by the Wethersfield company, under the Command of Capt. Chester, entered the Town of Charlestown, and marching slowly through it, halted at the Ferry, where, upon a Signal being given, Major Moncrief landed from the Lively, in order to receive the Prisoners, and see his old Friend, General Putnam. Their meeting was truly cordial and affectionate.

The wounded Privates were soon on board the Lively; but Major Moncrief, and the other Officers, returned with General Putnam and Dr. Warren to the House of Dr. Foster, where an Entertainment was provided for them.

About 3 o'Clock a Signal was made by the Lively, that they were ready to deliver up our Prisoners; upon which General Putnam and Major Moncrief went to the Ferry, where they received Messrs. John Peck, James Hews, James Brewer, and Daniel Preston, of Boston, Messrs. Samuel Frost and Seth Russell, of Cambridge, Mr. Joseph Bell, of Danvers, Mr. Elijah Seaver, of Roxbury, and Caesar Augustus, a Negro Servant to Mr. Tileston, of Dorchester, who were conducted to the House of Dr. Foster, and there refreshed; after which the General and Major returned to their Company, and spent an Hour or two in a very agreeable Manner.

Between 5 and 6 o'Clock Major Moncrief, with the Officers that had been delivered to him, were conducted to the Ferry, where the Lively's Barge received them; after which General Putnam, with the Prisoners who had been delivered to him, &c. returned to Cambridge, escorted in the same manner as before.

The whole was conducted with the utmost Decency and good Humour. The Regular Officers expressed themselves as highly pleased; those who had been Prisoners politely acknowledged the genteel, kind Treatment they had received from their Captors. The Privates, who were all wounded Men, expressed in the strongest Terms, their grateful Sense of the Tenderness which had been shown them in their miserable Situation; some of them could do it only by their Tears.

It would have been to the honour of the British Arms, if the Prisoners taken from us could with Justice have made the same acknowledgement. It cannot be supposed that any Officers of Rank, or common Humanity, were knowing to the repeated cruel Insults that were offered them; but it may not be amiss to hint to the *Upstarts* concerned, two Truths, of which they seem to be totally ignorant, viz. That Compassion is as essential Part of the Character of a truly brave Man as daring; and that Insult offered to a Person entirely in the Power of the Insulter, smells as strong of Cowardice as it does Cruelty.

Recreated from The Hartford Courant, June 12, 1775.

Extract of a Letter from HARTFORD, *June 5.*

"Mr. Hide, the Boston post, reports that a vessel bound to London, on board of which Mr. Robert Temple, a high flying Tory, was passenger, sprung a leak soon after her departure and put into Plymouth (New England) to refit, that the people took Temple prisoner, sent him to the camp at Cambridge, secured his papers, and opened a great number of letters, many of which were from officers of the army at Boston. Those letters in general are full of complaints and expressions of uneasiness. Some of the officers desire and entreat to sell out, others say they are fighting in a bad cause, and apprehensive of mutiny; others mention a difference between the General and the Admiral, and that the army in general are disheartened and uneasy; other letters are full of invectives against the poor *Yankees*, as they call us. We hear the Provincial Congress will keep Temple as an hostage; but I hope they will let the vessel go with the above letters."

Recreated from The Pennsylvania Gazette, June 21, 1775.

LORD DUNMORE FLEES.

WILLIAMSBURG, *June* 8.—This morning the Right Honourable, the Earl of Dunmore, with his Lady and family, and Captain Foy, attended by some of his Lordship's domestics, left this city, and are now on board the Fowey man of war, lying in York river. His Lordship urges, in vindication of this precipitate retreat that he was apprehensive his life was in absolute danger from the infatuated and inflamed minds of the people. His Lordship says, it is not his intention to impede or obstruct the business of the Assembly; so far from it, that he hopes the gentlemen who compose the house, will proceed in the great business which they have before them with diligence and effect.

He farther says, that he shall endeavour to make access to him easy and safe, that the necessary communication between him and the house may be attended with the least inconvenience possible. His Lordship declares that he is still perfectly disposed to contribute all in his power to restore that harmony, the interruption of which is likely to cost so dear, to the repose, as well as to the comfort, of every individual.

In consequence of these declarations, the house immediately resolved themselves into a Committee, to take the same under consideration; who, after a mature deliberation, appointed a number of gentlemen to draw up an address to his Excellency; which being prepared and approved by the house, and concurred in by his Majesty's Council, two of that Hon. Board, and four members, were desired to wait upon his Excellency with the same; the purport of which was that the house were exceedingly concerned that his Lordship should even suspect that they would meditate a crime so horrid and atrocious as was couched in his message; that they were sorry his Lordship should leave the seat of government, as it might conduce to that great uneasiness which hath of late so unhappily prevailed in this country; that they think his Lordship ought to have communicated the grounds of his uneasiness to them, as, from their zeal and attachment to the preservation of order and good government, they should have judged it their indispensable duty to have endeavoured to remove every cause of disquietude; that they will cheerfully concur in any measures for the security of his Lordship and family; that the apprehensions of his amiable lady are productive of the greatest pain to them, and that they should think themselves happy in being able to restore tranquility to her; that they are proud his Lordship is willing for them to continue the business of the country; but think it almost impracticable, whilst his Lordship is absent, especially at this time, when the season of the year is so far advanced. This address concludes, with intreating his Lordship's return, with his lady and family, to the palace; which they are persuaded will be the most likely means of quieting the minds of the people.

The gentlemen appointed to wait on the Governor arrived at the Capitol between 1 and 2 o'clock, and were delivered this verbal message from his Excellency, "that, as the subject of their address was of the utmost concern to himself and his family, he would take time to consider, and return an answer, in writing, after he had maturely deliberated upon its contents." His Lordship behaved with the utmost politeness, and held a friendly conference with the deputies.

Recreated from The Pennsylvania Gazette, June 21, 1775.

NEW YORK, *June* 12.

We hear from Albany, that the General Committee for that City have resolved to raise 800 Men for the Defence of American Liberty; and that as soon as said Resolve was made public, three Companies were immediately inlisted, who have since marched for the Defence of the important Fortresses of Ticonderoga and Crown-Point.

The Provisional Congress of New Hampshire have voted 2000 Men to join the American Forces.

A Gentleman that left Boston about 6 days ago, asserts for Fact, that he saw landed on Long Wharf at that Place, out of one Boat alone, no less than 64 dead Men, that had been killed by the Provincials at the late Attack at Noddle's and Hog Islands.

Recreated from The Pennsylvania Gazette, June 14, 1775.

ARMY NEARLY COMPLEAT.

CAMBRIDGE, *June* 8.—We have the pleasure to inform the public, that the grand American army is nearly completed. Great numbers of the Connecticut, New Hampshire, and Rhode Island troops are arrived; among the latter is a fine company of artillery, with four field pieces. Many large pieces of battering cannon are expected soon from different places; 12 pieces, 18 and 24 pounders with a quantity of ordnance stores, we are informed, are already arrived from Providence.

NEW LONDON, *June* 9.—We hear that all the men of war which were in the harbours near Boston, have been called to that place, and that every method is taken to strengthen the town. The entrenchment at the fortification is now extended quite across the neck, by which the town is become an island. General Gage, by all his late conduct, appears to be greatly alarmed.

Recreated from The Maryland Gazette, June 22, 1775.

THE YANKOOS.

PHILADELPHIA, *June* 12.—We are favoured with the following etymology of the word YANKEE.

When the New England colonies were first settled, the inhabitants were obliged to fight their way against many nations of Indians. They found but little difficulty in subduing them all, except one tribe who were known by the name of the YANKOOS, which signifies *invincible*. After the waste of so much blood and treasure, the YANKOOS were at last subdued by the New Englanders. The remains of this nation (agreeable to the Indian custom) transferred their name to their conquerors. For a while they were called YANKOOS; but from a corruption, common to names in all languages, they got through time the name of YANKEES. A name which we hope will soon be equal to that of a Roman, or an *ancient* Englishman.

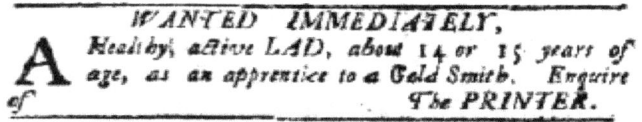

Recreated from The Hartford Courant, June 12, 1775.

COL. WASHINGTON TO COMMAND.

Extract of a letter from one of the VIRGINIA *delegates, to his friend now in* WILLIAMSBURG, *dated June* 14, 1775.

"Col. Washington has been pressed to take the supreme command of the American troops encamped at Roxbury, and I believe will accept the appointment, though with much reluctance, he being deeply impressed with the importance of that honourable trust, and diffident of his own (superiour) abilities.

"We have determined to keep 10,000 men in Massachusetts Bay, and 5000 in different parts of New York government, at the expense of the continent; and probably a large sum of money will be emitted, in order to carry on the war, preparations for which go rapidly on in this place.

"It seems likely that some of the newly arrived Generals were intended for the southern colonies, but no troops can be spared from Boston. The Provincials talk much of storming that town, and it is expected by many.

"The Congress will sit long. Adjusting the expenses of each colony for the common cause, and settling proper funds for the army, are subjects fruitful of debate, and of the utmost consequence."

Recreated from Purdie's Virginia Gazette, June 23, 1775.

BRITISH SEIZE SHIPS.

NEWPORT, *June* 12.—Last Tuesday a schooner from Philadelphia, loaded with provisions, bound to Nantucket, was brought here by one of the men of war's tenders. We hear the provisions in this vessel belong to near seventy poor men at Nantucket, and the chief their families had to depend on for a considerable time to come.

Last Saturday Capt. Cahoone, of this place, arrived here from Virginia, in a sloop loaded with Indian corn, &c. The vessel and cargo were taken into custody, by the man of war in the harbour.

The above vessels, it is supposed, will be sent to Boston.

Recreated from The Pennsylvania Packet, June 26, 1775.

BATTLE at BUNKER'S HILL.

From Capt. Elijah Hide, of LEBANON, *a spectator on* WINTER'S HILL, *during the whole action.*

ON Friday night, the 16th inst. 1500 of the Provincials went to Bunker's Hill, in order to intrench there, and continued intrenching till Saturday, 10 o'clock, when two thousand Regulars marched out of Boston, landed in Charlestown, and plundering it of all its valuable effects, set fire to it in ten different places at once; then dividing their army, part of it marched up in the front of the provincial intrenchment and began to attack the Provincials at long shot; the other part of their army marched round the town of Charlestown under cover of the smoke occasioned by the fire of the town.

The Provincial centries discovered the regulars marching upon their left wing. Upon notice of this given by the centry to the Connecticut forces posted on that wing, Capt. Nolton, of Ashford, with 400 of said forces, immediately repaired to, and pulled up, a post and rail fence, and carrying the posts and rails to another fence, put them together for a breast-work. Capt. Nolton gave orders to the men not to fire until the enemy were got within fifteen rods, and then not till the word was given. At the word's being given the enemy fell surprisingly; it was thought by spectators who stood at a distance that our men did great execution.

The action continued about two hours, when the Regulars on the right wing were put into confusion and gave way; the Connecticut troops closely pursued them, and were on the point of pushing their bayonets, when orders were received from General Pomeroy, for those who had been in action for two hours to fall back, and their places to be supplied by fresh troops.—These orders being mistaken for a direction to retreat, our troops on the right wing began a general retreat, which was handed to the left, the principal place of action, where Captains Nolton, Chester, Clark and Putnam, had forced the enemy to give way, and were before them for some considerable distance, and being warmly pursuing the enemy, were, with difficulty persuaded to retire; but the right wing, by mistaking the orders, having already retreated, the left, to avoid being encircled, were obliged to retreat also with the main body.

They retreated with precipitation across the causeway to Winter's Hill, in which they were exposed to the fire of the enemy from their shipping and floating batteries.—We sustained our principal loss in passing the causeway. The enemy pursued our troops to Winter's Hill, where the Provincials being reinforced by General Putnam, renewed the battle with great spirit, repulsed the enemy with great slaughter, and pursued them till they got under the cover of their cannon from the shipping.

When the enemy returned to Bunker's Hill, and the Provincials to Winter's Hill, where, after intrenching and erecting batteries, they on Monday began to fire upon the Regulars on Bunker's Hill, and on the ships and floating batteries in the harbour.

Then number of Provincials killed is between 40 and 70; 140 are wounded. Of the Connecticut troops, 16 were killed:—No officer among them was either killed or wounded, excepting Lieutenant Grosvenor, who was wounded in the hand. A Colonel, or Lieutenant Colonel of the New Hampshire forces, is among the dead. It is also said that Dr. Warren is undoubtedly among the slain.

The Provincials lost three iron six pounders, some intrenching tools, and a few knapsacks. The number of Regulars which first attacked the Provincials on Bunker's Hill was not less than 2000. The number of Provincials was only 1500, who it is supposed would soon have gained a complete victory had it not been for the unhappy mistake already mentioned. The Regulars were afterwards reinforced with a thousand men.

It is uncertain how great a number of Regulars were killed or wounded, but it is supposed by spectators who saw the whole action, that there could not be less than 400 or 500 killed. Mr. Gardner, who got out of Boston on Sunday evening, says, that there were 500 wounded men brought into that place the morning before he came out.

Recreated from The Pennsylvania Packet, June 26, 1775.

The following Account came to Hand last Saturday Night, by Post from WATERTOWN, *about 10 Miles from* BOSTON, *taken from a Paper printed at that Place, by Mr. Benjamin Edes, formerly a Printer in* BOSTON.

WATERTOWN, *June 19.*—Friday Night last a Number of the Provincials intrenched on Bunker Hill in Charlestown; and on Saturday about Noon a large Number of Regulars from Boston came across Charles's River, and landed a little below the Battery near the Point, when a bloody Battle commenced, many being killed and wounded on both sides.

The very heavy Fire from the Shipping, the Battery on Copp's Hill, Boston, together with the Train of the Enemy, obliged the Provincials to retreat a little this Side Charlestown Neck about Sunset, when the Enemy took Possession of our Entrenchment; after which they set the Town of Charlestown on Fire, beginning with the Meeting-House, and we hear they have not left one Building unconsumed.

The engagement continues on this Publication, 9 o'Clock, with Intermissions. The Confusion of the Times render it impracticable to give a particular Account of what has already occurred, but hope to give a good one in our next. The Provincials are in high spirits.

Recreated from The Pennsylvania Gazette, June 28, 1775.

JAMES GEDDY, GOLDSMITH, near the Church, Williamsburg,

HAS now on hand an assortment of JEWELLERY, which he would sell at an unusual low price for ready money.

N. B. He has just procured by the *Bland*, Capt. *Danby*, from *London*, a WATCH FINISHER, who will repair and clean repeating, horizontal, and plain watches, very reasonably, and warrant them twelve months, accidents excepted.

Recreated from Purdie's Virginia Gazette, June 2, 1775.

GEN. WASHINGTON BIDS ADIEU.

Extract of a Letter from GENERAL WASHINGTON, *dated the 20th of June, at* PHILADELPHIA, *to the independent companies of Fairfax, Prince William, Fauquier, Spotsylvania and Richmond,*

"GENTLEMEN,

"I am now about to bid adieu the companies under your respective commands, at least for a while. I have launched into a wide and extensive field, too boundless for my abilities, and far, very far, beyond my experience. I am called, by the unanimous voice of the colonies, to the command of the Continental Army; an honour I did not aspire to, an honour I was solicitous to avoid, upon a full conviction of my inadequacy to the importance of the service. The partiality of the Congress, however, assisted by a political motive, rendered my reasons unavailing; and I shall, to-morrow, set out for the camp near Boston. I have only to beg of you, therefore, before I go (especially as you did me the honour to put your companies under my direction, and know not how soon you may be called upon in Virginia for an exertion of your military skill) by no means to relax in the discipline of your respective companies."

NEW YORK, *June 19.*

Friday last the Mercury frigate, Capt. M'Carthy, arrived at Sandy Hook, in fourteen days from Boston. He was dispatched from thence by General Gage, to order whatever troops might arrive here (from England or Ireland) for Boston; and last Wednesday he luckily fell in with a transport from Cork, with part of the 44th regiment, bound into this place, but she soon stood to the eastward, and Capt. M'Carthy now waits at the Hook to give the like orders to the rest of the fleet that may arrive there.

Three or Four Hundred Wharff Logs
ARE WANTED.
Any Persons having such to dispose of, may be informed of a Purchaser, by applying to MATTHEW CLARKSON, or EDWARD BONSALL.

Recreated from The Pennsylvania Gazette, July 26, 1775.

AMERICANS RETRIEVE VESSELS.

NEWPORT, *June* 19, 1775.

LAST Friday evening when the men of war on our harbour were shifting their watches, a number of musket balls were fired into the town, one of which entered a closet window of a house on Gravelly point, just to the northward of the Long wharff, went through the closet door, and made a considerable dent in the opposite corner of the room, adjoining the closet; by which one or two persons narrowly escaped being killed or wounded.

Last Saturday, it being reported that two American Vessels of Force were lying in Narraganset Bay, Capt. Wallace, of the ship Rose, Capt. Ayscough, of the Swan, and a Tender, came to sail, and first beat out within about two miles from the light-house, when they bore away, and ran up the river as far as Connanicut point, and took a peep down Narraganset Bay, but not discovering any vessels, they returned to their station in this harbour. While they were on this short and unsuccessful cruize, a number of people boarded and carried off five vessels, which those men of war had taken, and left lying in the road.

By two Gentlemen, who left Charlestown and Cambridge last Wednesday, we are assured, that last Sunday, Monday, Tuesday and Wednesday morning, 22 transports arrived at Boston, with near 200 horses, and 'twas supposed not exceeding 2000 troops, chiefly new recruits, who made a poor appearance; and that 15 horses died on the passage.

Recreated from The Pennsylvania Gazette, June 28, 1775.

On Colonel HANCOCK'*s being asked to review the three battalions of the* PHILADELPHIA *militia.*

WHILE FREEDOM's daughters all their aid afford,
   And deck the warrior with the gorgeous sword;
Do THOU, great HANCOCK, all their ranks inspire,
With PATRIOT virtues, and the HEROES fire.
Form'd by THY blest example——they shall claim,
The FAIR one's fondness, and the conqueror's fame.

Recreated from The Virginia Gazette, June 24, 1775.

DR. WARREN KILLED.

WATERTOWN, *June* 20.—We have just received an Account by a Man, who is said to have swam out of Boston, that we killed and wounded 1000 of the Ministerial Troops, among the first of which is a General, Majors Sheriff and Pitcairn, and 60 other Officers; 70 Officers wounded.

In this Action fell our worthy and much lamented Friend Dr. Warren, with as much Glory as a Wolfe, after performing many Feats of Bravery, and exhibiting a Coolness and Conduct, which did Honour to the Judgement of his Country in appointing him, a few Days before, one of our Majors General.

Recreated from The Pennsylvania Gazette, June 28, 1775.

WASHINGTON REVIEWS TROOPS.

PHILADELPHIA, *June* 21.—Yesterday morning the Three Battalions of this City and Liberties, together with the Artillery Company, a Troop of Light-horse, several Companies of Light Infantry, Rangers, and Rifle-men, in the Whole about 2000, marched out to the Commons, and, having joined in Brigade, were reviewed by General WASHINGTON, who is appointed Commander in Chief of all the North American Forces by the Honourable CONTINENTAL CONGRESS, when they went through the Manual Exercise, Firings, and Manoeuvres, with great Dexterity and Exactness.

Recreated from The Pennsylvania Gazette, June 21, 1775.

Extract of a letter from Wethersfield, June 22.

"Last Friday afternoon orders were issued for about 1800 provincial troops, and 200 of the Connecticut, to parade themselves at six o'clock, with one day's provision, equipped with packs, blankets, &c. Their orders were given at 9 o'clock, and they marched with their teams, trenching tools, &c. on Bunker's Hill, to heave up an entrenchment, which you are sensible is near the water, ships, &c. They worked most surprisingly that night, and were discovered at sunrise by a sailor from the mast-head.

"The British army began a heavy fire from Copp's Hill, near Cutler's Church, in Boston, and from all the ships which could be brought to play, which continued till near night

"About 1 o'clock, A.M. the Americans at Cambridge heard that the regulars were landing from their floating batteries, the alarm was sounded, and they were ordered down to the breast-work at Charlestown; and Capt. Chester writes me, that before it was possible for him to get there, the battle had begun in earnest, and cannon and musket balls were plenty about their ears. Chester and my brother were both in the engagement. They reinforced our men that had left the breast-work in fine order, tho' they passed thro' the cannonading of the ships, bombs, chain-shot, ring-shot, &c. but then their superior number of artillery and men, for they were three to two, forced our men to retreat, after a warm engagement of an hour and a half.

"Thank Heaven, but a few of our men fell, considering the advantages they had over us, our men being much fatigued with working at the entrenchments, and I believe not in the best preparation to meet the enemy. The British troops, to their eternal disgrace, shame and barbarity, set Charlestown on fire with torches.

"My brother says we were obliged to retreat to Prospect Hill (alias Winter's Hill) where we made a stand, and declared we would all die, before we would retreat any further; but the British troops did not think fit to come out from under the protection of their shipping. The loss of Americans is said to be, of wounded, missing and slain about 120. A large, genteel, well dressed Gentlemen, who first mounted our brest-work, was overset by one of our impudent Americans, who took so good aim as to prevent his ever mounting another, as he tumbled him into the entrenchment just as he cried, *The day is our own.*

"We greatly rejoice to hear of the coming of the good, brave and great General Washington, and shall receive him with *open arms*."

Recreated from The Pennsylvania Gazette, June 28, 1775.

TORIES REBUFFED.

CAPTAIN OF TENDER KILLED.

WATERTOWN, *June 24.*—A letter from Machias was this Day laid before the Provincial Congress containing Advices that in Consequence of an Application to that Place from Ichabod and Stephen Jones of Boston and Casco Bay, for lumber to supply the Navy and Army, the last mentioned Person was arrested by the Inhabitants, and put under Guard, while the other made his Escape into the Woods. That the Captain of a Tender sent to protect two Sloops which the Traitors aforesaid intended to have loaded, put Springs to his Cables, and threatened to burn the Town unless the Prisoners were released. That an Engagement between the People on Shore and the Crew on board the Tender took Place, and the latter were obliged to put to Sea. The Inhabitants immediately manned the Sloops, and arming themselves with Fire Arms, Swords, Axes and Spears, came up with the Tender & engaged her a second time. That an obstinate Resistance was made, but that the Tender was obliged to yield. That the Capt. of the Tender was mortally wounded, and died the next Morning; five of the Crew were wounded, and one Marine killed; two of our Men were killed, and five wounded.

Mr. Robert Avery of Norwich, in Connecticut, who was on the Tender, as a prisoner, was unhappily killed.

Recreated from The Hartford Courant, July 3, 1775.

For SALE at *Tappahannock*,

AN exceeding likely young negro man, who is a very good house servant, understands taking care of horses, and is a tolerable good cook. If the purchaser is not perfectly satisfied with him after a month's trial, he may return him if in health.
(tf.) ARCHIBALD M'CALL.

Recreated from Purdie's Virginia Gazette, June 23, 1775.

THE GREATEST SCENE.

Extract of a letter from General Burgoyne *to a noble lord, dated* BOSTON, *June 25.*

BOSTON is a peninsula, joined to the mainland only by a narrow neck, which on the first troubles general Gage fortified. Arms of the sea and harbour surround the rest on the other side; one of these arms to the north is Charlestown, or rather was, for it is now rubbish, and over it a large hill, which is also (like Boston) a peninsula. To the south of the town is a still larger scope of ground, containing three hills, joining also to the main by a tongue of land, and called Dorchester Neck; the heights, as above described, both north and south (in the soldier's phrase) command the town; that is, give an opportunity of erecting batteries above any that you can make against them, and consequently are much more advantageous.

It was absolutely necessary we should make ourselves masters of these heights, and we proposed to begin with Dorchester, because, from a particular situation of batteries and shipping (too long to describe, and unintelligible to you if I did) it would evidently be effected without any considerable loss. Everything was accordingly disposed; my two colleagues and myself (who, by the by, have never differed in one jot of military sentiment) had, in concert with general Gage, formed the plan. Howe was to land the transports on the point, Clinton in the center, and I was to cannonade from the causeway, or the neck, each to take advantage of circumstances, the operations must have been very easy; this was to have been executed on the 18th.

On the 17th, at dawn of day, we found the enemy had pushed entrenchments, with great diligence, during the night, on the heights of Charlestown, and we evidently saw that every hour gave them fresh strength; it therefore became necessary to alter our plan, and attack on that side. Howe, as second in command, was detached with about two thousand men, and landed on the opposite side of the peninsula, covered with shipping, without opposition. He was to advance from thence up the hill which was over Charlestown, where the strength of the enemy lay. He had under him brigadier general Pigot; Clinton and myself took our stand (for we had not any fixed post) in a large battery directly opposite Charlestown, and also reaching the heights above it, and thereby facilitating Howe's attack. Howe's disposition was exceedingly soldier-like, in my opinion it was perfect.

As his first arm advanced up the hill, they met with a thousand impediments from strong fences, and were much exposed. They were also exceedingly hurt by musquetry from Charlestown, though Clinton and I did not perceive it till Howe sent us word by a boat, and desired us to set fire to the town, which was immediately done. We threw a parcel of shells, and the whole was instantly in flames. Our battery afterwards kept up an incessant fire on the heights; it was seconded by a number of frigates, floating batteries, and one ship of the line.

And now ensued one of the greatest scenes of war that can be conceived. If we look to the height, Howe's corps, ascending the hill in the face of entrenchments, and in a very disadvantageous ground, were much engaged; to the left, the enemy pouring in fresh troops by thousands, over the land, and in the arm of the sea our ships and floating batteries cannonading them; strait before us a large and noble town in one great blaze; the church steeples, being of timber, were great pyramids of fire above the rest; behind us the church steeples and heights of our own camp, covered with spectators of the rest of our army which was not engaged, the hills round the country covered with spectators, the enemy all in anxious suspense, the roar of cannon, mortars, and musquetry, the crush of churches, ships on the stock, and whole streets falling together in ruins to fill the ear; the storm of the redoubts, with the objects above described, to fill the eye, and the reflection that perhaps a defeat was a final loss to the British empire in America, to fill the mind, made the whole picture a complication of horror and importance beyond any thing that ever came to my lot to be witness to.

I much lament Tom's absence; it was a fight for a young soldier that the longest service may not furnish again, and had he been with me he would likewise been out of danger, for except two cannon balls that went an hundred yards over our heads, we were not in any part of the direction of the enemy's shot.

A moment of the day was critical. Howe's left was staggered, two battalions had been sent to reinforce them, but we perceived them on the beach, seeming in embarrassment what way to march. Clinton, then next for business, took the part without waiting for orders, to throw himself into a boat to head them, and arrived in time to be of service. The day ended with glory, and the success was most important, considering the ascendancy it gave the regular troops; but the loss was uncommon in officers for the numbers engaged.

Recreated from Rind's Virginia Gazette, December 6, 1775.

ON HIS WAY TO BOSTON.

PHILADELPHIA, *June 26.*—On Friday morning the Generals WASHINGTON and LEE set off from this city to take the command of the American army at Massachusetts Bay. They were accompanied from town by the troop of the light horse, and by all the officers of the city militia on horseback, who attended them about five miles, when they returned, but the former continued with them, and how far they will go is uncertain.

Major THOMAS MIFFLIN is appointed Aid de Camp to General Washington, and accompanies the General to the camp near Boston. The active and successful part which this Gentlemen has taken in the civil and military affairs of the province of Pennsylvania, had endeared him so much to his fellow citizens, that few men have ever left us more universally beloved or regretted.

A PLACE in the Country is wanted for a likely, active NEGRO GIRL, who is about nine years old, and has had the small pox; she is to be bound until twenty-four years old.— For further particulars enquire of the Printer.

Recreated from The Pennsylvania Packet, June 26, 1775.

FOR SALE,

A NEW BRIGANTINE, now rigging, and may be soon got ready for Sea, Burthen 122 Tons. She is a handsome well calculated Vessel, built of excellent Materials, ornamented with a Figure Head and other carved Work. Credit will be allowed for one Half of the Money on giving proper Security. If not sold shortly, would accept of a Freight. Apply to Capt. *Wills Cowper*, Merchant, who will be at the Merchants Meeting, or to me in *Suffolk*.

SAMUEL COHOON.

For CHARTER *to any Part of* BRITAIN,

AN EXCEEDING GOOD

VESSEL,

Burthen about 500 Hogsheads.

FOR TERMS APPLY TO

Greenwood, Ritson, & Marsh.

NORFOLK, May 1, 1775.   (tf)

THE Volunteer Company of *Dinwiddie* County would willingly engage with an expert ADJUTANT to instruct them in military Discipline.

TO BE SOLD,

At HANOVER TOWN, on THURSDAY *the 15th of this Instant* (JUNE) *at the Shop of the deceased Dr.* JOHN WALKER,

A large Assortment of MEDICINES, TOGETHER with an elegant and complete Set of SHOP FURNITURE, SURGEON's and MIDWIFERY INSTRUMENTS, and many valuable MEDICAL BOOKS.— An Inventory of the Whole may be seen at any Time before the Sale, in the Hands of   THOMAS SIMPSON. Adm'r.

HANOVER TOWN, *June* 1, 1775.   (2)

To be sold by Auction,

At the Meeting of the Merchants in *May* next, for Cash or short Credit, about 600l. Sterling Worth of

EUROPEAN GOODS.

Recreated from The Virginia Gazette, June 10, 1775.

GEN. WASHINGTON AT NEW YORK.

June 26.—Yesterday arrived here from Philadelphia, in their way for the camp at Boston, Gen. Washington, appointed by the Hon. the Continental Congress, Commander in Chief of all the Provincial Troops in North America, attended by the Generals Lee and Schuyler. They were escorted by a party of Light Horse. The generals landed at the Seat of Col. Lispenard about 4 o'Clock Yesterday Afternoon, from whence they were conducted by 9 Companies of Foot, in their Uniforms, and a greater Number of the principal Inhabitants of this City than ever appeared here on any Occasion before.

Recreated from The Pennsylvania Gazette, June 28, 1775.

The Address of the PROVINCIAL CONGRESS *of the Colony of* NEW YORK,

To his Excellency GEORGE WASHINGTON,

AT a time when the most loyal of his Majesty's subjects, from a regard to the laws and constitution by which he sits on the throne, feel themselves reduced to the unhappy necessity of taking up arms to defend their dearest rights and privileges; while we deplore the calamities of this divided empire, we rejoice in the appointment of a Gentleman, from whose abilities and virtue we are taught to expect both security and peace.

Confiding in you, Sir, and in the worthy Generals, immediately under your command, we have the most flattering hopes of success in the glorious struggle for American Liberty, and the fullest assurances that, whenever this important contest should be decided, by the fondest wish of each American soul, an accommodation with our Mother Country, you will cheerfully resign the important deposit committed into your hands, and re-assume the character of our worthy citizens. *June 26, 1775.*

P.V.B. LIVINGSTON, President.

HIS EXCELLENCY'S ANSWER.

GENTLEMEN, *June 26, 1775.*

AT the same time with you, I deplore the unhappy necessity of such an appointment, as that with which I am now honoured, I cannot but feel sentiments of the highest gratitude, for this affecting instance of distinction and regard.

May your warmest wishes be realized in the success of America, at this important and interesting period; and be assured, that every exertion of my worthy colleagues and myself, will be equally extended to the re-establishment of peace and harmony between the Mother Country and these Colonies. As to the fatal but necessary operations of war, when we assumed the soldier we did not lay aside the citizen, and we shall most sincerely rejoice with you, in that happy hour, when the establishment of American Liberty, on the most firm and solid foundation, shall enable us to return to our private stations, in the bosom of a free, peaceful, and happy Country.

G. WASHINGTON.

Recreated from The Pennsylvania Gazette, July 5, 1775.

HARTFORD, *July* 3.—On Friday last passed through this Town for the Camp at Charlestown, his Excellency General Washington, appointed by the Hon. Continental Congress, Commander in Chief of all the Provincial Troops in North America.

Twelve companies of Rifle Men, consisting of 64 men each, exclusive of officers, are on their march from Philadelphia, to join the American army at Cambridge and Roxbury.

Recreated from The Hartford Courant, July 3, 1775.

WATERTOWN, *July* 3.—The Hon. George Washington, Esq., appointed by the Continental Congress General and Commander in Chief of all the New England forces, passed through this town yesterday, on his way to Cambridge, attended by a Committee from the Provincial congress, and a train of other gentlemen, escorted by a company of horse from Marlborough.

WASHINGTON ARRIVES AT CAMP.

Extract of a letter from CAMBRIDGE, *July 3.*

"The greatest civility and attention was paid to the Generals on their arrival at the camp, which was on Sunday about noon. When they were within 20 miles of the camp, they received an express that the Parliamentary troops had, on Sunday morning, about 6 o'clock begun a very heavy cannonading on the town of Roxbury, which continued better than two hours, without intermission, tho' with little or no loss on the side of the Provincials, and they expected a general attack on Sunday, about 2 o'clock, at the time of high water; that we had confirmed, and this I believe was prevented by a heavy rain, which began at half past 12, and continued till late at night.

"The Generals have spent this whole day in reviewing the troops, lines, fortification, &c. They find the troops to be 15,000 strong, and the works to be in as good order as could be expected. The Regulars have been sounding the shore this afternoon, and we are in some expectation of a visit at the next high water. Our men are all in good spirits, and wish they may come out. The best account we can get of the late engagements, that the Regulars lost more than 800 in the field, and 700 wounded.

"Among the slain are Col. Williams, Major Pitcairn, and Major Sheriffe. It remains a matter of doubt whether or not General Burgoyne is among the dead; this we are certain of, that General Howe commanded the first division, of 1700, and General Burgoyne the second, of 1300, and since the battle he has not been seen in Boston; 'tis given out that he is gone to England."

TO BE SOLD,

TWO valuable NEGROES, a Man and his Wife, both young and hearty, have had the Small-pox, and been bred up in the Country, the Man to Farming and the Woman to Housewifery, sold for no Fault but Want of Employ. They have a fine promising Male Child, two Years old, that has had the Small-pox, likewise to be sold with them, if the Purchaser chooses. Enquire of the PRINTERS.

IN CONGRESS.

July 4, 1775.

RESOLVED. *That the two acts passed in the first session of the present Parliament, the one intituled, "an act to restrain the trade and commerce of the province of Massachusetts Bay and New Hampshire, and colonies of Connecticut and Rhode Island, and Providence Plantation, in North America, to Great Britain, Ireland, and the British islands in the West Indies; and to prohibit such provinces and colonies from carrying on any fishery on the banks of Newfoundland, or other places therein mentioned, under certain conditions and limitations;" the other intituled, "an act to restrain the trade and commerce of the colonies of New Jersey, Pennsylvania, Maryland, Virginia, and South Carolina, to Great Britain, Ireland, and the British islands in the West Indies, under certain conditions and limitations," are unconstitutional, oppressive and cruel, and that the commercial opposition of these colonies, to certain acts enumerated in the association of the last Congress, ought to be made against these until they are repealed.*

CHARLES THOMPSON, *Secretary.*

CHARLESTOWN, South Carolina, *June 27.*—The Provincial Congress have requested, by public advertisement, that men of every denomination and persuasion would carry with them, to all places of divine worship, loaded fire-arms, which, on Sunday last, was almost generally complied with.

Recreated from The Pennsylvania Gazette, July 12, 1775.

MORE TROOPS ARRIVE.

NEW YORK, *July 3.*—Since our last, nine transports with troops, of the second embarkation from Cork, have arrived at Sandy Hook, and agreeable to orders there received, sailed last Friday for Boston, under convoy of his Majesty's ship of war Nautilus. The regiments on board the transports are the 22d, 40th, 44th, and 45th.

Recreated from The Pennsylvania Gazette, July 5, 1775.

In Congress.

A DECLARATION *by the* REPRESENTATIVES *of the United Colonies of North America, now met in* GENERAL CONGRESS *at Philadelphia, setting forth the* CAUSES *and* NECESSITY *of their taking up* ARMS, *July 6, 1775.*

IF it was possible for men who exercise their reason to believe, that the Divine Author of our existence intended a part of the human race to hold an absolute property in, and an unbounded power over others, marked out by his infinite goodness and wisdom, as the objects of a legal domination, never rightfully resistable, however severe and oppressive, the inhabitants of these Colonies might at least require from the Parliament of Great Britain some evidence, that this dreadful authority over them has been granted to that body. But a reverence for our great Creator, principles of humanity, and the dictates of common sense, must convince all those who reflect upon the subject, that government was instituted to promote the welfare of mankind, and ought to be administered for the attainment of that end.

The legislature of Great Britain, however stimulated by an inordinate passion for a power not only unjustifiable, but which they know to be peculiarly reprobated by the very constitution of that kingdom, and desperate of success in any mode of contest, where regard should be had to truth, law or right, have at length, deserting those, attempted to effect their cruel and impolitic purpose of enslaving these Colonies by violence, and have thereby rendered it necessary for us to close with their last appeal from reason to arms. Yet, however blinded that assembly may be, by their intemperate rage for unlimited rule, so to slight justice and the opinion of mankind, we esteem ourselves bound by the obligation of respect to the rest of the world, to make known the justice of our cause. Our forefathers, inhabitants of the island of Great Britain, left their native land, to seek on these shores a residence for civil and religious freedom.

At the expense of their blood, at the hazard of their fortunes, without the least charge to the country from which they removed, by unceasing labour and an unconquerable spirit, they effected settlements in the distant and inhospitable wilds of America, then filled with numerous and warlike nations of barbarians. Societies or governments, vested with perfect legislatures, were formed under charters from the crown, and an harmonious intercourse was established between the colonies and the kingdom from which they derived their origin. The mutual benefits of this union became in a short time so extraordinary, as to excite astonishment.

It is universally confessed, that the amazing increase of the wealth, strength and navigation of the realm, arose from this source; and the ministers who so wisely and successfully directed the measures of Great Britain in the late war, publicly declared, that these colonies enabled her to triumph over her enemies. Towards the conclusion of that war, it pleased our Sovereign to make a change in his counsels. From that fatal moment, the affairs of the British empire began to fall into confusion, and gradually sliding from the summit of glorious prosperity to which they had been advanced by the virtues and abilities of one man, are at length distracted by the convulsions, that now shake it to its deepest foundations. The new Ministry finding the brave foes of Britain, though frequently defeated, yet still contending, took up the unfortunate idea of granting them a hasty peace, and of then subduing her faithful friends.

These devoted colonies were judged to be in such a state, as to present victories without bloodshed, and all the easy emoluments of stauteable depredation. The uninterrupted tenor of their peaceable and respectful behaviour from the beginning of colonization, their dutiful, zealous and useful services during the war, though so recently and amply acknowledged in the most honourable manner by his Majesty, by the late King, and by Parliament, could not save them from the meditated innovations. Parliament was influenced to adopt the pernicious project, and assuming a new power over them, have in the course of eleven years given such decisive specimens of the spirit and consequences attending this power, as to leave no doubt concerning the effects of acquiescence under it.

They have undertaken to give and grant our money without our consent, though we have ever exercised an exclusive right to dispose of our own property; statues have been passed for extending the jurisdiction of courts of Admiralty and Vice Admiralty beyond their ancient limits, for depriving us of the accustomed and inestimable privilege of trial by jury in cases affecting both life and property; for suspending the legislature of one of the colonies; for interdicting all commerce of another; and for altering fundamentally the form of government established by charter, and secured by acts of its own legislature solemnly confirmed by the crown; for exempting the "murderers" of colonists from legal trial, and, in effect, from punishment; for erecting in a neighbouring province, acquired by the joint arms of Great Britain and America, a despotism dangerous to our very existence; and for quartering soldiers upon the colonists in time of profound peace. It has also been resolved in Parliament, that colonists, charged with committing certain offences, shall be transported to England to be tried.

But why should we enumerate our injuries in detail? By one statute it is declared, that Parliament can "of right make laws to bind us IN ALL CASES WHATSOEVER." What is to defend us against so enormous, so unlimited a power? Not a single man of those who assume it is chosen by us; or is subject to our control or influence. But on the contrary, they are all of them exempt from the operation of such laws; and an American revenue, if not diverted from the ostensible purposes for which it is raised, would actually lighten their own burdens in proportion as they increase ours. We saw the misery to which such despotism would reduce us. We for ten years incessantly and ineffectually besieged the throne as supplicants; we reasoned, we remonstrated with Parliament in the most mild and decent language.

But Administration, sensible that we should regard these oppressive measures as freemen ought to do, sent over fleets and armies to enforce them. The indignation of the Americans was roused it is true; but it was the indignation of a virtuous, loyal, and affectionate people.

A Congress of Delegates from the united colonies was assembled at Philadelphia, on the fifth day of last September. We resolved again to offer an humble and dutiful petition to the King, and also addressed our fellow-subjects of Great Britain. We have pursued every temperate, every respectful measure, we have even proceeded to brake off our commercial intercourse with our fellow-subjects, as the last peaceable admonition, that our attachment to no nation upon earth should supplant our attachment to liberty. This, we flattered ourselves, was the ultimate step of the controversy. But subsequent events have shown, how vain was this hope of finding moderation in our enemies.

Several threatening expressions against our colonies were inserted in his Majesty's speech; our petition, though we were told it was a decent one, that his Majesty had been pleased to receive it graciously, and to promote laying it before his Parliament, was huddled into both Houses amongst a bundle of American papers, and there neglected. The Lords and Commons in their address, in the month of February, said, that "a rebellion at that time actually existed within the province of Massachusetts Bay, and that those concerned in it had been countenanced and encouraged by unlawful combinations and engagements, entered into by his Majesty's subjects in several other colonies; and therefore they besought his Majesty, that he would take the most effectual measures to enforce due obedience to the laws and authority of the supreme legislature." — Soon after the commercial intercourse of whole colonies, with foreign countries and with each other was cut off by an act of Parliament; by another, several of them were entirely prohibited from the fisheries in the seas near their coasts, on which they always depended for their sustenance; and large reinforcements of ships and troops were immediately sent over to General Gage.

Recreated from The Pennsylvania Gazette, July 12, 1775 (cont'd).

Fruitless were all the entreaties, arguments and eloquence of an illustrious band of the most distinguished Peers and Commoners, who nobly and strenuously asserted the justice of our cause, to stay or even to mitigate the heedless fury with which these accumulated and unexampled outrages were hurried on. Equally fruitless was the interference of the city of London, of Bristol, and many other respectable towns in our favour. Parliament adopted an insidious manoeuvre calculated to divide us, to establish a perpetual auction of taxations where colony should bid against colony, all of them uninformed what ransom would redeem their lives, and thus to extort from us at the point of the bayonet, the unknown sums that should be sufficient to gratify, if possible to gratify, ministerial rapacity, with the miserable indulgence left to us of raising in our own mode the prescribed tribute.

What terms more rigid and humiliating could have been dictated by remorseless victors to conquered enemies? In our circumstances to accept them would be to deserve them.

Soon after the intelligence of the proceedings arrived on this continent, General Gage, who, in the course of the last year, had taken possession of the town of Boston, in the province of Massachusetts Bay, and still occupied it as a garrison, on the 19th of April, sent out from that place a large detachment of his army, who made an unprovoked assault on the inhabitants of the said province, at the town of Lexington, as appears by the affidavits of a great number of persons, some of whom were officers and soldiers of that detachment, murdered eight of the inhabitants, and wounded many others. From thence the troops proceeded in warlike array to the town of Concord, where they set upon another party of the inhabitants of the same province, killing several and wounding more, until compelled to retreat by the country people suddenly assembled to repel this cruel aggression. Hostilities thus commenced by the British troops, have been since prosecuted by them without regard to faith or reputation.

The inhabitants of Boston being confined within that town by the General, their Governor, and having in order to procure their dismission entered into a treaty with him, it was stipulated that the said inhabitants having deposited their arms with their own Magistrates, should have liberty to depart, taking with them their other effects. They accordingly delivered up their arms, but in open violation of honour, in defiance of the obligations of treaties, which even savage nations esteem sacred, the Governor ordered the arms deposited as aforesaid, that they might be preserved for their owners, to be seized by a body of soldiers; detained the greater part of the inhabitants in the town, and compelled the few, who were permitted to retire, to leave their most valuable effects behind.

By this perfidy, wives are separated from their husbands, children from their parents, the aged and the sick from their relations and friends, who wish to attend and comfort them; and those who have been used to live in plenty, and even elegance, are reduced to deplorable distress.

The General, further emulating his ministerial masters, by a proclamation, bearing date on the 12th day of June, after venting the grossest falsehoods and calumnies against the good people of these colonies, proceeds to "declare them all either by name or description to be rebels and traitors, to supercede the course of the common law, and instead therefore to publish and order the use and exercise of the law martial."

His troops have butchered our countrymen; have wantonly burnt Charlestown, besides a considerable number of houses in other places; our ships and vessels are seized; the necessary supplies of provisions are intercepted, and he is exerting his utmost power to spread destruction and devastation around him.

We have received certain intelligence, that General Carleton, Governor of Canada, is instigating the people of that province and the Indians to fall upon us; and we have but too much reason to apprehend, that schemes have been formed to excite domestic enemies against us.

In brief, a part of these Colonies now feels, and all of them are sure of feeling, as far as the vengeance of administration can inflict them, the complicated calamities of fire, sword and famine. We are reduced to the alternative of choosing an unconditional submission to the tyranny of irritated ministers, or resistance by force. The latter is our choice. We have counted the cost of this contest, and find nothing so dreadful as voluntary slavery. Honour, justice and humanity, forbid us to surrender that freedom which we received from our gallant ancestors, and which our innocent posterity have a right to receive from us. We cannot endure the infamy and guilt of resigning succeeding generations to that wretchedness which inevitably awaits them, if we basely entail hereditary bondage upon them.

Our cause is just. Our union is perfect. Our internal resources are great, and, if necessary, foreign assistance is undoubtedly attainable. We gratefully acknowledge, as signal instances of the Divine favour towards us, that his Providence would not permit us to be called into this severe controversy, until we were grown up to our present strength, had been previously exercised in warlike operations, and possessed of the means of defending ourselves. With hearts fortified with these animating reflections, we most solemnly, before GOD and the world, declare, that, exerting the utmost energy of those powers, which our benificient Creator hath graciously bestowed upon us, the arms we have been compelled by our enemies to assume, we will, in defiance of every hazard, with unabating firmness and perseverance, employ for the preservation of our liberties, being with one mind resolved to die Freemen, rather than to live Slaves.

Lest this declaration should disquiet the minds of our friends and fellow-subjects in any part of the empire, we assure them, that we mean not to dissolve that union which has so long and so happily subsisted between us, and which we sincerely wish to see restored. Necessity has not yet driven us into that desperate measure, or induced us to excite any other nation to war against them.

We have not raised armies with ambitious designs of separating from Great Britain, and establishing independent states. We fight not for glory or for conquest. We exhibit to mankind the remarkable spectacle of a people attacked by unprovoked enemies, without any imputation, or even suspicion of offence. They boast of their privileges and civilization, and yet proffer no milder conditions than servitude or death.

In our own native land, in defence of the freedom that is our birthright, and which we ever enjoyed till the late violation of it—for the protection of our property, acquired solely by the honest industry of our forefathers and ourselves, against violence actually offered, we have taken up arms. We shall lay them down when hostilities shall cease on the part of the aggressors; and all of the danger of their being renewed shall be removed, and not before.

With an humble confidence in the mercies of the supreme and impartial Judge and Ruler of the universe, we most devoutly implore his divine goodness to conduct us happily through this great conflict, to dispose our adversaries to reconciliation on reasonable terms, and thereby to relieve the empire from the calamities of civil war.

By order of Congress,
JOHN HANCOCK, *President.*

Attested, CHARLES THOMPSON, Secretary.

PHILADELPHIA, *July* 6, 1775.

Recreated from The Pennsylvania Gazette, July 12, 1775.

CONGRESS VOTES FOR AN ARMY.

WILLIAMSBURG, *July* 7.—The following intelligence may be depended on as authentick, viz. That the General Congress have voted an army of 15,000 men to be forthwith raised, which it is expected will be augmented, and TWO MILLIONS of DOLLARS to be struck.

Recreated from Purdie's Virginia Gazette, July 7, 1775.

A CURIOUS PHENOMENON.

Extract of a Letter from PHILADELPHIA, *July 6.*

"A few minutes past, a curious Phaenomenon appeared at the door of the Congress—a German Hussar, a veteran in the wars in Germany, in his uniform, and on horseback, a forlorn cap upon his head, with a streamer waving from it half down to his waistband, with a death's-head painted in front, a beautiful hussar cloak ornamented with lace and fringe and cord of gold, a scarlet waistcoat under it, with thinning yellow mettle buttons—a light gun strung over his shoulders—a turnpike sabre, much superior to an highland broad sword, very large and excellently fortified by his side—holsters and pistols upon his horse—in short, the most warlike and formidable figure I ever saw. He says he has fifty such men ready to enlist under him immediately, who have been all used to the service as hussars in Germany, and desirous to ride to Boston immediately, in order to see Burgoyne's light horse.

Recreated from The Hartford Courant, July 31, 1775.

LADY DUNMORE SAILS TO ENGLAND.

WILLIAMSBURG, *July 7.*

LAST Sunday the Fowey man of war returned to her moorings before York town, with LORD DUNMORE and Captain Foy on board; having only proceeded as far as the capes with the Magdalen schooner, which carries LADY DUNMORE, and the rest of the Governor's family, immediately to England.

JUNE 26, 1775.

THE delegates appointed by the counties and corporations of the colony are defired to meet at the town of *Richmond*, in the county of *Henrico*, on Monday the 17th of *July* next.

PEYTON RANDOLPH, Prefident.

Recreated from Purdie's Virginia Gazette, July 7, 1775.

TROOPS DRIVE THE ENEMY.

Extract of a Letter from CAMBRIDGE, *July 9.*

"Two hundred volunteers, from the Rhode Island and Massachusetts forces, undertook to burn a guard-house of the regulars on the neck, within three hundred yards of the enemy's principal works. They detached six men, about ten o'clock in the evening, with orders to cross on a marsh up to the rear of the guard-house, and there to watch for an opportunity to fire it, the remainder of the volunteers secreted themselves in the marsh, on each side of the neck, about two hundred yards from the house; two pieces of brass artillery were brought softly on the marsh within three hundred yards, and upon a signal from the advanced party of six men, two rounds of cannon shot were fired through the guard-house; immediately the regulars, who formed a guard of forty-five or fifty men, quitted the house, and were then fired on by the musquetry, who drove them with precipitation into their lines. The six men posted near the house set fire to it, and burnt it to the ground.

"After this they burnt another house nearer the enemy, without losing a man. They took two musquets and accoutrements, a halbert, &c. all which were bloody, and showed evident marks of loss on the part of the regulars. The houses had been a long while made use of by the regulars as an advanced post, and gave them an opportunity of discovering our operations at Roxbury.

"Yesterday afternoon some barges were sounding the river of Cambridge, near its mouth, but were soon obliged to row off by our Indians (fifty in number) who are encamped near that place."

PROVIDENCE, *July* 15.—Tuesday night a party of the Americans went in boats to Long Island, in Boston Bay, and brought off 18 horned cattle, 40 sheep, 3 hogs, a horse, and some valuable goods, the property of our enemies; they likewise brought 17 men, and a negroe, that had been making hay for the regular army.

Recreated from The Pennsylvania Gazette, July 26, 1775.

DISPOSITION OF FORCES.

Extract of a Letter from CAMBRIDGE, *July* 11.

"The General's express, that ought to have left there this four days ago, is not yet gone.—I therefore sit down to give you some description of our situation here, and that of the enemy.—The enemy are situated on Bunker's and Breed's hills, both on the Peninsula, where the late town of Charlestown stood, and within reach, and under the cover of the guns, from the batteries in the town of Boston and the ships in the harbour, and of a number of floating batteries, which they have built, that carry two guns in their bows, two in their sterns, and one on each side.

"Our people are situated from Charles river, about 200 rods below the College, where we have a redoubt; which begins the line; then about 60 rods from that another redoubt, and lines continued near 100 rods; then at Charlestown road on the west side of the road, at the foot of Prospect hill, another redoubt, and strong fortification; then on Prospect hill is Putnam' post, a very strong fortification; then between that and Winter hill a redoubt.

"On Winter hill, a strong citadel, and lines, over Charlestown road to Mistick; then in Mr. Temple's pasture, a strong redoubt, that commands to Mistick river, so that we have a compleat line of circumvallation from Charles river to Mistick river; our main fortress on Prospect hill; the enemy's main fortress on Bunker's hill; within cannon shot of each other; a hill between these two posts, a little to the eastward of Prospect hill, called Cobble hill, I expect will soon cost us a squabble, which shall have it, our people or theirs, nor do I expect it will be many days before the contest begins, which will probably bring on a general engagement; if they let us alone four or five days more, we shall be well prepared, and shall not care how soon they come, the sooner the better.

"At Roxbury side the enemy have dug across the neck, and let water through, and our people in turn have entrenched across the outer end of the neck, and are strongly fortified there, and on the hill by the meetinghouse, so strong, that I believe every man in Boston, and at Bunker's hill and Breed's hill must fall, before they could force a passage that way into the country.

"General Burgoyne sent a trumpet yesterday with a letter to General Lee, wishing a composition of the unhappy differences, &c. and says the Parliament will certainly give up all right or pretence of taxation, if that will do, and wishes a conference. This letter is sent to the Congress for their opinion, and for them to appoint a person whom they can confide in to attend the conference, and hear what passes, if they judge it best to have a conference. Major Gates is arrived, and we are getting into order and regularity fast. Last night our people at Roxbury fired the remainder of Brown's buildings on Boston neck, and have drove the enemy's guards back to their lines."

Recreated from The Pennsylvania Gazette, July 26, 1775.

INSTRUCTIONS FOR RECRUITING.

Instructions for the officers of the several regiments of Massachusetts Bay forces, who are to immediately go upon the recruiting service.

YOU are not to enlist any deserter from the ministerial army, nor any stroller, negro, or vagabond, or person suspected to be an enemy to the liberty of America, nor any under 18 years of age. As the cause is the best that can engage men of courage and principle to take up arms, so it is expected that none but such will be accepted by the recruiting officers. The pay, provision, &c. being so ample, it is not doubted but the officers sent upon this service will, without delay, compleat their respective corps, and march their men forthwith to camp.

You are not to enlist any person who is not American born, unless such person has a wife and family, and is a settled resident in this country.

The persons you enlist must be provided with good and compleat arms.

Given at the HEAD QUARTERS, *at* CAMBRIDGE, *this 10th day of July*, 1775.

HORATIO GATES, adj. general.

Recreated from Rind's Virginia Gazette, August 10, 1775.

THREE SMUG GENERALS.

LONDON, *July* 8.—It is said, that General Gage has written in the most pressing terms, either to be recalled or have 15,000 men sent to him.

July 12.—On Monday arrived at Dover the Polly, Thompson, and the Mary, Turrel, both from New York. They have brought over several of the most capital families, who have left New York on account of the troubles that subsist there, which are not likely to end till that once flourishing city is laid in ruins, which was daily expected when the above ships sailed from thence.

The people of Ireland, it is said, are exceedingly uneasy, and very apprehensive that the Spaniards mean to pay them a visit, as they are at present totally incapable of resisting them, for when the next American embarkation takes place, it is computed that there will not be then 4000 effective men in the whole kingdom, many of the regiments of foot scarcely amounting to 180 men.

July 13.—We are informed, that should the disturbances in New England continue till the next sitting of Parliament, an act will be passed to make it lawful to try, by a court-martial, all such persons as shall be taken in arms after the promulgation of a proclamation, on a day to be specified in the act.

Others affirm, that a court of Oyer and Terminer shall be established for the special purpose of trying the rebels at Boston; and that no person, suspected by the King's Council as disaffected to the supremacy of Parliament over America, shall be permitted to sit upon any jury. This measure will be less liable to objections than the bringing of the culprits to be tried in this country.

It is said that the reason for delaying the 5000 men, which the Ministry designed to send to America, is, that the three generals lately arrived at Boston have sent it home, as their opinion, that they may be able to defeat the Provincials without further assistance, though General Gage thinks 15,000 men absolutely necessary for the reduction of New England.

Recreated from The Pennsylvania Gazette, September 13, 1775.

LEE DECLINES CONFERENCE.

CAMBRIDGE, *July* 13.—Last Sabbath a Trumpeter came from the Enemy's Army with a Letter from General Burgoyne to General Lee, and was conducted, blindfolded, by our Guards, to the head quarters in this Town. After delivering the Letter he was permitted to return. The Content of this Letter has occasioned much Speculation, and variously reported; but we hear the substance of it is nothing more than this: That General Burgoyne laments his being obligated to act in Opposition to a Gentleman, for whom he has formerly entertained a great Veneration; but that his Conduct proceeds from Principle, & doubts not General Lee is actuated by the same Motive; that he wishes Affairs might be accommodated, and desires to have a Conference with General Lee.

We are informed General Lee has returned an Answer, in which he declines complying with General Burgoyne's desire of holding the proposed Conference.

LEE'S LETTER TO BURGOYNE.

CAMBRIDGE, Head Quarters, *July* 11.

General LEE's compliments to General Burgoyne. Would be exceedingly happy in the interview he so kindly proposed; but as he perceives that General BURGOYNE has already made up his mind on this great subject, and as it is impossible that he (General Lee) should ever alter his opinion, he is apprehensive that the interview might create those jealousies and suspicions so natural to a people struggling in the dearest of all causes, that of their liberty, property, wives, children, and their future generation. He must therefore defer the happiness of embracing a man whom he most sincerely loves, until the subversion of the present tyrannical ministry and system, which he is persuaded must be in a few months, as he knows Great Britain cannot stand the contest. He begs General Burgoyne will send the letters which his aid-de-camp has for him. If Gardiner be his aid-de-camp, he desires his love to him."

Recreated from The Hartford Courant, July 17, 1775.

BRITISH IN GREAT DISTRESS.

Extract of a Letter from Roxbury, July 13.

"Our troops are in good spirits and health. By a gentleman of undoubted veracity, who came out of Boston yesterday, we are informed, that the troops in Boston are in the greatest *distress* imaginable, for want of fresh provisions; that a flux rages among them, which sweeps off commonly 25 men a day; that old Ruggles had attempted to raise a company in Boston, but at most could not enlist more than 30 men; that several of our friends had been committed to close confinement."

The number of inhabitants remaining in the town of Boston is said to be 6,500. Number of the army and navy, including men, women and children, 13,600. There are about 300 Tories who do military duty in Boston.

Recreated from The Pennsylvania Gazette, July 26, 1775.

GENERAL GAGE'S BOSTON.

Extract of a letter from Braintree, Massachusetts Bay, July 16.

"I am much surprised that you have not been more accurately informed of what passes in the camps. As to intelligence from Boston, it is but seldom we are able to collect any that may be relied on, and to repeat the vague flying rumours would be endless. I heard yesterday by one Mr. Roulston, a goldsmith, who got out of Boston in a fishing schooner, that their distress increases upon them very fast; their beef is spent, their malt and cider all gone. All the fresh provisions they can procure they are obliged to give to the sick and wounded. That 13 of our men who were in jail, and were wounded at Charlestown, are dead. That no man dared to be seen talking to his friend in the street. That they are obliged to be at home every evening by ten o'clock, according to martial law; nor can any inhabitant walk the street after that time, without a pass from Gage. That Gage has ordered all the molasses to be distilled into rum, for the soldiers. That he has taken away all licenses for selling of liquors, and given them to his creatures. That he has issued an order that no one else shall sell liquors, under a penalty of 10l. That the spirit which prevails among the soldiers is that of malice and revenge, and that there is no true courage to be observed among them. That their duty is hard, always holding themselves in readiness for an attack, which they are in continual fear of. That doctor Elliot was not on board of a man of war, as was reported. Mr. Lovel and Leach, with many others, are certainly in jail. That last week a poor milch cow was killed in the town, and sold for 1s. sterling a pound. That the transports from Ireland and New York arrived last week, but every additional man adds to their distress."

THE ship MOLLY, *John Cowan* commander, will sail for *London* on or before the first of *September* next.

WANTED,

A PERSON who can play upon the FIFE. Such a one who can play the field duty will meet with great encouragement by applying to *Warner Lewis*, esq; in *Gloucester*, to *Thomas Davis*, adjutant, or the printer.

FREDERICKSBURG, *August* 2, 1775.

I INTEND to leave the colony in a few weeks.

JOHN TAILYOUR.

DUMFRIES, *July* 25, 1775.

WILLIAM CARR will attend at *Westmoreland* court, on *Tuesday* the 29th of *August*, to have payment for the servants sold on board the *Caroline*, last *February*.

Recreated from Purdie's Virginia Gazette, August 18, 1775.

PHILADELPHIA.
In CONGRESS, *July* 18, 1775.

Resolved,

THAT it be recommended to the inhabitants of all the United English colonies in North America, that all able bodied effective men, between 16 and 50 years, of age, in each Colony, immediately form themselves into regular companies of militia, to consist of one Captain, two Lieutenants, one Ensign, four Sergeants, four Corporals, one Drummer, one Fifer, and about forty-eight Privates.

THAT the officers of each company be chosen by the respective companies.

THAT each soldier be furnished with a good musket, that will carry an ounce ball, with a bayonet, steel ramrod, worm, priming wire and brush, fitted thereto, a cutting sword or tomahawk, a cartridge box, that will contain twenty-three rounds of cartridges, twelve flints, and a knapsack.

THAT the companies be formed into regiments or battalions, officered with a Colonel, Lieutenant Colonel, two Majors, an Adjutant or Quarter Master.

THAT all Officers above the rank of a Captain be appointed by their respective Provincial Assemblies or Conventions, or in their recess by the Committees of Safety appointed, by said Assemblies or Conventions.

THAT all Officers be commissioned by the Provincial Assemblies or Conventions, or in their recess by the Committees of Safety appointed by said Assemblies or Conventions.

THAT all militia take proper care to acquire military skill, and be well prepared for defence, by being each man provided with one pound of good gunpowder and four pounds of ball fitted to his gun.

THAT one-fourth part of the militia in every Colony be selected for minute men, of such persons are willing to enter into this necessary service, formed into companies and battalions, and their officers chosen and commissioned as aforesaid, to be ready on the shortest notice to march to any place where their assistance may be required for the defence of their own or a neighbouring Colony; and as these minute men may eventually be called to action before the whole body of militia are sufficiently trained, it is recommended that a more particular and diligent attention be paid to their instruction in military discipline.

THAT such of the minute men, as desire it, be relieved by new draughts as aforesaid from the whole body of the militia once in four months.

As there are some people, who from religious principles cannot bear arms in any case, this Congress intend no violence to their consciences, but earnestly recommend it to them to contribute liberally in this time of universal calamity to the relief of their distressed brethren in the several Colonies, and to do all other services to their oppressed country, which they can consistently with their religious principles.

THAT it be recommended to the Assemblies or Conventions in the respective Colonies to provide, as soon as possible, sufficient stores of ammunition for their Colonies; also that they devise proper means for furnishing each with arms such effective men as are poor and unable to furnish them themselves.

THAT it be recommended to each Colony to appoint a Committee of Safety, to superintend and direct all matters necessary for the security and defence of their respective Colonies, in the recess of their Assemblies and Conventions.

THAT each Colony, at their own expense, make such provision by armed vessel or otherwise, as their respective Assemblies, Conventions, or Committees of Safety shall judge expedient and suitable to their circumstance and situations, for the protection of their harbours and navigation on their sea-coasts, against all unlawful invasions, attacks and depredations, from cutters and ships of war.

THAT it be recommended to the makers of arms for the use of the Militia, that they make good substantial muskets, with barrels three feet and a half in length, that will carry an ounce ball, and fitted with a good bayonet and steel ramrod, and that making such arms be encouraged by these United Colonies.

Where in any Colony a Militia is already formed under Regulations approved of by the Convention of such Colony, or by such Assemblies as are annually elective, we refer to the discretion of such Convention or Assembly, either to adopt the foregoing Regulations in the whole or in part, or to continue their former, as they, on consideration of all circumstances, shall think best.

A true Copy from the MINUTES,
  CHARLES THOMPSON, Secretary.

Recreated from The Pennsylvania Gazette, July 26, 1775.

1043 BRITISH DEAD AT BUNKER'S HILL.

Extract of a letter from CAMBRIDGE, *July* 21.

"We have been in a state of perfect quiet for several days, both armies being so well entrenched that they may look with confidence at each other. Doctor Winship, who attended the sick and wounded after the battle at Charlestown, and lived in the same house with the commanding officer of the marines, has given us a precise account of the number of killed and wounded on the side of the enemy. He assures us we may depend on its being more, not less, than 1043, of whom 300 fell on the field, or died in a few hours; many of the wounded have since died, through confinement to salt provisions.

"Beef, of the most miserable kind, is eagerly bought up at 1s. sterling per pound. Fish they have in general plenty, but all accounts agree in a great mortality in their army by fevers and fluxes. On our side, we are amply provided with fresh and salt provisions, and all manner of vegetables; the army is in high spirits, and eager to retrieve the honour they lost on Bunker's hill."

CAMBRIDGE, *July* 27.—Last Tuesday came to town from Philadelphia, and joined the army of the united colonies, a company of 106 rifle-men. Many hundreds more are daily expected.

Recreated from Purdie's Virginia Gazette, August 18, 1775.

THREE HUZZAS!

CAMBRIDGE, *July* 21.—Last Saturday, the several Regiments quartered in this Town being assembled upon the Parade, the Rev. Dr. Langdon, President of the College, read to them—

"A Declaration by the Representatives of the United Colonies of North America, now met in General Congress at Philadelphia, setting forth the Causes and Necessity of taking up Arms."

It was received with great Applause, and the Approbation of the Army, with that of a great Number of other People, was immediately announced by three Huzzas. His Excellency the General with several other Officers, &c. were present on the occasion.

AN APPEAL TO HEAVEN.

A Gentleman has favoured us with the following Account of the Declaration being read upon Prospect Hill.

Last Tuesday Morning, according to Orders issued the Day before, by Major-General Putnam, all the Continental Troops under his immediate Command assembled on Prospect Hill, when the Declaration of the Continental Congress was read, after which an animated and pathetic Address to the Army was made by the Rev. Mr. Leonard, Chaplain to General Putnam's Regiment, and succeeded by a pertinent Prayer; when General Putnam gave the Signal, and the whole Army shouted their loud Amen by three Cheers; immediately upon which a Cannon was fired from the Fort, and the Standard lately sent to General Putnam was exhibited flourishing in the Air, bearing on one side this Motto, AN APPEAL TO HEAVEN—and on the other Side, QUI TRANSTULIT SUSTINET.

The whole was conducted with the utmost Decency, good Order, and Regularity, and to the universal Acceptance of all present. And the Philistines on Bunker's Hill heard the Shout of the Israelites, and being very fearful, paraded themselves in Battle Array.

Recreated from The Hartford Courant, July 24, 1775.

NEW YORK, July 21.

YESTERDAY, agreeable to the recommendation of the delegates in the Honourable Continental Congress, was observed with the utmost solemnity, by fasting, abstinence, and devotion. In all the churches were large congregations, and excellent discourses delivered from the several pulpits, expressive of the truly calamitous situation of this unhappy continent.

An exact account of the troops under general Gage, and of the provincials.

Regulars now at Boston,	5000
One regiment of tories and negroes,	500
Light-horse, about	200
4 regiments expected, said to amount to	3000
Marines unknown, perhaps	800
Total of ministerialists,	9500
Massachusetts forces at Cambridge, Roxbury, and out posts.	13,600
Connecticut forces at ditto,	3000
New Hampshire ditto, at ditto,	1800
Rhode Island ditto, at ditto	1300
Total of provincials,	19,790

Besides several companies from Connecticut, on their way.

WILLIAMSBURG, August 4, 1775.

RUN away, a mulatto woman slave named JENNY, about 5 feet 5 or six inches high, and was formerly the property of mr. *Eaton*. She has some marks in her face, that appear blacker than her skin. I hereby forewarn all persons from harbouring or employing her, on any account. Very likely she may pass for a free woman. Whoever brings her to the subscriber shall receive 20s.

JOHN CARTER.

Recreated from Purdie's Virginia Gazette, August 4, 1775.

LONDON.

July 22. There is at present such a universal stagnation of trade, that there is no less than 200 merchantmen in the river, bound to different ports, which cannot obtain freight.

A gentleman is arrived from India. It is said he comes from the Company's servants, and inhabitants of Bengal, with a formal refusal of submission to the commissioners or judges lately arrived there, and also brings an account that the resignation of the Company's servants will be the consequence of their being continued, by which the Company's affairs will be greatly injured, and the government of the country much endangered.

July 25. Notwithstanding all the pains taken by the hirelings of government to blacken the Americans, it does not appear even from the partial account in the gazette of the action of the 17th of June, that they were either cruel, unskillful or cowardly. They fought it out bravely to the last, carried off their dead, nay, buried them in spite of their enemies utmost efforts. They have killed and disabled above a thousand of the King's troops, who have gained a dear bought victory by their own confession. For what have they done? By the help of the artillery, and the assistance of the men of war, they have been enabled to dislodge the provincials from a post, which in all probability they have regained by this time. The enemies of administration cannot wish them a greater misfortune than such another victory.

It is now confidently asserted that Lord North insists upon his Majesty's permission to resign, but offers to give every substantial assistance in his power, as much as if he had still continued in office.

July 27. England and Ireland groan under the weight of heavy taxations and unconstitutional pensions. Will the burden be lighter should we humble the Americans? No. But there will then be places on the continent for our ministers to dispose of; and the world will then be convinced, that in these men self-interest has the precedency of public good.

We are well assured that the most effectual and vigorous measures will be pursued with the provinces of New England, both on the account of their own signal demerits, and as an example to the other Colonies. The Parliament is to meet in the first week of November, in which a motion will be made for a bill of general forfeiture of the lands of all such as shall not surrender themselves on or before the first of February, 1776; and the lands so forfeited will by the same authority be distributed by debentures to such volunteers as shall join themselves, at their own expense (but with the aid of government) to effectuate the entire conquest and absolute subjection of the country.

July 31. We hear that a great personage, when he first read General Gage's Letter on the late action, exclaimed, "I am sorry for the loss of my Subjects, but the laws of my country must be supported."

The Government contractors have received orders to furnish winter camp clothing and utensils for 10,000 men, which are to be shipped off immediately for Boston.

JUST PUBLISHED, and to be SOLD by
JAMES HUMPHREYS, junior,
The Corner of Black-horse-alley, Front-street,

The Speech of Edmund Burke, Esq;
On moving his Resolutions for Conciliation with the Colonies,
March 22, 1775.
And shortly will be published, and to be sold by said *Humphreys*,

Mr. Burke's Speech in 1774.
Also the SPEECHES upon the Taxation of the *American* Colonies, delivered in the last Session of Parliament, by Governor Johnston; Mr. Hartley; Mr. Lutterell; Col. Achland, &c.

GOOD TALLOW CANDLES,
At Nine-pence per Pound, by the Box or Dozen,
TO BE SOLD BY
JOHN PURDON,
In Front-street, near the Drawbridge, Philadelphia.

3000 Bushels of good Indian CORN,
TO BE SOLD BY
JOHN SNOWDEN,
In Front-street, below the Drawbridge. *Sept.* 23, 1775.

Recreated from The Pennsylvania Gazette, October 11, 1775.

FORAY ON LONG ISLAND.

CAMBRIDGE, *July* 27.—Last Wednesday fe'nnight embarked from Dorchester Neck, Colonel Greaton, with 96 men in ten Whale Boats, for Long Island, in order to remove from thence some Stock and Hay. On his Way he was fired upon by the Men of War lying near said island, but notwithstanding the very heavy fire from the Ships, he proceeded, when not finding any Stock on the Island, he fired the Barns, in which was a quantity of Hay, he not being able to remove it; as he perceived several Barges, Cutters, and an armed Schooner coming upon him.

Having executed his Designs, so far as to deprive our Enemy of the Advantage they might receive from the Hay, &c. which he destroyed, he retreated, and when on board, he found himself again beset by the Savage Enemy, who perhaps would have taken some of the hindermost Boats, had it not been for the good Conduct of the Commander, and a Party from Squantom, posted on the shore, who by a warm fire drove off the Enemy; they killed one of our Men on the shore, and it is asserted by one in a Boat that there were two of the Enemy killed. The House that catched fire from the Barns was consumed.

LEATHER BREECHES,
MADE in the neatest and strongest manner, and on the most reasonable terms, by the subscribers at their shop a few rods north of the court-house and next door to Wid. Collyer's tavern in *Hartford*. As they served a regular apprenticeship to the Breeches Making business, they flatter themselves that their work will meet with general approbation---As they intend to continue in this town, they will make it their greatest study to merit the favour of the public. All orders will be strictly observed, and the least favour gratefully acknowledged by the public's most obedient humble servants,
Hartford, June 23, 1775.   JOHN HILL
    CHARLES WRIGHT.

Recreated from The Hartford Courant, July 31, 1775.

GENERAL HOWE TO COMMAND ARMY.

GATES TO REMAIN CIVIL GOVERNOUR.

Extract of a Letter from the Camp, at CAMBRIDGE, *dated July* 28, 1775.

"Within a day or two we have had five deserters from the advanced posts of the enemy; two of them are sensible and honest looking fellows; one that came in this morning particularly so. They have brought a return of the enemy killed and wounded, amounting to 1052; most of the wounded are dead or in a dangerous way. They have had no fresh provisions since the affair of Noddle's Island; and are not likely to have any without fighting for it.

"One of the deserters went off last night, with leave, to Philadelphia; he is a grenadier of the Royal Irish. The deserters say that yesterday morning General Gates surrendered, in the orders of the day, his command of the army to General Howe, and now acts only as civil Governor. That he is lampooned and despised by the whole army. That Howe is much censored for his mode of attack on our lines last month. That their artillery was wretchedly served; and what is more strange that all their spare cartridges which they brought out, were twelve pounders, and they took out only nine pounders cannon, so that when our people were obliged to quit their lines the enemy had not one round of artillery.

"That young Richardson was the first person who mounted our parapet; you know him well, he is of the 18th, or Royal Irish; he is dangerously wounded. That their number of effective men is 4000 in Boston, and 2200 on Bunker's hill. That they despair of forcing our lines; but talk of getting round us *if they can.*

"That eight sail of transports and one frigate are gone to Fisher's Island and other places in the sound marauding with 100 men. That they have erected a large bomb battery on Bunker's hill, and amongst others two 18 inch French mortars. That our morning gun, yesterday, threw an 18 pound shot into their incampment on the top of Bunker's hill."

Recreated from The Pennsylvania Packet, August 14, 1775.

IN WOMEN'S CLOTHING.

WORCESTER, *July* 26.—Information is given to Gen. Gage of matters in our army, &c. by persons in women's clothing, who or what they were is not known to our informant. Gage's army was thought to be 9000 strong but greatly intimidated. The regiments that arrived last at Boston, were as follows, viz: Light Dragoons 17th, Col. George Prestons, 120 men; Foot, 35th, Col. Henry Campbell; 49th, Alexander Maitland; 63rd, Francis Grant; 420 men each. Regiments destined for New York, but ordered to Boston by Gage, 22d, Gen. Tho. Gage; 40th, Sir Robert Hamilton; 44th, James Abercrombie (killed at Bunker's Hill); 45th, William Haviland; 420 men each. The whole number of King's troops lately arrived at Boston, 3060.

BRITISH WON'T FIGHT.

PROVIDENCE, *July* 26.—A gentleman from Cambridge informs, that advice had been received there, by several regular soldiers who have deserted, that it had been determined to attack the lines of the American army on Sunday last, but that not more than one quarter of the troops destined for the attack could be prevailed on to come out, the others declaring they would rather die within their own lines than turn out to be slaughtered; and that Gage had been, in consequence, obliged to lay aside the project. Some movements made at Bunker's Hill, and the landing of a number of troops at Charlestown, on Sunday, corroborates this intelligence.

WILLIAMSBURG, *July* 29.

Information having been received that a man of war's people carried off a sum of money from the custom house at Hamilton, amounting to upwards of 900l., a party of volunteers in this city went and secured the following sums of public money, viz. 360l. in the Receiver and Auditor General's offices; 314l. 14s. post-office money; and about 1000l. in the naval office of the upper district of James river.

TERROR OF A DEFENCELESS TOWN.

NEWPORT, *July* 31.—From last Tuesday, about 2 o'clock, till near the same hour on the next day, this town was threatened to be fired upon from three ships of war in this harbour, viz. the Rose, capt. Wallace, the Swan, capt. Ayscough, and Kingfisher, capt. Montague, and also a tender; for which purpose these ships were brought close in with the north-west part of the town, on Tuesday, toward night. Their tomkins were immediately taken out, and all the apparent preparations made for cannonading the town, which greatly terrified women and children, especially those who were with child. In the evening lanthorns and men were placed at the guns, and the most hostile appearance kept up which it was possible for them to exhibit; and many women and children were running about, wringing their hands and crying, in the greatest distress.

About half past 9 at night a cannon was discharged from the Rose, when the women really thought the firing on the town was begun, many of whom fainted away, and went into fits; and a number, we are told, absolutely miscarried by the fright. However, this gun was loaded with powder only, and the men of war gave out to a number of persons, whom, they had stopped coming down the river, that they should not beat the town down till next morning, when they would certainly do it.

In the morning the like terrific scene was opened by firing another cannon, and seizing on four ferry-boats, one passenger-boat, with a number of passengers, and two wood sloops. The Swan moved down toward the south part of the town, where she anchored, with her guns pointing diagonally across the wharves, so as to rake them from thence up to the parade and court-house. Here again all the tomkins were out; quantities of tar, and other inflammatory and combustible matter, were put into the ferry-boats, in order, as was said, with horrid cursing and damning, to set on fire, and send into the town to burn it, as a more expeditious way of destroying the town than by cannon only.

At the same these boats were to be sent into the town, a number of men were to be landed at the south end, to set fire on that part. Thus the most warlike and hostile parade was kept up to the highest degree, till near 2 o'clock on Wednesday; when, all at once, the boats were discharged, the ships weighed anchor, and stood up the river. The same evening the Rose got ashore, on the north part of the island; but by taking out her guns, &c. she was got off, and the next day they all came down again to their old station.

We know not of even the shadow of a just reason for the above inhuman conduct. If the captains of said ships have any reason to offer, we should be very glad to publish them to the world. The story about two of the Swan's men being seized by a mob in this town, gagged, carried to a Bristol jail, &c. had it not been absolutely disproved, would have been a most wretched pretext for firing on a defenceless town, in which there were not less than 6000 women and children. This story we hope to publish more at large, when we can obtain the letters which passed, and the affidavits which were taken, concerning the same.

N.B. It must have been well known to the commanders of these ships, that there was not a single cannon in this town mounted for its defence.

Recreated from Purdie's Virginia Gazette, August 18, 1775.

LONDON.

July 28. Major Pitcairn, of the marines, who was killed in the late action in America, has left 7 children. Four balls were lodged in his body, and he was taken off the field upon his son's shoulders.

The Americans load their rifle-barrel guns with a ball slit almost in four quarters, which when fired out of those guns, breaks into four pieces, and generally does great execution.

The provincials fight in regimentals, which are red, faced with blue, green, and orange colour. General Putnam's regimentals are faced with orange colour, and in his hat he wears an orange coloured feather and cockade.

Recreated from Rind's Virginia Gazette, October 19, 1775.

CREEPING ON HANDS AND KNEES.

RIFLE-MEN KILL SEVERAL.

Extract of a Letter from CAMBRIDGE, *dated July 31, 1775.*

"Last Friday we were informed by our out-centries at the foot of Bunker's Hill, that the enemy had cut down several large trees, and were busy all night in throwing up a line and abbatis in front of it.

"In the evening orders were given to the York county Rifle company to march down to our advanced post on Charlestown Neck, to endeavour to surround the enemy's advanced guard, and to bring off some prisoners, from whom we expected to learn the enemy's design, in throwing up the abbatis on the neck.

"The Rifle company divided, and executed their plan in the following manner. Captain Dowdle, with 39 men, filed off to the right of Bunker's Hill, and creeping on their hands and knees, got into the rear of the enemy's centries, without being discovered; the other division of 40 men, under Lieut. Miller, were equally successful in getting behind the centries on the left, and were within a few yards of joining the division on the right, when a party of regulars came down the hill to relieve their guard, and crossed our Rifle-men under Capt. Dowdle, as they were lying on the ground in an Indian-file. The regulars were within 20 yards of our Rifle-men before they saw them, and immediately fired. The Rifle-men returned the salute, killed several, and brought off two prisoners and their muskets, with the loss of Corporal Creuse, who is supposed to be killed, as he has not been heard of since the affair.

"In return for this, the enemy alarmed us all night in their turn. At one o'clock this morning a heavy firing of small-arms and cannon occasioned our drums to beat to arms; the army was immediately ordered under arms to their posts. The firing continued in three different quarters, Roxbury, Sewell's Point at the mouth of Cambridge river, and at the advanced posts on Charlestown Neck."

Recreated from The Pennsylvania Gazette, August 9, 1775.

AN INVETERATE ENEMY.

HARTFORD, *July* 31.—Last Wednesday week major Skeene came to town, from Philadelphia; and in the evening, he, with his son, who has been some time past in this place, took leave of the town without liberty. We hear they have taken a house in Middletown, near the water side. As the major appears to be an inveterate enemy to us, and will doubtless watch every opportunity to make his escape, it is hoped our friends in that place will keep a watchful eye over him.

Yesterday major Clark's company of volunteers passed through this town, to join the American army at Cambridge. They are the first company of the last recruits raised by this colony that have marched for their station, and are provided with excellent fire-arms, &c. made in the town of Farmington, to which they belonged.

Last Wednesday major Skeene was removed from Middletown to a very commodious and peacefully situated house in the West Society, in this town.

Recreated from Purdie's Virginia Gazette, August 18, 1775.

NEW YORK, *July* 27.—On Tuesday and Wednesday a large detachment from the camp at Harlaem, consisting of about 1000 men, under the command of Colonel Waterbury, marched for Albany. It is said they are intended as a reinforcement of Ticonderoga, where Major General Schuyler commands.

WHEREAS Abigail my wife, has without any cause or provocation deserted my bed and board, and has and still doth refuse to return and live with me; I do therefore strictly forbid all and every person or persons harbouring, or in any way entertaining or detaining her, or crediting her on my account, or having any deal whatsoever with her: And I do now stand ready to receive her if she will return, and provide for her to the utmost of my abilities, and in every respect treat her as a kind and tender husband. TIMOTHY HUBBARD, jun.
Wethersfield, July 3, 1775.

Recreated from The Hartford Courant, July 31, 1775.

PERMITTED TO LEAVE BOSTON.

CAMBRIDGE, *August* 3.—Last Monday morning, near Charlestown Neck, a warm fire began between our advanced parties and those of the enemy's works on Bunker's Hill. We made two marines prisoners, and killed several of the regulars, with the loss of one man, belonging to Marblehead who was killed with a cannon ball.

We hear that the enemy are about dismantling Castle William.

On Thursday last notifications were posted up in the town of Boston, the purport of which was to inform all such inhabitants as were desirous of quitting the town, that they might give in their names to the town Major; great numbers immediately applied, and several have had permission to come out. The reason of this permission is owing to the scarcity of provisions. Gage thinking he must be obliged to furnish them out of the King's stores, or let them starve.— They were not permitted to bring out their effects.

Recreated from The Pennsylvania Packet, August 14, 1775.

IRELAND, *August* 2.

CARLOW.—Saturday fe'nnight SIR Vesey Colclough, Bart. apprehended at the Pattern of Kilmeshan, in the County of Wexford, one Daggon, commonly called Captain Cropper, a noted White Boy, and lodged him in the Wexford gaol. He has made several useful discoveries, by which it is hoped that there will shortly be a stop put to the outrages of this lawless banditti.

The people of this kingdom are under the greatest apprehensions between the dread of internal annoyance from the White Boys and an invasion from the Spaniards.

The former assemble in great numbers in different parts of the kingdom. They are all composed of poor ignorant Roman Catholics, who fancy that their misery and poverty spring from the present form of government, so that our wise ministry will probably repent too late their temerity in furnishing them with arms against themselves.

Recreated from The Pennsylvania Gazette, October 18, 1775.

PAINTED LIKE INDIANS.

Extract of a letter from a gentleman at FREDERICK TOWN, *dated, August 1, 1775.*

"Notwithstanding the Urgency of my Business, I have been detained three Days in this Place by an Occurrence truly agreeable. I have had the Happiness of seeing Captain Michael Cressap, marching at the Head of a formidable Company, of upwards of 130 Men from the Mountains and back Woods, painted like Indians, armed with Tomahawks and Rifles, dressed in hunting Shirts and Mockasons, and tho' some of them had travelled near 800 Miles from the Banks of the Ohio, they seemed to walk light and easy, and not with less Spirit than in the first Hour of their March. Health and Vigour, after what they had undergone, declared them to be intimate with Hardship and familiar with Danger. Joy and Satisfaction were visible in the Crowd that met them. Had Lord North been present, and assured that the brave Leader could raise Thousands of such like to defend his Country, what think you, would not the Hatchet and the Block have intruded upon his mind?"

NORFOLK, *August* 2.

This town and neighbourhood have been much disturbed lately with the elopement of their Negroes, owing to a mistaken notion, which has unhappily spread amongst them, of finding shelter on board of the men of war in this harbour, notwithstanding the assurances given by the commanding officers that not the least encouragement should be shown them.

On Friday last a deputation from the common-hall of this borough waited upon Captains Macartney and Squires, of the men of war now lying here, with the thanks of the Corporation for their conduct, in discountenancing the runaway slaves that have made application for service on board.

TO BE SOLD,
A NEGROE WENCH, strong and healthy, a very good Cook, and capable of any Kind of House-work. Enquire of the PRINTERS.

Recreated from The Pennsylvania Gazette, August 16, 1775.

News From London.

MAKING READY FOR WAR.

August 3. Twenty thousand stands of arms were shipped yesterday morning at the Tower for America.

General Clinton writes to a friend in the following terms: "We are in tolerable good spirits, but we have no victuals, nor no money to buy any with."

On the late survey made of the Royal Navy, it appears that there are 87 ships fit for service, including those already in commission, and also several frigates.

August 4. Yesterday the Lady of Earl Dunmore, lately arrived from Virginia, and the Lady of Governor Johnson, from Minorca, were severally presented to the Queen.

Eight men of war, from 40 to 50 guns each, are ordered for the American station, the other ships now there being ordered home as too large for the service.

August 5. We hear that the men of war now getting ready for America, when finished and manned, are to sail with five transports to Ireland, which it is expected will be in three weeks at farthest, and there to take on board 900 men; which replacement, with those from England (wind and weather permitting) will join General Gage in October next; and that several sergeants in the guards are to be promoted, and sent to America as subaltern officers to that body of men, which is to be new raised.

On Saturday in the afternoon, several thousand weight of gunpowder, soldiers accoutrements, bedding, and stands of arms, were shipped at the Tower for North America.

The 27th ult. fifty silk weavers enlisted at Dublin, as volunteers, with the party of marines recruiting in that city.

Fourteen thousand suits of green regimentals are ordered to be made up with expedition, and sent for the use of the regulars at Boston. All are to be faced with red, and the difference will be only in trimming the button holes with various colours. Officers and private men will be alike.

Orders are sent to Cork and Kinsale, to provide quarters immediately for eight regiments of foot, which are to be quartered there for the greater convenience of embarkation.

Orders are sent to Dock, near Plymouth, for the regiment lying there in barracks at that place to hold themselves in readiness to embark for America on the shortest notice.

A letter from Boston concludes thus, "The Provincials, I am clear, will never stand us in a fair line, but behind hedges, walls or breast-works, their fire is truly formidable, and their rifles peculiarly adapted to take off the officers of a whole line as it marches to attack. Our three Generals came over in high spirits, and expected rather to punish a mob than fight with troops that would look them in the face; but there is an air of dejection through all our superiors, which forbodes no good, and does not look as things ought to do after victory."

August 7. The Parliament will assemble much earlier than was at first imagined; some say about Michaelmas, but it is believed at all events by the second week in October. And the principal motives assigned for this unprecedented and unexpected early meeting, are the following: To grant money for the purpose of raising and paying new levies. To authorise his Majesty, in case of necessity, to take sixteen thousand Hanoverians into pay. To grant money to embody and keep in pay one half of the militia throughout England; and in case the Americans should show a disposition to return to their duty, to consult Parliament on the conditions proper to be granted them.

It is whispered that government has ordered Gen. Gage to offer five thousand pounds to any person or persons, who will bring him Gen. Putnam's head. This has been privately communicated to most of the Royalists in and about Boston, who could be confided in.

August 8. Orders are given for the cruisers on the American station to take all ships, of what nation soever, which are found within a certain distance of the ports there, which are now shut up.

Recreated from The Pennsylvania Gazette, October 11, 1775.

GOV. MARTIN SHUNNED.

IN COMMITTEE, NEWBERN, N.C.

Aug. 5. From the late conduct of Gov. Martin at Fort Johnston, and intelligence since by this committee, it appears, he intends erecting the king's standard, and commencing hostilities against the people of this province. It is therefore resolved, that no person or persons whatsoever have any correspondence with him, either by personal communication or letter, on pain of being deemed enemies to the liberties of America, and dealt with accordingly. And that no person or persons presume to remove him or themselves from hence to Core sound, or any other part of the province where the governor resides, without leave of this committee, as he or they will not be suffered to return here.

By order,
    R. COGDELL, chairman.

AMERICANS BURN FORT JOHNSTON.

By a gentleman just come to town from Cape Fear, we have a certain account that the armed force which lately went down to burn Fort Johnston have effected the same by destroying all the houses and rendering the fortifications entirely useless. Capt. Collet, who commanded that fort, 'tis said, had a number of slaves which he had instigated to revolt from their masters, actually concealed in the fort, which were again recovered by their several owners; for this treachery they burnt his dwelling-house with all his furniture, and every thing valuable he had not time to get on board the men of war.

TO BE SOLD,
A PAIR of very fine charriot geldings, full 15 hands high. Enquire at Mr. Browns, at Annapolis.   tf

---

Recreated from The Maryland Gazette, August 24, 1775.

DR. FRANKLIN TO BE POST-MASTER.

THE HONOURABLE CONTINENTAL CONGRESS have established a Continental Post Office, and appointed Dr. BENJAMIN FRANKLIN, to be the Post-Master, with a Salary of 1000 Dollars a year.

We are informed that the hon. Continental Congress, after resolving to meet again at Philadelphia, have adjourned to the 5th of September; during their recess, it is said that a committee, chosen from the Delegates, will sit during the summer, and that their residence will be to the eastward of the city.

Recreated from The Hartford Courant, August 7, 1775.

WORCESTER, *August* 2.—Several men of war and two or three transports, sailed last week from Boston, where they were bound was not certainly known, but it is conjectured they are gone in search of fresh provisions.

NEW YORK.—A letter from Oyster Pond, August 3, says, "Thirteen sail of the ministerial fleet is arrived off Gardiner's Point. A boat belonging to them has taken 20 sheep out of a boat that Mr. Rufus Tuthill was carrying sheep in from Plum Island to Long Island; he had landed 30 head a little before he was attacked by the boat from one of the men of war."

NEWPORT, *August* 7.—A gentleman from the American Camp, says—Last Wednesday, some riflemen, on Charlestown side, shot an officer of note in the ministerial service, supposed to be Major Small or Bruce, and killed three men on board a ship in Charlestown Ferry, at the distance of full half a mile.

That General Gage had lately sent armed schooners to Machias, or to some place near it, with cash to buy live stock, and gave orders to take the stock by force, if the inhabitants would not sell it, which they did refuse, when the schooner's people attempted to take off the stock; upon which the inhabitants rose, made all the men prisoners, seized on the schooners and cash, and shared about 5l. sterling a man.

Recreated from The Pennsylvania Gazette, August 16, 1775.

HANG SOME CANADIANS.

King's Troops at St. John's.

Extract of a letter from Ticonderoga, *dated August 4, 1775.*

THREE weeks ago an attempt was made to force the Canadians to take up arms, and they were about to hang some in every parish, when the Canadians arose in a body of near 3000 men, disarmed the officer that was after recruits, and made him flee, being determined to defend themselves in the best manner they could by a full resistance, rather than be forced to arm against the colonies. The common people there cannot bear to have the old French laws take place again amongst them, as they will be thereby plunged into enormous taxes.

Two persons who have lately come from St. John's, being examined under oath before the general, give accounts that the King's troops are well fortified at St. John's; that there is at that place 470 regulars, and 110 at Chamblee, about 12 miles distant, about 20 at Montreal, and one company at Quebec; 40 Indians at St. John's.

Colonel Guy Johnson and colonel Claus, with 500 Indians, just arrived at Montreal, and are just going to join the English rebels against us.

One of these men was at Montreal, and saw Johnson and his Indians. They appear to be two sensible men, and gave a very direct account. There are two large and strong vessels nearly finished at St. John's, to carry about 14 or 15 carriage guns each, and they are every day in expectation of being joined by about 4000 regulars that are come into the river, and then to come against us, unless forced by a formidable army.

We had a few days ago two men, who went down to the lake with an Indian boy from Dr. Wheelock's college, intending to land him about 30 miles this side of St. John's, who are taken by a scout of the enemy, and held prisoner.

THE subscriber intends to leave the colony immediately.
RICHARD POOK.

Recreated from Rind's Virginia Gazette, August 31, 1775.

MOST OF THE WOUNDED DEAD.

George Tavern Burnt.

Extract of a letter from Cambridge, August 5.

"Since I wrote you last, our troops have had several skirmishes with the enemy, in all of which we have had the better of them. We have burnt the light-house twice. The last time Major Tupper with three hundred men went down to effect it; he found the party there had repaired the building and lighted it the night before. The party consisted of about fifty marines and tories, a master carpenter from New York among the latter. Our people were fired on by the party on the island before they landed. However, they landed and finally carried the island, took what was valuable, burnt the building, killed the Lieut. who commanded and eight others, and took the rest prisoners, and also burnt one sloop and one schooner, and got off with the loss of one man killed, one wounded dangerously, and one boat lost.

"Last Sunday evening the enemy sallied from the neck on our out-sentries, drove them back to our main guard without the George Tavern, and before our main guard turned out and reached them, set fire to the George, which was burnt down; but our men from the main guard soon drove them back quite into their lines, killed one officer and several men, without one of ours killed or wounded.

"For some days past Gen. Gage has been permitting the people to come out of Boston, stripped of every thing, and what they call a pocket sergeant to search every person's pocket, that no one carries with him or her more than five pounds. The inhabitants are extremely distressed, and the troops almost as much. Almost all their wounded at Bunker's Hill and elsewhere are dead, and all the Provincials who were prisoners with them, are dead. They say our balls were poisoned, but the bad provisions and the scurvy, which prevails among them, is a more probable and charitable way of accounting for the death of the wounded. Certainly there never was any poisoned balls used.

"Some of their officers are still very angry, talk high and big, but the more sensible men among them are dispirited, and say that it is in vain to attempt any thing, for if they should attempt our lines, success is uncertain; and should they succeed, the enemy will rally again on the next hills, and increase in number and in rage, and will harass them to death, and those that may happen to survive the conflict at the lines; that they cannot do as in Europe, fight one or two battles in a season, and then lie still and quiet, and refresh on good provisions, forage, &c. and get recruited from the neighbourhood; here they cannot be succoured in the course of months.

"The troops are universally disheartened; both officers and men heartily cursing Mr. Gage and the Tories; not one of the latter dare be seen among them. It has been seriously talked of to plunder the town of Boston, and desert it if they are not soon recruited, I shall not be disappointed at the sight. Eight or ten of their men have lately deserted to us, and say, hundreds will do the same at the first opportunity. By deserters, inhabitants of Boston, &c. it is agreed that the enemy have not so many men now as at the first of April. Their losses killed and wounded have been great, and by sickness greater still.

"Those troops, who have been here three or four years have not been so sickly, but those who have come lately have been very sickly indeed, and now remain so. I believe most of them will be swept off by sickness, if we lie still, and only look on, and keep them from fresh provisions, &c."

The Address to the Soldiers, which has been printed at Cambridge, and dispersed among the ministerial troops, has the following indorsement.

PROSPECT HILL.	BUNKER'S-HILL.
I. Seven doll. a month.	I. Three pence a day.
II. Fresh provisions, and in plenty.	II. Rotten salt pork.
III. Health.	III. The Scurvy.
IV. Freedom, ease, affluence, and a good farm.	IV. Slavery, beggary, and want.

Recreated from The Pennsylvania Packet, August 14, 1775.

WATERTOWN, *August* 5.

We are credibly informed that general Burgoyne has lately shown every appearance of a deep settled melancholy; he is continually walking the streets of Boston with his arms folded across his breast, and talking to himself.

We are also informed, that general Gage and admiral Greaves have publickly quarrelled. Admiral Greaves having told Gage it was a cowardly action to burn Charlestown. Gage sharply replied, he should not consult him in such matters.

Recreated from Purdie's Virginia Gazette, August 18, 1775.

NEWPORT, *August* 7.

Last week a gentleman came from Connecticut, who exhibited several examples of salt petre, of excellent quality, lately made in that colony, where, as well as in other colonies, a number of works are erecting for making that useful article, and it is not doubted but there will soon be a sufficient quantity procured to supply the whole continent for making as much gunpowder as will be wanted.

Recreated from The Pennsylvania Gazette, August 23, 1775.

HARTFORD, *August* 7.

Since our last, nine Companies of Rifle-Men from Virginia, Maryland, and Pennsylvania, have passed through this town on their Way for the Head Quarters at Cambridge; they are an exceeding fine Body of Soldiers, commanded by very able and experienced Officers, and to a Man appear determined to defend their Rights and Privileges, in Connection with their Brethren of the Northern Colonies, against those who attempt barbarously to deprive us of them. We hear many of the private Soldiers in the above Companies, are Gentlemen of large Fortunes in the Southern Provinces.

We can't yet learn that a single Tribe of Savages on this Continent have been persuaded yet to take up the Hatchet against the Colonies, notwithstanding the great Pains made Use of by the vile Emissaries of a savage Ministry for that purpose.

Recreated from The Hartford Courant, August 7, 1775.

PHILADELPHIA.

To the SPINNERS in this City, the Suburbs and Country.

YOUR services are now wanted to promote the American Manufactory at the corner of Market and Ninth streets, where cotton, wool, flax, &c. are delivered out. Strangers who apply are desired to bring a few lines by way of recommendation from some respectable person in their neighbourhood.

One distinguishing character of an excellent woman, as given by the wisest of men is, "That she seeketh wool and flax, and worketh willingly with her hands—she layeth her hands to the spindle, and her hands holdeth the distaff."—In this time of public distress you have now each of you an opportunity, not only to help sustain your families, but likewise to cast your mite into the Treasury of the public good. The most feeble effort to help to save the state from ruin, when it is all you can do, is, as the widow's mite, entitled to the same reward as they who of their abundant abilities have cast in much.

Recreated from The Pennsylvania Gazette, August 9, 1775.

JUNTO DISAPPOINTED.

LONDON, *August* 9.—Nothing can prove more strongly the despair of the administration of ever executing their wicked schemes against America, than the late provision for Mr. Jenkinson. A year ago they thought themselves sure of having all the lands in Massachusetts Bay as forfeitures, out of which Mr. Jenkinson was promised a princely portion.

This was a principal motive with the Buckingham-house junto, of which he is the leader, for involving the nation in the unnatural and ruinous civil war with America; but the bravery of Americans having rendered these fruits distant and problematical, Mr. Jenkinson is in the mean time provided for, by the clerkship of the Pells in Ireland.

Recreated from The Pennsylvania Gazette, October 18, 1775.

BOSTON ENCIRCLED.

Extract of a letter from a Gentleman of this City, dated, CAMBRIDGE, *August* 9, 1775.

"We waited on General Washington, who I have the pleasure to inform you is much beloved and admired for his polite condescension and noble deportment. His appointment of the Chief Command has the general suffrage of all the ranks of people here, which I think is no bad omen.

"We viewed the lines, and were truly amazed at the extent and grandeur of the works, considering the short time in which they have been erected. The whole works, from Winter Hill to Dorchester Neck, form a kind of semi-circle around Boston, Winter Hill belong the northernmost; next comes Prospect Hill, very properly named from the fine prospect it affords (from its summit) of the towns of Boston and Charlestown, the latter now in ashes, and nothing to be seen of that fine town but chimnies and rubbish, having been burnt as you know about the 20th of June by the British barbarians; it affords also a distinct view of Bunker's Hill, about one mile distant therefrom.

"To the southward of this hill is a chain of breastworks and redoubts till you come to Cambridge river, from whence it is continued along by Roxbury and Dorchester Neck, being in the whole extent, as near as I can judge, about eight miles. The two hills appear to me almost impregnable, having forts within breast-works strongly picketed, and in many places planted with heavy cannon—add to these their natural strength from their great elevation. To the eastward of Winter Hill lies Penny ferry, where the said barbarians, out of mere wantonness, burnt a house a few days since, without any prospect or advantage to themselves.

"This day they have been blowing up the Castle, the explosions we could see from an high hill in the neighbourhood of Winnisimet ferry. The people bear their misfortunes with astonishing patience and magnanimity. It is no uncommon thing to see those who have lost one or two houses, and nearly all their effects, and some who have lost their all, yet you would discover nothing of this by their behaviour or countenances.

"Gage has again agreed to let the people come out of Boston, but will not suffer more than two small boats to ply, which bring out bout 12 or 15 in a day. The people say great pains are taken to persuade them to stay, by telling them that 30,000 Hanoverians, 30,000 Hessians, and as many Russians, are shortly expected, when they shall destroy all the rebels at once.

"We have an account from the eastward of our people having taken a man of war's tender, and one or two transports—the particulars are difficult to gather or ascertain; however, seven marine officers are brought prisoners here, and are secured. There has just arrived an account of an engagement between our people and a man of war at Cape Anne, wherein our people had the advantage, but no particulars that can be relied on are come to hand."

Recreated from Purdie's Virginia Gazette, August 11, 1775.

RIFLEMEN AT CAMBRIDGE.

August 10.—Since Monday last eight companies of Rifle-men, of about 100 men each, have arrived from the southward. Four more are daily expected.

Col. Thompson of the Pennsylvania regiment of rifle-men, and a number of young gentlemen, volunteers, from Philadelphia, are arrived. Also Capt. Morgan's company in 3 weeks from Virginia, being 600 miles.

WILLIAMSBURG, *August* 11.—Colonel Benjamin Harrison, and Thomas Jefferson, esq., arrived a few days ago from Philadelphia, and are now at the convention in Richmond.

It was last Wednesday determined upon in Convention, that only 1000 regular forces shall at present be raised, who will be assisted, as exigencies may require, by 8000 minute men to be kept in training in the several counties.

Recreated from The Pennsylvania Gazette, August 23, 1775.

REINFORCEMENTS FOR CANADA.

NEW YORK, *August* 10.—Last Tuesday the first division of Col. M'Dougall's battalion of provincial troops sailed, under the command of Lieut. Col. Ritzema, to join Gen. Schuyler at Ticonderoga. They will be followed immediately by the second, under Major Zedwitz; and their Colonel is preparing immediately to follow with the third and last division.

Last Sunday an express arrived from Suffolk County, on Long Island, with information that a number of transports, with a considerable body of troops from Boston, under convoy of five ships of war, had appeared off Montock Point; that an officer landed, and requested to purchase a number of cattle and sheep, which was refused. The particulars of the proceedings in consequence of this demand must be deferred, till more authentic accounts are received.

We hear that the officers of the county militias marched a large body of men to the place of their landing; and on Tuesday last Maj.-Gen. Wooster, with the Connecticut forces, left their encampment at Harlaem, crossed the East River to HOORN'S HOOK and marched with expedition to act in concert with the militia.

Recreated from The Pennsylvania Gazette, August 16, 1775.

NEW YORK, *August* 10.—"The express, who was sent by the Congress, is returned here from the Eastward, and says he left the Camp last Saturday; that the Rifle-Men had picked off ten men in one day, three of whom were *Field Officers*, that were reconnoitering; one of them was killed at a distance of 250 yards, when only half his head was seen."

Extract of a letter from the Hague.

"From the many warlike preparations now making by the Emperor of Germany, and the King of Prussia, between whom there is the strictest unity and alliance, it is imagined that they will shortly put in force their favourite scheme of annihilating the ancient system of Government in Germany, and establish out of its ruins two formidable monarchies."

Recreated from The Pennsylvania Packet, August 14, 1775.

ENEMY CANNONADE TOWN.

ALMIGHTY ON OUR SIDE.

GLOUCESTER,—On the 9th inst. the Falcon sloop of war, Capt. Linzee, hove in sight, and seemed to be in a quest of two schooners from the West Indies bound to Salem, one of which he soon brought to, the other taking advantage of a fair wind, put into our harbour; but Linzee having made a prize of the first, pursued the second into the harbour, and brought the first with him. He anchored and sent two barges with fifteen men in each, armed with muskets and swivels, these were attended with a whale boat, in which was the Lieutenant and six privates; their orders were to seize the loaded schooner, and bring her under the Falcon's bow.

The Militia and other inhabitants were alarmed at this daring attempt, and prepared for a vigorous opposition. The barge men under the command of the Lieutenant boarded the schooner at the cabin windows, which provoked a smart fire from our people on the shore, by which three of the enemy were killed, and the Lieutenant wounded in the thigh, who thereupon returned to the man of war. Upon this Linzee sent the other schooner and a small cutter he had to attend him, well armed, with orders to fire upon the damn'd rebels wherever they could see them, and that he would in the mean time cannonade the town; he immediately fired a broad side upon the thickest settlements, and stood himself with a diabolical pleasure to see what havock his cannon might make.

"Now, (said he) my boys, we will aim at the damn'd Presbyterian Church—Well, my brave fellows, one shot more and the house of God will fall before you."

While he was thus venting his hellish rage, and setting himself as it were against Heaven, the Almighty was on our side, not a ball struck or wounded an individual person, although they went through houses in almost every direction then filled with women and children.

Under God our little party at the water side performed wonders, for they soon made themselves masters of both the schooners, the cutter, the two barges, the boat, and every man in them, and all that pertained to them. In the action, which lasted several hours, we lost but one man, two others wounded, one of which is since dead, the other very slightly wounded. We took of the man of war's men 35 prisoners, several were wounded and one has since died; 24 were sent to head-quarters, the remainder being impressed from this and the neighbouring towns, were permitted to return to their friends. Next day Capt. Linzee warped off with but half his men, never a prize, boat nor tender, except a small skiff the wounded Lieutenant returned in.

We are informed that amongst the prisoners taken at Cape Ann, is one Budd, Gunner of the Falcon sloop of war, who was some time ago taken at Machias, with a number of others, and brought to this town, and upon being released from close confinement, took an opportunity of running off with a few of our town gentry, and got on board the Falcon again. It is hoped this fellow, if retaken, will be better secured.

How is the glory of Britain departed! Her army, which not long since was the terror of many nations, is now employed in cutting the throats of his Majesty's loyal subjects, and SHEEP STEALING! *Felons indeed!*

TO BE SOLD, A NEGROE MAN, named TOM, 22 or 23 years of age, can talk English and Dutch, has had the small-pox and measles; he can plough, sow, reap and mow, and can do as much in a day as any man that I have seen.

HORSES TAKEN IN AT ANTHONY FORTUNE's LIVERY STABLE, at the Sign of the Horse and Groom, in Shippen-street, the second House from Third-street, near the New-market, Philadelphia. Horses at Twenty-two Pounds per Year Travellers Horses at One shilling per Night, good and convenient Grass Lots, well watered, for Pasture, on the lowest Terms. ¶ 6 W.

Recreated from The Pennsylvania Gazette, August 30, 1775.

THE PLUNDERING ENEMY.

The following is the best account we are able to collect, of the late expedition of the Piratical Regular traitors to the English constitution, and the British Colonies, in plundering Fisher's, Gardiner's, Plum and Block Islands, of stock, provisions, &c.

The design of the regulars to plunder these islands having been communicated to the inhabitants and proprietors of the Congress of New York, and other intelligences, as early as Tuesday the 8th, there was time to have taken off all the stock; and some was actually taken off. But some differences having arisen between the proprietors and the Committees, concerning the expence of the business, before any thing could be determined, the ships of the enemy appeared in sight.

Dispatches were immediately sent to alarm and assemble the people on the Connecticut and Long Island shores, who, notwithstanding the utmost haste they could then make, were too late to prevent the execution of the felonious design of the enemy; who on Friday the 11th, approached Gardiner's island with the following vessels and forces, viz. 7 transport ships, 2 brigs, 2 men of war, 1 snow of 10 guns, 1 armed schooner of 17 men and 200 regulars, as reported by the sailors, landed on the island, and assisted by 10 villainous tories from South-Hold, &c. took off the following stock, &c.

By the account of Benjamin Miller, the overseer, 1000 sheep, 30 hogs, 13 geese, 3 calves, 1000lb. cheese, 7 tons hay, were taken off, and much damage done to gardens, fences, fowls, &c. When they went away, they left on the table half a guinea and a pistareen.

Signed by, Benjamin Miller.

TO BE SOLD BY ISRAEL PEMBERTON, AN ENGLISH SERVANT LAD, who hath upwards of five Years to serve; he writes a good Hand, and has worked some Time at the Shoemaker's Trade.

The following letter was left by the Commanding Officer, and gives reason to suspect that the expedition (as to Gardiner's Island) was preconcerted with the proprietor, or manager.—The following is an exact copy, viz.

SIR, As we have got loaded all the vessels, I can't come to your house according to promise, I send you account of what I have got off your island; sheep, 823; fat cattle, 59; cows, 3; calves, 3; one of the calves got away. The cheese I will take account of. Send me some pigs, fowls and potatoes, and ducks, and some bread, and when you come to Boston, I will secure your interest to you if in my power. I am very sorry it is not in my power to come to your house, but so good a wind we can't stay. The hay you must send an account of by Captain Lawrence.

Sir, I am your's, Abijah Willant.

August 11, 1775, 12 o'clock at night.

Besides the aforementioned stock from Gardiner's island, we are informed, that the same crew of free booters took from Fisher's island 26 fat cattle, and about 1000 sheep; also from Plum island 14 fat cattle. At this last island they had only one prize wood boat, and a transport brig. On their arrival and landing on one side of the island, they were fired upon by about 100 of Col. Wooster's Provincials, who had landed on the other side. But it being represented to the commanding officer, that the island was nearly surrounded by a number of the enemy's armed vessels who would be likely to cut off their retreat, they fired but one volley, which did not appear to have done any execution, and the retired to the main land, when the 14 cattle were taken off.

After these exploits, 3 more transports appearing in sight, on Tuesday morning, the Rose and Swan sloops of war sailed to meet them, in order to make a descent upon and plunder Block Island; the success of which attempt we have not yet heard.

Recreated from The Pennsylvania Gazette, August 23, 1775.

DELEGATES ARRIVE HOME.

WHITHER GO DUNMORE?

WATERTOWN, *Aug.* 14.—The Hon. John Hancock, Samuel Adams, and John Adams, Esqrs., three of the Delegates of this colony, at the Continental Congress, arrived here in good health on Friday last.

We hear that last Thursday afternoon a number of Riflemen killed two or three of the Regulars as they were relieving the centries at Charlestown lines.

WILLIAMSBURG, *August* 12.—Intelligence was received this morning, that a brig, which was lately taken with provisions, and carried into Boston by the ministerial pirates, returned from thence to Norfolk last Wednesday, having on board 7 officers of the regular army. We do not hear that any soldiers are come with them, or are to follow; but it is certain that the Earl of Dunmore's ship is now compleated for an expedition, and that his Lordship has fitted up thirteen field pieces for service. It is apprehended he intends to commence hostilities upon York or James river very soon.

* * * *

Friday last was conducted to this town by an escort, commanded by Captain Melcher, the officers and crew of the armed cutters Margaretta, Diligent, and their tender, taken at Machias, together with that noted friend to government, Ichabod Jones, formerly of Boston, and a staunch friend to that infernal traitor to his country, T. Hutchinson. Capt. Moore, of the Margaretta, was killed in the engagement. Capt. Knight, Lieut. Spry, five Midshipmen and Warrant Officers, together with 17 Privates belonging to the above vessels, we hear are ordered to the more interior parts of this colony.

NEWPORT, *Aug.* 14.—Fifteen transports and ships of war passed by this harbour last Saturday, supposed to be bound to Boston with the sheep, oxen, &c. from Fisher's and Gardiner's Island.

Recreated from The Pennsylvania Gazette, August 23, 1775.

ARMY IN PERFECT HARMONY.

WILLIAMSBURG, *August* 18.—Letters from the camp at Cambridge say, that his Excellency General Washington, as well as General Lee, have been indefatigable, ever since their arrival, to put the army under the best regulation, which is now very strongly intrenched, remarkably healthy, being abundantly supplied with provisions, and that the most perfect harmony subsists between the officers and men. The ministerial camp is likewise strongly fortified, so that there was no likelihood of there being a general engagement soon.

We can assure the publick that forty tons of GUNPOWDER have been lately imported into Philadelphia, six tons and a half of which were sent to the continental camp, and one ton to Virginia; also, that the colonies may depend upon a constant supply of that very useful commodity, at this juncture.

Thomas Nelson, Thomas Jefferson, George Wythe, and Francis Lightfoot Lee, esquires, are chosen delegates to represent this colony in the General Congress, on the 5th of next month.

In the room of his Excellency General Washington, commander in chief of the continental army, Patrick Henry, esq., has been appointed to the command of the troops to be raised for the defence of this colony.

Recreated from Purdie's Virginia Gazette, August 18, 1775.

SLAVES DISCHARGED FROM SHIP.

NORFOLK, *Aug.* 16.—Last week several slaves, the property of a gentleman in this town, were discharged from on board the Otter, where it is now shamefully notorious many of them for weeks past have been concealed, and their owners in some instances ill-treated for making applications for them. The publick, it is generally thought, is indebted for this discharge to a higher power than any on board that vessel.

The officers that lately arrived in a vessel from Boston still continue at Gosport. Two of them, as we hear, are captains, one a lieutenant, three of them ensigns, and one a surgeon.

Recreated from Purdie's Virginia Gazette, August 25, 1775.

CAMBRIDGE, *August* 21.—Accounts mention that the Capts. Perceval and Sabine, of the marines, Capt' Le Moine, of the royal artillery, and a number of privates, of Gen. Gage's army, in all about 90, were lately killed by the rifle men, &c. from the Provincial lines.

● ● ● ●

In a letter dated April 23, from an officer in Lord Percy's regiment at Boston, is the following:—"Our business was to seize a quantity of military stores, and the bodies of Messieurs Hancock and Adams, who are both attainted, and were at the place enforcing, with all their influence, the rebellious spirit of the Provincial Congress."

Recreated from The Pennsylvania Gazette, August 23, 1775.

WILLIAMSBURG, *July* 20, 1775.

THERE is now living in my family, adjoining to this city, a negro girl called SARAH, who is about 14 years old, near 4 feet 7 inches high, somewhat slender made, and is very black; she says she is a *Mundingo*, but cannot tell her owner's name. I have been informed she was purchased by some person of *Carolina*, at *Suffolk* in *Nansemond*, and that she was in jail there since, consequently must have been advertised, as she was taken out to be sold for prison fees, but was turned loose at *Smithfield*, without any thing being farther done. She was there taken in by sundry families, as an object, and maintained for what little service she could do, being often troubled with choaking fits, which deprive her of the use of her limbs, as well as her senses. Her owner is desired to apply for her to me, at *Whaley's* free-school.

SAMUEL WALLACE.

Recreated from Purdie's Virginia Gazette, August 11, 1775.

INDIANS OFFER SERVICES.

WATERTOWN, *August* 21.—Yesterday fe'nnight arrived at the camp in Cambridge, Swashan the chief, with four other Indians of the St. Francois tribe, conducted thither by Mr. Reuben Colburn, who has been honourably recompensed for his trouble. The above Indians came hither to offer their service in the cause of American liberty, have been kindly received, and are now entered the service. Swashan says he will bring one half of his tribe, and has engaged 4 or 5 other tribes, if they should be wanted. He says the Indians of Canada in general, and also the French, are greatly in our favour, and are determined not to act against us.

Last Monday morning came to town, from Ipswich, 20 of the prisoners taken at Cape Anne the Tuesday before; who, together with the marines, &c. are gone forward.

We hear that General Gage's lady and family, with a number of other people, are sailed from Boston for England.

We hear a number of officers' ladies have lately arrived at Boston, from England, Ireland, &c. and on their landing they were to a woman, widows.

PROVIDENCE, *August* 19.—We hear a detachment from the American army has marched for Cape Anne, to repel any attempts that may be made in that quarter by the ministerial troops or ships.

BALTIMORE, *August* 22.—By a letter from York Town, in Pennsylvania, we learn, that the inhabitants of that town and county, who early distinguished themselves in support and defence of our inestimable rights and liberties, have now formed a battalion of 500 minute men, to be ready to march to such place as may be deemed necessary for the protection and defence of these colonies—that they are all become military men, and have 3400 able bodied men associated in the county, and public arms, &c. and are preparing as fast as possible.

Recreated from The Pennsylvania Gazette, August 30, 1775.

LONDON.

August 21.—Wednesday a small ship from Bristol to America was stopped in the Bristol channel, on an information given that she was carrying out some warlike ammunition to the provincials, and on searching her there were found 30,000 muskets.

The Sphynx, a snow, Parks, from Ireland, with salt provisions for Boston, is said to be lost in the passage, and all on board perished.

Recreated from Purdie's Virginia Gazette, November 17, 1775.

LONDON, *August* 22.—By a letter from Clonmel, Ireland, to a gentleman in Dublin, in the said kingdom, we learn, that the White-boys assembled on the common in Loughrick, on Monday evening, the 9th instant, in their usual uniforms, and proceeded to the house of one Mulally, a Proctor, dragged him out of his bed, cut off his ears, took the tythe book out of his desk, and hanging it about his neck, brought him to an adjacent wood, where they dug a whole and set him upright in it about his neck, stopping it up, and laid a great stone on his head, in which condition he was found dead the next morning.

August 24. It is reported, "that no answer has yet been given, to the petition of the Continental Congress, as it is thought beneath the dignity of the government to treat with or acknowledge an Assembly, which has no constitutional existence."

It is said that Governor Dunmore had sent to the people of Norfolk (Virginia) to supply the shipping with provisions, for which they were to be paid; but if this was not complied with, orders would be issued to burn the town.

Recreated from The Pennsylvania Gazette, November 1, 1775.

Extract of a letter from Glasgow, August 22.

"The old Highland Watch, who were stationed in Ireland, upon being ordered to Boston, they all refused going, to a man, and declared they would not go and fight against their brethren, who last fought and conquered by their side."

Recreated from The Pennsylvania Gazette, November 29, 1775.

A PROCLAMATION
by the KING.
For Suppressing Rebellion and Sedition.

GEORGE R.

WHEREAS many of our subjects in divers parts of our colonies and plantations in North America, misled by dangerous and ill designing men, and forgetting the allegiance which they owe to the power that has protected and sustained them, after various disorderly acts committed in disturbance of the public peace, to the obstruction of lawful commerce, and to the oppression of our loyal subjects carrying on the same, have at length proceeded to open and avowed rebellion, by arraying themselves in hostile manner to withstand the execution of the law, and traiterously preparing, ordering, and levying war against us; And whereas there is reason to apprehend that such rebellion hath been much prompted and encouraged by the traiterous correspondence, counsels, and comfort of divers wicked and desperate persons within this realm. To the end therefore that none of our subjects may neglect or violate their duty through ignorance thereof, or through any doubt of the protection which the law will afford to their loyalty and zeal, we have thought fit, by and with the advice of our Privy Council, to issue this our royal Proclamation, hereby declaring that not only all our officers civil and military are obliged to exert their utmost endeavours to suppress such rebellion, and to bring the traitors to justice; but that all our subjects of this realm, and the dominions thereunto belonging, are bound by law to be aiding and assisting in the suppression of such rebellion, and to disclose and make known all traiterous conspiracies and attempts against us, our crown and dignity; and we do accordingly strictly charge and command all our officers as well civil as military, and all our obedient and loyal subjects, to use their utmost endeavours to withstand and suppress such rebellion, and to disclose and make known all treasons and traiterous conspiracies which they shall know to be against us, our crown and dignity, and for that purpose, that they transmit to one of our principal Secretaries of State, or other proper officer, due and full information of all persons who shall be found carrying on correspondence with, or in any manner or degree aiding or abetting the persons now in open arms and rebellion against our Government, within any of our colonies and plantations in North America, in order to bring to condign punishment the authors, perpetrators, and abettors of such traiterous designs.

Given at our Court, at St. James's, August 23, 1775, *in the fifteenth year of our reign.*

GOD SAVE THE KING.

Recreated from The Pennsylvania Gazette, November 1, 1775.

PEYTON RANDOLPH RECOVERED.

WILLIAMSBURG, *Aug.* 25.—Last Saturday, about 2 o'clock, the hon. PEYTON RANDOLPH, esq., with his Lady, arrived at his house in this city from Richmond, the gentlemen of the Convention having recommended it to him to retire for the present from the fatigue of business, on account of his being much indisposed, and as the time of his departure for the General Continental Congress was nearly approaching.

He was escorted into town by a troop of the Williamsburg volunteers, and received at the college by all the volunteer companies now here under arms, who, as well as a great number of the inhabitants, attended him to his own door, where they gave him three cheers, wishing him and his lady an uninterrupted enjoyment of every felicity.

We have the pleasure to inform the publick, that his Honour is greatly recovered since his return home, and intends setting out next Sunday morning for Philadelphia.

ROBERT CARTER NICHOLAS, esq., was unanimously elected President of the Convention, during the indisposition or absence of the hon. Peyton Randolph, esq.

Recreated from Purdie's Virginia Gazette, August 25, 1775.

Just Published——*Price one Shilling,*

The MANUAL EXERCISE

As ordered by his Majesty in the Year 1764,

WITH

EXPLANATIONS of the Method generally practised at Reviews and Field-Days.

TO WHICH IS ADDED,

The RULES and ARTICLES ordered by the General Congress, to be attended to, and observed for the better Government of the *American* Army.

Also, just published,——*Price one Shilling,*

THE

Sentiments of a Foreigner,

On the Disputes of GREAT BRITAIN with AMERICA.—Translated from the *French.*

Likewise——*Price fifteen Pence,*

A SERMON

On the present Situation of AMERICAN Affairs, preached on the 23d of *June* last, at the Request of the Officers of the THIRD BATTALION of the City of *Philadelphia,* by WILLIAM SMITH, D. D. Provost of the College of that City.

AUGUST 2, 1775.

THE Medicines, Shop Utensils, and Books, belonging to the Estate of Dr. *John Walker,* will certainly be disposed of to the highest Bidder, at *Hanover* Town, on *Friday* the 18th Instant.

2   THOMAS SIMPSON.

Recreated from The Virginia Gazette, August 12, 1775.

A SECOND EXPEDITION.

NEW YORK, *Aug.* 31.—*On Tuesday last the following was published in a hand bill through this city.*

SIR,   OYSTER PONDS, *August* 27.

Your favour of the 11th instant came duly to hand, and I should have sailed for Haerlem without loss of time, had I not received the following important intelligence from Gen. Washington, viz.

August 23. "Yesterday I received advice from Boston, that a number of transports have sailed on a second expedition, for fresh provisions. As they may pursue the same course, only advancing farther, we think Montaug Point, or Long Island, a very probable place of their landing; I have therefore thought best to give you the earliest intelligence; but I do not mean to confine your attention or vigilance to that place; you will please to extend your views as far as the mischief may probably extend."—Thus far from the intelligence, I will further inform you, that the King Fisher last Wednesday went up the Sound, with several small cutters, reconnoitering the north side of the island; and Thursday there followed past this place two top sail vessels, which I apprehended to be transports, as they fired two signal guns when they went through the Race.—I would therefore recommend it to the Provincial Congress, to keep a good guard upon Queen's county, as I imagine their design is to get stock from Huntington, Lloyd's Neck, or Flushing; and as we hope to secure all the stock upon this part of the island, you may expect the Boston fleet will proceed farther up the Sound.

I am, Sir, your most obedient humble servant,
DAVID WOOSTER.

WORCESTER, *August* 23.—General Gage, we hear, has seized the donation stores in Boston, and placed a strong guard over the same.

It is said for a certainty that the enemy have dismantled the part of Castle William which commands the harbour of Boston, and blowed up the walls.

BRITISH FAIL AT PROVIDENCE.

We hear from Providence, that on Tuesday, the 22d instant, his Majesty's ships the Rose, Swan and Glasgow, attempted to go to Providence, and got within 8 miles of the town, when two of them ran ashore, and the other came to anchor. Soon after arrived a brig and a sloop inward bound from the West Indies, these were immediately charged by the men of war's barges and three cutters, till they ran ashore at Warwick, where they were boarded by the men of war's men, in sight of a great number of people who had assembled on the shore

There were in the harbour two armed schooners fitted out by the town of Providence for the protection of their trade, and were going to convoy a small fleet down the river. A smart engagement then began and lasted three hours and a half, during which an incessant fire was kept up between the schooners and the brig and sloop, which the people on board attempted to get off, but as often were driven from the windlasses. But at last they cut the brig's cable and carried her off, with the Captain on board, who refused to quit her; the sloop we re-took, and brought her into the harbour, though fired upon by the man of war as we passed them. We had not one man killed or wounded, which is surprising. Upwards of thirty cannon balls were picked up on the shore. It is supposed many of the enemy were killed. The men of war are at present in Bristol harbour, where they have begun to rob and plunder the plantation of Mr. William Wessals.

WATERTOWN, *August* 28.—Yesterday another company of Riflemen, commanded by Captain Michael Cressap, arrived in this town on their way to join the Grand American Army. Some of this company, we hear, have travelled from the Mississippi.

IRISH LINENS, of various Prices, TO BE SOLD, on reafonable Terms, for Cash, by THOMAS M'GLATHRY, At Mr. ROBERT HUNTER's, in Second-ftreet, between Cheftnut and Market-ftreet.

JOHN HANCOCK MARRIES.

Last evening, the 28th instant, was married, by the Rev. Mr. Elliot, The HONOURABLE JOHN HANCOCK, Esq., President of the Continental Congress, to MISS DOROTHY QUINCEY, daughter of EDMUND QUINCEY, Esq., of Boston.

Florus informs us, that "in the second Punic war, when Hannibal besieged Rome, and was very near making himself master of it, a field upon which part of his army lay, was offered for sale, and was immediately purchased by a Roman, in a strong assurance that the Roman valour and courage would soon raise the siege."

Equal to the conduct of that illustrious citizen was the marriage of the HON. JOHN HANCOCK, Esq., who, with his amiable Lady, has paid a great compliment to American valour, and discovered equal patriotism, by marrying now while all the colonies are as much convulsed as Rome when Hannibal was at her gates.

40 HOUSES KNOCKED DOWN.

Extract of a letter from New London, to a merchant in New York, dated August 31.

"Yesterday morning there was a tender came into Stonington, and fired on the town, and then went out again and returned with the Rose man of war and two other tenders, who immediately began to fire directly into the houses; the ship came to an anchor, but the tenders kept under sail, standing close in, tacking, and firing, &c. the whole day, and this morning the fire is begun again. I soon expect them here.

"By express from there, we find we have two men killed. Great numbers from all parts are going there. The tender first chased two small sloops in, who had men on board to go on Block Island to prevent their taking the stock off. The men landed in Stonington, and as soon as the tender got within good shot, they fired on the people."

We hear the men of war and tenders have knocked down 40 houses in Stonington.

LIBERTY TREE CUT DOWN.

BOSTON, *August* 31, 1775.

The Enemies to Liberty and America, headed by Tom Gage, lately gave a notable specimen of their Hatred to the very Name of Liberty. A Party of them, of whom one Job Williams was the Ringleader, a few Days since, repaired to a Tree at the South End of Boston, and armed with Axes, &c. made a furious Attack upon it. After a long Spell of laughing and grinning, sweating, swearing, and foaming, with Malice diabolical, they cut down a Tree because it bore the Name of Liberty.

But, be it known to this infamous band of Traitors, that the GRAND AMERICAN TREE OF LIBERTY, planted in the Center of the United Colonies of North America, now flourishes with unrivaled, increasing Beauty, and bids fair, in a short Time, to afford, under its wide spreading Branches, a safe and happy Retreat for all the Sons of Liberty, however numerous and dispirited.

Recreated from The Pennsylvania Gazette, September 6, 1775.

In COMMITTEE OF SAFETY *of New Jersey.*

Princeton, August 31, 1775.

WHEREAS the public roads of this province are observed to abound with strollers and vagabonds, and many servants have run away from their masters, and horse stealing and other robberies are become very frequent: Therefore it is resolved, that it be recommended to the good people of this province, that they do strictly examine all suspicious persons passing to and fro through the different parts thereof; and if, upon such examination, they do not give a satisfactory account of themselves, they do proceed to deal with them according to the laws of this province.

A true copy of the minutes,
WILLIAM PATTERSON, *Secretary*.

Recreated from The Hartford Courant, September 4, 1775.

A WARNING.

WILLIAMSBURG.

IN consequence of a report last Tuesday morning that a certain Joshua Hardcastle, of this city, had the preceding evening been guilty of uttering expressions highly degrading the good people who compose the several companies now in this place; and moreover, that he had frequently spoke of the cause of America in a most disgraceful and menacing manner; the volunteers, exasperated at this insulting behaviour, and thinking themselves bound, by the ties of honour and love of country, to enquire into the nature of the offence, accordingly waited upon the said Hardcastle, and conducted him to the *Grove* (the habitation of the soldiers) where the officers and men were immediately drawn up.

They then proceeded to his trial, and after a candid, mature, and deliberate examination of the witnesses, found him guilty of the facts laid to his charge. One of the principal officers then made the following propositions: Whether the said Hardcastle should be *complimented* with a coat of *thickset*; whether he should be *drummed* through the city; or whether he should make *public concessions*. The officers then divided, when ten were for DRUMMING, and a like number for CONCESSIONS.

However, they at last agreed that he should only ask pardon of all the officers and soldiers present, and give his promise that he never again would be guilty of a like offence, and also be published in the Virginia gazettes, as a warning to those who may hereafter sport with the great and glorious cause of America.

COMMITTED to the gaol of Middlesex, on the 6th instant (*Augusta*) a negro man named WILL, who says he belongs to Mr. *George Dabney*, of *King William*. He is cloathed in negro cotton, and has on an oznabrig shirt. The owner is desired to apply for him, and pay charges.

JOHN CRAINE, gaoler.

Recreated from Rind's Virginia Gazette, September 7, 1775.

OUR VASTLY SUPERIOR NUMBERS.

Extract of a letter from PROSPECT HILL, *dated August* 31, 1775.

"Last Saturday evening a party of 1000 men, attended by a picquet guard of 2000 Provincials and 400 Riflemen, were ordered to throw up an entrenchment on the Plow'd Hill, which lies on Charlestown Neck, about half a mile from Bunker's Hill. They had their works considerably advanced before dawn, at which time they expected to be attacked, but the Regulars observed a profound silence till about 10 o'clock, when they began a heavy cannonade on the hill, which continued pretty constantly the whole day. An Adjutant and a private soldier of the Massachusetts men had their heads shot off, and one volunteer in the rifle battalion, of the name Simpson, received a wound in his leg, of which he has since died.

"They remained quiet all Sunday night, but on Monday morning we were alarmed by a signal from Chelsea, and presently perceived that the enemy were drawn up and in motion on the side of Bunker's Hill facing that way. It was immediately conjectured that they intended to attack us at high water, and in a short time 5 or 6000 of our men were marched to the entrenchments on Plow'd Hill, and on the Charlestown road.

"We there waited till near 3 o'clock in the afternoon, whilst the most awful silence was observed by both sides, until some of our men, straggling along the walls, fired upon the Regular centries, which brought on several shots from the floating batteries, with the loss of one of the Bay soldiers. Since that time they have thrown between 20 and 30 bombs, and a vast number of cannon ball, but without doing any injury to our people.

"Unless very large reinforcements soon arrive, there will not be another engagement this year, as we have so vastly the superiority in point of numbers. At present they lie tolerably still, except disturbing us at night with their bombs."

SKIRMISH NEAR ST. JOHN'S.

Extract of a letter from a Gentleman at ALBANY, *dated, September* 2, 1775.

"By an express arrived last evening we hear there has been a skirmish near St. John's, between a reconnoitering party of our men in a boat, and a boat of Regulars, Canadians and Indians. The General's letter on the occasion mentions, that the Captain of our party was killed, (one Baker) and a number of Whites and two Indians of the enemy were slain; that General Montgomery, with 1200 men, set off the first of the week for St. John's and were to muster on the Isle of Noe until joined by General Schuyler, who, with about as many more men, has by this time arrived, so that within a very few days it is possible the blow will be struck, which shall determine the fate of three provinces; and here I must wait, an idle listener to news, merely because hard necessity ties me down, as our men cannot yet march for want of their campaign equipage."

From the same Gentleman, September 5.

"Before you get this you will hear of the unhappy Affair of Captain Baker, near St. John's: It seems Baker had often been sent out by General Schuyler, to make Observations, but always with strict Orders never to molest either Canadians or Indians. The last Tour he made was without any orders from the General, and landing somewhere on the Shore of the Lake, he indiscreetly, or wickedly, snapped his Firelock at some Indians he saw near him; immediately he was fired at and slain, on which his People returned the Fire, and killed two of the Savages. This Matter was immediately represented in its true Colours by the Commissioners of Indian Affairs, to the Six Nations, now on Congress in this City, who thanked them for their Candour; and in order to put out the Flame which the unhappy Affair could not help kindling, a Lieutenant sets out To-day with four Mohawk Indians, and an Interpreter, to join General Schuyler, wherever he shall be, to endeavour to make up Matters."

ON July last, twenty-first day,
My servant John Smith ran away;
Age twenty-five years and no more,
I think his height is five feet four;
Black curled hair and slender made,
And is a weaver to his trade;
His breeches drilling, also white,
His coat and jacket coloured light;
A plated buckle, had but one,
With blue ribb'd hose, his hat Athlone;
And further yet I'll let you know,
He has two shirts, one of them tow:
Loom, shears, and brushes, with him took,
His trade in some place to set up;
Should any person him conceal,
No doubt with them I think to deal.
Last fall from Newry came in brief,
In the ship Renown, with Captain Keith;
Certificates in plenty had,
Each of them calls him a good lad;
I think of them he is full saucy,
One of them signed by Parson Lasley:
If any man will him secure,
That of the youth I may be sure,
Six lawful Dollars I will pay,
I live in Salsbury, Pequea;
And further to oblige you still,
My name is junior JOHN WHITEHILL.

Chester County, September 7, 1775.

The Committee of Chester County are desired to meet at the sign of the Turk's Head, in the township of Goshen, on Monday, the 25th instant, at 10 o'clock, A. M. on business of consequence; at which time and place the Board of Commissioners and Assessors are requested to attend. *By order of the Committee,*
ANTHONY WAYNE, *Chairman.*

Recreated from The Pennsylvania Gazette, September 13, 1775.

AID SAILS TO GAGE.

The following letter was lately intercepted in the brig Dolphin, Capt. Wallace, from Quebec to Boston.

SIR,   Quebec, *September* 6, 1775.

I HAVE the honour to inform your Excellency, that by General Carleton's orders I have taken up a vessel to transport a quantity of cattle, sheep, &c. a present from the province of Quebec to the sick and wounded soldiers of his Majesty's forces at Boston; bills of lading for which, together with the charter party, I have enclosed to Major Sheriff.

I still continue to send (by order of General Carleton) as many bullocks and sheep as the deck of each transport will contain, which I hope meets with your Excellency's approbation. I could wish the cattle were better, but in general they are very poor and small in this country. General Carleton has given me direction to contract for some forage, in order to be in readiness to load the transports he expects you will send to Quebec this fall; and I am in hopes I shall be able to procure a quantity of oats and hay, in time enough to dispatch the transports you may think proper to send.

I hope you will pardon me for reminding you of my situation; my length of service, and pretensions as an officer, I took the liberty to set forth in a memorial I transmitted to your Excellency by the last Transport that sailed; and I shall only add, that when a proper Opportunity offers, I hope you will take the Prayer of it into Consideration, and grant me either the purchase of a Company, or one in a new Corps; which ever your Excellency should think most proper.

No prospect yet of the Militia being embodied here; nor do I think they will; General Carleton I am apt to think is afraid to give the order lest they should refuse to obey; and I believe this year will pass over without the Canadians doing anything in favour of Government; this day's post has brought an account that the rebels have taken the post at Point O'Fare, with a body of troops; if so, they may have thoughts of advancing into this Province; two small vessels of ours were launched at St. John's yesterday; we are told here that Mr. Schuyler is building four at Ticonderoga; in short, Sir, you must look for no diversion in favour of the army immediately under your Excellency's command this year from Canada; the language here being only to defend the province; and it is generally thought here, that if the rebels were to push forward a body of four or five thousand men, the Canadians would lay down their arms, and not fire a shot. I know you will pardon my thus writing so freely, and not impute it to presumption, as it is merely intended to let your Excellency into a true state of facts; as from many other quarters you may have interested accounts.

Your Excellency's most Obedient humble Servant,
             THOMAS GAMBLE.
To his Excellency General Gage.

Recreated from The Pennsylvania Gazette, October 18, 1775.

THE MINISTERIAL TOOLS.

Worcester, September 6.—Notwithstanding the heavy fire of the enemy from Boston Neck, Bunker's Hill, and their floating batteries upon our army at Plough and Prospect Hills, Roxbury, Dorchester, &c. for the week past, they have killed only six men, four at Plough Hill and two at Roxbury.

The following may serve as a specimen of the humanity of the ministerial tools in Boston. A soldier's wife was sick in a house upon Noble's wharf, and hired another soldier's wife to tend her, to whom she gave two dollars, upon receiving which she left the sick woman to tend herself.

The neighbours knowing the woman lived there, and observing for some days that no person went in or out of the house, they went in, when to their great amazement they found the woman dead, and by the putrefaction of her body must have been dead for several days, a little tender infant with all the horrors of death in its face was sucking the dead mother's breast, the rats had eaten into the bowels of the dead corpse; they applied to the selectmen, but as the affair was not in their department, they sent them to Gage, who at first refused having anything to do with it, but after some time sent a number of soldiers, who dug a hole by the front door of the house and flung in the body, hardly covering it with earth, which made such a stench as caused another application from the neighbours, when a coffin was made and the dead body taken up and buried.

Recreated from The Pennsylvania Packet, September 18, 1775.

In COMMITTEE OF SAFETY *of New Jersey,*
Princeton, August 31, 1775.

Resolved, That the several Officers and Privates who embody themselves as Minute-men in this province, be, and they hereby are directed, for the sake of distinction and convenience, to adopt, as their uniform, hunting frocks, as near as may be familiar to those of the Rifle-men now in the Continental service.

A true copy from the minutes,
WILLIAM PATTERSON, Secretary.

PHILADELPHIA, *September* 6.

Yesterday the Hon. JOHN HANCOCK, Esq., and his LADY, arrived here from New York.

Last Saturday night and Sunday morning we had a hard gale of wind from N.E. to S.E. which occasioned a prodigious tide, so that many stores on the wharffs were overflowed, and great quantities of sugar, &c. very much damaged. We hear of great devastation in the country, by the washing away of banks, overflowing meadows, carrying away bridges, mill-dams, mills, stores, &c.

During the storm a number of vessels lying at Reedy-island, outward bound, parted their cables and drove on shore on the marshes at high water, where some of them must be entirely unloaded before they can be got off.

Recreated from The Pennsylvania Gazette, September 6, 1775.

A NEW FORT AT NEW HAMPSHIRE.

CAMBRIDGE, *September* 7.—The people of New Hampshire are building a strong fort on Pierce's Island, in Piscatagua River, in order to prevent their capital, the town of Portsmouth, from being attacked by the piratical ships of war, which now infest this coast.

It is said the enemy, since we began our works on Plow'd Hill, have thrown from their several batteries above 300 shells, not one of which has occasioned the least hurt to a single man in our army.

A party of the enemy, who came out last Saturday, with a design to throw up a battery or entrenchment, near where Mr. Brown's house lately stood, on Boston Neck, were drove back with the loss, we hear, of several killed. We also, it is said, had two men killed at the same time.

Two deserters from the enemy came to Roxbury camp last week. It is said a number more endeavoured to come off with them, but were prevented.

Extract of a Letter from CAMBRIDGE, *Sept.* 10.

"We are at present in our camp in tolerable security. Ploughed Hill may bid defiance to all their malice. And what is more amazing, they have suffered our men to throw up an entrenchment below the George tavern, and within musket shot of their last entrenchment, and have scarce honoured us with a cannon.

"We were last night under some apprehensions of an attack; General Ward sent a letter to his Excellency, informing him, that he had seen (or his people had seen) a number of men parading on Bunker's Hill, and our army was kept during the night under arms, in order to give them a genteel reception. They have since been seen with their knapsacks on their backs, and from good accounts from Boston, we are convinced they have sent a party of men, either (which is most probable) to reinforce the garrison at Quebec, or to New York. Three men of war have gone out of the harbour, for what purpose we cannot tell."

Recreated from The Pennsylvania Gazette, September 20, 1775.

NO MORE TROOPS FROM IRELAND.

WATERTOWN, *September* 11.

We hear that Captain Malbone arrived at Newport last Tuesday, in about six weeks from Ireland, and brings advice that the Parliament of Ireland have resolved that no more Troops should be sent to America; and also that no more Provisions should be shipped from thence. Several recruiting Parties in attempting to inlist men there had been killed.

A ship of about 260 Tons, commanded by Capt. Flagg, laden with Lumber, &c. which sailed from Portsmouth the beginning of last Week, for the West Indies, was met with and taken by the Lively Man of War, the Capt. of which put two Officers and five Sailors on board her, in order to carry her to Boston. Soon after a Privateer from Beverly luckily came across the Ship, as she was going to Boston, retook and carried her into Cape Anne.

CAMBRIDGE, *September* 14.

On Monday last a Regular soldier, from the besieged Army in Boston, went off in a Canoe, with a Design, as it is supposed, of deserting; being discovered, a Sergeant and four Men hastened in pursuit of him; but he had reached so near Dorchester Point before they overtook him, and having an unwieldy Boat to manage, and the Wind against them, they could not recover the Wharf again.

Lieut. Sparrow, of Col. Cotton's Regiment, marched down with a small Party, and by his Dexterity soon got within Musket Shot, and threatened to Fire in Case they attempted to escape, they all surrendered themselves Prisoners. The boats were immediately secured. The same Day the six Prisoners were brought under Guard to Head Quarters in this Town.

"To be given away, a very likely, healthy female Negro child, of a good breed, is about five months old, any person inclining to take it, may be further informed by applying to the Printer."

Recreated from The Hartford Courant, September 18, 1775.

NEWS FROM LONDON.

Sept. 15. This day arrives here the Charming Nancy, Davidson, from Boston; she was only 24 days on her passage; General Gage's lady came passenger in her. This ship has brought home 170 sick and wounded soldiers and officers. By her there is an account that no action had happened between the Regulars and the Provincials, since the 17th of last June, nor did the General think it proper to hazard an engagement till re-inforced by a body of fresh troops.

Sept. 21. There are letters in town by the Charming Sally, from Boston, which mention, that the Provincials have made themselves masters of some important posts, which they have intrenched in a manner far beyond conception; and that the talk among the King's officers, of attacking them when the reinforcements arrive, is now entirely dropped, as they confess they could not come to an engagement even supposing their number to be equal, without a material disadvantage.

• • • •

In future times it will be asked, how such a separation happened, as that between England and America? Nor will it ever be remembered, without solemn execrations on the framers and perpetrators of this disunion. The old men will shake their heads, and tell their children, "that an inordinate lust of power, and enmity to liberty, generally, and in *particular* in America, made a wretched administration, like the dog in the stable, snap at the shadow, and lose the substance."

• • • •

Authentic intelligence has been received, that General Schuyler had left a garrison in Ticonderoga, and was in full march into the heart of Canada. The inhabitants of that province, it is said, have expressed a wish to join the American Confederacy. General Carleton is at Montreal; but his force is so inconsiderable, that several of the friends of government here already confess they are in pain for Canada.

Recreated from The Pennsylvania Gazette, December 13, 1775.

STENCH OF THE SICK AND WOUNDED.

A letter from Plymouth, dated Sept. 17, says:

"This day the transport from Boston came into Catwater, and a few of the men came on shore, when hardly ever were seen such objects! Some without legs, and others without arms; and their clothes hanging on them like a loose morning gown, so much are they fallen away by sickness and want of proper nourishment. There were near 60 women and children on board, widows and children of the men who were slain. Some of these I have met in the street, and they exhibit a most shocking spectacle; and the vessel itself, I am told, though a very large one, yet is almost intolerable, from the stench arising from the sick and wounded, for many of them are hardly cured yet. There are two more transports daily expected with invalids, who sailed from Boston with the above."

PRISONERS DESIRE TO STAY.

Extract of a letter from Plymouth, Sept. 17.

"We learn here, by the sick and wounded soldiers who are landed, that there are not above 2000 soldiers, including officers, at Boston, fit to do duty, and these are averse to the service. They declare, that 60,000 men would not be able to bring the Americans under subjection. They farther say, that the provincials used the prisoners so well that most of them desire to continue where they are. All of the soldiers speak well of the Americans, for their great humanity. In short, many who were against the Americans are now in favour of them."

By the latest advices government have received, there is every reason to believe that the Americans, if they have not effected, have yet meditated, the capture of Canada.

Three merchant ships, freighted on account of generals Howe, Clinton, Percy, and Burgoyne, laden with live-stock, pease, flour, and porter, sailed yesterday from the river for Boston.

Recreated from Purdie's Virginia Gazette, January 5, 1776.

BRITISH REGULARS DEJECTED.

Extract of Letter from a Gentleman in Roxbury, dated September 20, 1775.

"General Gage, they say, has taken down some houses in the Hay-market, in Boston, and designs to erect a fortification thereabout from shore to shore, and build a fort in that square. I think it not unlikely. I hear the Regulars have cut down all, or almost all the trees in town, and that they went to cut down some at Dr. Elliot's, upon which he came out, and entreated that they would not; they thereupon damned him, and bid him be gone, or they would do so by him, or words of that import.

"Last Saturday I saw a gentleman who got out of Boston the Thursday before. I could only ask him two or three questions; he says the insults and abuses offered the inhabitants are intolerable; but that the Regulars seem to be now rather dejected, and that in general they wish the dispute was at an end."

COL. ARNOLD SAILS FROM NEWBURY-PORT.

CAMBRIDGE, *September* 21.—Last Saturday afternoon the enemy with their cannon fired briskly from their Lines on Boston Neck, but without doing us any damage. The next morning the firing was returned, and, as we have since heard, with success; two of the enemy being killed, and several wounded. The cannonading has been continued on both sides almost ever since, without any loss on our side. The enemy, we hear, had a Lieutenant shot on Monday by one of our cannon balls.

We hear that the colony troops destined for Canada, under the command of Col. Arnold, sailed from Newbury-Port last Tuesday morning.

Five or six impressed seamen, we are informed, had the good fortune to make their escape from the enemy last Monday night. One of them informs that the sailors on board the men of war are very sickly, and almost all of them very feeble and greatly emaciated, owing to bad provisions.

Recreated from The Pennsylvania Gazette, October 4, 1775.

GAGE TO BE LORD LEXINGTON.

LONDON, *September 20.*

Most of the officers, particularly the field-officers and captains, of the regiments in Ireland ordered to go to America (except those of the 46th) have presented memorials, soliciting leave of absence, alleging sickness, &c.

Government have contracted with Mr. Mellish to supply the troops at Boston with a very considerable number of oxen, and 14,000 sheep, the largest and fattest that can be procured. Several of the oxen, and 4000 of the sheep, are ordered to be sent over immediately, alive, and the remainder as soon as they can be purchased.

Boston is said to be no longer tenable. The government troops will, in consequence, retire to Long Island.

We hear that general Gage, on his arrival in England, is to be created lord Lexington, and baron of Bunker's Hill.

On Sunday evening arrived in town general Gage's lady from Salisbury, and immediately waited on their majesties at Kew, where she was most graciously received, and had a conference for upwards of an hour, after which she returned to town.

The government have contracted with Felix Calvert and Henry Thrale, esqrs., to furnish 5000 butts of strong beer each, to be shipped with all possible despatch for the use of his Majesty's troops at Boston. A contract is also entered into with Mr. Sladem to furnish 5000 cauldrons of coals; and Mr. Duffy, of Tooly street, a very large quantity of potatoes; and on Monday a quantity of faggots were shipped on board several transports at Deptford. Happily there is a very large fleet of colliers in the river, or it is imagined the above extensive contract would greatly enhance the price of coals, as they are all taken at the market price, which is a sufficient proof of the necessities of government.

Thirteen surgeons have received orders to embark for Boston, by the first ship that sails for that port.

Recreated from Purdie's Virginia Gazette, January 5, 1776.

BRITISH FIRE ON HOLME'S HOLE.

Extract of a Letter from a Gentleman, dated EDGERTON, *(Martha's Vineyard) Sept.* 18, 1775.

"On the 10th Instant, his Majesty's ship Swan, Capt. Ascough, lay at Holme's Hole at Anchor, with a Tender. Said Tender being observed to take on board a number of Marines from the ship, and pursue several boats as they passed, and frequently running backward and forward by the Point of said Harbour.

"The People suspecting they were on no good Design, kept a Guard of 12 Men to watch their Motions; said Tender discovering 3 Men leaning on a Fence near my House, they stood far inshore, as near as they could, and instantly fired their Guns, about 2 pounders, with grape shoot, which was followed immediately with several volleys of small Arms from the Marines, which put the Women and Children in grave confusion. Said Guard running directly for the shore, the Tender instantly stood off, and before they could get to the shore, by reason of a Pond, she was out of shot. Although the shot flew very thick, a number of Women and Children escaped without hurt."

Recreated from The Hartford Courant, October 2, 1775.

PATRICK HENRY ESCORTED.

WILLIAMSBURG, *September 23.*

Thursday last arrived here PATRICK HENRY, Esq., Commander in Chief of the Virginia forces. He was met and escorted to town by the whole body of volunteers, who paid him every mark of respect and distinction in their power, in testimony of their approbation of so worthy a Gentleman to the appointment of that important trust, which the convention has been pleased to repose in him.

The Mercury Man of War is sailed under the command of Lieutenant Graham of the Admiral's ship, having on board Captain Macartney under arrest, to be conducted to Boston, and tried by a Court-martial. What charge is against him we have not been able to learn.

Recreated from The Pennsylvania Gazette, October 4, 1775.

ARNOLD 20 DAYS FROM CANADA.

Letters have been received at Cambridge from Colonel Arnold, who commanded the detachment which lately went from that place for Canada, dated at Fort Western, the 28th September, in 20 days from which time the Colonel expected to arrive in Canada. The detachment was then in three divisions; the first of which was to march the next day, the second and third the two following days. A spy that had been sent out to reconnoitre, reported that the ways were passable. The troops were in the greatest health, and the greatest harmony subsisted among the officers.

Recreated from The Pennsylvania Gazette, October 18, 1775.

MONTGOMERY TO ATTACK ST. JOHN'S.

A Gentleman arrived here yesterday morning from the camp at the Isle aux Noix, which place he departed from the 16th ult. where he left General Montgomery with about 3000 men, who intended the next day to make an attack on St. John's, which was defended by Col. Templer and about 600 regulars with some Indians; he says a large schooner of sixteen guns lay within a half mile of the fort, but she could not get into the lake so as to annoy our troops, by reason of a large boom being laid from the Isle aux Noix to the opposite shore; that Colonels Allen and Brown had got into Canada, where they were joined by 500 men at Le Praire and Chamblee, and had cut off an escort of thirteen waggon loads of provisions intended for St. John's, and were determined to prevent any supplies being sent to that post; that in the first skirmish our people were up to their waists in water, but being animated by their brave General, and other worthy officers, who exposed themselves much on the occasion, they soon made the enemy retreat, with the loss of their Commander William Johnson; that in the boat which was sunk by the Gondola, there were a number gentlemen from Quebec and Montreal, who all perished.

Recreated from The Pennsylvania Gazette, October 4, 1775.

MONTGOMERY SKIRMISHES REGULARS.

ST. JOHN'S, Canada.—By an express from Ticonderoga, we are informed that General Montgomery, on the 18th of September, marched with 500 of the forces under his command round St. John's, and had a light skirmish with a party of the regulars; and a further account that General Montgomery had summoned the commanding officer at St. John's, *Prescott*, to surrender; he for the present declined.

Extract of a Letter from Schenectady, Sept. 26.

"This afternoon an express arrived from Albany from our army, which mentions they had met with great success; had taken a schooner well manned and armed, killed all the people on board, and possessed themselves of a twelve pounder. The companies of New England men landed at St. John's, and engaged a party of regulars going to the fort with carts, cattle, and provisions, which they took, and defeated the regulars. Capt. Yates, commander of a company of Germans, and one Lieut. Van Slyk, of this town, have greatly distinguished themselves, which has recommended them to the notice of General Montgomery. Five Hundred Canadians have voluntarily joined our army."

ST. JOHN'S BESIEGED.

Extract of a Letter from General Schuyler, dated Ticonderoga, September 29, 1775.

"I am still confined with the remains of an inveterate disorder. I have this moment received a line from General Montgomery; he holds St. John's besieged. The Canadians are friendly to us, and join us in great numbers. We have taken fifteen prisoners, seven of which are soldiers, and the rest unfriendly Canadians and Scotchmen, in the service of the Ministry."

WORCESTER, *September* 29.

Yesterday a waggon load of money passed through this town, from Philadelphia, for the use of the continental army.

Recreated from The Pennsylvania Gazette, October 11, 1775.

GEN. WASHINGTON'S INTENTIONS.

CAMBRIDGE, *September* 28.

The following address will be published in CANADA, *on the arrival there of* Col. ARNOLD.

To the INHABITANTS of CANADA.

THE unnatural contest between the English Colonies and Great Britain has now risen to such a heighth, that arms alone must decide it. The Colonies, confiding in the justice of their Cause, and the Purity of their Intentions, have reluctantly appealed to that Being, in whose Hands are all human Events. He has hitherto smiled upon their virtuous Efforts. The Hand of Tyranny has been arrested in its Ravages, and the British Arms, which have shone with so much Splendor in every Part of the Globe, are now tarnished with Disgrace and Disappointment. Generals of approved Experience, who boasted of subduing this great Continent, find themselves circumscribed within the Limits of a single City and its Suburbs, suffering all the Shame and Distress of a Siege. While freeborn Sons of America, animated by the genuine principles of Liberty and Love of their Country, with increasing Union, Firmness and Discipline, repel every Attack, and despise every Danger.

Above all, we rejoice, that our Enemies have been deceived with Regard to you. They have persuaded themselves, they have even dared to say, that the Canadians were not capable of distinguishing between the Blessings of Liberty, and the wretchedness of Slavery; that gratifying the Vanity of a little Circle of Nobility would blind the eyes of the People of Canada. By such Artifices they hoped to bend you to their Views, but they have been deceived, instead of finding you in that Poverty of Soul, and Baseness of Spirit, they see with a Chagrin equal to our Joy, that you are enlightened, generous and virtuous, that you will not renounce your own Rights, to serve as Instruments to deprive your Fellow Subjects of theirs. Come then, my Brethren, unite with us in indissoluble Union, let us run together to the same Goal.

We have taken up Arms in Defence of our Liberty, our Property, our Wives, and our Children, we are determined to preserve them or die. We look forward with Pleasure to that Day not far remote (we hope) when the Inhabitants of North America shall have one Sentiment, and the full Enjoyment of the Blessings of a free Government.

Incited by these Motives, and encouraged by the Advice of many Friends to Liberty among you, the Grand American Congress have sent an Army into your Province, under the Command of General Schuyler; not to Plunder, but to Protect you; to animate, and bring forth into Action those Sentiments of Freedom you have disclosed, and which the Tools of Despotism would extinguish through the whole of Creation. To co-operate with this Design, and to frustrate those cruel and perfidious Schemes, which would deluge our Frontiers with the Blood of Women and Children; I have detached Colonel Arnold into your Country, with a Part of the Army under my Command. I have enjoined upon him, and am certain that he will consider himself, and act as in the Country of his Patrons, and best Friends. Necessaries and Accommodations of every Kind which you can furnish, he will thankfully receive, and render the full Value. I invite you therefore, as Friends and Brethren, to provide him with such Supplies as your Country affords; and I pledge myself not only for your Safety and Security, but for ample Compensation.

Let no Man desert his Habitation. Let no one flee as before an Enemy. The Cause of America, and of Liberty, is the Cause of every virtuous American Citizen; whatever may be his Religion or his Descent, the United Colonies know no distinction but such as Slavery, Corruption and arbitrary Domination may create. Come then, ye generous Citizens, range yourselves under the Standard of general Liberty against which all the Force and Artifice of Tyranny will never be able to prevail.

G. WASHINGTON.

Recreated from The Hartford Courant, October 2, 1775.

WANTED immediately for the army, CAMP KETTLES, either of tin or brass, to hold about three gallons; a large quantity of DUCKING, or RUSSIA DRAB, for tents; OSNABRUGS, for hunting shirts; CHECKS, *coarse white* LINEN, or *country made* LINEN, for under shirts; also BLANKETS *and coarse* STOCKINGS. Any person who has any of the above articles for sale will be pleased to inform me by letter, per post, directed to be lodged at the post-office, *Aylett's*,—CANTEENS are also much wanted, and it is requested of the respective committees to make immediate inquiry after those taken from the magazine, and contrive them to the head-quarters; not omitting those that are damaged, which may be repaired.—I will also give ready money for any quantity of SALTPETRE, SULPHUR, or LEAD.

*** SPADES, SHOVLES, and MATTOCKS, are also wanted. Those who have them will apply as above.

WILLIAM AYLETT, contractor.

WANTED,

A GOOD negro BLACKSMITH, for whom a reasonable price will be given.—Also a HOUSEKEEPER, who is a single woman, and can come well recommended.—Inquire of the PRINTER.

Recreated from Purdie's Virginia Gazette, October 6, 1775.

HOWE SUCCEEDS GAGE.

CAMBRIDGE, *October* 5.—We hear that Gen. Howe, a besieged officer in Boston, was, on Saturday last, proclaimed Governor of the whole Province of Massachusetts Bay. The immaculate Gage, Howe's Predecessor in this mighty command, is ordered to return to England forthwith. Howe also succeeds to the Command of all the King's troops in America. Admiral Graves is also superceded but who is appointed in his room, we have not heard.

Recreated from The Hartford Courant, October 9, 1775.

NEW YORK, *October* 9.

We are informed from undoubted authority, that Lord WILLIAM CAMBELL, Governor of South Carolina, has fled with the utmost precipitation on board the Man of War in the harbour. The committee of Charlestown having very fortunately discovered that his Excellency had employed one CAMERON, an Indian Commissary in the interior parts of that province, to engage the Indians in the Ministerial service, who had actually inlisted 600 of them, and furnished them with every necessary in order to butcher back inhabitants. This plan was discovered by a gentleman, who seized the express on his way from said Cameron to the Governor, whom he knew to be disaffected to the American cause, and conveyed the dispatches to the Provincial Committee. The above gentleman disguised himself in a drover's habit, and attended the express to the Governor's house, and heard the conversation between them, and then discovered the whole plot to the Committee.

Recreated from The Pennsylvania Gazette, October 11, 1775.

CAMBRIDGE, *October* 13.

General Washington has heard from Col. Arnold, who had then passed the Carrying Place, and was going to embark on the river Chandiere, and writes that he was assured there were no forces of consequences to resist him at Quebec, where it is thought he is arrived.

Recreated from The Hartford Courant, October 23, 1775.

NO PROSPECT OF ACCOMMODATION.

Extract of a letter from the Camp at CAMBRIDGE, *from undoubted Authority, dated October 5th,* 1775.

"GENTLEMEN,

"By an intelligent Person from Boston, the 3d instant, I am informed that a Fleet consisting of one 64, and one 20 Gun Ships, two Sloops of 18 Guns, two Transports with 600 Men, were to sail from Boston as Yesterday; their Destination a profound Secret. That they took on board two Mortars and 4 Howitzers, with other Artillery, calculated for the Bombardment of a Town. I have thought it proper to apprise every considerable town on the Coast of this Armament, that they may be on their Guard. Should I receive any farther Account of their Destination, it shall be forwarded.

"The same Person also informs, that an Express Sloop arrived 4 Days before, from England, at Boston, which she left the 8th of August. General Gage and most of the Officers who were at Lexington are recalled, and sail this Day. General Howe succeeds in Command. Six Ships of the Line and two Cutters, under Sir Peter Dennis, are coming out. Five Regiments and 1000 Marines may be expected at Boston in 3 or 4 Weeks. No Prospect of Accommodation; but on the other Hand, every Appearance of the War being pushed with the utmost Vigour."

We hear from St. John's, that Captain Prescott, commander of the Fort, sent word to General Montgomery, that he would deliver it up to him, if he would permit him and the King's troops to march to Quebec, with their arms, stores and artillery, but, the General refused to comply with his request.

Governor Carleton, it is said, has brought up all the powder from the merchants at Quebec, and stored it there, the whole of which amounts to upwards of 10,000 barrels.

Since our last his Majesty's Sloop of War the Viper sailed on a cruize.

INHABITANTS FLEE BRITISH.

NEWPORT, *October* 9, 1775.

By the motions of some of the men of war and transports in this harbour, last Monday, it was suspected they intended to take off live stock from the farms of the south part of this island, called Brenton's Neck, the ensuing night; whereupon a number of persons went down in the evening, and brought off about 1000 sheep, and between 40 and 50 head of horned cattle from several farms. But there still remained a considerable number of cattle, sheep and hogs, on two farms belonging to Jaheel and Benjamin Brenton, great part of which 'tis supposed were by them there collected and sold to the men of war, to be sent to Boston, for the express purpose of supplying our inveterate enemies.

The next day the ships took off from said Brentons farms, about 35 head of cattle and 150 sheep; on Wednesday they took 5 or 6 more cattle. There being still left on the farms of James, Jaheel and Benjamin Brenton, between 60 and 70 head of cattle, on Wednesday and Thursday morning, about 300 Minute-men arrived here from the county of Providence, Tiverton and Little Compton, under the command of Cols. Eseck Hopkins and William Richmond, Esqrs., and as soon as they refreshed themselves, they marched into the Neck, and brought off 66 horned cattle, some sheep, hogs, and poultry, the ships the same time lying within gun shot, and discharged several cannon at them, but without any effect.

Recreated from The Pennsylvania Gazette, October 18, 1775.

THE GERMAN FLUTE, TAUGHT in the most approved and expeditious manner, and on the most reasonable terms, by JAMES CICERO, lately arrived here from Jamaica, where he taught that instrument for several years. Any Gentleman inclining to learn that instrument, will be waited on by leaving a line directed for him at Mr. William Bradford's Book-store, in Market-street.

Recreated from The Pennsylvania Packet, September 18, 1775.

BRITISH FIRE ON BRISTOL.

NEWPORT, *October* 9.

THIS town having been threatened to be fired on from the men of war, on account of the armed force which made its appearance here, sundry of the inhabitants moved part of their effects, and many left town. The carts, chaises, riding-chairs, and trucks, were so numerous, that the streets and roads were almost blocked with them. Thursday and Friday being rainy and muddy, the poor women and children were much exposed in looking for some place of safety; the people continued moving out very fast all Saturday and yesterday, with their effects.

Saturday afternoon the ships Rose, Glasgow, and Swan, a brig with six guns, and one or two small bomb mortars, three or four tenders, two transports, and several wood vessels, &c. making in all fifteen sail, weighed anchor, and went up the river, entered the harbour of Bristol, and demanded 300 sheep, which not being complied with, between 8 and 9 o'clock they began a very heavy fire upon the town, and continued it upwards for an hour; in which time a number of shots went through the houses of William Bradford, Esq., and Capt. Ingraham, damaged the church a little, and several shops, stables, &c. The women and children, in great distress, (dark and rainy as it was) were obliged to leave their habitations, and seek shelter in the adjacent country.

Between 9 an 10 o'clock a committee was appointed to go on board, who settled the matter, by giving or selling 40 sheep. In the small defenceless town of Bristol were near 100 persons very sick, and dead, at the time of this firing; and we are assured, that two sick persons actually died of fright.

Recreated from The Pennsylvania Gazette, October 18, 1775.

TAKEN UP, on the road between Philadelphia and Chesnut Hill, a Bag full of Empty Bags. Whoever has lost them, describing the mark and number, and paying charges, may have them again, by applying to the Printer hereof.

Recreated from The Pennsylvania Packet, September 18, 1775.

PRINTING PRESS REMOVED.

WILLIAMSBURG, *October* 7.—The following extract of a letter from Norfolk will serve to show the distressed situation that town is unhappily reduced to by the wanton, unjust, and cruel behaviour of the tools of tyranny and oppression on board the ships of war in that harbour. Various reports have been in circulation here, within a few days past, of a manoeuvre of the soldiery on the 30th ult. We are assured the letter contains an authentic account.

Extract from a letter from NORFOLK, *Oct.* 1.

"Yesterday came on shore about 15 of the King's soldiers, and marched up to the printing-office, out of which they took all of the types and part of the press, and carried them on board the new ship Eilbeck, in presence, I suppose, of between two and three hundred spectators, without meeting with the least molestation; and upon the drums beating up and down the town, there were only about 35 men to arms. They say they want to print a few papers themselves; and they looked upon the press not to be free, and had a mind to publish something in vindication of their own characters. But as they have only part of the press, and no ink as yet, it is out of their power to do any thing in the printing business. They have got neither of the compositors, but I understand there is a printer on board the Otter. Mr. Cumming, the bookbinder, was pressed on board, but is admitted ashore at times. He says Captain Squire was very angry they did not get Mr. Holt, who happened to be in the house the whole time they were searching, but luckily made his escape, notwithstanding the office was guarded all round. Mr. Cumming also informs, that the Captain says he will return every thing in safe order to the office, after he answers his ends, which, he says, will be in about three weeks. It was extremely melancholy to hear the cries of the women and children in the streets; most of the families are moving out of town, with the greatest expedition; the carts have been going all this day."

Recreated from The Pennsylvania Gazette, October 18, 1775.

MAN OF WAR GROUNDED.

CAMBRIDGE, *October* 12.

Last Tuesday one of the Privateers from Beverly, having been on a Cruize in the Bay, was followed on her Return into Port, by the Nautilus Man of War. The Privateer ran aground in a Cove a little without Beverly Harbour, where the People speedily assembled, stripped her, and carried her Guns, &c. ashore. The Man of War was soon within Gun shot, when she also got aground; she however let go an Anchor, and bringing her Broadside to bear, began to fire upon the Privateer. The People of Salem and Beverly soon returned the Compliment from a Number of Cannon on shore, keeping up a warm and well directed Fire on the Man of War for 2 or 3 Hours, and it is supposed did her considerable Damage and probably killed and wounded some of the Men; but before they could board her, which they were preparing to do, the Tide arose about 8 o'Clock in the Evening when she cut her Cable, and got off. Some of her shot struck one or two Buildings in Beverly; but no Lives were lost on our side, and the Privateer damaged very little, if any.

Recreated from The Hartford Courant, October 16, 1775.

WANTED to the battalion of minute, men in the lower end of the *Northern Neck*, an ADJUTANT who is well acquainted with the duty of that office, agreeable to the order or directions of his majesty in the year 1764. As this is the only officer in the minute service whose pay will be constant for nine months in the year, it is hoped such as are qualified will readily engage. Also wanted, a DRUMMER and FIFER, who can teach others the duty, to act as drum and fife-majors. The CHAPLAIN's place to said battalion is not yet engaged.

Recreated from Purdie's Virginia Gazette, October 13, 1775.

ETHAN ALLEN CAPTURED.

October 18. By accounts from Canada we learn, that on the twenty-fifth of September last, Col. Ethan Allen, prompted by ambition, had imprudently without orders crossed over from Longale with thirty of his own men and fifty Canadians, in order to get possession of Montreal. Col. Prescot, hearing of his coming, engaged a number of people from the suburbs, at a Half Joe per man, to join a party of regulars from the garrison, and to go out against him. They met about two miles from the town, when a smart engagement ensued, which lasted upwards of two hours. The enemy had two field pieces. After a long engagement our party were obliged to retire. Col. Allen and two or three of his men were taken prisoners, and about as many wounded, the rest returned to their friends. By the best accounts we learn, that a considerable number of the enemy were killed and wounded.

PHILADELPHIA.

COMMITTEE of SAFETY, *Oct.* 14.

Such humane persons who may have, and can spare, rags for lint, or old linen for bandages, and would choose to apply them for the use of the armed boats now employed for the defence of this province, are requested to send them to Capt. Henry Dougherty's store, on Mr. Cuthbert's wharf, where they will be received with gratitude, and be taken proper care of for the good purposes intended.

ROBERT MORRIS, President.

Extract of a Letter from CAMBRIDGE, *Oct. 16.*

"Dr. Church (Surgeon-General of the Army, and Chairman of the Committee of Safety at Watertown) having been found guilty of treacherous practices, in corresponding with the enemy, is put under arrest."

We are informed that Dr. Church is confined in a house opposite to the head quarters in Cambridge; his correspondence, it is said, was carried on in cyphers with a field officer in General Gage's army, in Boston.

Recreated from The Pennsylvania Gazette, October 18, 1775.

FORT CHAMBLEE SURRENDERS.

HARTFORD, *November*, 6.

Last Wednesday came to Town Mr. BENNET, *Post-Rider from the* NORTHERN ARMY *near* ST. JOHN'S, *which Place he left the* 23d *Ult. and brings the following intelligence, viz.*

That on the 16th of October, a Detachment of our Troops, under the Command of Maj. Brown, laid siege to the fortress of Chamblee, and on the 18th the garrison surrendered the fort with its contents to the American Arms. He likewise informs, that when the Garrison of St. John's received the above Account they immediately ceased Firing, and it was expected they would soon surrender.

Extract of a Letter from an Officer on Lake Champlain *before* ST. JOHN'S, *October* 20.

"We are arrived here, with our little army, for the third time, on Sunday the 17th of September and have kept our ground ever since. St. John's is a little, ugly place, well intrenched all round, with about 500 *red Lobsters* in it, who are constantly spitting their large *plums* and *chestnuts* at us, some of which are so hot as to crack almost where they choose, but have done us little harm. We have three batteries open, but the land here is so flat it is impossible at any place to overlook them; but as we so entirely surround them, they never dare to come to see us on any quarter, nor do they get provisions or intelligence from any place. They are like a fox in his hole, with a dog at the mouth, that barks every time he can see but so much as his ears. It appears as 'tho we must soon have them.

"At 8 o'clock yesterday morning, a party of our troops, with the Canadians, took possession of Chamblee, 12 miles north of St. John's, after a siege of 48 hours. We took in this garrison, 83 regulars, total of the prisoners (including women and children, which belong to the garrison at St. John's) 180; also 3 small Mortars, 11 Swivels, with a considerable quantity of artillery.

"The enemy here had a new Schooner of 12 guns, and a large Row Galley, which being unable to digest our *American plums*, grew *Sea sick*, and are gone to the bottom of the Lake. On the whole, I think we have taught them to be a little more *civil*, as they have been very silent for two days past. At the first of our acquaintance with them, they would be bawling, *Fire away, you Yankee beggars*. But their tune now is, *Why don't you go home? What do you come here for?*"

"P.S. Since I wrote the above, this afternoon, the prisoners are come from Chamblee; 83 regulars, one Major, two Captains, and 90 women and children. Also 120 barrels of powder."

The post-rider who brought the above, also informs, that those two arch plotters against the rights of America, *Guy Carleton* and *Guy Johnson*, (who in villainy exceed *Guy Faux*, that attempted to blow up the king and parliament) are both at Montreal; and that our people intend immediately to lay siege to that place. He also says, that the moment he came away, intelligence came in of the arrival of Col. Arnold, with his troops, in Canada.

DUNMORE MISFIRES.

WILLIAMSBURG, *October* 21.—Some time last week Lord Dunmore was alarmed with information that 19 pieces of cannon were fitted up, and would soon be placed on the wharves, &c. in Norfolk, to annoy the ships of war, and that a number of men were daily expected from Williamsburg, who were to fire them from behind hogsheads filled with sand.

Yesterday fe'nnight, in consequence of the above intelligence, his Lordship sent ashore a party of soldiers, under the command of two officers, who marched through Norfolk to the place where the cannon were, destroyed 17 of them and carried off two for their own use, without molestation. The above cannon we are confident were never intended for such a purpose; on the contrary, they belonged to sundry private gentlemen, who had them removed for their safety.

Recreated from The Hartford Courant, November 6, 1775.

SHOCKING OBJECTS.

Part of a letter from CAMBRIDGE, *October* 19.

"The great hurry and business of this morning, and the immediate departure of the post, almost deprives me of the satisfaction of communicating the news of the day, which to me is very affecting. We sent down two floating batteries from Cambridge to fire on the town of Boston, the night before last, being informed they opened their play-house that evening for the season. They fired seven shot apiece, and one of their cannon burst the eighth shot, tore off the side of one of the batteries, split her top of covering, sunk her, and wounded eight men with the Captain, one died that night, the others are in my hospital, and will do well, except one. They are burnt very much by the cannon cartridges that took fire on the burning of the cannon, and are shocking objects. We have recovered the battery and brought her up."

Recreated from The Pennsylvania Gazette, November 1, 1775.

CAPT. CRESSAP INTERRED.

NEW YORK, *October* 21.

ON Thursday was interred, at Trinity church, Michael Cressap, esq., captain of a company of riflemen, who died here on his way from Cambridge. His funeral was attended from his lodgings by the independent companies of militia, and the most respectable inhabitants, through the principal streets to the church. The grenadiers of the first battalion fired three volleys over his grave. The whole was conducted with great decency, and in military form. He was a gentleman universally esteemed by those who had the pleasure of his acquaintance, a worthy member of society, and a brave soldier. His loss is greatly lamented by every well-wisher to the liberties of this once happy country.

> MANCHESTER, July 28, 1775.
> A STOCKING WEAVER WILL MEET WITH ENCOURAGEMENT BY APPLYING TO
> ALEXANDER AND PETERFIELD TRENT.

Recreated from Rind's Virginia Gazette, November 9, 1775.

ANOTHER ARMY NECESSARY.

CAMBRIDGE, *October* 19.

Since our last, arrived in town the hon. Benjamin Franklin, Thomas Lynch, and Benjamin Harrison, Esquires, from Philadelphia, a committee from the Continental Congress; the hon. Matthew Griswold, Esq., Deputy Gov., and Nathaniel Wales, Esq., of Connecticut; the hon. Nicholas Cooke, Esq., Deputy Gov. and commander in chief of Rhode Island; and the hon. John Wentworth, Esq., President of the provincial congress of New Hampshire.

As the time for the present army is raised will expire in two or three months, these gentlemen, with the members of the honourable council of this colony, are appointed to meet and confer with his Excellency George Washington on the subject of forming and establishing another continental army, for the defence of the invaded rights of the united colonies.

Captain Coffin arrived last week, at Nantucket from London, has brought prints to the 9th of August, which are not yet come to hand. We hear he brings an account that five regiments were to embark for Boston, no more being called of; and that the public talk in the streets of London was for another OLIVER CROMWELL.

Recreated from The Hartford Courant, October 23, 1775.

BEWARE MORE TREACHERY.

WATERTOWN, *October* 23.—Tom Gage, before his departure, issued a commission, appointing Crean Brush, "Receiver of all such goods, chattels, and effects as may be voluntarily delivered into his charge, by the owners of such goods, or the persons whose care they may be left in, and to give a receipt for the same; and he is to take care of, and deliver said goods when called upon, to those whom he shall give a receipt for the same." FANEUIL HALL is provided for the reception of such goods, in order that they may be as compact as possible, in case of plunder!

BOSTONIANS! Have you forgot that your ARMS were most shamefully deposited there?

BURN ALL THE TOWNS.

SIR,   CAMP AT CAMBRIDGE, *Oct.* 24, 1775.

The inclosed information being of the highest importance, I thought it proper to transmit it to you with all dispatch. I am Sir, Your obedient Servant,

GEORGE WASHINGTON.

On the service of the United Colonies.

To the Hon. Nicholas Cooke, Esq.,

    Dep. Gov. of Rhode Island, at Providence.

• • • •

SIR,   PROSPECT HILL, *Oct.* 24, 1775.

By an express that arrived from Falmouth last night, we learn that the greatest part of the town is in ashes. The enemy fired about three thousand shot into it, and a large number of carcasses and bombs, which set the town on fire. The enemy landed once or twice to set fire to the stores; they lost eight or ten men in the attempt, and had one taken prisoner. The inhabitants got out a very considerable part of their furniture, no person was killed or wounded during the whole time of their firing; the enemy produced orders from Admiral Greaves, to burn all the towns from Boston to Halifax.

Capt. Mowat informed the Committee at Falmouth, there had arrived orders from England about ten days since, to burn all the seaport towns on the continent, that would not lay down and deliver up their arms, and give hostages for their future good behaviour; he also acquainted them that he expected the city of New York was in ashes.

By these accounts we may learn what we have to expect. I think Newport should be fortified in the best manner it can be. Doubtless the enemy will make an attempt to get the stock off the island. Provision should be made to defeat them. Death and desolation seem to mark their footsteps. Fight or be slaves is the American motto, the first is by far the most eligible. In haste, I am, with esteem,

"Your most obedient humble servant,

"NATHANIEL GREEN."

Recreated from The Pennsylvania Packet, November 6, 1775.

SURRENDER OR DIE.

[*The following is what* Capt. Mowett *sent the people of* FALMOUTH, *soon after his arrival before that Town.*]

• • • •

Canceaux, FALMOUTH, *October* 16th, 1775.

After so many premeditated attacks on the legal prerogative of the best of Sovereigns, after the repeated instances you have experienced in Britain's long forbearance of the rod of correction, and the manifest and paternal extension of her hands to embrace again and again, having been regarded as vain and nugatory; and in place of a dutiful and grateful return to your King and parent state, you have been guilty of the most unpardonable rebellion, supported by the ambition of a set of designing men, whose insidious views have cruelly imposed on the credulity of their fellow creatures; and at last have brought the whole into the same dilemma; which leads me to feel, not a little, the woes of the innocent of them particular, on the present occasion, from my having it in orders to execute a just punishment on the town of Falmouth, in the name of which authority, I previously warn you to remove without delay, all the human species out of the said town, for which purpose I give you the time of two hours, at the period of which, a red pendant will be hoisted at the main top gallant mast head, with a gun. But should your imprudence lead you to show the least resistance, you will in that case free me of that humanity so strongly pointed out in my orders, as well as in my inclination. I do also observe, that all those who did on occasion fly to the King's ship under my command for protection, that the same door is now open to receive them.

The officer who will deliver this letter, I expect to return immediately unmolested.

I am, &c.

H. MOWETT.

Recreated from The Hartford Courant, November 6, 1775.

DUNMORE LANDS NEAR HAMPTON.

WILLIAMSBURG, *October 27.*

After Lord Dunmore, with his troops, and the navy, had been for several weeks seizing the persons and property of his Majesty's peaceable subjects in this colony, on Wednesday night last a party from an armed tender landed near Hampton, and took away a valuable negroe man slave and a sail from the owner. Next morning there appeared, off the mouth of Hampton river, a large armed schooner, a sloop, and three tenders, with soldiers on board; and a message was received at Hampton from Capt. Squire, on board the schooner, that he would that day land and burn the town. On which a company of regulars, and a company of minute-men, who had been placed there in consequence of former threats denounced against that place, made the best disposition to prevent their landing, aided by a body of militia, who were suddenly called together on the occasion.

The enemy accordingly attempted to land, but were retarded by some boats sunk across the channel for that purpose. Upon this they fired several small cannon at the provincials, without any effect; who, in return, discharged their small arms so effectually, as to make the enemy move off with the loss of several men, as it is believed. But they had, in the mean time, burnt down a house belonging to Mr. Cooper, on that river. On intelligence of this reaching Williamsburg, about 9 o'clock at night, a company of rifle-men were dispatched to the aid of Hampton, and the Colonel of the 2d regiment sent to take command of the whole, who with the company arrived about 8 o'clock the next morning.

The enemy had, in the night, cut through the boats sunk, and made a passage for their vessels, which were drawn close up to the town, and began to fire upon it soon after the arrival of the party from Williamsburg; but as soon as our men were so disposed as to give them a few shot, they went off so hastily that our people took a small tender with five white men, a woman, and two slaves, six swivels, seven muskets, some small arms, a sword, pistols, and other things, and several papers belonging to Lieutenant Wright, who made his escape by jumping over board and swimming away with Mr. King's negroe man, who are on shore, and a pursuit it is hoped may overtake them. There were two of the men in the vessel mortally wounded.

The vessels went over to Norfolk, and we are informed the whole force from thence is intended to visit Hampton this day. If they should, we hope our brave troops are prepared for them; as we can, with pleasure, assure the public, that every part of them behaved with spirit and bravery, and are wishing for another skirmish.

Recreated from Purdie's Virginia Gazette, October 27, 1775.

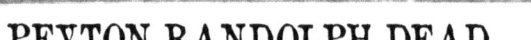

PEYTON RANDOLPH DEAD.

PHILADELPHIA, *October 28.*

LAST Sunday died, of an apoplectic stroke, in the 53d year of his age, the honourable PEYTON RANDOLPH, esquire, of Virginia, late president of the continental congress, and speaker of the house of burgesses of Virginia; a gentleman who possessed the virtues of humanity in eminent degree, and, joining with them the soundest judgement, was the delight of his friends in private life, and a most valuable member of society, having long filled, and with great ability and integrity discharged, the most honourable public trusts. To the truth of this his family, friends, and his country, bear mournful testimony.

And yesterday afternoon his remains were removed from Mr. Benjamin Randolph's to Christ church, where an excellent sermon on the mournful occasion was preached by the reverend Mr. Duche, after which the corpse was carried to the burial ground, and deposited in a vault, till it can be conveyed to Virginia.

Recreated from Rind's Virginia Gazette, November 9, 1775.

A PROCLAMATION.

By his Excellency the Honourable WILLIAM HOWE, Major General *and* Commander in Chief *of all his Majesty's Forces within the Colonies laying on the Atlantic Ocean, from* NOVA SCOTIA *to* WEST FLORIDA *inclusive,* &c. &c. &c.

WHEREAS several of the inhabitants of this town have lately absconded to join, it is apprehended, His Majesty's Enemies assembled in open rebellion:

I DO, by Virtue of the Power and Authority in me vested by His Majesty, forbid any Person or Persons whatsoever, not belonging to the Navy, to pass from hence by Water or otherwise, from the Date hereof, without my Order or Permission given in Writing.

Any Person or Persons detected in an Attempt, or who may be retaken, upon sufficient Proof thereof, shall be liable to military Execution; and those who escape shall be treated as Traitors, by Seizure of their Goods and Effects.

All Masters of Transports or other Vessels sailing from hence, unless under the immediate Order of Samuel Graves, Esq., Vice Admiral of the White, &c. &c. &c. or Officer commanding His Majesty's Ships of War on this Service for the Time being, are hereby strictly forbidden to receive any Person or Persons on board without my Order or Permission in Writing. Any Master or others detected disobeying this Proclamation shall be liable to such Fine and Imprisonment as may be adjudged.

Given at Head Quarters in Boston, this Twenty-eight Day of October, 1775.

By his Excellency WILLIAM HOWE, &c.

WHEREAS there is Reason to believe, that many Persons leaving this Town by Permission have, contrary to Orders, conveyed away large Sums in Specie, to the great Inconvenience of this Garrison, and Detriment of his Majesty's Service in general:

I DO hereby give Notice, that any Person, having leave to depart from hence, by Water or otherwise, who shall be detected in an Attempt to carry away more than Five Pounds in Specie, as heretofore allowed, without first obtaining my particular Permission for so doing, shall forfeit the whole Sum discovered; and suffer such other Fine and Imprisonment as may be adjudged, according to the Degree of the Offence.

And, for the more effectual Discovery of those who shall presume to act contrary to this Proclamation, I do hereby Order that one half of the Monies duly detected on Information, be given to the Informers.

Given at Head Quarters in Boston, Oct. 28, 1775.

By his Excellency WILLIAM HOWE, &c.

WHEREAS it is become the indispensable duty of every loyal and faithful citizen, to contribute all in his power for the preservation of order and good government within the town of Boston:

I DO hereby command, that the inhabitants do immediately associate themselves, to be formed into companies under proper officers, selected by me, from among the associators, to be solely employed within the precincts of the town. and for the purposes above mentioned.

THAT this Association be opened in the Council Chamber, under the Direction of the Honourable Peter Oliver, Foster Hutchinson and William Brown, Esquires, on Monday, the thirteen Day of October, 1775, and continued for four Days following, that no one may plead ignorance of the same.

Out of the Number of Persons voluntarily entering into this Association, all such as are able to discharge the duty required of them, shall be properly armed, and an Allowance of Fuel and Provisions be made to those requiring the same, equal to what is issued to His Majesty's Troops within the Garrison.

Given at Head Quarters in Boston, Oct. 28, 1775.

Recreated from The Hartford Courant, November 6, 1775.

KING TO INCREASE FORCES.

LONDON, *October* 28, 1775.

YESTERDAY, about noon, his majesty went from the queen's palace to St. James's, attended by only two footmen behind his coach. About ten minutes before two o'clock his majesty got into the state coach, attended by the duke of Ancaster and lord Bruce, and proceeded to the House of Peers, where, being seated on the throne, and a message having been sent to the Commons, requiring their attendance, his majesty opened the present session of parliament with the following speech:

"My Lords and Gentlemen,

"THE present situation in America, and my constant desire to have your advice, concurrence, and assistance, on every important occasion, have determined me to call you thus early together. Those who have long too successfully laboured to inflame my people in America, by gross misrepresentations, and to infuse into their minds a system of opinions repugnant to the true constitution of the colonies, and to their subordinate relation to Great Britain, now openly avow their revolt, hostility, and rebellion. They have raised troops, and are collecting a naval force; they have seized the publick revenue, and assumed to themselves legislative, executive, and judicial powers, which they already exercise, in the most arbitrary manner, over the persons and properties of their fellow-subjects. And although many of these unhappy people may still retain their loyalty, and may be too wise not to see the fatal consequence of this usurpation, and wish to resist it, yet the torrent of violence has been strong enough to compel their acquiescence till a sufficient force shall appear to support them.

"The authors and promoters of this desperate conspiracy have, in the conduct of it, derived great advantage from the difference of our intentions and theirs. They meant only to amuse by vague expressions of attachment to the parent state, and the strongest protestations of loyalty to me, whilst they were preparing for a general revolt.

"On our part, though it was declared in your last session that a rebellion existed in the province of Massachusetts Bay, yet even that province we wished rather to reclaim rather than subdue. The resolutions of parliament breathed a spirit of moderation and forbearance, conciliatory propositions accompanied the measures taken to enforce authority, and the coercive acts were adapted to cases of criminal combinations amongst subjects not then in arms. I have acted with the same temper, anxious to prevent, if it had been possible, the effusion of the blood of my subjects, and the calamities which are inseparable from a state of war, still hoping that my people in America would have discerned the traiterous vies of their leaders, and have been convinced, that to be a subject of Great Britain, with all its consequences, is to be the freest member of any civil society in the known world.

"The rebellious war now levied is become more general, and is manifestly carried on for the purpose of establishing an independent empire. I need not dwell upon the fatal effects of the success of such a plan.

"The object is too important, the spirit of the British nation too high, the resources with which GOD has blessed her too numerous, to give up so many colonies, which she has planted with great industry, nursed with great tenderness, encouraged with many commercial advantages, and protected and defended at much expense of blood and treasure.

"It is now become the part of wisdom, and (in its effects) of clemency, to put a speedy end to these disorders, by the most decisive exertions. For this purpose, I have increased my naval establishment, and greatly augmented my land forces, but in such a manner as may be the least burdensome to my kingdoms.

"I have also the satisfaction to inform you, that I have received the most friendly offers of foreign assistance; and if I shall make any treaties in consequence thereof, they shall be laid before you.

"And I have, in testimony of my affection for my people, who can have no cause in which I am not equally interested, sent to the garrisons of Gibraltar and Port Mahon a part of my electoral troops, in order that a larger number of the established forces of this kingdom may be applied to the maintenance of its authority; and the national militia, planned and regulated with equal regard to the rights, safety, and protection of my crown and people, may give a farther extent and activity to our military operations.

"When the unhappy and deluded multitude, against whom this force will be directed shall become sensible of their error, I shall be ready to receive the misled with tenderness and mercy; and in order to prevent the inconveniences which may arise from the great distance of their situation, and to remove, as soon as possible, the calamities which they suffer, I shall give authority to certain persons upon the spot to grant general or particular pardons and indemnities, in such manner, and to such persons, as they shall think fit, and to receive the submission of any province or colony which shall be disposed to return to its allegiance. It may be also proper to authorise the persons so commissioned to restore such province or colony, so returning to its allegiance, to the free exercise of its trade and commerce, and to the same protection and security as if such province had never revolted.

Philadelphia Constitutional Post-Office.

October 10, 1775.

NOTICE is hereby given, that a Post will leave this Office, on Thursday next, for New-York, and continue to go three Times a Week, between Philadelphia and New-York, setting out every Tuesday, Thursday and Saturday, and twice every Week to the Eastward, as far as Portsmouth, in New-Hampshire. A Post also sets out every Tuesday and Saturday to the Southward, and proceeds as far as Savannah, in Georgia.

R. BACHE, Post-Master.

N. B. The Office is kept on the West Side of Front-street, a few Doors Southward of the Coffee-House.

Philadelphia, October 4, 1775.

LOST last Monday, in Philadelphia, a shagreen studded WATCH CASE. Whoever will bring it to the PRINTERS, shall have TEN SHILLINGS reward.

"*Gentlemen of the House of Commons,*

"I have ordered the proper estimates for the ensuing year to be laid before you, and I rely on your affection to me, and your resolution to maintain the just rights of this country, for such supplies as the present circumstances of our affairs require.

"Among the many unavoidable ill consequences of this rebellion, none effects me more sensibly than the extraordinary burden which it must create to my faithful subjects.

"*My Lords and Gentlemen,*

"I have fully opened to you my views and intentions. The constant employment of my thoughts, and the most earnest wishes of my heart, tend wholly to the safety and happiness of all my people, and to the re-establishment of order and tranquility through the several parts of my dominions, in a close connection and constitutional dependence. You see the tendency of the present disorders, and I have stated to you the measures which I mean to pursue for suppressing them. Whatever remains to be done, that may farther contribute to this end, I commit to your wisdom. And I am happy to add, that, as well from the assurances I have received, as from the general appearance of affairs in Europe, I see no probability that the measures which you may adopt will be interrupted by disputes with any foreign power."

Recreated from The Pennsylvania Gazette, January 10, 1776.

TO BE SOLD,

A YOUNG HEALTHY NEGROE WENCH, about 20 Years of Age, with one Male Child, about two Years and two Months old; she can be recommended for her Honesty and Sobriety, and is disposed of only for Want of Employment. Enquire of the PRINTERS.

TO BE SOLD,

A neat, light, second-hand Post Coach, Not much the worse for wear.

Any person inclining to purchase, may apply to DANIEL SMITH, at the City Tavern, or to JOHN HALE, in Lombard-street.

Recreated from The Pennsylvania Gazette, October 18, 1775.

ETHAN ALLEN'S MISFORTUNE.

Extract of a letter from an officer of rank, dated, camp before St. John's, *November 1, 1775.*

COLONEL Allen's misfortune happened by reason of his not being joined, as was agreed, by 400 men, which undoubtedly would have enabled him to have stood the party that attacked him, they being only 300 strong. Colonel Allen withstood them an hour and a quarter with only 40 men. At first he had 40 men exclusive of seventy Canadians.

When the party from Montreal were marching down to give Colonel Allen battle, he retreated to an advantageous spot of ground, where he made a stand, and soon saw a party of the enemy filing off to surround him; whereupon he sent off about half his men, under the command of captain Youngs, to annoy them, but neither Youngs nor any of his party fired a single gun, for reasons best known to themselves, and Allen was left with about 35 men, as most of the Canadians left him on the first fire from the enemy. Allen had but one man killed in the skirmish. Seventeen of the enemy were killed, among whom are major Carden, who commanded the party, and several principal tory merchants of Montreal.

Several Canadians were taken prisoner with Colonel Allen, whom the regular officers said they would put to death; on which Allen stepped up, opened his breast, and said the Canadians were not to blame; that he brought them there, and that if anybody must be murdered, let it be him. This got him great credit with all the officers at Montreal, and General Carleton himself said it was a pity a man of Allen's spirit should be engaged in so bad a cause, as he calls it. Colonel Allen is prisoner on board the Gaspee brig before Montreal.

General Schuyler has offered to give up any officer he has in exchange for him, but has not as yet received an answer."

Recreated from Rind's Virginia Gazette, December 16, 1775.

WOMEN PERISH IN FLAMES.

Charles-Town, *October 26, 1775.*—A most melancholy accident happened last night near this place. The dwelling house, kitchen, and a negroe-quarter, belonging to Mrs. Key, on the place called Carpenter's Point, together with almost all her furniture, were reduced to ashes. But what in a peculiar manner rendered the scene distressing was, two women who perished in the flames. Mrs. M'Alwain, a young married lady from Frederick county, who, a few days before, had come to Mrs. Key's (with whom she lived when a girl) with an intention of lying in with her first child. The other was a white girl, who slept in the chamber with her, in the character of a servant.

The roof of the house beginning to fall in near to where a labouring man slept, was the first thing which gave the alarm. He with difficulty got down stairs and waked Mrs. Key, who, notwithstanding the utmost danger of being buried in the flames, went to the chamber where Mrs. M'Alwain slept, and seizing her by the hand, endeavoured to wake her; begging that she would come down, the house being all on fire. At that instant, the flames began to beat on the stair case, and Mrs. Key, not without being scorched, rushed down.

It appears probable, that Mrs. M'Alwain never got out of her bed, although she answered Mrs. Key, and said she was coming, as her remains were found the next morning in the cellar just under where her bed stood, and the child of which she was big, about half consumed, at a little distance from her. By what accident, or in what manner the fire at first broke out, is as yet wholly unknown. There is some reason to believe it was done designedly, and some of Mrs. Key's own negroes are not altogether unsuspected.

TO BE SOLD,
THE Time of an English Servant young WOMAN, who has three Years and an Half to serve. She understands Housework, and is a good plain Cook. Enquire of the PRINTERS.

Recreated from The Pennsylvania Gazette, November 8, 1775.

St. JOHN'S SURRENDERS.

HARTFORD.—*Yesterday an Express from the Northern Army passed through this Town, to his Honour Governor Trumbull, with the glorious News that on Friday the 3rd Inst., the strong Fortress of* St. JOHN's *was surrendered to the American Arms, the Particulars of which happy Event we have not yet been able to obtain.*

Recreated from The Hartford Courant, November 13, 1775.

HONOURS OF WAR GRANTED.

Extract of a letter from Fort St. John's.

"The 28th ult. the remainder of our army, on the south-west side of the fort, of which our regiment composed a part, marched round St. John's to the north side of it, and encamped there with the main body.

• • • •

"*Oct.* 29. I went in the evening with 200 men, and compleated a battery within 250 yards of the fort. The fort kept a continual fire upon us all night.

• • • •

"*Oct.* 30. The army busily employed in preparing for a cannonade, and an assault if necessary. This day we received news that 700 of our men, near Longue Geel, about 18 miles from hence, had repulsed Governor Carleton, who intended to raise the siege at St. John's with 800 men. Our green Mountain boys did this business. The Governor had 25 men killed, and 50 wounded, besides several prisoners, among whom are two Indians. Carleton retreated to Montreal.

• • • •

"*Nov.* 1. Our gun and mortar battery on this side, and the four gun batteries on the east side, kept an incessant fire all day on the garrison, the garrison kept up a very brisk fire. In the evening General Montgomery sent a flag into the fort, with a letter to Major Preston, by one of the prisoners taken at Longue Geel, informing him of Carson's defeat, and that he had now no longer any reason to flatter himself with relief from that quarter, and that therefore to prevent the farther effusion of blood, which a fruitless and obstinate defence would cause, he recommended to him a surrender of the fort.

"Major Preston in return to General Montgomery's letter, sent Capt. Stuart of the 26th, with a drum into our camp, that the general should have a full answer to his letter in the morning, that in the mean time hostilities should cease on both sides.

• • • •

"*Nov.* 3. Capt. Stuart and Capt. Williams, of the Train, came about 8 o'clock in the morning, with a Flag into our Camp, with an answer from Major Preston, to General Montgomery's letter of yesterday, requesting of the General to wait four days, to see whether no relief could come to the garrison in that time, if not, that then they would make proposals for a surrender. The general returned an answer, that from the advanced season of the year, he could not give the garrison the time it requested, and that they must immediately surrender as prisoners of war, otherwise that if any fatal consequences should ensue, from their needless defences in the weak state they were in, they must charge themselves with it.

"The General also referred them for the truth of Carleton's defeat, to another prisoner on board of our sloop, whom they might have access to examine; and that whenever they choose to renew hostilities, they should give a signal, by firing a cannon without a ball.

"In the evening the above gentlemen returned into our Camp from the Fort, with articles of Capitulation, some of which were agreed to by us, others rejected, which, as amended, were sent back to the Fort, and agreed to, the sum of which were: That the Garrison should march out of the Fort to-morrow morning, with the honours of war, and then lay down their arms, be prisoners of war, and be sent to Connecticut. A great quantity of military stores are taken, the details of which are not yet ascertained; about 600 men are prisoners. This day detachments from every regiment in our army took possession of the Fort, and the prisoners are embarked for the place of their detention."

Recreated from The Pennsylvania Gazette, November 15, 1775.

GEN. MONTGOMERY AT ST. JOHN'S.

Extract of a Letter from General MONTGOMERY, *near* ST. JOHN'S, *November 3, 1775.*

MY DEAR GENERAL,

I have the pleasure to acquaint you the garrison surrendered last night. This morning we take possession. To-morrow I hope the prisoners will set off. Enclosed you have the capitulation, which I hope will meet with your approbation, and that of Congress. I have ventured to permit an officer or two to go to their families, which are in some distress at Montreal, upon their parole. They cannot do us any harm, and there would have been a degree of inhumanity in refusing them.

When we had played on the fort some hours from our battery of four twelve pounders on the N.W. and another of two twelve pounders and two four pounders on the East side, some prisoners arrived, who had been taken in an action with Governor Carleton at Longueile.

He made an attempt to land with thirty-four boats full of men. Warner's detachment, consisting of the Green Mountain Boys and second regiment of Yorkers, repulsed them with loss, took two Indians and two Canadians prisoners. We have buried three Indians, and it is supposed many in the boats must have been killed. We had not a man even wounded. This I believe is his last effort.

One of the above mentioned prisoners I sent into the fort, to inform Major Preston of the circumstances of the action, that he might judge what prospect he could have of relief. It had the desired effect. The garrison having been on half allowance for some time.

I am making the necessary preparations to proceed immediately down to Montreal by way of La Prairie, as the enemy have armed vessels in the Sorel.

Several men of rank in Canada are among the prisoners. I have permitted them to remain at Crownpoint, till the return of two gentlemen they sent to their friends for money, &c. They pleaded hard to return home, but they are too dangerous to let loose again.

Col. Easton and Major Brown with that corps, and Mr. Livingston, with I believe a thousand Canadians, are going towards the mouth of the Sorel, and pushing Col. Allen M'Clean before them. M'Clean had many Canadians, but they joined through fear of fire and sword.

I send you a list of the artillery, a good deal of artillery stores, but we have not time to ascertain them. I am, &c.   RICHARD MONTGOMERY.

Recreated from The Pennsylvania Gazette, November 22, 1775.

WANTED immediately, A Number of FIRELOCKS with BAYONETS, to be made agreeable to a Pattern. Any Person or Persons willing to undertake the compleating a Quantity will meet with proper Encouragement, by applying to the Commissioners and Assessors of the County of Philadelphia.   October 21, 1775.

WHERE IS HIS EAR?

WILLIAMSBURG, *November 3.*—The rifle-men and soldiers of Hampton desire their compliments to Capt. Squire and his squadron, and wish to know how they approve the reception they met with last Friday. Should he incline to renew his visit, they will be glad to see him; otherwise, in point of complaisance, they will be under the necessity of returning the visit. If he cannot find the *ear* that was cut off, they hope he will wear a *wig* to hide the mark; for perhaps it may not be necessary that all should know *chance* had effected that which *the laws* ought to have done.

• • • •

AS saltpetre is an article much wanted in America, the Committee of Safety earnestly recommend it to the planters of tobacco in this colony to cut down and preserve all their tobacco suckers, and also to preserve the trash, stalks, and sweepings of their tobacco-houses, which are found to be exceedingly useful in the production of that necessary article.   *By order of the committee:*
     JOHN PENDLETON.

Recreated from Purdie's Virginia Gazette, November 3, 1775.

A PROCLAMATION.

AS I have ever entertained hopes that an accommodation might have taken place between Great Britain and this colony, without being compelled, by my duty, to this most disagreeable, but now absolutely necessary step, rendered so by a body of armed men, unlawfully assembled, firing on his majesty's tenders, and the formation of an army, and that army now on their march to attack his majesty's troops, and destroy the well disposed subjects of this colony: To defeat such treasonable purposes, and that all such traitors, and their abettors, may be brought to justice, and that the peace and good order of this colony may be again restored, which the ordinary course of the civil law is unable to effect, I have thought fit to issue this my proclamation, hereby declaring, that until the aforesaid good purposes can be obtained, I do, by his majesty, determine to execute martial law, and cause the same to be executed throughout this colony. And to the end that peace and good order may the sooner be restored, I do require every person capable of bearing arms to resort to his majesty's *standard*, or be looked upon as traitors to his majesty's crown and government, and thereby become liable to the penalty the law inflicts upon such offences, such as forfeiture of life, confiscation of lands, &c. &c. And I do hereby farther declare all indented servants, negroes, or others (appertaining to rebels) free, that are able and willing to bear arms, they joining his majesty's troops, as soon as may be, for the more speedily reducing this colony to a proper sense of their duty to his majesty's crown and dignity. I do farther order and require all his majesty's liege subjects to retain their quitrents, or any other taxes due, or that may become due, in their own custody, till such time as peace may be again restored to this at present most unhappy country, or demanded of them for their former salutary purposes, by officers properly authorized to receive the same.

November 7, 1775.   DUNMORE.

FORTY SHILLINGS REWARD.

RUN away from the subscriber. living in Reedy-Island-Neck, New-Castle county, on the 28th of July last, a NEGROE man, named *Jacob Purkins*, about 26 years of age, 5 feet 9 inches high, of a yellowish colour, he chews tobacco and is very apt to ask any person he sees use it, for a chew; he had an iron collar about his neck, when he went away, a pair of old striped holland trousers, an old felt hat, and an old blue coat. Whoever secures the said Negroe, so his master may have him again, shall be paid the above reward, and reasonable charges, by

WILLIAM M'KEAN.

LOST from the subscriber, living on Raccoon creek, in Woolwich township, Gloucester county, West New Jersey, in the night between the 9th and 10th of this instant October, an indentured Female Child, her name is Polly Murphy, very near five years of age, pretty tall for her age, of a fair complexion, had ruddy cheeks, grey eyes, light hair, and a small scar on her forehead; had on an almost new homespun lincey petticoat, with red, brown and yellow stripes, turned up round-about, a red, ragged woolen short gown, and a coarse ozenbrigs shirt. It is supposed she has been taken away by her parents, who stayed that night with the subscriber, and with the child disappeared in the morning. The father's name is Henry Sharff, has a lean face and thin hair, and had on an old worn-out blue coat; the mother is a lusty hearty woman, of a fair complexion, has thick lips, and black hair, and is big with child. Whoever takes up the said persons with the above described child, and secures them; so that the subscriber may have the child again, and the parents convicted of the theft, shall have FIVE POUNDS reward, or for the child alone THREE POUNDS, and all reasonable charges paid by

ANDREW MINTS.

Recreated from The Pennsylvania Gazette, November 1, 1775.

ETHAN ALLEN'S LETTER.

LONDON, *November* 8.

The following is the copy of a letter from Mr. ETHAN ALLEN, the person who commanded the Provincials near Montreal, and who was also taken prisoner, to Gen. PRESCOTT, on the General's ordering him into irons, and to be closely confined.

"Honourable SIR,

"In the wheel of transitory events I find myself prisoner, and in irons. Probably your Honour has certain reasons to me inconceivable, though I challenge an instance of this sort of economy of the Americans during the late war towards any officers of the crown.

"On my part, I have to assure your Honour, that when I had the command, and took Capt. Delaplace and Lieut. Felton, with the garrison of Ticonderoga, I treated them with every mark of friendship and generosity, the evidence of which is notorious even in Canada. I have only to add, that I expect an honourable and humane treatment, as an officer of my rank and merit should have, and subscribe myself your Honour's most obedient humble servant,

"ETHAN ALLEN."

Recreated from The Pennsylvania Gazette, January 31, 1776.

PHILADELPHIA.

In CONGRESS, *Wednesday, November* 8, 1775.

Resolved, That all letters to and from the Delegates of the United Colonies during the sessions of Congress, pass, and be carried free of postage; the members having engaged upon their honour, not to frank or enclose any letters but their own.

Recreated from The Hartford Courant, November 20, 1775.

WORCESTER, *November* 10.

We are credibly informed that the assembly of Rhode Island have passed an act, making it death for any person or persons to supply our worse than savage enemies, the ministerial army and navy, with provisions and other necessaries.

Recreated from Rind's Virginia Gazette, November 30, 1775.

BRITISH ATTACK FAILS.

MORE ENEMY TROOPS ARRIVE.

Extract of a letter from CAMBRIDGE, *Nov.* 9.

"We had an account of the Regulars landing at Lechmere's Point, about a mile and a half from Cambridge; about 300 of the Regulars landed, from Boston, on the above mentioned point, under cover of a very heavy and continual fire from their batteries on Bunker's, Breed's, Copp's and Beacon Hills; as also from a frigate which lay within 300 yards of the point on which they landed. They had possession of the hill for nearly an hour before they could be obstructed, owing to a very high tide, which prevented our people crossing a causeway, which was overflowed, and the only way to get at the enemy.

"During this time they were shooting horses and cows, with an intent of taking them off; but a battalion of rifle-men, under command of Col. Thompson, disregarding danger and difficulty, took to the water, which was then up to their middles, and a quarter of a mile over, and notwithstanding the Regulars had lodged themselves behind stone walls, and in an orchard, where they might have done our people much damage, yet on Col. Thompson's approach they fled to their boats in great confusion, but not without a warm serenade from the rifle-men, who fired at a great distance, when they found them retreating, and ran up with all speed in hopes of bringing them to an engagement before they reached their boats.

"All this time the unceasing warm fire was kept up from the before mentioned forts and ships, and from the soldiers and their boats. Our loss is 1 killed and 3 wounded; their loss uncertain, but have since heard three of their men were found dead on the field. One of the enemy's boats was sunk from our fort on Prospect Hill by a 24 pounder, and the enemy were beat off the ground about 2 o'clock, and landed at Charlestown.

"During the engagement, 22 large ships hove into sight, with troops from England and Ireland."

GOD'S HOUSE FOR HORSES.

A GENTLEMAN who lately came out of Boston, assures, that the ministerial rebels in Boston, by order of their General Howe, have taken down the pulpit and all the pews in the old south meetinghouse, and are using it for a riding school. This he saw. Thus we see the house once set apart for the true worship and service of GOD, turned into a den for thieves!

IRELAND FOR AMERICA.

WATERTOWN, *November* 13.—Wednesday last Captain Robbins, bound from Ireland for Boston, in a schooner laden with beef, tongues, butter, potatoes and eggs, (all much wanted for the butchering assassins there) was taken by a privateer from Beverly and carried in there. Capt. Robbins, who has been brought to town, informs us, that he left Ireland the 24th of September, at which time five regiments were embarking on board seven ships and one brig, for Boston.

Captain Robbins brought papers to the 16th of September, which are not come to hand. He says the common people of Ireland were almost unanimous in favour of the Americans, and that only those in favour of government appeared against us.

Recreated from The Pennsylvania Gazette, November 22, 1775.

IN COMMITTEE of SAFETY.

PHILADELPHIA, *November* 11, 1775.

"*Resolved*, That Capt. Shee, Capt. Wilcocks, and Capt. Cadwalder, be authorised to contract for and provide any number of Firelocks and Bayonets, not exceeding 1000, to be made agreeable to a pattern which this Board will deliver to them, and for a price which shall not exceed what is given by the Commissioners and Assessors of the county where they shall make such a contract. That the said Firelocks, before they are accepted, shall be proved by Robert Towers, Commissary. And this Board do agree to advance such sums of money, as may be necessary to expedite and complete the said business."

IN PURSUANCE of the above Resolve of the Committee of Safety, we hereby give notice to all persons in this and the neighbouring provinces, who can execute any of the branches in said business, to apply immediately to the subscribers, who will afford them the best encouragement. Makers of Gunlocks will be more particularly wanted.

JOHN SHEE, JOHN WILCOCKS, LAMBERT CADWALDER.

Recreated from The Pennsylvania Gazette, December 6, 1775.

DUNMORE INTERCEPTS MILITIA.

WILLIAMSBURG, *November* 17.

COL. HENRY received an express yesterday morning with the following intelligence, viz. that lord Dunmore, having received advice that about 200 Princess Anne militia were on their march to join the troops destined for the protection of the lower parts of the country, marched from Norfolk last Tuesday, about 10 P.M. to intercept them; who, not having the least intelligence of his lordship's approach, were obliged to engage under every disadvantage, both as to the enemy's superiority in point of numbers, and the situation on the ground, being hemmed in by a fence. Our people fought a considerable time, and it is thought did great execution; but were at last over-powered, and forced to retreat, with the loss of Mr. John Ackiss in the minute service, killed on the spot, and col. John Hutchings, and one Mr. Williams, wounded. The publick, no doubt, will be exceedingly incensed on finding that lord Dunmore has taken into his service the *very scum* of the country to assist him in his diabolical schemes against the good people of this government, all well attached to his majesty, but mortal enemies to his infamous ministry and their subordinate tools; but it is to be hoped his sphere of mischief will soon be circumscribed within narrow bounds, as col. Woodford, with about 800 as brave troops as the world can produce, are now on their march to Norfolk, and, should his lordship incline to give them battle, we have not the smallest doubt we will give a very satisfactory account of him.

Recreated from Purdie's Virginia Gazette, November 17, 1775.

[*The following* LETTERS *are published by order of the* HON. CONTINENTAL CONGRESS.]

To General Schuyler.

MONTREAL, *Nov.* 17, 1775.

My dear General,

With great pleasure I transmit you a letter from Col. Arnold for Gen. Washington, together with the copy of his letter to me. Col. Easton has six guns mounted on shore, three twelve pounders, one nine ditto, and two sixes, at the Sorrel, and the two row gallies. Mr. Carleton, with his 11 sail, has not yet been able to pass him by. Indeed Easton has obliged him twice to weigh anchor, and remove higher up the river. I am making all dispatch to attack him on my side, with field artillery mounted in batteaus. I have had great difficulty about the troops. I am afraid many of them will go home; however, depending on my good fortune, I hope to keep enough to give the final blow to ministerial politics in this province, and I hope effectual measures will be taken to prevent their laying hold of it again.

I must beg the boats may be sent back, if possible, which take up the discharged men. Some of them might be left at the Point au Fere. I am exceedingly hurried, and have not done half my business with you. I shall establish a post, which will set out next Monday for Ticonderoga. Will you appoint a Post-Master there? May you enjoy your better health. I am, &c.

RICHARD MONTGOMERY.

To the Hon. John Hancock, Esq., &c. &c.

TICONDEROGA, *Nov.* 22, 1775, 9 *o'clock*, P.M.

SIR,

I sent off the express about noon to-day, who brought me your favour of the 9th. Since his departure, I received a letter from General Montgomery, inclosing a copy of one from Col. Arnold. Copies of both I do myself the honour to transmit to you.

If general Carleton had reached Quebec before Col. Arnold, it is probable the latter might have met with more difficulties than he expected, from the reinforcement the former carried with him, but I hope by this time that our troops are in barracks at Quebec.

Col. Arnold's march does him great honour. Some future historian will make it the subject of admiration to his readers. I am, Sir,

Your most obedient and most humble servant,

P.H. SCHUYLER.

Nov. 23. The frost has been so severe last night, that the lake, as far down towards Crown Point as we can see, which is about three miles, is intirely closed.

To Brig. Gen. Montgomery.

ST. MARIA, *two leagues and a half from* POINT LEVY, *November* 8, 1775.

Dear Sir,

Your favour of the 29th ult. I received at ten o'clock this morning, which gave me much pleasure. I heartily congratulate you on your success thus far. I think you have great reason to be apprehensive for me, the time I mentioned to General Washington being so long since elapsed. I was not then apprised, or indeed apprehensive of one half of the difficulties we had to encounter, of which I cannot at present give you a particular detail. I can only say we have hauled our batteaus up over falls, up rapid streams, over carrying places, and marched through morasses, thick woods, and over mountains about three hundred and twenty miles, many of which we had to pass several times to bring over our baggage. These difficulties the soldiers have with the greatest fortitude surmounted, and about two thirds of the detachment are happily arrived here, and within two days march, most of them in good health and high spirits.

The other part, with Col. Enos, returned from the Dead River contrary to my expectation, he having orders to send back only the sick, and those that could not be furnished with provisions.

I wrote Gen. Schuyler the 13th of October, by an Indian I thought trusty, inclosed to my friend in Quebec, and as I have had no answer from either, and he pretends being taken at Quebec, I make no doubt he has betrayed his trust, which I am confirmed in, as I find they have been some time apprised of our coming to Quebec; and have destroyed all the canoes at Point Levy, to prevent our passing. This difficulty will be obviated by birch canoes, as we have about twenty of them, with forty Savages who have joined us, and profess great friendship, as well as the Canadians, by whom we have been very friendly received, and who will be able to furnish us with a number of canoes.

I am informed by the French there are two frigates and several small armed vessels lying before Quebec, and a large ship or two lately arrived from Boston; however, I propose crossing the St. Lawrence as soon as possible, and if any opportunity offers of attacking Quebec with success, shall embrace it, otherwise will endeavour to join your army in Montreal. I shall as often as in my power advise you of my proceedings, and beg the favour of hearing from you by every opportunity.

The inclosed letter to his Excellency Gen. Washington, beg the favour of your forwarding by express. I am, dear Sir, your most obedient humble servant,

P.S. Since my writing the above, I have seen a friend from Quebec, who informs me a frigate of 26 guns, and two transports, with 150 recruits, arrived from St. John's, Newfoundland, last Sunday, which, with the inhabitants who have been compelled to take up arms, amount to about 300 men. That the French and English inhabitants in general are on our side, and that the city are short of provisions; I shall endeavour to cut off their communication with the country, and make no doubt, if no more recruits arrive, to bring them to terms soon, or at least keep them in close quarters until your arrival here, which I wait with impatience, but if St. John's should not have surrendered, and you can possibly spare a regiment this way, I think the city must of course fall into our hands.

B. ARNOLD.

POINT LEVY, *Nov.* 14, 1775.

Dear Sir,

The foregoing is a copy of my last, by the two Indians you sent express the 29th ult. who, I hear this moment, are taken five leagues above this, since which I have waited two or three days for the rear to come up, and in preparing ladders, &c.

The wind has been so high these three nights, that I have not been able to cross the river. I have near forty canoes ready; and, as the wind has moderated, I design crossing this evening. The Hunter sloop and Lizard frigate lie opposite to prevent us, but make no doubt I shall be able to avoid them. I this moment received the agreeable intelligence (via Sorrel) that you are in possession of St. John's, and have invested Montreal. I can give no intelligence, save that the merchant ships are busy day and night in loading, and four have already sailed.

B. ARNOLD.

Recreated from The Pennsylvania Gazette, December 13, 1775.

HIS MAJESTY DEMURS.

PHILADELPHIA, IN CONGRESS, *Nov.* 9.

On the 21st of August a copy of the petition to the king, which was sent from the Congress by mr. R. Penn, was sent to the Secretary of State for America, and on the first of September, the first moment that was permitted, the original was presented to him, which his lordship promised to deliver to his majesty.

His lordship was pressed to obtain an answer, but those who presented it were told, *That as his majesty did not receive it on the throne, no answer would be given.*

CHARLES THOMPSON, *secretary.*

Wanted to hire or purchase,
A GOOD *NEGRO BLACKSMITH.*
Inquire of the printer.

Recreated from Purdie's Virginia Gazette, November 24, 1775.

LONDON.

Nov. 18. The following ships are now fitting out at this port, with all possible dispatch for America, viz. Jersey 60 guns, Ifis 50, Brune 32, Blond 32, Repulse 32, Flora 32, Emerald 32, Milford 28, and Carysfort 28.

The seven regiments said to be sailed for Ireland are, it is said, gone with seven men of war to Virginia, to resent the treatment of Lord Dunmore. They are to burn every place within shot of the ships on the coast.

* * * *

Nov. 25. The new plan of the American war in the spring, is to burn everything on the coast, to withdraw the army, and interrupt all vessels that trade thereto.

Letters of marque are now said to be making out at the Admiralty office, ready to sign as soon as ever the new America bill takes place.

* * * *

Nov. 28. The 33d regiment of foot, of which Lord Cornwallis is Colonel, is ordered for America, instead of the 53d. Lord Cornwallis is to command the expedition to South Carolina and Virginia.

A letter from Dublin says, "By letters from Sligo we have the melancholy account of several ships wrecked upon the north coast of this kingdom, and among the number a transport, which contained three companies of the 46th regiment, bound for America."

* * * *

Dec. 1. It is confidently reported, that General Gage advises an immediate reconciliation with America by all means, and that General Burgoyne seconds this opinion.

* * * *

Dec. 7. It is said that General Gage has been offered a Peerage, but that he has declined accepting it, till he shall have rendered some farther public service, that my entitle him to such an honour.

* * * *

Dec. 8. The clause in the American restraining bill, which occasioned the greatest debate at its second reading, was at length settled as follows:

"And be it further enacted by the authority aforesaid, that this act, so far as the same relates to the capture and forfeiture of ships and vessels belonging to the inhabitants of the above mentioned colonies, shall commence and be in force from and after the first of January, 1776; and so far as the same relates to the capture and forfeiture of all ships and vessels that shall be found going in or at any of the said colonies, from and after the first of next March; and so far as the same relates to the capture and forfeiture of all ships and vessels that shall be found trading in or at any of the said colonies, or bound and trading from any port or place in the same, from and after the first of June next; and shall continue to be in force so long as any of the said colonies shall remain in a state of rebellion and disobedience."

Another amendment we hear is, that all seamen who are taken on board American vessels made prizes, are to be entered into his Majesty's service as part of the crew of the ship of war by which they are taken, instead of being made prisoners.

* * * *

Dec. 9. Yesterday Lord Cornwallis took leave of his Majesty, he being in a few days to set out to embark for Virginia.

Orders are sent to the victualling office to get ready, by the latter end of January, such a quantity of beef and pork as will victual a considerable fleet for eight months; and this week they will begin to kill, several new hands being engaged for that purpose.

The troops going to Virginia are to be commanded by Gen. Clinton, from Boston.

Lord Cornwallis, who goes out commander of the troops, is to resign the command when at Williamsburg (if they ever arrive there) to Gen. Clinton; and is there to act under that officer, or command a detachment, as the exigency of affairs may require.

* * * *

Dec. 11. Eight sail of the line, and 5000 soldiers, are to be employed in reducing the Southern Colonies, while the main fleet and army are to occupy Boston. This is the new disposition for the spring.

Recreated from The Pennsylvania Packet, March 4, 1776.

GENERALS WATCH FROM PROSPECT HILL.

PHILADELPHIA, November 27.

Extract of a letter from an officer in one of the rifle companies to his friend in this city, dated PROSPECT HILL, *November* 11, 1775.

"Since you left us, nothing particular happened till about twelve o'clock on Thursday last, we were alarmed by the landing of a number of boats on Litchmore's Point, in order to take off some cattle that were then on the Point; our brigade repaired immediately to the alarm-post, and we saw the enemy drawn up (to the number, as nearly as I can say, of 300) behind the stone wall that surrounds the orchard, and their out-guards driving the cattle.

"I mention the particular places as you know them all. They landed at a very high tide, which surrounded the whole Point; and, in the opinion of most people, made it impossible to get over to attack them, as there was no way to get on but by a narrow causeway that leads from Patterson's encampment to Litchmore's Point, and the water on that four or five feet high.

"Colonel Thompson asked General Greene's permission to cross the causeway, but he refused, as he was informed, he said, by people that knew the place well, that it was impossible to effect it; but Colonel Mifflin coming up, persuaded the General to order us to march, which was cheerfully obeyed, and we passed the bridge, headed by our brave Colonel, without any loss, but exposed to a very heavy fire from the mill near Charleston Neck, the small redoubt near the water side, and two floating batteries off the Point, besides the fire of small arms in front.

"We formed after passing the bridge, and advanced in two columns up the hill with an Indian halloo, and in a few minutes drove the enemy from their post and forced them to their boats; they made a most inglorious retreat, for they were posted as advantageously as possible, and their number, I think, superior to ours, as there did not a man advance but part of our six companies, the rest being on guard.

"We received a very heavy fire of cannon ball and grape-shot as we got over the stone wall, but providentially we had only two men wounded, one mortally; what the enemy suffered I can't pretend to say, as they were in the boats before we could get a fair shot at them, and if there were any killed, they took them off; our regiment met with universal applause.

"All the generals were in the fort on Prospect Hill the whole time, and it was generally thought we would all be cut off, as they supposed that there were a large body of men behind the hill to attack us as we came up. Generals Lee and Greene waited on Col. Thompson in the evening to thank him for the conduct of his regiment, and we had the Commander in Chief's thanks in general orders."

Recreated from The Pennsylvania Packet, November 27, 1775.

GAGE TO WINTER AT BOSTON.

BOSTON, *November* 17.—Before Gen. Gage left Boston it was determined that the troops should winter there, instead of going to Halifax; in consequence of which the provincial army have thatched their tents (or hutted, as they term it) to guard against the inclemency of the weather, by which measure they intend to keep the King's troops within their lines, and prevent their foraging in the neighbouring country.

Recreated from The Pennsylvania Gazette, January 31, 1776.

COL. ALLEN TO ENGLAND?

NEW YORK, *November* 20.—By a person who left Montreal the 4th of last month, we learn, that Col. Guy Johnson had sailed from that place for Quebec, with an intent to proceed from thence for England; and that Col. Allen, with his party, taken prisoners some time ago, were put on board a man of war. The same person also informs, that it was believed the town of Montreal would not be ale to hold out many days against General Montgomery, as most of the Indians had actually gone to their respective towns.

Recreated from The Pennsylvania Packet, November 24, 1775.

GEN. MONTGOMERY AT MONTREAL.
COL. ARNOLD AT QUEBEC.

Copy of a letter from his EXCELLENCY GENERAL SCHUYLER, *Ticonderoga, November 18, 1775.*

SIR,

You will be pleased to communicate to the Committee of the city and county of Albany the farther success of our arms. General Montgomery possessed himself of Montreal on the 13th instant. Colonel Arnold is arrived at Quebec, so that in all probability the entire province of Canada, as formerly limited, will be in our possession soon, if not already. Events which I hope will have a tendency to bring the Ministry of our Sovereign to reasonable terms.

That Heaven may again, and speedily, re-unite us in every bond of affection and interest; that the British empire may become the envy and admiration of the universe, and flourish until the omnipotent Master thereof shall be pleased to put his fiat on all earthly empires, is the sincere wish of, Sir, your most obedient humble Servant,

PHILLIP SCHUYLER.

Recreated from The Pennsylvania Gazette, December 6, 1775.

FORCED MARCH TO SUFFOLK.

CAMP, 5 *miles below* COBHAM, *Nov.* 21.—Colonel Woodford having received an express last night from Suffolk, with intelligence that lord Dunmore was expected to be there this night or to-morrow, in order to destroy the provisions, recruit, and publish *his* proclamation, &c. this morning, at reveille beating, detached a party of 215 privates (103 of them good rifle-men) under the command of lieutenant-colonel Scott and major Marshall, with their other proper officers, to make a forced march, without any other baggage than their blankets, to prevent the farther progress of our enemies till we can get down. They will be at Suffolk before they sleep, which is 35 miles distant.

Recreated from Purdie's Virginia Gazette, November 24, 1775.

COL. ARNOLD ARRIVES AT QUEBEC.

Extract of a letter from a volunteer with Col. Arnold, to his friend in this city, dated Point aux Tremble, 21 miles from Quebec, Nov. 21, 1775.

WE arrived before Quebec the 15th instant, after a severe march of about 600 miles. When we left Cambridge we were 1100 strong; about half way Col. Enos got frightened, and with three companies, and the sick, which together was about half our number, and the greatest part of the provision, *turned back!* May shame and guilt go with him, and wherever he seeks shelter may the hand of *justice* shut the door against him. Perhaps I have said too much; but a man that has suffered by him can hardly refrain speaking. We were about two months on our march, 32 days of which we did not see a house, and at short allowance, six days of which we were at half pound of pork and a half pound of flour per man a day; after which, for four days, we had only half a pound of flour per day, our pork being gone; two days of which we lost ourselves, marched 40 miles, and were but ten miles on our way. Our whole stores was then divided, and it was about four pints of flour per man; a small allowance for men near 100 miles from any habitation, or prospect of a supply. After having travelled 50 or 60 miles on this scanty allowance, we came to a river, which we were told was only eight miles from the inhabited parts. Here I sat down, baked and eat my last morsel of bread; but think what was my distress, when I found, after crossing the river, that I had 30 miles to travel before I could expect the least mouthful. However, my dread was soon removed by the return of Col. Arnold, who, with a small party, had made a forced march, and returned to us with some cattle he had purchased of the inhabitants. On these we made a voracious meal, and renewed our march with new courage to Point Levi, from there we were transported in birch canoes to the Plains of Abraham, and from thence retreated to this place to wait for General Montgomery.

Recreated from The Virginia Gazette, January 20, 1776.

MONTGOMERY TO ASSIST ARNOLD.

By a letter from St. John's, dated November 24, we are informed, that the Continental troops have received intelligence, that there were concealed under ground, about ten tons of gunpowder, and 7000 stands of small arms, that were to be put into the hands of the Canadians and Indians, to assist the ministerial troops, and that they were digging for them, had found several chests of small arms, and likewise had fished out of the lake a royal standard, and a number of muskets.

Saturday night arrived here from our army in Canada, Lieut. Norton, of Col. Clinton's regiment, Mr. Bean, gunner, and Mr. Phineas Chapman; who bring us the agreeable news that all the shipping that lay at Montreal had fallen into the hands of General Montgomery, among them the Gaspee brig of war, with all the prisoners (Col. Allen excepted) lately taken near St. John's.

The fleet with Governor Carleton on board, had sailed for Quebec, but was intercepted by a Gondola, and a battery erected by Col. Easton, near the river Sorrel, and there taken, with about 130 soldiers, &c. among them Col. Prescot, &c. who were arrived at Ticonderoga, a few days ago, on their way to Connecticut. That Carleton, Luke La Corne, and two others went off in a boat from the fleet before it struck, but were taken prisoners by Col. Arnold, near Quebec; that Gen. Wooster, was left to command Montreal, and Gen. Montgomery was gone to assist Col. Arnold to secure Quebec.

Recreated from The Pennsylvania Gazette, December 20, 1775.

THE GENERAL'S LADY.

PHILADELPHIA, *November* 22.—Yesterday the Lady of his Excellency General WASHINGTON arrived here, upon her way to New England. She was met at the Lower Ferry by the officers of the different battalions, the troop of light horse, and the light infantry of the second battalion, who escorted her into the city.

Recreated from The Pennsylvania Gazette, November 22, 1775.

DUNMORE'S DRAUGHT.

Copy of Lord Dunmore's orders to the Militia Captains.

IT being requisite to raise a body of men in this county, for the immediate protection of the lives and property of his Majesty's loyal subjects, inhabitants thereof, now exposed to the lawless violence of those who are meditating their destruction, and that of the most excellent constitution, under which they have hitherto enjoyed perfect tranquility, I require of you, therefore, to call together, at the most convenient place, the company of militia under your command, on Monday, the 27th instant, and draught out of it 15 young men, or more, capable to bear arms, to serve as soldiers for six months, and send them, with a list of their names, to me, in Norfolk, on or before Wednesday next following.

And although this measure is adopted merely for their own defence, I am willing, for the encouragement of such persons, to allow them the same pay and provisions which his Majesty's troops now have, with one guinea and a crown bounty money, in hand paid to them; and good clothing, viz. a coat, waistcoat, breeches, and a hat, which you are hereby authorized to assure them of.

Being also desirous to study the inclinations, together with the interests of the people, under my government, you are desired to return me the names of such persons as you think proper to serve as officers, and are agreeable to the persons they are to command.

Given under my hand, on board the William, the 24th day of November, 1775.

To Capt. William Hodges, DUNMORE.

JUST PUBLISHED, And to be SOLD by the PRINTERS hereof, POOR RICHARD'S ALMANACK, For the YEAR 1776.

Recreated from The Pennsylvania Gazette, December 13, 1775.

A DECLARATION.

WHEREAS divers reports have been propagated, that the army destined to guard and protect the inhabitants of the counties of *Norfolk* and *Princess Anne*, and the parts adjacent, were empowered and directed to destroy the houses and properties of particular persons in some of the towns in those parts, who have been justly alarmed by such false and malicious reports; in order, therefore, to do justice to the publick in general, and to satisfy all private persons in particular, the Committee of Safety think it necessary to declare, in the most solemn manner, that the above mentioned reports have been propagated without having the least foundation in truth, it having been determined, and the army aforesaid being instructed, particularly to support and protect the persons and properties of all friends to *America*, and not wantonly to damage or destroy the property of any person whatsoever.

By order of the committee,
EDMUND PENDLETON, president.

Recreated from Purdie's Virginia Gazette, November 24, 1775.

HEADQUARTERS, WILLIAMSBURG, *Nov.* 19.

General Orders. All the troops being now quartered in this city, it will highly behove them to be careful and guarded in their conduct, so that all offence be avoided toward the citizens. The officers and soldiers will remember, that their profession is to defend and protect the citizens, and all others who are in the American interest. A modest respectful behaviour towards our friends, it is hoped, will characterise all our troops, and that no condition, age, or sex, will justly charge them with licentiousness or immorality.

GEORGE MUTER, Sec'ry, C.C.

• • • •

CARTER BRAXTON, Esq., is appointed, by the Hon. Convention, a Delegate to the Congress in room of the late Hon. Peyton Randolph, Esquire.

Recreated from The Virginia Gazette, December 16, 1775.

SURRENDER OF MONTREAL.

NEW YORK, *November* 27.—About 11 o'clock yesterday afternoon Capt. Henry Livingston arrived here from Montreal and informs us of the surrender of that city to General Montgomery, on Monday the 13th instant, on condition, that the inhabitants have the full enjoyment of their religion as usual, and their property secured from plunder.

We also learn that Governor Carleton was gone off for Quebec, with several vessels and a large quantity of gunpowder, &c. but it was expected the whole would fall into the hands of Col. Arnold, who, we hear, was arrived before Quebec, and no doubt would very soon reduce that place.

Every necessary requisite for supplying the army under General Montgomery was found in Montreal, and on the most moderate terms, and where they will find very comfortable winter quarters, after an amazingly fatiguing campaign.

The garrison of fort St. John, which surrendered to General Montgomery, was arrived at Fort George. They amounted, it is said, to 652, besides women and children, and will be removed to the towns of York, Lancaster, and Reading, in Pennsylvania.

PHILADELPHIA, *November* 29.—On Monday last, the Lady of His Excellency General WASHINGTON, the Lady of General GATES, J. CURTIS, Esquire, and Lady, and WARNER LEWIS, Esquire, set out for Cambridge. They were escorted by the Officers of the First and Second Battalions, the Light Infantry of the First and Third Battalions, and by the Troop of Horse.

Recreated from The Pennsylvania Gazette, November 29, 1775.

CAMBRIDGE, *November* 24.—LAST Thursday the noted Dr. Church, some time since detected in attempting to carry on a traiterous correspondence with the ministerial rebels in Boston, was carried from this town, under a strong guard, and conducted to the interior part of the country.

Recreated from The Pennsylvania Packet, December 11, 1775.

COLONEL WOODFORD AT SUFFOLK.

WILLIAMSBURG, *November* 29.

By advices from the army we learn, that Col. Woodford arrived at Suffolk on the 25th instant; and that Col. Scott, with his detachment, had advanced within seven miles of the great bridge. He has taken several tory prisoners, particularly one Ives, who has been a very active person, and informed, that Lord Dunmore had withdrawn most of his troops from the bridge, which is only guarded by tories and slaves.

Several persons lately from Norfolk inform that Lord Dunmore was preparing barracks for his army near the distillery, and begun to intrench between the two rope walks; and that several Scotch tories in that borough command black companies, who speak, with much confidence, of beating us, with the odds of five to one.

The Committee of Safety of N. Carolina have offered Col. Woodford the assistance of their troops, who are now at Currituck, about a day's march from the great bridge.

By a gentleman from Norfolk we learn, that the prison of that borough was burnt down last Sunday night, by some accident, but that the prisoners were all taken out safe. We also hear, that sundry houses in the environs of Norfolk had been set on fire by Lord Dunmore's order, to prevent our troops from occupying them.

Lord Dunmore's cruel policy begins at length to be discovered by the blacks, who have lately deserted from him to a considerable number. When his Lordship first went down to Norfolk, he gave great encouragement to unwary Negroes, but, such was his baseness, some of them, it is confidently said, he sent to the West Indies, where these unfortunate creatures were disposed of to defray his Lordship's expenses; and others, such as he took any dislike to, he delivered up to their masters, to be punished. Since our troops under Col. Woodford's command began their march, Lord Dunmore issued a proclamation inviting the slaves of rebels, as he pleased to say, to repair to his standard. A considerable number at first went to him, but upon their masters taking the oath of allegiance, they were immediately told they must return. Some runaways, however, remained, but these were kept constantly employed in digging entrenchments in wet ground, till at length the severity of their labour forced many of them to fly. Those that were left behind have made several attempts to get off, but such is the barbarous policy of this cruel man, he keeps these unhappy creatures not only against their will, but intends to place them in the front of the battle, to prevent their flying, in case of an engagement, which, from their utter ignorance of firearms, he knows they will do.

Last Tuesday night a party of men, chiefly blacks, from a tender, came up to Mr. Benjamin Wells's, at Mulberry island, pillaged his house of every thing valuable, such as bedding, wearing apparel, liquors, a watch, the stock of poultry, and carried off two negro girls. They told Mrs. Wells, that they had orders to burn the house; which they would certainly have put into execution had it not been for her earnest entreaty to spare it that time, as she had some sick children in bed, who must perish in the flames.

Recreated from The Pennsylvania Gazette, December 13, 1775.

WILLIAMSBURG.

Twenty men, just returned from off guard, made application to colonel Scott for liberty to fire their wet guns at lord Dunmore's entrenchment, which he granted, not thinking they intended it in reality. They, however, advanced within 70 yards of the entrenchment, and began to fire their rifles, which the enemy returned, with the loss of one man on our side. The fire was kept up on both sides for two hours; our men then retreated, and brought off their dead man with them. It is supposed that some of the enemy are killed, as the rifle-men had many fair shots at them.

Eleven negroes are now in the great gaol in this city for attempting to get to lord Dunmore. They were discovered making off in boats when our people attacked them. They made very little resistance.

Recreated from Rind's Virginia Gazette, November 30, 1775.

In COMMITTEE of SAFETY.

Philadelphia, *November* 30, 1775.

ALL persons who are willing to supply the officers and men employed in the armed boats with the following rations, viz. Seven pounds of bread per week, or six pounds of flour.—Ten pounds of beef, mutton or pork.—The value of six pence per week in roots and vegetables, salt and vinegar.—Three pints and a half of rum, or beer in proportion, are desired to send in their proposals to this Committee, on or before the 6th day of December inst. when the same will be considered.

The contract to commence on the 11th of December, and continue for the space of three months, if the men are not sooner discharged.

WILLIAM GOVETT, *Secretary.*

Boston, *December 1.*—General Howe sent 300 men, women and children, poor of the town of Boston, over to Chelsea, without any thing to subsist on, at this inclement season of the year; having, it is reported, only six cattle left in the town for Shubael Hewes, Butcher-Master-General, to kill.—*A very sufficient excuse for a General of an army to dispose of HIS prisoners.*

New York, *December 4.*—Wednesday evening last arrived at Newark, in their way to the Provincial Camp at Cambridge, the Lady of his Excellency General Washington, the Lady of Adjutant-General Gates, John Curtis, Esq., and his Lady, and Warner Lewis, Esq. They were escorted from Elizabeth Town by the company of light horse, and most of the principal gentlemen of that borough; and on their arrival at Newark, the bells were set ringing, and Col. Allen's company of minute men immediately mounted guard.

About 10 o'clock on Thursday morning Lady Washington and Lady Gates, &c. escorted by a party of Elizabeth Town light horse, and a great number of ladies and gentlemen from Newark, set out for Dobb's ferry, in order to pass the North river at that place, in their way to the Provincial Camp.

Recreated from The Pennsylvania Gazette, December 6, 1775.

TRANSYLVANIA.

A COMPANY *of Gentlemen, of North Carolina, having for a large and valuable consideration, purchased from the Chiefs of the Cherokee Indians, with the advice and consent of the whole nation, a considerable tract of their lands, now called Transylvania, hereby inform the Public, That any person who will settle on said land, before the first day of June 1776, shall have the privilege of taking up and surveying for himself five hundred acres, and for each male person, above 16 years of age, he shall carry with him and settle there, two hundred and fifty acres, on the payment of fifty shillings sterling, per hundred acres, subject to an yearly quitrent of two shillings sterling, to commence in the year 1780.—Such person as incline to become purchasers, may correspond with Colonel Richard Menderson, at Boonsborough, in Transylvania, or with William Johnston, Esq., at Hillsborough, North Carolina.*

N. B. This country lies on the south side of the river Ohio and Louisa, or Kentucke, in a temperate and healthy climate; it has several rivers, up which vessels of considerable burden may come with ease.—In different places of it are salt springs, where the making of salt has been tried with success, and where any quantity needed may be made.—It has extensive quarries of lime stone, and abundance of iron ore.—The fertility of the soil and goodness of the range, almost surpass belief, and it is at present well stored with buffaloe, deer, elk, bear, beaver, &c. and the rivers abound with fish of various kinds. Many people are daily flocking to it, and gentlemen of the first rank and character have purchased lands in it, so that there is all appearance of a rapid settlement, and that it will soon become one of the most agreeable countries in America.

Recreated from The Pennsylvania Packet, December 4, 1775.

A copy of the OATH *extorted from the people of* NORFOLK *and* PRINCESS ANNE, *by Lord* DUNMORE.

WE the inhabitants of _____ , being fully sensible of the errors and guilt into which this colony hath been misled, under colour of seeking redress of grievances, and that a set of factious men, styling themselves Committees, Conventions, and Congresses, have violently, and under various pretenses, usurped the legislative and executive powers of Government, and are thereby endeavouring to overturn our most happy constitution, and have incurred the guile of actual rebellion against our most gracious Sovereign. We have therefore taken an oath abjuring their authority, and solemnly promising, in the presence of Almighty God, to bear faith and true allegiance to his sacred Majesty George the third; and that we will, to the utmost of our power and ability, support, maintain, and defend his crown and dignity, against all traiterous attempts and conspiracies whatsoever.

TO BE HIRED

For the ensuing Year, at KING WILLIAM *Courthouse, on Friday the 29th Instant (*DECEMBER*) if fair, otherwise next fair Day.*

ABOUT fifty likely *Virginia* born NEGROES, consisting of Men, Women, Boys, and Girls, several of which are good House Servants, being Part of the Trust Estate of Col. *Philip Johnson*. Bond and Security will be required, to carry Interest from the Date if not punctually discharged.

All Persons who hired the above Negroes last Year are desired to return them at the Place and Day above-mentioned, properly clothed; and as the Bonds for their Hire will carry Interest from the Date if not immediately discharged, it is expected all possible Payments will be made, in Order to prevent that Inconvenience. Those in Arrears for old Hire will be pleased to pay their respective Balances as soon as possible, to

4   JOHN WATKINS, for the Trustees.

THE Subscriber intends to leave the Colony soon, and to return in a few Months.

NINIAN MINZIES.

And whereas armed bodies of men are collected, in various parts of this colony, without any legal authority, we wish them to be informed, that however unwilling we should be to shed the blood of our countrymen, we must, in discharge of our duty to God and the King, and in support of the constitution and laws of our country, oppose their marching into this county, where their coming could answer no good end, but, on the contrary, must expose us to the ravages and horrors of a civil war; and, for that purpose, we are determined to take advantage of our happy situation, and will defend the passes into our county, and neighbourhood, *to the last drop of our blood.*

....

WILLIAMSBURG, *December* 2.—Since Lord Dunmore's proclamation made its appearance here, it is said he has recruited his army, in the counties of Princess Anne and Norfolk, to the amount of about 2000 men, including his black regiment, which is thought to be a considerable part, with this inscription on their breasts:—"Liberty to Slaves."—However, as the rivers will henceforth be strictly watched, and every possible precaution taken, it is hoped others will be effectually prevented from joining those his Lordship has already collected.

The army that went down last week, under the command of Col. Woodford, to obstruct Dunmore's progress of enlisting men in the lower counties, fell in with a party of 12 or 13 of Dunmore's friends, and made them all prisoners. Lieut. Col. Scott, with the advanced guard, upon his arrival at the Great Bridge, found the enemy entrenched there, and it is said a smart firing began by some of the riflemen, which was returned, and continued a considerable time on both sides, but to what effect we know not. It is also said, that Thursday last was fixed upon by our troops to begin a general attack; they were healthy, in good spirits, and had a great prospect of success.

Some accounts from Norfolk are, that Dunmore's party has demolished several houses back of the town, and fortified themselves.

Recreated from The Virginia Gazette, December 2, 1775.

4000 DEAD AT HALIFAX.

December 4. A person lately from Halifax to Cape Cod reports, that he saw at Halifax a particular account of the loss in the several harbours of Newfoundland, on the 9th of September, amounting in the whole to 4000 men, who had nearly finished their fishing voyages, intending to go not more than one or two trips, and then the greater part of them to enlist into the regular service, there being at that time a lieutenant there, on the recruiting service, who had enlisted 120 men, which he afterwards brought to Halifax, and on his arrival there, in the hearing of the person who gives this account, declared that he was determined to sell or resign his commission, as the winds, the seas, the people, and GOD ALMIGHTY, were against them, he would not be concerned in such a damned cause. It was said at Halifax, that the loss in ships, fish, oil, and merchandise of various kinds, was computed to amount to 140,000*l*. sterling. An account from Boston confirms the foregoing, and mentions that nearly all the shallops employed in that fishery, as well as other vessels, were wholly lost.

SHIPS STRUCK WITH LIGHTNING.

Yesterday fortnight a large ship being near the light off Cape Ann, was struck with lightning which set her on fire, and burnt to the water's edge, until she sunk. A number of cannon were heard to go off, while she was on fire, and it was thought at first that she was at least a 20 gun ship; but we have an account from Boston, that it was the Juno transport ship from London, laden only with hay for Burgoyne's heavy horse at Boston, which will soon become light, if forage fails at this rate.

At the same time a sloop being near her laden with wood and hay, bound also for Boston, was likewise struck with lightning, which so disabled her that she put into the Gurnet, when our people went and took possession of her, and carried her into Plymouth. One Hull is master of the sloop.

Recreated from Purdie's Virginia Gazette, December 29, 1775.

HEAVY FIRE AT GREAT BRIDGE.

Extract of a letter from lieutenant-colonel Scott, *to his friend in* WILLIAMSBURG, *dated* GREAT BRIDGE, *Dec.* 4, 1775.

"Since I wrote you, which was about two days ago, we have been well informed that we killed 16 negroes and 5 white men the first day we got to this place. The next day, lieutenant Tibbs, who had the command of the boat guard, about 5 miles from this place, was attacked by a party of the King's troops, and several negroes, upon which some of our people gave ground; but Mr. Tibbs, with 4 of his people, maintained his post until I reinforced him with 50 men under capt. Nicholas, who were obliged to pass through a very heavy fire from the enemy. Before they got to the place, Mr. Tibbs had beat off the enemy, and killed 7 of their men, amongst whom was the commander of the party.

"We still keep up a pretty heavy fire, between us, from light to light. We have only lost two men; and about half an hour ago one of our people was shot through the arm, which broke the bone near his hand.

"Last night was the first of my pulling off my clothes for 12 nights successfully. Believe me, my good friend, I never was so fatigued with duty in my whole life; but I set little value upon my health, when put in competition with my duty to my country, and the glorious cause we are engaged in.

"The Carolina forces are joining us. One company came in yesterday, and we expect 800 or 900 of them by to-morrow, or next day at farthest, with several pieces of artillery, and plenty of ammunition and other warlike stores.—A gun fired—I must stop."

"P.S. Since I finished my letter, we saw a large pile of buildings at the far end of this town all in flames, between which and the fort we had four sentinels, who can give no account of how it happened. As I mentioned above, the fire was discovered when the gun fired; and by the time the men got paraded a volley of small arms was fired from the fort, mixed with now and then a cannon shot. About 11 at night it ceased for about half an hour, when, to our great surprise, we saw several houses in blaze, which are just now consumed. It is now 10 o'clock. I shall lie down until the next alarm."

Extract of a letter from the same gentleman, dated GREAT BRIDGE, *Dec.* 5.

"Since my last, we have sent a party of 100 men, under the command of col. Stevens, of the minute battalion, over the river, who fell in last night, about 12 o'clock, with a guard of about 30 men, chiefly negroes. They got up close to the sentinel undiscovered; the sentinel challenged, and was not answered, upon which he fired. Our people, being too eager, began the fire immediately, without orders, and kept it up very hot for near 15 minutes. We killed one, burnt another in the house, and took two prisoners (all blacks) with 4 exceeding fine muskets, and defeated the guard. There is hardly an hour in the day but we exchange a few shot. I am, &c."

Recreated from Purdie's Virginia Gazette, December 8, 1775.

ADVERTISEMENTS.

AS the Revenue arising from the 2 s. per Hogshead on Tobacco, will not be sufficient to defray the Expences of Government, and it is expected no further Payments will be made during the Continuance of the present Troubles, I think it proper to inform such Officers and others, who have been usually paid out of that Fund, that the whole of the Revenue to the 25th of October last will be exhausted by the Payment of such Salaries, as are authorised by his Majesty's immediate Warrants.

RICHARD CORBIN, D. R. G.

Recreated from The Virginia Gazette, December 9, 1775.

QUEBEC SURRENDERS.

NEW YORK, *December* 6.

YESTERDAY we were favoured with the following intelligence from several gentlemen who left Albany last Friday: That, as they were coming away, a sergeant-major belonging to gen. Wooster, just arrived from Montreal, informed them that, just before he left, an express arrived from Quebec, which brought the agreeable news of its having surrendered to col. Arnold; and a party was detached to cut off Carleton's retreat with a number of gondolas, and that the express heard the firing, but what was the success of the attempt was not known.

Recreated from The Maryland Gazette, December 14, 1775.

ENEMY LOSSES AT GREAT BRIDGE.

WILLIAMSBURG, *December* 9.—We learn from Great Bridge, that the enemy have kept an incessant cannonading upon our troops for several days past, from a stockade fort which the Governor has erected there, and that two men were killed. A Gentleman from thence mentions some part of their fortifications to be in possession of our men, and that they had taken several prisoners, with a considerable umber of arms. It is said the enemy have met with great loss from our rifle-men, &c. and that Lord Dunmore's friends are deserting daily.

Several companies from North Carolina, have joined our troops under Col. Woodford at Great Bridge. It is said they are commanded by Col. Howe, and have several field-pieces with them. We hourly expect to hear of the total overthrow of Lord Dunmore's forces.

A few days ago one of the men of war fell in with a ship load of servants, from Great Britain and Ireland, whom his Lordship has taken into his service.

RICHMOND, November 17, 1775.
I INTEND TO LEAVE THE COLONY for a few Months.   Wm. CUTHBERT.

Recreated from The Virginia Gazette, December 9, 1775.

FATAL BRITISH ATTACK.

GREAT BRIDGE,
near NORFOLK, *December 9, 1775.*

THE enemy were reinforced about 3 o'clock this morning with (as they tell me) every soldier of the 14th regiment, at Norfolk, amounting to 200, commanded by capt. Leslie; and this morning, after reveille beating, crossed the bridge, by lying down some plank, and made an attack to force our breast-work (the prisoners say the whole number amounted to 500, with volunteers and blacks) with two pieces of cannon, but none marched up but his majesty's soldiers, who behaved like Englishmen. We have found of their dead captain Fordyce and 12 privates, and have lieutenant Battit, who is wounded in the leg, and 17 privates prisoners, all wounded.

They carried their cannon back under cover of the guns of the fort, and a number of their dead. I should suppose (to speak within compass) their loss must be upwards of 50. Some powder and cartridges were taken. I sent an officer to inform them if they would not fire upon our people they should collect the dead and wounded. This they agreed to, and there has been no firing since. We are now under arms, expecting another attack. There is but one man of ours hurt, and he is wounded in the hand. The prisoners inform that lord Dunmore has got a reinforcement of highlanders; they, I expect, will be up next.

Recreated from Rind's Virginia Gazette, December 13, 1775.

CAROLINE, *November 14, 1775.*

WHEREAS a Certain *William* and *James Sutton*, of this County, have, by the Assistance of a Negro Fellow who worked some Time with me, made a Number of Spinning-Wheels, the Work of which is very bad, and have travelled about the Country, calling themselves my Sons, and selling the same in my Name; this is to acquaint the Public that the said Wheels are not of my Make, and that in future I will sell none but what is branded with the Initials of my Name, I D. I also forewarn the said *Suttons*, and every other Person, from selling any Spinning-Wheels in my Name, at their Peril.

JOSEPH DEJARNATT, Senior.

Recreated from The Virginia Gazette, December 9, 1775.

BURGOYNE SAILS FOR ENGLAND.

PROVIDENCE, *December 9.*

LAST night a gentleman arrived here, who has just made his escape from Boston, he informs that the Boyne Man of War, of 70 guns, with General Burgoyne on board, sailed for England on Wednesday last; she likewise carried, it is said, a number of Masters and Mates of vessels, that had been taken by the enemy.

CAPT. MANLY'S 3 PRIZES.

WATERTOWN, *December 9.*—We have just received certain intelligence, that on Saturday last Captain Manly, of the Lee privateer, took and carried into Beverly a large ship of 300 tons burthen (mounted with two double fortified 6 pounders, and 6 blunderbusses, with 18 men before the mast) bound from London for the ministerial army at Boston, loaded with coals and provisions, consisting chiefly of porter, cheese and 40 live hogs, 30 more have died on the passage. Although fuel and the above articles are no rarity to the army of the United Colonies; yet so far as they are distressing to their enemies, it must be acknowledged they are an advantage to us. The above ship had 7 weeks passage, and brought papers to the 16th of October, which, together with the letters, we are informed the Captain hove overboard after he was taken.

The same day Captain Manly also took and carried in there, a brig of about 150 tons burthen, from Antigua for Boston (consigned to one Brimer, for the use of the ministerial navy) loaded with about 130 puncheons of rum, besides 100 cases of gin, some cocoa, and a cask of oranges, to please the delicate appetite of my Lord How!—Which however may possibly be more acceptable to our army than any other provision.

Last Saturday fortnight, a ship from Scotland, bound to Boston, laden with about 350 chaldron of coal, and a quantity of bale goods, taken by Captain Manly, was carried into Salem. She is about 200 tons burthen, and is almost a new ship.

Recreated from The Pennsylvania Gazette, December 20, 1775.

BRITISH RAID CONANICUT.

NEWPORT, *December* 11.

About one o'clock yesterday morning, the bomb-brig, a schooner, and two or three armed sloops, left this harbour, went to Conanicut, and landed upwards of 200 marines, sailors and negroes, at the East-ferry, marched in three divisions immediately over to the West-ferry, and set the several houses on fire which were near the ferry place, then retreated back, setting fire to almost every house on each side of the road, and several houses and barns some distance on the North and South side of the road, driving out the women and children, swearing they should be burnt in the house if they did not instantly turn out.

Widow Hull lost one house, John Clarke, Esq., two houses and one barn, Thomas Fowler one house, barn and crib full of corn, Benjamin Ellery two houses, a store and a barn, Benjamin Remington two houses, John Gardner, Esq., one house and tanyard, Thomas Hutchinson one house, Widow Franklin two, Abel Franklin one, Benedict Robinson one. All of the above houses were plundered of beds, wearing apparel, and such household furniture as could be conveniently carried off, the rest were consumed. Some women, we are told, were stripped of some of their best clothes they had on. 'Tis said Capt. Wallace commanded on this HUMANE expedition.

A company of minute men had left Conanicut the afternoon before, so that there were but 40 or 50 soldiers on the island, most of whom had been inlisted but a few days, and arrived there but the evening before, in miserable condition for such a sudden attack; but notwithstanding, it is said, there is certainly one officer of marines killed, and 7 or 8 badly wounded. There was not one Provincial either killed or wounded, except Mr. Joseph Martin, who was shot in his belly standing unarmed in his door. The above vessels brought off about 30 head of oxen and cows, a few sheep and hogs, most of which they killed before they took them on board. They left Conanicut yesterday, and came to this harbour again about noon.

Recreated from The Pennsylvania Gazette, December 20, 1775.

TORIES HANDCUFFED TO NEGROES.

Extract of a letter from col. Scott to captain Southall, dated GREAT BRIDGE, *Dec.* 12, 1775.

"We are now about to finish the work that we came down about. We sent a detachment of 400 men to Kemp's Landing last night to take possession of that place, which they did without interruption. The inhabitants of Norfolk are daily sending petitions to us for protection. We have not yet answered them. We have taken up some of the worst of the tories, and coupled them to a negro with handcuffs. I expect a flag of truce here every moment. We have just received a letter from lord Dunmore, desiring to exchange the prisoners. I do not expect we shall agree to do it without consulting the convention. Four of the prisoners are dead since taken. We are well informed that the governor has disarmed the negroes, and taken all the troops, together with a number of Scotchmen, on board. I am your most obedient servant, "C. SCOTT."

"P.S. The flag I mentioned above has since come to our camp, in order to exchange prisoners. They behaved exceeding well, and were discharged about 11 o'clock at night, but it is expected we shall hear again from them so soon as our express returns from Williamsburg."

Recreated from Rind's Virginia Gazette, December 16, 1775.

Just come to Hand, and to be SOLD *at this* PRINTING-OFFICE, A large and exact VIEW of the late BATTLE at CHARLESTOWN, Elegantly coloured, Price one Dollar. Also an accurate MAP of *The present* SEAT *of* CIVIL WAR, Taken by an able Draughtsman who was on the Spot at the late Engagement. Price one Dollar.

Recreated from The Virginia Gazette, December 9, 1775.

BRITISH DEFEATED AT GREAT BRIDGE.

From a correspondent, December 13.

"We have just been favoured with an extract of a letter from colonel Woodford, dated December 11, at the Great Bridge, by which we learn that the enemy lost, in their attempt on our trenches, 102 killed and wounded, that 65, dead and wounded were counted, when they were carried over in boats to Norfolk; that but 11 of Fordyce's grenadiers escaped; that we have, since the last account, found 2 more of their dead, that the breast-works at Norfolk were abandoned; that the Scotch tories had fled, with all their effects, on board the vessels in the river; that the Norfolk people were preparing a petition to colonel Woodford, who had dispatched colonel Stephens, with 6 companies, to Kemp's landing; that he himself was preparing to follow, with all his forces and baggage, as soon as possible; and that lord Dunmore raved like a madman, on hearing of the defeat of his forces, and swore he would hang the boy who had deserted him, and informed that there were 300 shirtmen at the bridges, on whose information he had ordered the attack. We are well assured that there were but about 60 or 70 of our men at the breast-work; the rest were stationed at proper places, and intervals, to cover them, in case they had been forced from their entrenchments. So that this affair was truly (as colonel Woodford, in a letter to a friend, expresses it) *Bunker's Hill slaughter*; adding, there never was more execution done by fewer men."

WHY THEY DESERT.

A few days ago six of lord Dunmore's men deserted from the Otter. They met some of our men, on their way to this city, by whom they were treated with the utmost hospitality; in return, they assisted us, with the highest pleasure, in stowing away our baggage, and expediting our troops to their destined place. When they were asked what induced them to leave Dunmore, they answered, "Hungry bellies, naked backs, and no fuel; besides, in other respects, the most cruel and inhuman treatment."

Recreated from Rind's Virginia Gazette, December 13, 1775.

DUNMORE ABANDONS NORFOLK.

WILLIAMSBURG.—Colonel Howe and colonel Woodford have entered Norfolk with their forces. Lord Dunmore had abandoned the town, and several of the tories had fled on board their vessels, with all their effects; others of them are applying for forgiveness to their injured countrymen.

FOR GOD'S SAKE, DO NOT MURDER US.

A CORRESPONDENT, on whose information we may depend, informs us that our soldiers showed the greatest humanity and tenderness to the wounded prisoners. Several of them ran through a hot fire to lift up and bring in some that were bleeding, and who they feared would die, if not speedily assisted by the surgeon. The prisoners expected to be scalped, and called out, FOR GOD'S SAKE, DO NOT MURDER US.

One of them, who was unable to walk, calling out in this manner to one of our men, was answered by him, put your arms around my neck, and I'll show you what I intend to do. Then taking him with his arm over his neck, he walked slowly along, bearing him up with great tenderness to the breast-work. Captain Leslie seeing two of our soldiers tenderly removing a wounded regular from the bridge, on which he lay, stepped up on the platform of the fort, and bowing with great respect, thanked them for their kindness. These are instances of a noble disposition of soul. Men who can act thus must be invincible.

• • • •

On Wednesday the 13th instant a sloop belonging to captain Mallory, and a schooner belonging to captain Brown, bound to Smithfield, from sea, were taken by a tender, which put a midshipman, two sailors, and a negro pilot on board, with orders to carry them to Norfolk; but last night the captains of the vessel, by a promise of 43 dollars, and a passage back, prevailed on them to join them in re-taking the vessels, which they accordingly did, and have now got them within the creek, with two thousand bushels of salt on board.

Recreated from Rind's Virginia Gazette, December 23, 1775.

A WAR BELT AND THE HATCHET.

Extract of a letter from general Schuyler, dated Albany, December 14.

"The Indians delivered us a speech on the 12th, in which they related the substance of all the conferences col. Johnson had with them the last summer, concluding with that at Montreal, where he delivered to each of the Canadian tribes a war belt and the hatchet, who accepted it; after which they were invited to *feast on a Bostonian and drink his blood.* An ox being roasted for that purpose, and a pipe of wine given to drink, the war song was sung. One of the chiefs of the Six Nations, that attended at that conference, accepted a very large black belt with a hatchet depictured on it; but would neither eat, nor drink, nor sing the war song. This famous belt they have delivered up, and we have now a full proof that the ministerial servants have attempted to engage the savages against us."

MUSKETS STOCKED in the best and neatest manner, by EDWARD POLE, In Market-street, near the Court-house, Philadelphia;

WHERE may be had, the best kind of wires and brushes for firelocks, priming flasks and oil bottles to fit in the cartouch boxes, musket and pistol balls, musket and pistol cartridges, and cartridge formers. Also cartridges made up on moderate terms, by the hundred or larger quantity.

N. B. A very neat cutteau de chase, a small sword and a fusee, to be sold at the above place.

WHALE OIL, In TIERCES and BARRELS, To be SOLD for CASH only, by CHARLES EDDY, In Second-street, between Market and Chesnut-streets, Philadelphia.

Recreated from The Pennsylvania Packet, December 25, 1775.

SMALL POX AT BOSTON.

Extract of a letter from CAMBRIDGE, *Dec. 15.*

THE smallpox is in every part of Boston. The soldiers who have never had it are under inoculation, and considered as a security against any attack by the provincials. A third ship-load of the inhabitants is come out to Point Shirley.

It is thought almost impossible to keep the smallpox out of the camp and country adjacent, but every precaution is taken which prudence can suggest.

OUR ARMY IS COMFORTABLE.

Extract of a letter from CAMBRIDGE, *Dec. 13.*

"I have the satisfaction to tell you, things wear a better complexion here than they have done for some time past. The army is filling up, the barracks go on well, firewood comes in, and the soldiers are made comfortable and easy; our privateers meet with success in bringing in vessels that were going to the relief of Boston, which town is in great distress; besides wanting almost every necessary, they are inoculating for the smallpox, and the disentry and black jaundice prevails, which makes the officers uneasy. No troops are yet arrived from Ireland. The three men of war which appeared off Marblehead are since gone off, without doing any damage."

WILLIAMSBURG, *Jan.* 12, 1776.

ON the 6th of this instant was stolen, from a soldier of my company, a RIFLE GUN, her stock made of persimmon tree, iron mounted, has a pistol lock, the box lid lost, and her bore very small. Any person producing said gun to me, at this place, shall have two dollars reward, and no questions asked.

(1) WILLIAM CAMPBELL.

Recreated from Purdie's Virginia Gazette, January 12, 1776.

CARLETON REFUSES FLAG.

Extract of a Letter from a Gentleman in the Continental Service, before QUEBEC, *Dec.* 16, 1775.

"General Carleton escaped Montreal by paddling with his hands by our men in the night, and got safe to Quebec, where he gave immediate orders for all that would not take up arms to leave the city.

"We have upon the Plains of Abraham, a battery of gabines [sic] filled with snow, and water poured on it till it froze quite hard, which does very well, and we have some mortars in St. Roc, behind a Tory's house, at a little distance from the Palace gate, from both of which we have put them into some confusion, and set the town on fire in several places; we have roused them up these five nights successively, and I believe they are almost tired out. Yesterday we sent a flag of truce to them, which they would not receive, and it was with great difficulty the raw sailors could be prevented from firing on the person who carried it. General Montgomery, in that, offered a safe convoy to Carleton, but he would not read it.

"Last Saturday night we made the Indians fire several letters into the town with bows and arrows, which were found by the inhabitants, and are circulating through the town. One was directed to the inhabitants, informing of our requests, and the consequence of a refusal; and another to Carleton, threatening him with immediate death, unless he gave up the city."

Recreated from The Pennsylvania Gazette, January 17, 1776.

NEW YORK, *December* 18.

Died on the 9th instant the Hon. Mr. Justice Livingston, at Claremont, in the Manor of Livingston. The event was so sudden, that he retired from company to his bed, and in a few minutes after expired from an apoplectic fit. He was in the 58th year of his age, and has left a numerous family. His eldest son is a member of the present Continental Congress; Gen. Montgomery's Lady is his eldest daughter; and his second son is now serving in the rank of Major in Canada.

Recreated from The Pennsylvania Gazette, December 20, 1775.

ABSURDITY OF RESISTANCE.

NEW YORK.

Copy of a letter from General Montgomery to General Carleton, dated Holland House, (near Quebec) Dec. 16, 1775.

"SIR,

"Notwithstanding the personal ill treatment I have received at your hands, notwithstanding the cruelty you have shown to the unhappy prisoners you have taken, the feelings of humanity induce me to have recourse to this expedient, to save you from the destruction which hangs over your wretched garrison. Give me leave to inform you that I am well acquainted with your situation. A great extent of works, in their nature incapable of defence, manned with a motley crew of sailors, most of them our friends; of citizens, who wish to see us within the walls; a few of the worst troops that call themselves soldiers; the improbability of relief, and the certain prospect of wanting every necessary of life, should your opponents confine themselves to a simple blockade, point out the absurdity of resistance—such is your situation.

"I am at the head of troops accustomed to success, confident of the righteousness of the cause they are engaged in, inured to danger and fatigue, and so highly incensed at your inhumanity, illiberal abuse, and the ungenerous means employed to prejudice them in the minds of the Canadians, that it is with difficulty I restrain them, till my batteries are ready, from assaulting your works, which would afford them a fair opportunity of ample vengeance, and just retaliation.—Firing upon a Flag of Truce, hitherto unprecedented, even among savages, prevents my following the ordinary mode of conveying my sentiments; however, I will at any rate acquit my conscience. Should you persist in an unwarrantable defence, the consequences be upon your own head. Beware of destroying stores of any fort, as you did at Montreal, or in the river; if you do, by Heavens there will be no mercy shown."

Recreated from The Pennsylvania Gazette, January 24, 1776.

DELEGATES ELECTED.

CAMBRIDGE, *December* 28.

LAST week both Houses of Assembly came to the choice of five Delegates to represent this colony in the American Congress, for the year 1776, by joint ballot, and the following Gentlemen were chosen, viz. The HON. JOHN HANCOCK, Esq., SAMUEL ADAMS, Esq., JOHN ADAMS, Esq., ROBERT TREAT PAINE, Esq., ELBRIDGE GERRY, Esquire.

Kent County, on Delaware.

On the 23d ult., a day remarkably cold and gloomy, Miss REBECCA KILLEN, the third daughter of WILLIAM KILLEN, Esq., of Dover, in the sixteenth year of her age, walked out, a little before noon, to a neighbouring house about a quarter mile distant from the town. The minute she entered the door, and approached to the fire, so extremely had the chillness of the air affected her, that she sunk down in a fainting posture. As soon as it was practicable, she was conveyed home; retaining yet some symptoms of life, which did not indeed entirely disappear for ten or eleven hours after. During all this time, every medical method and appliance was made use of that two very skillful physicians attending could devise—while Hope and deep Anxiety stood looking on;—but all appliances and means proved ineffectual.—Endued with a temper meek and exceeding kind; possessing a share of prudence and discretion above her years; having a peculiar happy turn for retirement and sweet domestic usefulness; she delighted to fulfil the pious duties of a *Daughter*, and all the *Sister's* endearing offices.—Called off so early—so very unexpectedly, from this tender department! no wonder, if the loss of such a one should be lamented.—But still, this consolation the dear departed *Innocent* hath left for her afflicted father, and the remaining children of the family—*the memory of her blooming virtues.*

GENERAL LEE TO NEWPORT.

Extract of a letter from a gentleman at the camp at Cambridge, to his friend in New York, dated Dec. 22, 1775.

"We have no news here at present worthy of note, the enemy continue bombarding our people, but with no effect; yesterday they threw a bomb within half a mile of the house we live in, which I believe is the farthest they can throw them; it will be our turn by and by. By an express from Newport, we hear that six companies of the royal Irish, and some of the light horse, were sailed from Boston, it is supposed to take possession of that island. General Lee, with a small escort, set off immediately to take command of the troops there, to oppose their landing; the event we are impatient to hear."

NEW YORK, *January* 1.—A gentleman arrived here last Saturday night from New London, by water, which place he left the Thursday before, where he saw the post from Rhode Island, who informed him, General Lee was arrived at that place from Boston, with an escort of about eighty men, in order to defend that island against any attempt made thereon by the troops that lately sailed from Boston.

Recreated from The Pennsylvania Gazette, January 10, 1776.

LONDON.

Dec. 29. It was decided in Council to send ships to the relief of Quebec, but was given up as impracticable at this season—so that the first news likely to come from that quarter will be that all Canada is in the hands of the United Colonies.

When all the intended reinforcement arrives in America, the Provincial Camp will not be attacked. The plan laid down is said to be this: To destroy every town on the coast, to draw their army from one place to another, and harass and starve them if possible; but to be very careful about coming to a general engagement. But if by any means the Provincial Army can be divided, then the Regulars are to attack them.

Recreated from The Pennsylvania Gazette, March 13, 1776.

NORFOLK BURNT BY BRITISH.

A letter from Cols. Howe and Woodford to the Convention, dated NORFOLK, *Jan.* 1, 1776.

BETWEEN 3 and 4 o'clock a severe cannonade began from all the shipping, under cover of which they landed small parties, and set fire to the houses on the wharves. The wind favours their design, and we believe the flames will become general. In the confusion which they supposed would ensue, they frequently attempted to land; but this, by the bravery of our officers and men, we have hitherto prevented, with only a few men wounded on our side, and we persuade ourselves with a good deal of loss on theirs. Their efforts and our opposition, still continue. We have stationed ourselves in such a manner as will, we believe, render everything but burning the houses ineffectual.

Extract of a letter from col. Howe, to the President of the Convention, Jan. 2.

"The burning of the town has made several avenues, which yesterday they had not, so that they may now fire with greater effect. The tide is now rising, and we expect at high water another cannonade. I have only to wish it may be as ineffectual as the last; for we have not one man killed, and but a few wounded. I cannot enter into the melancholy consideration of the women and children running through a crowd of shot to get out of town, some of them with children at their breast. A few have, I hear, been killed. Does it not call for vengeance, both from God and man! It is but justice to inform you, that I had the pleasure to find every officer ready to execute orders at a moment's warning, and that the men behaved with steadiness and spirit. Col. Stevens went down at my command, and headed some men near the water, where he engaged a party who had landed, with the spirit and conduct of a good officer. Of my friend col. Woodford, I cannot avoid expressing, that I received from him every assistance which conduct and spirit could give me."

Recreated from Purdie's Virginia Gazette, January 5, 1776.

100 CANNON FOR 25 HOURS.

By an express from Norfolk, and letters from colonel Howe, we learn, that all the ships and tenders which had been drawn up close began a heavy fire at 3 o'clock in the evening of Monday last, that after about an hour's firing, a few boats were sent ashore under cover of the cannon, and concealed by their smoke, which was blown in on the shore, and several houses were set on fire in different places along the river, that this was done so suddenly, and amidst so much smoke and noise, that it was impossible to prevent it; that the wind being favourable to their design, the flames spread with great rapidity, and when the fire had run to a great extent, and our enemies imagined they had spread confusion and terror amongst our young troops, by such an incessant cannonade as they have kept up, and by the conflagration around them, they attempted to land a number of men in different parts of the town, but were repulsed with considerable loss in every attempt; all our centinels and guards kept their posts notwithstanding, and had pretty smartly chastised those who set fire to the houses; they were reinforced by lieutenant col. Stevens, with about two hundred marksmen, who behaved with great bravery.

Six of the enemy were left dead on the shore, and great numbers were supposed to be carried off in their boats. We did not lose a man; but had six or seven wounded. Some poor woman was killed in endeavouring to move out of town. It was a shocking scene to see the poor women and children running about through the fire, and exposed to the guns from the ships, and some of them with child at their breasts. Let our countrymen view and contemplate this scene!

Col. Howe speaks highly of col. Woodford, col. Stephens, and all the officers and men. The cannonade had lasted twenty-five hours when the express came away, and the flames were raging (it being impossible to extinguish them on account of the heavy fire from the ships) and had consumed two thirds of the town. Our men, notwithstanding this, still kept their posts.

The ships which fired were the Liverpool, Kingfisher, and Otter, men of war, lord Dunmore's large ships, the William and Eilbeck, the store ships, and all the tenders. It is affirmed that one hundred cannon played on the town almost incessantly for twenty-five hours, and the express says he heard the firing all the way down the road. Notwithstanding this heavy firing, and the town in flames all around them, our men had the resolution to maintain their posts, and the coolness to *aim* as usual. They seem animated in their glorious cause, and appear to be shielded as the favourites of Heaven.

Upwards of thirty of Jack Dunmore's *hopeful gang*, consisting of soldiers, sailors, and negroes, arrived here yesterday as prisoners under a strong guard. They are taken *proper care* of.

Recreated from Rind's Virginia Gazette, January 6, 1776.

BRITISH FEMALE RECRUITS.

CORK, (IRELAND) *January* 4.—It is confidently asserted, that the Ministry having experienced the inefficiency of the measures hitherto adopted to subjugate the Americans, and finding that the number of men for that service is yet very inadequate to carry into execution their grand designs, have determined upon making up the deficiency with females, from whose arms the greatest success is expected, and that there are already arriving in this city, recruiting officers of that sex to beat up for volunteers.

• • • •

WATERFORD, (IRELAND) *January* 9.—By a letter from an Officer at Boston, dated December 3, 1775, we learn, that a vessel arrived at that port from Canada, brought an account of Quebec being taken by the Provincials. If this intelligence be true, the Americans are masters of the entire province of Canada.

• • • •

CLONMEL, (IRELAND) *January* 8.—Yesterday was committed to jail by Daniel Graham, Esq., Maurice Ryan, charged on oath with being a White Boy.

Recreated from Finns Leinster Journal, Ireland, January 10, 1776.

CHAINED TO RING BOLTS.

NEW YORK.

January 1, 1776. We are assured that the emigrants from Scotland, who lately put in here, to this their port of destination, and who were sent from hence against their will to Boston, have been all forced into the ministerial service, which act of compulsion was not effected without many of them undergoing the greatest tortures, such as their being chained down on their backs to the ring bolts, and fed with bread and water; several of them suffered this torture for three days before they could be brought to yield, and sign the paper of their inlistment. Many of them openly professed their resolution of firing upon their enemies in action, if reduced to that necessity, declaring they could never look upon the people of this country, among whom they hoped for an asylum from heavy taxes and oppression, in any other light than friends, and therefore could never think of treating them as enemies.

January 4. A gentleman from Hispaniola informs, he left that place but 14 days ago, that 7000 French troops and 9 sail of the line were arrived there; that two vessels belonging to North America were at that place, but not having any credentials from Congress, the inhabitants refused to trade with them; and that the Congress was in high esteem there.

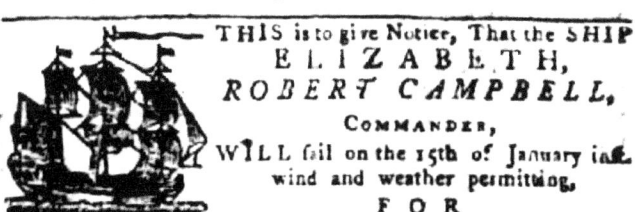

Recreated from The Pennsylvania Gazette, January 10, 1776.

BRITISH FLEET ON THE MOVE.

UNION FLAG ON PROSPECT HILL.

By authentic advices from the Camp at Cambridge, of the 3d and 4th instant, we learn, that the bay and harbour of Boston still continue open; that a man of war is so stationed as to command the entrance of Salem, Beverly, and Marblehead harbours; that 500 fresh troops had arrived from Ireland, two regiments had gone to Halifax, and two had pushed into the river St. Lawrence, in hopes of getting to Quebec, which was very doubtful; that the two regiments that had arrived in Boston were the 55th and 17th; that Admiral Shuldham was also arrived.

An intelligent person got out of Boston on the 3d instant, who informed Gen. Washington, that a fleet, consisting of nine transports, containing 360 men, were ready to sail under convoy of the Scarborough and Fowey men of war, with two bomb vessels and some flat bottomed boats; their avowed destination in Boston was to Newport, but it was generally supposed to be Long Island or Virginia; that a number of other transports are taking in water, and they are baking large quantities of biscuit in Boston, some say for the use of the shipping, who are to lay in Nantucket road on account of the ice, while others believe a more important movement is in agitation.

This person also informs, that they have not the least idea in Boston of attacking our lines, but will be very thankful to be permitted to remain quiet. That before General Burgoyne's departure it was circulated thro' the army, in order to keep the soldiery quiet under their distress, that the disputes would soon be settled, and that he was going to England for that purpose. That they had intelligence at Boston of four vessels having sailed from Hispaniola for this Continent some time ago, laden with arms and ammunition.

CARTRIDGE PAPER, By the Ream, Quire, to be SOLD by JOHN DUNLAP.

Our advices conclude with the following anecdote: That upon the King's Speech arriving at Boston, a great number of them were reprinted and sent out to our lines on the 2d of January, which being also the day of forming the new army, the great Union Flag was hoisted on Prospect Hill, in compliment to the United Colonies—this happening soon after the Speeches were delivered at Roxbury, but before they were received at Cambridge, the Boston gentry supposed it to be a token of the deep impression the Speech had made, and a signal of submission. That they were much disappointed at finding several days elapse without some formal measure leading to a surrender, with which they had begun to flatter themselves.

When these accounts came away the army were all in barracks, in good health and spirits. That 5000 Militia had taken the places of those soldiers who would not stay beyond their time of service; that they were good troops, and the whole army impatient for an opportunity of action.

Recreated from The Pennsylvania Packet, January 15, 1776.

CAMBRIDGE, *January 4.*

On Wednesday, the week before last, Major General Lee set out for Rhode Island. He was attended from hence by his guard and a party of rifle-men; and from Providence, by the cadet company of that place, and a number of minute-men. He entered the town of Newport the Monday following, preceded by the cadets, his guard, and the rifle-men. While there, he called before him a number of obnoxious persons, to whom he tendered an oath of fidelity to the country, which was taken by all of them, excepting Col. Joseph Wanton, and, Nicholas Lechemere and Richard Beale, two custom-house officers, who refused taking it; upon which they were put under guard, and brought to Providence. The General, after having viewed the island, and given directions for erecting some fortifications, set out for Providence on Wednesday from whence he came to town last Saturday.

Recreated from The Pennsylvania Gazette, January 17, 1776.

HANOVER TOWN, January 10, 1776.

I intend to leave the Colony immediately. (2)   JOSEPH WRIGHT.

FREDERICKSBURG, Jan. 10, 1776.

I intend to leave the Colony very soon.   WILLIAM HORNER.

RICHMOND, January 11, 1776.

I intend to leave the Colony soon. (1)   JAMES M'DOWALL.

RICHMOND, January 11, 1776.

I intend to leave the Colony soon. (1)   GEORGE WEIR.

RICHMOND, January 11, 1776.

I intend to leave the Colony soon. (1)   ROBERT BURTON.

HANOVER TOWN, January 13, 1776.

THE SUBSCRIBER intends to sail for Britain early next Month.
    ARCHIBALD GOVAN.

MANCHESTER, January 8, 1776.

I intend to leave the Colony immediately. (1)   JOHN CAMPBELL.

MANCHESTER, January 8, 1776.

I intend to leave the Colony immediately. (1)   ROBERT DONALD.

ELIZABETH CITY COUNTY, Jan. 9, 1776.

I INTEND to leave the COLONY soon
    GEORGE GRAHAM.

BEDFORD, January 8, 1776.

I intend to leave the Colony immediately. (1)   THOMAS MONTGOMERIE.

Recreated from The Virginia Gazette, January 20, 1776.

GEN. MONTGOMERY DEAD.

[Tuesday Morning. We have stop'd the Press, to give the Public the following.]

Extract of a Letter from Gen. Wooster, *to* Col. Warner, *dated,* MONTREAL, *January* 6, 1776.

"Dear Sir, With the greatest distress of mind I now sit down to inform you of the event of an unfortunate attack made upon Quebec, between the hours of 4 and 6 in the morning of the 31st of December; unfortunate indeed for us: in it fell our brave General Montgomery, his Aid de Camp, Mr. McPherson, Capt. Chelmsford, Capt. Hendrick, of the Rifle-men, and two or three Subaltern officers, and between 60 and 100 privates, the number not certainly known, and about 300 Officers and Soldiers taken prisoners, among them are Lieut. Col. Green, Major Bigelow, and a number of Captains and under Officers. Col. Arnold was wounded in the leg in the beginning of the action, as was Major Ogden in the shoulder, and brought off to the general hospital. I have not time to give you all the particulars."

Recreated from The Hartford Courant, January 15, 1776.

HEAD QUARTERS.
CAMBRIDGE, 6*th Jan.* 1776.

All officers, non-commissioned officers, and soldiers, belonging to any of the regiments, or corps of the army of the United Colonies, under the immediate command of his Excellency General Washington, who are absent upon furlough, recruiting, or by permission of their commanding officers, are to join their respective regiments by the first day of February next. If any officer neglects to pay due obedience to this order, he will be immediately cashiered, and any non-commissioned officers, or soldiers, offending therein, will be tried and punished as deserters.

By his Excellency's command,

HORATIO GATES,
Brigadier and Adjutant General.

Recreated from The Pennsylvania Packet, January 29, 1776.

GENERAL ARNOLD WOUNDED.

Extract of a letter from COLONEL (BRIGADIER-GENERAL) ARNOLD, *dated Camp before* QUEBEC, *Jan. 6, 1776.*

"Before this reaches you, I make no doubt you will have heard of our misfortune of the 31st ult. and will be anxious for my safety. I should have wrote you before, but a continual hurry of business has prevented me. The command of the army, by the death of my truly great and good friend General Montgomery, devolved on me; a task I find too heavy under my present circumstances. I received a wound by a ball through my left leg, at the time I had gained the first battery, at the Lower Town, which by the loss of blood rendered me very weak.

"As soon as the main body came up, with some assistance, I returned to the Hospital, near a mile, on foot, being obliged to draw one leg after me, and a great part of the way under the continual fire of the enemy from the walls, at no greater distance than 50 yards. I providentially escaped, though several were shot down at my side. I soon learned of the death of our General, who attacked the town at the side opposite to me. He behaved heroically—marched up in the face of their cannon, and when he had nearly gained the pass—received the fatal shot—or the town would have been ours.

"This occasioned the disaster that afterwards happened to my detachment, which, after the general defeat, had the whole garrison to encounter, under every disadvantage of ground, &c. To return was impossible, as the route was within 50 yards, and exposed to the fire of the whole garrison, who had brought several field pieces out of one of the gates, which our people would have been obliged to pass. In this situation they maintained their ground near three hours, but being overpowered with numbers, were obliged at last to lay down their arms; about 300, including Capt. Lamb of New York, and part of the Train, were taken prisoners, and as near as I can judge about 60 killed and wounded.

"Capt. Oswald is among the prisoners, he was with me in a selected party of about 25, who attacked the first battery. He behaved gallantly, and gained much honour. The prisoners are used politely, and supplied with everything the garrison affords. Governor Carleton sent to let me know, that the soldiers baggage, if I pleased, might be sent to them, which I shall immediately send. Though the enemy now are double our number, they have as yet made no attempt to come out. We are as well prepared to receive them, as we can possibly be in our present situation, divided at a distance of two miles.

"I expect General Wooster from Montreal in a few days with a reinforcement. I hope we shall be properly supplied with troops by the Congress. I have no thoughts of leaving this proud town, until I first enter it in triumph. My wound has been exceeding painful, but is now easy, and the Surgeons assure me will be well in 8 weeks. I know you will be anxious for me.—That providence which has carried me through so many dangers is still my protection. I am in the way of my duty, and know no fear."

PHILADELPHIA.—We hear that among other honours decreed to the memory of GENERAL MONTGOMERY, by the Honourable *Continental Congress*, they have appointed a FUNERAL ORATION; which is to be composed by Dr. SMITH, and will be delivered on Monday next, at eleven o'clock in the forenoon.

Recreated from The Pennsylvania Gazette, February 14, 1776.

THIS DAY IS PUBLISHED, and now selling, by ROBERT BELL, in Third-street,

PRICE TWO SHILLINGS,

COMMON SENSE; addressed to the Inhabitants of AMERICA, on the following interesting Subjects. 1. Of the Origin and Design of Government in general, with concise Remarks on the English Constitution. 2. Of Monarchy and Hereditary Succession. 3. Thoughts on the present State of American Affairs. 4. Of the present Ability of America, with some miscellaneous Reflections.

Man knows no Master save creating HEAVEN,
Or those whom choice and common good ordain.
THOMSON

Recreated from The Pennsylvania Gazette, January 10, 1776.

FLASHING OF MUSQUETRY.

Extract of a letter from CAMBRIDGE, *January* 9.

"Last evening General Putnam achieved what our friend on Winter Hill attempted; Major Knowlton commanded the party; Minchin, and a deserter who lately came out, were the guides; about 130 men passed, near nine o'clock, over the mill-dam; Majors Cary and Henly had each a party, and the former was to push to the farthest house; (if you recollect, there was to your right from Cobble Hill, when you looked towards Bunker Hill, about 15 houses, which had escaped the conflagration on the 17th of June) the plan was to surprise these houses, set them on fire, and bring off the guard, which we were informed consisted of an officer and 30 men, but the information was wrong, as there was only a sergeant and five men. The persons appointed to set fire to the houses nearest the dam, had orders not to execute it until Cary had returned from the furthest, but, eager to fulfill what they had undertaken, they were the first that appeared in flames; some time after, the whole was one blaze of fire.

"Had I Burgoyne's knack at description, I assure you a picture might be drawn that would afford great horror, and at the same time great entertainment. Bunker's Hill took the alarm—the flashing of the musquetry, from every quarter of that fort, showed the confusion of its defenders—firing some in the air—some into Mystic River—in short, they fired at random, and thought they were attacked at every quarter, which, you may suppose, gave no small pleasure to the General, and a number of us, who were spectators of the scene from Cobble Hill. Ten of the houses were soon in ashes. The sergeant and four of the men, with one woman, were brought off prisoners; one poor wretch made some resistance, and was killed.

"It is the opinion of many, that, if there was a vigorous attack made, the hill might be carried with little loss; but it was not designed, of course no preparations were made for such a push."

Recreated from The Pennsylvania Gazette, January 24, 1776.

IN CONGRESS.

January 11, 1776.

WHEREAS it appears to this Congress, that several evil disposed persons, in order to obstruct and defeat the efforts of the United Colonies in defence of their just rights, have attempted to depreciate the BILLS of CREDIT emitted by the authority of this Congress.

Resolved therefore, That if any person shall hereafter be so lost to all virtue and regard for this country, as to refuse to receive the said bills in payment, or obstruct or discourage the currency or circulation thereof, and shall be duly convicted by the Committee of the city, county, or district, or in case of an appeal from their decision, by the Assembly, Convention, Council, or Committee of Safety of the colony where he shall reside, such person shall be deemed, published, and treated as an enemy of his country, and precluded from all trade or intercourse with the inhabitants of these colonies.

Extracted from the minutes,
Published by order of Congress,

CHARLES THOMPSON, Secretary.

Recreated from The Pennsylvania Gazette, January 17, 1776.

A MATCH FOR OUR RIFLE-MEN.

LONDON, *January* 10.

The following intelligence was communicated by an officer of rank in the army: "Government have sent over to Germany to engage 1800 men, called Jagers, people brought up in the use of the rifle barrel guns in boar hunting. They are amazingly expert. Every petty Prince, who hath forests, keeps a number of them, and they are allowed to take apprentices, by which means they are a numerous body of people. These men are intended to act next campaign in America, and our ministry plume themselves much in the thought of their being a complete match for the American rifle men."

Recreated from The Hartford Courant, May 27, 1776.

SNOW FOUR FEET DEEP.

Extract of a letter from Col. ARNOLD, *before* QUEBEC, *January* 14.

"The charge which has devolved upon me has been a most arduous task. Our last disaster so disheartened the troops, that I have had the greatest difficulty to keep them together. Our whole force, since the attack, amounts to no more than 700 men. We were for some time in expectation of an attack from the garrison, which consisted of 1500, but they have yet thought proper to continue in their strong hold, and we have effectually blockaded them up.

"General Wooster, whom I for some time expected, acquaints me he cannot leave Montreal, but will send me a reinforcement as soon as possible. Our duty has been extremely hard and fatiguing in this inclement climate, where the snow is now 4 feet deep on a level; but what cannot soldiers do who are fighting for liberty and their country? I make no doubt of a large reinforcement being sent us, as early as possible, and of being in Quebec before the spring."

Recreated from The Virginia Gazette, March 2, 1776.

CAMBRIDGE, *Jan.* 14.

A Gentleman who came passenger in a transport, arrived at Boston last week from London, informs, that 26 sail of vessels laden with stores and provisions were, when he left England sailed or setting out for Boston, for the support of the garrison the present winter; but that no troops may be expected before the spring; and that 110 fine large sheep were brought out in the vessel in which he came passenger, but that *only two* of them were carried into Boston alive.

Recreated from The Virginia Gazette, January 27, 1776.

Extract of a letter from the WEST INDIES, *Jan.* 15.

"I suppose that France will make an excursion in your favour in the spring, as we are well assured that Martinico and Guadaloupe have been lately reinforced with 10,000 men, and are strengthening with new works."

Recreated from The Pennsylvania Packet, February 19, 1776.

GEN. LEE COMING TO NEW YORK.

Extract of a letter from NEW YORK, *Jan.* 17.

"General Lee is coming here with a body of armed men. A gentleman of this city, who is just returned from Connecticut, tells me, General Washington has wrote to Governor Trumbull, informing him, that a fleet has left Boston; that he conjectures they are bound for New York; given him their size and strength as nearly as he could; informed him that General Lee was coming along with 90 rifle-men, and desired he would order a number of men to be immediately raised to come with him to this city. That in consequence thereof, Governor Trumbull had assembled the Committee of Safety, and they advised him to issue his warrant, ordering two regiments to be raised (about 1500 in both) to be commanded by Cols. Waterbury and Ward, under the direction of General Lee; and to come to this city. Another gentleman, who is just come from Camp, told me, that General Lee was to bring with him an engineer and artillery men.

"The Eastern post told me, he left General Lee at Hartford on Monday."

OUT of the press, and now selling by ROBERT BELL, in Third-street, [*Price Two Shillings.*] The SECOND EDITION of COMMON SENSE; Addressed to the INHABITANTS of AMERICA, on the following interesting SUBJECTS.
I. Of the origin and design of Government in general, with concise remarks on the English Constitution.
II. Of Monarchy and Hereditary Succession.
III. Thoughts on the present state of American Affairs.
IV. Of the present ability of America, with some Miscellaneous Reflections.
WRITTEN BY AN ENGLISHMAN.
Man knows no Master save creating HEAVEN,
Or those whom choice and common good ordain.
THOMSON.

Recreated from The Pennsylvania Packet, January 29, 1776.

TWO PRIZES SEIZED.

NEWBURY-PORT, *January* 19.

ON Monday last a brigantine from Ireland, burthen about 90 tons, Engs, Master, laden with provisions for the ministerial army at Boston, was taken and bro't into this port, the particulars of her cargo are as follows, viz. 29 tierces, 18 barrels, and 31 half barrels of best beef; 150 sirkins and 72 casks of butter; 64 sirkins, 1 barrel and 10 half barrels of tongue; 10 puncheons of claret; 1 tierce, 11 barrels, and 9 half barrels of best pork; 8 puncheons of oats; 2 sirkins of lard; 19 kegs of tripe; two casks of peas; and 109 hampers of potatoes.

On the same evening a ship from London, burthen about 200 tons, Bowie, Master, owned at London, out 12 weeks, with the following articles on board, intended for the same use as the brig's cargo, viz. 52 chaldron of coals, 86 butts and 30 hogsheads of porter, 20 hogsheads of vinegar, 16 hogsheads of sour grout, and 23 live hogs, was brought here.

Recreated from The Pennsylvania Packet, February 5, 1776.

CARLETON ATTACKS HOSPITAL.

QUEBEC, *January* 20.—By a letter from an officer in the continental army before Quebec, dated January 20, we learn, that gen. Carleton sallied out with a party to attack our hospital; on which our people engaged them, and drove them into the town, killed 16 of the enemy, and took 12 prisoners. Our loss was only 4 killed, and 3 taken prisoner.

Recreated from The Pennsylvania Packet, February 19, 1776.

To be SOLD, for ready money, at King William courthouse, on Thursday the 15th of February 1776, being court day,

ALL the remaining slaves of the estate of col. John Martin, deceased, late of the said county, by

ELIZABETH MARTIN, executrix.

WILLIAMSBURG, *Jan.* 13.

The following Gentlemen are chosen, by the Hon. the Convention, FIELD OFFICERS of seven more regiments that are immediately to be raised for the defence of the colony.

Reg't.	Colonels.	Lieutenant Colonels.	Majors.
3d.	Hugh Mercer,	George Weedon,	Tho. Marshall.
4th.	Adam Steven,	Isaac Read,	Robert Lawson.
5th.	William Peachey,	Wm. Crawford,	Josiah Parker.
6th.	Mordecai Buckner,	Thomas Elliott,	James Hendricks.
7th.	Wm. Daingerfield,	Alex. M'Clanahan,	William Nelson.
8th.*	Peter Muglenburg,	Abraham Bowman,	P. Helvenstone.
9th.†	Thomas Fleming,	George Matthews,	M. Donavon.

* (or German regiment.) † To be raised upon the Eastern Shore, and stationed there.

Recreated from The Virginia Gazette, January 13, 1776.

ARCHIBALD DIDDEP, TAILOR, WILLIAMSBURG,

RETURNS *his employers in general, and his old customers in particular, the most cordial thanks for past services, and shall always be ready to execute any command which they may hereafter intrust him with. As his family is extensive, journeymens wages very high, and his creditors exceedingly solicitous for their due, he hopes those whose accounts have been long standing will not take it amiss should he earnestly entreat them to make immediate payment; and those for whom he shall in future do business, it is expected, will not hesitate to tender down the cash so soon as their work is done. Ladies riding habits are still made by him, on the shortest notice. He remains the publick's most obedient humble servant,*

FRANCIS STREET, *January* 25. 1776.

Recreated from Purdie's Virginia Gazette, February 7, 1776.

AMERICAN DEFEAT AT QUEBEC.

AMERICA THE NURSERY OF HEROES.

Our readers will expect that we should give some account of so interesting a piece of intelligence as the late unsuccessful but brave attempt made by the Continental Congress to storm the town of QUEBEC. The following is the best we have been able to collect, and we have reason to think contains the most material facts.

General Montgomery had determined to storm the town as soon as a good opportunity offered, and his plan was to attack the upper and lower town at the same time; but several of his soldiers having deserted, he was induced to alter his design, and thought it most prudent to make two different attacks upon the lower town, the one at Cape Diamond, and the other at St. Rock's. The former was conducted under the immediate command of the General himself; but here a most unfortunate event early took place, viz. the fall of that gallant and able commander, which no doubt damped the ardour of his troops, and was the occasion of a repulse, though not till they had passed the first barrier, and were preparing to attempt the second.

The other attack was conducted by Colonel (now Brigadier-General) Arnold, with his own detachment from New England, and Captain Lamb's company of artillery from New York. They pressed through the St. Rock's, and approached near a two gun battery, without being discovered, and attacked it; the enemy bravely defended it above an hour, but it was carried.

In this attack General Arnold was shot through the leg, and was obliged to be carried to the hospital, as was also Brigade Major Ogden, who, after a spirited and soldier like conduct, received a wound in his shoulder. The command of the detachment now devolved on Lieutenant Colonel Green of Rhode Island, who, after gaining the battery, pushed on to a second barrier which they took possession of; at the same time the enemy sallied out from Palace gate, and attacked them in the rear.

A field piece, which the roughness of the road would not permit their carrying on, fell into the enemies hands. The communication between the two detachments was by this means cut off; and after a resolute push for the lower town, these brave soldiers were forced to yield to superior numbers with superior advantage, and submitted themselves prisoners. Capt. McPherson and Capt. Cheeseman fought and fell by the side of their General. The officers distinguished themselves by their good conduct. and Lt. Col. Green, Majors Bigelow and Meiggs, and Captains Oswald and Burr, are particularly mentioned as having done themselves great honour.

The loss of General Montgomery, who well understood the duties of the soldier and the citizen, and generously endured the fatigues of the one for the sake of securing the right of the other, is greatly regretted by every lover of mankind; but our enemies will soon find that America is become the nursery of heroes, and that while we are struggling in so glorious a cause as that of LIBERTY and VIRTUE, she will not want for Generals to lead forth her armies, and direct them to victory and triumph.

GEORGE HAUGHTON, UPHOLSTERER, Next the City Vendue Store, Front-street,

CONTINUES to make all kinds of Upholstery furniture, in the genteelest manner, and at the most reasonable rates; likewise informs the public in general, that he makes and sells every article in the military way, such as drums, colours, camp bedsteads and furniture, camp chairs, stools, tables, and mattrasses of all sorts, and begs to recommend himself to the several Committees and the Military Gentlemen to make markees and all sorts of tents, on the most approved method and quickest dispatch. All orders from the country strictly complied with.

⁎ The PHYSICIANS appointed by the COMMITTEE OF SAFETY to examine the young Gentlemen, who intend to offer themselves for Surgeons in the new Battalions, have fixed Tuesday, the 13th of February, for that purpose.

⁎ The Township Committees are requested to compleat their Collections for the Relief of the Poor of Boston, and pay their respective Balances into the hands of Mr. Edward Milnor, in Philadelphia.

Recreated from The Pennsylvania Gazette, January 24, 1776.

WHITHER BOUND GEN. CLINTON?

Extract of a letter from Cambridge, Jan. 23.

"I have been informed, by a Gentleman who left Boston last Saturday, that General Clinton has gone on board a 20 gun ship, and is bound with a number of transports, having on board two regiments (about 600 men) to some distant place, where he expects to meet five or six other regiments from Europe; some suppose he is going to Virginia. A 40 gun ship of war arrived there last week; she left England the 27th of November. Nothing has transpired, but that General Gage arrived 13 days before she sailed."

CAMBRIDGE, *January* 25.

Last Thursday one of our cruisers, Capt. Mascolt, carried into Cape Anne, a ship of 250 tons. She was from England, bound to Boston, and had on board, besides other valuable articles, 1500 blankets, 100 bolts of oznabrigs, 100 casks of oat meal, a large number of shoes, and a quantity of coal.

NEW LONDON, *January* 26.

We hear, that on the report of our unsuccessful attempt upon Quebec, about 5000 men from the back parts of Massachusetts Bay, Connecticut, and New York, immediately marched off, determined to force their way into Quebec, and drag out the infamous Carleton and his Banditti, or nobly perish in the attempt.

A VERY BRITISH FARCE.

Extract of a letter from CAMBRIDGE, *Jan. 28.*

"It would now be no news to acquaint you with the burning of the houses at Charlestown, or rather at the fort at Bunker's Hill, but the circumstances being odd and humorous, we shall give them to you; when 200 of our people (Col. Mifflin in the number) were performing their business, the regulars were acting a play called the Busy Body; that being finished, the scenes were hoisted to perform a farce (wrote by the officers) called the Blockade of Boston.

"General Washington, with a large wig and a long rusty sword, had just appeared on the stage, together with his orderly sergeant, who had a rusty gun of seven feet long on his shoulder; at that instant one of the sergeants came running (almost out of breath) on the stage, on which he threw his bayonet, and hallowed out, *Boston is on fire and attacked in fifty places*; those who were unacquainted with the farce, thought this part of it, but General Howe cried out, *Officers to your alarm posts*, which changed the act to shrieking, crying, fainting, &c. and indeed the troops on Bunker's Hill were not much less frightened than they were in Boston, for notwithstanding the officers ordered the men to preserve their fire, they kept up a continual blaze all round the hill."

Recreated from The Virginia Gazette, February 24, 1776.

ETHAN ALLEN IN IRONS.

Extract of a letter from a gentleman of the Continental Congress to a friend.

"Poor Allen, with his party, who were taken at Montreal, is certainly sent to Great Britain in irons by general Prescott, who was the commanding officer at the fortress; and shall this injury go unpunished? No, I think I can venture to say that the congress will order Prescot into irons, to remain in them until we have favourable accounts of our colonel and his men. Montgomery, hearing of the treatment of our people, refused to see general Prescot when he was taken, which was showing a soldier-like spirit.

"Howe is carrying on the war at Boston in a manner that would disgrace savages. The very great scarcity of provisions in the town has obliged them to turn several of the inhabitants out, and, to his eternal shame be it spoken, he had them inoculated for the small pox a short time before they were to come out, in hopes of spreading it among our troops. Is this not as bad as poisoning waters? But not withstanding this vile scheme, by the vigilance of our people the disorder has been prevented from spreading."

Recreated from The Maryland Gazette, January 25, 1776.

SOME MATTERS WITH TORIES.

Extract of a letter from MONTREAL, *Jan. 27.*

"The remnant of our battalion are to hold themselves in readiness, and expect marching orders tomorrow. I am for some time to be stationed at the Three Rivers, some matters being necessary to be settled with the tories, who, in different parts begin to be insulting, since our late misfortune at Quebec. This makes the third visit I have had among this kind of people. I expect soon to be called down to Quebec.

"Our blockade at Quebec is yet maintained. On the 25th instant Capt. Seaborn, from the Massachusetts, the first hero that has appeared to our assistance since the repulse at Quebec, arrived with 27 men. His arrival had a very good effect, for in the morning of the same day, was found at the church door, an anonymous seditious paper, very artfully written, calculated to stimulate the inhabitants to rise and cut us all off. However, I believe few of them had as much courage as the writer had ingenuity. They are now convinced the lakes are frozen, and think the Bostonians are coming as thick as the trees in the woods. The tories now seem quite crest fallen."

WITH THE HELP OF GOD.

Extract of another letter.

"Let no one small disaster among so many noble deeds discourage the SONS OF LIBERTY, especially considering how the small remnant of the army left before Quebec, dare to stand their ground, and form a blockade against that almost impregnable fortress. But I perceive it is open over head, and with the help of God, and a speedy reinforcement, we shall yet catch the fox in his den."

A Few copies of that justly esteemed pamphlet, called, COMMON SENSE; addressed to the Inhabitants of America; are to be sold at the Printing-Office.

Recreated from The Hartford Courant, February 19, 1776

WILLIAMSBURG, *Jan. 27.*

An express arrived here on Tuesday, with advice, that last Sunday morning near a hundred of the enemy landed at Norfolk, from the men of war, under heavy firing of cannon, which continued when the express came away. They had set three houses on fire, but were soon forced to retire; the loss they sustained was then uncertain. Three of our men were killed by cannon shot, two of whom, it is said, belonged to Capt. Bleuford's company of minute-men.

On Wednesday evening last six waggons arrived here from Philadelphia, loaded with arms and ammunition.

TO BE SOLD,

THE Schooner PEGGY, Burthen about 110 Tons, lying in HAMPTON Creek, a new vessel, has made but one Voyage (to *St. Vincent's*) and is as good a Vessel as hath been built on the Continent, is a very fast Sailer, and built of Cedar, Mulberry, and Locust to her Keel, except a few of her flat Floors, which will not rot in thirty Years. For Terms, inquire of the Subscriber, or the Printers.

4   MAXIMILIAN CALVERT.

SURRY, *January 25, 1776.*

WHEN the Troops were ordered to the Battle at *Hampton*, a HORSE of mine was pressed into the Service, rode down there, and lost. He had on a *Virginia* made Saddle very little worn, with a large blue striped Saddle-Cloth, a half-cheek'd double rein'd Bridle, and a new Surcingle. The Horse is an Iron Gray, 13 or 14 Hands high, about 10 Years old, and canters exceeding well. As he was a very short Time in my Possession, I do not sufficiently know his Marks to give a more particular Description of him. Whoever delivers the said Horse, Saddle, Bridle, &c. to me in *Cobham*, shall have 10s. Reward.

tf   ANTHONY DEGGE, Junior.

TWENTY VERY FINE
S L A V E S
To be SOLD for ready Money,
At the *Rocky Ridge*, on *Thursday* the 1st of February next.   (2)

Recreated from The Virginia Gazette, January 27, 1776

LEE MUST REACH NEW YORK.

Extract of a letter from CAMBRIDGE, *Feb.* 1.

"This serves to acquaint you, that by desire of Gov. Tryon, gen. Clinton has sailed for New York, with nineteen companies, ten of which are grenadiers and light infantry. As gen. Lee must reach New York before the ministerial invaders, I think he will give them a warm reception. The Scarborough man of war gave chase to one of our privateers a few days since—he fired 180 shot without doing any execution. The Chicknawaga Indians are to set off in a day or two, they have given gen. Washington much satisfaction, and assured him they will appear before Quebec in a very short time at the head of 500 Indians."

CAPT. MANLY TAKES MORE PRIZES.

CAMBRIDGE, *February* 1.—Last Thursday morning, Capt. Manly, being on a cruize in the Bay, discovered a ship a league or two S.E. of Boston lighthouse, which he immediately gave chase to, and took her within sight of the ships in Boston harbour. He then stood for a snow, which he espied off Cohasset, and soon coming on her, she struck to him without hesitation. Just as Capt. Manly had manned his last prize, a schooner of eight carriage guns, with many swivels, and full of men, convoying two little provision vessels from Halifax, came up, and began an engagement with Capt. Manly; but being soon convinced of her error, she sheared off for Boston. Capt. Manly would undoubtedly have taken her also, with the two provision vessels, had not his crew (which was at first much short of the complement) been weakened by manning the two prizes. In the engagement, his gunner was wounded, and his rigging something damaged. We have not heard what loss the enemy sustained. Both of the prizes, which were loaded with coal from Whitehaven, in England, Capt. Manly got safe into Plymouth in the ensuing night.

It is said about 100 sail of transports may be soon expected on the coast from England.

Last Monday one of the Continental Cruizers got into a harbour to the eastward, after having been chased by the Lively man of war, who fired about 170 shots at her.

Last Tuesday an express arrived from Canada, with dispatches for his Excellency the General, dated the 15th ult.—We have the pleasure to hear that our army, not withstanding the loss sustained in the unfortunate attack upon Quebec, still continues the blockade of that city; and we have good grounds to hope that the reduction of that capital will be compleated before spring, as we have authentic intelligence that reinforcements from various quarters have been poured in to the assistance of our brave little army.

Recreated from The Pennsylvania Gazette, February 14, 1776.

QUEBEC UNDER SIEGE.

Extract of a letter from MONTREAL, *Feb.* 4.

"Quebec is inclosed by a considerable body of forces under Brigadier General Arnold. They hope to avoid storming, and thereby prevent effusion of blood on both sides. The garrison consists of the seamen belonging to the two frigates, and the merchantmen that winter at Quebec, two companies of wretched emigrants raised from the outskirts of the suburbs, the dependants of government, and a few citizens whose exposed effects obliged their remaining to preserve. In the whole, we estimate from 1200 to 1300 men capable to bear arms; a body not sufficient to do the daily duty of guards only. To this may be added the want of wood to the degree that (by a deserter just escaped) without destroying the houses, there remained not fuel for five days. These circumstances we flatter ourselves will engage General Carleton (out of humanity) to offer terms before the season becomes so advanced as to oblige the Continental Army to force their admittance."

The report that the Mercury Man of War was taken by the American fleet, on board which was Gen. Clinton, is not yet confirmed.

Recreated from The Hartford Courant, March 4, 1776

Wednesday's Post.

D. LONDON, *Tuesday*, Feb. 6.

1. Yesterday at the levee, Lord Howe kissed the King's hand upon being appointed commander in chief of his Majesty's forces in North America.

2. Count Leipe is certainly to command the foreign troops against America; they are all ready for orders to sail, amounting to 22,000, which, with 28,000 English forces, will make an army of 50,000 men in America.

3. The public may be assured, that the following is the disposition of the ensuing campaign in America: Up the river St. Lawrence 12,000 men, under Gen. Carleton.—In Virginia and Carolina 11,000, commanded by Gen. Clinton and Lord Cornwallis. In New-York about 12,000, with Gen. Howe at their head.—At Boston no army will be encamped, but a strong garrison left, sufficient to defend it.—The above bodies are to be re-inforced occasionally by detachments from a corps-de-reserve, the station of which is not yet fixed upon, nor is the number it is to consist of determined; but it will certainly be considerable.—The naval armament is to be composed of 80 sail, from 50 guns down to cutters.—The different armies are to begin their operations as nearly as possible at the same time, and to march almost strait forwards from the coast, so as to cut off all communication between the several detached bodies of the Provincial forces.

4. Letters received by Capt. Abbot mention, that the Hannah, Capt. Foster, from London to Boston, laden with provisions, is taken by the Provincials, and carried into Marblehead, with several others, whose names are not mentioned.

H. Ireland.

1. *Cork, Jan.* 22. Early last Thursday morning the house of Miss Mary Kennedy, in Mallow-lane, was broke into by four persons armed, who forcibly took Miss Kennedy out of bed, and carried her off, with intent, as is supposed, to marry her to one of the party.

Recreated from The Ipswich Journal, England, February 10, 1776.

LEE AND CLINTON ARRIVE AT NEW YORK.

Extract of a letter from NEW YORK, *Feb. 5.*

"Yesterday, about the same time, Generals Lee and Clinton arrived. The Committee of Safety met immediately, and we expected something like a commencement of hostilities to-day. The Mayor went on board, and the Governor and General both assured him not a man was to be landed here. A 20 gun ship, said to be the Mercury, and a transport, came into the harbour yesterday. Clinton came in the frigate, and is going to the southward, I believe to Virginia. Lee says he will send word on board the man of war, that if they set a house on fire, in consequence of his coming, he will chain an hundred of their friends together by the neck, and make the house their funeral pile."

NO TROOPS WILL LAND.

Extract of a letter from NEW YORK, *Feb.* 7.

"The Governor sent for the Mayor, and desired him to assure the publick, that General Clinton was only come to pay him a visit on his way, and that the troops should not land here; nevertheless it is thought necessary to keep a strict look out, for fear they should land by surprise; in consequence of which half of our battalion kept guard all night, the other half the next, and the second battalion are doing the same. Nothing hostile has yet commenced, but God knows how soon it may. The ice obliges the ships to warp close to the wharf. This day the ice in large cakes was chock from side to side, and many people upon it."

Extract of another letter from NEW YORK, *February* 7, 1775.

"The town is in great confusion. The Congress have recommended for the inhabitants to move out. The Mercury man of war has demanded three months provision, which is refused. Lord Sterling came to town this morning with Jersey forces."

Recreated from The Pennsylvania Packet, February 12, 1776.

CAPT. MANLY SURVIVES 400 BALLS.

CAMBRIDGE, *February* 8.

We hear, that as Capt. Manly was coming out of Plymouth, January 30, an armed brig (which went from Boston for the purpose of taking him, as is supposed) gave him chase; upon which he ran his vessel on shore a little south of the North river in Scituate. The brig came to anchor, and fired not less than four hundred times at the privateer; but very remarkably, no man was even wounded. One ball entered the stern, and passed about six inches from Capt. Manly, who was confined by sickness in his cabin. The next day 130 balls were found on the adjacent shore.

After the brig ceased firing, she manned her boats, boarded Capt. Manly's vessel (the people being on shore) and endeavoured to set her on fire; but seeing our people coming upon them, they were glad to get off without effecting their design. She has since been got off, is refitting, and nearly ready for another cruise.

Recreated from The Pennsylvania Gazette, February 14, 1776.

PRESCOTT REMOVED TO GAOL.

PHILADELPHIA, *February* 5. Last Monday Brigadier General Prescot was removed from his apartments in the city tavern, to the new gaol, by order of the Honourable Continental Congress. It is said he was guilty of cruelly treating the prisoners taken from the continental army in Canada, particularly Col. Allen, lately sent home to England in irons.

Recreated from The Virginia Gazette, February 24, 1776.

In the Press, and will be published as soon as possible, and sold by W. and T. BRADFORD, at the London Coffee-house, in Philadelphia,

A NEW EDITION OF
COMMON SENSE:

Addressed to the INHABITANTS of AMERICA, with large and interesting additions by the author, as will be expressed at the time of publication, among which will be a seasonable and friendly admonition to the people called QUAKERS.

Several hundreds are already bespoke, 1000 for Virginia. A German edition is likewise in the press.

Recreated from The Pennsylvania Gazette, February 14, 1776.

BRITAIN'S NEW PLAN.

Extracts of letters from several eminent gentlemen in London to their friends in America, dated February 7 and 14, 1776.

"Lord George Germain, or Sackville, is made minister for the American war. Lord Howe is appointed commander in chief of the fleet, the commander at land is not yet determined. Lord Cornwallis is now ready to sail from Cork with 3000 men for Virginia to meet General Clinton. The plan is to march through that colony and attack Philadelphia by land, if impracticable by sea; they reckon upon paper to have an army of 30,000, mostly Germans, in America by June. Burgoyne is to retake Canada with 10,000 men."

Recreated from The Hartford Courant, May 20, 1776.

OUR MEN ARE WELL TREATED.

WORCESTER, *February* 9.—An officer from Quebec informs us, that he saw Major Meiggs (who came out on his parole to carry in the prisoners baggage) who told him that our men were all well treated; that the officers were lodged in the cathedral, and the soldiers in dwelling houses in the city; that they were permitted to walk about and take the air, and a straw bed and three blankets allowed to every two men, and porter or wine given them once in a day, that our field officers were invited by turns to dine with Gen. Carleton; that flour was very scarce in the city; but every thing, provisions in particular, very plenty among our army on the out side, and our troops, though few in number, in high spirits. Our informant, on his journey hither, saw about eight hundred men on their way to Montreal. Capt. Hubbard of this town is among the prisoners; he was wounded in the ankle, but likely to do well. There is not the least communication between our little army and the city, since Major Meiggs went in.

NEW YORK, *February* 2.—The Governor of Nova Scotia has issued a Proclamation, publishing MARTIAL LAW in that colony.

Recreated from The Pennsylvania Packet, February 26, 1776.

THE FIRST AMERICAN FLEET.

NEWBERN (N. Carolina), *Feb.* 9. By a Gentleman from Philadelphia we have received the pleasing account of the actual sailing from that place of the first American fleet that ever swelled their sails on the western ocean in defence of the rights and liberties of the people of these colonies, now suffering under the persecuting rod of the British Ministry, and their more than brutish tyrants in America.

This fleet consists of five sail, fitted out from Philadelphia, which are to be joined at the Capes of Virginia by two ships more from Maryland, and in command of Admiral Hopkins, a most experienced and venerable sea Captain.

The Admiral's ship is called the Columbus, after Christopher Columbus, the renowned discoverer of this western world, and mounts 36 guns, 12 and 9 pounders, on two decks, 40 swivels, and 500 men; the second ship is called the Cabot, after Sebaston Cabot, who completed the discoveries of America made by Columbus, and mounts 32 guns; the others are smaller vessels, from 24 to 14 guns.

They sailed from Philadelphia amidst the acclamation of many thousands assembled on the joyful occasion, under the display of a union flag with 13 stripes in the field, emblematic of the Thirteen United Colonies; but unhappily for us, the ice in the river Delaware, as yet, obstructs the passage down, but the time will now soon arrive when this fleet must come to action. Their destination is a secret, but generally supposed to be against the ministerial Governors, those little petty tyrants that have lately spread fire and sword through these southern colonies. For the happy success of this little fleet, three millions of people offer their most earnest supplications to Heaven.

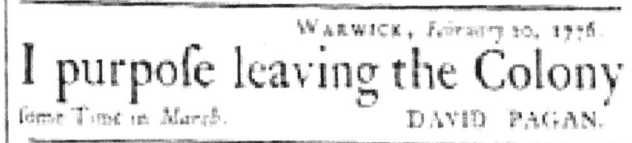

Recreated from The Virginia Gazette, March 2, 1776.

ENEMY ABANDONS NORFOLK.

WILLIAMSBURG, *February* 9.

By advices from the army under col. Howe, we learn that they abandoned Norfolk last Tuesday, after removing the poor inhabitants, with what effects they could carry along with them, and demolished the intrenchments which lord Dunmore threw up a little before he fled on board the fleet now lying before that place. What few houses remained after the late bombardment were likewise destroyed, after being valued, to prevent our enemies taking shelter in them. Thus, in the course of five weeks, has a town which contained upwards of 6000 inhabitants, many of them in affluent circumstances, a place that carried on an extensive trade and commerce, consequently affording bread to many thousands, being reduced to ashes, and become desolate, through the wicked and cruel machinations of lord North and the junto, aided by their *faithful servants*, by lord Dunmore with his motley army, and the *renowned* capt. Bellew, commodore of his Britannic majesty's fleet in Virginia, and his *generous* and *valiant* crew. Truly may it be now said,

Never can true reconciliation grow where
Wounds of deadly hate have pierc'd so deep.

The troops are now stationed at Kemp's landing, the Great Bridge, and in and about Suffolk.

The cannonading heard last Thursday fortnight, at Norfolk, was occasioned by a detachment of our troops, under major Eppes, attacking a number of black and white people from the men of war, who had landed to steal tobacco. Major Eppes drove them back, after killing four negroes, and two white men, upon which the ships began to fire.

We hear lord Dunmore and his friends are exceedingly uneasy, and a good deal frightened, upon hearing that the continental fleet is designed against them; and indeed they have very good reason, for as sure as a rifle (and that, they will know, is pretty true) commodore Hopkins will pay them a visit as soon as he is joined by the Maryland squadron.

Recreated from Purdie's Virginia Gazette, February 9, 1776.

QUEBEC BLOCKADE CONTINUES.

A Gentleman from Montreal, which place he left the 11th of February, informs us, that just as he came away, an express arrived from Quebec, who said our little Army still maintained their Blockade against that City, were in high Spirits, and that Recruits from the Colonies were daily coming in to their Assistance. The same Gentleman likewise informs us, that while he was at Montreal, about 1000 Men, of the Pennsylvania and New Jersey Battalions, arrived at that Place, on their way to join Gen. Arnold at Quebec.

Recreated from The Hartford Courant, February 26, 1776.

THE Committee of Safety wish to contract with proper persons for supplying the troops with provisions to be stationed between York river and Rappahannock, also one regiment to be stationed in the lower part of the Northern Neck, for one year. Any persons willing to enter into such a contract are desired to communicate their proposals as soon as possible, either personally to the Committee, or by letter to the President.

JOHN PENDLETON, jun. clerk.
February 9, 1776.

NORFOLK, Feb. 1, 1776.
I INTEND to leave the colony for a few months.
ARCHIBALD CAMPBELL.

CULPEPER, Jan. 21, 1776.
I INTEND to leave the colony immediately.
ROBERT BOYD.

Recreated from Purdie's Virginia Gazette, February 9, 1776.

MORE SHIPS AT NEW YORK.

NEW YORK, February 10.—Yesterday arrived here a transport, with a number of troops on board; it is said there is a man of war and more transports below, as a considerable firing was heard at the Narrows yesterday afternoon.

Extract of a letter from NEW YORK, *Feb.* 10.

"Yesterday the ship Kitty, with two companies of light infantry, arrived here from Boston; they sailed in company with Clinton. Governor Tryon assures the people that they will sail the first fair wind, it is believed they are bound for Virginia, and to await the arrival of the troops from England. It is expected Lee will entrench next week, but in what part he will break ground no one knows. Last night a great number of carts were pressed and placed at the battery, it was expected the guns were to be taken away.

Recreated from The Pennsylvania Packet, February 19, 1776.

FROM THE SOUTHERN DEPARTMENT.

Extract of a letter from NEWBERN *Feb.* 13.

"An express arrived here yesterday from the back country, informing us that the regulators and tories were making head there, and intend marching to Cross Creek, and from thence to Cape Fear. I am of the opinion they will get well flogged before they reach Cape Fear, provided they will fight.

"Our minute men, and a part of the militia, march to-morrow, and will join col. Caswell in Dobb's county, from which place he will march in two or three days with near a thousand men under his command.

"Col. Rutherford informed me this day, that col. Ashe, in New Hanover county, was on his march two days ago against the regulators, &c. with near two thousand men. If three or four more of our colonels, in this province, raise as many men, which I expect will soon be the case, they will be able to attack ten thousand regulars, and beat them too, I think, as our men will fight with great resolution."

Recreated from The Maryland Gazette, March 14, 1776.

BRITISH INTENTIONS.

Extract of a letter from LONDON, *February* 13, 1776.

"You will be anxious to know what are the ministerial intentions, and their forces for the next campaign; the following is their army upon paper; Hessians, 12,000; Brunswickers, Wolfenbatlers and Waldeckers, 5000; six regiments under Lord Cornwallis, 3000; eight more to sail in the spring, 4000; Highlanders, 2000; now in America, 8000.

"The sailing and destination of this armament is thus: Those under General Cornwallis are now embarked at Cork, and wait for sailing orders; their destination Virginia. By the treaty now signed, the Germans are to be ready the 27th of this month to march to the sea coast and embark, but for what part of America is not exactly known. The march by land is near six weeks, so that they cannot sail before April.

"The second embarkation from Cork will be about the same time, and it is probable that their destination will be against Canada, under Gen. Burgoyne, who is soliciting that command; in the mean time, the 19th regiment, with General Carleton's brother, is to sail from hence immediately, to reinforce Quebec, supposing that they can get high enough up the river, as far as the isle of Orleans, to make good their march by land.

"Lord Howe is appointed to command at sea, but the commanders at land are not known; certain, however it is, that there are two Lieut. Generals, and one of them old, who go with the Germans, so that it must be some one of great reputation and old in the service to command over them; it is therefore conjectured that Count La Lippe will be the man; he commanded the army in Portugal the last war.

"They are taking up East India men for the transport service, supposing they will be able to beat off the cruizers. A great number of artillery and waggon horses are to be sent, and a train of large battering cannon are preparing, which it would seem can only be intended against Quebec, should it be taken by General Montgomery.

"The English and Irish troops go with infinite resistance, and strong guards are obliged to be kept on the transports to keep them from deserting by wholesale.

"The Germans, too, I am well informed are almost mutinous; but the Landgrave of Hesse is an absolute tyrant, and must be obeyed. It is therefore conceived, that if the Congress have proposals prepared in English and German to distribute among them when they land, which no precautions can prevent, multitudes will desert.

"Upon the whole, the ministry, if every thing favours them, may have about thirty thousand men in America the latter end of June. They will have no horse but two regiments of light dragoons, that are now there, and Burgoyne's, which is to go.

"If the Americans have horses well trained to the woods, it will harass such an army infinitely; and if they act upon the defensive, intrench well, harass them continually, cut off their convoys, and if ever they hazard an engagement, make their push upon one wing, it is imagined here, that no General upon earth can make the campaign decisive and it is hardly possible that this country can stand another.

"They have found it impossible to recruit in England, Ireland or Scotland; though the leading people of the last are violently against America; they have therefore been obliged to draught from other regiments to compleat those who are going; so that when the whole are embarked, there will scarce be 2000 men remaining in Ireland, and as many in England, besides the foot guards and cavalry. I am well assured that the French government will wink at the exportation of arms and ammunition.

"God bless you, and prosper your undertakings."

Recreated from The Hartford Courant, June 3, 1776.

NEW YORK, *February* 15.—A few days ago arrived here from New Jersey, the Right Hon. the Earl of Stirling, with about 1000 men; 2000 are daily expected from Pennsylvania; and there are great numbers hourly arriving from the several counties of this, as well as of the neighbouring provinces.

Recreated from The Hartford Courant, February 19, 1776

GEN. CLINTON IN HAMPTON ROAD.

WILLIAMSBURG, *February* 14.—GENERAL Clinton and Lord Percy are arrived in Hampton road, in the Mercury, it is reported they have with them the grenadier and light companies of four regiments, amounting to about 600 men, but have not landed them. If the General has an intention, as some think, of striking a blow in this colony, he certainly expects a reinforcement from England, and that must be a large one too; otherwise, he will hardly be able to penetrate this length, and to hold it for any space of time. There are now six King's ships within the capes, and most of the shipping under their protection have moved out of the harbour of Norfolk into the road.

Recreated from The Hartford Courant, March 18, 1776.

NEW LONDON, *February* 16.—By Captain Arthur from Guadaloupe, we learn, that a French frigate had arrived at that island from France, with reports that the French had made a demand on the British court of fifty millions of livres, as a restitution for vessels taken by the English before the declaration of the last war. He also informs us that there is not so many English cruisers off the foreign ports in the West Indies as has been represented.

Recreated from The Pennsylvania Packet, February 26, 1776.

WANTED for the army, a large number of SHOES, for which ready money will be given; and I will engage to take any quantity that can be furnished, throughout the year, from any part of the colony. Such persons as can supply me, and are willing to engage, will meet with proper encouragement by applying to the subscriber, or mr. *Wm Armistead* at the regimental store in *Williamsburg*.
WILLIAM AYLETT.

Recreated from Purdie's Virginia Gazette, March 1, 1776.

1000 ENEMY ON DORCHESTER POINT.

CAMBRIDGE, *Feb.* 16.—"Yesterday morning about 4 o'clock, the enemy landed 1000 men, with two field pieces, on Dorchester Point, and burnt all the houses on that Point, except three, which were saved by our people. A Captain and 70 men, who were on the Point, retired to a height, between two causeways, which adjoins Roxbury, and there defended themselves until they were reinforced by Col. Reid, with 1000 men. The enemy, after setting the houses on fire, retreated to the Castle in boats. We lost two men, taken prisoners."

Recreated from The Hartford Courant, March 4, 1776.

PHILADELPHIA, *February* 17.—Last night Capt. Souder arrived here from Grenada. On his passage he spoke a vessel from Cork, the master of which informed him that 25 transports, with 4000 troops on board, had sailed from Cork for America.

Recreated from The Hartford Courant, February 26, 1776.

PHILADELPHIA, *February* 19.—Upon the news of general Clinton's attempt to land at New York, col. Dickinson, with two companies from the three first battalions of the Philadelphia militia, prepared to march to New York, at the request of general Lee, but were countermanded on Thursday, by an account that the king's troops had left that city without effecting a landing. The competition and spirit which appeared among the officers and privates upon this occasion indicated that the citizens of Philadelphia are on a footing with the foremost of the colonies in resolving to die freemen rather than to live slaves.

To be RENTED,
THE SWAN TAVERN in the town of *Falmouth*, which may be entered upon in *April* next. For farther particulars inquire of the subscriber, or proprietor in said town.
WILLIAM SMITH.

Recreated from Purdie's Virginia Gazette, March 1, 1776.

DIRECTIONS HOW TO PERFORM MANUAL EXERCISE BY MUSIC FOR THE BRITISH ARMY.

FIRST, let a march, such as God Save the King, Carbiner's, or the Dorseshire, be fixed upon for the above purpose; but any other tune may do that is set to music on common time, i.e., having four crotchets (or other notes equal thereunto) in a bar.

• • • •

2dly, Order one of these tunes to be blown either on the trumpet, fife, clarinet, or on some other wind instrument, and set those whom you would first learn by this method to march without arms for some time by the said tune, in order to ground them thoroughly in the several beats of the same, till they can march by them with ease and without constraint.

• • • •

3dly, Now you may venture to let them take up their arms, and shoulder; then order the first strain, or part, of the tune to be played in piano, or soft, the men standing fast.

• • • •

4thly, The music to begin the second time, forte, or loud; at the same instant the manual exercise to begin, and be continued till the whole is ended, keeping the same exact time between each motion as was done in marching.

5thly, An exception or two must be made to the last general rule, viz. when the ramrod is half drawn out, and seized back-handed, double time, or two beats, is to be allowed in clearing it off the pipes, turning, and pointing in the barrel.

• • • •

6thly, The same portion of time is likewise to be allowed for drawing it out of the barrel, turning and guiding it down the loops.

• • • •

7thly, In the second motion of charging bayonets, the music must dwell a little on that note (called a hold) in order to gain time to bring the firelock down to its proper attitude.

• • • •

It is practical to bring, not only a battalion or a regiment to exercise by the aforesaid rules, but a whole army, consisting of at least 50,000 men, and with such accuracy and perfection in point of time, as cannot be executed by any other method hitherto found out; the due performance of which will most pleasingly affect the glowing breast of every spectator, as can be better felt than demonstrated.

Recreated from The Pennsylvania Gazette, March 13, 1776.

TO BE SOLD

At BLANDFORD, on FRIDAY the 1st of MARCH next, to the highest Bidders,

ELEVEN valuable NEGRO FELLOWS, among whom is a very good Ship Carpenter. Also two SCHOONER FLATS, one 85, the other 70 Hogsheads Burthen, with their BOATS, and two smaller FLATS Burthen 35 and 32 Hogsheads. Twelve Months Credit will be allowed the Purchasers, on giving Bond, with approved Security, to

THOMAS CRAWFORD.
JOSHUA POYTHRESS, Jun.

THE SCHOONER REBECCA,

JOHN HARVEY Commander,

NOW lying in *Wycomico*, near the Mouth of *Potowmack* River, well fitted, will take in Passengers for any Part of BRITAIN, and will sail by the Middle of *April*. She will be prepared to receive conveniently 25 Passengers. Those inclinable to go had better make Application as soon as possible, either to Mr. *Thomas Reid* of *Northumberland*, or to the Captain on Board the said Schooner. Each Passenger to pay twenty Guineas, and find his own Bedding.

Recreated from The Virginia Gazette, February 24, 1776.

COMMON SENSE.

INTRODUCTION.

Perhaps the sentiments contained in the following pages, are not yet sufficiently fashionable to procure them general favour; a long habit of not thinking a thing wrong, gives it a superficial appearance of being right, and raises at first a formidable outcry in defense of custom. But the tumult soon subsides. Time makes more converts than reason.

As a long violent abuse of power is generally the Means of calling the right of it in question (and in matters to which might never have been thought of, had not the Sufferers been aggravated into the inquiry) as the King of England hath undertaken in his own Right, to support the Parliament in what he calls Theirs, and as the good people of this Country are grievously oppressed by the combination, they have an undoubted privilege to inquire into the pretensions of both, and equally to reject the usurpation of either.

In the following sheets, the author hath studiously avoided every thing which is personal among ourselves. Compliments as well as censure to individuals make no part thereof. The wise, and the worthy, need not the triumph of a Pamphlet; and those whose sentiments are injudicious, or unfriendly, will cease of themselves unless too much pains are bestowed upon their conversion.

The cause of America is in a great measure the cause of all Mankind. Many circumstances have, and will arise, which are not local, but universal, and thro' which the principles of all Lovers of mankind are affected, and in the Event of which, their Affections are interested. The laying of a Country desolate with Fire and Sword, declaring war against the natural rights of all Mankind, and extirpating the Defenders thereof from the Face of the Earth, is the Concern of every Man to whom Nature hath given the Power of feeling; of which Class, regardless of Party Censure, is the **AUTHOR.**

IT IS TIME TO PART.

HARTFORD, *February* 19.

THE pamphlet entitled Common Sense, (says a correspondent) is indeed a wonderful production. It is completely calculated for the meridian of North America. The author introduces a new system of politics as widely different from the old, as the Copernican system is from the Ptolemaic. The blood wantonly spilt by the British troops at Lexington, gave birth to this extraordinary performance, which contains as surprising a discovery in politics as the works of SIR ISAAC NEWTON do in philosophy.

This animated piece dispels, with irresistible energy, the prejudice of the mind against the doctrine of independence, and pours in upon it such an inundation of light and truth as will produce an instantaneous and marvelous change in the temper, in the views and feelings of an American. The ineffable delight with which it is perused, and its doctrines imbibed, is a demonstration that the seeds of independence, though imported with the troops from Britain, will grow surprisingly with proper cultivation in the fields of America.

The mind indeed exults at the thought of a final separation from Great Britain; whilst all its prejudices and enchanting prospects in favour of a reconciliation, like the morning cloud, are chased away by the heat and influence of this rising luminary, and although the ties of affection and other considerations have formerly bound this country in a threefold cord to Great Britain, yet the connexion will be dissolved, and the gordion knot be cut: *"For the blood of the slain, the voice of weeping nature cries it is time to part."*

Recreated from The Hartford Courant, February 19, 1776

NEW YORK, *February* 22.—We are informed that the Continental Congress have ordered General Lee to take command of the forces in Canada, and that General Schuyler is to succeed in the command in this city.

Recreated from The Pennsylvania Packet, February 26, 1776.

MINUTE-MEN ARRIVE.

NORTHAMPTON COUNTY, *Feb.* 22, 1776.

ABOUT a week ago two minute men companies arrived here from Maryland, one from Kent county, under the command of capt. William Henry, the other from Queen Anne, under the command of capt. James Kent. They are two very fine companies, extremely well armed, have amongst them many fine gentlemen of family and fortune, and are examples of good discipline and subordination. The day after their arrival the committee met, and addressed them as follows:

To capt. WILLIAM HENRY, *and capt.* JAMES KENT, *and the troops under their command.*

THE committee of Northampton county beg leave to congratulate you upon your safe arrival into this county, after a fatiguing march, at this rigorous season.

When gentlemen of easy fortunes, such as the companies we have seen from your province, and who can enjoy at home every convenience and elegance of life, enter themselves voluntarily to serve their country, by undertaking a tedious march at an inclement season, and cheerfully submitting to every inconvenience consequent thereto, it cannot be doubted that they are actuated by the noblest principles. They are justly entitled to the thanks of their country, and we hope Providence will ever crown them with honour and success.

The peaceful state which this once happy county enjoyed, till the present unnatural though unavoidable contest, renders us totally unprovided for the proper reception of a number of armed men; and we hope, gentlemen, you will consider the very indifferent accommodations which you meet with here as solely owing to this cause, and not from want of respect and attention to your circumstances. We however beg leave to assure you, that nothing in our power shall be wanting to promote your convenience and happiness, which the situation of our county will permit; in full confidence, that you will at all times, during your residence amongst us, cheerfully co-operate with this committee in maintaining good order and regularity in this place, and in opposing the dangerous designs of all the secret and avowed enemies of American liberty.

The committee received the following reply.

HEAD QUARTERS, Northampton Courthouse, Feb. 22, 1776.

Mr. president and gentlemen of the committee for Northampton *county*, Virginia,

We return thanks for your very polite address to us, and the companies under our command, upon our arrival at this place, as also for your attention in making the necessary provision for our reception. Impressed with a lively sense of the duty we owe to our country, and animated with the glorious cause of American liberty, we cheerfully left our habitations, thinking no difficulties too much for a people to encounter who were *determined to die or live free*, and shall esteem ourselves happy in proportion to the services we shall be able to render the colony, and this county in particular.

We are not insensible of the many inconveniences attending the accommodation of soldiers in a country hitherto a stranger to war, and with pleasure we find your assiduity has conquered the difficulties, and made our residence easy and agreeable.

Be assured, gentlemen, we shall be always ready to give you any assistance in our power, consistent with our duty, to preserve good order and regularity; and shall be at all times thankful for your advice and directions in the execution of the trust reposed in us, especially as we are strangers to what is and may have been transacted in this place. We beg leave to subscribe ourselves, with the greatest respect, gentlemen, your obedient servants,

WILLIAM HENRY.
JAMES KENT.

Recreated from Purdie's Virginia Gazette, March 1, 1776.

In Congress.

PHILADELPHIA, *February 23, 1776.*

RESOLVED, That a Committee of five be appointed to contract for the making of MUSKETS and BAYONETS for the use of the United Colonies, and to consider of further ways and means of promoting and encouraging the manufacture of FIRE ARMS in the United Colonies. The Members chosen—Mr. *Paine*, Mr. *Wilson*, Mr. *Huntington*, Mr. *Lee*, Mr. *L. Morris*. *Extract from the Minutes*,

CHARLES THOMPSON, Secretary.

• • • •

IN pursuance of the above Resolve, the said Committee hereby notify all persons who are disposed to contract for the making of Muskets and Bayonets, that they make known their proposals as soon as possible to them at Philadelphia, or to the Assemblies, Conventions, or Committees of Safety in the Colonies where they live, in order to be transmitted to the said Committee.

R.T. PAINE, *per Order.*

Recreated from The Pennsylvania Packet, March 4, 1776.

WILLIAMSBURG, *February* 26.—By Mr. Hancock Lee, lately from Kentucky, we are informed, that the Indians have scalped two or three white people on the Ohio, and the commanding officer at Detroit offers them 10l. for every scalp. Capt. Neaville, at Fort Pitt, writes his friend in Frederick to the same purpose, but says a reward is 30l. a scalp.

Recreated from The Pennsylvania Gazette, March 13, 1776.

Extract of a letter from MONTREAL, *Feb.* 26.

"We have nothing material new, from Camp before Quebec, except a few deserters now and then, who report, that there is a scarcity of provisions, and that Gen. Carleton has promised the sailors in town one hundred pounds each, and 200 acres of land, wherever they choose it, if they will defend the town till a reinforcement comes in the spring."

Recreated from The Hartford Courant, March 18, 1776

IRISH FETE ETHAN ALLEN.

Extract of a letter from CORK, *February* 27.

"When Col. Ethan Allen, with about 50 other prisoners, arrived in the Solebay, two gentlemen went on board to enquire into their situation, and to assure them of the disposition of several gentlemen in this city to alleviate their distresses. Col. Allen was so affected with this instance of unexpected generosity, that the expression of his gratitude could hardly find utterance.

"His treatment on board the Solebay is far different from the barbarous and cruel usage he experienced in his passage from Quebec, being then handcuffed and ironed in the most dreary part of the vessel, and basely insulted with cruel and unmanly reflections by some officers of the ship, whom he challenged in Cornwall, without receiving satisfaction.

"A subscription was begun this morning among some friends of the cause, and near fifty guineas collected to buy clothes for his men, and necessaries for himself; and if liberty can be got of Captain Williams to put livestock on board, I can assure you, Col. Allen will be exceedingly well provided.

"We this day sent a hamper of wine, sugar, fruit, chocolate, &c. on board, for his immediate use, and to-morrow intend to prepare the sundry articles of which he sent a list. I inclose you a rough copy of his answer to our letter. Should he have permission to come on shore, he will be entertained by some of the first gentlemen of this city. I have not been refused by a single person on the subscription."

Copy of Allen's note.

"GENTLEMEN,

"I have received your generous present this day with a joyful heart. Thanks to God, there are still the feelings of humanity in the worthy citizens of Cork towards those of your bone and flesh, who, through misfortune from the present broils in the empire, are needy prisoners.

"*Dated* COVE, *January* 24, 1776."

Recreated from The Pennsylvania Gazette, May 8, 1776.

WORK ON DORCHESTER NECK.

Extract of a letter from CAMBRIDGE, *Feb.* 29.

"Preparations were still making for getting to work on Dorchester Neck and Boston; that the enemy were well acquainted with their designs, and had lately thrown up several works to weaken our fire; that on the 28th, they (the enemy) compleated a bomb battery and a gun ketch opposite Lechemere's Point, and promise our folks a visit as soon as they break ground on Dorchester; that the principal part of their heavy cannon, hospital stores, &c. are on board ship; all the square rigged vessels in the harbour are taken up, and received two months advance to transport the troops and tory inhabitants, if necessary, to a less hostile shore; that Monday or Tuesday next will be the important day; that we have forty-five batteaus, each to carry eighty men, and two floating batteries, stationed at the mouth of Cambridge river; if the enemy make a serious affair of Dorchester, we may rush into the west part of Boston; the enemy's strength (marines, tories and negroes included) about 7000—ours about 20,000; that two of our privateers had fallen in with an armed brig of 13 guns, engaged her for three hours, and sent her off on a careen."

Recreated from The Virginia Gazette, February 17, 1776.

Extract of a letter from Cambridge, Feb. 22.

"Captain Manly has refitted his schooner, and will sail in a day or two.—The Fowey man of war, lately stationed off Marblehead, Salem, Beverly, &c. returned to Boston on Monday.—It is said that four smaller vessels are to be sent in her stead, to block up those ports.—We have six mortars fitted to their beds, 10 twelve pounders and 6 eighteen pounders, and 12 field pieces, of different calibres (all from Ticonderoga) mounted. The remainder will be fit for service in a week."

On Saturday last, David Rittenhouse, Esq., was chosen Burgess for this city, in the room of Dr. Franklin, who is appointed upon an embassy to Canada by the Congress.

Recreated from The Pennsylvania Gazette, March 6, 1776.

WIDOW MOORE'S CREEK.

Extract of a letter from col. Caswell, *Feb.* 29.

I have the pleasure to acquaint you, that we had an engagement with the Tories, at Widow Moore's Creek bridge on the 27th current. Our army was about 1000 strong, consisting of the Newbern battalion of minute men, the militia from Craven, Johnston, Dobbs, and Wake, and a detachment of the Wilmington battalion of minute men, which we found encamped at Moore's creek the night before the battle, under the command of col. Lillington.

The Tories, by common report, were 3000 strong; but general M'Donald, whom we have a prisoner, says there were about 15 or 1600; he was unwell that day, and not in battle. Capt. M'Cleod, who seemed to be the principal commander, with capt. John Campbell, are among the slain. The number killed, and mortally wounded, from the best accounts I was able to collect, was about 30, most of whom were shot on their passing the bridge. Several had fallen into the water, some of whom, I am pretty certain, had not risen yesterday evening, when I left the camp. Such prisoners as we have made say, there were at least fifty of their men missing.

The Tories were totally put to rout, and will certainly disperse. Col. Moore arrived at out camp a few hours after the engagement was over; his troops came up that evening, and are now encamped on the ground where the battle was fought; and col. Martin is at or near Cross Creek, with a large body of men. Those, I presume, will be sufficient effectually to put a stop to any attempts to embody again. I therefore, with col. Moore's consent, am returning to Newbern with the troops under my command, where I hope to receive your orders to dismiss them.

There I intend carrying the general. If the Council should rise before my arrival, be pleased to give orders in what manner he shall be disposed of. Our officers and men behaved with the spirit and intrepidity becoming freemen, contending for the dearest privileges. I have the honour, &c.   R. CASWELL.

Recreated from The Pennsylvania Gazette, March 27, 1776.

AMERICAN FLEET AT NASSAU.

We have certain intelligence, by express, that on the 2d instant the American fleet, commanded by Admiral Hopkins, put into the island of New Providence, and took possession of 280 pieces of cannon from 6 to 18 pounders, and a large quantity of ball and other warlike stores, which they found in the town and fortification of Nassau; but the Governor being advised of their approach, had secured all the powder except 17 barrels, by sending it off in the night. The Admiral ordered the Governor and Council, the Collector of the Customs, and the Judge of the Supreme court, to be confined to their houses till the stores should be got in; but suffered no injury to be offered to the persons or property of any of the inhabitants. It was imagined the fleet would be ready to sail in two or three days.

Recreated from The Virginia Gazette, March 30, 1776.

FOREIGN TROOPS TO AMERICA.

GAGE AND BURGOYNE TO RETURN.

LONDON, *March* 2.—The Generals Gage and Burgoyne are both to return to America to their respective commands, in a very short time.

This week the following forces are to be agreed to in Council to be sent to America this spring: Hessians, 12,000, Brunswickers, 4000, Walders, 2000, British, 37,000; total, 55,000.

The treaty with the Duke of Brunswick was signed by Col. William Fawcitt, the 6th of January, 1776. By this treaty 3964 men are taken into the pay of Great Britain; also, 336 light cavalry, dismounted. Half to be ready to march the 13th of February, and to arrive at the place of embarkation the 25th; the other half to begin their march the last week in March; levy money to be paid to the Duke thirty crowns each, at 4s. 6d. 1/4. The King to pay the Duke a subsidy of 64,500 German crowns a year, while in pay; and double that for two years after the troops return.

The treaty with the Landgrave of Hesse, was signed at Cassel, by the same Gentleman, the 13th of January; by it 12,000 Hessians are hired; a part to begin their march the 27th of February, and the remainder within four weeks after; twenty crowns banco to be paid for levy money for each man; the subsidy to be 45,000 crowns banco, per annum, at 4s. 9d. 1/4. The treaty to continue at least one year after the troops arrive back in the dominion of Hesse.

That with the Count of Hanau was signed the 5th of February, for 669 infantry to begin their march the 20th of March. Levy money thirty crowns; the annual subsidy to be 35,000 crowns. It is calculated that the ensuing campaign against the American colonies will cost Great Britain at least four millions.

Several of Sir Peter Parker's fleet, which sailed from Cork the 12th ult. we learn, were seen bearing away for Lisbon, having lost main top masts, sails, &c. and it is imagined that most of the men of war had got into the above place.

March 12. It is reported that his Majesty will go to Plymouth to take a survey of the fleet before they sail for America.

The officers who are ordered for America are to wear the same uniform as the common soldiers, and their hair to be dressed in like manner, so that they may not be distinguished by the rifle-men, who aim particularly at the officers.

To be SOLD, for ready Money, to the highest Bidder, at my STORE in GLOUCESTER County, on THURSDAY the 13th Instant (if fair, otherwise next fair Day)

A QUANTITY of *German* OSNABRUGS, TICKLINGBURGS, CHECKS, SHEETINGS, WHITE LINENS, LEATHER BREECHES, HATS, WRITING PAPER, CARPENTERS TOOLS, NARROW HOES, COFFEE, SNUFF, and a great Number of other Articles, too tedious to mention.

M. ANDERSON, Junior.

☞ I have about 1500 Weight of BAR IRON, which will likewise be sold that Day, if not before.

A VALUABLE Library of Books to be sold. For a Catalogue, and Terms, apply to the Printers. (4)

Recreated from The Virginia Gazette, June 8, 1776.

BRITISH CLEAR BUNKER'S HILL.

March 1. We are told by a gentleman who came out of Boston last Friday, that the enemy have taken away their mortars from Bunker's Hill, and carried them to Boston; that a council of war had been held in Boston for several days, that General Howe had advised the Mandamus Counsellors to go to England, and the tories to leave the town; that all the vessels in the harbour that were not in the King's service were taken up to transport the tories and their effects; and that it was surmised in Boston, that should another battle ensue, and the regulars be defeated, they would set fire to the town, and remove to some other part of the continent. It is a prevailing opinion that something extraordinary will turn up in the course of a few days.

Recreated from The Hartford Courant, March 4, 1776

WILLIAMSBURG, *March* 2.—Monday morning last General Clinton, with two men of war, the Mercury and Kingfisher, three transports and four tenders, put out to sea, destined, it is imagined, for Charlestown, South Carolina; and on Thursday another King's ship left Norfolk, supposed to be the Liverpool bound out upon a cruise, accompanied with a tender.

Sixty men of war are ordered out upon the American station, and it is probable, unless the Russian's join, that they will only annoy us with their shipping.

Recreated from The Virginia Gazette, March 2, 1776.

PHILADELPHIA.—The sloop Fanny, Captain Hayman, arrived here from Ocracock, in North Carolina, which he left about the 1st instant. By him we learn, that Governor Martin, at the head of 700 Regulators and Tories, had got between the two Provincial Armies, commanded by the Colonels Ash and Caswell, in order to prevent their joining, but it was thought he would not be able to accomplish this design, as great numbers from all parts were daily going to the assistance of the Colonels. He also informs, that the Tories and Regulators had not been joined by any considerable number of Scotch settlers, as was expected.

Recreated from The Pennsylvania Gazette, March 13, 1776.

AMERICANS ON DORCHESTER HEIGHTS.

HOWE SENDS FLAG OF TRUCE.

Intelligence is received from the camp at Cambridge, that a cannonading and bombardment had begun on the night of Saturday the 2d instant, and continued the two following nights; during which time a vast number of shot and shells were thrown into the town, under cover of which the General possessed himself of the heights of Dorchester.

On the enemy's perceiving this on Thursday morning, they were in the greatest confusion, hurry, and bustle, and embarked their troops in order to attack us before we had made our lodgements; but the violent storm which came on that day, prevented them from receiving, and us from the honour of giving them a good drubbing. Our troops are now forming a battery on Nook's hill, which commands the south of Boston, and to which their shipping lie much exposed.

General Howe in his great tenderness to preserve the town of Boston from destruction, has, by a flag of truce sent out by the selectmen, asked permission to embark his troops, and sail without molestation. The permission it is possible he may obtain, on condition that he leaves his whole artillery, and military stores behind him. It is supposed that General Howe intends to remove his quarters to the city of New York; and it is hoped that every proper measure will be taken for his reception.

NEW LONDON, *March* 1.—We hear that about 190 cannon, of various sizes, have been taken from Fort George, in New York, and that part of the fort next to the city is destroyed. Numbers of cannon are mounted on different wharfs in that city.

CAMBRIDGE, *March* 9.—Capt. Manly has taken another transport, 400 tons burthen, laden with peas, potatoes, pork, sour grout, 10 packages of medicine, 6 carriage guns, 4 swivels, 3 barrels of powder, &c. and carried her into Newbury.

Recreated from The Virginia Gazette, March 30, 1776.

THE SIEGE OF BOSTON.

CAMBRIDGE, *March* 6.—The Continental Army, assisted by a large body of militia, are now carrying on the siege of Boston with great vigour. Last Saturday night our artillery at the fortresses of Cobble Hill and Lechemere's Point, below this town, and at Lamb's dam in Roxbury, bombarded and cannonaded the town; the following night the same was continued with briskness; and the whole of Monday night the artillery from all the above fortresses played incessantly. Our shot and shells were heard to make a great crashing in the town, but we have not learnt any execution done thereby.

The enemy returned the fire, from their batteries at West Boston, and from their lines on the Neck, very vigorously. They threw many shells into the battery at Lechemere's Point, one into the fort on Prospect Hill, and one or two as far up as fort No. 2, within a quarter of a mile of the college. On Monday night we had two killed, Lieut. Mayo at Roxbury, by a cannon ball; and a man at Lechemere's Point by a shell, which, with one or two wounded is all the loss, of any consequence, that we have sustained. We have had but little firing since Tuesday morning.

On Monday night a body of the Continental troops took possession of two large hills at Dorchester, about a mile from the south part of Boston, where they are now strongly fortified. These are two of the heights which General Burgoyne said, in a letter to a noble Lord, commanded the town of Boston, and which, he also said, it was absolutely necessary the British troops should be possessed of.

• • • •

Yesterday was the anniversary of Preston's massacre, in King-Street Boston, 1770, where Grey, Maverick, Caldwell, Carr and Attucks, were cruelly murdered by a band of ruffians, sent hither by George III, brutal tyrant of Britain, in order to execute his infernal plans for the enslaving of a free people.

HARTFORD, *March* 11.—Last week General LEE set out from New York for Virginia.

Recreated from The Hartford Courant, March 11, 1776.

REGALING THE SHARKS.

WILLIAMSBURG, *March* 9.—We have intelligence that the jail distemper rages with great violence on board lord Dunmore's fleet, particularly among the negroe forces, upwards of 150 of whom, it is positively affirmed, have died within a short time, and who, as fast as they expired, are tumbled into the deep, to regale the sharks, which it seems swarm thereabouts, and no doubt keep as sharp a look-out, for all such sorts of provision, as land animals do for fresh pork, good mutton, poultry, &c.

Twelve deserters have come into Suffolk within these few days, from the fleet at Norfolk, viz. a sergeant and corporal, with five marines, and five common sailors, who all confirm the miserable situation of the people on board, occasioned by the jail fever breaking out among them; and one of the marines declared, that he firmly believed the captain would come on shore likewise, had he a good opportunity.

Last Tuesday fortnight, capt. William Deane (some time ago sent prisoner to Boston by lord Dunmore, but re-taken by capt. Manly of the Lee privateer) had the misfortune to have his vessel seized, the sloop John, from Cape Anne, about six miles below York, by one of the ministerial tenders. The captain, with his people, escaped in their boat; and, had it not been calm, and the tide against him, he would have saved his vessel likewise.

We have the pleasure to assure the publick, that the recruiting service in this colony has met with the greatest success, all the nine regiments being at this time nearly completed, with able-bodied men; and there is not the smallest doubt, should the war continue (which, from appearances, is most likely to be the case) but our troops may be increased to any number the legislature shall judge necessary for the support of the rights of America, as well as to repel every hostile invasion.

A number of troops have lately arrived in this city and more are daily expected.

Recreated from Purdie's Virginia Gazette, March 8, 1776.

AN ACCOUNT FROM MOORE'S CREEK.

GOV. MARTIN THREATENS WILMINGTON.

Extract of a letter from a Gentleman in NORTH CAROLINA, *to his friend in* PHILADELPHIA, *March 10, 1776.*

"I have it in my power to give you a few lines by the express.—Yesterday afternoon we received a letter from Col. Caswell, giving an account, in a full manner, of a battle between his troops, Col. Lillington's, off Cape Fear, and the Highlanders and Regulars, about twenty miles above Wilmington, at Moore's creek bridge, which is between the North West and North East rivers. The insurgents had made many attempts to escape the vigilance of our troops, and get down to Governor Martin. Col. Caswell was after them many days; at length they made an attempt to cross at this pass, about the break of day, on Tuesday, the 27th of last month.

"Col. Caswell had very wisely ordered the planks to be taken off the bridge, so that in passing it they met with many difficulties; a very heavy firing came on. Our troops reserved their fire till within a small distance, which did great execution. Many passed the bridge. Gen. M'Cleod and Captain Campbell were instantly shot dead. M'Cleod had nine bullets and twenty-four swan shot through him and into his body.

"Twenty-eight more are killed and mortally wounded; and between twenty and thirty prisoners, amongst them is his Excellency General Donald M'Donald, who is on his way to us, and is expected here to-morrow. We had only two men wounded, one of them mortally. The insurgents retreated with the greatest precipitation, leaving behind them some waggons, &c. They cut the horses out of the waggons, and mounted three upon a horse. Many of them fell into the creek and were drowned. Tom Rutherford ran like a lust fellow, he and Felix Kenan of Duplin county were in arms against us; they by this time are our prisoners, as is Lieutenant-Colonel Cotton, who ran the first fire. The battle lasted only three minutes.

"The Colonels Caswell and Lillington had under their command 1000 men. The Highlanders and Regulars 1600. The account is certain as to the number of the insurgents, for Col. Caswell had it from Gen. M'Donald himself. Col. Moore sent off expresses to the main army, consisting of between five and six hundred men, under Cols. Martin, Polk, Thackston, and Long, in and about Cross creek, to secure the whole of the Highlanders and Regulators; not a man of them has a probability of making his escape.

"Governor Martin has threatened the destruction of Wilmington, if they do not supply him with provisions. The town has spiritedly refused to supply him, with a single mouthful, notwithstanding that a cruizer and three armed vessels lay opposite it; and they have told the Governor he may do as he pleases, as they are determined to resist to the last.

"They have a good battery there, and four hundred chosen men, under the command of a brave Irishman, Col. William Purviance, who is determined to see it out with them. The women and children are all sent out of town. The Tories are all secured in Wilmington jail, to the number of twenty-five. Captain Parry, of the cruizer, has meanly begged a few quarters of beef, which the town has refused him, and the vessels dare not begin the attack, though we daily expect to hear of an engagement, as they are starving.

"It was humorous enough to the inhabitants of Wilmington, when the Governor haughtily demanded one thousand barrels of flour, after answering him fully on that head, they then went immediately into the insurrection, and what a hopeful situation he had reduced his friends to, that were surrounded by large, spirited and powerful armies, who were determined to make short work with them.

"We now have in arms, to the southward of this town nine thousand four hundred men. Gen Clinton we expect to hear every moment, is landed at Cape Fear, with the troops under his command. As soon as we learned he had sailed from Virginia, we sent off an express instantly to our commanding officer there to be ready for him."

Recreated from The Pennsylvania Gazette, March 27, 1776.

LEE TO COMMAND SOUTHERN DEPARTMENT.

WILLIAMSBURG.

ON Saturday, the 9th instant, an express arrived to the Committee of Safety, from the General Congress, enclosing commissions for col. ANDREW LEWIS, and col. ROBERT HOWE, to rank as brigadier-generals in the continental army. The express continued his route to North Carolina, and we learn carried with him a brigadier-general's commission for col. JAMES MOORE of that province.

Private letters by the same express mention, that major general LEE was appointed commander in chief of the southern department; although letters, since received, say, he had marched for Quebeck, at the head of 8000 men, to reduce that important fortress.

Recreated from Purdie's Virginia Gazette, March 15, 1776.

A PROCLAMATION.

By his Excellency WILLIAM HOWE, Major General, *at* BOSTON, *March* 10, 1776.

AS LINEN and WOOLEN GOODS are articles much wanted by the rebels, and would aid and assist them in their rebellion, the Commander in Chief expects that all good subjects will use their utmost endeavours to have all such articles conveyed from this place. Any who have not opportunity to convey their goods under their own care, may deliver them on board the Minerva, at Hubbard's wharff, to Crean Brush, Esq., marked with their names, who will give a certificate of the delivery, and will oblige himself to return them to the owners, all unavoidable accidents excepted. If, after this notice, any person secrets or keeps in his possession such articles, he will be treated as a favourer of the rebels.

Recreated from The Pennsylvania Gazette, April 17, 1776.

For SALE, *by the Printers,*

FINE polished Steel INSTRUMENTS, with Ivory Handles, for drawing Teeth, also Temple Spectacles, with double and single Joints.

Recreated from The Virginia Gazette, March 2, 1776.

REGULARS ARE EMBARKING.

WATERTOWN, *March* 11.

After Monday night there was a cessation of firing on both sides till last Saturday evening, when the bombardment and cannonading was greater than heretofore. Through the imprudence of five of our people who went on Dorchester Neck, near Boston, and made a fire, four of them were killed, among which we hear was Dr. Dole, of Cocksett, the names of the three others we have not heard; this is all the loss we have sustained. We have not heard what loss they have met with in Boston, but we heartily sympathise for our distressed friends there.

It is reported the regulars are embarking. Our friends on the continent, we hope, will be on their guard.

BRITISH EVACUATING BOSTON.

CAMBRIDGE, *March* 14.

The common topic of conversation, since last Friday, has been, the evacuation of the town of Boston by King George's plundering, murdering army, under General Howe. On that day a paper was brought out by a flag of truce, to which was affixed the names of sundry inhabitants, among which were those of some of the late Selectmen; advising that they were permitted by General Howe, on behalf of the town, to notify our army that if the firing into the place was discontinued, the British troops would leave the same in three or four days, without destroying it. Though the enemy might really be preparing to leave the town, this paper was thought worthy of little attention, as being nothing more than a mere finesse, to induce a relaxation in our proceeding. Sundry persons, since the above paper came out, have escaped from the town, and inform, that the enemy are very busy in moving their effects on board the transports; and that there is great appearance of their going off very speedily. And yesterday it was reported, that they were plundering the town, breaking and destroying everything they cannot carry away.

Recreated from The Hartford Courant, March 18, 1776

PEACE IN HIS POCKET?

NEW YORK, *March* 13.—On Sunday last the Swallow packet, capt. Copeland, arrived at Sandy Hook with the mail, in nine weeks from Falmouth. The letters not being come on shore, we can only favour the publick with the following accounts from several gentlemen that came passengers, viz.

That the Restraining Bill (whereby all American property, wherever found, would be confiscated) had passed both Houses, and had come in this vessel to the respective governors.

That the French ambassador had informed the ministry, that, although his master had only been a spectator of the differences with the colonies, yet, if Great Britain took foreign troops into pay, they might be assured his master would take an active part in the matter.

General Burgoyne, on his arrival at Portsmouth, reported, that he had brought peace in his pocket from the Americans, which is supposed to be the letters passed between him and our general while in Boston. The people of England are very desirous of peace, and the minority increasing very fast.

The brave col. Allen, with about 30 others, who was unfortunately taken prisoner by general Carleton, were confined in Pendenness castle; but were ordered onboard to work their passage, and do duty on board the fleet that sailed about the time this packet did, with seven regiments from Cork for Virginia, under the command of general Cornwallis, and escorted by 12 frigates.

By the Restraining Act, all vessels belonging to America, whether taken at sea, in harbours, or at docks, are to be made prizes, and all the men taken in them entered on the ship's books, as volunteers, and their desertion punished accordingly.

TWENTY fine SLAVES for sale at Hanover courthouse, the first Thursday in April, for ready money.

Recreated from Purdie's Virginia Gazette, March 29, 1776.

IN CONGRESS.

March 14, 1776.

RESOLVED, that it be recommended to the several Assemblies, Conventions, and Councils or Committees of Safety of the United Colonies, immediately to cause all persons to be disarmed within their respective colonies who are notoriously disaffected to the cause of America, or who have not associated, and refuse to associate, to defend, by arms, these United Colonies against the hostile attempts of the British fleets and armies, and to apply the arms taken from such persons in each respective colony, in the first place, to the arming the continental troops raised in said colony; in the next, to the arming such troops as are raised by the colony for its own defence, and the residue to be applied to the arming the associators: That the arms, when taken, be appraised by indifferent person, and such as are applied to the arming continental troops to be paid by the Congress; and the residue by the respective Assemblies, Conventions, or Councils or Committees of Safety.

Extract from the minutes,
CHARLES THOMPSON, Secretary.

Recreated from Purdie's Virginia Gazette, April 12, 1776.

PHILADELPHIA.

March 12. Last Saturday evening baron de Woedlke, formerly a general in the Polish service, arrived here.

March 16. A sea captain arrived in one of the last vessels from Martinico, says that the French in that island speak highly in favour of the colonies; and several principal persons informed him, that they only wanted for us to declare independency to attack the English islands with their whole force, which is much greater than has ever yet been reported here.

ESSEX county, March 26, 1776. WE intend to leave the colony immediately. *John Shedden, Robert Paul, Thomas Hannay,* and *James Patoun.*

Recreated from Purdie's Virginia Gazette, March 29, 1776.

In CONGRESS.

Saturday, *March* 16, 1776.

IN times of impending calamity and distress, when the liberties of America are imminently endangered, by the secret machinations and open assaults of an insidious and vindictive administration, it becomes the indispensable duty of these hitherto free and happy colonies, with true penitence of heart, and the most reverent devotion, publickly to acknowledge the over-ruling providence of GOD, to confess and deplore our offences against him, and to supplicate his interposition for averting the threatened danger, and prospering our strenuous efforts in the cause of FREEDOM, VIRTUE, and POSTERITY.

The Congress THEREFORE, considering the warlike preparations of the British ministry to subvert our invaluable rights and privileges, and to reduce us, by fire and sword, by the savages of the wilderness, and our own domesticks, to the most abject and ignominious bondage; desirous, at the same time, to have people of all ranks and degrees duly impressed with a solemn sense of GOD's superintending providence, and of their duty devoutly to rely in all their lawful enterprises on his aid and direction, do earnestly recommend that Friday the 17th day of May next be observed, by the said colonies, as a day of HUMILIATION, FASTING, and PRAYER, that we may, with united hearts, confess and bewail our manifold sins and transgressions, and by a sincere repentance, and amendment of life, appease his righteous displeasure, and, through the merits and mediation of JESUS CHRIST, obtain his pardon and forgiveness: Humbly imploring his assistance to frustrate the cruel purposes of our unnatural enemies, and, by inclining their hearts to justice and benevolence, prevent farther effusion of kindred blood; but if, continuing deaf to the voice of reason and humanity, and inflexibly bent on desolation and war, they constrain us to repel their hostile invasions by open resistance, that it may please the *Lord of Hosts, the God of Armies*, to animate our officers and soldiers with invincible fortitude, to guard and protect them in the day of battle, and to crown the continental arms by sea and land with victory and success: Earnestly beseeching him to bless our civil rulers, and the representatives of the people in their several Assemblies and Conventions, to preserve and strengthen their union, to inspire them with an ardent disinterested love of their country, to give wisdom and stability to their councils, and direct them to the most efficacious measures for establishing the rights of America on the most honourable and permanent basis: That he would be graciously pleased to bless all the people in these colonies with health and plenty, and grant that a spirit of incorruptible patriotism, and of pure undefiled religion, may universally prevail; and this continent be speedily restored to the blessings of PEACE and LIBERTY, and enabled to transmit them inviolate to the latest posterity. And it is recommended to Christians of all denominations to assemble for publick worship, and abstain from servile labour on that day.

By order of Congress,
JOHN HANCOCK.

FOUND near *Williamsburg*, by a negro fellow, a RIFLE GUN stamped on the top of the barrel CRW in a triangle, the spring of the box out, and is rifled with twelve rifles. The owner may have her by applying to capt. *Dickinson*, and paying the expense of advertising.

Essex county, March 26, 1776.

WE intend to leave the colony immediately. *John Shedden. Robert Paul. Thomas Hannay. James Patoun.*

Recreated from Purdie's Virginia Gazette, April 5, 1776.

HOWE'S FRUITLESS FEINT.

NEW YORK, *March* 20.

BY an express arrived last night from Cambridge, which place he left the 14th instant, we learn that General Howe intended a feint of embarkation, in order to draw off our troops from Dorchester point, who intended to attack his lines, which at the same time were doubly manned. The bait did not take, General Washington having secured the heights with 7000 men; and a reserve of 5000 were ready at Roxbury to sustain them, in case of need. Our army was soon increased to the amount of 30,000 men; every thing conspired to render General Howe's designs fruitless, and he has at length been obliged to turn his feint into a real embarkation. He can no longer stay here, as he is enfiladed on every side.

The admiral's ship, and a number of transports, had left the harbour, and were in Nantasket road; the rest of the army embarking as fast as possible, and there is no doubt but their destination is New York.

General Washington has already detached six regiments for this place, who are already advanced 100 miles towards it; 2000 men from Connecticut are coming, 13 other regiments will soon be here, so that we shall in a few days have an army of at least 20,000 men to oppose our enemies, and we have a train of 200 pieces of canon ready to salute them.

Extract of a letter from NEW YORK, *March 16.*

"Yesterday several cannon were sent across the river to the fortification at Brooklyn ferry, and one third of the citizens were ordered out to erect new works. They began a fort upon mr. Bayard's mount, near the Bowery, and another all round the hospital. To-day another one third is gone out. Every street in the city is to be barricaded."

Extract of a letter from NEW YORK, *March 18.*

"No news, only 5000 regulars embarked at Boston on the 10th instant; have no account of their sailing."

I GIVE YOU JOY!

Extract of a letter from CAMBRIDGE, *March* 18.

"I give you joy of Boston's being evacuated. Saturday night our people began firing upon the hill next the point; about midnight the regulars began firing upon them, and continued it until morning, but did not hurt any one. After that the ministerialists hurried on board as fast as they could. They did not set fire to the town, but they have done much mischief, and though the soldiers were not authorised to plunder, they were not hindered from doing it. Many of the officers have been as bad as the privates, and carried off the furniture from the houses of those gentlemen who had left the same, and accommodated them therewith. The British troops are disgraced. This change in our affairs has been produced by the movements on Dorchester Neck. Almost all the tories are gone off, and are in a dreadful situation; should it be long before they can be put to sea, they will be half-starved."

• • • •

We hear the humane General Howe has burnt the pretty little town of Nantasket, in Boston harbour, and that many of the Tories, not being able to get off with the fleet, have thrown themselves on the mercy of their countrymen.

Part of a Letter from a Gentleman in St. Mary's County, *to a Friend in* BALTIMORE, *March 14.*

"We have just taken an oyster boat, with six men on board, and on search, found five British muskets concealed in the boat; the men have been strictly examined, and it appears they came from Virginia, and were bound to Baltimore, and had oysters on board to further their intended purpose, being employed by that infamous tool of Government, Lord Dunmore, as spies, to collect information from and enquire into the situation of your town, and take a view of your fortifications, &c.—They are all properly confined—It is hoped you will keep a good look out, and carefully examine all suspected vessels and men."

Recreated from The Pennsylvania Gazette, March 27, 1776.

BURGOYNE SAILING TO QUEBEC.

BRITAIN'S DESIGN.

We learn by the extracts from the St. James's Chronicle, of the 19th of March, inserted in the Halifax gazette, that Gen. Burgoyne was to sail for Quebec with 10,000 troops, and retake it if in the hands of the rebels, and then proceed to Montreal, St. John's, &c. That Gen. Gage, and Lord Howe, with 7000 troops, were to join General Howe at Boston, at which place it is supposed there is 8000. Gage to remain as Governor of Massachusetts, while the Generals Howe are to attack and beat the rebels from their posts; they are then to secure their embarkation and proceed to New York, land there, and occupy Hudson's river, and proceed up and join General Burgoyne from Quebec, and establish a chain of forts round New England. Also that one hundred sail of frigates and sloops of war are to line our coast (it is said three deep) to cut off all communication between the colonies. That the above troops are to be Hessians, who enter into pay before they march, and Hanoverians and British; the foreign States are subsidized for two years after the troops shall be returned to their own land again, if ever that should be.

FOUND, by a Negro Servant of the Subscriber's, at Bland's Ordinary, in Prince George, a TWO POUND BILL. Whoever claims it within three Months from the Date hereof, and properly describes the Bill, shall have it delivered on paying the Charge of this Advertisement, otherwise I shall deliver 35s. to the Negro who found it. (June 6, 1776.) (s) THOMAS FENNER.

TO BE SOLD, for ready Money, at Amelia Courthouse, on Thursday the 27th Instant (June) being Court Day, a Parcel of Ivory handled Swords, elegantly mounted with Silver, also a Number of the best Kind of Rifles, with Bullet Moulds, &c. by
(1f) BENJAMIN WARD.

FOUR very stout good MULES to be sold, or exchanged for able Plough Horses or Mares that will suit the Mountain Lands. Inquire of Mr. William Ruffell, Williamsburg.

Recreated from The Virginia Gazette, June 8, 1776.

In CONGRESS.

March 20, 1776.

WHEREAS, in the execution of the resolve of Congress of the fourteenth of March respecting the disarming disaffected persons, many fire arms may be taken which may not be fit for use, to arm any of the troops mentioned therein, therefore *Resolved*, That all the fire arms so taken, be appraised according to said resolve, none of them shall be paid for but those that are fit for the use of such troops, or that may conveniently be so made, and the remainder shall be safely kept by the Assemblies, Conventions, Councils or Committees of Safety for the owners, to be delivered to them when the Congress shall direct.

March 21, 1776.

Resolved. That it be recommended to the several Assemblies, Conventions and Councils, or Committees of Safety, and Committees of Correspondence and Inspection, that they exert their utmost endeavours to promote the culture of HEMP, FLAX and COTTON, and the growth of WOOL, in these United Colonies.

Resolved. That it be recommended to the said Assemblies, Conventions and Councils, or Committees of Safety, that they take the earliest measures for erecting and establishing, in each and every colony, a Society for the improvement of agriculture, arts, manufactures and commerce; and to maintain a correspondence between such Societies, that the rich and numerous natural advantages of this country, for supporting its inhabitants, may not be neglected.

Resolved. That it be recommended to the said Assemblies, Conventions and Councils, or Committees of safety, that they forthwith consider ways and means of introducing the manufacture of DUCK and SAIL CLOTH, and STEEL, into such colonies where they are not now understood; and of encouraging, increasing and improving them where they are.

Extracts from the minutes,
CHARLES THOMPSON, Secretary.

Recreated from The Pennsylvania Gazette, March 27, 1776.

WASHINGTON TO LORD STIRLING.

MOST ACTIVE EXERTIONS.

An express arrived from BOSTON, *which place he left on the* 19*th instant, with a letter from his* Excellency General **WASHINGTON** *to* Brigadier General **LORD STIRLING**, *at* NEW YORK, *of which the following is a copy.*

CAMBRIDGE, 19th *March*, 1776.

MY LORD,

I AM now to acknowledge the receipt of your favour of the 11th instant, to give you my congratulations upon your appointment by the Honourable Congress. If the intelligence is true, and to be depended on, which was brought by the Gentleman to New York, I think with you, that we shall have an opportunity of securing, and putting the continent in a tolerable posture of defence; and that the operations of the summer's campaign, will not be so terrible as we were taught to expect from the accounts and denunciations which the ministry have held forth to the public.

I have the pleasure to inform you, that on the morning of the 17th instant, General Howe, with his army, abandoned the town of Boston without destroying it; an event of much importance, which must be heard with great satisfaction; and that we are now in full possession. Their embarkation and retreat were hurried and precipitate, and they have left behind them stores, of one thing and another, to a pretty considerable amount, among which are several pieces of heavy cannon, and one or two mortars, which are spiked. The town is in a much better situation, and less injured than I expected, from the reports I have received; though to be sure, it is much damaged, and many houses despoiled of their valuable Furniture.

The fleet is still in King and Nantasket roads, and, where they intend to make a descent next is altogether unknown; but, supposing New York to be an object of great importance, and to be in their view, I must recommend your most strenuous and active exertions in preparing, to prevent any designs or attempts they may have formed or make against it. I have detached the rifle-men, and five battalions from hence to your assistance, which will be followed by others as circumstances allow.—These, with what forces you have, and can assemble, if there should be any occasion, I trust, will be sufficient to hinder the enemy from possessing the city, or making a lodgement, till the main body of this army can arrive.

I am, my Lord, with great esteem,
Your most obedient and humble Servant,
G. WASHINGTON.

The courier, who was himself in Boston, reports, we hear, that the enemy left about *forty* horses almost starved, and that before they went off, they dismasted all the vessels in the harbour. General Putnam was arrived at New Haven, on his way to New York.

20 BRITISH SAIL OFF MONTOCK.

By an EXPRESS *just arrived, we have the following intelligence.*

EAST HAMPTON, *March* 22. This day about ten o'clock in the forenoon, our guard stationed at Montock saw 20 sail of square rigged vessels, five of them appeared to be large, and two sloops, bearing about S.S.E. from the point of Montock, about 9 or 10 miles to sea, the wind S.S.E. the weather forming thick and hazy, steering about N.E. by N. and sailed to the east end of Long Island, and supposed by the course they steered, they were going into Rhode Island; this is all the information we can give you concerning them, as about one o'clock they disappeared behind Block Island, and they saw them no more.

WHEREAS *AGNES DODS*, wife of the subscriber, hath eloped from him; these are to forewarn all persons from trusting her on his account, as he will pay no debts of her contracting after this 3d day of February, 1776.
¶ *JOHN DODS.*

Recreated from The Pennsylvania Gazette, March 27, 1776.

GENERAL WASHINGTON'S ORDERS.

By his Excellency GEORGE WASHINGTON, General and Commander in Chief of the Forces of the United Colonies.

WHEREAS the Ministerial Army have abandoned the town of Boston; and the forces of the United Colonies, under my Command, are in possession of the same:

I HAVE heretofore thought it necessary for the Preservation of Peace, good Order and Discipline, to publish the following ORDERS, That no Person offending therein may plead ignorance as an Excuse of their Misconduct.

All Officers and Soldiers are hereby ordered to live in the strictest Peace and Amity with the Inhabitants; and no Inhabitant, or Person employed in his lawful Business in the Town, is to be molested in his person or property on any Pretence whatsoever. If any Officer or Soldier shall presume to strike, imprison, or otherwise ill treat any of the Inhabitants, they may depend on being punished with the utmost severity. And if any Officer or Soldier shall receive any insult from any of the Inhabitants, he is to seek redress in a legal way and no other.

Any Non-commissioned Officer, Soldier, or others under my command, who shall be guilty of robbing or plundering in the Town, are to be immediately confined, and will be most vigorously punished. All Officers are therefore ordered to be very vigilant in the Discovery of such Offenders, and report their Names and Crimes to the Commanding Officer in the Town, as soon as may be.

The Inhabitants, and others, are called upon to make known to the Quarter-Master General, or any of his Deputies, all Stores belonging to the Ministerial Army, that may be remaining or secreted in the Town: Any Person or Persons whatever, who shall be known to conceal any of the said Stores, or appropriate them to their own Use, will be considered an Enemy of America, and treated accordingly.

The Selectmen, and other Magistrates of the Town, are desired to return to the Commander in Chief, the Names of all or any Person or Persons they may suspect of being employed as Spies upon the Continental Army, that they may be dealt with accordingly.

All Officers of the Continental Army, are enjoined to assist the Civil Magistrates in the Execution of their Duty, and to promote Peace and good Order. They are to prevent as much as possible, the Soldiers from frequenting Tippling Houses, and strolling from their posts. Particular Notice will be taken of Officers as are inattentive and remote in their Duty; and on the contrary, such only who are active and vigilant, will be entitled to future Favour and Promotion.

Given under my Hand at Head Quarters *in* CAMBRIDGE, *this* 21st *Day of March*, 1776.
GEORGE WASHINGTON.

Recreated from The Hartford Courant, April 8, 1776

ROUSE YOUR RESENTMENT.

NEWBERN, *March* 22, 1776.

THE Committee of Safety for this district have ordered col. Caswell, commanding officer of the Newbern battalion of the minute men to march immediately to Brunswick, to join the other forces of this province in opposing general Clinton, who is arrived there with considerable force. The committee have also ordered 750 of the militia of the several counties in this district to march under col. Caswell, and we expect in 12 or 15 days to have 15,000 men embodied against governor Martin's cut-throat army; for by a deposition of a master of a vessel who lately fell into the hands of capt. Collett, *that little atrocious villain*, he told him general Clinton's army was to spare neither age nor sex, except a few young ladies, who were to be saved for their private pleasures.

Americans, *rouse, rouse your resentment* against the savage brutes, and let your indignation fall with tenfold vengeance on the heads of these murderers, the pious troops of George III, *the father of his people.*

Recreated from Purdie's Virginia Gazette, April 12, 1776.

BRITISH QUIT IN DISGRACE.

CAMBRIDGE, *March* 21.

Last Sabbath the British army in Boston, under Gen. Howe, consisting of upwards of 7000 men, after suffering an ignominious blockade for many months past, disgracefully quitted all their strong holds in Boston and Charlestown, and fled before the army of the United Colonies, and took refuge aboard their ships.

The most material particulars of this signal event are as follow: About 9 o'clock a body of the enemy were seen to march from Bunker's Hill, and at the same time a very great number of boats, filled with troops, put off from Boston, and made for the shipping, which mostly lay before the Castle.

On the first discovery of these movements, the Continental Army immediately paraded, several regiments embarked in boats, and proceeded down the river from this place. About the same time two men were sent to Bunker's Hill, in order to make discoveries. They proceeded accordingly, and when arrived, making a signal that the fort was evacuated, a detachment was immediately sent down from the army to take possession of it.

The troops in the river, which were commanded by General Putnam, landed at Sewell's Point; where they received intelligence that all the British troops had left Boston; on which a detachment was sent to take possession of the town, while the main body returned up the river. About the same time General Ward, attended by about 500 troops from Roxbury, under the command of Col. Ebenezer Learned, who unbarred and opened the gates, entered the town on that quarter, Ensign Richards carrying the standard.

The command of the whole thing then being given to General Putnam, he proceeded to take possession of all the important posts, and thereby became possessed, in the name of the Thirteen United Colonies of North America, of all the fortresses in that large and flourishing metropolis, which the flower of the British army, headed by an experienced general, and supported by a formidable fleet of men of war, had, but an hour before, evacuated in the most precipitate and cowardly manner. God grant that the late worthy inhabitants, now scattered abroad, may speedily reoccupy their respective dwellings, and never more be disturbed by the cruel hand of tyranny; and may the air of that Capital be never again contaminated by the stinking breath of Toryism.

The joy of our friends in Boston, on seeing the victorious and gallant troops of their country enter the town almost at the heels of their barbarous oppressors, was inexpressibly great. The mutual congratulations and tender embraces, which soon after took place between those of the nearest connections in life, for a long time cruelly rent assunder by the tyranny of our implacable enemies, surpasses description. From such a set of beings the preservation of property was not expected. And it was found that a great part of the evacuated houses had been pillaged, the furniture broke and destroyed, and many of the buildings greatly damaged.

It is worthy of notice, however, that the buildings belonging to Mr. Hancock, particularly his elegant mansion house, were left in good order. All the linen and woolen goods, except some that might be secreted, were carried off by the enemy. All the salt and molasses, which they could find, were destroyed. The enemy also destroyed great quantities of effects belonging to themselves, which they could not carry away, such as gun carriages, and other carriages of various kinds, house furniture, &c. together with a quantity of flour and hay.

All their forts, batteries, redoubts and breast works, remain entire and complete; they left many of their heaviest cannon, mounted on carriages, and several of them charged; all of them were either spiked or had a trunnion beat off. They also left several of their largest mortars. Quantities of cannon shot, shells, numbers of small arms, and other instruments of war, have been found in many parts of the town, thrown off the wharffs, concealed in vaults, or broken in pieces.

THE TORIES ARE UNDONE.

In the fort on Bunker's Hill several hundred good blankets were found. It is said, about 15 or 20 of the King's horses have been also taken up in town; and it is thought about the same number of Tories remain behind, all the rest being gone with the fleet.

We are told that the Tories were thunderstruck when orders were issued for evacuating the town, after being many hundred times assured, that such reinforcements would be sent, as to enable the King's troops to ravage the country at pleasure. Thus are many of those deluded creatures, those vile traitors to their country, obliged at last, in their turn, to abandon their once delightful habitations, and go they know not where. Many of them, it is said, considered themselves as undone, and seemed, at times, inclined to throw themselves on the mercy of their offended country, rather than leave it. One or more of them, it is reported, have been left to end their lives by the unnatural act of suicide.

SOME INHABITANTS UNAWARE.

The enemy, previous to their going off, scattered great numbers of crows feet on Boston Neck, and in the streets, in order to retard our troops in case of pursuit; and with such silence and precaution did they embark, that a great part of the inhabitants did not know it till after they were gone. The prisoners, who were long confined in gaol, were cruelly carried off in irons.

To the wisdom, firmness, intrepidity and military abilities of our amiable and beloved General, his Excellency George Washington, Esq., to the assiduity, skill and bravery of the other worthy Generals and Officers of the army; and to the hardiness and gallantry of the Soldiery, is to be ascribed, under God, the glory and success of our arms, in driving from one of the strongest holds in America, so considerable a part of the British army as that which last week occupied the capital of this province.

The enemy's fleet, consisting of about 100 sail, still lie between the Castle and Nantasket.

Recreated from The Pennsylvania Gazette, April 3, 1776.

ABSOLUTE UNCONDITIONAL SUBMISSION.

Extract of a letter from BRISTOL, ENGLAND, *March* 22, 1776.

"The wind has been so long to the westward, that the fleet of transports have been retarded, some of them a full two months. The newspapers will give you all the information it is in my power farther to present, or furnish. The design of administration is declared to be, absolute, unconditional submission, on your part; and, to effect this, they are straining every nerve. It is the opinion of some of the most intelligent, that if you are successful in this campaign (and it is most devoutly to be wished) you may bid defiance to any future effort to subdue you. The expenses attending this merciless business are already enormous, and at the close of the year the national debt will be as great as at the close of the last war. Many manufacturers are loudly complaining, and the Coventry trade is in a state of stagnation.

"We have the news confirmed of the unfortunate defeat at Quebec. We hope, however, it may yet be subdued, before any succour can arrive from hence. The 29th regiment was sent, with Carleton's brother, some weeks ago; but it is still at Portsmouth, detained by contrary winds.

"It has been a matter of astonishment that the town of Boston has not been destroyed. We imagine it might have been burnt long since. It would have been a happy circumstance if the troops could have been dispossessed of it. They would have then had no place of security. The burning of Norfolk has made serious impressions, and the like fate to a few towns more will increase the number of those who have long lamented and exclaimed against such unexampled cruelty.

"Sir Peter Parker's squadron was entirely dispersed. Many are put back, some into French ports, and others into Lisbon; and as the wind is now likely to come about, they will again be collected together. Sir Peter, with lord Cornwallis, did not put back, so that they probably weathered the storm."

Recreated from Purdie's Virginia Gazette, June 21, 1776.

In Congress.

March 23, 1776.

WHEREAS the Petitions of these United Colonies to the King, for the Redress of great and manifest grievances, have not only been rejected, but treated with Scorn and Contempt; and the Opposition to Designs evidently formed to reduce them to a State of servile Subjection, and their necessary Defence against hostile Forces, actually employed to subdue them, declared Rebellion: And Whereas an unjust War hath been commenced against them, which the Commanders of the British Fleets and Armies have prosecuted, and still continue to prosecute, with their utmost Vigour, and in a cruel manner; wasting, spoiling and destroying the Country, burning Houses and defenceless Towns, and exposing the helpless Inhabitants to every Misery from the Inclemency of the Winter, and not only urging Savages to invade the Country, but instigating Negroes to murder their Masters: And Whereas the Parliament of Great Britain hath lately passed an Act, affirming these Colonies to be in open Rebellion; forbidding all Trade and Commerce with the Inhabitants thereof, until they shall accept Pardons and submit to despotic Rule, declaring their Property, wherever found upon the Water, liable to Seizure and Confiscation; and enacting that what had been done there, by Virtue of the Royal Authority, were just and lawful Acts and shall be so deemed: From which it is manifest, that the iniquitous Scheme, concerted to deprive them of the Liberty they have a right to by the Laws of Nature and the English Constitution, will be pertinaciously pursued. It being, therefore, necessary to provide for their Defence and Security, and justifiable to make Reprisals upon their Enemies and otherwise to annoy them, according to the Laws and Usages of Nations; the CONGRESS, trusting that such of their Friends in Great Britain (of whom it is confessed there are many intitled to Applause and Gratitude for their Patriotism and Benevolence, and in whose favour a discrimination of Property cannot be made) as shall suffer by Captures, will impute it to the Authors of our common Calamities, DO DECLARE AND RESOLVE as followeth, *to wit.*

• • • •

RESOLVED, That the Inhabitants of these Colonies be permitted to fit out armed Vessels to cruise on the Enemies of these United Colonies.

RESOLVED, That all Ships and other Vessels, their Tackle, Apparel and Furniture, and all Goods, Wares and Merchandizes, belonging to any Inhabitant or Inhabitants of Great Britain, taken on the high Seas, or between high and low water Mark, by any Armed Vessel, fitted out by any private Person or Persons to whom Commissions shall be granted, and being libelled and prosecuted in any Court erected for the Trial of Maritime Affairs in any of these Colonies, shall be deemed and adjudged to be lawful Prize, and after deducting and paying the Wages which the Seamen and Mariners on board of such captures as are Merchant Ships and Vessels shall be intitled to, according to the Terms of their Contracts, until the time of the Adjudication, shall be condemned to and for the Use of the Owner or Owners, and the Officers, Marines and Mariners of such Armed Vessel, according to such Rules and Proportions as they shall agree on. *Provided* always That this Resolution shall not extend, or be constructed to extend, to any Vessel bringing Settlers, Arms, Ammunition, or Warlike Stores to and for the Use of these Colonies, or any of the Inhabitants thereof who are Friends to the American Cause, or to such Warlike Stores, or to the Effects of such Settlers.

RESOLVED, That all Ships or Vessels with their Tackle, Apparel and Furniture, Goods, Wares and Merchandizes, belonging to any Inhabitant of Great Britain, as aforesaid, which shall be taken by any of the Vessels of War of these United Colonies, shall be deemed forfeited, one third after deducting and paying the Wages of Seamen and Mariners, as aforesaid, to the Officers and Men on board, and two thirds to the use of the United Colonies.

RESOLVED, That all Ships or Vessels with their Tackle, Apparel and Furniture, Goods, Wares and Merchandizes, belonging to any Inhabitants of Great Britain as aforesaid, which shall be taken by any Vessel of War fitted out at the Expense of any of the United Colonies, shall be deemed forfeited, and divided, after deducting and paying the Wages of Seamen and Mariners as aforesaid, in such manner and Proportions as the Assembly or Convention of such Colony shall direct.

RESOLVED, That all Vessels, their Tackle, Apparel and Furniture, and Cargoes belonging to Inhabitants of Great Britain, as aforesaid, and all Vessels which may be employed in carrying Supplies to the Ministerial Armies, which happen to be taken near the Shores of any of these Colonies, by the People of the Country or Detachments from the Army, shall be deemed lawful Prize, and the Court of Admiralty within the said Colony is required, on Condemnation thereof, to adjudge that all Charges and Expences which may attend the Capture and Trial be first paid out of the Monies arising from the Sales of the Prize, and the Remainder equally among all those who shall have been actually engaged and employed in taking the said Prize. *Provided*, That where any Detachments of the Army shall have been employed as aforesaid, their Part of the Prize Money shall be distributed among them in Proportion to the Pay of the Officers and Soldiers so employed.

Extract from the Minutes,
CHARLES THOMPSON, SECRETARY.

DAVID REID, GARDENER and SEEDMAN, from London, living in Spring-Garden.
WILL supply any Gentleman or other person with any quantity of Garden Seed, which he will warrant to be of good quality: They may be had at his stall at the Court-house every day of the week (sundays excepted) or at the Widow Lawrence's in Second-street, near the Market, Philadelphia.

Recreated from The Pennsylvania Packet, April 1, 1776.

BRITISH FLEET NOT FIT FOR SEA.

CAMBRIDGE, March 25.

BY a letter, of the best Authority, from Cambridge, dated March 25, 1776, we are informed, that the Ministerial troops have blown up, burnt and demolished the Castle totally; that they have been in Nantasket Road ever since their embarkation, their stay there is judged necessary to prepare for sailing, as neither the vessels themselves, nor, as loaded, were fit for sea, being loaded in great haste and disorder; this account is confirmed by a deserter, who says they have yards, booms, bowsprits, &c. to fix. Some conjecture they mean to give the Provincial troops a parting blow, as their whole force is now collected, 15 vessels having arrived with troops from the West Indies since their flight from Boston.

Six regiments of the Continental troops have marched to New York; ten regiments of the militia were to be discharged the first of April. As soon as the fleet had sailed from Nantasket General Washington proposed setting out for New York. The Provincial troops are now fortifying Fort Hill, and demolishing the lines on Roxbury Neck, which are a defence against the country only.

Recreated from Purdie's Virginia Gazette, April 3, 1776.

TROOPS ARRIVING FAST IN CANADA.

Extract of a letter from the camp before QUEBECK, *dated March* 28, 1776.

"We have great hopes of taking the town soon, the troops arriving so fast, and two batteries being almost ready to play upon the town; and they begin to be in want of provisions, their allowance being only four ounces a day, and they only receive two.

"There have been orders sent to the country to raise the inhabitants of the parishes below and, having forged a number of lies, they have been able to raise about 250 men, but they have already been beat by our troops, and the principals of their officers taken."

Recreated from Purdie's Virginia Gazette, May 24, 1776.

CARLETON SHOOTS HIS OWN MEN.

New York, *March* 28.—By the Albany post we are informed that letters had just come to hand in Albany, informing that governor Carleton, one morning, had shot 17 of his men, for refusing to fight; that the few forces under his command, as well as the people in general in Quebeck, were much divided; that our forces amounted to 5700 men, and many on their march, which, when joined, would augment our army to upwards of 6000, and that our troops were to storm the city the 20th of March.

Recreated from Purdie's Virginia Gazette, April 12, 1776.

FLEET BOUND TO HALIFAX.

Cambridge, *March* 28.—Near or quite all the enemy's fleet lay below the Castle till Tuesday last, when a considerable part of them (said to be about one half) put to sea. Near all the remainder sailed yesterday afternoon.

The general opinion is, that the enemy's fleet and army, lately fled from Boston, are bound to Halifax.

Recreated from The Pennsylvania Packet, April 8, 1776.

LEE & CLINTON IN THE SOUTH.

March 29. There is a report that general Clinton is arrived at Cape Fear, North Carolina, with troops brought with him from Boston, and that he has since been joined by 12 or 1500 from England or the West Indies. We likewise hear that the provincial troops are in motion, and marching from all quarters to attack him; so that we may soon expect to hear of another battle in that province, which we hope will prove equally glorious to the American arms as that which was, but a few weeks ago, so successfully fought by the brave col. Caswell.

This day his excellency Charles Lee, major-general in the continental army, arrived at head-quarters in Williamsburg, to take command of the Virginia troops, attended by Otway Bird and Lewis Morris, esqrs., his secretary, Mr. Nourse, and mons. Le Braun, engineer.

Recreated from Purdie's Virginia Gazette, March 29, 1776.

NEW GOVERNMENT. NO INDEPENDENCY.

Extract of a letter from Charlestown, South Carolina, *March* 30, 1776.

"We have adopted a new form of government in this colony. A President, Vice-President, Privy Council, Upper and Lower House of Assembly, Chief Justice, Judges, Attorney General, Judge of the Admiralty, Secretary, Sheriffs, Register, &c. are all appointed. John Rutledge is President, Henry Laurens Vice-President, W.H. Drayton Chief Justice, &c. Thursday was the day of inauguration, when there was a grand procession from the State House to the Exchange, where the President and Vice-President's commissions were read and approved of by the acclamations of hundreds, firing of cannon, &c. The new constitution is said only to be a temporary expedient. This form is much approved of, as matters are expected to go on nearly in the old channel; but I do not think *independency* will ever go down here."

Recreated from The Virginia Gazette, May 11, 1776.

NOVA SCOTIA WON'T FIGHT.

Providence, *March* 30.—By several gentlemen lately arrived from Checonecto, in the province of Nova Scotia, we have undoubted intelligence that the government had endeavoured to enlist part of the inhabitants to act against their American brethren, which they nobly refused; in consequence whereof the governor had ordered the militia to be called together, and a number to be draughted, when the officers were told by the men, that if they attempted to draught they would fire upon them; this stopped their proceeding any farther, and the men clubbed their muskets and marched home.

AMERICAN FLEET BUILDING.

Watertown, *April* 1.—The man of war building at Portsmouth for the Continental service, will, it is said, be ready to launch in about a month.

Recreated from The Pennsylvania Gazette, April 10, 1776.

PREPARE TO MEET THE STORM.

Extract of a letter from PHILADELPHIA, *April* 2.

"From the French islands we learn, that they have been hitherto prevented from getting supplies for us from Old France by British assurances that the quarrel was quickly to be made up; but, now that this is discovered to be all finesse, they say we may rely on speedy and large supplies from them. The King's friends (as they are called) in parliament, have declared, that the plan is to subdue America before they even offer pardons, and then it is to be with such exceptions as they choose. We learn that a pretty strong attack is intended to be made in Virginia this spring. It behooves you, therefore, to be prepared to meet the storm, with firmness and effect."

The Hon. the Congress have ordered reprisals to be made upon the vessels and cargoes of all inhabitants of Great Britain, and permit the fitting out of armed vessels to cruise on the enemies of the United Colonies.

Recreated from Purdie's Virginia Gazette, April 12, 1776.

NEW YORK, *April* 3.

By letters from Montreal, we are informed that the troops were coming in very fast, and filing off for Quebeck in great spirits, not doubting of being able shortly to reduce that place; as, by deserters daily coming out, their situation is known to be very bad, on account of fuel, &c. so that they are burning the lower part of the town, in order to save the upper. And that many of the inhabitants are compelled, much against their will, to take up arms, and wish to be relieved.

Recreated from Purdie's Virginia Gazette, April 19, 1776.

Extract of a Letter from NEW YORK, *April* 1.

"Out of 106 Cannon, found at the Castle at Boston, only five 32 pounders, two 24 pounders, and one 12 pounder can be made serviceable. One 24 pounder was turned on a Man of War, and our People were getting ready to fire; she saw it, and fell Half a Mile lower down."

Recreated from Purdie's Virginia Gazette, April 3, 1776.

LECTURE IN COUNCIL CHAMBER.
SUP AT BUNCH OF GRAPES.

CAMBRIDGE, *April* 4.—Thursday last the Lecture, which was established, and has been observed from the first settlement of Boston, without interruption, until these few months past, was opened by the Rev. Dr. Elliot. His Excellency General Washington, the other General Officers and their suites, having been previously invited, met in the Council Chamber, from whence, preceded by the Sheriff with his Ward, attended by Members of the Council who had had the Small Pox, the Committee of the House of Representatives, the Select Men, the Clergy, and many other Gentlemen, they repaired to the Old Brick Meeting House, where an excellent and well adapted Discourse was delivered from the 33. chap. Isaiah, 20 verse.

After Divine Service was ended, his Excellency attended and accompanied as before, returned to the Council Chamber from whence they proceeded to the Bunch of Grapes Tavern, where an excellent Dinner was provided at the Public Expense; after which many very proper and pertinent Toasts were drank.

Joy and gratitude sat, on every countenance, and smiled in every eye. The whole was conducted and concluded to the satisfaction of all.

DR. FRANKLIN TO QUEBEC.

NEW YORK, *April* 4.—On Saturday last arrived here from Cambridge, the Hon. Brigadier-General Heath, with about 3000 of the continental troops under his command.

Yesterday Brigadier-General Baron De Woedlke, and the Hon. Benjamin Franklin, set off from this place for Albany, on their way to Quebeck.

Last Tuesday afternoon five battalions of the continental troops were reviewed by his Excellency General Heath, on the Green, near the Liberty Pole; they made a very martial appearance, being excellently well armed, and all of them hearty young men. They went thro' their exercise with surprising activity.

Recreated from The Hartford Courant, April 8, 1776

GEN. WOOSTER ARRIVES AT QUEBEC.

Extract of a letter from MONTREAL, *April 6.*

"A number of Canadians, at the instigation of the priests, rose with a design to cut off our guards at Point Levi. A party under major Dubois attacked their advanced guard, killed seven, wounded five, and took about fifty prisoners, 25 of which arrived here last evening.

"Gen. Wooster arrived before Quebeck on Monday last. The battery opened at Point Levi on Tuesday morning. One of capt. Lamb's company made his escape from Quebeck, and informs, that the soldiers and prisoners are at an allowance of three ounces of pork per day.

"A Canadian, who brought letters from Carleton to the inhabitants, is made prisoner, and says that the inhabitants, as well as soldiers, have risen in a body and gone to Carleton, and that he promised, if he did not get assistance in 14 days, to deliver up the town."

Recreated from Purdie's Virginia Gazette, May 24, 1776.

FLEET SAILS FOR AMERICA.

Extract of a letter from BRISTOL, *April 13.*

"This morning arrived here the Hibernia, Knethell, from Cork, who sailed from thence the 9th instant and informs, that the men of war, with upwards of forty sail of transports under their convoy, sailed the 8th from the Cove; and as the wind blew fresh at N.E. and continued so for many days, it is imagined they must be got quite clear. The Tartar, Capt. Russell, and the Friendly Trader, with several volunteers on board, sailed from this place for Cork and America."

April 11. A Council has lately been held at St. Janes's on a very extraordinary occasion; no less, it is said, than a representation of the Commander in Chief, and the rest of the General Officers in America, containing their reasons against the prosecution of the war, and demonstrating the impracticability of carrying it into execution with any prospect of success.

A new corps of Roman Catholics, and said to consist mostly of White Boys, have been raised in Ireland, and are called the Limerick volunteers.

Recreated from The Virginia Gazette, July 29, 1776.

CAPTAIN BARRY ENGAGES SLOOP.

Copy of a Letter from Captain John Barry, *in sight of the Capes of* VIRGINIA, *April 7, 1776.*

GENTLEMEN,

I HAVE the pleasure to acquaint you, that at 1 P.M. this day, I fell in with the sloop Edward, belonging to the Liverpool frigate. She engaged us near two glasses. They killed two of our men, and wounded two more. We shattered her in a terrible manner, as you will see. We killed and wounded several of her crew. I shall give you a particular account of the powder and arms taken out of her, as well as my proceedings in general. I have the happiness to acquaint you, that all of our people behaved with much courage.

I am, gentlemen, your humble servant,
JOHN BARRY.

Extract of a letter from CAMBRIDGE, *April 7.*

"Captains Manly and Waters have lately taken a brig, 15 leagues off Cape Anne eastward, richly loaded with English goods and other merchandise. On board were one Brush, formerly of New York, but lately a most bitter refugee in Boston, and William Jackson, the noted importer, who had of his own property in said brig to the value of £24,000 sterling. A sergeant and 12 soldiers were likewise in her. She made resistance, but being the least able to defend herself of any that went off with the fleet, she was obliged to yield, tho' in sight of two of the King's ships."

Recreated from The Pennsylvania Gazette, April 17, 1776.

HARTFORD, *April 8.*

The Report, for several Days past, that the City of Quebec had surrendered to General Arnold, wants Confirmation.

• • • •

A favourite toast, in the best companies, is, "May the INDEPENDENT principles of COMMON SENSE be confirmed throughout the United Colonies."

Recreated from The Hartford Courant, April 8, 1776

SAILORS POPPED OFF.

Extract of a letter from NEW YORK, *April 8.*

"Yesterday the Viper's boat went ashore on Staten Island to get water; a party of the riflemen who were posted there attacked her, and took all hands prisoners, some say 8, others 14. The man of war fired; the riflemen returned it. They were at it all day. The man of war was obliged to cut her cables and run. It is said she fell down with her sails furled; and when the men went up to loose them, the riflemen popped them off. Cannot get at particulars yet. Our people have since taken up the anchor and 80 fathom of cable."

MAN OF WAR AT NEWPORT.

Extract of a letter from Cambridge, per express.

"This instant an express arrived from Governor Cooke with an account that a man of war was just arrived in the harbour of Newport, and that 27 sail of vessels, supposed to be part of the fleet from Boston, are within Seconet Point. General Sullivan's brigade, which left Cambridge the 29th of March, was ordered to file off immediately for Providence, and General Greene's, which was to march the first of April, was ordered to repair immediately to the same place."

NEW YORK, *April 8.*

Wednesday night last arrived here, from the camp at Cambridge, Brigadier Gen. Putnam; and the evening before Col. Mifflin, Quarter-Master Gen. of the American army, arrived here from the same place.

A sloop of war, supposed to be the Nautilus, is arrived at the Narrows.

TO BE SOLD,
A SULKEY, with a Canvas Top.
Enquire of WILLIAM RUSH, at the Corner of Third and Race-streets, or BENJAMIN DAVIDS, at the George, in Arch-street. *April 8, 1776.* ¶

Recreated from The Pennsylvania Gazette, April 10, 1776.

WILLIAMSBURG, *April 13, 1776.*

IT being thought necessary for the publick Service to keep a Body of SHIP CARPENTERS in constant Employment, this is to give Notice, that TWO COMPANIES, consisting of one CAPTAIN and thirty MEN each, are to be raised. The Captain is to have ONE DOLLAR *per Diem*, the Men HALF a DOLLAR, their Provisions and Rum. They are to find their own Tools and Arms. Such as are willing to engage may repair to *Williamsburg,* or *Suffolk.*

AS GENERAL LEE *must in great measure regulate the motions of the continental troops under his command according to the internal force of the colony, the committees of the different counties are requested to send into head-quarters a return of their minute-men, with the state and condition of their arms.*

Williamsburg, *April 8, 1776.*

⁂ I have a set of SURGEONS CAPITAL INSTRUMENTS, which I would part with on very reasonable terms.

Recreated from Purdie's Virginia Gazette, April 19, 1776.

ADMIRAL HOPKINS'S REPORT.

Extract of a letter from ESECK HOPKINS, *Esq., Commander in Chief of the American Fleet, to the President of the Congress, dated on board the ship Alfred, New London Harbour, April 9.*

"When I put to sea, on the 17th February, from Cape Henlopen, not thinking we were in a condition to keep on a cold coast, I appointed our rendezvous at Abacco, one of the Bahama islands.

"I arrived at the rendezvous, in order to wait for them fifteen days, agreeable to orders. I then formed an expedition against New Providence, which I put in execution the third of March, by landing two hundred marines under the command of Lieut. Weaver, of the Cabot, who was well acquainted there.

"The same day they took possession of a small fort, of seventeen pieces of cannon, without any opposition, save five guns which were fired at them without doing any damage. I received, that evening, an account that they had two hundred and odd men in the main fort, all inhabitants.

"I then caused a manifesto to be published, the purport of which was, that the inhabitants and their property should be safe, if they did not oppose me in taking possession of the fort and King's stores. This had the desired effect, for the inhabitants left the fort almost alone. Captain Nicholas, by my order, sent to the Governor for the keys of the fort, which were delivered, and the troops marched directly in, where we found the several warlike stores agreeable to the inventory inclosed; but the Governor sent one hundred and fifty barrels off in a small sloop the night before. I have taken the Governor, Montford Brown, the Lieut. Governor, who is a half pay officer, and Mr. Thomas Arwin, who is a Counsellor and Collector of his Majesty's quit rents in South Carolina; and it appears, by the Court Calendar, that he is also Inspector General of his Majesty's Customs of North America. Since we came out, we have lost company with the Wasp.

"The 4th instant we fell in with the east end of Long Island, and took the schooner _____, commanded by young Wallace, of six carriage guns and eight swivels; and the 5th we took the bomb brig of eight guns and two howitzers, ten swivels and forty-eight hands, well found with all sorts of stores, arms, powder, &c. The sixth in the morning we fell in with the Glasgow, and her tender, and engaged her near three hours. We lost six men killed, and as many wounded. The Cabot had four men killed, and seven wounded, the Capt. is among the latter. The Columbus had one man who lost his arm. We received a considerable damage in our ship, but the greatest was in having our wheel ropes and blocks shot away, which gave the Glasgow time to make sail, and I did not think it proper to follow, as it would have brought on an action with the whole of their fleet, and I had upwards of thirty of our best seamen on board the prizes. I therefore thought it most prudent to give over the chase, and secure our prizes, and having taken the Glasgow's tender, arrived the 7th with all the fleet."

HEAD QUARTERS,
NEW YORK, *April 8, 1776.*

THE General informs the inhabitants, that it is become absolutely necessary that all communication between the ministerial fleet and shore should be stopped,—for that purpose he has given positive orders that the ships should no longer be furnished with provisions. Any inhabitant, or others, who shall be taken that have been on board (after the publishing of this order) or near any of the ships, or going on board, will be considered as enemies, and treated accordingly.

All boats are to sail from Beekman's Slip, Capt. James Alner is appointed Inspector, and will give permits for oystermen. It is expected and ordered that none attempt going without a pass.

ISRAEL PUTNAM,
Major-General in the Continental Army, Commander in Chief of the Forces in New York.

WHEREAS I the subscriber have endeavoured to persuade the good people in my neighbourhood to refuse signing the association drawn up by the Assembly, and oppose the payment of the fines laid on non-associators, from a mistaken opinion that it would be sufficient for them to form an independent company for the defence of our liberties, to discharge them from said fines, I do therefore hereby promise and engage for the future to support the said association as much as in my power, and do ask pardon for my former conduct, which I am convinced was greatly amiss, and tended to disturb the public union so necessary at this critical time. Witness my hand, April 4, 1776. JACOB RIETH.

Published by order of the Committee,
COLLINSON READ, Secretary.

Gloucester County, April 11, 1776.
In COMMITTEE of INSPECTION and OBSERVATION.
WHEREAS the Continental Congress did lately resolve, " That if any person shall be so lost to all virtue and regard for this country, as to refuse to receive the BILLS of CREDIT emitted by the authority of Congress, or should obstruct or discourage the currency thereof, and be convicted by the Committee of the city, county or district, where he should reside, such person should be deemed, published and treated as an enemy of this country, and be precluded from all trade or intercourse with the inhabitants of these colonies." And whereas LUCAS GIBBS, of the township of Deptford, in the county of Gloucester, blacksmith, being charged with a breach of this resolve, in refusing to receive the above Bills of Credit, and the said Lucas Gibbs appearing before the Committee of the county aforesaid, and being charged with said breach, acknowledged the same, and alledged, in his defence, scruples of conscience thereupon, as being money emitted for the purpose of carrying on war against government.

The Committee, pursuant to the trust reposed in them, proceeded to consider the charge and defence, were of opinion, that as such charge appears to be true, and there being no exception made by Congress, and as such conduct tends to subvert the most essential rights and liberties of their fellow-citizens and the freedom of America, and by destroying the means of defence, to expose their lives and properties to unavoidable ruin, it ought not to be admitted. And it appearing by his own acknowledgment, that he has heretofore received, and still continues to receive, Bills of Credit emitted in this and the neighbouring provinces, though frequently issued for the purpose of war, his objection being ill-founded, and the present pretence inconsistent with his former conduct.—This Committee do unanimously hold up to the world the said LUCAS GIBBS as an ENEMY to his country, and PRECLUDED from all TRADE or INTERCOURSE with the inhabitants of these colonies.

By Order of the Committee,
JOSEPH HUGG, Clerk.

Recreated from The Pennsylvania Gazette, April 17, 1776.

NORTH CAROLINA FOR INDEPENDENCY.

IN CONGRESS, *April* 12, 1776.

Resolved, That the Delegates for this colony in the Continental Congress be empowered to concur with the Delegates of the other colonies in declaring independency, and forming foreign alliances, reserving to this colony the sole and exclusive right of forming a constitution and laws for this colony, and of appointing Delegates from time to time (under the direction of a general representation thereof) to meet the Delegates of the other colonies for such purposes as shall be hereafter pointed out.

The Congress taking the same into consideration, unanimously concurred therewith.

By order,
JAMES GREEN, jun. Secretary.

Recreated from The Virginia Gazette, June 22, 1776.

AMERICAN PROPERTY SEIZED.

WILLIAMSBURG.—Lord Dunmore has issued a proclamation forbidding goods of any kind being sold to persons on shore, on penalty of imprisonment to the seller, and forfeiture of the vessel and cargo to which they belonged. He has also, in obedience to the late act of parliament, seized a great deal of American property, and sold it at publick auction; for this very singular reason, because the owners did not incline to stay on board his fleet and starve, or run the risk of falling victims to jail distemper.

REPRISALS APPLICABLE.

The doctrine of reprisals appears to be now very applicable, and there is no doubt but its influence will extend to the securing of all British property throughout the colonies, to compensate for the many heavy losses we have sustained, by burning of towns, &c. &c. &c. and the damages likely to accrue from the piratical war now carrying on under the sanction of our *gracious king* and his *obedient and loyal parliament*.

Recreated from Purdie's Virginia Gazette, April 12, 1776.

WARM FOR INDEPENDENCE.

Extract of a letter from PETERSBURG, *April* 12.

"In my way through Virginia I found the inhabitants warm for independence. I spent last evening with Mr. _____ from South Carolina. He tells me that the people there have no expectation of ever being reconciled with Britain again but only as a foreign state. They have formed a government for themselves. John Rutledge, Esq., is appointed president.

"From several letters I have received from North Carolina, since that convention met, I find they are for independence, as they either have or intend to repeal the instructions that were given to their delegates, and to leave them the liberty to vote upon every occasion, as they may think fit. Mr. _____ was some little time at Halifax; he says they are quite spirited and unanimous; indeed I hear nothing praised but Common Sense and Independence.

"The people of North Carolina are making great preparations, and say they are determined to die hard. I assure you, my good sir, the vehemence of the southern colonies will require all the coolness of the northern ones to moderate their zeal. I suspected when I was with you, that whenever they were urged, they would go great lengths."

Recreated from The Maryland Gazette, May 2, 1776.

GENERAL WARREN INTERRED.

Extract of a letter from BOSTON, *April* 13.

"Last Monday the remains of the brave General Warren were interred at Boston. Col. Phinney's regiment marched first, with drums and fifes in mourning; then the Free Masons, the remains, the relations, friends, and town's people. They repaired to the King's chapel. Dr. Cooper prayed. Mr. Morton delivered a funeral oration, closed with a solemn funeral dirge. The General's remains were known by two artificial teeth fastened in with gold wire, and by being found under the remains of a person buried in trousers, agreeable to the accounts given by one who was well acquainted with that circumstance."

Recreated from The Virginia Gazette, May 11, 1776.

PROVIDENCE, *April* 13.—Capt. Cook, from Belfast, informs, that recruiting parties had been beating up there from September till January, to reinforce the ministerial army in America, but that they had only inlisted ten men. He further informs, that the ministry's plan of sending commissioners to America is dropt.

WATERTOWN, *April* 15.—We hear, that on Wednesday last, the rev. president, fellows and overseers of Harvard college, waited on his Excellency General Washington, with an address, conferring on him the degree of doctor of laws.

HARTFORD, *April* 15.—By a gentleman from Albany, who came to town yesterday, we are informed that all the troops destined for Quebec, who had been detained at Albany some time past, not being able to cross the lakes, had marched for the place of their destination. The battalion from this colony marched on Wednesday fortnight; and the first and second battalions of Pennsylvania, and the Jersey blues, on Thursday, Friday, Saturday, and Sunday following, and that the general officers, appointed to the northern department, together with the commissioners from Philadelphia had passed through Albany for Canada.—Nothing material from Quebec.

Part of a letter from PHILADELPHIA, *April* 22.

"This morning we received an account, that capt. Barry has taken another tender, and sent her into Egg harbour; she is a schooner of six guns, fitted out by the Phoenix; she hove her guns overboard and ran ashore, but capt. Barry soon got her off. The captain got intelligence of another tender of 10 guns which he is gone after. We hope we shall soon clear our coast of those little pirates who have done so much mischief."

NEW YORK, *April* 25.—On Sunday brigadier general Thompson set out for Canada, with Paterson's. Bond's Greighton's and Poor's regiments of the continental troops that lately arrived here from Cambridge.

Recreated from The Maryland Gazette, May 2, 1776.

WASHINGTON AT NEW YORK.

NEW YORK, *April* 15. Saturday last his Excellency General Washington arrived here from Cambridge, attended by Mr. Palfrey and Mr. Moyland, his aids-de-camp, Horatio Gates, Esq., adjutant-general, and several other gentlemen of distinction.

Admiral Hopkins, with the continental fleet under his command, arrived at New London last Saturday morning from a cruise, and brought in with him a large quantity of cannon, mortars, &c. which he took at New Providence, as also the governor of that island. He also carried in with him a bomb brig and three tenders belonging to capt. Wallace's fleet, which he took off Block island; and we hear the Admiral, and some part of the fleet, fell in with his majesty's ship the Glasgow of 20 guns, the morning before he arrived, with whom he had a very hot engagement.

April 18. Since our last a considerable number of troops have arrived from New England. As great numbers of the inhabitants have moved into the country, many of their houses are taken up for the soldiers. The behaviour of the New England soldiers is decent, and their civility to the inhabitants very commendable; they attend prayers, with their chaplain, evening and morning regularly, in which their officers set the example. Our Lord's day they attend publick worship twice, and their deportment in the house of God is such as becomes the place.

The first division of the ministerial fleet, consisting of the Fowey and Nautilus, with 68 transports, from Boston, sailed for Halifax on the Monday preceding the 1st of April. The second division, consisting of Admiral Schuldham in the Chatham, the Centurion, and the Lively, with 62 transports, sailed the Thursday after, for the southward, not half manned, and had but short allowance for 14 days. The Renown, of 50 guns, the Senegal, of 28, and the Hope, of 16, remain below; but have moved from their station in King road, off the lighthouse, for fear of our fire rafts.

Recreated from Purdie's Virginia Gazette, May 3, 1776.

TROOPS EAGER FOR ACTION.

Extract of a letter from an officer at FORT GEORGE, *April* 20, 1776.

"We came here two days ago, and found the lake still closed with ice. Yesterday it all vanished, when doctor Franklin and the other delegates immediately embarked on board batteaus and crossed the lake. Our regiment, with sundry other troops from New England and the Jerseys, sets out at daybreak tomorrow morning. The whole of the troops that are now on the lake, and here, will amount to upwards of 1500 men; so that I think we should make a very respectable figure before Quebec when we all arrive; and I hope we shall not lie long there, but endeavour immediately to see what the inside is made of."

Recreated from Purdie's Virginia Gazette, May 24, 1776.

A circular letter sent by order of his Excellency the General to the commanders of the several battalions.

SIR,

YOU'LL please to give orders to the several recruiting officers of your regiment, not to take any natives of Great Britain or Ireland as recruits, unless they have been some time residents in the country, have wives and children, or unless they can bring a strong and sufficient recommendation. As this, sir, is a matter of no small importance, a colonel will be appointed to examine and pass all the fresh recruits; and whoever does not come under this predicament will be thrown on the officer's hands.

By the General's orders.
THOMAS BULLITT, D. A. G.

Recreated from Purdie's Virginia Gazette, April 26, 1776.

As an army without cavalry is, in all countries, a very defective machine, but in this province, circumstanced as it is, it is impossible to carry on the service, with any tolerable degree of credit and success, without a certain proportion of this species of troops, general LEE begs leave to address himself to the young gentlemen of the different counties, entreating that they will form themselves into companies of LIGHT DRAGOONS, consisting of one captain, one lieutenant, one cornet, two serjeants, two corporals, and a trumpet or horn sounder. As it is intended, and hoped, that the whole will be composed of GENTLEMEN VOLUNTEERS, it will not be expected that they should receive any pay; but, at the same time, as it is not reasonable that they should put themselves to the expense of maintaining their horses, they are to be allowed rations for them, as well as for themselves. Their arms should be, a *short rifled carbine*, a *light pike*, of eight feet long, and a *tomhawk*. General LEE is confident, if the young gentlemen approve and adopt this scheme, they will not only do very great honour to themselves, but very important service to their country.

Recreated from Purdie's Virginia Gazette, April 19, 1776.

AMERICAN FLEET AT NEW LONDON.

NEW YORK, *April* 22. Wednesday last the Lady of his Excellency General Washington, arrived here from Boston. Brig. General Greene's brigade arrived from Cambridge by way of New London the same day.

The following is a list of the continental fleet at New London, April 18: Ship Alfred, Hopkins, 32 guns. Ship Columbus, Whipple, 28 guns. Brig Cabot, Hopkins, jun. 14 guns. Brig Andrew Doria, Biddle, 14 guns. Sloop Providence, Hazard, 12 guns. Bomb brig (prize retaken) 10 guns. Schooner (prize retaken) 8 guns. Sloop (prize retaken) 6 guns. New Haven brig, 16 guns. Total guns 140. In Rhode Island, two row-gallies, two 18 pounders, and four 9 each.

April 25. We have information from good authority, that the ministerial fleet is arrived at Halifax; and that the Tories are in the greatest distress, and can scarcely get shelter from the weather.

We hear from Sandy Hook, that sixteen men from one of the ships of war, having landed there in order to get water, they had all got into an upper room in the light-house, where they were carousing, when a party of the New Jersey militia surprised them, and, raking away the lower part of the stairs, made them all prisoners, burnt their boat, and filled up the well.

Commodore Hopkins, with his fleet, has left New London on a cruise.

Recreated from The Virginia Gazette, May 11, 1776.

Extract of a letter from Boston, April 22.

"They are fortifying and putting the harbour, &c. in the best posture of defence they can. To-morrow they talk of sinking hulks by the castle, and erecting a battery at Camp hill, on Noddle's island. Our small privateers run in and out by Pulling's point, without any regard to the enemy."

We hear that it is the determination of the Continental Congress to fortify New London harbour, in the best and most effectual manner, it being judged a good and convenient rendezvous for the continental fleet.

Recreated from Purdie's Virginia Gazette, May 17, 1776.

BRITISH SHIPS AT CAPE FEAR.

WILLIAMSBURG, *April 27.*

Thirty-eight sail of the men of war and transports destined for North Carolina, from England, are said to be arrived at Cape Fear, and that they took on the passage a large French ship with arms & ammunition.

• • • •

There have, within these two or three weeks, been taken and brought into Norfolk, by the tenders, &c. the following vessels, viz. The sloop Congress, with 110 barrels of gun powder, and a large quantity of cloth, linens, oznabrigs, &c. A schooner with a very large cargo of medicines, particularly jesuit's bark. A large new ship from Baltimore, bound to Liverpool, with 1900 barrels of flour and bread, and 5000 bushels of wheat; this last taken by old Goodrich, who commands a privateer, fitted out by himself, and has likewise fitted out two others, one commanded by his son William, the other by a certain William Picket. A brig outward bound, loaded with provisions. And a New England schooner, supposed to be bound for Maryland. There were taken and brought in, some little time before, three vessels with gun powder, about 5000 stand of arms, &c.

Recreated from The Hartford Courant, May 27, 1776.

NEW YORK, *May 1.*

BRIGADIER-general Sullivan, with six regiments now here, are to set out for Canada in a day or two; and we hear the remainder of his army will encamp this week, near the city.

We hear from Albany, that general Thompson's brigade, arrived there on Tuesday last. We also hear, that the first division of general Sullivan's brigade was seen at Poughkeepsie, on Tuesday evening, on their way to Albany.

NEW LONDON, *April 26.*—We hear that the continental currency is received in payment, and passes very freely, among the inhabitants of the French West India islands.

Recreated from Purdie's Virginia Gazette, May 17, 1776.

DR. FRANKLIN REACHES MONTREAL.

Extract of a letter from MONTREAL, *May 1.*

"On Sunday last arrived here, Baron Woedlke, and Colonel De Haas, with Mr. Joseph Terry, of this place, accompanied by several other gentlemen of the army; and on Monday, the Committee of the Hon. Continental Congress, for establishing and regulating the Continental affairs in this province, with the celebrated Dr. Franklin at their head. They were received on the beach at the port de Vaudreuil by General Arnold, and the friends to liberty, and a salute was fired from the Citadel; being escorted to head-quarters, they and a number of friends to liberty spent the evening with decent mirth."

Recreated from The Hartford Courant, May 27, 1776.

Extract of a letter from SAMUEL CHASE, *Esq., one of the continental commissioners in* CANADA, *dated* MONTREAL, *May 1, 1776.*

"On this day week our party left Ticonderoga, and arrived at St. John's on Saturday. On Monday we came to this city, by way of La Praire, where we were politely received at our landing by general Arnold; he is not only the brave, active, and experienced soldier, but the polite, accomplished gentleman."

BOSTON, *May 9.*—Almost every able-bodied inhabitant of this place has voluntarily engaged to work two days in a week, for six weeks, on the fortifications carrying on here for the general defence. They began to fortify Noddle's island last week, since which they have been joined by several of the neighbouring towns, and it is not doubted but others will follow the laudable example.

Recreated from Purdie's Virginia Gazette, May 31, 1776.

BOSTON, *April 25.*—William Jackson of this town, and Crean Brush of New York, who were on board a brig taken by Captain Manly, are now imprisoned in the gaol of this town.

Recreated from The Pennsylvania Gazette, May 8, 1776.

TROOPS RETREATING FROM QUEBEC.

To CONGRESS, *dated* MONTREAL, *May* 10.

"By Col. Campbell, who arrived here early this morning, from Quebec, we are informed that two men of war, two frigates, and one tender, arrived there early Monday the 6th instant. About 11 o'clock the enemy sallied out, to the number, it is supposed, of 1000 men. Our forces were so dispersed at different parts, that not more than 200 could be collected at head quarters. This small force could not resist the enemy. All our cannon, 500 muskets, and about 200 sick, unable to come off, have fallen into their hands. The retreat was made with the utmost precipitation and confusion. However, col. Campbell informs us that he imagines we have lost very few men, except the sick above mentioned.

"General Thomas was last Thursday evening at Dechambeau. At a council of war it was determined to retreat to the mouth of the Sorel. This day General Arnold goes down there, and if he can get information of the enemy's real strength, and it should be found inconsiderable, perhaps a council of war, or reconsideration, may think proper to march the army back to Dechambeau, which is now strengthened by Col. Gratton's, Burrel's, and Sinclair's regiments. Besides the above losses, one batteau loaded with powder, supposed to contain 30 barrels, and an armed vessel, which the crew were obliged to abandon, were intercepted by one of the enemy's frigates."

THE College of WILLIAM & MARY has been lately cleaned, and will be immediately plaftered and whitewafhed, to render it fit for the Reception of the Profeffors, Students, Grammar Scholars, and Servants; and the feveral Schools will be opened at the Beginning of Trinity Term, namely, on *Monday* the 17th of next Month. (4) EMMANUEL JONES, Clk.

WILLIAMSBURG, *June* 1, 1776.

LEFT in the Neceffary Houfe at the *Raleigh*, on *Monday* laft, a SILVER STOP WATCH, Maker's Name *Prentis*, LONDON, No. 112, with two Seals fet in Gold, one of them a Cypher, the other a Coat of Arms. Whoever delivers them to the Printers, or the Bar-Keeper at the *Raleigh*, fhall have forty Shillings.

Recreated from The Virginia Gazette, June 1, 1775.

From the LONDON GAZETTE *of May* 3, 1776.

WHITEHALL, *May* 3.—GENERAL HOWE, Commander in Chief of his Majesty's forces in North America; having taken a resolution on the 7th of March to remove from Boston to Halifax with the troops under his command, and such of the inhabitants, with their effects, as were desirous to continue under the protection of his Majesty's forces, the embarkation was effected on the 27th of said month, with the greatest order and regularity, and without the least interruption from the rebels. When the packet came away the first division of the transports was under sail, and the remainder were preparing to follow in a few days; the Admiral leaving behind as many of the ships of war as could be spared from the convoy, for the security and protection of such vessels as might be bound to Boston.

WHITEHALL, *May* 5.—The King hath been pleased to order letters patent to be passed under the Great Seal of Great Britain, constituting and appointing Richard Lord Viscount Howe, of the kingdom of Ireland, and the Hon. William Howe, Esq., Major of his Majesty's forces, and General of his Majesty's forces in North America only, to be his Majesty's Commissioners for restoring peace to his Majesty's Colonies and Plantations in North America; and for granting pardons to such of his Majesty's subjects there, now in rebellion, as shall deserve the royal mercy.

LONDON, *May* 4.—In a letter from a Hessian soldier, going to America, to his friend in town, is the following remarkable passage: "We are all coming to England, and shall be happy if I have an opportunity of coming to London to see you; if not, you will do me a particular pleasure if you will come down to the port where we shall lay till we embark for America; for most probably I shall never have another opportunity of seeing you again, as I intend to reside in America; and many hundreds of my countrymen have resolved to do the same, having taken leave of their country and friends for ever."

Recreated from The Hartford Courant, August 12, 1776.

[*The following was from a manuscript from* NORTH CAROLINA, *and is inserted to show our readers what sort of* COMMISSIONERS *we are to expect. Our troops, however, in that province being in good spirits, as well as sufficient in point of number, we may venture to predict that* CLINTON *and his* COMMISSIONERS *will be* TREATED *very roughly.*]

By Major General CLINTON, commander of his Majesty's forces in the southern provinces of NORTH AMERICA.

A PROCLAMATION.

WHEREAS a most unprovoked and wicked rebellion hath for some time past prevailed, and doth now exist, within his Majesty's province of North Carolina, and the inhabitants (forgetting their allegiance to their Sovereign, and denying the authority of the laws and statutes of the realm) have, in a succession of crimes, proceeded to the subversion of all lawful authority, usurping the powers of government, and erecting a tyranny in the hands of Congresses and Committees of various denominations, utterly unknown and repugnant to the spirit of the British constitution; and divers people, in avowed defiance to all legal authority, are now actually in arms, waging unnatural war against their King; and whereas all attempts to reclaim the infatuated and misguided multitude to a sense of their error have unhappily proved ineffectual: I have it in my command to proceed forthwith against all such men, or bodies of men in arms, and against all such Congresses and Committees thus unlawfully established, as against open enemies to the state. But, considering it a duty inseparable from the principle of humanity first of all to forewarn the deluded people of the miseries ever attendant upon civil war, I do most earnestly entreat, and exhort them, as they tender their own happiness, and that of their posterity, to appease the vengeance of an injured and justly incensed nation, by a return to their duty to our common Sovereign, and to the blessings of a free government, as established by law; hereby offering, in his Majesty's name, free pardon to all such as shall lay down their arms and submit to the laws, excepting only from the benefit of such pardon Cornelius Harnett and Robert Howe. And I do hereby require, that the Provincial Congress, and all Committees of Safety, and other unlawful associations, be dissolved, and the judges allowed to hold their Courts according to the laws and constitution of this province; of which all persons are required to take notice, as they will answer the contrary at their utmost peril.

Given on board the Pallas, in Cape Fear river, in the province of North Carolina, the 5th day of May, 1776, in the *sixteenth* year of his Majesty's reign.

H. CLINTON.

To the Magistrates of the province of NORTH CAROLINA, *to be by them made public.*

Recreated from The Virginia Gazette, June 8, 1776.

By a letter from head-quarters, at Williamsburgh, in Virginia, dated May 10, 1776.

We learn, that an express was arrived there from General Moore, in North Carolina, acquainting the committee, that 2000 men, under the command of General Cornwallis, was arrived at Wilmington, on Cape Fear river, from England; and that Sir Peter Parker was daily expected at the same place with 8000 men; that the inhabitants of North Carolina were assembling in great numbers, and were determined to give General Cornwallis a warm reception.

PROVIDENCE, *May* 25.—Tuesday last Captain Horn arrived here from Charles-Town, South Carolina, which place he left the 12th inst. He informs that 17 sail of transports from Ireland, with 7 regiments, consisting of about 5000 men, arrived at Long Bay, near Cape Fear, the 1st inst. and that they were in great want of water, but had not got any supply when he sailed. He further informs that Brigadier General Armstrong was arrived at Charlestown, from Philadelphia, and that our brethren at the southward are in high spirits.

Recreated from The Hartford Courant, June 3, 1776.

AMERICANS ABANDON QUEBEC.

Extract of a letter from General SCHUYLER, *at* FORT GEORGE, *May* 13, 1776.

"Some ships of war, with troops, arrived the 4th instant at Quebec, which obliged our troops to raise the siege. We left about 200 of the sick, too ill to be removed, and a few others, who were out on detached parties, and a few cannon."

Recreated from The Virginia Gazette, June 1, 1775.

THE SICK WE LEFT BEHIND.

Extract of a letter from LIEUTENANT CLAGBORN, *in* CAPTAIN STODDARD'S *Company, to his friend in Salisbury, dated, Sorel, May* 12, 1776.

"I arrived here this day and am in perfect health, though something lame in my feet, occasioned by my sudden and unexpected retreat, of which I am unable to give you a very particular account, being in the utmost hurry. We arrived at Quebec the last of March, and the whole company were soon taken with the small pox; we lay in plain sight of the city, where we could see their motions, they kept up a heavy fire the greatest part of the time. Our army seemed totally neglected; we were wanting of men, and had not sufficient provisions for those that were present, and our supply of warlike stores was very inconsiderable.

"On Monday morning last the enemy were reinforced with 3 men of war and their tenders, upon which orders were given to make a speedy retreat, and about one o'clock afternoon, the enemy sallied out upon us and knowing the situation of our little distressed army, determined to drive all before them. The whole of our army fled that were able to travel. The sick we left behind to share the fate of being killed or taken prisoners. About 23 of our company are left behind, among whom are Lieut. Convers and Ensign Holcomb; sergeant Whiney and Elija Collins, of our company, and Joseph Moseley, of Capt. Stanton's company, are dead. Our battalion came 40 miles from Quebec, where our rear made a stand."

Recreated from The Hartford Courant, June 3, 1776.

WOMEN TREATED BARBAROUSLY.

Extract of a letter from WILMINGTON, *May* 13.

THEY having landed at General Howe's plantation, on Sunday morning, between 2 and 3 o'clock, about 1000 troops, under the command of Generals Clinton and Cornwallis, the sentry posted on the river bank immediately gave the alarm to the guard, who only had time to collect their horses, and throw down the fences to let a few cattle out, which they drove off before the enemy surrounded the house.

On their march up the causeway from the river, part of the guard kept up a fire on them, which the enemy returned. A few women, who lived in the house, were treated with great barbarity; one of whom was shot through the hips, another stabbed with a bayonet, and a third knocked down with the butt of a musket. The enemy had two men killed, several wounded, and a sergeant of the 33d regiment taken prisoner. They proceeded on their march to Orton Mill, with a design to surprise Major Davis, who commanded a detachment of about 90 men, stationed at that place. In this they failed, as the Major had received the alarm from the guard, and had retired, with his baggage and two small swivels, in very good order, unpursued by the enemy. They have burned the mill, and retreated to their vessels at the fort. Upon the whole, the Generals had very little to boast of, they having got, by this descent, three horses and three cows. We had not a man killed or wounded.

Recreated from The Virginia Gazette, June 29, 1776.

COUNTERFEITING CONTINENTAL MONEY.

NEW YORK, *May* 15.—Friday last information was given to our Congress, that some men on Long Island were counterfeiting continental money, also, Massachusetts, Connecticut, and New York currency. A party of minute men were ordered out the same day in search of them, and they were all taken, with what cash they had struck off, likewise their press, tools, &c. They were yesterday brought to town, and committed to jail.

Recreated from Purdie's Virginia Gazette, May 31, 1776.

ADVERTISEMENTS.

PHILADELPHIA, May 8, 1776.

MADE his escape, from the jail of this city, yesterday in the evening, a certain MOSES KIRKLAND, called colonel KIRKLAND, belonging to South Carolina, confined in the said jail by order of the Honourable Congress, for practices inimical to this country. He is a stout corpulent man, between 50 and 60 years of age, about 5 feet 10 inches high, of a swarthy complexion, fresh coloured, and wears his own gray hair tied behind. He had on a green coat faced with blue velvet, a blue velvet waistcoat, and brown velvet breeches; had also a brown coat and waistcoat, and may possibly have taken other clothes with him. It is said he crossed over Delaware at Cooper's ferry last night, and it is supposed will either endeavour to get on board one of the men of war in the river, or at Sandy Hook. The publick are earnestly desired to endeavour to apprehend this dangerous enemy to the American cause, and a reward of TWO HUNDRED DOLLARS is hereby offered to any person, or persons, that shall take and bring him back to the jail of this city, and all reasonable charges paid.

THOMAS McKEAN.
ELRIDGE GERRY.
T. LYNCH, jun.

Recreated from Purdie's Virginia Gazette, May 17, 1776.

FORTIFYING THE SOREL.

Extract of a letter from the mouth of the Sorel, dated May 14, 1776.

"We have here Generals Wooster, Arnold, the Prussian General, and about 1500 good troops. Two battalions are just arrived from Cambridge, and one gone to Montreal. Colonel Poor and his battalion are expected every minute, with General Thompson. Here is to be our grand stand. We are now fortifying, but the main body is not yet come up from Dechambeau. There are six battalions more on their way to this place. This fortification is at the mouth of the Sorel on the river St. Lawrence, where our provisions and stores come down into Canada. As soon as the six battalions arrive, I hope we shall be able to drive them faster than they drove us."

Recreated from The Virginia Gazette, June 22, 1776.

PURSUANT to powers received from the Hon. the Continental Congress, the Committee of Safety are ready to grant commissions for making reprisals upon the property of the people of *Great Britain*, at sea, or in the rivers, below high-water mark, to any persons who shall apply for them, and comply with the terms mentioned by Congress.

EDMUND PENDLETON, president.

THE Committee of Safety desire the commanding-officers of the several minute battalions to procure and return, without delay, an exact list of the number of men in each company, and how they are furnished with arms, that the same may be laid before the Convention.

EDMUND PENDLETON, president.

Recreated from Purdie's Virginia Gazette, May 10, 1776.

VIRGINIA URGES INDEPENDENCE.

In CONVENTION, May 15, 1776.

FORASMUCH as all the endeavours of the UNITED COLONIES, by the most decent representations and petitions to the King and Parliament of Great Britain, to restore peace and security to America under the British government, and a reunion with that people upon just and liberal terms, instead of a redress of grievances, have produced, from an imperious and vindictive administration, increased insult, oppression, and a vigorous attempt to effect our total destruction. By a late act, all these colonies are declared to be in rebellion, and out of the protection of the British crown, our properties subjected to confiscation, our people, when captivated, compelled to join in the murder and plunder of their relations and countrymen, and all former rapine and oppression of Americans declared legal and just. Fleets and armies are raised, and the aid of foreign troops engaged to assist these destructive purposes.

The King's representative in this colony hath not only withheld all the powers of government from operating for our safety, but, having retired on board an armed ship, is carrying on a piratical and savage war against us, tempting our slaves, by every artifice, to resort to him, and training and employing them against their masters. In this state of extreme danger, we have no alternative left but an abject submission to the will of those overbearing tyrants, or a total separation from the crown and government of Great Britain, uniting and exerting the strength of all America for defence, and forming alliances with foreign powers for commerce and aid in war:

Whereof appealing to the SEARCHER OF HEARTS for the sincerity of former declarations, expressing our desire to preserve the connexion with that nation, and that we are driven from that inclination by their wicked councils, and the eternal laws of self-preservation,

RESOLVED, *unanimously*, that the delegates appointed to represent this colony in General Congress be instructed to propose to that respectable body TO DECLARE THE UNITED COLONIES FREE AND INDEPENDENT STATES, absolved from all allegiance to, or dependence on, the Crown or Parliament of Great Britain; and that they give the assent of this colony to such declaration, and to whatever measure may be thought proper and necessary by the Congress for forming foreign alliances, and A CONFEDERATION OF THE COLONIES, at such time, and in the manner, as to them shall seem best. Provided, that the power of government for, and the regulations of the internal concerns of each colony, be left to the respective colonial legislatures.

• • • •

RESOLVED, *unanimously*, that a committee be appointed to prepare A DECLARATION OF RIGHTS, and such a plan of government as will be most likely to maintain peace and order in this colony, and secure substantial and equal liberty to the people.

EDMUND PENDLETON, *President.*

A HANDSOME COLLECTION.

In consequence of the above resolution, universally regarded as the only door which will lead to safety and prosperity, some gentlemen made a handsome collection for the purpose of treating the soldiery, who next day paraded in Waller's grove, before brigadier-general Lewis, attended by the gentlemen of the Committee of Safety, the members of the General Convention, the inhabitants of the city, &c. &c.

The resolution being read aloud to the army, the following toasts were given, each of them accompanied by a discharge of the artillery and small-arms, and the acclamations of all present:

1. *The American independent states.*
2. *The Grand Congress of the United States, and their respective legislatures.*
3. *General Washington, and victory to the American arms.*

The UNION FLAG of the American States waved upon the Capital during the whole of this ceremony, which being ended, the soldiers partook of the refreshment prepared for them by the affection of their countrymen, and the evening concluded with illuminations, and other demonstrations of joy; every one seeming pleased that the domination of Great Britain was now at an end, so wickedly and tyrannically exercised for these twelve or thirteen years past, notwithstanding our repeated prayers and remonstrances for redress.

Recreated from The Pennsylvania Packet, June 3, 1776.

MIDAS, a remarkable large jack ass, imported last fall from *Malta*, by *Philip Mazzei*, esq; stands at my plantation in *Prince George* county, and covers at two dollars the leap, 40s. the season, and 3l. to ensure.---It may not be amiss to inform the publick, that, from the difficulty of obtaining and the expense attending the importation of an ass of this kind, his price for covering is necessarily much higher than any one of the common breed, but it will be amply compensated by the size and strength of the mules he gets.

THEODORICK BLAND, jun.

FOUND in this city, a THREE POUND BILL. Whoever can prove his property, by giving an account of the emission and number, shall have it delivered to him on paying the charge of this advertisement. N. B. Inquire of the Printer.

Recreated from Purdie's Virginia Gazette, May 24, 1776.

"ADOPT SUCH GOVERNMENT"

IN CONGRESS, PHILADELPHIA, *May* 15, 1776.

WHEREAS his Britannic Majesty, in conjunction with the Lords and Commons of Great Britain, has, by a late act of Parliament, excluded the inhabitants of these United Colonies from the protection of his crown.

• • • •

AND WHEREAS no answers whatsoever, to the humble petition of the Colonies for redress of grievances and reconciliation with Great Britain, has been, or is likely to be given, but the whole force of that kingdom, aided by foreign mercenaries, is to be exerted for the destruction of the good people of these colonies.

• • • •

AND WHEREAS it appears absolutely irreconcilable to reason and good conscience, for the people of these Colonies now to take the oaths and affirmations necessary for the support of any government under the crown of Great Britain; and it is necessary that the exercise of every kind of authority under the said crown should be totally suppressed, and all the powers of government exercised under the authority of the people of the Colonies for the preservation of internal peace, virtue, and good order, as well as for the defence of our lives, liberties and properties, against the hostile invasions and cruel depredations of our enemies.

• • • •

Therefore Resolved, That it be recommended to the respective assemblies and conventions, of the United Colonies, where no government sufficient to the exigencies of their affairs has been hitherto established, to adopt such government as shall, in the opinion of the representatives of the people, best conduce to the happiness and safety of their constituents in particular, and America in general.

By order of the Congress,
JOHN HANCOCK, President.

Recreated from The Hartford Courant, May 27, 1776.

REGULATIONS FOR ALL PERSONS TAKEN ON BOARD PRIZES.

In CONGRESS.

May 21, 1776.

Resolved, That all persons taken in arms on board any prize be deemed prisoners, to be taken care of by the supreme executive power in each colony to which they are brought, whether the prize be taken by vessels fitted out by the Continent, or by others.

That such as are taken be treated as prisoners of war, but with humanity, and be allowed the same rations as the troops in the service of the United Colonies; but that such as are officers supply themselves, and be allowed to draw bills to pay for their subsistence and clothing.

That officers made prisoners in the land service be allowed the same indulgence.

That the officers be not permitted to reside in or near any sea-port town, nor public post road, and that the officers and privates be not suffered to reside in the same places.

That in case the officers cannot draw or sell their bills, the Congress will allow for each of them Two Dollars a week, for board and lodgings, to be repaid by said officers before they are released from their captivity.

That no tavern-keepers supply any officers who are prisoners, on the credit of the Continent.

That the capitulations entered into with prisoners at the time of their surrender be punctually observed.

That such officers as surrender prisoners of war be put on their parole, unless Congress shall otherwise direct.

TO BE SOLD,
A DUTCH SERVANT WOMAN, who has two years and eleven months to serve; she understands town or country work, can spin, knit, and dairy; she is sold for no fault, only for want of employ since her master's decease. Enquire of the PRINTERS.

That the FORM of the PAROLE be as follows:

I _____ being made prisoner of war, by the army of the Thirteen United Colonies in North America, do promise and engage, on my word and honour, and on the faith of a gentleman, to depart from hence to ____, in the province of ____, being the place of my destination and residence, and there, or within six miles thereof, to remain during the present war between Great Britain and the said United Colonies, or until the Congress of the said United Colonies, or the Assembly, Convention, or Committee or Council of Safety of the said Colony shall order otherwise; and that I will not directly or indirectly give any intelligence whatsoever to the enemies of the United Colonies, or do or say any thing in opposition to, or in prejudice of the measures and proceedings of any Congress for the said Colonies during the present troubles, or until I am duly exchanged or discharged. Given under my hand, this day of ____, A.D. 1776.

That the said Parole be signed by the officers.

That such as refuse to subscribe the parole be committed to prison.

That the women and children belonging to prisoners be furnished with subsistence and supplied with firing and other things absolutely necessary for their support.

That no prisoners be enlisted in the Continental Army.

That the prisoners be permitted to exercise their trades, and labour in order to support themselves and families.

That a list of the prisoners in each Colony be made out by the Committees of the counties, towns, or districts, where they reside, and transmitted to the Assembly, Convention, or Council or Committee of Safety of such Colony respectively, who shall send a copy thereof to Congress.

By Order of the Congress,
CHARLES THOMPSON, Secretary.

Recreated from The Pennsylvania Gazette, June 5, 1776.

THIRTEEN UNITED COLONIES.

United, we stand---Divided, we fall.

ANY young, healthy, and strong man, not under 5 feet 7 inches high, that is free and willing to enlist as a MATROSS in my company of artillery, will please to repair to my quarters in Williamsburg, where he will be kindly received, have 3 l. advance money paid to him, besides new clothes, and 2 s. per day, for one, two, or more years, if not sooner discharged.

God save the Congress.

DOHICKY ARUNDEL.

Recreated from Purdie's Virginia Gazette, May 24, 1776.

A FRESH PARCEL OF
KEYSER's famous PILLS
Just come to Hand,
And selling by Dixon & Hunter, in Boxes at 10s. 20s. and 40s.
ALSO A FEW BOTTLES OF
Maredant's antiscorbutic Drops.

Recreated from The Virginia Gazette, June 22, 1776.

10,000 BRITISH AT NEW YORK.

Extract of a letter from PHILADELPHIA, *to a Gentleman in* WILLIAMSBURG, *May 20, 1776.*

"A gentleman arrived from New York this day, who informs, that 70 sail of transports, with 10,000 men, are arrived before that place, and that an express is coming to Congress from the general with an account of it. We are well prepared to receive them there, being strongly fortified; and, though not more than 8000 regular troops are in the works, yet we can speedily throw in 10 or 12,000 militia, so that we have no doubt of giving a good account in that quarter."

Recreated from Purdie's Virginia Gazette, May 31, 1776.

IN VIRGINIA CONVENTION.

Tuesday, May 21, 1776.

RESOLVED, That such Indian warriors, of the neighbouring tribes, as are willing, be engaged in the service of this country, provided the number so to be engaged doth not exceed two hundred, and to be marched down to the assistance of the regular forces on the eastern quarter.

Resolved, That John Gibson, Esq., be desired to negotiate with the Ohio or Western Indians, and inform them of the friendly sentiments of this country towards them, and of the purport of the foregoing resolution for calling in their assistance, and that the same is warranted and directed by the resolution of the General Congress of the first day of July last.

Resolved, That the militias of all the frontier counties ought to be got in readiness for action, without loss of time; and, for this purpose, the several militia officers ought to use their utmost exertion in their several departments, as there is too much reason to apprehend the wicked attempts of our enemies, to excite an Indian war, may involve us in calamities inseparable therefrom.

Recreated from The Pennsylvania Packet, June 3, 1776.

THE BRAVE CAPTAIN MUGFORD.

THE VENGEANCE OF OUR ENEMY.

BOSTON, *May 23*, 1776.

EARLY last Friday morning, the Franklin schooner, one of the continental cruizers, commanded by Capt. James Mugford, of Marblehead, fell in with one of the enemies transport ships from Cork, bound directly into this harbour, the captain not knowing that the place had been evacuated by the British fleet and army. Notwithstanding she appeared to be an armed ship, and was in sight of the enemy's man of war laying in Nantasket, Capt. Mugford resolutely bore down upon her, and took her without opposition. She mounted six carriage guns, a number of swivels, and 18 men. The Franklin, at that time, had only 21 men.

Capt. Mugford, determining to bring her into this harbour, the inhabitants, on leaving their respective places of worship after forenoon's service (it being the day of the continental fast) had the pleasure of seeing the most valuable prize taken since the commencement of the war entering the harbour. But it being ebb tide, she run ashore in Pulling point gut, where she lay till the ensuing night. As her cargo was of almost inestimable value to these colonies, it was thought prudent to bring up to town the greatest part of it in boats; and a large number being immediately dispatched, the same was soon safely landed and properly deposited.

The ship is about 300 tons burthen, Alexander Lumsdale master. She had five weeks passage; and sailed from Cork in company with 12 or 13 other transports, all bound to this place, from which she parted a few days before she was taken. The others, it is concluded, hearing of the evacuation of the town from one of their cruizers, steered for Halifax.

The captain brings no material advices.

The following is an inventory of the cargo of the above mentioned prize ship, taken and bro't in here last Friday, viz.

Carbines, with bayonets, scabbards and steel rammers	1000
Carbine cartouch boxes	1000
Slings	1000
Spare travelling carriages---24 pounder, heavy,	1
12 do.---light	4
Traversing handspikes for do.	8
Handsaws	84
Sand bags---bushel 5000, half bushel 5000,	10,000
Mantelets of cured hides	200
Broad axes	144
Hand hammers	50
Grindstones, with troughs	15
Felling axes	300
Hand hatchets	500
Hand bills	500
Barrows---wheel 268, hand 150	418
Spades---common 1000, ditching 250	1250
Shovels---shod 750, iron 250	1000
Carpenters tools---sets	6
Handsaws, whet and set, 6; tennant do. 6; turning do. 6; broad axes, helved, 6; adzes, helved, 6; penmauls, helved, 6; hammers, claw 6, rivetting 6; chizzels, broad helved 6, scribing 6, heading 12, paring 6, firmer 36, mortice 24, and large 12; gouges, helved, firmer 36, pecking 6, and trunnion 12; piercers or pads, stocks and springs, 6; bitts for do. 72; draw borers, helved, 24; pairs of pincers 6; iron squares 6; brass chalk line, rolls 6; chalk line, knots 12; iron compasses, pairs 6; engineers augers, 8 to a set, sets 6; thrifts for do. 48; two feet rules 6; black lead pencils, dozens 6; stones, rub 6, rag 6, Turkey oil 6; rasps 12; saw setts 6; files for do. 18; gimblets, sorted 144, large spike 12; glue 12lb. copper glue pots 6; fish skins 6; mallets 6; beetles, or small iron crows 6; planes of all sorts 132; Hambro' line, skains 50; spikes, from 5 to 8 & an half inch, 29C. 3qr. 0lb. nails, 24d. 38,500; pick-axes with helves 500; hammers with helves, sledge, 25; augers with thrifts 75:	
Rope, tarred, from 2 to 4 1-half inch coils	5
Do. white, from 1 1-half to 5 2 half inch coils	4
Powder, copper hooped, whole barrels,	1500

The enemy, on board the men of war below, intolerably vexed and chagrined that the above ship should be taken and unloaded in their open view, formed a design of wreaking their vengeance on the gallant Capt. Mugford, who took her.

The Sunday following, Capt. Mugford, in company with Capt. Cunnigham, in the Lady Washington, a small privateer armed with swivels, blunderbusses, and musquets, fell down in order to go out in the bay. The enemy observed their sailing, and fitted out a fleet of boats for the purpose of surprising and taking them in the night; and the Franklin's running aground in the gut, gave them a good opportunity for executing their plan. The Lady Washington came to anchor near Captain Mugford; and between 9 and 10 o'clock he discovered a number of boats, which he hailed, and received for answer, that they were from Boston. He ordered them to keep off, or he would fire upon them. They begged him, for God's sake not to fire, for they were going on board him.

Capt. Mugford instantly fired, and was followed by all his men; and cutting his cable brought his broadside to bear, when he discharged his cannon, loaded with musquet ball, directly in upon them. Before the cannon could be charged a second time, two or three boats were along side, each of them supposed to have as many men on board as the Franklin, which were only 21, including officers.

By the best accounts, there were not less than 13 boats in all, many of them armed with swivels, and having on board, at the lowest computation, 200 men. Capt. Mugford and his men plied those along side so closely, with fire arms and spears, and with such intrepidity, activity and success, that two boats were soon sunk, and all the men either killed or drowned.

But while the heroic Mugford, with out stretched arms, was righteously dealing death and destruction to our base and unnatural enemies, he received a fatal ball in his body, which in a few minutes put a period to his life, from which, had it been spared, his oppressed country would undoubtedly have reaped very eminent advantages.

After our brave men had maintained this unequal contest for about half an hour, the enemy thought proper to retire. The carnage among them must have been great; for, besides the two boat loads killed and drowned, many were doubtless killed and wounded on board the others. Great execution was done by the spears. One man, with that weapon, is positive of having killed nine of the enemy.

The number of boats which attacked the Franklin was about 8 or 9. The remainder, to the number of 4 or 5, at the same time attacked Capt. Cunningham, in the Lady Washington, who then had on board only 6 men, besides himself. This brave little company gave the boats such a warm reception, that the enemy were soon glad to give over the contest, after suffering, it is thought, considerable loss.

The remains of Capt. Mugford have been carried to Marblehead for interment. No other life, on our part, was lost.

Recreated from The Hartford Courant, May 27, 1776.

WILLIAMSBURG, *May* 18.—Twelve hundred men from this colony are ordered for North Carolina, to reinforce the troops collected at Cape Fear to oppose General Clinton. It is not certain what number of the ministerial troops are arrived; report says 5000.

We have within our Capes the Fowey man of war, 24 guns, the Nautilus, 16 guns, and the Otter, 10 guns.

Recreated from Purdie's Virginia Gazette, May 31, 1776.

WATERTOWN, *May* 20.—Since our last a quantity of powder has been received at the powder house in this town from France.

The fortifications at Fort Hill in Boston, at Governor's Island, Dorchester Point, and at the Castle, we hear, are near compleat.

A TURNER of Metal or Hard Wood will meet with good encouragement by the subscribers, at the Metal Button Manufactory, in Second-street, near the Dock.
THOMAS BRAMALL.
JAMES GREGRON.

Recreated from The Pennsylvania Packet, June 3, 1776.

DUNMORE'S ARMY BOARDS FLEET.

Williamsburg, Virginia, *May* 24.—Last night an express arrived from col. Woodford, at Kemp's landing, with advice that Lord Dunmore's motley army, after dismantling their intrenchment at the mills, and setting fire to the barracks and other buildings they had erected there for their convenience, had retired on board the fleet, which, to the amount of 70 odd sail, were in motion yesterday morning, and appeared to be bound for sea.

They supplied themselves with wood, from a number of houses at the distillery, which they demolished for that purpose; and it was given out, that they intended for Halifax in Nova Scotia, with intent, it may be presumed, to enjoy the free exercise of their limbs and a vegetable diet, and undergo a complete scouring from the filth in which they have been involved for a long while past. They destroyed between 40 and 50 sail of small vessels, after taking out what they deemed to be valuable, but suffered all the salt on board to go to the bottom.

Recreated from Purdie's Virginia Gazette, May 24, 1776.

Extract of a letter from Major Hendricks *to* General Lewis, *dated* Hampton, *May 23.*

"I wrote you this morning that 30 sail of the enemy fleet were moved down the river, since which it appears that their whole fleet is in motion. From our church steeple I can see 60 or 70 sail of vessels of different kinds, hovering about the mouth of James River. What they mean is impossible to tell."

Recreated from The Pennsylvania Packet, June 3, 1776.

MORE SHIPS AT CAPE FEAR.

By a gentleman from North Carolina, we learn that the remainder of the fleet destined for Cape Fear had arrived, and that the number of troops now with general Clinton was supposed to be about 4000, none of which had yet landed; and it was even suspected they had a design upon some other quarter, and would not land there at all.

Recreated from Purdie's Virginia Gazette, May 24, 1776.

GEN. ARNOLD PURSUING THE ENEMY.

Extract of a letter from Montreal, *May 17.*

"I wrote you last from Dechambeau, where we remained four or five days on a very short allowance, and left it with half an allowance of flour, and no pork to serve the men to Trois Rivieres, two good days march. It has since been concluded on to keep no detachment for the present below the Sorel, as the army have been living from hand to mouth for some time past, the supplies of provisions from the other side of the Lakes being but small, and very little to be procured without force, or paying hard money for it. The common people in general, though they will probably take the stronger side, do, I have no doubt from all the observations I have made, wish well to us and our cause, and would be very glad we should succeed.

"Forty or fifty men of the 18th regiment commanded by Captain Foster, joined by three hundred Indians, and two hundred and fifty Canadians, had (hearing, it is supposed, that this place was in a defenceless situation) come down within twelve miles of this, having made prisoner of a Major Sherbourne and three hundred of our men on their way thither; but being informed that a reinforcement was arrived, they have retreated.

"General Arnold is in pursuit of them with nine hundred men, four hundred of whom he has sent to endeavour to cut off their retreat, while he pursues them with the utmost expedition, with the remainder.

"Provisions, as I mentioned before, are so very scarce that we are absolutely obliged to seize flour and wheat, pledging the faith of the United Colonies for the payment of the market price. General Thomas is very ill with the smallpox at Chamblee, taken in the natural way."

N. B. There are five instead of three hundred of our people made prisoners. There is a report that General Arnold has beat the enemy, but no account is yet arrived from himself.

Recreated from The Virginia Gazette, June 22, 1776.

ENEMY ATTACKS AT THE CEDARS.

GENERAL ARNOLD IN FULL HEALTH.

BY a gentleman who left Montreal on the 24th May, we have the following intelligence, viz.

That Col. Beadle with a party of 200 men, some of whom were the Caughnawaga Indians, were posted at a place called the Cedars, 45 miles above Montreal. That a number of the aforesaid Indians who had been up the river in a canoe informed the Colonel that a party of Indians consisting of about 500, with 40 regulars, were coming down the river to destroy him and his men, on which he sent immediately to Montreal for more help. And the before mentioned gentleman says, that a party of 14 men under the command of a sergeant being sent forward to the relief of Col. Beadle with some provisions and ammunition were intercepted and fell into the hands of the enemy.

Soon after which the party at the Cedars were attacked, and a skirmish ensued; after which our people abandoned their post and were retreating, when General Arnold came up with about 700 men and reinforced them.

Matters being thus circumstanced they pushed immediately for the Cedars, and with redoubled fury attacked the enemy, killed great numbers, took 60 or 70 prisoners, and routed the whole party, forcing them to fly, leaving their bag and baggage behind them. The spoil consisted of 600 firearms, large quantity of musquet ball, a considerable quantity of ammunition, a number of blankets, hatchets, &c. He further says, that General Arnold has perfectly recovered his health, and that the Prussian General who speaks the French language, has great influence over the Canadians, who offer him every assistance in their power.

Recreated from The Hartford Courant, June 10, 1776.

PHILADELPHIA, *May* 23.—This afternoon, about two o'clock, his Excellency General Washington arrived in this city, from New York.

Recreated from The Virginia Gazette, June 8, 1776.

THE KING'S MAJESTY DENIED.

BALTIMORE, *May* 28.

WHEREAS his Britannic Majesty, King George, has prosecuted, and still prosecutes a cruel and unjust war against the British Colonies in America, and has acceded to acts of Parliament declaring the people of the said Colonies in actual rebellion, and whereas, the good people of this province have taken up arms to defend their rights and liberties, and to repel the hostilities carrying on against them, and whilst engaged in such a contest, cannot with any sincerity of heart, pray for the success of his arms.

Therefore Resolved, that every prayer and petition for the King's Majesty in the book of common prayer and administration of the sacraments and other rights and ceremonies of the church of England, except the second collect for the King in the communion service, be henceforth omitted in all churches and chapels in this province, until our unhappy differences are ended.

Extract from the Minutes, G. DUVALL, Clerk.

TOWN VOTES FOR INDEPENDENCE.

HARTFORD, *May* 27.—We hear the town of Canterbury, in a full meeting, have unanimously adopted the principles of independence contained in Common Sense; and also voted, that the Delegates for the Continental Congress ought to be elected by the freemen of the Colony, and not by their representatives.

CONTINENTAL SHIP LAUNCHED.

PROVIDENCE, *May* 27.—Wednesday the 15th inst. was launched at Providence, the Continental ship America, of 32 guns, esteemed a very fine vessel.

The Coxswain of a barge belonging to one of his Majesty's ships now at Nantasket road, came to town yesterday from that place, and reports, that he, with the crew were sent on shore for milk, but rather than return on board the ship, delivered themselves up to the people of Boston, where they were kindly received.

Recreated from The Pennsylvania Packet, June 3, 1776.

DUNMORE AT GWYNN'S ISLAND.

WILLIAMSBURG, *May* 31.

LAST Sunday lord Dunmore, with his whole fleet, left Hampton road, and came up the bay to Gwynn's island, in Gloucester county, where we understand he has landed his black and white troops, to the number of about 500, and is intrenching. This island contains about 2000 acres, occupied by several families, who are possessed of a considerable quantity of stock, and is well watered. A body of regulars and militia, to the amount of 2000 men, quickly assembled, and are watching their motions and, if opportunity suits, will very likely attempt to beat up their new quarters.

CLINTON LANDS TROOPS.

By a gentleman from North Carolina, we learn that general Clinton has landed 1300 of his troops near Wilmington, and was intrenching. Brigadier-general Moore, with 5000 men, is close by, ready to receive him, should he attempt marching into the country; and we are well assured, that he may be reinforced, in a few days, with twice that number.

Recreated from Purdie's Virginia Gazette, May 31, 1776.

GENERAL ARNOLD MORTIFIED.

Part of a letter from Gen. ARNOLD, *May* 28.

"I have only one minute to acquaint you I am well, tho' much fatigued, having this morning returned from an expedition fifteen leagues above this, at a place called St. Ann's, where we have lately had near five hundred of our men made prisoners, by a number of regulars and savages; you will see a particular account soon of the agreement I have made with them for an exchange of prisoners. I was never more mortified in not having it in my power to revenge the cruel and perfidious treatment of our enemies; humanity forbad the step; and tho' I had a sufficient force, my hands were tied."

Recreated from The Pennsylvania Gazette, June 19, 1776.

To be SOLD, pursuant to an order of the Hon. Committee of Safety, for ready money, on *Saturday* the 15th instant (*June*) before the Raleigh tavern, in the city of *Williamsburg*,

A GENTEEL CHARIOT *and* HARNESS, also two HORSES, lately the property of a certain mr. Logan, and condemned under the ordinance of Convention for punishing the enemies of America.—— At the same time will be sold a likely young NEGRO MAN, who is a very good tailor, has been used to waiting on gentlemen, and taking care of horses, and is a remarkable active well disposed lad.

(1)   WILLIAM AYLETT.

To be SOLD for ready money, at Amelia court-house, on Thursday the 27th instant (June) being court day,

A PARCEL of ivory handled SWORDS, elegantly mounted with silver; also a number of the best kind of RIFLES, with bullet moulds, &c. by

1   BENJAMIN WARD.

FREDERICKSBURG, *May* 15, 1776.

THE present situation of York having occasioned me to remove my family to this town, I shall open a large and fresh assortment of MEDICINES, in the shop formerly occupied by doctor Mercer, where will attend to practise.

THOMAS POWELL.

Recreated from Purdie's Virginia Gazette, June 7, 1776.

FLEET SAILS FROM CAPE FEAR.

WILLIAMSBURG, *June* 8.—By an express which arrived in town this evening from Cape Fear, with letters from his Excellency General Lee, to Brigadier General Lewis dated the 1st inst. we learn, that the whole fleet of the enemy had sailed from that place, the first division on Wednesday the 29th of May, the last on the Friday following. It was uncertain which way they had steered their course, although it was generally believed for South Carolina, while others were of opinion they were bound for Virginia.

Troops are stationed on the sea coast of North Carolina from the Virginia line to Cape Fear, for the purpose of preventing the British plunderers from being supplied with live stock.

By advices from Martinico, we learn, that the French General and Admiral in the West Indies, will commence hostilities against Great Britain the moment that the independence of the American Colonies is authenticated to them.

LEFT INFECTED BLANKETS BEHIND.

Extract of a letter from Wilmington, May 30.

"This day Capt. Alfred Moore came from Fort Johnstone, and says all the English forces are gone on board, and upwards of thirty sail gone over the bar. They left behind them some blankets, with an intention, it is thought, of spreading some infectious disorder among us."

Recreated from The Hartford Courant, July 8, 1776.

PERSONS *held up to* PUBLIC VIEW, *as* ENEMIES *to their* COUNTRY.
JONATHAN HILL, *Alford, Massachusetts-Bay.*
DAVID VAUGHN, *Jericho, Massachusetts-Bay.*
BENJAMIN KILLBORN, *Litchfield, Connecticut.*
Lieut. EBENEZER ORVIS, *Farmington, ditto.*

☞ CONFESSION, ONE DOLLAR.

Recreated from The Hartford Courant, May 27, 1776.

Mr. PURDIE,

UNDERSTANDING that the army is suffering for want of tents, and that the country has ordered a number of wooden ones to be made, which the carpenters cannot supply them with for want of NAILS, and being informed there was a considerable number imported by the college for the purpose of building an addition to it, and as that design seems at present to be laid aside, I cannot see any reason why the Convention should not order those nails to be taken for the use of the army, more especially, as, I am credibly informed, one of the professors has taken two barrels for his own use (one of 10d. the other of 8d.) containing many thousands, and carried them to Gloucester, unknown to the president, who, when he comes to hear of it, I make no doubt will order them to be brought back, and not suffer the college to be plundered by one of its professors.

Please to insert the above intelligence in your paper, for the benefit of the country, and you will oblige your constant reader.

A FRIEND *to* AMERICA.

THE gentleman who advertised for a person to teach English, Writing, and Arithmetick, may hear of one, properly qualified, by applying to the Printer.

Recreated from Purdie's Virginia Gazette, June 7, 1776.

TROOPS MARCHING TO CHARLESTOWN.

WILLIAMSBURG, *June* 22.—Last Monday an express arrived at head-quarters from General Lee, who left his Excellency the 6th of June at Little River, on the road to Charlestown, with three battalions of the North Carolina troops, marching with all possible expedition to the assistance of that place; General Clinton, with upwards of 50 sail of men of war and transports, having appeared off the bar the Tuesday before, where they cast anchor. Two other North Carolina regiments, and Col. Muhlenburg's Virginia battalion, were likewise on their march for Charlestown; with whose assistance it is not doubted but our brethren in South Carolina will be able to defeat any attempts of their enemies, and, when under the conduct of so able and experienced a commander, give them that chastisement which they are so richly entitled to.

Recreated from The Pennsylvania Gazette, July 3, 1776.

ETHAN ALLEN AT NEW YORK.

Extract of a letter from NEW YORK, *June* 7.

"General Sullivan writes the General that ten of our friendly Oneida Indians had waited on him and stayed but two hours, going amongst the Canadian tribes to use their influence in preventing them from joining with the British troops, which they were afraid they would.

"I saw a letter at General Putnam's yesterday, from the Colonel stationed at the Hook, informing of two or three vessels being arrived there, and that two or three deserters informed him that Sir Peter Parker was arrived at North Carolina with 3500 troops under convoy of a 50 gun ship, a 28, and 20 (the names I forgot). That Colonel Ethan Allen is on board the Mercury at the Hook, and captain Proctor of your city in irons on board the same. A Gentleman just come up says, a very large ship arrived yesterday, not less than a 74, but supposed a 90 gun ship; so that there are now at the Hook 10 ships, a brig, &c."

Recreated from The Virginia Gazette, June 22, 1776.

AMERICAN SHIP LAUNCHED.

WATERTOWN, *June* 10.

On Monday the 3d instant, one of the Continental frigates of 24 guns, built at Newbury Port, under the direction of the Hon. Thomas Cushing, Esq., was launched in view of a great number of spectators, she is highly approved of by all who are judges as a very fine ship, she is built with the very best of timber, and the workmanship is compleat.

Thursday last was sent into Cape Ann, a large Jamaica man, with 500 hogsheads of sugar, besides other valuable goods, and a large sum of specie. She was taken by one of the Continental cruizers, who put the Captain, his Lady, and all the hands (which did not voluntarily enter on board the cruizers) ashore at New Providence. The prize master of the ship, on his passage from the West Indies, met with a Scotch vessel of force with 90 soldiers, bound for Boston, on board of which he breakfasted, and told the Scotch Captain he was destined from Jamaica for London, but as he thought sugars would bear a better price at Boston, he had thoughts of trying that market first. The Scotchman being a stranger to this coast desired the prize master to pilot him in, which he agreed to, and conducted him almost into Cape Ann, when he observing two of our privateers appearing in sight, discovered the trap, and being considerably to the windward, made the best of his way off.

Part of a letter from ALBANY, *June* 12, 1776.

"I was this moment informed by General Schuyler, that about 300 of the regular troops came up the river St. Lawrence as far as the Three Rivers, where they were busy intrenching themselves, at which time General Sullivan, with his brigade, arrived at the Sorel; he immediately ordered 2000 of his troops, under general Thompson, to march down to dislodge them, and by appearance there is not the least doubt but he will effect his purposes; should he succeed in this, he is determined to march his army to Quebec, as the enemy have no sufficient force to withstand them."

Recreated from The Pennsylvania Gazette, June 19, 1776.

A WARNING TO NEW YORK.

Copy of a letter from the Hon. JOHN HANCOCK, *President of the* CONTINENTAL CONGRESS, *to the Convention of this city, dated* PHILADELPHIA, *June 11, 1776.*

THE Congress have this day received advice, and are fully convinced, that it is the design of General Howe, to make an attack upon the city of New York as soon as possible; the attack they have reason to believe will be made within ten days; I am therefore most earnestly to request you, by order of Congress, to call forth your Militia, as requested in my letter of the 4th instant, and to forward them with all dispatch to the city of New York; and that you direct that they march in companies, or any other way that will hasten their arrival there. The important day is at hand that we will decide not only the fate of the city of New York, but in all probability of the whole province. On such an occasion there is no necessity to use arguments with Americans; their feelings, I well know, will prompt them to their duty, and the sacredness of the cause will urge them to the field. The greatest exertions of vigour and expedition are requisite to prevent our enemies from getting possession of that town; I must therefore again most earnestly request you, in the name and by the authority of Congress, to send forward the Militia, agreeable to the requisition of Congress, and that you will do it with all the dispatch which the infinite importance of the cause demands.

I have the honour to be, Gentlemen, your most obedient humble servant,

JOHN HANCOCK.

Recreated from The Pennsylvania Packet, June 24, 1776.

NEW YORK, *June* 10.

The Mercury man of war, and an armed sloop, sailed for Halifax, from Sandy Hook, last Friday, having two vessels under convoy.

Thursday afternoon his Excellency George Washington arrived in town from Philadelphia.

Recreated from The Virginia Gazette, June 22, 1776.

At a meeting of the president and masters of the College, June 25, 1776.

WHEREAS, upon an inquiry, it appears to this meeting that mr. Emmanuel Jones, sen. master, has removed one cask of nails, No. 5, the property of the president and masters, as a publick body, out of their storehouse in the College, to his own plantation in Gloucester, under a mistaken notion, that any one of the professors is at liberty to borrow out of this storehouse what goods or chattles he thinks fit, without consulting the proprietors thereof; and whereas this transaction seems to have had its source more in the want of due consideration than evil design, and since mr. Jones intended to restore the nails immediately, but cannot now do it, as they have been seized for the use of the country: It is therefore ordered, that no farther notice be taken of this affair, provided that these proceedings be immediately published in the same printer's paper wherein mr. Jones endeavoured to avail himself of a custom, which, as far as we know, or believe, never existed, and has unjustly, as well as weakly, attempted to make an arraignment of the conduct of his brethren serve as an apology for his own erroneous practice.

(By order of the society)

EMMANUEL JONES, clerk.

Recreated from Purdie's Virginia Gazette, June 28, 1776.

THE GRAND QUESTION.

PHILADELPHIA, *June* 11—Monday the first of July is fixed upon to decide the grand question of AMERICAN INDEPENDENCE, in General Congress.

Part of a letter from PHILADELPHIA, *June* 11.

"The owners of two small six gun privateers have got, by the capture of three Jamaica-men (British property), 5000l. each, and the common sailors 500l. each. A few days will make East India property equally liable."

Recreated from Purdie's Virginia Gazette, June 21, 1776.

DECEIVED AT THREE RIVERS.

Extract from a letter to GENERAL SCHUYLER, *dated Sorel, June* 12, 1776.

"On the 6th inst. about 2000 men, under the command of Gen. Thompson, marched to attack the enemy at Three rivers. They designed to have surprised them at day break on the 8th inst. but the guide led them into a morass, returning from which took them two hours; they then had to pass through a long swamp, in the face of the enemy, who had a large reinforcement arrived very unhappily that evening, and landed in sight of our men. Being well equipped they gave General Thompson's party so warm a reception, he thought prudent to retreat; in the mean time a body of 600 were sent off from the enemy to cut off our retreat, and destroy our batteaus, which they could not effect; and our batteaus were all saved but one, out of which the men escaped.

"General Thompson, Colonel Irvine, Dr. M'Kennie, Parson M'Auley, Lieutenants Bird and Currey, and about 40 men are prisoners, and about 150 more are missing.

"It is supposed that Gen. Burgoyne has with him the whole reinforcement designed for Canada. Our army are more than half sick with the small pox, the other part have an enemy of more than three times their number—may they be recruited—but I fear the usual slowness will prevent it."

Recreated from The Pennsylvania Gazette, July 3, 1776.

A TURN TO INDEPENDENCE.

PHILADELPHIA, *June* 12.—Last Saturday the Hon. House of Assembly gave the following INSTRUCTIONS to their Delegates in CONGRESS.

WHEN, by our instructions of last November, we strictly enjoined you, in behalf of this Colony, to dissent from and utterly reject any proposition, should such be made, that might cause or lead to a separation from Great Britain, or a change of the form of this government, our restrictions did not arise from any diffidence of your ability, prudence or integrity, but from an earnest desire to serve the good people of Pennsylvania with fidelity, in times so full of alarming dangers and perplexing difficulties.

The situation of public affairs is since so greatly altered, that we now think ourselves justifiable in removing the restrictions laid upon you by those instructions.

The contempt with which the last petitions of the Hon. Congress have been treated; the late act of parliament declaring the just resistance of the Colonists, against violences actually offered, to be rebellion, excluding them from the protection of the Crown, and even compelling some of them to bear arms against their countrymen; the treaties of the King of Great Britain with other Princes for engaging foreign mercenaries, to aid the forces of that kingdom, in their hostile enterprise against America, and his answer to the petition of the Lord Mayor, Aldermen and Commons of the city of London, manifest such a determined and implacable resolution to effect the utter destruction of these Colonies, that all hopes of a reconciliation, on reasonable terms, are extinguished. Nevertheless, it is our ardent desire that a civil war, with all its attending miseries, should be ended by a secure and honourable peace.

We therefore hereby authorize you to concur with the other Delegates in Congress, in forming such farther compacts between the United Colonies, concluding such treaties with kingdoms and states, and in adopting such measures as shall be judged necessary for promoting the liberty, safety and interests of America; reserving to the people of this colony the sole and exclusive right of regulating the internal government and police of the same.

The happiness of these colonies has, during the whole course of this fatal controversy, been our first wish. Their reconciliation with Great Britain our next. Ardently have we prayed for the accomplishment of both. But if we must renounce the one or the other, we humbly trust in the mercies of the Supreme Governor of the Universe, that we shall not stand condemned before his throne, if our choice is determined by that over-ruling law of self-preservation, which his divine wisdom has thought fit to implant in the hearts of his creatures.

Recreated from The Pennsylvania Gazette, June 12, 1776.

BRITISH ABANDON BOSTON HARBOUR.

Disgraceful Precipitate Flight.

Last Thursday, the 13th instant, the inhabitants of the town of Boston were made acquainted, by beat of drum, that an expedition was to be undertaken against our enemy's ships in Nantasket Road, and for erecting proper fortifications in the lower harbour. Accordingly, detachments from the colonial regiments commanded by the Cols. Marshall and Whitney; and a battalion of train commanded by Lieut. Col. Crafts, were embarked on board boats at the Long Wharf, together with cannon, ammunition, provisions, intrenching tools, and every necessary implement, and proceeded for Pettick's Island and Hull, where they were joined by some continental troops, and sea coast companies, so as to make near 600 men at each place; a like number of the militia from the towns in the vicinity of Boston harbour, with a detachment from the train, and some field pieces, took post at Moon Island, Hoff's Neck, and Point Alderton.

At the same time a detachment from the continental army under the command of Col. Whitcomb, with two 18 pounders, one 13 inch mortar with the necessary apparatus, intrenching tools, &c. were embarked for Long Island, to take post there. The troops did not arrive at their several places of destination till near morning, occasioned by a flat calm; notwithstanding, such was the activity and alertness of our men, that they had the cannon planted, and a line of defence hove upon Long Island and Nantasket Hill in a few hours, when a cannon shot from Long Island announced to the enemy our design; upon which a signal was immediately made for the whole fleet, consisting of eight ships, 2 snows, 2 brigs, and 1 schooner, to remove and get under way

The Commodore bore our fire, and returned it with spirit. Our shot from Long Island pierced the upper works of his ship, when he immediately unmoored or cut his cables and got under sail, and happy for him that he did so, for in a small space of time afterwards, a shell from our works fell into the very spot he had but just before quitted.

Unhappily our cannon did not arrive at Pettick's Island and Nantasket as soon as might have been wished, but the fire from the latter place being properly pointed against the Commodore's ship, who came to the Light-House channel, is apprehended to have done considerable execution.

In short, the enemy were compelled once more to make a disgraceful precipitate flight; and we have it now in our power to congratulate our readers on our being in possession of the lower harbour of Boston; and had the wind have been to the eastward, we are confident we should have had the much greater pleasure of giving them joy on our being in the possession of many of their ships. Through divine Providence, not one of our men were hurt.

Four different views of the battle of Lexington and Concord, neatly engraved from original paintings, taken on the spot, to be SOLD, by ENOS DOOLITTLE, Under the Printing Office, Hartford; who has likewise a quantity of crucibles for sale.

Recreated from The Hartford Courant, June 24, 1776.

BRITISH DROVE FROM BOSTON HARBOUR.

Extract of a letter from BOSTON, *June* 17.

"I have the pleasure to acquaint you of the piratical fleet being drove from this harbour a few days ago by our people. They placed a number of cannon on the heights below, and had prepared a number of flat bottomed boats, &c. but the cannon only did the business, and they pushed off with great precipitation both men of war and transports.

"Last evening came into the harbour two transports, a ship and a brig, from the enemy's land, say England, &c. in expectation of finding the fleet that had been so lately driven away, and to their great disappointment were followed in by several privateers, amongst which was the Connecticut brig, and on there coming up with Point Alderton, they were fired on by the cannon there, when they both struck; and sent on shore a boat load of their men. Night coming on soon, they attempted their escape by going through Broad Sound, when the privateers attacked them again, and a very severe engagement ensued for three quarters of an hour.

"The enemy had a Major and seven men killed, and several wounded; all the rest, consisting of 210 Highland regular rebels, with all their equipment, taken prisoners, amongst whom is a Colonel Campbell. They are now on their way up from Nantasket to this town, all in safe custody. The transports were loaded with provisions and baggage; the ship mounted six 6 pounders, and the brig two. While I am writing this they are all in sight. We had three men wounded in the engagement, one mortally, which is all the loss we sustained."

WILLIAMSBURG, *June* 15.—We learn from Gloucester, that Lord Dunmore has erected hospitals upon Gwynn's island; that his old friend Andrew Sprowle is dead, and that they are inoculating the blacks for the smallpox. His Lordship, before the departure of the fleet from Norfolk harbour, had two of those wretches inoculated and sent ashore, in order to spread the infection, but it was happily prevented.

One day this week a small vessel belonging to the enemy, with five hands on board, ran aground on the Gloucester shore, within musket shot, and was taken. The crew jumped overboard, two swam to Gwynn's island, one was shot, and the other two drowned.

We hear the Honourable Continental Congress have appointed Col. Hugh Mercer, of the 3d regiment, to the rank of Brigadier General in the service of the United Colonies, and that he will set out immediately for New York.

Recreated from The Pennsylvania Gazette, June 26, 1776.

Part of a letter from CAPT. SETH HARDING, *Commander of the brig* Defence, *in the Continental service, to the* HON. GOVERNOR TRUMBULL, *dated* BOSTON, *June* 19, 1776.

"I sailed on Sunday last from Plymouth. Soon after we came to sail, I heard a considerable firing to the northward. In the evening I fell in with four armed schooners, near the entrance of Boston harbour, who informed me they had been engaged with a ship and brig, and were obliged to quit them. Soon after I came up into Nantasket road, where I found the ship and brig at anchor, I immediately fell in between the two, and came to anchor about 11 o'clock at night. I hailed the ship, who answered, "from Great Britain." I ordered her to strike her colours to America. They answered, asking,—"What brig is that?"—I told them,—The Defence.—I then hailed him again and told him, I did not want to kill his men, but would have the ship at all events, and again ordered them to strike; upon which the Major (since dead) said, "yes, I'll strike," and fired in a broadside upon me, which I immediately returned, when an engagement began, which lasted three glasses when the ship and brig both struck. In this engagement I had 9 men wounded, but none killed. The enemy had 18 killed, and a number wounded. My officers and men behaved with great bravery, none could have outdone them. We took out of the above vessels 210 prisoners, among whom is Col. Campbell, of Gen. Frazer's regiment of Highlanders. The Major was killed in the engagement.

"Yesterday a ship was seen in the Bay, which came towards the entrance of Boston harbour; upon which I came to sail, with four schooners in company; we came up with them, and took them without an engagement; there were on board 112 Highlanders. As there are a number more of the same fleet expected every day, and the General urges me to stay, I shall tarry a few days, and then proceed for New London. My brig is much damaged in her sails and rigging. I am, with great respect,

"Your Honour's most humble servant,
"SETH HARDING."

PHILADELPHIA, June 19.

Yesterday the Deputies from the Counties of this Province met in PROVINCIAL CONFERENCE in this city, in consequence of the Resolution of the Continental Congress of the 15th of May, declaring it *"to be necessary that the exercise of any kind of authority under the Crown of Great Britain should be totally suppressed, and all the powers of government exerted under the authority of the people."*

BOSTON, June 24.

'Tis worthy of special notice, that the 14th of June, 1774, was the last day allowed for trading vessels to leave or enter the port of Boston, through the cruelty of a British Act of Parliament; and that on the 14th of June, 1776, through the blessing of God upon the operations of a much injured and oppressed people, was the last day allowed for British men of war or ministerial vessels to remain or enter within the said port, but as American prizes, Thus has Providence retaliated.

We have now upwards of 400 Highlanders confined in the Work-house and Alms-hose, who we hear are soon to be distributed in country towns.

Yesterday afternoon 13 large ships were seen standing in for Boston, thought to be the remainder of the Scotch fleet, with their convoy.

217 SCOTCH HIGHLANDERS TAKEN.

WILLIAMSBURG, *June* 22.—This morning Capt. James Barron came to town from Jamestown, with the agreeable news that he and his brother, in two small armed vessels, were safe arrived there with the Oxford transport from Glasgow, having on board 217 Scotch Highlanders, with a number of women and children, which they took last Wednesday evening on her way up to Gwyn's island, to join lord Dunmore.

The people on board inform, that they are part of a body of 3000 troops which sailed from Glasgow for Boston but upon hearing that place was in our possession, they steered their course for Halifax; that they had been taken by the Andrew Doria, one of the Continental fleet, who after disarming them, and taking out all the principal officers, with such of the transport's crew as were acquainted with navigation, put eight of their own hand on board to bring her into port, but that the carpenter of the transport formed a party and rescued the vessel from them, and was conducting her into Hampton road when the two Captain Barrons very fortunately came across them, and moored them safe in Jamestown, where they are now disembarking, and are expected in town this day.

• • • •

Yesterday the Hon. Convention made the choice of the following gentlemen to represent this dominion in General Congress, for one year, viz. GEORGE WYTHE, THOMAS NELSON, jun., RICHARD HENRY LEE, THOMAS JEFFERSON, AND FRANCIS LIGHTFOOT LEE, Esquires.

Recreated from The Pennsylvania Gazette, July 3, 1776.

Just published and to be sold by JOHN DUNLAP, in Market street, Philadelphia,
EXTRACTS,
From the JOURNALS of
CONGRESS,
RELATIVE TO THE
Captures and Condemnation of PRIZES, and the fitting out PRIVATEERS; together with the Rules and Regulations of the NAVY, and Instructions to the Commanders of private SHIPS of WAR.

Recreated from The Pennsylvania Packet, June 17, 1776.

PLOT TO KILL GEN. WASHINGTON.

Extract of a letter from NEW YORK, *June* 24.

"My last to you was by Friday's post, since which a most barbarous and infernal plot has been discovered among our Tories, the particulars of which I cannot give you, as the Committee of Examination consists of but three, who are sworn to secrecy. Two of Washington's guards are concerned, the third they tempted to join them made the first discovery: The general report of their design is as follows: Upon the arrival of the troops, they were to murder all of the Staff Officers, blow up the magazines, and secure the passes of the town.

"Gilbert Forbes, Gunsmith, in the Broadway, was taken between two and three o'clock on Saturday morning, and carried before our Provincial Congress, who were then sitting, but refusing to make any discovery, he was sent to gaol, and put in irons. Young Mr. Livingston went to see him early in the morning, told him he was sorry to find he had been concerned, and, as his time was very short, not having above three days to live, advised him to prepare himself. This had the desired effect; he asked to be carried before the Congress again, and he would discover all he knew. Several have been since taken, between 20 and 30, among them our Mayor, who are all now under confinement. It is said their party consisted of about 500.

"I have just heard the Mayor has confessed bringing money from Tryon, to pay for Rifle guns that Forbes had made. Burgoyne is arrived at Quebec with his fleet."

Recreated from The Pennsylvania Gazette, June 26, 1776.

IN CONGRESS, *June* 26, 1776.
RESOLVED, that a bounty of TEN DOLLARS be given to every non-commissioned officer and soldier who will enlist to serve for the term of three years.

Extract from the minutes.
CHARLES THOMPSON, *Secretary*.

Recreated from Purdie's Virginia Gazette, July 12, 1776.

AN ACCOUNT FROM THREE RIVERS.

A letter from PHILADELPHIA, *dated June* 25.

"An express this moment came to Congress, informing us of general Thompson and col. Irwin being totally defeated by general Burgoyne. Thompson and Irwin had been detached with 700 men to dislodge a party who had taken post on the Three Rivers. The guide deceived the general, and led him into a swamp, the crossing of which exposed him to a cannonade from the ships of war. It seems, the very day before, Burgoyne arrived with 70 transports of troops. Thompson's expedition was known; he was met and totally routed, he himself taken prisoner, with col. Irwin, and 150 privates and officers, killed, wounded, or taken prisoners, that number being missing; the rest of the detachment have gotten back. It is conjectured that Burgoyne has brought with him 10,000 men, but this is not probable. We killed and wounded about 30."

Recreated from Purdie's Virginia Gazette, July 5, 1776.

WILLIAMSBURG, *June* 29.

ON Sunday last a man of war and two merchantmen went up to Gwyn's island, from sea. And on Wednesday the Highlanders taken by Captain Barron set out on their march into the back country, under a strong guard.

ALBEMARLE, *May* 12, 1776.

CAME to my House, this Day, TWO MULATTO BOYS about 13 Years of Age, who say they are Twins, their Names *Thomas Hill* and *James Hill*, Children of *Susanna Hill*, a free Woman, who lived at *Fredericksburg* with one *Thomas Mitchell*, a Scotch Merchant, and went away with him either to *Scotland* or Lord *Dunmore* (as they understand) about two Months and a Half past. They claim Freedom, and say they never were bound to any Person: But as they may be Slaves to Somebody, I have thought it prudent to publish this Advertisement, that their Master (if they have any) may get them again. (§) JOSEPH WOOLING.

WILLIAM & MARY *College, June* 21, 1776.

THOSE young Gentlemen who have a Right to their Maintenance in the College, commonly styled Foundationers, are desired to return to the College as soon as possible, unless they choose to have their Places filled up by other Persons.

By Order of the President and Masters.
EMMANUEL JONES, Clerk.

Recreated from The Virginia Gazette, June 29, 1776.

FURIOUS BATTLE AT FORT SULLIVAN.

ASTONISHING AMERICAN BRAVERY.

Extract of a letter from his EXCELLENCY MAJOR GENERAL LEE, *to the* HON. EDMUND PENDLETON, *esq., President of the Convention, dated* CHARLESTOWN, *June* 29, 1776.

YESTERDAY, about 11 o'clock, the enemy's squadron, consisting of one 50 and one 40 gun ship, and six frigates, came to anchor before fort Sullivan, and began one of the most furious cannonades I ever heard or saw. Their project was apparently, at the same time, to land their troops on the east end of the island. Twice they attempted it, and as often were gallantly repulsed. The ships continued their fire on the fort till 11 at night. The behaviour of the garrison, both men and officers, with col. Moutrie at their head, I confess, astonished me. It was brave to the last degree.

I had no idea that so much coolness and intrepidity could be displayed, by a collection of raw recruits, as I was witness of in this garrison. Had we been better supplied with ammunition, it is most probable this squadron would have been utterly destroyed. However, they have no reason to triumph. One of their frigates is now in flames, another lost her boltsprit. The commodore and a 40 gun ship had their mizzens shot away, and are otherwise much damaged. In short, they may be said, in this their first essay on South Carolina, to have been worsted; but, I presume, they will make another attempt. Our loss is 10 killed and 12 wounded, 7 of whom have lost their legs or arms. The defences of the fort have received no injury; only one gun dismounted.

I shall write, when the affair is finished, a more accurate relation to your Convention, and to the Congress. In the mean time, I think it but justice to publish the merits of col. Moutrie and his brave garrison. Colonel Thompson, of the South Carolina rangers, acquitted himself most nobly in repulsing the troops who attempted to land at the other end of the island.

I know not which corps I have the greatest reason to be pleased with, Muhlenburg's Virginians, or the North Carolina troops; they are both equally alert, zealous and spirited.

I shall not write to Congress till the operations of the enemy are brought to something more like a decision. If you, Sir, think this short relation of importance sufficient, you will of course transmit it.

The frigate that was on fire is this moment blown up.

Recreated from Purdie's Virginia Gazette, July 19, 1776.

A PLOTTER EXECUTED.

NEW YORK, *July* 1.—Last Friday in the forenoon was executed in a field between the colonels M'Dougall and Huntington's camp, near the Bowery-lane, (in the presence of near twenty thousand spectators) a soldier belonging to his Excellency General Washington's guards, for mutiny and conspiracy, being one of those who formed, and was soon to have put in execution, that horrid plot of assassinating the staff officers, blowing up the magazines, and securing the passes of the town on the arrival of the hungry ministerial myrmidons. It is hoped the remainder of those miscreants, now in our possession, will meet with a punishment adequate to their crimes.

July 4.—It is currently reported that our cruisers have taken thirteen sail of transports to the eastward.

Recreated from The Virginia Gazette, July 20, 1776.

HIGHLANDERS FOOLED.

We hear that some of the Highlanders, lately taken, assert, that they were told before they sailed, that they were sent hither to take possession of forfeited farms, the rebels having been drove by the King's troops several hundred miles into the country. One or more of them also declare, that, out of the number inlisted in Scotland for the American service, 400 deserted on their march from Perth to Greenock.

Recreated from The Pennsylvania Packet, July 1, 1776.

GLORIOUS NEWS.

IT is with much satisfaction the printer can entertain his readers with the following account of an engagement which happened at Charlestown the 28th of last month, between his Britannick majesty's fleet commanded by sir Peter Parker and our gallant brethren of that city. A letter from his excellency general LEE, dated July the 3d, says, "that the affair is much more important than he at first imagined; and that the enclosed is the narrative of some deserters, one of whom is a very intelligent fellow; that he thinks it is his duty to send the account in its proper form, without adding or curtailing a single circumstance; and congratulates the Hon. President of the Convention, and the publick, on an event which certainly does great credit to the American arms, and, he hopes, must be attended with very great advantages."

NARRATIVE by Thomas Bennet of col. Damilton's Massachusetts regiment, Daniel Hawkins of Boston, Robert Scott and Edmond Alston of New Hampshire, and James Scott of Virginia, deserters from the fleet which attacked and were beaten off by the brave garrison in fort Sullivan, under the command of col. Moutrie, on Friday the 28th of June, 1776. [They are all Americans, and had been taken by the enemy at sea.]

THE Bristol of 50 guns, commanded by sir Peter Parker, is greatly damaged in the hull, large knees and timbers shot through, and smashed. If the water had not been very smooth, it would have been impossible to have kept her from sinking. All the carpenters in the fleet had been called to her assistance. Her mizzen-mast shot away, main-mast badly wounded by three several shot, fore-mast by two, and her rigging, sails, and yards, much damaged.

The captain of the commodore lost his left arm, above the elbow. He was sent yesterday (June 30) to England, in a brigantine. The commodore had his breeches tore off, his backside laid bare, and his thigh and knee much wounded. He walks only when supported by two men.

There are 44 men killed, and 30 wounded, among whom were many midshipmen and petty officers; 20 of the wounded died since the action. It was talked in the fleet, that the two large ships would go over the bar again, and proceed to English harbour, in Antigua, to be repaired. The Bristol, when lightened as much as possible, drew 18 feet 7 inches water.

The Experiment of 50 guns, on two decks, all twelve pounders, a slighter vessel than the Bristol, exceedingly damaged in her hull, several ports beat in, one of her mizzen-masts hurt, but uncertain of particulars. Killed 47, of whom the captain was one. Wounded 30; several since dead. Draws, when lightest, 17 feet water. The general opinion, that neither of these large ships will go safely over the bar again.

Solebay, 28 guns, two men killed, and four wounded. Active 28 guns, the lieutenant killed, and four men wounded. Actaeon 28, Sphynx 20, Syren 28, all got aground; the first in coming up, the two latter in running away. The Sphynx cut away her boltsprit; the Syren got off. The Actaeon, by the assistance of a friendly English seaman, remained fast; burnt, and blown up by her own people. [Whilst she was on fire, capt. Milligan, one of our marine officers, and a party of men, boarded her, brought off her colours, the ship's bell, and as many sails and stores as three boats could contain.]

The Thunder bomb lay at a considerable distance, throwing shells at the fort; and, by overcharging, had shattered the beds and damaged the ship so much as to render it necessary for her to go into dock before she can act again.

The Friendship, a hired armed vessel of 26 guns, of various sizes, covered the bomb, as did the Syren, which also fired very briskly at the fort. The whole fleet badly manned, and sickly, particularly the Syren's crew; at two thirds short allowance of provision and water, and no fresh meat since their arrival, June the 1st.

Lord William Campbell had been very anxious for the attack, and proposed taking all the forts with only the Syren and Solebay.

Lord Cornwallis has the chief command of the land forces; he and general Clinton are both ashore with the troops at Long Island. His lordship had some time ago urged sir Peter Parker to attack on the sea side, otherwise he would march up, attack, and take the fort, and complain of sir Peter's tardiness. The commodore replied, "Lord Cornwallis might march his troops where he pleased, but the fleet required fair wind; the first that happened, he would proceed against the fort." The general at that time believed we had no troops out of the garrison, but he was soon better informed, being since repulsed, and drove back with loss. He remained quiet, and left the commodore to enjoy the glory of being defeated alone.

When the fleet sailed from Ireland, the number of troops was about 4000; but 11 transports had been separated from the rest, and have not been since heard of. Some of the deserters, who had seen all the land forces, said the amount was from 1300 to 2000 most.

Between 9 and 10 o'clock, The Actaeon, the commodore, and other ships, began to steal away. They made no piping, nor waited to heave up their anchors, but slipped their cables. The commodore has only one anchor and cable left.

About 2 o'clock on Friday, when the fort was waiting for a supply of powder, some of the men of war's men, mistaking the unavoidable silence for surrender, cried out, The Yankies had done fighting. Others replied, By God we are glad of it, for we never had such a drubbing in or lives. We had been told the Yankies would not stand two fires, but we never saw better fellows. All the common men in the fleet spoke loudly in praise of the garrison, brave fine fellows!

NEW YORK, June 26.

YESTERDAY the Hon. major-general Gates set off for Canada, being appointed, we hear, commander in chief for the northern department.

PHILADELPHIA, July 3.

Yesterday the CONTINENTAL CONGRESS declared the UNITED COLONIES FREE and INDEPENDENT STATES.

Recreated from The Pennsylvania Gazette, July 3, 1776.

WANTED,

SEVERAL SURGEONS for the NAVY. Such as incline to enter into the service will please to apply to the commissioners, now sitting in *Williamsburg*.

AMHERST, July 5, 1776.

NOTICE is hereby given, that I shall attend at the courthouse of this county on the first *Monday*, and at *Bedford* courthouse on the fourth *Monday*, in *August*, being court days, to purchase HORSES for the third troop to be raised pursuant to a late ordinance of General Convention. Any horses four feet ten inches high, at least, will be received, and a good price given for them.

WILLIAM PENN.

YORK, July 5, 1776.

WANTED immediately, to mount the sixth troop, a number of HORSES, either bays, browns, sorrels, or chestnuts, from 4 to 7 years old, and not under 14 hands high. I will give ready cash for all such as shall suit the purpose they are intended for.

JOHN NELSON.

Recreated from Purdie's Virginia Gazette, July 12, 1776.

THE MOST IMPORTANT EVENT.

The first instant was rendered remarkable by the most important event that ever happened in the American Colonies, an event which will doubtless be celebrated through a long succession of future ages, by anniversary commemorations, and be considered as a grand Era in the history of the American States.

On this auspicious day, the Representatives of the Thirteen United Colonies, by the providence of God, unanimously agreed to, and voted a Proclamation, declaring the said Colonies FREE and INDEPENDENT STATES, which was proclaimed at the State House in Philadelphia, on Monday last, and received with joyful acclamations. Copies were also distributed to All the United Colonies.

On Wednesday last it was read at the head of each Brigade of the Continental Army posted at and near New York, and every where received with loud hoozas, and the utmost demonstrations of joy.

The same evening the equestran statue of George III, which Tory pride and folly raised in the year 1770, was, by the Sons of Freedom, laid prostrate in the dirt, the just desert of an ungrateful tyrant! The lead wherewith this monument was made, is to be run into bullets, to assimilate with the brain of our infatuated adversaries, who to gain a pepper corn, have lost an Empire.

Lord Clare, in the House of Commons, declared that a pepper corn, in acknowledgement of Britain's right to tax America, was of more importance than millions without it.

BOSTON, *July* 15.—The General Court have passed an Act allowing of innoculation with Small Pox in the Town of Boston till next Monday the 15th Instant, after which Time it is forbidden on severe Penalties both on the Innoculator and Innoculated. And the Selectmen are impowered and directed to remove all Persons such with the Small Pox on the third of August next, in Order that the Town may be cleared of all Infection immediately after.

Recreated from The Hartford Courant, July 15, 1776.

INDEPENDENCE DECLARED.

Abstract from the minutes of the GENERAL CONGRESS, *of Thursday the* 4th *instant, declaring the* UNITED COLONIES *free and independent states*:

IN every stage of these oppressions, we have petitioned for redress in the most humble terms. Our repeated petitions have been answered only by repeated injury. A prince whose character is thus marked, by every act which may define a TYRANT, is unfit to be the ruler of a FREE PEOPLE.

Nor have we been wanting in attentions to our British brethren. We have warned them, from time to time, of attempts by their legislature to extend an unwarrantable jurisdiction over us. We have reminded them of the circumstances of our emigration and settlement here. We have appealed to their native justice and magnanimity, and we have conjured them by the ties of our common kindred to disavow these usurpations, which would inevitably interrupt our connexions and correspondence. They too have been deaf to the voice of justice and consanguinity. We must therefore acquiesce in the necessity which denounces our separation, and hold them (as we hold the rest of mankind) enemies in war; in peace, friends.

We therefore, the representatives of the UNITED STATES OF AMERICA, in General Congress assembled, appealing to the Supreme Judge of the world for the rectitude of our intentions, do, in the name and by the authority of the good people of these colonies, solemnly publish and declare, that these United Colonies are, and of right ought to be, FREE and INDEPENDENT STATES, they have full power to levy war, conclude peace, contract alliances, establish commerce, and to do all other acts and things which INDEPENDENT STATES may of right do. And for the support of this declaration, with a firm reliance on the protection of Divine Providence, we mutually pledge to each other our lives, our fortunes, and our sacred honour.

Signed by order and in behalf of the CONGRESS,

JOHN HANCOCK, president.

Recreated from Purdie's Virginia Gazette, July 19, 1776.

July 10, 1776. NUMB. 2481.

The PENNSYLVANIA GAZETTE

Containing the Freſheſt Advices, Foreign and Domeſtic.

IN CONGRESS, JULY 4, 1776.
A DECLARATION
By the REPRESENTATIVES of the UNITED STATES of AMERICA, in GENERAL CONGRESS aſſembled.

WHEN, in the Courſe of human Events, it becomes neceſſary for one People to diſſolve the political Bands which have connected them with another, and to aſſume among the Powers of the Earth, the ſeparate and equal Station to which the Laws of Nature and of Nature's God entitle them, a decent Reſpect to the Opinions of Mankind requires that they ſhould declare the cauſes which impel them to the Separation.

We hold theſe Truths to be ſelf-evident, that all Men are created equal, that they are endowed by their Creator with certain unalienable Rights, that among theſe are Life, Liberty, and the Purſuit of Happineſs—That to ſecure theſe Rights, Governments are inſtituted among Men, deriving their juſt Powers from the Conſent of the Governed, that whenever any Form of Government becomes deſtructive of theſe Ends, it is the Right of the People to alter or to aboliſh it, and to inſtitute new Government, laying its Foundation on ſuch Principles, and organizing its Powers in ſuch Form, as to them ſhall ſeem moſt likely to effect their Safety and Happineſs. Prudence, indeed, will dictate that Governments long eſtabliſhed ſhould not be changed for light and tranſient Cauſes; and accordingly all Experience hath ſhewn, that Mankind are more diſpoſed to ſuffer, while Evils are ſufferable, than to right themſelves by aboliſhing the Forms to which they are accuſtomed. But when a long Train of Abuſes and Uſurpations, purſuing invariably the ſame Object, evinces a Deſign to reduce them under abſolute Deſpotiſm, it is their Right, it is their Duty, to throw off ſuch Government, and to provide new Guards for their future Security. Such has been the patient Sufferance of theſe Colonies; and ſuch is now the Neceſſity which conſtrains them to alter their former Syſtems of Government. The Hiſtory of the preſent King of Great-Britain is a Hiſtory of repeated Injuries and Uſurpations, all having in direct Object the Eſtabliſhment of an abſolute Tyranny over theſe States. To prove this, let Facts be ſubmitted to a candid World.

He has refuſed his Aſſent to Laws, the moſt wholeſome and neceſſary for the public Good.

He has forbidden his Governors to paſs Laws of immediate and preſſing Importance, unleſs ſuſpended in their Operation till his Aſſent ſhould be obtained; and when ſo ſuſpended, he has utterly neglected to attend to them.

He has refuſed to paſs other Laws for the Accommodation of large Diſtricts of People, unleſs thoſe People would relinquiſh the Right of Repreſentation in the Legiſlature, a Right ineſtimable to them, and formidable to

For oppoſing our own Legiſlatures, and declaring themſelves inveſted with Power to legiſlate for us in all Caſes whatſoever.

He has abdicated Government here, by declaring us out of his Protection and waging War againſt us.

He has plundered our Seas, ravaged our Coaſts, burnt our Towns, and deſtroyed the Lives of our People.

He is, at this Time, tranſporting large Armies of foreign Mercenaries to compleat the Works of Death, Deſolation and Tyranny, already begun with Circumſtances of Cruelty and Perfidy, ſcarcely paralleled in the moſt barbarous Ages, and totally unworthy the Head of a civilized Nation.

He has conſtrained our Fellow-Citizens, taken captive on the High Seas, to bear Arms againſt their Country, to become the Executioners of their Friends and Brethren, or to fall themſelves by their Hands.

He has excited domeſtic Inſurrections amongſt us, and has endeavoured to bring on the Inhabitants of our Frontiers, the merciless Indian Savages, whoſe known Rule of Warfare is an undiſtinguiſhed Deſtruction of all Ages, Sexes and Conditions.

In every Stage of theſe Oppreſſions we have petitioned for Redreſs in the moſt humble Terms: Our repeated Petitions have been anſwered only by repeated Injury. A Prince, whoſe Character is thus marked by every Act which may define a Tyrant, is unfit to be the Ruler of a free People.

Nor have we been wanting in Attentions to our Britiſh Brethren. We have warned them from Time to Time of Attempts by their Legiſlature to extend an unwarrantable Juriſdiction over us. We have reminded them of the Circumſtances of our Emigration and Settlement here. We have appealed to their native Juſtice and Magnanimity, and we have conjured them, by the Ties of our common Kindred, to diſavow theſe Uſurpations, which would inevitably interrupt our Connections and Correſpondence. They too have been deaf to the Voice of Juſtice and of Conſanguinity. We muſt, therefore, acquieſce in the Neceſſity, which denounces our Separation, and hold them, as we hold the reſt of Mankind, Enemies in War, in Peace, Friends.

We, therefore, the Repreſentatives of the UNITED STATES OF AMERICA, in GENERAL CONGRESS Aſſembled, appealing to the Supreme Judge of the World for the Rectitude of our Intentions, do, in the Name and by Authority of the good People of theſe Colonies, ſolemnly Publiſh and Declare, That theſe United Colonies are, and of Right ought to be, FREE AND INDEPENDENT STATES; that they are abſolved from all Allegiance to the Britiſh Crown, and that all political Connection between them and the State of Great Britain, is and ought to be totally diſſolved; and that as FREE AND INDEPENDENT STATES, they have full Power to levy War, conclude Peace, contract Alliances, eſtabliſh Commerce, and to do all other Acts and Things which INDEPENDENT STATES may of right do. And for the Support of this

juſt publiſhed, and to be ſold by JOHN DUNLAP, in Market-ſtreet, Philadelphia,

OBSERVATIONS ON THE
Nature of CIVIL LIBERTY, the Principles of GOVERNMENT, and the Juſtice and Policy of the WAR with AMERICA.

To which is added,
An APPENDIX, containing a State of the National Debt, an eſtimate of the Monies drawn from the Public by the taxes, and an account of the National Income and Expenditure ſince the laſt War.

By RICHARD PRICE, D.D. F.R.S.

*** This learned, judicious and liberal author had the thanks of the Common Council, and the Freedom of the City of London preſented to him in a gold box, for this his much admired and excellent pamphlet on Civil Liberty.—And for which he alſo deſerves the united thanks of America.

July 8, 1776.

SEVEN POUNDS Reward.

RUN away, laſt Sunday night, from the ſubſcriber, living in Cheſter county, the two following ſervants, viz. Edward Gray, about 5 feet 6 inches high, pock-marked, freckle faced, about 26 years of age, ſays he was born in London, was bound his time with William Hoskins, in New-Caſtle county, underſtands all ſorts of plantation work, and ſays he worked at the Miller's buſineſs two years with one Reynolds, in Northampton; had on, when he went away, white country linen ſhirt and trouſers, new coat tow jacket, and a leather apron, took with him a ſcythe and hangers. Said Gray, was talked out of gaol by the ſubſcriber, and for no ſecurity eſcaped thereto him; it is hoped that every honeſt perſon will endeavor to apprehend ſaid Gray, as for the reward that be in order to bring him to juſtice. The other, named John Duffy, about 25 years of age, born in New-England, a ſtout well ſet fellow, about 5 feet 8 or 9 inches high, with dirty coloured hair, his face with wide apart; ſays he belongs to the Row-galleys, and has been, ſeen about Port-Penn; had on, when he went away, white ſhirt and trouſers, a red under jacket, without ſleeves, no ſhoes nor ſtockings; he is fond of ſtrong drink, and company, and a very great liar. Whoever takes up the ſaid runaways, and ſecures them, ſo as the ſubſcriber gets them again, ſhall have Five Pounds for Gray, and Forty Shillings for Duffy, and reaſonable charges for both, paid by WILLIAM KERLIN.

N.B. Duffy ran away the 21ſt of June.

Paxton, July 2, 1776.

BY virtue of a writ to me directed, will be expoſed to ſale, on the premiſes, on Tueſday, the 30th day of July inſtant, at 2 o'clock in the afternoon, two certain tracts or parcels of land, ſituate in Donegal townſhip, in the county of Northampton, one of them bounded by the lands of Reuben Haines, Henry Prouſt and John Pople, etc. containing 207 acres, whereon are a large tenement and log tenement, a large log barn, ſtables and other out-houſes, and a conſiderable quantity of good meadow; and the other of the ſaid tracts bounded by the land of Peter Haas and the ſaid Haines, and containing 95 acres uncleared, lies the property of Henry Shultz, ſeized and

BRITISH FLEET AT NEW YORK.

July 4, 1776.

LAST Thursday arrived at the Hook (like a swarm of locusts escaped from the bottomless pit) a fleet said to be 130 sail of ships and vessels from Halifax, having on board General Howe, &c. sent out by the tyrants of Great Britain, after destroying the English constitution there, on the pious design of enslaving the British colonies and plundering their property at pleasure, or murdering them at once, and taking possession of all, as Ahab did of Naboth's vineyard.

On Monday about 1000 of them landed on the west end of Long Island, but soon embarked again; and seeing a party of riflemen, said to be about 1000, gave them three huzzas, which they returned with the Indian war whoop. On Tuesday morning some of them appeared coming up, and before night about 45 sail came above the Narrows and anchored at and near the Watering Place, where they fired about 50 cannon shot, of which we have not heard the occasion, and landed many of their men, whom we could plainly see exercising and parading.

It was apprehended they intended to penetrate into the interior parts of the island; or to some of the neighbouring towns; but it does not appear that they have yet attempted it, or done any thing on shore, except taking up a little bridge in the causeway between the landing and the highlands, at the ferry. We hear general Mercer, with a detachment, was yesterday despatched to watch their motions, and act as occasion might require.

TO BE SOLD,

A HOUSE and LOT situate in Germantown, opposite the White Horse; the house is new, two stories high, with a good garret, two rooms on a floor, and cellar under the whole, all well finished; the lot is 55 feet front on the street, and 118 feet deep. For terms apply to the subscriber, living in Germantown.

§   HENRY FRAILY.

Recreated from The Pennsylvania Packet, July 8, 1776.

AMERICANS LEAVING CANADA.

Extract of a letter from CROWN POINT, *July 3.*

"We left Sorel the 14th of June, and arrived at Isle aux Noix the 18th, after having burnt and destroyed two gondolas, two schooners and a sloop, which we could not get over the Rapids, together with the forts of Chamblee and St. John's, and Col. Hazen's house. While we lay at Isle aux Noix, eight officers and four privates, of the 6th battalion, went out with their arms to a French house on the opposite shore, about a mile from the encampment, in order to get spruce beer, where they were attacked by a number of Indians, who killed and scalped Captain Adams, Ensign Culbertson, and two privates, and took prisoners Capt. M'Lane, Lieutenants M'Farran, M'Callister and Hog, and two privates; Captain Rippey and Ensign Rush made their escape. As soon as the firing was heard, a boat was sent to their assistance, but too late."

Recreated from The Pennsylvania Gazette, July 17, 1776.

Extract of a letter from WILLIAMSBURG, *July 4.*

"Our Convention is not yet broke up; they have appointed PATRICK HENRY, Governor, and chosen a council of eight members, which is to be the executive power; the legislative consists of a House of Burgesses or Delegates, the other consists of 24 members called Senators, to be chosen by the Freeholders as soon as the Colony is laid out in districts; the House of Burgesses to be elected as customary. Governor not to continue more than three years, and annually elected."

ALL Persons having PROVINCIAL ARMS not fit for Service, are desired to bring them forthwith to the GUN-LOCK FACTORY, in Cherry-Alley, to be put in good Order.

THE SALE of the Ship JUNO's Cargoe, consisting of Jamaica Spirits, Sugar, Fustick, &c. will begin this Day, at Ten o' Clock A. M. N. B. The Sugar and Spirits will be sold by the single Hogshead.

Recreated from The Pennsylvania Gazette, July 10, 1776.

TROOPS ON MOVE TO NEW YORK.

Extract of a letter from PHILADELPHIA, *July* 6.

Saturday morning.—"General Howe has landed a great body of troops on Staten Island; his forces cannot be ascertained. General Washington and his troops are in high spirits. The strength of our army at New York cannot be ascertained; the militia pour in so fast that it is impracticable. The Jersey militia, amounting to 3500, have acquired great honour in forming and marching with such alacrity and expedition. They have for some time past got over to New York. The battalions of this city (every one of them) are marching to Trenton and Brunswick, in the Jerseys. The rifle battalion, in the pay of this province, marched yesterday for the same places.

"The militia in the counties are also ordered to march. Out of these bodies they mean to form their quota of the flying camp, to be posted in the Jerseys, and to be at the command of General Washington. It is expected that the Lower Counties and Maryland will immediately march their quotas of militia, to compose the flying camp to this city, to defend it in the absence of its own battalions.

"Your hour of trial is come; your plighted faith, your publick honour, the love of your country, and its dearest liberties, in this moment of imminent danger, demand that you instantly fly to the assistance of a sister colony."

Saturday noon.—"An express is just arrived from General Washington. Howe's army is not yet arrived, but hourly expected with 150 sail, having on board 20,000 troops. The enemy's grand army will consist of 30,000. The whole militia of this province are ordered to the Jerseys. We are in anxious expectation to hear from Maryland, nor can we for a moment entertain a doubt that our brethren will desert us in the day of our distress. The farmers have left their harvest, and cast away the scythe for the musket. I should rejoice to hear you have imitated so laudable, so glorious an example."

Recreated from Purdie's Virginia Gazette, July 19, 1776.

PHILADELPHIA, *July* 8, 1776.

This day, at 12 o'clock, the declaration of INDEPENDENCE will be proclaimed at the statehouse.

ANNAPOLIS, *July* 11.

YESTERDAY evening six companies of the first battalion of Maryland troops stationed in this city, commanded by col. William Smallwood, embarked for the head of Elk in high spirits; and three companies of the same battalion, stationed in Baltimore town, embarked yesterday morning for the same place, from whence they are to proceed to Philadelphia.

Recreated from Purdie's Virginia Gazette, July 19, 1776.

TRENTON, *July* 8, 1776.

THE declaration of independence was proclaimed here, together with the new constitution of the colony of late established, and the resolve of the Provincial Congress, for continuing the administration of justice during the interim.

The members of the Provincial Congress, the Gentlemen of the committee, the officers and privates of the militia under arms, and a large concourse of the inhabitants attended on this great and solemn occasion. The declaration and other proceedings were received with loud acclamations.

The people are now convinced of what we ought long since to have known, that our enemies have left us no middle way between perfect freedom and abject slavery. In the field we hope, as well as in council, the inhabitants of New Jersey will be found ever ready to support the freedom and independence of America.

Extract of a letter from PRINCETON, *July* 10.

"Last night Nassau Hall was grandly illuminated, and INDEPENDENCY proclaimed under a triple volley of musketry, and universal acclamation, for the prosperity of the UNITED STATES. The ceremony was conducted with the greatest decorum."

Recreated from The Virginia Gazette, July 29, 1776.

THE WHOLE FLEET AT ANCHOR.

BRITISH TROOPS ON STATEN ISLAND.

NEW YORK, *July* 8, 1776.

THE fleet from Halifax, we informed our readers, in our last, was arrived at Sandy Hook, to the amount of 113 sail. It is difficult, from their situation, to ascertain their number, but we suppose it does not exceed 130 sail. Monday it came up into Yakes's Bay, below the Narrows; Tuesday several ships came to at the Watering-Place; and by Thursday noon the whole fleet was at anchor in a line from Kill Van Kull to Simonson's ferry, on the east side of Staten Island.

The Asia brought up the rear of the fleet, and in the Narrows was fired at from a small battery on Long Island, which compliment was returned by about forty 24 pounders, and one which lodged in the wall of the house of Mr. Bennet, but did no hurt to the family; and three shot had near done much mischief to the house and family of Mr. Dennise, one of them narrowly missing the kitchen, wherein was a number of the family; a second struck the barn, and the third destroyed much of the fence of the garden opposite the front door of the mansion house.

Part of the army is now encamped on Staten Island, and we have not the least reason to doubt will endeavour to secure the north side thereof by entrenchments, while the shipping protects the other parts of it.

As soon as the troops landed, they paraded the north shore, and on Wednesday morning made their appearance near Elizabeth Town Point; but the country being soon alarmed, they retreated, took up the floor of the draw-bridge in the Salt Meadows, and immediately threw up some works. Their near approach to Elizabeth Town Point greatly alarmed the inhabitants of Essex county, and particularly the people of Elizabeth Town and Newark, but they are now in a condition to receive them wherever they may think proper to approach.

Two young men from Elizabeth Town crossed the river in a canoe last Thursday, and fired upon the regulars; but a number of them rushing out of the woods, they were obliged to retreat and cross the river again.

We hear two men of war now lay near Amboy, in order, it is supposed, to stop all navigation that way.

Major Lamb, Captain Oswald (late Aid de Camp to General Arnold) and Captain Burr, we hear are on board the fleet in our port. These intrepid men were taken prisoners at Quebec, when the most noteworthy asserter of our noble rights and privileges (Gen. MONTGOMERY) fell a victim to ministerial vengeance.

The number of Highlanders lately taken prisoners in the different vessels from Scotland amounts to about 750.

Yesterday seven seamen belonging to the Killingsworth transport, of 700 tons, were brought to town from Long Island, having deserted the ship the night before. They say the number of soldiers with the fleet is about 8500, who are all encamped; and that many of the seamen intend to desert the fleet when an opportunity presented.

Recreated from The Pennsylvania Gazette, July 10, 1776.

WILLIAMSBURG, *July* 12, 1776.

The postmaster in Fredericksburg writes, of last Wednesday, that, by a gentleman just arrived from Philadelphia, he had seen an Evening Post of the 2d instant, which mentions that the Hon. the Continental Congress had that day declared the *United Colonies free and independent state*s.

WANTED,

SEVERAL surgeons for the NAVY. Such as incline to enter into the service will please to apply to the commissioners, now sitting in *Williamsburg*.

Recreated from Purdie's Virginia Gazette, July 12, 1776.

LORD DUNMORE WOUNDED.

Extract of a letter from WILLIAMSBURG, *July* 13.

"A battery of two 18 pounders was opened on the enemy's fleet on Tuesday morning, whilst another of four 9 pounders played on their works and camp on Gwynn's Island. In a short time the whole fleet was forced to tow out of reach of the battery; their fire ceased after a few rounds. Their camp was thrown into confusion, and in the night, before we could procure boats to carry over our men, they removed all their tents except one, their cannon except one, and all their stores, &c.

"There were three tenders in the haven, which attempted to prevent our passage. Their works were still manned, as if they meant to dispute their ground, but as soon as our soldiers put off in a few canoes they retreated precipitately to their ships. The tenders fell into our hands, one they set on fire, but our people boarded it and extinguished the flames. The enemy burnt two small vessels, and the night following a very large ship, supposed to be the Dunmore, for she was very much damaged, having received four 18 pound shot through her sides, and a double headed one through her stern, which raked her. Her mate was killed, a sailor had his arm taken off, and Lord Dunmore had his leg wounded by this shot.

"The fleet has sailed from the island, which we are in quiet possession of. From their works, and preparations for others, and stocks of cattle left on the island, it is evident they left it much against their inclination, and long before they expected it. We found 150 graves, and 12 dead negroes lying in the open air. They have had a dreadful fever amongst them, and the small-pox; I wish our army may not catch the infection. The Roebuck was at the mouth of Rappahanock. The Fowey and Otter did not choose to come to the assistance of the Dunmore, which, unfortunately for her, had changed stations with the Otter, and by this means came into the jaws of our battery which was concealed. We did not lose a man."

Recreated from The Pennsylvania Gazette, July 24, 1776.

GEN. SULLIVAN TO CROWN POINT.

Extract of a letter from an Officer at FORT GEORGE, *to an Officer in* NEW YORK, *July* 14, 1776.

"I never knew the fatigues of a campaign till I arrived in Canada. The most shocking scenes that ever appeared in a camp were constantly exhibited to view. When General Sullivan arrived in Canada the army was torn in pieces by sickness and other unaccountable occurrences. A whole regiment was not to be found together. General Sullivan, with his usual activity and alertness, collected together a debilitated and dispirited army; tried the strength of the enemy, who were at least four to our one, and performed one of the most remarkable retreats that ever was known.

"No person who was not present can conceive a tenth part of the difficulties attending it; the enemy at our heels, 3000 of our men sick of the small-pox, those who were most healthy like so many walking apparitions. All our baggage, stores and artillery to be removed, officers as well as men all employed in hauling cannon, &c. Our batteaus loaded were all removed up the Rapids six miles, one hundred of them were towed up by our poor wearied men, up to their arm-pits in water.

"This was performed in one day and an half; our sick and baggage all safely landed at St. John's, and from thence at Crown Point, with the loss of three cannon only, which were poor ones. All this was accomplished thro' the amazing exertions of General Sullivan, who performed what appeared to be almost impossible to have been done by mortal man! He is now on his way to New York."

New London Township, Chester County, July 1, 1776.

WHEREAS my wife SARAH, at the inftigation of her children (as I fuppofe) has refufed to cohabit or live with me as a wife ought to do with her hufband, and threatens to run me in debt; it puts me under the difagreeable neceffity of thus publicly advertifing all perfons not to truft her on my account, as I will pay no debt of her contracting after this date. JAMES PURTLE. †

Recreated from The Pennsylvania Gazette, July 31, 1776.

PLOT TO BURN ALBANY.

Extract of a letter from ALBANY, *July* 15.

"Last Saturday evening a plot was discovered here, (by confession of two Tories) that this week the city was to be set on fire in different places, and the magazine blown up. Yesterday between two and three hundred men went out with their arms to take up these scoundrels, who, by information, were skulking in the woods, &c. and they have taken several of them. As there are no soldiers in town, the inhabitants watch 24 hours round to guard the Tory goal, magazine, &c."

Recreated from The Pennsylvania Gazette, July 24, 1776.

LORD HOWE AT SANDY HOOK.

NEW YORK, *July* 15.—Last Friday morning it was reported in town, that Lord Howe was arrived at Sandy Hook, with a large fleet from England. Between one o'clock and two o'clock P.M. two ships hove in sight and joined the fleet at the watering place; about an hour after, a ship supposed to be the Phoenix, of 44 guns, a frigate of 28, and three tenders, got under way at Staten Island, and stood up for this city.

The army soon took alarm, and in a few minutes every man was at his station, well provided with all necessaries for a vigorous defence; but as soon as the ships came near Bedlow's island, they inclined towards the Jersey shore, to avoid our batteries that then began to play upon them from every quarter on both sides of the river; and notwithstanding they must have received considerable damage, they stood their course up Hudson's river, firing several broadsides as they went along, without either killing or wounding any of our people, who on this occasion behaved with uncommon bravery.

A strong southerly wind, and the tide of flood facilitated the ships getting above the batteries near the town, but we hear they were roughly handled about 12 miles up river, from whence they have not yet attempted to return, but we hear laid at Tarry town, about 50 miles up the river, on Saturday evening.

HOWE'S FLAG REFUSED.

Extract of a letter from a Gentleman at NEW YORK, *to his friend in* PHILADELPHIA, *July* 15.

"Yesterday Lord Howe sent up a flag, with the Captain and Lieutenant of the Eagle man of war, the Adjutant General met them after some little ceremony, but as their letter was directed for George Washington, Esq., he could not receive it; the officers insisted much on his receiving it, saying it was of a civil nature, his Lordship being invested with unlimited powers, and was sorry that he had not arrived a few days sooner.

"On Tuesday another flag from the fleet appeared, and was met as before, when a letter was again offered, but for the same reason as the former, rejected."

IN CONGRESS, *July* 17, 1776.

Resolved, that General WASHINGTON, in refusing to receive a letter said to be sent from Lord Howe, addressed to GEORGE WASHINGTON, ESQUIRE, acted with a dignity becoming his station; and therefore this Congress do highly approve the same, and do direct, that no letter or message be received, on any occasion whatever, from the enemy, by the Commander in Chief, or the other Commanders of the American army, but such as shall be directed to them in the characters they respectively sustain.

By Order of CONGRESS,
JOHN HANCOCK, President.

WILLIAMSBURG, *August* 2, 1776.

THE Ship *Oxford*, a Prize of 200 Tons Burthen, with her Tackle, Apparel, Rigging, and Furniture, all in excellent Order, will be sold at public Sale, for ready Money, on Monday the 19th Instant, before the Raleigh Tavern in Williamsburg, at 6 o'Clock in the Afternoon. The Ship, with her Furniture, may be seen by applying to Capt. *James Gregory* of *Prince George*, who has an Inventory of the same. (2)   JAMES HUBARD.

Recreated from The Virginia Gazette, August 3, 1776.

BRITISH SHIPS UNDER WAY.

New York, *July* 22.—Wednesday several ships, to the number of about 16 or 20, part of the fleet at Staten Island, got under way and stood through the Narrows, but we have not been able to get any certain intelligence of their destination. Some conjecture that they are bound to the eastward, to attempt an entrance through the Sound; should that be the case, it affords us pleasure to think we are in a fit condition there also to give them a suitable reception.

Thursday last the Declaration of INDEPENDENCY of the *United States of* AMERICA, was published at the Court-house; where a number of people, true friends to the rights and liberties of this country, attended, and signified their approbation to it by loud acclamations; after which the coat of arms of his Majesty George III, was torn to pieces, and burnt in the presence of the spectators.

NORTHERN ARMY RETREATS.

General Sullivan, with the whole northern army, we hear is retreated to Ticonderoga, (165 miles from Albany, and 265 from this city) a very advantageous spot, and where it is believed he will in a short time be sufficiently reinforced and fortified to withstand any attack that may be made by our cruel unrelenting enemies.

• • • •

Thursday the first day of August is appointed, by authority, to be observed as a day of Humiliation, Fasting and Prayer, throughout the state of Massachusetts.

• • • •

The ships up the Hudson's river, that passed our batteries the 12th instant, prove to be the Phoenix, Captain Parker, and the Rose, commanded by the infamous Wallace. We have not learnt that they ventured to approach nearer our forts than the distance of eight miles; and from the mustering of the militia in that quarter, it is not doubted they will be prevented from committing any depredations on the inhabitants

STORY OF THE FLAGS.

Yesterday fe'nnight, in the afternoon, a barge from the fleet appeared in our bay with a white flag, and there was met with several gentlemen of the army on board. The flag was sent by Lord Howe, with a letter to his Excellency George Washington. But as the letter was improperly directed, it was not received, though much solicited by the officer, who, we hear, said it contained nothing of a hostile nature. That Lord Howe came over possessed of unlimited power, and was much concerned he had not arrived a few days sooner, which would have effected a reconciliation, &c. However, it seems his unlimited power did not extend even to the necessary preliminaries of a negociation—an acknowledgement of the right of the persons to whom he came to treat with him.

On Tuesday another flag from the fleet appeared, and was met as before, when a letter was again offered, but for the same reason as the former rejected.

On Friday a third flag from the fleet appeared, which we hear brought only an open letter directed to Miss Margaret Moncrieffe.

Saturday forenoon our people discovered a fourth flag of truce, whereupon the Mechanics barge was sent to meet it, and conducted the officer (said to be Adjutant General of the forces under the command of Lord Howe) to the dwelling of Colonel Knox, in this city, where his Excellency General Washington, attended by his body guards, waited his arrival, which was a little past one o'clock. The interview was short, and the particulars we believe are as yet not made known; we can therefore only say, that at parting much courtesy was seen to pass between the gentlemen who bore the flag, and those of the continental forces who had the honour to be present.

Yesterday several discharges of cannon and musquetry was heard in this city, and by the appearance of a cloud of smoke over Bergen Point, it is imagined our people on the Jersey shore have had a skirmish with the enemy from Staten Island.

Recreated from The Pennsylvania Gazette, July 24, 1776.

In CONGRESS.

July 22, 1776.

RESOLVED, That the several Commanders in Chief in each department be directed to exchange any Officer in the British service, now a prisoner in any of these States, of or under the rank of Colonel, for Colonel ETHAN ALLEN.

Resolved, That the persons taken prisoners with Colonel Ethan Allen be put upon the same footing as those in the Continental service, and exchanged accordingly, as opportunity presents.

By Order of CONGRESS,
JOHN HANCOCK, President.

[*All the Printers are desired to publish the above Order, for the benefit of Colonel Allen, who has suffered much in the cause of his country.*]

Recreated from The Pennsylvania Gazette, July 31, 1776.

In COUNCIL.

WILLIAMSBURG, *July* 20, 1776.

Ordered, That the two printers publish in their respective gazettes the DECLARATION of INDEPENDENCE, made by the Honourable the CONTINENTAL CONGRESS; and that the sheriff of each county in this Commonwealth proclaim the same at the door of his courthouse, the first court day after he shall have received the same.

ARCHIBALD BLAIR, C.C.

N.B. *The Declaration of Independency may be seen at full length in our gazette of the 20th instant.*

ABLE SEAMEN

WANTED for a new Ship, lying at *Edenton, North Carolina.* Extraordinary Wages will be given. Apply to Capt. *Alexander Thompson* on Board, or to the Subscriber at *Miner's.*

NANSEMOND, *July* 16.   MICHAEL WALLACE.

Recreated from The Virginia Gazette, July 29, 1776.

ENEMY DRIVEN OFF BERGEN POINT.

NEW YORK, *July* 25.—Our troops, stationed on Bergen Point, give the ministerial fleet and army some uneasiness, by firing at the tenders, boats, &c. It so galls and provokes them, that they return the fire with great fury, but have not done the least damage to our people.

Last Lord's day, a great many shot were heard in the city from Bergen Point. The occasion was this, a barge from the fleet, full of men, landed on the Point, but were opposed and driven off with precipitation by our troops; a smart fire ensued from a tender for a considerable time, without doing any injury. By two deserters, we are informed, that a Captain and two privates were killed on board their barge.

WOMEN WORKING THE HARVEST.

We hear from New Jersey and Connecticut, that a great part of the men being absent on military service, and the time of harvest coming on, the women, assisted by the elderly men, whose age rendered them unfit for the army, have so effectually exerted themselves, that they have generally got in the harvest completely, the laudable example being set by the ladies of the first character in each place. And we are credibly informed, that many of them have declared, that they will take the farming business upon themselves, so long as the rights and liberties of their country require the presence of their sons, husbands, and lovers in the field.

PHILADELPHIA, *July* 29, 1776.

On Friday evening arrived in this city from Canada, Brigadier General SULLIVAN.

We hear that one of the Continental Frigates lately launched in this city is called the DELAWARE, an the other the RANDOLPH, in honour of the late illustrious senator of that name.

Yesterday Brigadier General EWING set off from this city to join the Flying Camp in New Jersey.

Recreated from The Pennsylvania Packet, July 29, 1776.

MISCREANTS THWARTED.

It is reported that Lord Dunmore's miscreants, since they were driven from Gwynn's island, have received a severe drubbing on the Maryland shore of the Potowmack, where they landed in hopes of procuring some necessaries, but were disappointed, and forced away after losing ten or more privates of the 14th regiment, who were killed; that the shipping are gone up the river, all in mourning, supposedly for some of the leaders of the gang, or perhaps the *magnanimous* Chief himself. Two tenders, it is also said, are burnt, and their crews taken, about 50 in all. Our gallies and other armed vessels will soon be able to meet them.

WILLIAMSBURG, *July* 27.

THURSDAY the 25th instant, the DECLARATION of INDEPENDENCE of the UNITED COLONIES was proclaimed here, and received with universal applause, under a discharge of cannon, firing of small arms, illuminations in the evening, &c. &c.

Recreated from The Virginia Gazette, July 29, 1776.

NEW YORK, *July* 29, 1776.

Several cannon were fired last Thursday afternoon, from our battery at Amboy, at a number of boats from Staten Island, bound to Sandy Hook; this brought on a cannonade from the encampment of regulars near Billop's point, on the island, which continued very hot on both sides for near an hour; the boats got clear, but many of the regulars were seen to fall, and several carried off, supposed to be wounded.

On our side a soldier, belonging to one of the Philadelphia Battalions, was killed, and one wounded; a horse in a carriage had his head shot off in the street, and some damage was done to the houses.

SEAMEN.

WANTED immediately, some able-bodied Seamen, to whom good Encouragement will be given by Col. *Fielding Lewis* in Fredericksburg, Mr. *Joshua Storrs* near Richmond, and Mr. *Aaroyd* in Williamsburg.

(1)

Recreated from The Pennsylvania Gazette, July 31, 1776.

AMERICAN GALLIES ON THE LAKE.

CARPENTERS AT SKENESBOROUGH.

Extract of a letter from TICONDEROGA, *July* 30.

"We have no certain accounts of the strength of the enemy, who are at St. John's building boats and vessels, in order to take the Lake.

"A number of ship carpenters from Philadelphia have arrived at Skenesborough, where they are building gallies, that in a short time we shall have a strong force on the lake. Some companies of militia from New England have also arrived there.

"We are impatiently expecting the return of a flag, sent by General Gates to Carleton, with the declaration of independency; also a requisition for the delivery of Forster and his party, that they may receive such punishment as their conduct merits, in suffering the Savages inhumanely to butcher the captives, in direct violation of the capitulation entered into by General Arnold at the Cedars."

"It is reported that General Carleton has used the Canadians who favoured us very barbarously, which has provoked them very much. Some deserters have come over, and some of the foreign troops are said to be desirous of deserting."

Another letter from the same place, July 29.

"We are hard at work every day repairing the old French lines, that have once already been very fatal to the British army; and if they will but let us alone for two weeks, I think they will meet with as warm a reception here as ever they did. We have a General that is at once the soldier and the gentleman and a parcel of men that are determined to defend this place; so that let the enemy come when they will, they will get what they little expect."

Philadelphia, *August* 20, 1776.

WANTED, A QUANTITY of white WAMPUM; also a GUNSMITH to work by the Year, or as may be agreed on. Apply to the Committee of Congress for Indian Affairs, or to GEORGE MORGAN, Arch-street.

Recreated from The Pennsylvania Gazette, August 21, 1776.

OUR CAUSE WILL PREVAIL.

August 2, 1776.—By private letters from Philadelphia, we learn that a reinforcement has been sent to General Clinton from Staten Island, where both Lord Howe and his brother the general waited the arrival of the men of war and transports from England; so that we may look for important news from that quarter by every post, which, considering the justice of our cause, the integrity and abilities of our noble general, joined to the zeal and alacrity of our northern brethren to protect their liberties, there is the greatest reason to believe will be propitious to America.

WILLIAMSBURG, *August* 2, 1776.

THE ship *Oxford*, a prize of 200 tuns burthen, with her rigging, tackle, apparel, and furniture, all in excellent order, will be sold at publick sale on Monday the 19th instant, before the *Raleigh* tavern, in *Williamsburg*, for ready money; the sale at 6 o'clock in the afternoon precisely. Any person, by applying to capt. *James Gregory* of *Prince George*, may be shewn the ship with her furniture, who has an inventory of the same.

(2)   JAMES HUBARD.

WANTED *for the Continental Hospital in* Williamsburg, *some* NURSES *to attend the sick. Any such, coming well recommended, will have good encouragement by applying to the Director of the Hospital.*

Recreated from Purdie's Virginia Gazette, August 2, 1776.

[*The following letters and orders are published by order of the Hon. Congress of the American States.*]

His Excellency General CARLETON's ORDERS.

QUEBEC, *August 4, 1776.*

THE Commanding Officers of corps will take especial care that every one under their command be informed, that letters or messages from rebels, traitors in arms against the King, rioters, disturbers of the public peace, plunderers, robbers, assassins, or murderers, are on no occasion to be admitted; that should emissaries from such lawless men again presume to approach the army, whether under the name of a flag of truce-men or ambassadors, except when they come to implore the King's mercy, their persons shall be immediately seized and committed to close confinement, in order to be proceeded against as the law directs, their papers and letters, for whomsoever, even for the Commander in Chief are to be delivered to the Provost Marshall, that, unread and unopened, they may be burned by the hands of the common hangman.

At the same time the Commander in Chief expects that neither the assassination of Brigadier General Gordon, nor the late notorious breach of faith, in resolving not to return the troops and Canadians taken at St. John's, in exchange for those rebels who fell into the hands of the savages at the Cedars and Quinchin, purchased from them at a great price, and restored to their country on those express conditions, be imputed to the provincials at large, but to a few wicked and designing men, who first deceived, then step by step misled the credulous multitude to the brink of ruin, afterwards usurped authority over them, established a despotic tyranny over them not to be borne, and now wantonly and foolishly endeavour to provoke the spilling of blood of our unhappy countrymen of this continent, in hopes of covering their own guilt, or confirming their tyranny, by the general destruction of their country.

Let their crimes pursue those faithless, bloody minded men, who assert that black is white and white black; it belongs to Britons to distinguish themselves not less by their humanity than their valour; it belongs to the King's troops to save the blood of his deluded subjects, whose greatest fault perhaps is having been deceived by such men to their own destruction; it belongs to the Crown, it is the duty of all faithful servants of the Crown, to rescue from oppression, and restore to liberty, the once happy, free, and loyal people of this continent.

All prisoners from the rebellious provinces, who choose to return home, are to hold themselves in readiness to embark at a short notice. The commissary (Mr. Murray) shall visit the transports destined for them, and see that wholesale provisions, necesary clothing, and all possible convenience for their passage, be prepared for the unfortunate men.

They are to look on their respective provinces as their prison, and there remain until farther enlarged, or summoned to appear before the commander in chief of this province, or any other commander in chief for his Majesty for the time being, which summons they shall obey.

General Howe will regulate the place of their landing.

FRANCIS CARR, *clerk*,

Aide de Camp to Lieutenant General Burgoyne.

WILLIAMSBURG, *August* 31, 1776.

A Person in this City would give ready Money for one or two NEGRO BOYS that are fit to be put to Trades. Inquire of the Printers of this Paper. (tf)

WILLIAMSBURG, *August* 14, 1776.

JOURNEYMEN GUNSMITHS and BLACKSMITHS will meet with good Encouragement from the Subscriber. Likewise are wanting 8 or 10 healthy BOYS as Apprentices. (tf)   JAMES ANDERSON.

Recreated from The Virginia Gazette, September 7, 1776.

LORD DUNMORE PUTS TO SEA.

WILLIAMSBURG, *August* 9, 1776.—By advices from Hampton, we learn that last Wednesday morning the Right Hon. the Earl of Dunmore, Viscount Fincastle, and Barron Murray of Blair, Mouilli, and Tillimet, after dividing his fleet, and burning ten or a dozen vessels, took leave of the Capes of Virginia, where he has, for more then twelve months past, perpetrated crimes that would even have disgraced the noted pirate **BLACK BEARD**. One part of the fleet was seen to stand to the southwards, it is imagined for South Carolina, the other to the northward, supposed for New York.

Their strength, from the information of two negroe deserters who came up to Hampton in the evening, amounts to near 400, regulars, negroes, and Tories; that they were now tolerably healthy, and had lately got a supply of provisions, which they took from a Rhode Island vessel. So *respectable* a band will, no doubt, be a most valuable acquisition to the generals Howe and Clinton!

Colonel WILLIAM CHRISTIAN is appointed commander of the expedition against the Indians, and it is hoped he will be able to root out those treacherous devils in human shape.

We have the pleasure to inform the publick, that the first regiment have nobly re-enlisted for three years longer, and are on marching orders for New York.

WILLIAMSBURG, *August* 9, 1776.

THE *building of a sufficient number of* WOODEN BARRACKS *to hold* 1000 *troops, also of a large* STABLE *for the horses belonging to the army, will be let to the lowest bidder on Saturday the* 17th *instant, at 3 o'clock in the afternoon, before the* Raleigh *tavern.*

WILLIAM FINNIE, D. Q. M. G.

Recreated from Purdie's Virginia Gazette, August 9, 1776.

FUNERAL of GEORGE III.

SAVANNAH, (Georgia) *August* 10.—A Declaration being received from the Honourable John Hancock, Esq., by which it appeared that the Continental Congress, in the name, and by the authority of their constituents, had declared, that the United Colonies of North America are, and of right ought to be, Free and Independent States, and absolved from all allegiance to the British crown, his Excellency the President, and the Honourable Council met in the Council Chamber, and read the Declaration. They then proceeded to the square before the Assembly House, and read it likewise to a great concourse of people, when the grenadier and light infantry companies fired a general volley.

After this, they proceeded in the following procession to the Liberty Pole: The grenadiers in front; the Provost Marshall, on horseback, with his sword drawn; The Secretary with the Declaration; His Excellency the President; the Honourable the Council and gentlemen attending; then the light infantry, and the rest of the militia of the town and district of Savannah. At the Liberty Pole they were met by the Georgia battalions, who, after the reading of the Declaration, discharged their field pieces, and fired in platoons. Upon this they proceeded to the battery, at the Trustees Garden, where the Declaration was read for the last time, and the cannon of the battery discharged.

His Excellency and Council, Col. Lachlan M'Intosh, and other gentlemen, with the militia, dined under the cedar trees, and cheerfully drank to the United, Free, and Independent States of America. In the evening the town was illuminated, and there was exhibited a very solemn funeral procession, attended by the grenadier and light infantry companies, and other militia, with their drums muffled, and fifes, and a greater number of people than ever appeared on any occasion before in this province, when George the Third was interred before the court-house in the following manner:

"Forasmuch as George the Third, of Great Britain, hath most flagrantly violated his coronation oath, and trampled upon the constitution of our country, and the sacred rights of mankind, we therefore commit his political existence to the ground, corruption to corruption, tyranny to the grave, and oppression to eternal infamy; in sure and certain hope that he will never obtain a resurrection to rule again over these United States of America; but, my friends and fellow citizens, let us not be sorry, as men without hope, for TYRANTS that thus depart; rather let us remember that America is free and independent, that she is, and will be, with the blessing of the Almighty, GREAT among the nations of the earth. Let this encourage us in well doing, to fight for our rights and privileges, for our wives and children, for all that is near and dear to us. May God give us his blessing, and let all the people say AMEN."

Recreated from The Pennsylvania Gazette, October 9, 1776.

FIRE-SHIPS GRAPPLE THE ENEMY.

NEW YORK, *August* 14.—Last Friday two fire-ships, commanded by Capts. Fosdyke and Thomas, (gentlemen volunteers of rank in the army of the United States) proceeded up the North river with intent to give a suitable warming to those piratical gentry that have infested it since the 12th of July last. The night was dark and favourable to the design, and the enemy did not perceive our vessels till they were near aboard them. Captain Fosdyke grappled the Phoenix; but as the fire not commencing so soon as was expected, she disentangled herself in about 20 minutes, after sustaining considerable damage in her rigging.

Captain Thomas fell on board one of the tenders, which was soon consumed; and we are truly sorry to inform the public, that this intrepid commander is yet missing. This gallant enterprise struck so great a panic upon the enemy, that they thought it prudent to quit their station; and yesterday, taking the advantage of a fresh wind at S.E., attended with considerable rain, they ran the gauntlet thro' a great number of well-directed shot from our batteries in and near this city, which undoubtedly, must have damaged them much.

Our gallies played smartly, and followed the ships a considerable distance into the bay. The enemy's fire seemed to be mostly directed upon the city, as the tops of the houses were crowded with spectators, but very little damage was done to the buildings, nor any lives lost upon the occasion.

Recreated from The Pennsylvania Packet, August 27, 1776.

ENCOURAGEMENT given by the province of SOUTH CAROLINA for raising a REGIMENT of ARTILLERY.---25l. South Carolina currency as a bounty, a full suit of regimentals every year, a cap, a blanket, and tents. Serjeants 12s. Corporals 11s. Drummers 11s. Fifers 11s. Gunners 10s. Matrosses 7s. 6d. each per day. Soldiers who are ordered upon fatigue duty have 5s. allowed them extraordinary. Rations, one pound and a half of beef, and a pound of bread; or 18 ounces of pork, and a pint of rice. Each man is allowed a pint of vinegar, one pint of salt, and two pounds of pepper, every month. The soldiers receive their pay regularly once a fortnight, and are enlisted for two years only. Recruits who bring a blanket to head-quarters will receive one dollar as a present.

Recreated from Purdie's Virginia Gazette, August 9, 1776.

HESSIAN FORCES ARRIVE.

Extract of a letter from NEW YORK, *Aug.* 15.

"I have just time to inform you that, by a deserter who came over to us last night, we have this intelligence, that the enemy's reinforcement of Hessians has arrived; they are not suffered to land, but have taken three days fresh provisions on board. The troops on the island began yesterday morning to embark, the boats, &c. are all prepared to land them, with sand bags for their protection; that we may hourly expect an attack. Their numbers, in the whole, amount to 25,000.

"There are various conjectures as to their intended descent. Some imagine it will be on Long Island, others about five miles above the city, and others up above General Mifflin's post. Our gallies went up yesterday again to try the Phoenix and Rose; we have not heard from them yet.

"If they wait a day or two longer we shall have near 2000 more of our Pennsylvania troops in."

Aug. 17. On Monday last, about 60 vessels (some say upwards of 90) came in from sea, and anchored at Staten Island. Some suppose them to be Lord Dunmore's fleet from Virginia, but it is most probable they are the fleet expected from England.

An attack from the piratical fleet and murderous army of Great Britain, is hourly expected here.

Recreated from The Virginia Gazette, August 31, 1776.

IN MENS CLOTHES.

RUN away the 30th of July last, from the Jerseys to Philadelphia or New-York, a MULATTOE Woman Slave, named *Maria*; had on a white or red and white jacket, white ticken breeches, white stockings, old mens shoes, and an old beaver hat; she is hardly discernable from a white woman, is rather thinish visage, middle size, thick legs, long black hair, and about 35 years old; she hath left behind her three young children, a good master and mistress, and is going towards New-York after a married white man, who is a soldier in the Continental service there. Whoever secures the said Mulattoe in goal, and will immediately advertise the same in this paper, shall have FOUR DOLLARS reward.

Recreated from The Pennsylvania Gazette, August 14, 1776.

AMERICA'S DECLARATION OF WAR.

LONDON, *August* 15, 1776.—Copies of the Declaration of War by the Provincials are now in town, and said to be couched in the strongest terms—that having now drawn the sword in defence of all that is dear to them, they are determined never to sheath it till a full compensation is made for the cruel oppressions they have sustained.

It is said the American provinces have not only declared themselves independent, but they have sent memorials thereof, and of their proceedings, to most of the Courts in Europe.

Tuesday a ship arrived from Quebec, which brings letters dated the 6th of July from thence, and of the 4th from Montreal; they inform us that Gen. Carleton had left 1000 of the foreign troops to garrison at Quebec, and as many at Montreal, and that the main army, consisting of 8000 regulars, and 2000 Canadians, with a large body of Indians, making twelve tribes, were getting and assembling the vessels and batteaus as fast as possible upon Lake Champlain, in the neighbourhood of St. John's (in which they had already made great progress) towards embarking the army, and proceeding to Crown Point in pursuit of the rebels, and from thence to enter the province of New York, &c. Mean while, nothing could exceed the eagerness of the British army in general to come up with the enemy; and several parties of Indians had already made excursions through the woods and swamps as far as Crown Point, and slain many of the scattered Provincials, and were frequently bringing in scalps, (although against Gen. Carleton's orders) nor is it possible for him to prevent it effectually, or those savages to desist from their cruel practices. The King's army are in great spirits, very healthy, and abound with all sorts of provisions.

On Tuesday afternoon died at his house in Grosvenor Place, the Right Hon. Lord Cathcart, lately appointed one of the Lords of his Majesty's bedchamber.

Recreated from The Pennsylvania Gazette, November 6, 1776.

CLINTON LEAVES SOUTH CAROLINA.

WILLIAMSBURG, *August* 16.—From undoubted authority we can assure the public, that 15,000 wt. of pure lead have been got from our mines in the back country; which, after being cast into bullets, we hope will be unerringly directed against our enemies.

An express from South Carolina arrived this morning, who brings advice that General Clinton with his troops, escorted by Sir Peter Parker's shattered squadron, parted from Charlestown on the 3d of this instant. They had been moving off for several days, and were supposed to be bound part for Virginia, the rest farther northward. In going over Charlestown bar, a row battery that was sent to annoy them made prize of a brig transport, having on board a whole company of the Royal Highland emigrants; the captain only escaped. The same day a boat from General Clinton's ship was taken, with nine sailors in her. General LEE is expected here in a few days.

INDIAN RAIDING PARTIES.

The advices since our last from the back country are, that the Cherokee and Creek Indians, to the number of between 6 and 700, are encamped in Carter's Valley, from whence they send out parties against the settlements, some of which had penetrated near 100 miles on this side of the Big Island, carrying destruction wherever they come, by burning houses, fences, fields of wheat and other grain, and turning droves of horses into the corn fields.

Upwards of 1000 head of horses have been drove off, and a great number of cattle; the sheep and hogs they shoot down. They had killed and scalped 18 men, one or two women, and several children; some of the people were most barbarously murdered, too shocking to relate. The ruined settlers had collected themselves together at different places, and forted themselves, 400 and upwards at Major Shelby's, about the same number at Captain Campbell's, and a considerable number at Amos Eaton's.

In all the skirmishes with the Indians, our people have continually worsted them, and, in the whole, have killed and scalped 27, and badly wounded several others, as was discovered by the tracks of blood.

A man from the frontiers of Georgia had arrived in Fincastle, who declared, upon oath, that he saw upwards of 100 people buried in one day, who were killed by the Creek Indians.

Recreated from The Pennsylvania Gazette, August 28, 1776.

INOCULATING FOR SMALL-POX.

THE small-pox has ever been a most formidable foe to New England and its armies. Our enemies knowing this, have taken inhuman pains to propagate it among us; for no barbarians could exceed them in the methods they have employed to distress and destroy us. In this, Heaven has permitted them to succeed, but at the same time has given us in inoculation an astonishing means of robbing this disease of its terror and fatality. At this critical season, we cannot be too speedy or diligent in every where applying this inestimable gift of Heaven for our own security.

The General Court has made provision that inoculating hospitals may be established through the colony, and appointed the Justices of several counties to superintend this affair. Many judicious persons, and some Gentlemen of the Congress in their letters have strongly urged that such a measure may be speedily carried into effect. It is not doubted then, that the Justices to whom this matter is committed, will consider the vast importance of it, and will without delay employ their utmost care and prudence for the establishing such hospitals in a proper number, and the most convenient places, and for introducing the most skilful physicians to attend them. They cannot in any way more essentially serve this colony, and the common cause of America. All friends to their country cannot fail to contribute their aid to a service of so much importance. A.B.

Recreated from The Hartford Courant, August 12, 1776.

By his Excellency GEORGE WASHINGTON, General, and Commander in Chief of the Army of the United States of NORTH AMERICA.

WHEREAS a bombardment and attack upon the city of New York, by our cruel and inveterate enemy may be hourly expected, and as there are great numbers of women and children, and infirm persons, yet remaining in the city whose continuance will rather be prejudicial than advantageous to the army, and their persons exposed to great danger and hazard, I Do, therefore, recommend it to all such persons, as they value their own safety and preservation, to remove with all execution, out of the said town, at this critical period—trusting, that with the blessing of Heaven, upon the American arms, they may soon return to it in perfect security. And I do enjoin, and require, all officers and soldiers, in the army, under my command, to forward and assist such persons in their compliance with this recommendation.

Given under my hand, at Head Quarters, NEW YORK, *August* 17, 1776.

GEORGE WASHINGTON.

Recreated from The Pennsylvania Packet, August 27, 1776.

DEATH of GEN. GORDON.

Extract of a letter from ALBANY, *August* 19.

"An officer, who went on a reconnoiter to St. John's and Chamblee, fell in with a regular officer on horseback alone, on the road between La Praire and St. John's, summoned him to surrender himself prisoner, but clapping spurs to his horse road off, the officer fired at and shot him. It turns out to be General Gordon."

The above letter was received since Carleton's orders were first published by order of Congress.

Col. Beadle and Major Butterfield, for bad conduct, are broke, and rendered incapable of holding a commission in the army of the United States; and Capt. Wentworth, for disobedience of orders is cashiered.

Recreated from The Virginia Gazette, September 7, 1776.

ACTION SOON ON THE LAKE.

Extract of a letter from an officer on board the Royal Savage, Lake Champlain, *Aug.* 21.

"To-morrow (wind and weather permitting) we sail towards St. John's, where we may soon expect to come to action. Our fleet consists of 1 sloop, 3 schooners, 4 galleys, and 7 gondolas, the whole well officered and manned, and under command of General Arnold. If we meet the enemy, doubt not we shall support our charge."

Recreated from The Maryland Gazette, September 12, 1776.

New York, *August* 22.—We can assure the public, that the foreigners, in Burgoyne's army, are beginning to desert in large numbers. About 60 of them, in a boat, came over to our troops the other day, at Ticonderoga.

Wednesday evening last we had here as violent a thunder-gust as has been remembered by the oldest man now living among us. The lightning struck a marque in General M'Dougall's camp, near the Bull's Head in the Bowery, and instantly killed Captain Van Wick and his two lieutenants, Versereau and Depyster.

Recreated from The Virginia Gazette, September 7, 1776.

Williamsburg, *August* 24.—A corespondent wishes some able hand would undertake to describe Gen. Lee's march from Boston to Charlestown, and would point out the remarkable circumstances of his meeting Gen. Clinton at New York the day he arrived there; of his finding him in Hampton Road when he came to Virginia; of Clinton's leaving Cape Fear just after his arrival in North Carolina, and of his *unlucky* meeting at Fort Sullivan. The world must have a high opinion of Gen. Lee's activity and vigilance, when they read of his march of more than 1100 miles, and of the circumstances attending it throughout; and Clinton himself must look on Gen. Lee as his evil genius, thus haunting him along a coast of such vast extent, and meeting him at last at *Philippi*.

Recreated from The Pennsylvania Gazette, September 4, 1776.

GERMAN TROOPS LANDED.

Philadelphia, *August* 20.—We are informed, by a Captain of a vessel belonging to this city, who escaped a few days ago from Staten Island, that the German troops lately arrived from Halifax are landed on the island, where it is said they are to wait the arrival of another reinforcement (which is hourly expected) before the attack will be made on New York. He adds, that the British troops speak with great contempt of General Washington's army, and are assured that they will have the pleasure of soon meeting and spending the winter with General Burgoyne and his troops in New York.

Recreated from The Virginia Gazette, August 31, 1776.

PHILADELPHIA, *August* 27.

From the best accounts we find the forces at Staten Island *to be as follows*:

General Howe from Halifax, with	8000
The Scotch, who embarked at Glasgow for Boston 3400, out of which 850 were taken by our cruisers	2350
The defeated troops under Cornwallis & Clinton, from South Carolina, supposed not more than	2500
The two divisions of Hessians, Waldeckers, and English guards, which arrived Monday the 12th inst.	9000
Lord Dunmore's scrubby fleet, about 30 fighting men, but with Negroes and Tories	150
Number of Marines unknown.	
Total	22,000

Ships, Asia and Eagle of 64 guns, the Roebuck and Phoenix of 44, one bomb, and about 20 frigates and sloops of war. They have also above 300 sail of transports, store ships, and prizes.

Recreated from The Virginia Gazette, September 7, 1776.

THE BATTLE OF LONG ISLAND.

Tuesday, the 21st instant, a number of ships with troops on board sailed from Staten Island out of the Narrows; next day they were followed by many more, and about 10 o'clock Thursday morning, about 10,000 men landed between New Utrecht and Gravesend, on Long Island. Friday a party of them came and took possession of Flat Bush, which immediately brought on a very hot fire from our troops, who are advantageously posted in the woods, and on every eminence around that place.

An advanced party of the regulars are encamped a little to the north-west of Flat Bush church, and have a battery somewhat to the westward of Mr. Jeremiah Vanderbelt's, from whence they continue to fire briskly on our people, who often approach and discharge their rifles within 200 yards of their works.

We have had only 4 men wounded since the enemy landed; but we are certain many of them fell. One, a Hessian, was killed last Friday; several dollars were found in his pocket, and he had an excellent rifle, and many of the regulars were in rifle dresses.

Recreated from The Pennsylvania Gazette, August 28, 1776.

RIFLE-MEN HARASS THE ENEMY.

Extract of a letter from General SULLIVAN *to* General WASHINGTON *at* NEW YORK, *dated* LONG ISLAND, *August* 23, 1776.

"This afternoon the enemy formed, and attempted to pass the road by Bedford; a smart fire between them and the riflemen ensued. The officer sent for a reinforcement, which I ordered immediately.

"A number of musketry came up to the assistance of the riflemen, whose fire, with that of our field pieces, caused a retreat of the enemy. Our men followed them to the house of Judge Lifford, where a number of them had taken lodgings, drove them out, burnt the house, and a number of other buildings contiguous.

"They think they killed a number, and an evidence of it they produce: three officers hangers, a carbine, and one dead body, with a considerable sum of money in his pocket. I have ordered a party out for prisoners tonight. We have driven them half a mile from their former station."

Recreated from The Virginia Gazette, September 7, 1776.

Extract of a letter from NEW YORK, *August* 27.

"I sit down in the midst of confusion to tell you that our people have been engaged with the enemy, on Long Island, all this morning. Those who have come over say, the enemy have lost the most men. Lieut. Col. Parry, of one of the Pennsylvania battalions, is killed; he died heroically, urging his men on against the enemy. Your kinsman, Hermanus Rutgers, was killed yesterday. Several of the enemy's ships have attempted coming up this morning, but both wind and tide a'head, and they are hitherto baffled. Our men on the island behave bravely. Heaven send them victory.

"Thirty-five minutes past twelve noon. Firing still continues with intermission. A man of war coming up, said to be the Roebuck, has just lost, by a flaw, all she gained last tack. Several fires have been kindled on the island. Capt. Farmer, of Col. Miles's regiment, is slightly wounded in the foot, and brought to this city. I think some men of war will be up next tide.

"P.S. The 1st battalion of New York, col. Luther, and the Pennsylvania and Maryland battalions, behaved with the greatest bravery, even to a fault. They were commanded by Lord Stirling. I fear some of our bravest officers from the southward are among the slain."

WANTED IMMEDIATELY,

A NUMBER of flaves, or freemen labourers, for the purpofe of carrying on a cannon foundery, at Antietam furnace in Frederick county. Good encouragement will be given by
w 4   DANIEL & SAMUEL HUGHS.

Recreated from The Maryland Gazette, September 5, 1776.

STORIES FROM THE BATTLE.

CONFLICTING ACCOUNTS GIVEN.

A letter from NEW YORK, *August 27, 8 p.m.*

"This minute returned from our lines, on Long Island, where I left his excellency the general. From him I have it in command to inform Congress, that yesterday he went there, and continued till evening, when, from the enemy having landed a considerable part of their forces, and many of their movements, there was reason to apprehend they would make, in a little time, a general attack. As they would have a wood to pass through, before they could approach the lines, it was thought expedient to place a number of men there on the different roads, leading from whence they were stationed, in order to harass and annoy them on their march.

"This being done, early this morning a smart engagement ensued between the enemy and our detachment, which being unequal to the force they had to contend with, having sustained a pretty considerable loss, at least many of our men are missing, among those that have not returned are gen. Sullivan and lord Stirling. The enemy's loss is not known certainly, but we are told, that such of our troops as were in the engagement, and that have come in, say that they had many killed and wounded. Our party brought off a lieutenant, serjeant, and corporal, with 20 privates, prisoners.

"While these detachments were engaged, a column of the enemy descended from the woods, and marched towards the center of our lines, with a design to make an impression, but were repulsed. This evening they appeared very numerous about the skirts of the woods, where they have pitched several tents; and his excellency inclines to think they mean to attack and force us from our lines by way of regular approaches, rather than in any other manner.

"To-day five ships of the line came up towards the town, where they seem very desirous of getting, as they turned a long time against an unfavourable wind; and on my return this evening, I found a deserter from the 23d regiment, who informed me, that they design, as soon as the wind will permit them, to come up to give us a severe cannonade, and to silence our batteries, if possible."

Extract of a letter from LONG ISLAND, *Wednesday, day-break.*

"I have the pleasure to inform you I have survived a very warm engagement yesterday. Our battalion has suffered much; a great number of both officers and men are killed and missing. We retreated through a heavy fire, and escaped by swimming over a river, or creek rather; my height was of service to me, as I touched almost all the way. Numbers of men got drowned. I have lost no officer and but few men. Capt. Veazy and lieut. Butler fell early in the engagement. We are now safe in our lines and forts. The affair yesterday was only a skirmish on the island, about three miles from our works. The particulars I cannot give you, but we were decoyed, and at once surrounded, I am convinced, with 10,000 men."

Extract of a letter from NEW YORK, *Aug. 28.*

"Yesterday proved a very distressing one on Long Island. Great numbers killed on both sides, and I fear (though we cannot get certain results) that numbers of our people are taken; however, I am told they continue in high spirits. The generals Sullivan, Stirling, and Parsons, went out of the lines too far, and were all missing this morning with many others.

"An intelligible man just now come over the ferry says, gen. Stirling is killed, but we don't know any thing of gen. Parsons. It appears as difficult getting certain intelligence here as it can be with you. On the whole, I believe our troops behaved with spirit, and have not yet given way in their skirmishing to any equal number of the enemy, and have kept them from getting up to their lines and forts, which are all well manned to receive them, should they get so far."

Recreated from The Maryland Gazette, September 5, 1776.

BATTALIONS SURROUNDED.

OUR LINES NOT TENABLE.

Extract of a letter from LONG ISLAND, *August* 28, 1776.

"Yesterday's occurrences no doubt will be described to you various ways. I embrace this leisure moment to give as satisfactory an account as I am able. A large body of the enemy landed some time since on Long Island, at the end of a beautiful plain, had extended their troops about six miles from the place of their first landing. There were at this time eleven regiments of our troops posted in different parts of the woods, between our lines and the enemy, through which they must pass if they attempted any thing against us. Early in the morning our scouting parties discovered a large body of the enemy, both horse and foot, advancing on the Jamaica road towards us. I was dispatched to General Putnam, to inform him of it. On my way back I discovered, as I thought, our battalion on a hill coming in, dressed in hunting shirts, and was going on to join them, but was stopped by a number of our soldiers, who told me they were the enemy in our dress. On this I prevailed on a serjeant and two men to halt and fire on them, which produced a shower of bullets, and we were obliged to retire.

"In the mean time, the enemy with a large body penetrated through the woods on our right, and center or front, and about nine o'clock landed another body on their right, the whole stretching across the fields and woods between our works and our troops, and sending out parties, accompanied with light horse, which harassed our surrounded and surprised new troops, who however sold their lives dear.

"Our forces then made towards our lines, but the enemy had taken possession of the ground before them by stolen marches. Our men broke through parties after parties, but still found the enemy's thousands before them. Col. Smallwood's, Atlee's and Hazlet's battalions, with General Stirling at their head, had collected on an eminence and made a good stand, but the enemy fired a field piece on them, and being greatly superior in number obliged them to retreat into a marsh, and finding it out of their power to withstand about 6000 men, they waded through the mud to a hill opposite them; their retreat was covered by the battalion which had got into our lines. Col. Lutz's and the New England regiments after this made some resistance in the woods, but were obliged by superior numbers to retire.

"Colonel Miles's and Broadhead's battalions, finding themselves surrounded, determined to fight and run; they did so, and broke through English, Hessians, &c. and dispersed horse, and at last came in with considerable loss. Colonel Parry was early in the day shot through the head, encouraging his men. Eighty of our battalion came in this morning, having forced their way through the enemy's rear, and came round by way of Hell-gate; and we expect more, who are missing, will come in the same way."

Extract of a letter from NEW YORK, *Aug.* 30.

"In a council of war held yesterday, it was determined that our lines on Long Island were not tenable, and therefore the council concluded to evacuate them.

"Lord Stirling and Gen. Sullivan are prisoners. Gen. Howe allowed Gen. Sullivan a flag, by which he informed us of this, and that he was politely treated."

Extract of a letter from an Officer in the PENNSYLVANIA *forces, dated* NEW YORK, *August* 31, 1776.

"I am but just come to this place, after a fatiguing time. Last Tuesday morning, at daylight, we found the enemy beginning their march for our lines; we with or little army went out to oppose them, on which a bloody battle ensued; we were surrounded by them on all sides, and had several times to fight our way through. It was a continued battle from a town about three miles off, called Flat-Bush, until we got to our lines."

Recreated from The Pennsylvania Gazette, September 4, 1776.

GUN-POWDER TO BE STAMPED 'U.S.A.'

In CONGRESS, *August* 28, 1776.

Resolved, That there be an Inspector or Inspectors sufficiently qualified to judge the goodness of gun-powder, who shall examine every cask of gun-powder manufactured, or to be purchased on account of the United States, by the mostapproved method of ascertaining the quality of gun-powder, the said Inspector or Inspectors to receive one eighth part of a dollar for every hundred weight of powder, he or they shall so examine.

That no gun-powder be received into the public magazine, for the use of the United States of America, or delivered for the powder mills for that purpose, but such as had been approved of by the public Inspector, as to its quickness in firing, dryness, and other necessary qualities.

That the Inspector mark each cask approved with the letters U.S.A. and such other marks as are necessary to distinguish the several sorts of gun-powder.

That every maker of gun-powder, mark every cask in which he shall pack his gun-powder with the first letters of his name.

That gun-powder be put into no cask, but such as are well seasoned and dry.

A Negro MAN, named LONDON, aged about 21 years, a well set fellow, about 5 feet 9 inches high, several negro scars in his face, speaks good English, had on when he went away a light colour'd coat and vest, with him one pair leather breeches, two pair trowsers, two pair shoes, and a buff cap, run away from the subscriber the 6th instant. Whoever shall take up and return said negro to me, shall have 5 dollars reward. SAMUEL HOOKER.
Kensington, Sept. 14, 1776.

CASH given for Sheep Skins, with the Wool on, by ELY WARNER, at the Goal in Hartford.

Resolved, That it be recommended to the Legislatures of the several States of America, to cause suitable Inspectors to be appointed to examine and determine the quality of all gun-powder manufactured within their Jurisdiction, and that no person be allowed to vend any gun-powder manufactured in any of the States of America, unless the same, in the judgment of such Inspector, shall be of sufficient quality, and to make such laws for executing this, or any other regulations for promoting the manufacture of good gun-powder, as to them may seem most convenient.

That the Continental Agents be impowered and required to Inspect or appoint some suitable person or persons to Inspect all gun-powder manufactured or purchased in, or imported into the respective States, wherein they reside, on account of the United States, except in those States where an Inspector is appointed by Congress.

By Order of CONGRESS,
JOHN HANCOCK, President.

Recreated from The Hartford Courant, September 16, 1776.

AMERICAN FLEET AT CANADA.

Extract of a letter, August 27, 1776.

"Our fleet, consisting of 3 schooners, a large sloop, 4 gondolas, and 4 galleys, now lie in Lake Champlain, near Crown Point, and expect to sail in 3 days, and lay in a narrow passage in the lake, to prevent the enemy from passing. We have information, that the enemy are on their way to this place from St. John's, they have no other craft than battoes; if they come, I trust we shall give them a warm reception, as our fleet is well fitted and manned. We have now at Ticonderoga about 3500 effective men, and more coming in daily; the fort and every height and point about it is well fortified; besides we have command of the lake."

Recreated from The Maryland Gazette, September 12, 1776.

LIBERTY DRAWING NEAR.

NEW YORK, *August 29, 1776.*

The great, the important day, big with the fate of America and Liberty seems to draw near! The British troops began to land on Long Island last Thursday, nearly their whole force, supposed to be more than 20,000 British and foreign troops. They marched through the small town of New Utrecht, in their way to Flat Bush, another town about five miles from this city, near which they encamped; but were much harassed by our riflemen. Scouting parties were sent from our army to the adjoining woods, but were rather scanty in their numbers considering the extent of ground they had to guard.

The British forces, in three divisions, taking three different roads, and the advantages of the night, almost surrounded the whole of our parties, who though encircled with more than treble their number, bravely fought their way through the enemy, killing great numbers of them, and brought off some prisoners. The New York first battalion behaved with great bravery. Lord Stirling's brigade sustained the hottest of the enemy's fire; it consisted of Colonel Miles's two battalions, Colonel Atlee's, Colonel Smallwood's and Colonel Hatch's regiments; they were all surrounded by the enemy, and had to fight their way through the blaze of their fire; they fought and fell like Romans!

Lieut. Colonel Barry, of the Pennsylvania musquetry, was shot through the head, as he was giving orders to, and animating his men. The major part of Colonel Atlee's and Colonel Piper's regiments are missing. Doctor Davis and his mate were both taken prisoners as they were dressing a wounded person in the woods. Colonel Miles is missing (a truly amiable character) and supposed to be slain. Generals Stirling and Sullivan are thought to be killed. General Parsons, with seven men, came in yesterday morning, much fatigued, being for ten hours in the utmost danger of falling into the enemy's hands.

General Grant, of the British troops, from good intelligence, is among the killed; his hat with his name on it, was found lying near the dead body; the bullet had gone thro' and thro' the hat, and carried some of his gray hairs with it. Thus fell the hero, who boasted in the British House of Commons, he would march thro' America with 5000 men, having only marched five miles on Long Island with an army four times the number. Our out guards have retreated to the main body of the army within the lines. The British army have two encampments about a mile from our lines, and by their manoeuvres, 'tis plain they mean to attack us by surprize, and storm our intrenchments. Our men show the greatest bravery, and wish to come to action. The firing continued yesterday all the day.

Recreated from The Hartford Courant, September 2, 1776.

SUDDEN RETREAT IN SECRECY.

Extract of a letter from NEW YORK, *Aug. 31.*

"You are no doubt surprised to hear of our sudden retreat from Long Island, but it was thought absolutely essential from our situation. We were under a necessity of marching out and attacking them upon their own ground, or suffering ourselves to be starved into a surrender.

"First, because they were entrenching within 500 yards of our lines, which were very weak and incapable of withstanding their heavy cannon, and our men from their situation, began to grow very uneasy; and secondly, because their shipping might have run up the East River, and cut off our resources of provisions and every other necessary.

"The retreat was conducted with the greatest secrecy, and by six o'clock in the morning we had every thing embarked. There never was a man that behaved better upon the occasion than General Washington; he was on horse back the whole night, and never left the ferry stairs till he had seen the whole of his troops embarked."

Recreated from The Pennsylvania Gazette, September 4, 1776.

WASHINGTON'S SAFE RETREAT.

Saturday's post brings us the agreeable intelligence of General Washington having effected a safe retreat for our army out of Long Island, in spite of the great numbers commanded by Howe. They have brought every thing off with them, except some very large cannon, which they spiked up, and a few out sentries. In the skirmishes, which have been for these several days past, the enemy have lost upwards of a thousand, and we not much more than five hundred.

They have sent a flag of truce, offering to exchange General Sullivan and Lord Stirling for two Generals they have missing, but as we have them not, it is supposed they are killed. The manner in which our retreat was performed reflects the highest credit on our commander in chief, and the officers in general.

Recreated from The Pennsylvania Packet, September 3, 1776.

GEN. SULLIVAN GOES TO CONGRESS.

PHILADELPHIA, *September 5.*—Monday last arrived here General Sullivan, who was taken in the late action on Long Island; he is permitted to come here by General Howe, to settle an exchange of prisoners.

Recreated from The Hartford Courant, September 16, 1776.

To be SOLD, on Thursday the 24th of October, at the town of Manchester, commonly called Rocky Ridge,

ABOUT 50 *Virginia* born NEGROES, belonging to the estate of *John Hylton,* deceased, among whom are some house servants, and a good carpenter. Twelve months credit will be allowed, the purchasers giving bond and good security to

(6)   FRANCIS EPPES, } executors.
             JOHN HYLTON,

Recreated from Purdie's Virginia Gazette, September 13, 1776.

HOWE'S POWERS.

[*Following is the purport of the message from* Lord HOWE *to* CONGRESS, *by Gen.* SULLIVAN.]

"That though he could not at present treat with Congress as such, yet he was very desirous of having a conference with some of the members, whom he could consider for the present only as private gentlemen, and meet them himself as such, at such place as they should appoint.

"That he, in conjunction with General Howe, had full powers to compromise the dispute between Great Britain and America, upon terms advantageous to both, the obtaining of which delayed him near two months in England, and prevented his arrival at this place before the Declaration of Independency took place.

"That he wished a compact might be settled at this time, when no decisive blow was struck, and neither party could say that they were compelled to enter into such agreement.

"That in case Congress were disposed to treat, many things, which they had not as yet asked, might and ought to be granted them; and that if, upon the Conference, they found any probable ground of an accommodation, the authority of Congress must be afterwards acknowledged, otherwise the compact could not be complete."

Extract from the Minutes,
CHARLES THOMPSON, Sec.

In CONGRESS.

September 5, 1776.

Resolved, That Gen. Sullivan be requested to inform Lord Howe, that this Congress, being the representatives of the free and Independent States of America, cannot with propriety send any of its members to confer with his Lordship in their private characters, but that, ever desirous of establishing peace on reasonable terms, they will send a Committee of their body, to know whether he has any authority to treat with persons authorised by Congress for that purpose, in behalf of America, and what that authority is, and to hear such propositions as he shall think fit to make respecting same.

Resolved, That to-morrow be assigned for electing the Committee.

September 6, 1776.

Resolved, That the Committee to be sent "to know whether Lord Howe has any authority to treat with persons authorised by Congress for that purpose, in behalf of America, and what that authority is, and to hear such propositions as he shall think fit to make respecting the same," consist of three.

The members chosen, Mr. Franklin, Mr. John Adams, and Mr. E. Rutledge.

Extract from the Minutes,
CHARLES THOMPSON, Secretary.

Recreated from The Pennsylvania Gazette, September 18, 1776.

COMMISSIONERS TO CONFER.

PHILADELPHIA, *September* 11.

Monday last the Hon. Benjamin Franklin, John Adams, and Edward Rutledge, Esquires, Members of the Hon. Congress, set off for New York in order it is said, to confer with Lord Howe, upon the subject of sundry propositions sent by his Lordship to the Congress by General Sullivan.

We hear that Lord Howe has consented to exchange General Sullivan and Lord Stirling for General Prescott and General M'Donald.

We hear from New York, that a few days ago a man of war of 40 guns came to anchor in Turtle Bay, upon which General Washington ordered two 12 pounders to be carried to a convenient piece of ground to attack her. They soon obliged the ship to retire, having hulled her twelve times.

Recreated from The Pennsylvania Gazette, September 11, 1776.

THE DEFENSIVE BATTERIES.

NEW YORK, *September* 9, 1776.

SINCE the retreat of our army from Long Island, the enemy have extended themselves a considerable length on the shore bordering the Sound; and on Tuesday a large number landed on Blackwell's island, about three miles from this city, but the shot from our batteries soon made them recross the river.

On Wednesday a ship from the fleet passed between Governour's island and Red Hook, and that night got up the Sound, abreast of the island the enemy had been drove from, when, under cover of her guns, they the next day came over to it in large bodies. This brought on a brisk cannonade for near two hours, in which the ship sustained so great damage, in her hull and rigging, as obliged her to move close in with the Long Island shore, for shelter from our shot and bombs.

At the same time of attack a firing also began from the enemy's batteries on Long Island, opposite the city, which was returned with such spirit by our people in their fortresses, at and about the shipyards, that they have given us little or no annoyance since from that quarter.

Several men of war now lie within gunshot of our main battery, and the greatest part of the fleet behind Governour's island, though they have lately had very favourable winds to come up to the city, which gives us reason to think they mean not to attack it by water till they know the success of their forces in attempting to land on this island.

Thursday a large barge was seen in the East river, sounding the channel where it is obstructed by scuttled vessels, but soon made off, as it is supposed she observed our people at the main fort, preparing to give her a suitable salutation.

Saturday night our guard boats for observing the motions of the fleet fell in with those of the enemy, when a smart attack began, and lasted for some time; but the latter being reinforced with several tenders, obliged ours to return to their station.

Recreated from Purdie's Virginia Gazette, September 27, 1776.

COMMITTEE REPORT TO CONGRESS.

The Committee, who were appointed to wait on Lord Howe, having returned to Congress, made their report in the following words:

"In obedience to the order of Congress, we have had a meeting with Lord Howe. It was on Wednesday last, upon Staten Island, opposite to Amboy, where his Lordship received and entertained us with the utmost politeness.

"His Lordship opened the conversation by acquainting us, that though he could not treat with us as a Committee of Congress, yet as his powers enabled him to confer and consult with any private gentlemen of intelligence in the colonies, on the means of restoring peace between the two countries, he was glad of this opportunity of conferring with us on that subject, if we thought ourselves at liberty to enter into a conference with him in that character. We observed to his Lordship, that as our business was to hear, he might consider us in what light he pleased, and communicate to us any propositions he might be authorised to make for the purpose mentioned; but that he could consider ourselves in no other character than that in which we were placed by the order of Congress.

"His Lordship then entered into a discourse of considerable length, which contained no explicit proposition of peace except one, viz. that the colonies should return to their allegiance and obedience to the government of Great Britain. The rest consisted principally of assurance that there was an exceeding good disposition in the King and his Ministers to make the government easy to us; with intimations that in case of our submission they would cause the offensive acts of Parliament to be revised, and the instructions to Governors to be reconsidered, so that if any just causes of complaint were found in the acts, or any errors in government were perceived to have crept into the instructions, they might be amended or withdrawn.

"We gave it as our opinion to his Lordship, that a return to the domination of Great Britain was not now to be expected.

"We mentioned the repeated humble petitions of the colonies to the King and Parliament, which had been treated with contempt, and answered only by additional injuries; the unexampled patience we had shown under their tyrannical government, and that it was not till the last act of Parliament which denounced war against us, and put us out of the King's protection, that we declared our independence.

"That this declaration had been called for by the people of the colonies in general, that every colony had approved of it when made, and all now considered themselves as Independent States, and were settling or had settled their governments accordingly; so that it was not in the power of the Congress to agree for them that they should return to their former dependent state.

"That there was no doubt of their inclination to peace, and their willingness to enter into a treaty with Britain, that might be advantageous to both countries.

"That though his Lordship had at present no power to treat with them as independent States, he might, if there was that same good disposition in Britain, much sooner obtain fresh powers from thence for that purpose, than powers could be obtained by Congress from the several colonies, to consent to a submission. His Lordship then, saying that he was sorry to find that no accommodation was likely to take place, put an end to the conference.

"Upon the whole, it did not appear to your Committee, that his Lordship's commission contained any other authority of importance, than what is expressed in the Acts of Parliament, viz. that of granting pardons with such exceptions as the Commissioners shall think proper to make, and of declaring America or any part of it to be in the King's peace upon submission.

"For as to the power of enquiring into the state of America, which his Lordship mentioned to us, and of conferring and consulting with any persons the Commissioners might think proper, and representing the result of such conversations to the ministry, who (provided the colonies would subject themselves) might after all, or might not, at their pleasure, make any alterations in the former instructions to Governors, or propose in Parliament any amendment of the acts complained of, we apprehend any expectation from the effect of such a power would have been too uncertain and precarious to be relied on by America, had she still continued in her state of dependence."

Recreated from The Pennsylvania Gazette, September 18, 1776.

ENEMY ATTACK EXPECTED.

Extract of a letter from NEW YORK, *Sept.* 14.

"The enemy, from their different manoeuvres and great preparations, intend soon to strike a decisive blow; their plan is to out-flank and hem us in, but I think they will be disappointed, for the heights above Harlem and Kingsbridge are strongly manned and fortified, and all the points up to Frog's securely picketed, the avenues blocked, and the roads cut up to prevent the approaches of their artillery."

ACTION AT HARLEM.

By several gentlemen arrived from the camp we collect the following intelligence, that on Monday, the 16th instant, General Washington being informed that an advanced party of the enemy was approaching his lines at Harlem, he intended to attack them with one party in front, whilst another attacked them in the rear, to prevent their retreat, which was nearly effected, when the enemy, after a smart engagement, secured their retreat under cover of their men of war in the East River.—Col. Nolton commanded one party, and Major Leech the other, the former killed and the latter wounded;—and that we had taken three field pieces.

We are further informed, that the evening before, our people sent down three fire-ships upon the enemy's fleet, one of which had grappled with a man of war, but she having a sporing in her cable, swung round with the tide and disentangled herself, and they burnt to the water's edge without having the desired effect.

Extract of a letter from Head Quarters at HARLEM, *September* 21, 1776.

"In the skirmish on Monday last we killed and wounded about 200 of the enemy; our loss was about 40 men killed and wounded; Col. Nolton among the slain, a brave officer, who, when he was expiring, asked, Do the enemy run? Do our men fight well? Upon being informed they did, he replied, well then, I die contented."

Extract of a letter from NEW YORK, *Sept.* 21.

"Last night a fire broke out in New York, and consumed all that part of the city near the North River. The enemy continue quiet and we are strengthening our lines; we shall soon be so strong that I think they cannot dispossess us."

Recreated from The Pennsylvania Gazette, September 25, 1776.

PHILADELPHIA, *September* 17.

On Thursday evening and Friday morning the Hon. Benjamin Franklin, John Adams, and Edward Rutledge, esquires, returned to this city from Staten Island, where they spent three hours in a conference with Lord Howe, upon the subject of his propositions to the Congress. We hear that his Lordship possesses no other powers to accommodate the dispute between Great Britain and the United States than those mentioned in the act of the British parliament for appointing commissioners to grant *pardons*, &c.

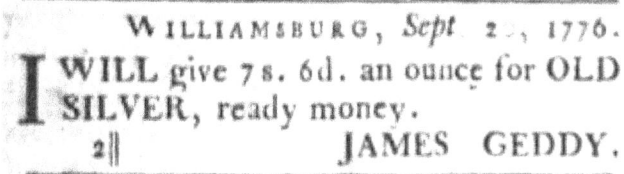

Recreated from Purdie's Virginia Gazette, September 27, 1776.

TROOPS REMOVING FROM NEW YORK.

Extract of a letter from HAERLEM, *seven miles from* NEW YORK, *Sept.* 16, 1776.

"Yesterday was unlucky for us. The enemy landed about 10 o'clock at Turtle Bay, below Hell Gate, under cover of many ships of war. The brigade under general Parsons was soon obliged to retire from the water side, and give ground for the enemy to land. General Mifflin immediately marched from Mount Washington, with 1000 men to the ground near and below this place, where he made a stand, threw up some works, rallied our retreating troops, and in an hour after had the principal part of our army (who were stationed below us) drawn up in good order on the heights. Generals Putnam and Scott were in New York, but made their way through the enemy's line with all their men, and the guards of the city. Col. Knox is missing, and supposed to be taken, as he was late in town, looking for a boat to cross the North river. Three days since it was resolved to quit the town, and we have been removing ever since. We have taken almost every thing out of the city, but lost some cannon and stores. New York never was tenable, and the holding of it obliged us to divide our army into many weak parts; but now I think we are in a good way, and only want two or three days to refresh our men, and secure the heights."

Recreated from Purdie's Virginia Gazette, October 4, 1776.

FIRING HEARD AT TICONDEROGA.

Sept. 16.—By a gentleman from Albany, since our last, we are informed, that General Schuyler had received intelligence by express from General Gates at Ticonderoga, that a heavy firing had been heard at that place, which continued, with some intermissions, for several days, supposed to be between General Arnold, at the head of the American fleet on that station, and a party of the enemy; but as no return had been made to the General when the express came away, no further particulars have as yet been obtained.

Recreated from The Pennsylvania Packet, September 24, 1776.

By Richard *viscount* HOWE, *of the kingdom of* Ireland, *and* William HOWE, *esq., general of his majesty's forces in* America, *the king's commissioners for restoring peace to his majesty's colonies and plantations in* North America, &c. &c. &c.

DECLARATION.

ALTHOUGH the Congress, whom the misguided Americans suffer to direct their opposition to a re-establishment of the constitutional government of these provinces, have disavowed every purpose of reconciliation not consonant with their extravagant and inadmissible claim of independence, the king's commissioners think fit to declare, that they are equally desirous to confer with his majesty's well affected subjects upon the means of restoring the publick tranquillity, and establishing a permanent union with every colony as a apart of the British empire.

The king being most graciously pleased to direct a revision of such of his royal instructions to his governors as may be construed to lay an improper restraint on the freedom of legislation in any of his colonies, and to concur in the revisal of all acts by which his majesty's subjects there may think themselves aggrieved, it is recommended to the inhabitants at large to reflect seriously upon their present condition and expectations, and judge for themselves, whether it be more consistent with their honour and happiness to offer up their lives as a sacrifice to the unjust and precarious cause in which they are engaged, or return to their allegiance, accept the blessings of peace, and to be secured in a free enjoyment of their liberties and properties upon the true principles of the constitution.

GIVEN *at* NEW YORK, *Sept.* 19, 1776.
HOWE.
W. HOWE.

Recreated from Purdie's Virginia Gazette, October 11, 1776.

NEW YORK IN FLAMES.

In our last we informed our readers, that the city of New York was in flames on Saturday morning the 21st instant, since which we have had many different reports concerning that melancholy affair; the most authentic of which we believe is as follows, viz. That the fire originated at or near Whitehall, soon extended to the Exchange, took its course up the west side of Broad-street, as far as Verlattenberg Hill, consuming all the blocks from the Whitehall up. The flames extended across the Broadway from the house of Mr. David Johnson, to Beaver Lane, or Fincher's Alley, on the west, and carried all before it, a few buildings excepted, to the house at the corner of Berkley-street, wherein Mr. Adam Vandenberg lived, sweeping all the cross streets in the way. The buildings left standing on the west side of the Broadway are supposed to be Captain Thomas Randall's, Captain Kennedy's, Dr. Maillat's, Mr. John Cortland's sugar-house and dwelling-house, Dr. Jones's, Hull's tavern, St. Paul's, Mr. Axtell's, and Mr. Rutherford's. The cause of the fire is not known. We imagine about a sixth part of the city is destroyed, and many families have lost their all.

ENEMY ATTACK AT POWLES HOOK.

Sunday last a number of the regulars embarked in boats from York Island near Greenwich, and it was supposed intended to attack Powles Hook, but in the afternoon they disembarked, and gave over the attempt for that time.

Monday the Roebuck and three other ships came opposite to our battery at that post, and after discharging about 100 cannon, landed near 500 men, our people having evacuated the place some hours before and carried off their artillery, &c. They are now advantageously posted on the heights at the mill about one mile from the enemy, and are busy throwing up entrenchments, having been reinforced with about 4000 men.

Wednesday last Brigadier General Sullivan, who was lately taken by the King's troops on Long Island, was exchanged for Gen. Prescott, who commanded at Chamblee. Gen. M'Donald would not be accepted for Lord Stirling.

BOSTON, *September* 19, 1776.

Monday last the new raised company of Independents, commanded by Henry Jackson, Esq., made their first appearance in their uniform (black, turned up with red) on the green in this town, where they were reviewed by the Hon. Major-General Ward, and his suite; some members of the Hon. Council of this State; a number of other gentlemen, and many ladies, &c. were present. They performed the exercise, various manoeuvres and firings, to the universal acceptance of the numerous spectators.

Recreated from The Pennsylvania Gazette, October 2, 1776.

BRITISH STRENGTH IN CANADA.

Extract of a letter from TICONDEROGA, *Sept.* 23.

"Our sick decrease fast, and the army is in high spirits; but whether we shall have the pleasure of giving Burgoyne a rap upon his knuckles is uncertain, as at present, he does not seem disposed to come this way. A serjeant who deserted from the British army at Point aux Trembles, between Montreal and Sorel, the 31st of August last, says, that col. Maclain's regiment was quartered at Point aux Trembles, 1200 foreigners are at Quebeck, all the 34th at Montreal, except two companies with col. Johnson, and his Indians at Le Chien; that he heard the officers compute their army at 7000, in which were the 9th, 20th, 21st, 24th, 29th, 31st, 34th, and 49th, and the Germans. There are none of the Canadians in the king of England's service; but they are in a worse situation than the children of Israel in Egypt, for the regulars have robbed them of every necessary of life, and now compel them to work without any prospect of reward."

Recreated from Purdie's Virginia Gazette, October 18, 1776.

Explanation of a late Declaration by Richard Viscount Howe, *of the Kingdom of Ireland, and* William, Howe, *esq., General of his Majesty's forces in America, the King's commissioners for deluding the good people of America by insidious offers of peace, or shedding their blood without mercy.*

DECLARATION.

ALTHOUGH the Congress, whom the much injured Americans suffer to direct their opposition to the establishment of tyranny, and an unconstitutional government over these provinces, have disallowed every purpose of reconciliation not consonant with that liberty to which they have the most clear and undeniable right, the king's commissioners aforesaid think fit to declare, that they are equally desirous to confer with his majesty's subjects (if any so weak and abandoned are to be found) upon the means of establishing a permanent tyranny over every colony, and fix them the everlasting slaves of the British empire.

The king being most graciously pleased to direct a revision of such of his royal instructions as may seem not to lay a sufficient restraint upon the freedom of legislation in any of the colonies, and to concur in the revisal of all acts by which his subjects there may think themselves aggrieved, for the better strengthening and confirming the same, it is recommended to the inhabitants at large to reflect seriously upon their present condition and expectations, and to judge for themselves, whether it be more consistent with their honour and happiness to risk their lives in defence of a glorious independency, or return to the galling yoke of tyrannick usurpation, and be deprived of every security in the enjoyment of their liberty and properties, upon the true principles of a wicked and destructive policy.

GIVEN at Philadelphia, *October* 1, 1776.

HOWE.

W. HOWE.

Recreated from The Pennsylvania Gazette, October 2, 1776.

GEN. ARNOLD'S FLEET READY.

By the Ticonderoga post, who left that place on Tuesday last, and came to town the Friday following, we are informed, that Lieut. Whitcomb, who killed Brig. Gen. Gordon near St. John's, (as lately mentioned) had arrived at Head Quarters, and brought with him two prisoners, one of whom was an Ensign, who informed that the enemy had got a 20 gun ship on the stocks, nearly compleated, together with several schooners that would carry 12 guns each, with a number of gondolas and flat bottomed boats.

That letters had been received by Gen. Gates from Gen. Arnold, informing that he expected the enemy would attempt to cross the Lake soon. That the health of our army in that department was greatly restored. That the main body was at Mount Independence, but were in daily expectation of being removed to Ticonderoga. That they were in general in high spirits, wishing for an opportunity to chastise the enemy for their intolerance.

Gen. Arnold, with the fleet under his command, is now in the Bay St. Anont, about half way between Crown Point and St. John's; and if the enemy attempt to cross the Lake this season, it is likely he will receive the first and most furious attack of our unnatural foe, and it is hoped he will be able to give a good account of both.

Recreated from The Hartford Courant, October 7, 1776.

HESSIANS PLUNDER ALL.

Extract of a letter from a gentleman at Harlem, *to his friend here, dated October* 8.

"The Hessians plunder all indiscriminately, tories as well as whigs; if they see any thing they want, they seize it, and say, "rebel, good for Hesse man." A tory complained to general Howe, that he was plundered by the Hessians; the general said he could not help it, it was their way of making war. So the 'friends of government' are protected! This is great encouragement for tories."

Recreated from The Maryland Gazette, November 21, 1776.

Bureau de la Guerre, le 14 Septembre, 1776.

De par l'Honorable le Congrés, il est ordonné, a tous les officiers et autre François, employez au service des etats de l'Amerique, de se rendre sans delay a leur postes.

RICHARD PETERS, Sec. de la Guerre.

War-Office, Sept. 14, 1776.

Congress having directed that the Board of War order all the French officers, who have received commissions in the service of the States, to repair immediately to their places of destination, the said officers are hereby required to repair to their posts without delay. RICHARD PETERS, Secretary.

A STATE of the Account of the battles, losses, &c. that have happened between the subjects of the King of Britain and the people of the United States, since the 19th of April, 1775.

The King of Britain, Dr.	Cr.
1. To the victory and rout at Lexington.	1. To the dear bought victory of Bunker's hill.
2. To the loss of Chamblee.	2. To the defeat before the walls of Quebec.
3. Ditto of St. John's.	3. To the defeat and captivity of Gen. Thompson at the Three Rivers.
4. Ditto of Montreal.	
5. To the defeat of General Macdonald.	4. To the disgraceful loss of a fort at the Cedars.
6. To the disgraceful captivity of Gen. Prescott, &c.	5. To the defeat near Flat-Bush, and evacuation of Long Island.
7. To the victory at the Great Bridge near Norfolk.	
8. To the evacuation of Boston.	
9. To the victory over land and sea forces at Sullivan's-Island.	

By this account it appears that there is a considerable balance in favour of the United States. D.

*** This afternoon, at One o'clock, at JONAS PHILLIPS's Vendue Store, begins the sale of a large assortment of MERCHANDIZE, amongst which are, cotton and linen stripes, checks, fine Brittanias, sheeting, linens and broadcloths, &c.

PHILADELPHIA, *October 1.*

At a general court-martial held at TICONDEROGA *the 26th day of July, 1776, by order of the hon. major-general* GATES.

Colonel POOR, president.

MEMBERS,

The four eldest colonels, the four eldest lieutenant-colonels, and the four eldest majors of the northern army.

CAPTAIN Wentworth was brought before the court, and accused of refusing to go on duty, when regularly warned by the adjutant of the regiment to which he belonged.

The court having considered the evidences, were of opinion that capt. Wentworth was guilty, and sentenced him to be cashiered, and advertised in the publick papers, as having wilfully neglected his duty, with a view of being discharged from the service.

Agreeable to this sentence, Jonathan Wentworth, of Somersworth, in Strafford county, New Hampshire, late captain in col. Poor's regiment, is published to the world as a *scoundrel*, guilty of neglecting his duty, evidently with a design of obtaining a discharge from the service of his country; a crime, till this day, unheard of!

His countrymen, it is hoped will treat him with the contempt merited by so infamous a conduct.

By the general's order.

JOHN TRUMBULL,

Dep. adjutant-general of the northern army.

Head Quarters, TICONDEROGA, *Aug. 25, 1776.*

[*All printers in the United States of America are desired to publish the foregoing in their respective papers.*]

CHARLOTTESVILLE, *Sept. 22, 1776.*

I INTEND to leave the colony very soon.

JAMES ROWAN.

DEFEAT ON LAKE CHAMPLAIN.

TROOPS REMOVE TO CROWN POINT.

That on the 11th instant, at 8 o'clock in the morning, the enemy's fleet on Lake Champlain, consisting of one ship mounting 16 guns, one snow mounting the same number, one schooner of 14 guns, two of twelve, two sloops, a bomb ketch, and a large vessel, (her force unknown) with fifteen or twenty flat bottomed boats or gondolas, carrying one 12 or 18 pounder in their bows, appeared off Cumberland Head. General Arnold with his forces immediately prepared to receive them.

At 11 o'clock the attack began, at half past 12 the engagement became general and very warm; some of the enemy's ships and all their gondolas beat up and rowed within musket shot of our fleet. They continued a very hot fire with round and grape shot till 5 o'clock, when they thought proper to retreat about six or seven hundred yards distance, and continued there until dark. Gen. Arnold and his troops conducted themselves during this action with great firmness and intrepidity, and made a better resistance than could have been expected against a force so greatly superior; the whole of our killed and wounded amounted to about 60. The Philadelphia gondola and a schooner were lost in the engagement, but all the men were saved. The enemy landed a large number of Indians on Schuyler's Island and on each shore, who kept up an incessant fire, but did little damage. The enemy had to appearance upwards of 1000 men in batteaus prepared for boarding.

The enemy's force being so greatly superior, it was determined in Council to remove to Crown Point, in order to refit and collect our force. At 2 o'clock, p.m. the 12th, our fleet weighed anchor, with a fresh breeze to the southward. The enemy's fleet at the same time got under way. In the evening the wind moderated, and we made such progress, that at six o'clock next morning we were about 28 miles from Crown Point.

Our troops are now busily employed in completing the lines, redoubts, &c. at Crown Point, expecting the enemy to attack them with their fleet and army. But as the season is now far advanced, and our men are daily growing in health, they have the most flattering expectations of maintaining their post against any force the enemy can bring.

Our commanders and men behaved most gallantly; some vessels having lost all their officers, fought notwithstanding, and refused to yield but with their lives.

Recreated from The Pennsylvania Gazette, October 23, 1776.

ADVERTISEMENT.

DIMSDALIAN INOCULATION.

THE *subscriber takes this method to inform the public, that he has opened a hospital in the town of Great Barrington, in the most healthful and delightsome situation, where he now carries on the inoculation for the small pox in the most gentle, safe and easy manner ever yet practiced, as many of his patients can witness. He practices exactly in the method of Doct. Dimsdale, whose great success for a number of years, has justly acquired him the greatest honour and reputation of any inoculator in Europe, many thousands of his patients (of the poorer sort) having been able to perform their daily labour through the course of the disease. The subscriber finds from his own experience, in this happy method of inoculation, his patients go through the (scarcely to be called) disease, including boarding, nursing, and every other necessary expense, from the time of their inoculation until they are pronounced clean, for the trifling some of eight dollars, which is less than any inoculator has heretofore demanded. Constant attendance on the business is given near the court house in Great Barrington, by the public's humble servant,*

WILLIAM WHITING,
GREAT BARRINGTON, *October* 15, 1776.

Recreated from The Hartford Courant, October 21, 1776.

THE TORY PRESS.

NEW YORK, *October* 7.

[*The following articles were taken from the New York Mercury, printed in* NEW YORK *at the office lately kept by* Mr. Gaine, *which we received via* LONG ISLAND]

HIS Majesty's forces are now in possession of the city of New York Island. They are also in possession of Powles Hook and command the East river and Connecticut sound. All this has been obtained with very little difficulty & loss on the part of the troops; the rebels, after the battle, or rather the ROUT of the 27th of August, having never attempted to face the soldiers but fled every way with the utmost precipitation. They quitted works, which they had been labouring upon during the whole summer without scarce the conflict of a day.

The King's forces are in remarkable good health and spirits, and seem resolved to convince the world that they not only bear the name, but the nature, of Britons; and while that they fight with their usual ardour in the cause of the King and Constitution they know how to treat even ungrateful rebels with pity and humanity. They consider that many of them are seduced and misled by designing men, who under pretence of patriotism, are sacrificing the interests and happiness of this whole continent to their own sordid interest and ambition.

The King's troops have not sustained the loss of 100 men; while the rebels, by the best accounts, cannot have lost fewer than between 4 or 5000 killed, wounded, and taken prisoners; to mention nothing of deserters, who leave them daily.

So vast a fleet was never seen together in this port, or perhaps in all America before. The ships are stationed up the East river or sound, as far as Turtle Bay; and, near the town, the multitude of masts carries the appearance of a wood. Some are moored up the North river; others lay in the bay between Red and Yellow Hook; some, again, off Staten Island; and several off Powles Hook, and towards the Kills. The men of war are moored chiefly up New York sound, and make, with the other ships, a very magnificent and formidable appearance. Five men of war have been detached from the squadron into the North river above Greenwich, probably to assist the operations of the army against the rebels, who still remain in the northern extremity of this island, and on the heights above Kingsbridge.

It is said, the Flora frigate of 32 guns, commanded by Capt. Brisbane, is preparing to sail, with several transports under convoy.

We are informed by a gentleman just escaped from New England, that the rebels have lately carried many hundred head of cattle from the East end of Long Island, to New London in Connecticut, and that their privateers are very busy in negotiating this kind of business, and have moreover committed some of their usual tyrannical and oppressive acts, upon several loyal subjects in those parts.

The savage burning of this city by the New England incendiaries, will be a lasting monument of their inveterate malice against the trade and prosperity of this colony, as well as rooted disaffection to British law and government. They had long threatened the performance of this villanous deed, and this is the best return that the people of property in this city, who have espoused their cause, are to expect for their heedless credulity.

On Thursday last arrived here from England, a number of transports under convoy, having on board the 27th Regiment of Light Horse, under the command of Lieutenant Colonel Harcourt.

[*Our readers will very much question the truth of the above account, when they are assured, that a letter from a person of distinction in New York, has been intercepted, the writer of which informs his friend that the regular army in the late encounters, have lost 1200 men and 100 officers killed.*]

Recreated from The Hartford Courant, October 21, 1776.

CROWN POINT EVACUATED.

BY our last accounts from Ticonderoga, we learn that on the defeat of our vessels on the lake under general Arnold, Crown Point, which was occupied as an out post, was evacuated by colonel Hartley, who commanded there with part of his battalion, who were all the troops he had with him. They brought off all of the cannon and military stores, and got safe to Ticonderoga in the evening of the 14th of October.

That colonel Waterbury, who, with a number of men, were taken in one of the gondolas on the lake, but were sent prisoners into their own states by Carleton, and general Arnold, with his party, got to Ticonderoga with colonel Hartley. We also learn, that our force at Ticonderoga is near 10,000 effective men, and that the enemy's force is about 7000, and that our people were in hourly expectation of an attack.

I HAVE received instructions from the CONGRESS to contract for supplying the continental troops with provisions for the ensuing year; the 2d and 7th regiments to commence the first day of December next, and the troops that are about to be raised as soon as they are collected. Those who are desirous to engage in this business are requested to meet me in the city of Williamsburg on Friday the 21st instant, with their proposals.

WILLIAM AYLETT, D. C. G.

ALEXANDRIA, October 10, 1776.

I INTEND to leave the colony immediately.

WILLIAM HUNTER, jun.

Recreated from Purdie's Virginia Gazette, November 15, 1776.

HOWE'S *Coup-de-Main.*

Extract of a letter from HARLEM, *October* 13.

"Yesterday morning about 4000 of the enemy landed at Fagg's or Frog's Point, in the sound, about six miles above us; a detachment was immediately sent to oppose them. The enemy got possession of the point, but as I was informed last night, had made no farther progress. Our people, I am told, had taken up a bridge which was there, and felled trees across the road, to obstruct them till a reinforcement could arrive.

"In the afternoon 42 sail passed the mouth of the Hudson river, in their way to the point; they consisted of sloops, schooners, brigs and 9 ships. I expect there will be bloody work there to-day. From the number of men landed and the ships which went up, I think this can be no feint, but that the main body of Howe's army must be there, and that there he intends to make his *Coup-de-Main.* This week will probably finish the campaign.

"Upon the arrival of the ships at Dobb's ferry they landed some men and plundered the store-house. I suppose those men who landed yesterday are to go across the country, and form a line from Flagg's point to Tarry town, four miles above Dobb's ferry, where the ships lie, but in this I expect they will be mistaken."

Recreated from The Pennsylvania Gazette, October 16, 1776.

ANY gentleman who has Muller's *New System of Mathematicks,* sometimes called Muller's *Elements of Mathematicks, Gunnery,* &c. 24 copperplates, 2 vols. of his *Conick Sections,* and his *Field Engineer,* will, if disposed to sell, receive double price for them, or any one of them, at mr. Purdie's printing-office; or, if any gentleman who has them is not willing to sell, a military gentleman would be glad to borrow for a few months.

Recreated from Purdie's Virginia Gazette, November 15, 1776.

URGENT CALL FOR MILITIA.

Copy of a letter from gen. SCHUYLER, *to the committee of the county of* BERKSHIRE, *Oct.* 16.

"Our fleet which suffered severely, in an engagement, on the 12th instant with the enemy, has been still more severely handled in a subsequent action, insomuch that the enemy are left masters of the Lake, and are marching on to attack our army at Ticonderoga; in this situation of our affairs, it is of the utmost importance that the militia of your county should immediately march to sustain the army, such as can march expeditiously, come by the way of Albany, should do so; and the others take the route to Skeensborough. Each man should come provided with as much provision and ammunition as possible.

"The commanding officer must send me information of his number and progress from time to time, I shall be either at Fort George or Skeensborough, but as I cannot determine which, it will be proper to send expresses to both places; and to forward copies of this to governor Trumbull, and to every committee in your state, that are in a situation of affording us assistance, as also to the neighbouring counties in the state of Connecticut; I must repeat, gentlemen, it is of great importance that I should be duly furnished with an account of the movements and number of the militia."

Your most obedient, humble servant,
PHI. SCHUYLER.

CONTINENTAL CURRENCY.

We hear that on the evacuation of our fortresses on Long Island, the continental currency sunk in its value one thousand per cent, but that now it has gained its nominal value, and passes currently among the British troops and tories as well as among our friends; what was the occasion of this strange turn is a matter of much speculation.

Recreated from The Maryland Gazette, November 14, 1776.

'TWILL BE FURIOUS.

Extract of a letter from TICONDEROGA, *Oct.* 20.

"The enemy are in possession of Crown Point, and we expect they may fancy this ground in a day or two. They must pay a great price for it however, as we value it highly. Fourteen boats or birch canoes, with Indians, were just now seen by our guard boats, five miles from here. We expect an attack every moment; whenever it comes, 'twill be furious, and the defences obstinate, cruelly obstinate."

Recreated from The Hartford Courant, November 4, 1776.

THE WIFE IS A SPY.

NEW LONDON, *Oct.* 18.—Last Saturday the wife and daughter of one John Hill, a prisoner confined in Boston goal, for being concerned with Crean Brush and others, in robbing the inhabitants of Boston, when that place was evacuated, came to this town from Providence by water, and were endeavouring to get a passage to the west end of Long Island, but were stopped by the Committee of this town, and on examination were found upon them sundry papers, containing matters of intelligence respecting the people, and state of the country, sent from said Hill and others in Boston, to be communicated to General Howe; it appeared from the papers found upon them, that they had been possessed of other papers, which they had secured or destroyed. They were both sent back with the papers, under a proper convoy, to the place from whence they came.

BOSTON, *October* 17, 1776.

On Wednesday last, was sent into Falmouth, Casco Bay, a large prize ship, with 16 carriage guns, and 10 swivels; her cargo consists of beef, pork, butter, pease, bread, oatmeal, flour, 20 casks and a half ditto powder, and 207 casks nails. Capt. English, the prize-master, took two brigs with raisins, beef, pork, butter and rice; but was obliged to dismiss one for want of hands.

Recreated from The Pennsylvania Gazette, November 6, 1776.

ARMY REMOVING FROM HEIGHTS OF HARLEM.

It has been determined in a Council of War at Head Quarters, to remove the army from the Heights of Harlem towards East and West Chester, in order to outflank the enemy, and disappoint their intentions.

In the night of the 15th instant General Mercer passed over to Staten Island with part of the troops posted at Perth Amboy, and advanced within a few miles of Richmond town, having been informed that a company of British troops, one of Hessians, and one of Skinner's militia lay there. Colonel Griffin was detached with Colonel Patterson's battalion, and Major Clarke at the head of some rifle-men, to fall in upon the east end of the town, while the remainder of the troops enclosed it on the other quarters; both divisions reached the town by break of day, but not before the enemy were alarmed; most of them fled after exchanging a few shot with Col. Griffin's detachment.

Two soldiers of the enemy were mortally wounded, and seventeen taken prisoners; with the loss of only two soldiers killed on our side. Col. Griffin received a wound in the foot from a musket ball, and Lieut. Col. Smith was slightly wounded in the arm. Amongst the prisoners taken in this action are eight Hessians. Our troops brought off from Staten Island 45 muskets, a number of bayonets, cutlasses, &c.

On Friday the 18th instant one of the enemy's advanced parties near East Chester fell in with part of Col. Glover's brigade, when a smart and close engagement ensued; in which our men behaved with great coolness and intrepidity, and drove the enemy back to their main body.

NEWPORT, *October* 11.—Last Monday the Continental sloop Providence, Capt. Jones, arrived at a safe port, having, in a cruise of six weeks, captured 16 sail of vessels, 6 of which he burnt; among the others is one ship with 3000 quintals of codfish, some smaller fishermen, and two West-Indiamen.

Recreated from The Pennsylvania Gazette, October 23, 1776.

200 SAIL ABOVE HELL GATE.

NEW HAVEN, *October* 23.—The enemy have extended themselves this way, as far as New Rochel, and small parties of them have advanced as far as Mareneck. In one of the churches at New Rochel, was stored more than two thousand bushels of salt, which has fallen into the hands of the enemy. It was owned by the state of New York.

Last Friday there was a small skirmish, near the above church, between a detached party of the enemy, and one from our army, in which we lost eight or ten men, and some wounded, among the latter was Col. Shepard of the Massachusetts's Bay, who was slightly wounded in the throat, and who commanded the party; the enemy's loss is not known.

We hear, that near 200 sail of the enemy's fleet, are this side of Hell Gate, the chief of them lying near Hart Island.

Recreated from The Hartford Courant, October 28, 1776.

AMERICANS AT WHITE PLAINS.

Extract of a letter from FORT LEE, *Oct.* 25.

"Head-Quarters is now above 20 miles from this place, and we have but little news we can depend upon till a day or two after the transaction. To-day indeed I heard the following, which may be worth communicating. One of the vessels up the North river came before Dobb's ferry with an intention to cut off our communication. She lay there one day undisturbed; but last night two field pieces were sent down, and early this morning began to play upon her. They hulled her 11 times out of 15. She hoisted sail, but could make no way for want of wind, and she was obliged to put out her boats and be towed off; all which time she was exposed to our fire. It is hoped this drubbing will prevent such manoeuvres for the future, and oblige the pirates to keep aloof. I am informed that several brigades of our army moved this day up to White Plains; so that almost all the army is now at that place.

"Little skirmishes happen almost every day; but they are thought so little of that they seldom are mentioned as news. The most considerable was that with Rogers's party, in which a number was killed and wounded, 36 taken prisoners, with 40 stand of arms. Two of the prisoners prove to be spies, and one a deserter from us. These I hope will be made examples of. Several Hessians have been taken since."

October 26. "P.S. Since I wrote the above, I learn that the enemy have got between Kingsbridge and White Plains. That ground was left vacant by the removal of the brigades I have mentioned. A captain's guard only was left over some provision till it could be moved. This day about noon the captain discovered about 100 light horse and as many infantry making that way towards him; he retreated to Fort Independence and the enemy continued their rout.

"Whether this was only a foraging party, or whether sent to take the ground which he had left, I cannot tell; if the latter, I believe it will not be disagreeable. It is probable the brigades were moved higher up on purpose to give the enemy an opportunity of getting in, when they will not be very likely to get out undisturbed."

Recreated from The Maryland Gazette, November 21, 1776.

THE BALL IS OPENED.

Colonel Smallwood Wounded.
Part of a letter from White Plains, *Oct.* 28.

"This morning information was received that the enemy appeared to be preparing for a general attack, and were advancing fast; proper preparations were made to receive them, and very soon the ball was opened with field-pieces on both sides. The enemy attacked our right wing, who defended themselves nobly. At the same time, a party of light horse filed off towards our center; a shot from one of our cannon forced them to wheel to the right about and retreat; it is said that this shot unhorsed two of them.

"About one o'clock one of the horse was brought in; his rider was killed; fighting still continues; it is now 3 o'clock p.m. and to-morrow I think will be the important day; no accounts can yet be given of the loss on either side. Our men are the most expert in the world at making breast-works; in an hour or two they made an amazingly long fence and covered it properly with earth.

"Yesterday we took 20 Waldeckers and regulars, 7 of the latter. Yesterday too the enemy attacked our lines at Harlem and Mount Washington at the same time, with two ships; they were repulsed in both places. This morning 45 tories, and some regular prisoners, passed through here, on their way to Fishkiln.

"Colonel Smallwood, of Maryland, is this moment come wounded to the house where I am. He is wounded in the arm and hip, but rode here on horseback, and can walk tolerably well."

Recreated from The Pennsylvania Gazette, November 6, 1776.

ANOTHER ATTACK EXPECTED.

Extract of another letter, dated in the evening of October 28, 1776.

"The post being detained by desire of the general gives me an opportunity (with a wooden pen on a drum head) to acquaint you that the part of our army which was engaged to-day was a brigade commanded by gen. M'Dougal, composed of Webb's, Ritzma's, Smallwood's, Haslet's and Brooks's regiments—Ritzma's and Smallwood's suffered most on this occasion, sustaining, with great patience and coolness, a long and heavy fire—and finally retreated with great sullenness, being obliged to give way to a superior force.

"The British army and auxiliaries are now encamped about one mile off our lines, and, make a formidable appearance, but, from the spirit and temper of our troops, I augur well of the event of another attack, which it is expected will commence to-morrow morning."

Recreated from The Maryland Gazette, November 7, 1776.

BRITISH SHIP HEAVILY DAMAGED.

Extract of a letter to CONGRESS, *from* FORT LEE, *dated, October* 28, 1776.

A ship moved up the river early in the morning, above our lower lines, right opposite to Fort No. 1, near old head-quarters at Morris's. She began a brisk cannonade upon the shore. Col. Magaw, who commands at Fort Washington, got down an 18 pounder, and fired 60 rounds at her; 26 went through her. The gun was mostly loaded with two balls. She was annoyed considerably by two 18 pounders from the shore. The confusion and distress that appeared on board the ship exceeds all description. Without doubt she lost a great number of men. She was towed off by four boats sent from other ships to her assistance. She slipped her cable, and left her anchor. Had the tide run flood one half hour longer, we should have sunk her.

At the same time the fire from the ships began, the enemy brought up their field pieces, and made a disposition to attack the lines; but col. Magaw had so happily disposed and arranged his men, as to put them out of conceit of that manoeuvre. A cannonade and fire with small arms continued almost all day, with very little intermission. We lost one man only. Several of the enemy were killed; two or three of them our people took and brought off the field, and several more were left there. The firing ceased last evening, and has not been renewed this morning. Troops (of our army) are in good spirits, and, in every engagement, since the retreat from New York, have given the enemy a drubbing.

Published by order of CONGRESS, *Oct.* 31, 1776.
CHARLES THOMPSON, sec'ry.

THE subscribers to the SLOOP PACKET are desired to meet at the *Raleigh* on *Friday* the 22d of this instant.

Recreated from Purdie's Virginia Gazette, November 15, 1776.

4000 LAND AT THREE MILE POINT.

By letters from Mount Independence of a late date, we are informed, that on the 28th of October a large body of the enemy appeared in boats coming down the lake, who soon after landed to the number of about 4000, on Three Mile Point in full view of Mount Independence. Soon after which, 2 or 3 boats came down from the main body, to reconnoitre and view the boom which our people have fixed across the lake from the old French lines to the eastern shore, to prevent their shipping from approaching our fortification; one of which boats came so near as to be within reach of our cannon, when she was so warmly fired upon from one of our redoubts, that she was obliged to quit her station, with the loss of one man killed, and several wounded.

In the evening after they landed they retired out of our sight, and by a gentleman from Albany, who came to town on Saturday last we are told, that the whole army under general Burgoyne have left the above place, as well as Crown Point, but what rout they have taken is not known.

Recreated from The Hartford Courant, November 11, 1776.

BASTARD NEGRO CHILD DEAD.

NEW HAVEN, *October* 30.—A surprising and instructive scene happened lately at Sunderland, in the State of Massachusetts Bay. One Fellows Billings, a noted tory, had a bastard negro child born in his house. The stupid ass, to insult the distress of this country, express his utter contempt of its sacred rights, and if possible to render himself more vile and infamous in the view of the people, named the child George Washington. The child, though healthy and well over night, was dead in the morning; and soon after two of the poor wretch's children, the only tender branches of his family, were lodged in the silent grave. A solemn lecture to those who sport with the sacred cause of LIBERTY.

Recreated from The Hartford Courant, November 4, 1776.

SIGNAL OF ENEMY'S APPROACH.

ACTION ON THE LAKE.

TICONDEROGA, *October* 31, 1776.

On Monday morning, between eight and nine o'clock, our advanced guard boat down the lake made the signal for the approach of the enemy's fleet. In about an hour five of the largest boats or gondolas appeared in sight, and a number of troops, Indians and Canadians, were seen landing upon Three Mile point. Soon after, two of the armed boats stood over to the east side of the lake, inclining upwards, as if sent to reconnoitre. When they came considerably within shot, they were fired upon from two redoubts very near the shore, and by a row galley that was stationed to cover the boom. They thereupon retired. In the mean time the enemy's troops were distinctly seen to land upon the back of the point, and presently after, thirteen small batteaus and birch canoes crossed from the west to the east side of the lake, into a bay about four miles below our redoubt.

Upon these threatenings of an attack, our lines, redoubts, and posts were all manned, and as the motions of the enemy seemed to indicate they were gathering their main force upon the west side of the lake, as if intending to make their push there, three regiments (Poor's, Read's and Greaton's) were ordered from Mount Independence to reinforce this side. The orders were instantly obeyed, and nothing could exceed the spirit and alertness which were shown by all officers and soldiers in executing every order that was given.

About four o'clock in the afternoon, the boats and canoes that had passed to the west side of the lake, returned, and the enemy were seen plainly to re-embark at the Three Mile point. The guard boat was immediately ordered to resume her station, and by sunset it was observed the body of the enemy had retired.

Published by order of CONGRESS,
CHARLES THOMPSON, Sec.

Recreated from The Pennsylvania Packet, November 19, 1776.

IN CONGRESS.

Copy of a letter to the president from major general GATES, *dated at* TICONDEROGA, NOV. 5.

SIR,

I have the honour to congratulate the Congress upon the retreat of lieutenant-general Sir Guy Carleton, with the fleet and the army under his command, from Crownpoint. Saturday last, the works being put in the best order, the boom and bridge of communication finished, and every necessary preparative for defence made, I determined to send a detachment down each side of the lake, to beat up the enemy's quarters of their advanced post on Putnam's point and the opposite shore. About eight at night the detachment, under the command of major Delap, proceeded down the east side of the lake, and the other, under col. Connor, down the west side. Sunday morning major Delap, with his detachment, took possession of Putnam's point, which the enemy had just abandoned; and immediately detached a subaltern, with a small party, to reconnoitre Crownpoint.

The officer, having returned, reported that he saw the enemy embark, a number of their vessels under sail, and the whole preparing to get under way. Col. Connor, on taking possession of the post opposite Putnam's point, found that likewise abandoned. Yesterday an officer, and a party whom I sent to Crownpoint returned, and reported he had been at Crownpoint with the inhabitants there; that the enemy were all gone from that post, and the inhabitants would come this day to Ticonderoga, to make their submission, and beg the protection of the United States.

I have the honour to be, &c.
HORATIO GATES.

P.S. This will be delivered to you by my first aid de camp, major Stuart, a deserving officer.

The foregoing is a copy of general GATES's *letter.*
JOHN HANCOCK, *president.*

Recreated from The Maryland Gazette, November 21, 1776.

The SPEECH of GEORGE III.

King of Great Britain, in his Parliament.

October 31, 1776.

My LORDS and GENTLEMEN,

NOTHING could have afforded me so much satisfaction as to have been able to inform you, at the opening of this session, that the troubles which have so long distracted my colonies in North America were at an end, and that my unhappy people, recovered from their delusions, had delivered themselves from the oppression of their leaders, and returned to their duty; but so daring and desperate is the spirit of their leaders, whose object has always been dominion and power, that they now have openly renounced all allegiance to the crown, and political connexion to this country. They have rejected, with circumstances of indignity and insult, the means of conciliation held out to them under the authority of our commission, and have presumed to set up their rebellious confederacies for independent states.

If their treason be suffered to take root, much mischief must grow from it to the safety of my loyal colonies, to the commerce of my kingdoms, and, indeed, to the present system of all Europe. One great advantage, however, will be derived from the object of the rebels being openly avowed and clearly understood; we shall have unanimity at home, founded on the general conviction of the justice and necessity of our measures. I am happy to inform you, that by the blessing of Divine Providence on the good conduct and valour of my officers and forces by sea and land, and on the zeal and bravery of the auxiliary troops in my service, Canada is recovered; and although, from unavoidable delays, the operations at New York could not begin before the month of August, the success in that province has been so important as to give the strongest hopes of the most decisive good consequences.

But, notwithstanding this fair prospect, we must, at all events, prepare for another campaign. I continue to receive assurances of amity from the several courts of Europe, and am using my utmost endeavours to conciliate the unhappy differences between two neighbouring powers; and still hope that all misunderstandings may be removed, and Europe continue to enjoy the inestimable blessings of peace. I think, nevertheless, in the present situation of affairs, it is expedient we should be in a respectable state of defence at home.

• • • •

Gentlemen of the House of Commons,

I will order the estimates of the ensuing year to be laid before you. It is a matter of real concern to me that the important consideration which I have stated to you must necessarily be followed by great expense. I doubt not, however, but that my faithful Commons will readily and cheerfully grant me such supply as the maintenance of the honour of my Crown, the vindication of the just rights of Parliament, and the public welfare, shall be found to require.

• • • •

My Lords and Gentlemen,

On this arduous contest, I can have no other object but to promote the true interest of all my subjects. No people ever enjoyed more happiness, or lived under a milder government, than those now revolted provinces. The improvements in every art, which they boast, declare it; their numbers, their wealth, their strength, by sea and land, which they think sufficient to enable them to make head against the whole power of the mother country, are irrefragable proofs of it. My desire is to restore to them the blessings of law and liberty equally enjoyed by every British subject, which they have totally and desperately exchanged for all the calamities of war, and the arbitrary tyranny of their chiefs.

Recreated from The Virginia Gazette, February 14, 1777.

THE MIGHTY BRITISH DEEDS.

Extract of a letter from NORTH CASTLE, *November 7, 1776.*

"Since I wrote you the other day an event has taken place which I think will finish this campaign; the enemy have suddenly and unexpectedly decamped. The general opinion is that they are going into winter quarters at New York, and indeed some of the deserters or prisoners told us this was what they intended, but I think the season is not yet so far advanced as to render this step immediately necessary. It is possible they will take Fort Washington in their return, or rather that our people will abandon it, by which means they will at last become masters of New York island. They have become possessed of more territory this campaign than the last, but they will derive very little, if any more advantage from it, than from their possessions in and about Boston—of *honour*, they will hardly gain so much, for they do not deserve it.

"Let us review their mighty deeds. Two hundred sail of British ships gained possession of Staten Island, a sandy spot of very small extent, inhabited by tories, who surrendered it to them without firing a gun. At Long Island they gained more credit, for by fighting they obtained a part of it, but much the largest part of it remains in our possession yet. The city of New York, and every other place the enemy became masters of, was evacuated by us, and not conquered by them, except a small hill at White Plains, which they bought and paid a high price for (by their own accounts) in British blood—this very hill they have now given up to us, as they did Bunker's last campaign. In every battle and skirmish, except at Long Island and the hill above mentioned, we have been victorious. Now what have they to boast of? Nothing but a little territory which we evacuated, and by evacuating it gained important advantages. Will this repay the expenses of the largest fleet and army Great Britain ever sent to America?

"Have all the enemy's exertions effected the so much talked of junction with Burgoyne, which was to produce wonders? Have they subjugated the "rebellious Americans,"—the grand design of their coming here? Nothing of all this, but to the eternal disgrace of lord and gen. Howe, impartial history will record that they crossed an ocean of 3000 miles, with a fleet of 3 or 400 sail, an army of near 30,000 men, and a very large train of artillery, to subdue men who had been declared in the British parliament to be '*cowards*,' and after all marched but *twelve* miles from their ships, during the whole summer and part of the fall, and then went into winter quarters. How is the glory of Britain fallen, how have her arms been sullied! I think gen. Howe must feel very much ashamed of himself. Six sailors and three soldiers (prisoners) are brought in this morning; the sailors were sent on shore to get wood. I have been talking with the prisoners. The soldiers say the talk in their camp is that the enemy intend attacking Fort Washington, and then retiring into winter quarters at New York."

Another letter from NORTH CASTLE, *Nov. 8.*

"The enemy's left wing is at Dobb's ferry, their right about three miles nearer New York. *Entre nous*, I think the enemy must try to strike some important stroke which will make a noise, before they go into winter quarters. From their lying along the river I suspect they intend either to enter New Jersey, or make a push up the North River. In either case we are ready for them."

Recreated from The Pennsylvania Gazette, November 13, 1776.

GOING HESSIAN HUNTING.

Extract of a letter from FORT LEE, *Nov. 8.*

"Our garrison at Fort Washington are in high spirits, and go a Hessian-hunting every day. Yesterday a serjeant and 15 men of col. Cadwallader's battalion, attacked an out-guard of 47 men, killed three, wounded several, and burnt the guard house."

Recreated from The Maryland Gazette, November 21, 1776.

ENEMY RETREAT TO NEW YORK.

Part of a letter from NORTH CASTLE, *Nov. 9.*

"The enemy are retreating towards New York; this is a very sudden manoeuvre of theirs, and occasions much speculation; some think they are going into winter quarters immediately, but the more judicious say General Howe cannot answer it if he does that, without performing some greater exploit than he has yet; and therefore they suppose he will attempt some strike in New Jersey. We watch his motions narrowly, and shall follow wherever he leads."

Recreated from The Pennsylvania Gazette, November 13, 1776.

Extract of a letter from FORT LEE, *Nov. 10.*

"The enemy have not decamped, as was reported, but are still at Dobb's ferry. Part of our army have come this side of the river. General Washington will cross to-day. Deserters confirm the suspicions of the enemy's design to pay us a visit in the Jerseys; but the attempt is so dangerous, and so long delayed, that I can scarcely believe it is in agitation. Yesterday col. Magaw's men killed thirteen Hessians and an officer, and stripped them; his little enterprise gives spirit to our men, and insensibly reduces the number of the enemy."

We hear that the fleet that left Sandy Hook on Wednesday last has since been seen standing to the eastward.

Recreated from The Maryland Gazette, November 21, 1776.

An easy Method to preserve Beef with a small quantity of salt.

TAKE four Gallons of Water, in which put four Pounds of common Salt, four Ounces of Salt-Petre, and two Pounds of brown Sugar, simmer them over a slow fire, and skim off the Scum till it is done rising; then let it stand until it is cold, and it will preserve a Barrel of Beef, for a Year.

Recreated from The Hartford Courant, November 4, 1776.

MOVEMENTS OF THE ENEMY.

HOWE MIGHT VISIT PHILADELPHIA.

PHILADELPHIA, *November* 13.—From the army in the province of New York we learn, that after the 27th of October nothing material happened, except some small skirmishes, in which we always came off victorious, and often took prisoners. That many deserters had come off to our army, among which were between 30 and 40 Hessians. That suddenly on the night of the 5th inst. the enemy filed off the right of their army to the East river, and the left, about 8 or 10,000 men, to Dobb's ferry. That general Washington, in the morning, sent several parties to harass their rear, who returned with a few prisoners and two or three baggage waggons. That on the 7th, the enemy's transports, 40 in number (being the same which landed the troops at Frogg's point) were seen going down the East river towards New York. That on the 10th, the party that filed off towards the North river lay between Dobb's ferry and Phillip's mills; that the general being apprehensive that they intended making an incursion into the Jerseys, had sent general Putnam with 4000 men across the river, to join general Green, who has 6000 men at Fort Lee, with an intention to stop their progress, should they attempt the same.

Several letters of the best authority from head quarters say, they have great reason to expect Howe will visit this city, therefore they urge us to be upon the watch, and be ready for them, should they attempt such a thing.

Recreated from The Maryland Gazette, November 21, 1776.

BROUGHT *from Hampton by mistake, a* BLANKET *when I returned from thence as a minute-man. Any person claiming the same may have it on proving his property, or be paid the value by*

R. WOOLFOLK.

BRITISH VIEW PHILADELPHIA.

To the ASSOCIATORS *of* PENNSYLVANIA.

CONGRESS have received intelligence that a fleet of the enemy, consisting of several hundred sail, were yesterday discovered near Sandy Hook, steering to the southward. It is highly probable that their destination is for Delaware and the city of Philadelphia. It is needless to observe that the utmost vigour and dispatch are necessary to counteract the designs of the enemy, and defend this city, the preservation of which is of very great importance to the general cause. Congress have directed us to co-operate within the council of safety of this state in concerting measures proper on the present emergency; and have invested us with their full power to carry such measures into execution.

In discharge of the trust committed to us, we think it our duty to recommend it to you, in the warmest and most earnest manner, immediately to put yourselves in array, and march, by companies and parts of companies, as you can be ready, with the utmost expedition to this city. Its safety and the interest of the United States point out the necessity of your strongest exertions.

General Washington, at the head of a considerable part of his army, is advancing southward; but, notwithstanding all the dispatch he can possibly make, the enemy may arrive before him. If they shall be opposed, with proper spirit and sufficient numbers, at their first approach, there is the greatest reason to expect that their views will finally be defeated; and they will experience, to their cost and disgrace, that on no part of the continent they can make an impression. They have been already obliged to abandon Crownpoint and retire into Canada.

It is vain to hope for lenity from your inveterate foes. Their tender mercies are cruelty. The property of those who acted as their friends is not safer than that of those whom they consider as their enemies. Devastation of every kind marks their footsteps.

Congress will do everything in their power to strengthen you. Expresses for this purpose are already set off to the neighbouring states. Every thing dear to freemen is now at stake. The freemen of Pennsylvania will undoubtedly discover the spirit and zeal, which their country expects and their critical situation demands.

BENJAMIN HARRISON,
JAMES WILSON,
EDWARD RUTLEDGE,
FRANCIS LIGHTFOOT LEE.
Attest, RICHARD PETERS, Secretary.
November 14, 1776.

Nov. 16. The fleet which lately sailed from New York, and took its course to the southward, with the appearance of a design to enter Delaware river, after keeping that course for some time, suddenly altered it, and are gone to the eastward, supposed to be bound for England. The apprehension, therefore, of an attack on this city, is now entirely removed, and the march of the associators is countermanded.

Part of a letter from PHILADELPHIA, *Nov.* 19.

"This moment an express arrived to Congress, with advice that the enemy's whole army, passing down to New York, attacked Fort Washington by storm, and carried it, but with what expense we cannot yet tell, as we have not the particulars; but as the firing continued long and heavy, it is supposed they met with great loss. This seems to be the last stroke left for general Howe this campaign. His manoeuvres must now end, and with disgrace, after the monstrous expense and enormous force of this year."

WANTED *on freight for* Europe *and the* West Indies, *suitable* VESSELS; *which, if required, will be ensured.*
JAMES & ADAM HUNTER.

Recreated from Purdie's Virginia Gazette, November 29, 1776.

THE REDUCTION OF MOUNT WASHINGTON.

In CONGRESS.

Intelligence received by Congress *concerning the reduction of* Mount Washington, *by the enemy on November* 16, 1776.

EARLY last Saturday morning col. Magaw posted his troops partly in the lines thrown up by our army on our first coming thither from New York, and partly on a commanding hill lying north of Mount Washington, the lines being all to the southward. In this position the attack began about 10 o'clock, which our troops stood, and returned the fire in such a manner as gave great hopes the enemy was entirely repulsed; but at this time a body of troops crossed Harlem river in boats, and landed within the second lines, our troops being then engaged in the first.

Col. Cadwallader, who commanded in the lines, sent off a detachment to oppose them; but they, being overpowered by numbers, gave way, upon which col. Cadwallader ordered his troops to retreat, in order to gain the fort, and the enemy, crossing over, came in upon them in such a manner that a number of them surrendered. At this time the Hessians advanced on the north side of the fort, in very large bodies. They were received by the troops posted there with proper spirit, and kept back a considerable time; but at length they were also obliged to submit to a superiority of numbers, and retire under the cannon of the fort.

The enemy having possessed themselves of the adjacent ground, which rendered the fort no longer tenable, the garrison surrendered.

The numbers killed or wounded, on either side, are not yet known; but, from the heaviness and continuance of the fire, it is supposed there must have been considerable execution.

Published by order of Congress,
CHARLES THOMPSON, Secretary.

Recreated from Purdie's Virginia Gazette, December 6, 1776.

FORT LEE EVACUATED.

New Haven, *November* 27.—The Tuesday following the Battle and Surrendery of Fort Washington, a large detachment from the enemy's army, supposed to be about 14,000 crossed North River, four or five miles above Fort Washington, to attack Fort Lee, but on their approach, the garrison marched out, and encamped about one mile from the fort, the next day they formed in order of battle, with an intention, it is said, to defend themselves against an attack of the enemy, but on their approaching, finding them much superior in number, they retired, and left them in possession of their tents, and other valuable field equipage. Our army on that side of the river is said to be about 6000 strong, and have with them Generals Washington, Putnam and Stirling; who, last Thursday, (when our informant came away) were at Hackinsack, about seven miles from Fort Lee.

RUSSIA AGAINST AMERICA.

Providence, *November* 23.—Thursday Capt. Avery, in a Schooner, arrived here from Nantz, in France, laden with Woolen, &c. on Account of the United States. He left Nantz the 11th of October, and informs, that the Empress of Russia had agreed to furnish Great Britain with a Body of Troops to serve against America. And that a great Naval Armament was preparing at Brest, said to be destined to intercept the Russian Fleet in the Baltic.

GATES JOINS CONTINENTALS.

Hartford, *December* 2.—Last week Gen. Gates, with about 3000 men from the Northern Army, joined the Continental Army near New York.

We hear that Generals Washington, Putnam, and Stirling, are at Elizabeth Town, in New Jersey, with about 6000 of the Continental Troops, and that they have lately been reinforced with 12 or 14,000 men from Pennsylvania and New Jersey, and more were continually coming in to their assistance.

Recreated from The Hartford Courant, December 2, 1776.

GENERAL HOWE ADVANCES.

Fort Lee, having been evacuated by our troops, and the stores removed to a place of security, part of the British army, we hear, took possession of it last Thursday.

We hear that part of general Howe's army has advanced a few miles into the state of New Jersey, and that he is preparing with the remaining body of his troops to effect a landing in that state. General Washington is busy preparing to receive them, and if properly reinforced with the militia of New Jersey, we hope will be able to check their progress. We also hear, that general Lee is advancing to join general Washington with a reinforcement from the continental army in the state of New York.

On Wednesday 100 sail of vessels left Sandy Hook and put to sea, but whether they have troops on board is uncertain. Various are the conjectures of their destination; but the prevailing opinion is, that they are empty transports, and are bound to Ireland for provisions, and for British troops.

THE marines belonging to my company who are now absent upon furlough, are ordered to repair to York garrison as soon as possible.

(2)   JOHN C. COCKE, capt. of marines.

Williamsburg, in Virginia, Dec. 3, 1776.

THE captains of the second *Georgia* battalion, now recruiting in this state, are requested to meet me on *Tuesday* the 20th instant, at *Charlottesville*, in *Albemarle* county.

2   S. J. CUTHBERT, major.

In COUNCIL of SAFETY.

PHILADELPHIA, *November* 24, 1776.

To the colonel or commanding officer of the _____ battalion of _____.

GENERAL HOWE, after having reduced Fort Washington, and obtaining possession of Fort Lee, is now directing his operations against New Jersey. There is much reason to believe that his views extend to the city of Philadelphia. The forces in New Jersey may be insufficient to oppose his progress. It is therefore indispensably requisite for the preservation of this State, and the support of the general cause, that troops be immediately raised to reinforce general Washington. The measures adopted for this purpose you will learn from the resolutions enclosed. In this time of danger, it is unnecessary to use arguments with freemen who are determined never to lose that character but with their lives. We have entire confidence that you, and the battalion under your command, will, upon this occasion, give the strongest proofs of vigour and patriotism.

A judicious choice of the officers will do honour to the volunteers, and produce essential advantages to the service; for it is our opinion that the volunteers ought to have the election of them, and we recommend to you the utmost circumspection and care, not only in the person you may recommend to them, but also in the manner of doing it. As this council can only have in view, and, as much as possible, to give satisfaction to the people.

A paymaster will be appointed for each battalion, and the volunteers may depend on having their pay regularly. The colonel or commanding officer ought to muster each company, and send a certificate thereof to this Board.

Money is forwarded to _____, in order to advance the month's pay. To him you will please to apply for what money will be necessary in your battalion for that purpose. By order of Council,

DAVID RITTENHOUSE, V. P.

Recreated from Purdie's Virginia Gazette, December 6, 1776.

In COUNCIL of SAFETY.

PHILADELPHIA, *Nov.* 30, 1776.

RESOLVED, that, in the present alarming situation of our affairs, it is highly expedient that no vessels should be suffered to depart this port until farther orders from this Board.

Extract from the minutes,
S. POWELL, secretary.

Recreated from Purdie's Virginia Gazette, December 13, 1776.

ACTION IN THE JERSEYS.

NEW HAVEN, *December* 4.—A gentleman directly from general Lee's Head Quarters, brings an account, that on Thursday last, there was a considerable action, in the Jerseys, between a large body of the militia belonging to that state, and Pennsylvania, and several thousands of the enemy, who were repeatedly repulsed as they attempted to cross the river at Aquinac Bridge. That those of them who got over, were either killed or taken prisoners; and that their loss is considerable, the particulars of which we hope will be in our next.

We hear that General Washington is at Newark, eight or ten miles from the above place of action.

Recreated from The Hartford Courant, December 9, 1776.

WE intend to leave the colony immediately.

WILLIAMSBURG,   ROBERT LAMB.
Nov. 20, 1776.   ADAM BELL.

⁂ Any veſſel, outward bonnd, in want of hands, may hear of two *SAILORS* by applying to the printer.

A SMALL *but uſeful collection of BOOKS,* on Phyſick, Surgery, &c. *to be ſold at this office, on reaſonable terms.*

Recreated from Purdie's Virginia Gazette, November 29, 1776.

HOWE'S ARMY AT BRUNSWICK.

Extract of a letter from TRENTON, *Dec.* 3.

On the 1st instant the enemy appeared on the opposite side of Brunswick river, and began to play on the town with their artillery, but did little damage. We returned the fire from our artillery with great briskness, which obliged the enemy to retreat two miles back. Our army are in high spirits, expecting to be reinforced to-morrow, from Pennsylvania, with a body of 3000 militia, a German battalion, and a number of field pieces. Howe's army is in a bad situation, and if they advance, which we are wishing for, we shall have a fair opportunity to give them a severe blow; particularly if general Gates joins general Lee, and comes on their backs, we have the greatest reason to hope for success. This day an express has been despatched to general Lee, to hasten his march. Expect in my next to give you some interesting and very agreeable intelligence.

Recreated from Purdie's Virginia Gazette, December 20, 1776.

60 MILES FROM PHILADELPHIA.

Extract of a letter from a gentleman in PHILADELPHIA, *dated December 2, 1776.*

We are here in a situation not very pleasant. The enemy's army are rapidly crossing the Jerseys, and are now at Brunswick, about 30 miles beyond the Delaware, and 60 from this city. General Washington has not above 5000 men between us and them, and is retreating as fast as he can.

We are not certain of general Lee's motions, but we understand he is on this side of the North river; his force is not known. The associators here are turning out to reinforce the general, but their motions are not so quick as could be wished. However, we hope they will be in time enough to prevent these foes to freedom from being gratified with the possession of this city, but if they should, it may hurt; but ten such cities would not ruin America, if her sons deserve the blessing they contend for.

I earnestly wish my countrymen would quit every other consideration but that of industriously arming themselves, and strain every nerve for the security of their country. All other questions, now, are vain and ruinous illusions.

The very latest intelligence from the French West Indies says that a war between France, Spain, and Great Britain, is inevitable, and must speedily take place. The latter has employed 12 Russian men of war to cruise off the French ports, to intercept the American trade; and France, with 30 sail of the line, are determined to prevent it.

GEN. WASHINGTON AT TRENTON.

We have advice from Philadelphia, by letters dated the 3d instant, that general Washington was retreated to Trenton, that the enemy had marched to Brunswick, were to continue their route to that place, and from thence to Philadelphia, unless our army should be able to drive them back.

It is said general Lee has passed the North river with 10,000 men, and expected to come up with the enemy's rear. If so, I hope we shall soon have a good account of the British plunderers. The inhabitants of Philadelphia have removed their most valuable effects into the country, and part of their militia have gone to join general Washington. General Gates is also on his march to join general Lee; so that we shall have, it is thought, an army equal to Howe's.

TWENTY likely *Virginia* born NEGROES, from 9 to 13 years of age, will be sold at *Fredericksburg*, for ready money, on the 10th day of *January* next. Mr. *James Lewis* will have the management of the sale.

ALEX: SPOTSWOOD.

Recreated from Purdie's Virginia Gazette, December 13, 1776.

BRITISH SHIPS AT NEW LONDON.

December 6.—Tuesday last this town was alarmed by the appearance of 11 ships from the eastward coming into the sound, most of which appeared to be men of war, who by their course, for some time, it was apprehended, might be bound into this place; but they went farther up sound, and towards evening anchored under Long Island shore, where they lay till yesterday morning, when being joined by other men of war and transports from New York, to the number of near 100, they came to sail, and anchored near Black Point, about eight miles from this harbour, where they remain at this publication. The appearance of such a formidable fleet, within one hour's sail of the town, has thrown the inhabitants into great confusion.

Recreated from Purdie's Virginia Gazette, January 3, 1777.

WILLIAMSBURG, *Dec.* 6, 1776.

THE officers and troopers belonging to the HORSE are to repair to this place by the 11th of the month, without fail, to join the regiment, which is ordered to march to reinforce his Excellency General WASHINGTON, or, after that day, to rendezvous at *Fredericksburg*, where the regiment will march from this place. Such soldiers as are, through sickness, unable to march, must certify the same to the commanding officer, under the hand of a magistrate of the county where he resides, or he must expect to be treated as a deserter.

THEODORICK BLAND,
major commandant.

Recreated from Purdie's Virginia Gazette, December 13, 1776.

CONGRESS MOVES TO BALTIMORE.

WILLIAMSBURG.—*His Excellency the Governour received the following letter, dated the 8th instant, by express from* BALTIMORE, *where the* Hon. CONTINENTAL CONGRESS *have adjourned from the city of* PHILADELPHIA.

The movements of the enemy's army in the Jerseys, by which the neighbourhood of Philadelphia had become the seat of war, determined Congress to adjourn from thence to this town, where publick business will be entered on the 20th instant, unless a sufficient number of members should be assembled to begin sooner. At this place the publick business may be conducted with more deliberation, and undisturbed attention, than could be the case in a city subject to perpetual alarm, and that had necessarily been made a place of arms. The propriety of this measure was strongly enforced by the continental generals Putnam and Mifflin, who commanded in Philadelphia, and who gave it as their opinion, that although they did not consider the town as liable to fall into the enemy's hands but by surprise, yet that possibility rendered it improper for Congress to continue there.

So long as the American army kept together, the enemy's progress was extremely limited, but they knew and seized the opportunity of coming forward, which was occasioned by the greater part of the army dispersing in consequence of short enlistments; and this indeed was a plan early founded on hopes of accommodation, and for the greater ease of the people.

When a new army is assembled, the enemy must again narrow their bounds; and this demonstrates the necessity of every state exerting every means to bring the new levies into the field with all possible expedition. It is the only sure means of placing America on the ground where every man would wish to see it.

The British army is at present stationed along the Delaware from above Trenton, on the Jersey side, to Burlington, about 20 miles above Philadelphia. General Washington, with near 6000 men, is on the river side, opposite to Trenton; and the gondolas, with other armed vessels are stationed from Philadelphia to Trenton, to prevent the passage of the Delaware. General Lee, with about 5000 men, remains on the enemy's rear, a little to the westward of their line of march through the Jerseys. In this state, if the country associators of Pennsylvania, and from this neighbourhood, reinforce the general with a few thousands, so as to enable him to press the enemy's front, it may turn out a happy circumstance that they have been encouraged to leave their ships so far behind.

Recreated from Purdie's Virginia Gazette, December 27, 1776.

DR. FRANKLIN ARRIVED AT FRANCE.

BORDEAUX, *Dec.* 13.—I have the pleasure of informing you, that the hon. BENJAMIN FRANKLIN, esq., arrived safe at Nantz on the 6th instant, and has set out for Paris. He took two prizes on the Cape loaded with wine and brandy, which he sent to Quiberoon bay, between this and Nantz. The people at large here are all your friends, and I believe the government of France are disposed to favour you. A war between the powers of France, Spain, and Great Britain, is said to be unavoidable. Great preparations for war are making all over Europe.

Recreated from Purdie's Virginia Gazette, March 14, 1777.

FLEET DISAPPEARS.

HARTFORD, *December 9.*—In consequence of the large fleet which appeared off New London last week, and came to anchor at Black Point, as mentioned under the New London head, his honour the governour, with the advice of the council of war, gave orders for the whole of the militia east of Connecticut river, with three regiments from the west side, immediately to march to that place; but the fleet having since disappeared, the orders are countermanded for the present.

GENERAL LEE TAKEN PRISONER.

Betrayed by a Judas.

HARTFORD.—On Friday the 13th instant, about 11 o'clock, his Excellency General Lee being at a house in Baskenridge, New Jersey, at a great distance from the enemy's army, the house was of a sudden surrounded by 60 of the light horse, who immediately fired 60 or 70 shot into the house, when his Excellency, seeing there was not a possibility of making his escape, surrendered himself a prisoner of war. Upon this, the enemy mounted him upon a horse, without hat or cloak, and rode off with the utmost expedition.

Intelligence of General Lee's unguarded situation was given to the enemy the evening before he was made prisoner, by an inhabitant of Baskenbridge, personally known to the General, and who had made great pretensions of friendship for the American cause, though at heart the greatest villain that ever existed. This Judas rode all the preceding night to carry the intelligence, and served as a pilot to conduct the enemy, and came personally with them to the house where the General was taken.

Recreated from The Pennsylvania Packet, January 22, 1777.

SHIPS PASS NEW HAVEN AT NIGHT.

WEDNESDAY evening, the 11th instant, a fleet of between 70 and 80 sail of men of war and transports were seen to pass Marineck, standing to the eastward, an account of which we received in the forenoon of the next day; and it is supposed they went by our harbour in the night, as nothing was seen of them here, and are the same mentioned under the New London head. We hear they left their station near Black Point on Saturday, and went out to sea through the Race, and that by the course they steered were bound to Rhode Island. It is uncertain what number of troops they have with them; some say about 5000.

Recreated from Purdie's Virginia Gazette, January 3, 1777.

TROOPS CROSS THE DELAWARE.

Extract of a letter dated Head Quarters, TRENTON FALLS, *December 12, 1776.*

"My last to you was by Capt. _____, of the 5th instant from Trenton, I was then in hopes my next would have acquainted you we were advancing on the enemy; my reason for presuming this, was a speedy arrival of General Lee, with his division of the army. Our enemy, knowing how far he was in the rear, and our weak situation, made a forced march to come up with us, and were within two miles of Princetown when Lord Stirling began his retreat with two brigades. Boats from every quarter were collected, and our stores, together with the troops remaining at Trenton, were immediately conveyed over the Delaware.

"On Sunday morning, having every thing over, we crossed the Delaware, and took our quarters about a half mile from the river. About 11 o'clock, the enemy came marching down with all the pomp of war, in great expectation of getting boats, and immediately pursuing; but of this we took proper care, by destroying every boat, shallop, &c. we could lay our hands on. They made forced marches up and down the river, in pursuit of boats, but in vain.

"This is Thursday; the enemy are much scattered, some in Trenton, directly opposite, from that on their left to Burdentown and Burlington, on the river banks. The enemy are at least 12,000 strong, determined for Philadelphia, for which purpose they are transporting flat bottom boats from Brunswick to Trenton by land."

The WATCH lost between Litchfield and Harwington, and advertised in written hand-bills, is found.---The owner may have it, by calling at the Printing-Office in Hartford, and paying charges.

A Few bushels of SALT to be exchanged for BUTTER.---Enquire of the Printer.

Recreated from The Hartford Courant, December 23, 1776.

ENEMY POSSESSES NEWPORT.

PROVIDENCE, *December* 14.—Saturday morning last Commodore Sir Peter Parker, with about 70 sail of Men of War and Transports, came into our bay from New York, and anchored above the harbour of Newport. On Sunday they landed a body of troops, under the generals Clinton and Piercey, who took possession of the town, the inhabitants having previously determined that the place was not defensible against the enemy's shipping.

The few troops we had on the island retreated to Bristol, leaving behind them some pieces of artillery. By the best accounts yet received, the enemy's troops do not consist of more than 5000 men; among them are a number of Hessians, some horse, and many invalids. They are intrenching, it is said, at a place called Meeting House Hill, three miles distant from Bristol ferry.

From the first appearance of the fleet, the militia and independent companies of this State have been in motion, and are since joined by a large body of troops, with some companies of artillery from the neighbouring States.

We hear that the enemy's troops were escorted into Newport by a set of well-known infamous tories, who have long infested that town, and who may yet meet with the fate justly due to their atrocious villainies.

We learn that two of the enemy's frigates lay at or near Seconet passage, another near Bristol, and a fourth at the North end of Prudence Island.

Some persons, it is said, have been taken up and committed to goal at Newport, for the heinous crime of bearing arms against the King of Great Britain.

Saturday last two frigates landed some men at one of the Elizabeth Islands, where they burnt two houses, and killed and carried off a few sheep. A number of our people landed soon after on the island, killed three of the pirates, and drove the rest on board their ships.

Recreated from The Hartford Courant, December 23, 1776.

BRITISH & HESSIAN BARBARIANS.

BUCKS COUNTY, *December* 14, 1776.

The progress of the British and Hessian troops through New Jersey has been attended with such scenes of desolation and outrage, as would disgrace the most barbarous of nations, Among innumerable other instances the following are authenticated in such a manner as leaves no doubt of their truth.

William Smith, of Smith's Farm near Woodbridge, hearing the cries of his daughter, rushed into the room and found a Hessian officer attempting to ravish her; in an agony of rage and resentment the injured father instantly killed him; but the officer's party soon came upon him, and he now lays mortally wounded at his ruined plundered dwellings.

On Monday morning they entered the house of Samuel Stout, in Hopewell, where they destroyed his deeds, papers, furniture and effects of every kind, except what they plundered; they took every horse away, left his house and farm in ruins, injuring him to the value of £2000 in less than three hours.

On Wednesday last three women came down to the Jersey shore in great distress, a party from the American army went and brought them off, when it appeared that they had been all very much abused, and the youngest of them, a girl about 15, had been ravished that morning by a British officer.

A number of young women in Hopewell, to the amount of sixteen, flying from the ravaging and cruel enemy, took refuge on the mountain near Ralph Hart's, but information being given of their retreat, they were soon brought down into the British camp, where they have been kept ever since.

The fine settlements of Maidenhead and Hopewell are intirely broke up; no age nor sex has been spared; the houses are stripped of every article of furniture, and what is not portable is entirely destroyed; the stock of cattle and sheep are drive off; every article of cloathing and house linen seized and carried away; hundreds of families are reduced from comfort and affluence to poverty and ruin, left at this inclement season to wander through the woods without house or cloathing. If these scenes of desolation, ruin and distress, do not rouse and animate every man of spirit to revenge their injured countrymen and countrywomen, all virtue, honor and courage must have left this country, and we deserve all that we shall meet with, as there can be no doubt the same scene will be acted in this Province upon our own property, and our beloved wives and daughters.

PHILADELPHIA, *Dec.* 18.—Since our last arrived here Maj. Gen. Putnam and Brig. Gen. Mifflin.

The main body of the enemy's force now lie at Trenton in New Jersey, from whence they send out parties of horse and foot to distress the country; about a week ago 500 Hessians with some light horse entered the city of Burlington, where, however, they staid not long, the gallies belonging to this state being ordered to fire on the town, they retired with precipitation in the night of the day on which they entered, and we hear have joined their main body. They have since sent a large body to Corell's Ferry, about five miles above Trenton, where, it is thought, they will attempt to cross the Delaware.

General Washington, with an army under his command, have been joined by General Lee, with a part of the Continental army from White Plains, who are encamped along the river to watch the motions of the enemy. The Militia from this city have joined our main army in Bucks county, and we hear the Militia of the different counties in this state are following the glorious example.

NEWPORT, *Nov.* 18.—Capt. Skimmer, in a Massachusetts sloop of war, has taken and carried into Boston, a ship bound to New York, having on board 17,000 suits of clothes, 30,000 shirts. 30,000 pair of stockings, 30,000 pairs of shoes, &c.

Recreated from The Pennsylvania Packet, December 18, 1776.

RUN away the 30th of *November* last, from the subscriber, in *Botetourt* county, *Fincastle* town, a negro fellow named *JOE*, about 46 years old, 5 feet 9 or 10 inches high, a slim straight fellow, who has a very smooth way of speaking, and when in liquor pretends to be very religious; he can read print very well, is a great liar, and will deceive any one that is not acquainted with him. He formerly ran away from *Virginia*, and was in most parts of *Carolina*, whither I have reason to think he is now gone, as one *Robinson*, who said he came from *Carolina*, that very night stole one of my neighbour's horses, and went off. The said *Robinson* I believe to be a great rogue, and may pretend the negro is his, to get him away. *Joe* stole from me a black horse about 14 or 15 years old, very gray about his ears, and paces naturally. He had on, when I saw him last, a pair of leather breeches, a hunting shirt, leggins, and old shoes; but as I believe he has been some time preparing for his journey, it is probable he has other clothes with him. Whoever takes up the said negro and horse, and secures them so as I get them again, shall have 40 s. reward, if taken in *Virginia*, and if in *Carolina* 5 l.

THOMAS BOWYER.

Recreated from Purdie's Virginia Gazette, January 3, 1777.

HOWE LEAVING TRENTON.

Extract from a letter from PHILADELPHIA, *December* 21, 1776.

"The troops under Howe and Cornwallis have left Trenton, and are moving towards New York. General Lee's division of troops, now commanded by general Sullivan, consisting of about 5000, have crossed the Delaware at Easton, and are marching to join general Washington, near Coryell's ferry, in Bucks county. More troops are on their way to join the commander in chief, whose army will be, in a short time, full 18,000.

"A fleet and army from New York have arrived at Newport. All New England is in motion; in consequence of this, 10,000 men are now in arms at or near Providence, for the purpose of defending the state of Rhode Island."

Major general Gates, and brigadier generals St. Clair and Maxwell, arrived a few days ago at general Washington's head quarters, from Ticonderoga.

A number of the Boston Tories have lately died, unpitied and unlamented, at Halifax in Nova Scotia. The *famous* general Brattle is among the number.

There is certain intelligence of our *quondam* governour, lord Dunmore, that celebrated chief, having at last taken his departure for England, to enjoy the smiles of his sovereign for the many signal services rendered to his august house while commander in chief in Virginia.

We also learn, that generals Burgoyne and Clinton have sailed for England. The latter, it is said, is recalled, to answer for his unsuccessful enterprise against Charlestown.

AN ARMORER is wanted for the *Hero* galley. Any perſon qualified, and willing to ſerve on board the ſaid galley in that capacity, will pleaſe apply to the captain at *Hampton.*

Recreated from Purdie's Virginia Gazette, January 3, 1777.

PRISONERS IN GREAT DISTRESS.

From a Gentleman of Honour and Distinction, a prisoner in NEW YORK, *December* 26.

"The distress of the prisoners cannot be communicated by words, 20 or 30 die every day, they lie in heaps unburied, what numbers of my countrymen have died by cold and hunger, perished for want of the common necessaries of life, I have seen it. This is the boasted *British clemency*, (I myself had well nigh perished under it).

"The New England people can have no idea of such barbarous policy, nothing can stop such treatment but retaliation. I ever despised *private* revenge, but that of the *public* must be in this case just and necessary, it is due to the names of our murdered countrymen, and that alone can protect the survivors. In the like situation, rather than experience again their barbarity and insults, may I fall by the sword of the Hessians."

I am, &c.

Recreated from The Hartford Courant, January 20, 1777.

WILLIAMSBURG.—No newspapers came by the post this week from Philadelphia, owing, we believe, to the printers (those important vehicles of intelligence) finding it necessary to quit their posts, with many other worthy inhabitants of that city, during the present troubles. We learn, that all the shops, storehouses, &c. are converted into prisons, and filled with the disaffected people in the state of Pennsylvania, who, more than probable, may very soon be made to repent their treachery and lukewarmness in their country's cause, especially if Americans, with a becoming and godlike spirit, are determined to support its liberties. The generals Washington, Lee, &c. are doing their utmost to counteract the designs of the enemy, those foes to freedom and mankind; and it is hoped, from their approved valour and capacity, that they will be able to render all their schemes abortive, and fix us, as we ought to be,

A FREE AND HAPPY PEOPLE.

Recreated from Purdie's Virginia Gazette, December 20, 1776.

BATTLE AT TRENTON.

Washington Crosses the Delaware.

Extract of a letter from an officer of distinction at Newtown, Bucks County, *dated December 27, 1776.*

"It was determined some days ago, that our army should pass over to Jersey, in three different places, and attack the enemy. Accordingly about two thousand five hundred men and 20 brass filed pieces, with his Excellency Gen. Washington at their head, and Majors Gens. Sullivan and Green, in command of two divisions, passed over on the night of Christmas, and about 3 o'clock, A.M., were on their march, by two routs towards Trenton.

"The night was sleety, and the roads so slippery that it was daybreak when we were two miles from Trenton. But happily the enemy were not apprised of our design, and our advance party were on their guards at half a mile from the town, when Gen. Sullivan's and Gen. Green's divisions came into the same road. Their guard gave our advanced party several smart fires, as we drove them; but we soon got two field pieces at play, and several others in a short time; and one of our Colonels pushing down on the right, while the other advanced on the left, into the town.

"The enemy, consisting of about fifteen hundred Hessians, under Col. Rohl, formed and made smart fires from the musketry and six field pieces, but our people pressed from every quarter, and drove them from their cannon. They retreated towards a field behind a piece of wood up the creek, from Trenton, and formed in two bodies, which I expected would have brought on a smart engagement from the troops, who had formed very near them, but at that instant, as I came in full view of them, from the back of the wood, with his Excellency Gen. Washington, an officer informed him that the party had grounded their arms, and surrendered prisoners. The others soon followed their example, except a part which had got off in the hazy weather, towards Princeton, and a party of their light horse which made off on our first appearance. Too much praise cannot be given to the officers of every regiment by their active and spirited behaviour, they soon put an honourable issue to this glorious day.

"I was immediately sent off with the prisoners to M'Conkey's Ferry, and have got about seven hundred and fifty in town and a few miles from here, on this side of the ferry, viz. one Lieutenant Colonel, two Majors, four Captains, seven Lieutenants, and eight Ensigns. We left Col. Rohl, the Commandant, wounded, on his parole, and several other officers and wounded men at Trenton.

"We lost but two of our men that I can hear of, a few wounded, and one brave officer, Capt. Washington, who assisted in securing their artillery, shot in both hands. Indeed every officer and private behaved well, and it was a most fortunate day to our arms, which I more rejoice at, having an active part in it. The success of this day will greatly animate our friends, and add fresh courage to our new army, which, when formed, will be sufficient to secure us from the depredations or insults of our enemy.

"Gen. Ewing's division could not pass at Trenton for the ice, which also impeded Gen. Cadwallader passing over with all his cannon and the militia, though part of his troops were over, and if the whole could have passed, we should have swept the coast to Philadelphia. We took two Standards and six regimental Colours, six fine brass cannon, and about one thousand stands of arms."

Published by the order of the Council of Safety.

G. BICKHAM, Secretary, pro tem.

THIS day is published (price two coppers … or one shilling and threepence per dozen) THE AMERICAN CRISIS, No. I. By the author of Common Sense. Printed and sold by STYNER … CIST, in Second street, six doors above Arch street, Philadelphia.

Recreated from The Pennsylvania Packet, January 4, 1777.

GREAT VICTORY AT TRENTON.

BALTIMORE, *Dec.* 31.—CONGRESS *received the following letter from* General WASHINGTON.

HEAD QUARTERS, NEWTOWN, *Dec.* 27, 1776.

SIR,

I HAVE the pleasure of congratulating you upon the success of an enterprise which I had formed against a detachment of the enemy lying in Trenton, and which was executed yesterday morning.

The evening of the 25th, I ordered the troops intended for this service to parade back of M'Conkey's ferry, that they might begin to pass as soon as it grew dark, imagining we should be able to throw them all over, with the necessary artillery, by 12 o'clock, and that we might easily arrive at Trenton by five in the morning, the distance being about nine miles; but the quantity of ice made that night impeded the passage of the boats so much that it was 3 o'clock before the artillery could all be got over, and near 4 before the troops took up their line of march.

I formed my detachments into two divisions, one to march up the lower or river road, the other by the upper or Pennington road. As the divisions had nearly the same distance to march, I ordered each of them, immediately upon forcing the out guards, to push directly into the town, that they might charge the enemy before they had time to form. The upper division arrived at the enemy's advanced post exactly at 8 o'clock, and in three minutes after, I found, from the fire on the lower road, that that division had also got up. The out guards made but a small opposition, though, for their numbers, they behaved very well, keeping up a constant retreating fire from behind houses.

We presently saw their main body formed, but from their motions they seemed undetermined how to act. Being hard pressed by our troops, who had already got possession of part of their artillery, they attempted to file off by a road, on their right, leading to Princeton; but perceiving their intention, I threw a body of troops in their way, which immediately checked them. Finding, from our disposition, that they were surrounded, and must inevitably be cut to pieces, if they made any farther resistance, they agreed to lay down their arms. The number that submitted in this manner was 23 officers and 886 men. Col. Rohl, the commanding officer, and seven others, were found wounded in the town. I do not know how many they had killed, but I fancy not above 20 or 30, as they never made any regular stand. Our loss is very trifling indeed, only two officers and one or two privates wounded.

I find that the detachment of the enemy consisted of the three Hessian regiments of Landspach, Kniphausen, and Rohl, amounting to 1500 men, and a troop of British light horse; but immediately, upon the beginning of the attack, all those who were not killed or taken pushed directly down the road towards Bordentown. These would likewise have fallen into our hands, could my plan have been completely carried into execution.

Gen. Ewing was to have crossed before day at Trenton ferry, and taken possession of the bridge leading out of town; but the quantity of ice was so great, that, though he did every thing in his power to effect it, he could not get over. This difficulty also hindered gen. Cadwallader from crossing with the Pennsylvania militia, from Bristol; he got part of his foot over, but finding it impossible to embark his artillery, he was obliged to desist.

I am fully confident, that could the troops under gens. Ewing and Cadwallader have passed the river, I should have been able, with their assistance, to have driven the enemy from all their posts below Trenton; but, the numbers I had with me being inferior to theirs below me, and a strong battalion of light infantry being at Princeton, above me, I thought it most prudent to return the same evening with the prisoners, and the artillery we had taken. We found no stores of any consequence in the town.

In justice to the officers and men, I must add, that their behaviour upon this occasion reflects the highest honour upon them. The difficulty of passing the river, in a very severe night, and their march through a violent storm of snow and hail, did not in the least abate their ardour, but when they came to the charge each seemed to vie with the other in pressing forward; and were I to give preference to any particular corps, I should do great injustice to the others.

Colonel Baylor, my first aid-de-camp, will have the honour of delivering you this, and from him you may be made acquainted with many other particulars, his spirited behaviour, upon every occasion, requires me to recommend him to your particular notice.

*I have the honour to be,
with great respect, Sir,
your most humble servant,*
G. WASHINGTON.

EXPORTS PROHIBITED.

IN CONGRESS, *December* 30, 1776.

IT appearing to Congress, that it will be extremely difficult, if not impracticable, to supply the army of the United States with bacon, salted beef, and pork, soap, tallow, and candles, unless the exportation thereof be prohibited:

Therefore resolved, that none of the said articles, except such as may be necessary for the crew, be exported from any of the United States after the 5th day of January next, until the first day of November next, or until Congress shall make farther order therein; and it is earnestly recommended to the executive powers of the several United States to see that this resolution be strictly complied with.

By order of the CONGRESS,
JOHN HANCOCK, President.

Recreated from Purdie's Virginia Gazette, January 10, 1777.

IN CONGRESS, *December* 27, 1776.

Resolved, That the Council of Safety of Pennsylvania be requested to take the most vigorous and speedy measures for punishing all such as shall refuse Continental Currency, and that the General be directed to give all necessary aid to the Council of Safety for carrying their measures on this subject into effectual execution.

By order of CONGRESS,
JOHN HANCOCK, President.

TRENTON, *January* 1, 1777.

HIS Excellency General Washington strictly forbids all the officers and soldiers of the continental army, of the militia, and all recruiting parties, plundering any person whatsoever, whether tories or others. The effects of such persons will be applied to public uses in a regular manner, and it is expected that humanity and tenderness to women and children will distinguish brave Americans, contending for liberty, from infamous mercenary ravagers, whether British or Hessians.
G. WASHINGTON.

Recreated from The Maryland Gazette, January 23, 1777.

PHILADELPHIA, *Jan.* 4.—By an authentic account received from Trenton, the following is a list of prisoners taken, viz. One Colonel, two Lieutenant Colonels, three Majors, four Captains, eight Lieutenants, twelve Ensigns, two Surgeon Mates, ninety-nine serjeants, twenty-five drummers, nine musicians, twenty-five servants, and seven hundred and forty privates.

Recreated from The Pennsylvania Packet, January 4, 1777.

A MOST GLORIOUS EFFECT.

Extract of a letter from PHILADELPHIA, *December 30, 1776.*

"The late enterprise of general Washington has had a most glorious effect; it animates the spirits of the friends of liberty amazingly. I firmly believe if he pursues the blow, which I believe he intends, he will take the greatest part of the enemy's army prisoners. It is said, when all our forces in Jersey join, they will amount to above 15,000 effective men."

Recreated from Purdie's Virginia Gazette, January 24, 1777.

WILLIAMSBURG, *Jan.* 7, 1777.

BY virtue of a decree of the Hon. Court of Admiralty of this state, will be sold for ready money, at publick vendue, in the town of *York*, 12 miles below the city of *Williamsburg*, on *Monday* the 20th instant, the ship *JANE*, about 120 tuns burthen, with her rigging, tackle, apparel, and furniture; also her cargo, consisting of 79 hogsheads and tierces of *BROWN SUGAR*, 21 puncheons and 3 barrels of *RUM*, 1 pipe, 8 hogsheads, and 12 quarter casks of very fine *Madeira WINE*, 13 bales of *COTTON*, and 80 tuns of *FUSTICK*, a wood very useful in dying. The cargo was shipped at *Tortola*, and intended for the *London* market, but brought in here by capt. *Thomas Lilly* of the armed brig *Liberty*. An inventory of the rigging, &c. belonging to the ship, may be seen by applying to capt. *Lilly* in *York*, or to the subscriber in this city.

BEN: POWELL, marshal.

Recreated from Purdie's Virginia Gazette, January 10, 1777.

AMERICANS TAKE PRINCETON.

Extract of a letter from a gentleman of great worth, in the AMERICAN *army, to the printer of this paper, near* PRINCETON, *January 7, 1777.*

"On the 2d instant intelligence was received, that the enemy's army was advancing from Princeton towards Trenton, where the main body of our forces was then stationed. Two brigades, under brigadier-generals Stephen and Fermoy, had been detached several days before, from the main body, to Maidenhead, and were ordered to skirmish with the enemy during their march and to retreat to Trenton, as occasion should require. A body of men, under the command of col. Hand, were also ordered to meet the enemy, by which means their march was so much retarded as to give ample time for our forces to form, and prepare to give them a warm reception upon their arrival.

"Two field pieces, planted upon a hill, at a small distance from the town, were managed with great advantage, and did considerable execution for some time; after which they were ordered to retire to the station occupied by our forces on the south side of the bridge, over the little river which divides the town into two parts, and opens at right angles into the Delaware. In their way through the town the enemy suffered much by an incessant fire of musketry, from behind the houses and barns.

"Their army had now arrived at the northern side of the bridge, whilst our army was drawn up, in order of battle, on the southern side. Our cannon played very briskly from this eminence, and were returned as briskly by the enemy. In a few minutes after the cannonade began a very heavy discharge of musketry ensued, and continued for ten or fifteen minutes. During the action a party of men were detached from our right wing, to secure a part of the river, which it was imagined, from the motions of the enemy, they intended to ford. The detachment arrived at the pass very opportunely, and effected their purpose.

"After this, the enemy made a feeble and unsupported attempt to pass the bridge, but this likewise proved abortive. It was now near six o'clock in the evening, and night coming on, closed the engagement. Our fires were built in due season, and very numerous, and whilst the enemy was amused by these appearances, and preparing for a general attack the ensuing morning, our army marched, about one in the morning, from Trenton, on the south side of the creek, to Princeton.

"When they arrived near the hill, about one mile from Princeton, they found a body of the enemy formed upon it, and ready to receive them; upon which a spirited attack was made upon them, with both field pieces and musketry, and after an obstinate resistance, and losing a considerable number of their men upon the field, those of them who could not make their escape surrendered prisoners of war. We immediately marched on to the centre of the town, and there took another party of the enemy, near the college.

"After tarrying a short time in the town, general Washington marched his army from thence towards Rocky Hill, and they are now at Morris town, in high spirits, and in expectation of a junction with the rest of our forces, sufficiently seasonable to make a general attack upon the enemy, and prevent, at least, a considerable part of them from reaching their asylum in New York.

"It is difficult, precisely, to ascertain the loss we have sustained in the two engagements; but, as near as I can judge, I think we have lost about 40 men killed, and had near double the number wounded. In the list of the former are the brave col. Hazlet, capt. Shippen, and capt. Neal, who fell in the engagement upon the hill near Princeton; amongst the latter was brigadier-general Mercer, who received seven wounds, five in his body, and two in his head, and was much bruised by the breech of a musket. His life was yesterday almost despaired of, but this morning I find him much relieved, and some of the most dangerous complaints removed, so that I still have hopes of his recovery, and of his being again restored to the arms of his grateful country. He is now a prisoner upon parole. The loss sustained by the enemy was much greater than ours, as was easily discovered by viewing the dead upon the field, after the action. We have near 100 of their wounded prisoners in the town, which, together with those who surrendered, and were taken in small parties, endeavouring to make their escape, I think must amount nearly to the number of 400, chiefly British troops. Six brass pieces of cannon have fallen into our hands, a quantity of ammunition, and several waggons of baggage.

"A capt. Leslie was found amongst the enemy's dead, and was this day buried with the honours of war. A number of other officers were also found in the field, but they were not known, and were buried with the other dead. According to information from the inhabitants of Princeton, the number which marched out of it to attack our army amounted to 13,000 men, under the command of general Cornwallis. This body, as soon as they discovered that they were out-generalled by the march of general Washington, being much chagrined at their disappointment (as it seems they intended to have cut our army to pieces, crossed the Delaware, and marched immediately, without any farther delay, to Philadelphia) pushed, with the greatest precipitation, towards Princeton, where they arrived about an hour after general Washington had left it; and imaging he would attempt to take Brunswick in the same manner, proceeded directly for that place.

"Our soldiers were much fatigued, the greatest part of them having been deprived of their rest the two preceding nights, otherwise, we might, perhaps, have possessed ourselves of Brunswick. The enemy appear to be preparing to decamp, and retire to New York, as they are much disgusted with their late treatment in New Jersey, and have a great inclination to rest themselves a little in some secure winter quarters."

Recreated from Purdie's Virginia Gazette, January 24, 1777.

4th CONTINENTAL FRIGATE.

PHILADELPHIA, *January* 4, 1777.

LATELY was launched at this port the fourth Continental Frigate, called the EFFINGHAM, in honour of the patriotic Earl of that name, who notably refused to draw his sword in support of British tyranny and usurpation.

Tuesday fe'nnight arrived here the Continental brig Andrew Doria, Capt. Robeson, from St. Eustatia and Martinico, laden with gun-powder, arms, and some woolen goods. On her passage she took two prizes—one a sloop of ten guns, fitted out by the Antelope man of war at Jamaica, and commanded by Lieut. Jones, of the Boreas frigate, who engaged Capt. Robeson near three glasses, in which he had two men killed and one wounded, and the sloop seven men and her commander wounded; the number killed unknown, as they were thrown overboard during the engagement. The other prize a brig mounting six carriage guns and six swivels, commanded by one Nicholson, bound from Jamaica to London; her cargo unknown. Capt. Robeson took fifty seamen out of the above vessels.

Recreated from The Pennsylvania Packet, January 4, 1777.

A PERSON properly qualified to direct the Business of a Rope-Maker, and can come well recommended, may be employed by applying to the Subscriber at *York* Town.
(tf)   WM. REYNOLDS.

NEWCASTLE, *January* 28, 1777.
THE Subscriber continues to keep public House at the Sign of two SYCAMORE TREES, where there will be good Entertainment for Man and Horse.
(1ʃ)   BENNETT WHITE.

ENEMY REMOVE TO BRUNSWICK.

CONGRESS *has received the following intelligence from the army at* PLUCKEMIN, *in the State of* NEW JERSEY, *January* 5, 1777.

ON the second instant the enemy began to advance upon us at Trenton; and, after some skirmishing, the head of their column reached that place about four o'clock, whilst the rear was as far back as Maidenhead. They attempted to pass Sanpinck creek, which runs through Trenton, at different places; but finding the ford guarded, they halted and kindled their fires. We were drawn up on the south side of the creek. In this situation we remained until dark, cannonading the enemy, and receiving the fire of their field pieces, which did but little damage.

"About 12 o'clock, after renewing our fires, and leaving guards at the bridge in Trenton, and other passes, on the same stream above, we marched by a round about road to Princeton. We found Princeton, about sunrise, with only three regiments, and three troops of light-horse in it, two of which were in their march to Trenton. These three regiments, especially the two first, made a gallant resistance; and, in killed, wounded, and prisoner, must have lost five hundred men. Upwards of one hundred of them were left dead on the field; and with those carried on by the army, and such as were taken in the pursuit, and carried across the Delaware, there are near three hundred prisoners, fourteen of whom are officers, all British.

"Colonels Hazlet and Parker, Captain Neal, of the artillery, Captain Fleming, who commanded the first Virginia regiment, and four or five other valuable officers, with about twenty-five or thirty privates, were slain in the field. Our whole loss cannot be ascertained, as many who were in pursuit of the enemy, whom they chased three or four miles, are not yet come in. We burnt the enemy's hay, and destroyed such other things as the occasion would admit.

"From the best intelligence we have been able to get, the enemy were so much alarmed at the apprehension of losing their stores at Brunswick, that they marched immediately thither from Trenton, without halting, and got there before day."

MORRIS TOWN, *January 7, 1777.*

"The enemy have totally evacuated Trenton and Princeton, and are now at Brunswick, and the several posts on the communication between that and Hudson's river, but chiefly at Brunswick. Their numbers and movements are variously reported; but all agree their force to be great. There have been two or three little skirmishes between their parties and some detachments of militia, in which the latter have been successful, and made a few prisoners; the most considerable was on Sunday morning, near Springfield, when 8 or 10 Waldeckers were killed and wounded, and the remainder of the party, 39 or 40, made prisoners, with 2 officers, by a force not superior in number, and without receiving the least damage."

Published by order of CONGRESS,
CHARLES THOMPSON, *Sec.*

Recreated from The Virginia Gazette, January 31, 1777.

ANECDOTE.—After the battle at Princeton on the 3d of this instant, General Washington perceived a wounded soldier belonging to the enemy laying on the field, came up to him, and after enquiring into the nature of his wound, commended him for his gallant behaviour, and assured him that he would want for nothing that his camp could furnish him.

After the General left him an American soldier who thought he was dead, came up in order to strip him; the general seeing it, bid the soldier begone, and ordered a sentry to stand over the wounded prisoner till he was carried to a convenient house to be dressed.

Recreated from The Pennsylvania Packet, January 22, 1777.

PRISONERS AT PHILADELPHIA.

January 4.—Last Monday morning the prisoners taken at Trenton, with a number of women and children, amounting in the whole to near one thousand, were brought to this city. The wretched condition of these unhappy men, most of whom were dragged from their wives and families by a despotic and avaricious Prince, must sensibly affect every generous mind with the dreadful effects of arbitrary power.

Col. Rohl died at Trenton on Thursday the 26th of December, of the wounds he received in the engagement that morning.

PROVIDENCE, *January* 4.—We learn that the enemy have sent a number of women and children from Newport to Narraganset.

Undoubted intelligence is received from Newport, that the enemy consider the inhabitants on the island as prisoners of war, and have absolutely refused to grant the benefit of their boasted pardons to a number who made application for the same.

It is said that the enemy's troops at Newport have received orders to hold themselves in readiness for embarkation at a moment's notice, but whether on board transports or their flat-bottomed boats is not mentioned. A number of carpenters have been fully employed in repairing the latter.

Recreated from The Hartford Courant, January 20, 1777.

HESSIAN OFFICERS ON PAROLE.

PHILADELPHIA, *January 4, 1777.*—Last Tuesday night col. George Weedon, of Virginia, arrived in the city with the Hessian officers taken at Trenton, in the action of the 26th. He this day delivered them to the Council of Safety, with six standards. They are allowed their parole of honour, and declare themselves perfectly satisfied with their fate. We hear the colonel sets off again, in a day or two, for the Continental army in Jersey.

Recreated from Purdie's Virginia Gazette, January 24, 1777.

COMMODORE HOPKINS DEFENDS PROVIDENCE.

Captain Josiah Arnold, just arrived here from Rhode Island, informs us, that about the 4th January, when he left that State, the enemy under the command of General Clinton, were in possession of the town of Newport, and that Sir Peter Parker's squadron were stationed in various parts of Narraganset Bay. That a number of small ships of war were sent by Sir Peter up the bay towards Providence, under the command of the noted Wallace, who finding Commodore Hopkins's squadron of five ships, one brig, one sloop, and two gallies lying across Providence river, six miles below the town, ready to receive him, Mr. Wallace thought proper to desist from any enterprise he may have had in contemplation, and came to anchor, at about two gun shots distance, where he continued when our informant came away.

Mr. Arnold further advises us, that the town of Providence has for its defence, in addition to the squadron, four respectable forts and batteries, a number of well constructed entrenchments, with 10,000 hearty fellows to man them, all in high spirits.

We hear that since the arrival of the enemy's ships of war in the bay, a number of perfidious people in the counties of Worcester and Somerset, on the eastern shore of this State, have assembled in hostile array, having, several months ago, been supplied with arms by the Congress to defend our liberties. They had been vapouring for some time; they are now so audacious as to erect a pole, with a rag upon it marked with the letters G.R. and are supposed to mean the sceptered miscreant, who, in violation of his coronation oath, is now, together with his venal Parliament, enslaving that people whom they are bound to make happy. It is said that General Smallwood is going, with a detachment of troops, to pay the banditti a visit, and, on his appearing, we prophecy, that their ignoble colours will be immediately lowered.

Recreated from The Virginia Gazette, February 21, 1777.

GENERAL MERCER DEAD.

PHILADELPHIA.—Last Sunday, the 12th instant, died near Princeton, of the wounds he received in the engagement at that place on the 3d inst., HUGH MERCER, Brigadier General in the Continental Army. On Wednesday his body was brought to this city, and yesterday buried at Christ Church yard with military honours, attended by the Gentlemen of the army now here and a number of the most respectable inhabitants of the city. The uniform character and exalted abilities of this illustrious officer, will render his name equally dear to America with the liberty for which she is now contending to the latest posterity.

Recreated from The Pennsylvania Packet, January 17, 1777.

Extract of a letter dated MORRIS-TOWN, *Jan.* 9.

"The two late actions at Trenton and Princeton have put a very different face upon our affairs. Great credit is due to the Pennsylvania militia; their behaviour at Trenton in the cannonade, and at Princeton, was brave, firm and manly; they were broken at first in the action at Princeton, but soon formed in the face of grape-shot, and pushed on with a spirit that would do honour to veterans; besides which they have borne a winter campaign with a soldier like patience. Gen. Cadwallader is a brave and gallant officer."

GEN. MAXWELL AT ELIZABETH TOWN.

By letters from gen. Washington's army of the 8th, 10th, and 11th instant, we have the following authentic intelligence, viz. That our army marched from Pluckemin, and arrived at Morris-town on the 6th; that gen. Maxwell, with a considerable body of Continental troops and militia, having marched towards Elizabeth-town, sent back for a reinforcement, which having joined him, he advanced and took possession of the town, and made prisoner 50 Waldeckers and 40 Highlanders, who were quartered there; and made prize of a schooner with baggage and some blankets on board.

Recreated from The Maryland Gazette, January 23, 1777.

OUR INHUMAN ENEMY.

Extracts of letters from PRINCETON *and* PHILADELPHIA, *January* 7, 14, *and* 15, 1777.

"Among the officers of the enemy killed at Princeton, is a Captain Leslie, nephew to General Leslie, and second son of the Earl of Leven. He was an accomplished officer. General Washington buried him with the honours of war.

"Princeton is indeed a destitute village. You would think it had been desolated with the plague and an earthquake, as well as with the calamities of war. The college and church are heaps of ruin. All the inhabitants have been plundered.

"The enemy in their advance upon our troops through the Jerseys, called them the rebel army; in their retreat through the same Jerseys, they called them the provincials, and sometimes the continental army.

"Major General Grant, who commanded at Brunswick, when Col. Rohl (who was killed at Trenton on the 26th of last month) wrote to him for more troops, to enable him to hold his posts on the Delaware, he laughed at his application, and sent him word that 'He could keep the whole Jerseys with a corporal and four men.'—N.B. *This same Mr. Grant was caned in South Carolina by Col. Middleton in the last war.*

"Lieutenant Yates, of Col. Read's Virginia regiment, died on Friday last at Princeton. The circumstances of his death merit attention. In the action on the 3d instant, he received a wound in his side which brought him to the ground. Upon seeing the enemy advance towards him, he begged for quarters; a British soldier stopped, and after deliberately loading his musket by his side, shot him through the breast. Finding he was still alive, he stabbed him in thirteen places with his bayonet; the poor youth all the while crying for mercy. Upon the enemy being forced to retreat, either the same or another soldier, finding he was not dead, struck him with the butt of a musket on the side of his head.

"He languished a week in the greatest anguish and then died (I declare it upon my honour as a man and physician) of the wounds he received after he fell and begged for quarters.

"The savages murdered a clergyman (chaplain to a regiment of militia) in cold blood at Trenton, after he had surrendered and begged for mercy; his name was ROSBOROUGH. It is a prostitution of language and truth to attribute a fibre of humanity to General Howe's heart. The name of the service he is engaged in has made him a mere Jeffries for every species of political inquiry. I write from good information, having picked up a number of anecdotes which justify the picture I have given of him."

Recreated from The Virginia Gazette, January 31, 1777.

DR. FRANKLIN AT PARIS.

Extract of a letter from PARIS, *Jan.* 9.

"Dr. Franklin is visited by many of the first rank of all nations, excepting the Scotch, and them he absolutely denies seeing, for he says those people were the sole cause for the ruin of his country. He has almost every day private conferences with the ministry, and great respect is paid him. The English ambassador looks on him with a jealous eye, and watches all his motions very strictly, but it is generally believed here, that whatever the Doctor asks of the court of France will be readily granted him. Many young gentlemen pay their court to him, in hopes of getting employment in the service of the provincials, most of whom have been taught the use of arms from their infancy. It is thought most of them will embark for America early in the spring."

Recreated from Purdie's Virginia Gazette, May 9, 1777.

THE CONTINENTAL LOAN-OFFICE
for this State,
IS removed to Dr. SHIPPEN's, Jun. in Fourth-street, where certificates of the United States, on interest, are given for Continental money, by
THOMAS SMITH, Loan Officer.

Recreated from The Pennsylvania Packet, February 4, 1777.

GENERAL MERCER INTERRED.

Part of a letter from PHILADELPHIA, *Jan.* 17.
"This day the body of the worthy and brave General MERCER was brought to this city, and interred with the military honours due to his rank and merit. In the death, or rather murder of this Gentleman, our country has lost a gallant officer and a virtuous citizen. His body, covered with wounds and mangled by our savage enemies, was exposed to public view. After he had surrendered himself, and had been carried into a house, he acquainted the enemy that he was a General in the service of the United States; deaf to the voice of humanity and the law of nations, they stabbed him with the bayonet, and with the butt end of a musket battered and disfigured his face. A Captain having received a bullet in each thigh, became a prisoner, but on being informed that he was an officer, he was shot in the breast, languished five days and then died, having testified an oath to this unmanly and barbarous conduct."

Recreated from The Virginia Gazette, January 31, 1777.

GEN. ARNOLD IN RHODE ISLAND.

PROVIDENCE, *January* 18, 1777.—Sunday last General Arnold arrived here from the westward.

Tuesday night last some men from the enemy's ships that lay at Prudence set fire to a house on that island, which was communicated to one or two other buildings, and gave rise to a report that the enemy had burnt the town of Newport. These were the only buildings that remained on the island after Wallace's expedition up the bay last winter.

Captain Ayres, who lately went with a flag of truce to Newport, returned on Wednesday, and brought with him about 50 Americans, in exchange for a number of prisoners he delivered there.

On Friday morning, last week, a party of our troops from Seconnet, with one 18 and one 12 pounder, drove the Cerberus man of war from Fogland ferry. She returned the fire briskly for some time, and slightly wounded one of our men; but was at length obliged to put to sea, and is since arrived at Newport. By certain accounts received from thence, we learn, that she was considerably damaged in her hull, and had six men killed, and a number wounded.

We hear that General Clinton has sailed from Newport for England in the Asia man of war, and that Earl Piercy (whom General Gage so highly commended for his *agility* in the Lexington retreat) now commands the ministerial troops at Rhode Island.

Recreated from The Virginia Gazette, February 28, 1777.

NEWS FROM RHODE ISLAND.

January 21, 1777.—By accounts from Rhode Island, we learn that soon after the arrival of six ships of the line, four frigates, and seventy transports, with twelve British and six Hessian regiments, amounting to between 6 and 7000 men, they took possession of the defenceless town of Newport and the island; that the expedition was carried on by Parker and Clinton; that Clinton is since gone home, and the command devolved to Lord Piercy; that major Prescot (late a prisoner in this state) is appointed governour of that small island, and one Kemble lieutenant governour; that they took on the few Tories who remained in the town not as friends, but as prisoners of war; that they rule them with a rod of iron; that they have seized all the sugar, &c. which they deem goods taken at sea by our privateers, and if a man says a wry word, he is hove into jail, a blessed specimen of English government; that they were in great distress for want of fuel, and had sent a number of transports to the east end of Long Island for wood; that in the night of the 7th instant the enemy embarked two regiments on board the transports, and it was said more were to follow, supposed for New York. We are told they propose drawing all their troops from thence, except a small garrison, which we hope, ere long, to inform our readers is in our hands.

Recreated from Purdie's Virginia Gazette, February 14, 1777.

BATTLE OF MILLSTONE.

Extract of a letter from General WASHINGTON *to* CONGRESS, *dated January 22, 1777.*

My last was on the 20th instant; since that, I have the pleasure to inform you that General Dickinson, with about 400 militia, has defeated a foraging party of the enemy of an equal number, and has taken 40 waggons, and upwards of 100 horses, most of them of the English draught breed, and a number of sheep and cattle which they had collected.

The enemy retreated with so much precipitation, that General Dickinson had only an opportunity of making nine prisoners; they were observed to carry off a good many dead and wounded in light wagons.

This action happened near Somerset courthouse, on Millstone river. General Dickinson's behaviour reflects the highest honour upon him, for though his troops were all raw, he led them through the river, middle deep, and gave the enemy so severe a charge, that although supported by three field pieces, they gave way and left their convoy.

I have not heard from General Heath, since the firing near Kingsbridge last Saturday, which I cannot account for, unless the North river should have been rendered impassable by the ice. But the account of his having surprised and taken fort Independence on Friday last, comes so well authenticated by different ways, that I cannot doubt it. It is said that he took 400 prisoners in that fort; and that he invested fort Washington on Saturday, which occasioned the firing.

Published by order of CONGRESS,
CHARLES THOMPSON, Secretary.

BAR IRON,
Of the First QUALITY,
TO BE SOLD BY
GEORGE MEADE, & Co.

In COUNCIL OF SAFETY.

PHILADELPHIA, *Jan.* 23, 1777.

ORDERED, *That the thanks of General Washington to the militia of Pennsylvania, transmitted to this Board, be published in the public papers of this city.*

"General Washington being informed that the time fixed by the Hon. Council of Safety of Pennsylvania for the service of part of the militia of that state is expired, and that some are desirous to return to Pennsylvania, agreeable to their engagements, the General takes the earliest opportunity of returning his most hearty thanks to those brave men, who in the most inclement season of the year nobly stepped forth in defence of their country.

"The General acknowledge with pleasure the signal services done by the militia of Pennsylvania, and has the best reason to expect the same spirit, zeal and activity, which lately brought them into the field, will induce them to come forth on every future occasion, when the security and happiness of America, and their own state in particular, demand it.

"The General acknowledges with additional satisfaction, the good services of the battalions who have determined to remain with him after the expiration of their times of service. He wishes not to detain them a minute longer than he thinks absolutely necessary to the security of their country, and will discharge them as soon as he finds his army in a condition to admit it."

Recreated from The Pennsylvania Packet, February 4, 1777.

To be SOLD at publick vendue, for cash, in the town of Alexandria, on Monday the 17th of February next,

ALL the sails, rigging, anchors, cables, &c. suitable for a brig of 150 to 175 tuns burthen.

Recreated from Purdie's Virginia Gazette, February 7, 1777.

BALTIMORE, *January* 28.

In CONGRESS, *November* 4, 1776.

Resolved, That any person who shall apprehend a deserter, and bring him to the regiment he belongs to, upon certificate thereof, by the Colonel or Commanding Officer of such regiment, shall be entitled to receive **FIVE DOLLARS**, and all reasonable expenses, from the Paymaster-General, or deputy Paymaster, which is to be deducted from the pay of such soldier.

That it be recommended to the several legislatures, Assemblies, or Conventions of the Colonies, to enact a law, or pass an ordinance, inflicting the following punishments upon such as harbour deserters, knowing them to be such, viz. A fine upon all such offenders, not less than thirty, nor more than fifty dollars; and in case of inability to pay the fine, to be punished with whipping, not exceeding thirty-nine lashes for each offense. Also, that they empower the Commander in Chief, or officers commanding a detachment, or any out post, to administer an oath, and swear any person or persons, to the truth of any information or intelligence, or any matter relative to the publick service.

Extract from the Minutes,
CHARLES THOMPSON, Secretary.

Recreated from The Pennsylvania Packet, February 4, 1777.

VIRGINIA, *Brunswick, Jan.* 30, 1777.

FERGUS KENNEDY, who was taken on board the *Oxford* transport from *Glasgow*, begs the favour of those gentlemen who are going to *Glasgow, North Britain*, that they will be kind enough to acquaint his wife, who lives in *Dunbarton*, that he is well, and that he is and has been treated with every mark of humanity ever since he was taken prisoner.

Recreated from Purdie's Virginia Gazette, February 7, 1777.

SKIRMISHES IN THE JERSEYS.

Extract of a letter from PHILADELPHIA, *dated, January* 25, 1777.

"Several successful skirmishes, but no considerable action, has very lately happened between our troops and the enemy; but from the movements of several large bodies of our forces in the Jersey State, it is conjectured that a grand assault will be speedily made upon Howe's panic-struck troops near Brunswick, &c. Apprehensive of this, the enemy have assembled a number of men of war and transports at Amboy, to facilitate the retreat, or rather escape, of their army, in case of a rout. We have had, within a day or two, several flattering accounts of the success of our arms in the State of New York; but we have nothing, as yet, well enough authenticated to publish."

Recreated from The Virginia Gazette, February 7, 1777.

BRITISH DEPREDATIONS.

How are the Mighty Fallen!

To the melancholy picture already exhibited of the brutal behaviour of the Britons, (who vainly boast being ever pre-eminent in Mercy) aided by Hessian and Waldeck mercenaries, in New York and New Jersey, it gives us pain to add, that they have not only outraged the feelings of humanity to many people, who were so unhappy as to fall into their hands, particularly the fair sex, but have degraded themselves beyond the power of language to express, by wantonly destroying the curious Water Works at New York, an elegant public Library at Trenton, and the grand Orrery, made by the celebrated Rittenhouse, which was placed in the College at Princeton; a piece of mechanism, which the most untutored savage, staying the hand of violence, would have beheld with wonder, reverence and delight! Thus are our cruel enemies warring against LIBERTY, VIRTUE, and the ARTS and SCIENCES. "How are the mighty fallen!"

Recreated from The Hartford Courant, January 20, 1777.

By his Excellency GEORGE WASHINGTON, Esq; General and Commander in Chief of all the forces of the UNITED STATES OF AMERICA.

PROCLAMATION.

WHEREAS several persons, inhabitants of the United States of America, influenced by inimical motives, intimidated by the threats of the enemy, or deluded by a Proclamation issued the 30th of November last, by Lord and General Howe, stiled the King's Commissioners for granting pardons, &c. (now at open war and invading these states) have been so lost to the interest and welfare of their country, as to repair to the enemy, sign a declaration of fidelity, and, in some instances, have been compelled to take oaths of allegiance, and to engage not to take up arms, or encourage others so to do, against the King of Great-Britain. And whereas it has become necessary to distinguish between the friends of America and those of Great Britain, inhabitants of these States, and that every man who receives a protection from and is a subject of any State (not being conscientiously scrupulous against bearing arms) should stand ready to defend the same against every hostile invasion, I do therefore, in behalf of the United States, by virtue of the powers committed to me by Congress, hereby strictly command and require every person, having subscribed such declaration, taken such oaths, and accepted protection and certificates from Lord or General Howe, or any person acting under their authority, forthwith to repair to Head-Quarters, or to the quarters of the nearest general officer of the Continental Army or Militia (until farther provision can be made by the civil authority) and there deliver up such protections, certificates, and passports, and take the oath of allegiance to the United States of America. Nevertheless, hereby granting full liberty to all such as prefer the interest and protection of Great Britain to the freedom and happiness of their country, forthwith to withdraw themselves and families within the enemy's lines.

And I do hereby declare that all and every person, who may neglect or refuse to comply with this order, within thirty days from the date hereof, will be deemed adherents to the King of Great Britain, and treated as common enemies of the American States.

Given at Heard-Quarters, MORRIS TOWN, *January* 25, 1777.

By his Excellency's command,

GEORGE WASHINGTON.

Recreated from The Pennsylvania Packet, February 4, 1777.

RECRUITING AT BOSTON.

Extract of a letter from a gentleman in BOSTON *to his friend, dated January*, 1777.

I HAVE the pleasure to inform you, that the recruiting for the service, for three years, and during the war, is uncommonly successful in this State. It swarms with recruiting officers, and many men of influence, not in the military line, exert themselves to promote the enlisting of men. They are confident of having their 15 regiments ready for the field by the middle of a March. Large quantities of barrelled beef are already provided, and on the way to Albany, for summer stores to the northern army; and, in short, a general spirit of activity, both in early procuring troops, clothing, tents, and provision, that presages our being able to open the campaign, with a numerous well appointed army. I hope Connecticut will exert itself with equal spirit.

Recreated from Purdie's Virginia Gazette, March 14, 1777.

WANTED for the publick service, 10 or 12 good WAGGONS and TEAMS, for which ready money will be given, by applying to the subscriber in Williamsburg.

WILLIAM AYLETT.

. Who has for sale a quantity of excellent SHIP BREAD.

Recreated from Purdie's Virginia Gazette, February 7, 1777.

ENEMY FORAGERS ATTACKED.

AMERICANS OBLIGED TO RETIRE.

PHILADELPHIA.—On Thursday, January 30, col. Parker, with 300 men, attacked a large foraging party near Quibble town, who had six pieces of cannon. He was obliged, by superiority of numbers, to retire with the loss of seven men. By a deserter and a prisoner we learn, that the enemy lost 25 men, and had a number wounded.

The report of the town of Newport (in Rhode Island) being destroyed, took its rise from some stacks of hay, on Prudence island, near that place, being burnt, supposed by accident.

Recreated from Purdie's Virginia Gazette, February 28, 1777.

In COUNCIL *of* SAFETY, *Philadelphia,*
January 14. 1777.

THE Officers of the Militia are desired, as soon as they arrive in town, to make a report thereof to the Council of Safety, and at the same time to deliver in a return of the number their party consists of, and of what arms and necessaries they stand in need of, that the Council may furnish them as soon as possible, it being the intention of the Council of Safety, as well as the General commanding here, not to march the militia from this city until they are equipped in the best manner the circumstances of the times will admit.

By order of the Council,
THOMAS WHARTON, Jun. President.

NOTICE is hereby given, to all persons who have HARD CASH to send to their friends who are Prisoners in New-York, That by leaving it with Mr. WILLIAM BRADFORD, at the London Coffee-house in Philadelphia, before the 5th day of next February, it will be conveyed by the subscriber, who will call for it.

MICHAEL SMYCER, Captain in the York County Battalion, Flying Camp.

Recreated from The Pennsylvania Packet, January 17, 1777.

BRITISH MURDER OUR WOUNDED.

VIRGINIA REGIMENT THE BRAVEST.

Extract of a letter from an officer of distinction, dated at CHATHAM *(between* MORRIS TOWN *and* ELIZABETH TOWN*) February 3, 1777.*

"We have hemmed the enemy in, and begin to pinch them. On the 23d ult. we trimmed two regiments near to Woodbridge, killed 30 privates, and several officers. Had col. Buckner, who commanded, behaved well, we should have destroyed one regiment. He is now under arrest. We lost no men that day.

"On the 1st instant, 3000 of the enemy, under command of Sir William Erskine, came out of Brunswick to forage. They had eight pieces of cannon. Several of our scouting parties joined, to the amount of 600 men, under command of col. Scott, of the 5th Virginia regiment. A disposition was made to attack the enemy. Col. Scott, with 90 Virginians on the right, attacked 200 British grenadiers, and drove them to their cannon. The other parties not marching so briskly up to the attack, the colonel was engaged ten minutes by himself; and 300 fresh men being sent against him, was obliged to give way, but formed again within 300 yards of the enemy. By this time two other divisions had got up with the enemy, but superior numbers at last prevailed. Our troops retreated about a quarter of a mile, formed again, and looked the enemy in the face until they retreated.

"The enemy had 36 killed, whom the country people saw, and upwards of 100 wounded. *We have lost 3 officers and 12 privates killed, and have about as many wounded.* Lieut. Gregory, from Charles City county, Virginia, a brave officer, and adjutant Kelly of the 5th Virginia regiment, one of the bravest men in the army, he was carried off the field with a flesh wound only, and five more Virginians; but the enemy coming on that ground, *murdered them, by beating out their brains, with a barbarity exceeding that of the savages.*"

Recreated from Purdie's Virginia Gazette, February 28, 1777.

300 DEAD LEFT ON THE FIELD.

Action at QUIBBLE-TOWN, *February* 8.

The Express Rider, who arrived here yesterday from Head Quarters, gives the following interesting intelligence, viz.

That when he came off with the dispatches from General Washington, Gen. Green brought in the following account, that 300 of our troops were stationed at Quibble Town, under the command of Col. Scott, that 3000 of the enemy attacked them, which obliged Col. Scott to retreat about a mile and a half, that being reinforced by a party of Lord Stirling's army, with four pieces of cannon, they renewed the engagement, obliged the enemy to retreat with the loss of 300 dead left on the field, and 100 taken prisoners; and were in pursuit of them when Gen. Green came away.

That deserters from the enemy inform, that their army are at half allowance, and their horses dying for want of fodder.

Recreated from The Hartford Courant, February 17, 1777.

GEN. LEE UNDER STRONG GUARD.

BALTIMORE, *February* 11.—By the last accounts from New Jersey we learn, that General Lee was still at Brunswick, under a strong guard, but that he was treated with great respect by most of the officers of the British army; that General Howe had refused to see him, and that he had treated him with several indignities; that he had, notwithstanding, a high sense of the General's military abilities, and wished for a pretext to excuse him from exchanging him; that General Lee retained his inflexible attachment to the liberties of America, and that he openly avowed it upon all occasions. It is impossible for an American to reflect upon the important services this illustrious General has rendered to the United States, by rousing and directing their military spirit in the controversy, by forming their armies, by exercising a spirit of emulation and laudable ambition among their officers, by his attention to the health, clothing, &c. of their soldiers, and, lastly, by his zeal in inculcating the principles of liberty and good government upon all orders and classes of men, without resolving to redeem him, or to retaliate, with tenfold vengeance, the least indignity or injury that is offered to his person or character.

Gen. LEE was some time since sent from Brunswick to New York, where he now remains, under a strong guard.

Recreated from The Hartford Courant, March 3, 1777.

WAR-OFFICE.

February 11, 1777.

THE Board of War having received information of the good success the recruiting officers meet with in raising the new levies; but that from a desire in the officers to have their battalions and companies entirely compleated before they join the army, great numbers of useful soldiers are idle in quarters, when their services are wanted in camp. I have it in direction to order and strictly enjoin all recruiting officers, in the service of the United States, on the western side of the North river, and in the middle States, forthwith to march their men to the several places of rendezvous appointed for assembling the regiments, as soon as thirty privates are raised in any company, leaving proper officers to complete the respective regiments and companies at the places of recruiting. And all officers commanding regiments who have recruiting parties out on service in the said Middle States, are directed to attend diligently to the equipping and sending off the companies to join General Washington, as speedily as possible, after their arrival at the places of rendezvous.

RICHARD PETERS, Secretary.

† *The printers of the several news papers in the middle department are desired to insert the above in their papers.*

Recreated from The Pennsylvania Packet, February 25, 1777.

GENERAL ORDERS.

Head Quarters, MORRIS-TOWN, *Feb.* 6, 1777.

THE General, informed that many frauds and abuses have been committed of late by sundry soldiers, who after inlisting in one regiment, and receiving the bounty allowed by Congress, have deserted, inlisted in others, and received new bounties, for prevention of such unjust and infamous practices, commands and strictly enjoins all officers of the Continental army to use their utmost endeavours to detect those who shall be guilty of such offences, and having them apprehended, they cause to be forthwith tried by a General Court Martial, that they may be dealt with according to their crimes.

The General thinks proper to declare, that this offence is of the most enormous and flagrant nature, and not admitting to the least palliation or excuse, whosoever are convicted thereof, and sentenced to die, may consider their EXECUTION certain and inevitable.

That such impositions may be less practicable, every officer engaged in the recruiting service is required to have a piece of blue, red or yellow ribband or tape fixed in the hat of each soldier recruited, at the time of inlistment; which he shall constantly wear, under pain of receiving thirty-nine lashes, till the regiment or corps to which he belongs is assembled, and joins the army.

G. WEEDON,
Adjutant-General.

Recreated from The Pennsylvania Packet, February 18, 1777.

PETERSBURG, *February* 10, 1777.

THE Subscriber has for Sale six three pounders CANNON, with Carriages, &c. some Bullets and Linstage. (2) RICHARD TAYLOR.

WILLIAMSBURG, *Feb.* 14, 1777.

A JOURNEYMAN Hair-Dresser will receive extraordinary Encouragement from LAFONG & WYLIE.

Recreated from The Virginia Gazette, February 14, 1777.

To be SOLD by the subscriber, in Smithfield, wholesale or retail, for ready money, a large assortment of the following articles, viz.

BROAD, narrow, and grubbing hoes, broad, narrow, and pole axes, ship carpenters axes and adzes, coopers axes, adzes, howells, and vices, crow irons, drawing knives, box irons and heaters, best steel plate and iron whip, cross cut, and hand saws, augers of all sizes, chisels, gouges, hinges of various sorts, iron and brass chaffing-dishes, tongs and shovels, hammers, shoe ditto, nippers, pincers, awl blades, copper, tin, and fish kettles, copper skillets and coffee pots, neat brass and iron candlesticks, sets of china tea cups and saucers, tin pots of several sorts, mens fine hats, womens plain furred and silk hats of various sorts and prices, womens stockings, patent stays, mens and womens gloves, ribands, tapes, garters, cap and black lace, shalloons, satin bonnets, velvet hoods, damascus, mozeens, corderoy, macaroni, tabby, manua, tafetas, pink, satin, and other silks, bombazeen, camlets, mens silk and worsted caps, saddle housings, a genteel cover for a lady's saddle, bridles and bridle bits, stirrup irons, saddle busses, pewter dishes, hard metal water plates, gallon, half gallon, quart, and pint pewter measures, tin lanthorns for ship and stable use, large and small tin funnels, large and small plates, japanned tea boards and waiters, large and small tin canisters and sugar boxes, silver and common shoe buckles, silver and gilt seals, watchkeys, thimbles, ladies and gentlemens stone shoe buckles, gold rings, gold bobs, earrings, egrets, hair pins, necklaces, common and pebble sleeve buttons, gold thread, fine ounce thread spectacles, decanters, wine and beer glasses, wash basons, queen's china plates and dishes, common and paper snuff boxes, best and common razors, hones, speaking trumpets, watering pots, a variety of books, among which are *Bunyan's* works in folio, pilgrim's progress, holy war, history of the bible in folio, history of *England* in ditto, bibles, prayer books, sermons, small histories, large legers and journals, &c. &c. brimstone, saltpetre, guns, swords, powder, white and red lead mixed in oil, rum, sugar, molosses, &c. &c.

LEWIS HANSFORD.

For SALE,

A YOUNG mulatto woman that has been used to the house, is a good sempstress, can wash and iron very well, and is a good pastry cook, also can spin and knit. Inquire of the printer.

Recreated from Purdie's Virginia Gazette, February 28, 1777.

A BRIGADE OF HONOUR.

Extract of a letter from a gentleman of distinction, dated CHATHAM, *February* 10.

MY brigade has behaved to admiration, most of the officers like heroes, and in a campaign or two will surpass any troops in the world for sobriety, orderly behaviour, and true courage. The 23d of January, we cut to pieces the 28th regiment of our enemies; and on the 1st instant, col. Scott, with only 600 men, and no artillery, attacked 3000 of the enemy, under lord Cornwallis, who had with him nine pieces of cannon. Col. Scott began the attack with 90 Virginians, and beat 230 British grenadiers; but not being seasonably supported, he was obliged to give way. The enemy butchered lieut. Kelly of the 5th regiment, a brave officer, and five others, who were wounded. I sent in major Bland with a flag, upbraiding them with savage cruelty, and threatening retaliation. On the 8th instant we were again engaged for four hours and compelled the enemy to retreat.

Lieut. Gregory, who was killed on the 1st instant, upon being brought out of the field, and about half an hour before he died, called the men to him, and said, "Countrymen and fellow soldiers, I shall leave you in a few minutes. All that I am sorry for is, that I did not live longer to be of service to my bleeding country. Be brave, my lads, and acquit yourselves like men! Maintain your own liberty, and that of your country." And immediately expired.

DESERTED from company, JOHN WEBSTER, of *Prince Edward*, about 22 years old, 5 feet 9 or 10 inches high, has blue eyes and light hair, his dress I cannot describe. I will give TWENTY DOLLARS for delivering him to me, or the commanding officer at *Williamsburg*. ABNER CRUMP, capt.

Recreated from Purdie's Virginia Gazette, March 14, 1777.

20 £ FOR EVERY SCALP.

General Carleton at Quebec.

A copy of a letter from a gentleman in Albany, *dated February* 15, 1777.

"Since I wrote the foregoing, an express arrived from Ticonderoga, at which place a captain in Livingston's regiment is just got in from Canada, from whence he had just made his escape. He tells the commanding officer on oath, that a scouting and scalping party of savages, to the amount of 80, together with some Canadians and regulars, to the amount of about 150, had set out from Canada; they were to have twenty pounds for every scalp they brought in. That col. Fraser commanded at Montreal, had with him 200 men, 150 men were at St. John's, and the like number at Chamblee; all the foreigners were at Three Rivers, had mutinied twice or thrice in such a manner as obliged the commanding officer to turn out the British troops and what Canadians they have, in order to quell them. That general Carleton was at Quebec, and that they were cutting wood on the Lake for three vessels. He further says, that the people in general are much more affected to our cause, than they were last year; and that what Canadians have joined the British army, are only the very lowest of the people; the troops take whatever they stand in need of from any person, just give them a certificate of having taken it, without any other satisfaction. Provision is very difficult to be had, by even the troops."

Recreated from The Pennsylvania Packet, March 11, 1777.

A MAJESTIC REWARD.

His Majesty, ever studious of rewarding exemplary merit, and particularly of signalizing martial prowess with the most distinguishing marks of his royal approbation, has sent over the Feather of a Peacock's tail of singular length and lustre; which was last week affixed to the cap of one of the Conquerors of America (an illustrious proof of his Majesty's deep sense of that hero's unparalleled exploits against the rebels!) with all the ceremony and splendour suitable to the pomposity of the occasion.

We hear from every part of the country, that the remarkable warm weather we have had during the present winter, the like of which was never known before, has caused the wool of all the American sheep to turn into hair, as is usual with that animal in warm climates.—*A manifest judgement of Providence to compel the rebels to return to their dependence upon Great Britain, or perish for want of clothing!*

It is generally supposed that if any thing besides the want of woolens, will obligate the Americans to sue for a reconciliation with the mother country, it will be the interposition of the Ladies, who have been so lavish in the monstrous size and longitude of their head-dress, that the materials of which their caps are composed (which are all British) will soon be expended: And then bare heads or peace upon any terms.

Recreated from The Pennsylvania Packet, February 18, 1777.

MORE ACTION AT QUIBBLE TOWN.

Extract of a letter from Morris Town, *Feb.* 21, 1777.

"Yesterday a party of our men near Quibble Town, took twenty of the enemy's waggons loaded with forage, drove in their picket guard, and sustained no loss. A soldier killed two light-horse men of the enemy, and narrowly escaped being taken; the horses and accoutrements were brought in.

"The same day a lieutenant of the enemy's artillery was taken and brought to General Sullivan's quarters, with seven other prisoners, most of them Highlanders. This morning twelve hundred men were detached to bring off forage from the enemy's lines, I hope they may prosper. A brigade of New England troops arrived this day from the White Plains."

Recreated from The Pennsylvania Packet, February 25, 1777.

THE 2d Regiment having marched to the Northward, all Officers to whom General *Lewis* gave Furloughs till last Spring, on Account of their ill State of Health, have my positive Orders to join their Regiment immediately. Those Officers who have been promoted by the Committees must still consider themselves as officers of the 2d Regiment until they have permission from General *Lewis* to resign, and are therefore ordered immediately to follow their Regiment with the Men they have recruited. ----- Lieutenant *Marks* is ordered to give *John Shelton*, a Fifer whom he recruited in *Williamsburg*, when the Regiment was discharged, a Pass to join his Regiment to the Northward. A. SPOTSWOOD, Lieut. Col. 2d Reg.

THE Continental Officers of the new raised Troops of the following Counties, *Augusta, Amherst, Fairfax, Culpeper, Orange, Spotsylvania, Fauquier, Cumberland, Caroline, Stafford,* and *King George,* are desired to take Notice, that by a Resolution of the Hon. the Governor and Council they are formed into a Battalion, to be under my Command; and as soon as any of them complete their Quota of Men, they are hereby desired to March immediately to *Fredericksburg,* where they will receive farther Instructions. It is recommended that the Men furnish themselves with every necessary that they possibly can for a Camp. (2) EDWARD STEVENS, Col. 10th Bat.

THE Subscriber, near *Warwick,* has for Sale, an Assortment of MEDICINES, consisting of Bark, Rhubarb, Jalap, Ipecacuanha, Glauber Salts, Calomel, and sundry other Mercurials, Senna, Manna, Emetic and soluble Tartar, Salt of Wormwood, Cream and vitriolated Tartar, crude and diaphoretic Antimony, Cinnabar, Golden Sulphur and Crocus of ditto, Squills, Valerian, Contrayerva, Gentian, Orange Peel, Camomile Flowers, Juniper Berries, Sugar of Lead, blue and white Vitriol, *Spanish* Flies, Bole Armenic, Dragon's Blood, Roch Allum, Lenitive Electuary, white Wax, Rosin, *Burgundy* Pitch, most Kinds of medicinal Gums, Balsams, Spirits, Salts, essential Oils, Extracts, Plaisters, &c. Syrup and Ointment Pots, double Flint Bottles, Gallipots, a Clyster Syringe, Clyster Pipes, a very large and Quart Marble Mortar, a large Bell Metal Mortar, a fine large Stove and Pipe, &c &c. Any Person who will purchase the Whole may have them at an Hundred *per Cent.* for each.
(2) SAMUEL NIVINS.

DUMFRIES, *February* 1, 1777.
THE Officers that are marching Men to the continental Army will be pleased to apply to the Commissaries at the following Places to draw Provisions, viz. Mr. *James Hunter,* Jun. at *Fredericksburg,* Mr. *Andrew Gifford* at *Dumfries,* and Mr. *Josiah Watson* at *Alexandria.* As Provisions are now laid in all along the Road to the Camp, there is no farther Occasion for Provision Waggons.
(6) RICHARD GRAHAM, Deputy Com. Gen.

Recreated from The Virginia Gazette, February 28, 1777.

IN CONGRESS. *Feb.* 24, 1777.
RESOLVED, that the Board of War be directed to send letters, by express, to the colonels or other commanding officers of the several regiments now raising and recruiting in the states of *Pennsylvania, Delaware, Maryland,* and *Virginia,* ordering them immediately to march the troops enlisted under their command, by companies and parts of companies, to join the army under general *Washington,* proper officers being left behind to recruit the companies or corps that are not yet completed, and to bring up the recruits.
Extract from the minutes.
CHARLES THOMSON, sec'y.

WILLIAMSBURG, *March* 13, 1777.
THE officers, especially the colonels of regiments for the continental service in this state, are directed to pay due regard to the above resolve, and to take with them what arms, blankets, and clothes, they can by any means obtain. The deficiency will be supplied either at *Philadelphia* or head quarters. The colonels will, without loss of time, report to me the present state of their respective regiments.
ANDREW LEWIS, brig. gen.

For SALE, at Fredericksburg.
ABOUT 1400 wt. of good GUNPOWDER, on reasonable terms.

Recreated from Purdie's Virginia Gazette, March 14, 1777.

AN EYE FOR AN EYE.

PHILADELPHIA, *February 26.*—*A copy of a letter to* Sir WILLIAM ERSKINE, *complaining of the savage cruelty of the British troops.*

SIR,

IT is told us that Sir William Erskine commanded the British troops covering the foraging party at Drake's farm, on Saturday the first instant. Is it possible that a gentleman, an officer so eminently distinguished for his bravery and experience, should allow the troops under his command to murder the wounded after the manner of savages! Until this time it was universally allowed that humanity was a certain concomitant of valour. It now appears that Britons, unhappily divested of many excellent qualities peculiar to their ancestors, are become strangers to humanity, and deaf to the entreaties of the brave, after the misfortune of having fallen wounded into their power. Mr. Kelly, a brave officer in my brigade, and five other Virginians slightly wounded in the muscular parts, were murdered, had their bodies mangled, and their brains beat out, by the troops of his Britannic majesty, on Saturday the first instant.

The cruelties exercised on the worthy general Mercer, near to Princeton, on the third of January, were equally barbarous. It gives pain to a generous mind, Sir William, to see you tarnish the laurels so honourably obtained last war, by permitting such savage barbarity in the troops under your command.

Such conduct, Sir William, inspires the Americans with a hatred to Britain so inveterate and insurmountable, that they never will form an alliance or the least connection with them.

I can assure you, Sir, that the savages, after general Braddock's defeat, notwithstanding the great influence on the French over them, could not be prevailed on to butcher the wounded, in the manner your troops have done, until they were made drunk. I do not know, Sir William, that your troops gave you that trouble.

So far does British cruelty, now a days, surpass that of savages! In spite of all the British agents sent among the different nations, we have beat the Indians into good humour, and they offer their services.

It is their custom in war to scalp, take out the hearts, and mangle the bodies of their enemies. This is shocking to the humanity natural to the white inhabitants of America. However, if the British officers do not refrain their soldiers from glutting their cruelties with the wanton destruction of the wounded, the United States, contrary to their natural disposition, will be compelled to employ a body of furious savages, who can, with an unrelenting heart, eat the flesh, and drink the blood, of their enemies.

I well remember that, in the year 1763, lieutenant Gordon of the Royal Americans, and eight more of the British soldiers, were roasted alive, and eat up, by the fierce savages that now offer their services.

The Americans have hitherto treated the wounded, and prisoners of the British troops, with that civility and tenderness natural to a brave and generous people, but should the inhuman cruelty of your men compel the American army to retaliate, let it be remembered that the British officers stand answerable to the world, and to posterity, for the many dreadful consequences.

I am &c.

————— —————, B.G.U.S.

Recreated from The Maryland Gazette, March 13, 1777.

GOODS PLENTY AND CHEAP.

WILLIAMSBURG, *Feb.* 28.—By a gentleman from the Northward, we learn that a number of vessels had arrived in the Delaware with a large quantity of salt, clothing for the army, and dry goods of all kinds; and we are also told, that at Charlestown there were upwards of 30 sail of vessels lying, from different ports, which had stocked the market there so plentifully with European goods, that all kinds sold full as cheap as before the war broke out.

Recreated from Purdie's Virginia Gazette, February 28, 1777.

BRITISH REINFORCEMENTS AT AMBOY.

Extract of a letter from MORRIS TOWN, *Feb.* 26.

"General Howe still continues to threaten your city. A reinforcement is arrived at Amboy, consisting of the 10th, 37th, 38th, and 52d regiments, one battalion of grenadiers, and one of light infantry, the whole amounting to about 2000 men. They were out on Sunday last, upon a foraging party, with three field pieces, when they were attacked by about 600 of our people at 11 in the morning near Spank town. The firing continued from, that time, with some short intermission, until night. By the best accounts we can get, the enemy's loss amounted to upwards of 100 men killed and wounded, and we took ten prisoners. Our loss was eight killed and wounded. They came with about 15 or 20 waggons, a considerable part of which were employed in carrying off their dead and wounded, and some of them so piled that the dead fell off, and were left in the road. A few such affairs will make them sick of foraging, at so expensive a rate.

"The enemy killed two of the inhabitants. One, with his protection in hand, had his brains blown out while he was offering it to an officer; the other was run through the body with a bayonet. Both were killed for not getting their waggons ready as speedily as they were wanted to remove the dead out of the way."

Recreated from Purdie's Virginia Gazette, March 25, 1777.

PROMOTED AMERICAN GENERALS.

BALTIMORE, *Feb.* 25.—The following gentlemen are promoted to the rank of Majors General in the army of the United States, viz. Lord Stirling, Thomas Mifflin, Arthur St. Clair, Adam Stephen, and Benjamin Lincoln, Esquires.

Colonels Enoch Poor, Glover, Patterson, Anthony Wayne, James Michael Varnum, John Phillip Dehass, George Weedon, Muhlenburg, John Cadwalader, and William Woodford, are also promoted to the rank of Brigadiers General.

Recreated from The Pennsylvania Packet, March 4, 1777.

PUT TO FLIGHT AT SPANK TOWN.

Extract of a letter from an officer in NEW JERSEY.

"The officer who commanded the 2000 British troops going as a reinforcement from Amboy to Brunswick, we hear, is under arrest for undertaking, like Don Quixote, to do impossibilities, and get himself a great and immortal name.

"For this purpose, he, instead of marching directly to Brunswick (which he might have done) must needs go 14 miles out of the direct road to take prisoners general Maxwell and his party at Spanktown, and to make his triumphant entry into Brunswick, leading his captives in chains, like an old Roman general, in which he found his fatal mistake when too late to remedy it, for he found that he had surrounded a nest of American hornets, who soon put his whole body to flight, pursued them to Amboy, and obliged them to get on board their ships again, since which they have never ventured a second time to reinforce their cooped up brethren in Brunswick."

Recreated from Purdie's Virginia Gazette, March 28, 1777.

CONGRESS ADJOURNS TO PHILADELPHIA.

BALTIMORE, *March* 4.—A gentleman from Philadelphia informs us, that it was reported there that general Arnold was preparing to make a descent on Rhode Island with about 4000 volunteers, in consequence of a considerable part of the British and Hessian troops having left it, to join Howe's army in Jersey.

On the 28th of January last, Daniel Strong, of Dutchess county, a spy from the enemy's army, was executed at Peek's Kill, pursuant to a sentence of a general court martial.

A few days ago the Continental Congress adjourned from this town to Philadelphia, for which place the members have mostly set out.

Last evening the Lady of his Excellency General Washington arrived in town from Alexandria.

Recreated from Purdie's Virginia Gazette, March 14, 1777.

FRENCH FLEET AT CHARLESTOWN.

BALTIMORE, *March* 18.—By mr. Charles Cook, a gentleman who arrived here last night in 12 days from Newbern, we have the following important intelligence, viz. That the day before he set out he saw a certain capt. Stedman, who commands a company in the 5th regiment of North Carolina troops, who was just returned from Charlestown, and there saw a large French fleet, consisting of 15 vessels of war, two of them 80 gun ships, and 40 merchantmen; that two of the armed vessels lay within the bar; that they had on board 200 pieces of brass cannon, 30,000 stand of small arms, and a great quantity of dry goods, for the use of the American states. Their destination was Chesapeake and Delaware bays. Mr. Cook declares that he himself heard capt. Stedman relate the above facts, and that capt. Stedman is a gentleman of undoubted veracity.

Recreated from Purdie's Virginia Gazette, March 28, 1777.

FRENCH SHIP AT PORTSMOUTH.

A letter from a gentleman at head quarters, dated, MORRISTOWN, *March* 29, 1777.

BRIGADIER general Knox does me the favour of transcribing part of a letter which he this moment received from col. Jackson, commanding one of the 16 additional battalions:

BOSTON, *March* 20, 1777.—News! glorious news! Last Tuesday a large ship arrived at Portsmouth from France; she has on board 1000 barrels of gunpowder, 12,000 stand of arms (I say 12,000 stand of arms) a complete set of cannon for the frigate at Portsmouth, and a very large quantity of linens, woolens, &c. &c. with a French general, colonel, and major. These gentlemen come well recommended by Dr. Franklin. She brings an account, that at the same time, and from the same port, a French 50 gun ship sailed for this place, with 50 brass field pieces, and other warlike stores. All, and every part of this, may be depended upon as a fact.

Recreated from Purdie's Virginia Gazette, April 11, 1777.

THE UNITED STATES OF COLUMBIA.

A correspondent proposes that the United States of AMERICA *should be called the United States of* COLUMBIA, *instead of* AMERICA, *and gives the following reasons for it.*

I. Columbus was the first discoverer of this quarter of the globe. He was illustrious for his virtues, and was requited for his unparalleled services to the great interests of humanity, which the most cruel and unjust persecution by the ungrateful monarch of Spain. Americus did not sail for this country till several years after its discovery, and afterwards obtained the honour of having it called after his name by fraud and injustice.

II. The name of an American, at this time, has nothing in it which distinguishes it from the vassals of Britain, Spain and Portugal, which inhabit those parts of this country, which do not belong to the Thirteen United States. The name of a Columbian, hereafter, will be characteristic of a citizen of the FREE STATES . . . the name of an American, of a subject of an European State.

Recreated from The Hartford Courant, March 3, 1777.

SHAMEFUL MISBEHAVIOUR.

COLONEL BUCKNER CASHIERED.

A GENERAL court martial was held upon col. Mordecai Buckner of the 6th Virginia regiment, the 8th ult., being accused of shamefully misbehaving before the enemy in an action on the 23d of January last, also quitting his post and party in time of engagement, and neglecting to bring up his men to action, when there was a prospect of defeating the enemy. The court found him guilty of the charge, and their sentence was, that he should be cashiered, and declared incapable of any military office in the service of the United States; which sentence was approved of by the general, and was ordered forthwith to depart the American army.

Recreated from Purdie's Virginia Gazette, March 7, 1777.

TEN POUNDS REWARD.

WILLIAMSBURG, February 14, 1777.

LOST, a Sum of *Virginia* Paper Money folded up in a square Piece of Parchment, supposed to be dropt last *Tuesday* on the Road between *Williamsburg* and *York*. The following are the Numbers of most of the Bills, viz.

Of TWELVE POUNDS each,

No.	98	101	153	8	148	273	7	148
	7798	10059	1528	753	14713	17222	625	14738

Of TEN POUNDS each,

No.	97	132	133	103
	9614	13172	13207	9955

Of EIGHT POUNDS each,

No.	23	16	31	14	88
	2213	1277	3096	1797	3725

Of FIVE POUNDS each,

No.	15	5	Old Emissions of do.	April 5th, No. 1728; March 1, No. 1701, April 1762, No. 1, April 1759, No. 1808.
	1444	623		

Of THREE POUNDS each,

No.	72	Old Emissions of do.	October 12th, No. 1040; April 1756, 1914; October 1758, No. 1685; 1760, No. 606; May 24th, No. 35
	7171		

Of TWO POUNDS each,

No.	55	Old Emission, November 1769, No. 57.
	5476	

Some 20 and 10 s. Bills, and four continental Bills of 30 Doll each.

If any of the Bills should be offered in Payment, it is hoped they be stopped, and Information given to the Subscriber, who will pay above Reward to any Person that delivers him the Money, or in Proportion for any Part of it. DAVID JAMESON.

TO be sold to the highest Bidder, at *York* Town, on *Monday* the 24th of *March*, a SLOOP, about 1800 Bushels Burthen. The Vessel may be seen by any Person inclined to purchase before, or on the Day of Sale.

W. REYNOLDS.

Recreated from The Virginia Gazette, March 14, 1777.

INDIANS DEMAND LANDS

CLAIM WRONGFULLY SETTLED.

Extract of a letter from PITTSBURGH, *dated* March 24, 1777.

"I must inform you that matters have a very gloomy aspect here. Daniel Sullivan has returned from the Indian country, and brings accounts of Indians being assembled, in order to attack the Kittanning and this post, and of several other things too tedious to mention.

"A few days ago the Indians killed one Andrew Simpson, and took or killed a brother of Captain Moorhead's, near Kittanning. They scalped Capt. Simpson, and left a tomahawk and war belt on him, and a piece of writing in his shot pouch, (dated Niagara, 8th February, 1777) from the Chiefs of the Mohawks, Onondagoes, Cayngas, Tuscaroras, Mistletoes, and Chippaws, to the Virginians and Pennsylvanians, now at Vanyngo, the purport of which is, that we have wrongfully settled their lands on the Ohio and Saskatchewan, and ordering us to quit them immediately, or abide by the consequences; that we have no foundation for our pretense (as they call it) of Col. Buder's [British Colonel John Buder] coming against us, as we know he has no army with him; they therefore think that our design is against them, but whether or not, they insist on our quitting their lands immediately, and not to make any excuse, by pretending to acquaint our Congress, &c. of their behaviour.

"In consequence of the before mentioned intelligence and depredations, a council of war was held at this place this day, in which it was determined that it would be most adviseable, for Col. Crawford's battalion, and two companies of Col. Wood's battalion, at Fort Pitt and Wheeling, not to march till further orders, and that 100 men should be immediately sent to Kittanning, and 25 men to attack the following places, viz. Logg's Town, Holliday's Cove, and Cox's."

Recreated from The Virginia Gazette, April 18, 1777.

BRITAIN'S CRUELTY!

AMERICANS IN IRONS AND EXILE.

The Deposition of Eliphalet DOWNER, Surgeon, *taken in the* Yankee *privateer, is as follows*:

THAT after he was made prisoner by Captains Ross and Hodge, who took advantage of the generous conduct of Captain Johnson of the Yankee to them his prisoners, and of the confidence he placed in them in consequence of that conduct and their assurances; he and his countrymen were closely confined, yet assured that on their arrival in port they should be set at liberty, and these assurances were repeated in the most solemn manner, instead of which they were, on their approach to land, in the hot weather of August, shut up in a small cabin; the windows of which were spiked down and no air admitted, insomuch that they were all in danger of suffocation from the excessive heat.

Three or four days after their arrival in the river Thames they were relieved from this situation in the middle of the night, hurried on board a tender and sent down to Sheerness, where the deponent was put into the Ardent, and there falling sick of a violent fever in consequence of such treatment, and languishing in that situation for some time, he was removed, still sick, to the Mars, and notwithstanding repeated petitions to be suffered to be sent to prison on shore, he was detained until having the appearance of a mortification in his legs, he was sent to Haslar hospital, from whence after recovering his health, he had the good fortune to make his escape.

While on board those ships and in the hospital he was informed and believes that many of his countrymen, after experiencing even worse treatment than he, were sent to the East Indies, and many of those taken at Quebec were sent to the coast of Africa, as soldiers.

The Deposition of Captain Seth CLARK, *of* NEWBURY PORT, *in the State of Massachusetts Bay, in* AMERICA, *is as follows*:

THAT on his return from Cape Nichola Mole to Newbury Port, he was taken on the 17th of September last by an armed schooner in his British Majesty's service,—Coats, Esquire, Commander, and carried down to Jamaica, on his arrival at which place he was sent on board the Squirrel, another armed vessel,—Douglas, Esquire, Commander, where, although master and half owner of the vessel in which he was taken, he was returned as a common sailor before the mast, and in that situation sailed for England in the month of November, on the twenty-fifth of which month they took a schooner from Port a Pe' to Charlestown, S.C., to which place she belonged, when the owner, Mr. Burt, and the master, Mr. Bean, were brought on board. On the latter's denying he had any ship papers, Captain Douglas ordered him to be stripped and tied up and then whipped with a wire cat of nine tails that drew blood every stroke and then on his saying that he had thrown his papers overboard he was untied and ordered to his duty as a common sailor, with no place for himself or his people to lay on but the decks. On their arrival at Spithead, the deponent was removed to the Monarch, and *there ordered to do duty as a foremast man*, and on his refusing on account of inability to do it, he was threatened by the Lieutenant, a Mr. Stoney, that if he spoke one word to the contrary he *should be brought to the gangway,* and there *severely flogged.*

After this he was again removed and put on board the Barfleur, where he remained until the tenth of February. On board this ship the deponent saw several American prisoners, who were *closely confined and ironed*, with only *four men's allowance to six.* These prisoners and others informed this deponent that a number of American prisoners had been taken out of the ship and sent to the East Indies and the coast of Africa, which he was told would have been his fate, had he arrived sooner.

This deponent further saith, That in Haslar hospital, to which place on account of sickness he was removed from the Barfleur, he saw a Captain Chase of Providence, New England, who told him he had been taken in a sloop of which he was half owner and master, on his passage from Providence to South Carolina, by an English transport, and turned over to a ship of war, where he was confined in irons thirteen weeks, *insulted, beat, and abused* by the *petty officers* and *common sailors*, and on being released from irons was ordered to do duty as a foremost man until his arrival in England, when being dangerously ill he was sent to said hospital.

PARIS, *March* 30, 1777.
Published by order of CONGRESS,
CHARLES THOMPSON, Sec

Recreated from The Pennsylvania Packet, August 5, 1777.

A BRITISH RUSE.

FRANCE AIDS AMERICA.

PHILADELPHIA, *April* 8.—A gentleman from camp informs, that the British troops at Perth-Amboy, in number about three thousand, last Tuesday morning, embarked on board several transports, sailed out of Sandy Hook, under convoy of three men of war, but in the evening they returned, and disembarked under cover of the night on Staten Island. This manoeuvre, it is supposed, was intended to make the appearance of a reinforcement from Europe, and which the Tories have industriously reported to be real.

By the last advices from France we learn, that Arthur Lee, esq., late of London, who is appointed by the United States to act in concert with Dr. Franklin, was arrived at that court, where, he, with the Doctor, were received and treated with all the respect shown to European Ambassadors, and that they already have negotiated a loan of two million of livres, for and on account of the United States.

Recreated from The Pennsylvania Packet, April 8, 1777.

SNUBBED.

From DR. FRANKLIN *and* SILAS DEANE, Esqs., *to* Lord STORMONT, *the English Ambassador.*

My Lord,   PARIS, *April* 2d, 1777.

We did ourselves the honour of writing some time since to your Lordship on the subject of exchanging prisoners; you did not condescend to give us any answer, we therefore expect none to this. We, however, take the liberty of sending you copies of certain Depositions which we shall transmit to Congress, whereby it will be known to your Court, that the United States are not unacquainted with the barbarous treatment their people receive when they have the misfortune of being your prisoners here in Europe; and that if your conduct towards us is not altered, it is not unlikely that severe reprisals may be thought justifiable, from the necessity of putting some check to such abominable practices.

For the sake of humanity, it is to be wished that men would endeavour to alleviate as much as possible the unavoidable miseries attending a state of war. It has been said, that among the civilized nations of Europe the ancient horrors of that state are much diminished; but the compelling men by chains, stripes and famine to fight against their friends and relations, is a new mode of barbarity which your nation alone has the honour of inventing; and the sending American prisoners of war to Africa and Asia, remote from all possibility of exchange, and where they can scarce hope ever to hear from their families, even if the unwholesomeness of the climate does not put a speedy end to their lives, is a manner of treating captives, that you can justify by no other Precedent or custom except that of the black Savages of Guinea.

We are, your Lordship's most obedient &c.
B. FRANKLIN.
S. DEANE.

The following insolent reply was made:

"THE King's Ambassador receives no letters from Rebels, except when they come to ask Mercy."

Recreated from The Pennsylvania Packet, August 5, 1777.

BRITISH BURN DANBURY.

HEADING TOWARDS TARRY TOWN.

PHILADELPHIA, *May* 1. The following accounts have been received by CONGRESS, relating to the enemy's attack upon the village of DANBURY in Connecticut.

Published by order of CONGRESS,
CHARLES THOMPSON, Sec.

• • • •

General ARNOLD *to* General M'DOUGAL, WEST-RIDING, *April* 27, 1777, X. *o'clock.*

"On Friday evening last the enemy landed about 2000 men at Compo, eight miles west of Fairfield, and on Saturday, two o'clock, P.M. reached Danbury, which was abandoned by a handful of our men. The enemy immediately began burning and destroying our magazines of provisions, &c.

"Last night, at half past eleven, General Wooster, General Stillman, and myself, with 600 militia, arrived at Bethel, eight miles from Danbury. The excessive heavy rains rendered their arms useless, and many of the troops were much fatigued, having marched 33 miles in the course of the day, without refreshment.

"At 6 this morning we divided the troops into two divisions, being uncertain if they would return by way of Fairfield or Norwalk. One division was stationed on each road, on a cross road, where they could support each other. We have this minute information that at nine this morning the enemy set fire to the meeting-house, and most of the buildings in town, and had taken the route to Newbury, leading either to Peck's Kill or Tarry Town. We imagine they are destined to the latter, as we hear they landed 800 men there yesterday morning. We propose following them immediately, in hopes of coming up with the rear, and hope you will be able to take them in front.

"I am, with esteem, Sir, &c.,
B. ARNOLD."

• • • •

PAUGATUCK, 3 *miles east of* NORWALK, *April* 28, 1777, 6 *o'clock*, P.M.

"Soon after I wrote you yesterday, I found the enemy was on their march for Ridgefield; at 11 o'clock we arrived, about an hour before them, with 500 men. We had little time to make a disposition of our troops, when a smart action began, which lasted abut an hour. Our troops were obliged to give way to superior numbers. I ordered a stand to be made at this place.

"At 11 o'clock this morning we met the enemy, with 500 militia, about two miles from this place, when a skirmishing began between the flanks, and soon became general, which continued until 5 o'clock, when the enemy gained an height, under cover of their ships, and embarked before night. At the beginning of the action Col. Huntington joined me with 500 men, and before it was over a small number of General Wadsworth's brigade. General Wooster, whose conduct does him great honour, was mortally wounded yesterday, Lieutenant Colonel Gold killed, and Colonel Lamb wounded. Our loss otherwise is not great, about twenty killed and wounded. The enemy's loss is uncertain, as they carried off most of their killed and wounded; several prisoners have fallen into our hands. As soon as the troops were embarked, the fleet got under way, and stood to the eastward.

B. ARNOLD"

To General M'Dougal.

BOSTON, *April* 24.—A State sloop of war arrived in port yesterday afternoon, from Martinico, having on board 1200 stands of arms, 13,000 weight of powder, a quantity of linen, and several hundred bushels of salt.

ARNOLD PROMOTED MAJOR-GENERAL.

May 7.—The Honourable the Congress have promoted Brigadier General Arnold to rank of Major General.

Recreated from The Virginia Gazette, May 23, 1777.

BARBARITY AT DANBURY.

LAST Friday afternoon upwards of 20 sail of men of war and transports appeared coming up the sound from New York, and soon after came to anchor near Fairfield, in Connecticut; and in the evening about 3000 of the enemy landed at a place called Compoo, about six miles west of Fairfield, and early next morning marched to Danbury, which place they set on fire, and a great part of it is entirely consumed.

They likewise took possession of the continental stores at that place, which were very considerable, and destroyed them. The enemy used some of the inhabitants with great barbarity. They were attacked in their retreat by a party of militia, and lost about 200 killed and taken prisoners.

General Wooster we are told, is badly wounded. General Arnold had his horse shot under him. Colonel Lamb is slightly wounded; and about 13 others killed, and some wounded, of our people. The enemy tarried all night in Danbury. Tryon told the people of the house where he lodged, that the troops would not have come there, had they not been conducted by our own people; meaning, no doubt, the Tories. The enemy had got back to their shipping before general M'Dongal could come up with them. We have not been able to learn farther particulars.

To the TORIES.

WANTED for his majesty's service, as an assistant to his excellency general Howe and Hugh Gaine, printers and publishers of the New York gazette, a gentleman who can lie with ingenuity. Inquire of Peter Numskull, compiler and collector of lies for their excellencies, at New York.

N. B. A good hand will receive the honour of knighthood.

Recreated from Purdie's Virginia Gazette, May 16, 1777.

GENERAL HOSPITAL.

May 17.—By a late resolve of Congress the pay of the regimental Surgeons has increased to two dollars per diem and four rations; and regimental Mates to one dollar and one third per diem, and two rations.

Any gentleman qualified for these places, may find employment by applying to the Director General.

Recreated from The Pennsylvania Packet, May 20, 1777.

TRAITORS.

BOSTON, *May* 22.—At a General Court Martial, held in this town last week by order of General Heath, Lieut. Col. Thomas Farrington, of Groton, State of Massachusetts, being found guilty of receiving and passing counterfeit money, knowing it to be such, was unanimously adjudged to be discharged from the army, and rendered incapable of acting any more as an officer in the continental service. He was committed to goal on Monday last, to be dealt with by the civil law, according to his atrocious crime.

Last Friday, one Hart, belonging to Duke's County, State of New York, was apprehended at Providence, being charged with bearing a commission under Mr. Howe, and was then recruiting. He was the same day tried, found guilty, and executed on Saturday following.

Last week a certain Rev. Martin, who is well known in this Town for boasting of his Exploits at Breed's Hill, on the 17th of June, 1775, on the part of the Americans, was taken up at Greenwich, State of Rhode Island, recruiting for the Enemy.

Just published, and now selling by
STYNER AND CIST,
In Second-street, six doors above Arch-street,

THE Love of our Country. A SERMON, Preached before the VIRGINIA TROOPS in New-Jersey. By JOHN HURT, CHAPLAIN.

Recreated from The Pennsylvania Packet, June 3, 1777.

AMBASSADORS FOR EUROPE.

All the courts of Europe, excepting Portugal, have, by letters, and personally by their ambassadors, made application to Dr. Franklin for ambassadors to be sent from us to their several courts, promising every honour to them as due to ambassadors of friends; that mr. Deane had set out for the Hague, mr. Lee for the court of Madrid, and that Congress will appoint the others; that all the ports in France were open to our shipping, and that several of our armed vessels, with their prizes, lay in the harbours of Brest and Nantz. That Dr. Franklin had purchased a 36 gun frigate, and was fitting her out; and that the bank for the Congress was increased to four millions.

Recreated from Purdie's Virginia Gazette, June 2, 1777.

FREE MONEY.

NEW YORK, May 23.—Sundry persons in the province of New York have been lately detected in attempting to pass counterfeit paper currency, having been tempted to follow the desperate employment by the terms offered in the following advertisement, taken from Hugh Gaine's gazette of the 14th ult. viz. "Persons going into the other colonies may be supplied with any number of continental Congress notes for the price of the paper per ream. They are so neatly and exactly executed, that there is no risk of getting them off, it being almost impossible to discover that they are not genuine. This has been proved by bills to a very large amount, which have been successfully circulated. Inquire for Q.E.D. at the coffeehouse, from 11 P.M. to 4 A.M. during the present month."

Recreated from The Virginia Gazette, May 23, 1777.

PHILADELPHIA, May 27.—We hear that Congress have ordered that an elegant Horse, properly caparisoned, be procured and presented to Major General Arnold, for his gallant behaviour against the enemy in their late expedition to Danbury, wherein he had one Horse killed and another wounded.

Recreated from The Virginia Gazette, June 6, 1777.

BRITISH LOSS AT SAAG HARBOUR.

CAPT. MEIG'S GREAT SUCCESS.

Extract of a letter from His Excellency General WASHINGTON *to* CONGRESS, *dated* Head Quarters, MIDDLE BROOK CAMP, 31st *May,* 1777.

"I have the pleasure to communicate a very agreeable piece of intelligence which I have received from General Parsons, of the destruction of 12 of the enemy's vessels at Sagg Harbour, upon the east end of Long Island. I give you his letter at length, which I think reflects high honour upon the conduct and bravery of Colonel Meigs, his officers and men."

NEW HAVEN, *May* 25, 1777.

DEAR GENERAL,

HAVING received information that the enemy were collecting forage, horses, &c. on the east end of Long Island, I ordered a detachment from the several regiments then at this place; consisting of 1 major, 4 captains, viz. Throop, Pond, Mansfield and Savage, 9 subalterns, and 220 non commissioned officers and privates, under command of Lieut. Col. Meigs, to attack their different posts on the island, and destroy the forage, &c. which they had collected.

Col. Meigs embarked his men here in 13 whale boats the 21st instant, and proceeded to Guilford; but the wind proving high, and the sea rough, could not pass the Sound until Friday the 23d. He left Guilford at one o'clock in the afternoon of the 23d with 170 of his detachment, under convoy of two armed sloops, and in company with another unarmed (to bring off prisoners) across the Sound to the North Branch of the island near Southold; where he arrived about 6 o'clock in the evening. The enemy's troops on this branch of the island had marched for New York two days before; but, about 60 of the enemy remaining at a place called Sagg Harbour, near 15 miles distant, on the South Branch of the island, he ordered the whale boats, with as many men as could be transported, across the Bay, over land to the Bay, where they re-embarked to the number of 130, and at about 12 o'clock arrived safe across the Bay, within about 4 miles of the Harbour; where having secured the boats in a wood under the care of a guard, Col. Meigs formed his little remaining detachment in proper order for attacking the different posts and quarters of the enemy, and securing the vessels and forage at the same time.

They marched in the greatest order and silence; and at two o'clock arrived at the Harbour. The several divisions, with fixed bayonets, attacked the guard and posts assigned them; whilst Capt. Throop, with the detachment under his command, secured the vessels and forage lying at the wharf. The alarm soon became general; when an armed schooner of 12 guns and 70 men, lying within 150 yards of the wharf, began a fire upon our troops (which continued without cessation for about three quarters of an hour) with grape and round shot; but the troops, with the greatest intrepidity, returned the fire upon the schooner, and set fire to the vessels and forage, and killed and captivated all the soldiers and sailors, except about six, who made their escape under cover of the night.

Twelve brigs and sloops, (one an armed vessel with 12 guns) about 120 tons of pressed hay, oats, corn, and other forage, 10 hhds. of rum, and a large quantity of other merchandize, were intirely consumed. It gives me great satisfaction to hear the officers and soldiers, without exception, behaved with the greatest bravery, order and intrepidity.

Col. Meigs having finished the business on which he was sent, returned safe with all his men to Guilford by 2 o'clock, P.M. yesterday with 90 prisoners; having, in 25 hours by land and water, transported his men full 90 miles, and succeeded in his attempt beyond my most sanguine expectations, without having a single man killed or wounded. It gives me singular pleasure to hear no disposition appeared in any one soldier to plunder the inhabitants, or violate private property, in the smallest degree; and that, even the cloathing, and other articles, belonging to the prisoners, the soldiers, with a generosity, (not learned from British troops) have, with great cheerfulness, been restored to them where they have fallen into their hands.

Major Humphry, who waits on your Excellency with the account, was in the action with Col. Meigs, and will be able to give you any further necessary information. A list of prisoners is inclosed.

I am, Your Excellency's
Most obedient humble servant,
SAM H. PARSONS.

Recreated from The Pennsylvania Packet, June 3, 1777.

WHERE IS THE BRITISH FLEET?

Extract of a letter from his Excellency *General* WASHINGTON, *Head Quarters, May* 31.

"I this morning received information, which I believe is not to be doubted, that on Saturday last a large fleet, said to consist of 100 sail, left New York, and stood out to sea. Whither they are destined, or what they had on board, remains to be known. If possessing Hudson's river should not be general Howe's first object, I should suppose his operations will be against Philadelphia, and that this fleet, if they have troops, are bound into Delaware Bay.

"Though my opinion is as above, yet I would take the liberty of suggesting, that it may be expedient to put your militia upon the most respectable footing that circumstances will admit, lest their destination should be more southern."

A NUMBER of good ARMORERS are immediately wanted to repair publick arms at *Richmond* town. Good wages will be given. Apply to col. *Turner Southall*.

Recreated from Purdie's Virginia Gazette, June 13, 1777.

WASHINGTON MOVES HEAD QUARTERS.

PHILADELPHIA, *June* 5.

WE can with pleasure inform our readers, that General Washington has now received such supplies of men, &c. that he has removed his head quarters from Morristown to Middle Brook, on the east side of the Rariton, within seven miles and a half of Brunswick, where his army (which is not composed of soldiers whose times of service are continually expiring, but of those enlisted for the war) are now encamped, and make a show that must please every person who is not a Tory. From our posts near Middle Brook we are able to see and watch the movements of the enemy, who are encamped on Brunswick hills, the west side of the Rariton.

By a gentleman from Charlestown, South Carolina, we learn that seven armed French vessels, one of them mounting 209 guns, arrived there about the 5th of May.

Part of a letter from BOUND BROOK, *May* 31.

"On Monday last we had a brush with the Philistines, killed three light horsemen, four Highlanders, and one lieutenant colonel; the latter was killed by a six pound shot. We had only two slightly wounded. The locusts have kept in, since they are not able to pay so dear for travelling so little a way. We have a pretty situation for our encampment, plenty of wood, and excellent water."

We hear the enemy at Brunswick have lately been reinforced with one brigade from Rhode Island and New York.

We can assure the publick, from good authority, that general Howe sends all the American soldiers who desert from the continental army to garrison Gibraltar, or some of the forts in the West India islands, where they will probably remain as slaves *in their army* for life, and that all the able bodied young men of York and Long Island are absolutely draughted to recruit mr. Howe's army.

PHILADELPHIA, *June* 7.—It is reported, and *believed*, that ammunition and clothing are deposited, by order of a *certain European court*, at New Orleans and the Havannah, with directions to lend them to such American vessels as may call for them.

MASSACHUSETTS ORDERS MILITIA.

The Massachusetts State have ordered that all their militia, from 16 years and upwards, immediately equip themselves with every thing necessary for immediate action, and hold themselves in readiness to march, at a minute's warning, to any place within their own territories, or to any of the United States that may hereafter be attacked by our unjust and cruel enemies.

Recreated from Purdie's Virginia Gazette, June 20, 1777.

ENEMY SIGHTS CROWN POINT.

BOSTON, *June* 5, 1777.—By a gentleman who arrived in town yesterday from Albany, we are informed, that an express passed through Pittsfield, last Friday, from Ticonderoga, which place he left yesterday fe'nnight, and advised, that the enemy had left St. John's, and were in sight of Crown Point when he came away, standing up the river, and it was expected that an engagement would ensue; however, should they risque an action, we have reason to think they will meet with a warm reception, as near three thousand men have already arrived at Ticonderoga, and many more are on their march for that place; artillery, stores, ammunition, &c. are going forward fast.

The enemy, are about 4000 strong; their magazines are almost all destroyed; seven different depositories of stores, provisions, &c. have been burnt; provisions are very scarce with them. Armed craft is building on lake George, for the security of the water.

Capt. Clouston, in a brig belonging to this State, has taken six prizes, and was left in chase of a seventh the 16th of April; the 6th prize, laden with salt, bread, &c.

bound from Topsham, in England, to Newfoundland, is arrived at a safe port; as is also a brig, bound from London to Guinea, laden with arms, powder, cordage, &c. A snow, from Newfoundland, for London, with fish; and a sloop, from Lisbon, with wine and lemons, are hourly looked for. Two brigs, laden with herrings, from Scotland, Capt. Clouston burnt.

By the prize from Topsham, which brings us the latest advices from England, we find no mention of General Burgoyne's coming to Boston with 13,000 men, as has been said in all our papers. Six thousand are reported in the London papers as a designed reinforcement for their whole army in America, but no place is specified where they are assembled, or where transports are ready to receive them.

The armaments of France and Spain are daily increasing—and the press in England hotter than ever. The assistance France has given by the supplies to the American States, appears to be thoroughly understood in England; accordingly, Lord Weymouth has pressed for an immediate declaration of war, but the Ministry dare not venture on so spirited a measure.

The Russians have taken the Precop from the Turks; and France, it is said, has found means to embroil again these two powers, to prevent Russia from aiding England in the American dispute. France is also applying to the States of Holland, to know what part they will take respecting the independency of America. It is evident they secretly wish to support it, and their merchants, and the body of the People speak openly and warmly for it. Indeed, the situation of Europe is such, that Britain, should she be able to raise a large body of troops in addition to what she has here, could not with safety to herself send them to America.

Our prospect brightens every day. A manly enduring for a little while some difficulties ever to be expected in such a struggle, and a few more spirited exertions, may, sooner than many are ready to imagine, place our country in the most happy security, and render it the praise of the whole earth.

Recreated from The Pennsylvania Packet, June 17, 1777.

THE HEALTH OF THE TROOPS.

Head Quarters, MIDDLE BROOK, *June* 4, 1777.

THE liberal provision made by Congress in the new medical arrangement, joined with a humane desire to prevent the repetition of the distresses which afflicted the brave American soldiers the last campaign, have drawn men of the first abilities into the field, to watch over the health and preserve the lives of the soldiers, many of them from very extensive and profitable practices, and every species of domestic happiness. Dr. William Brown of Virginia, Dr. James Craike of Maryland, and Dr. James Bond, jun. of Philadelphia, are appointed assistant directors general. Dr. Walter Jones of Virginia, and Dr. Benjamin Rush of Philadelphia, physician and surgeons general of the hospitals of the middle department. Under these, none but gentlemen of the best education, and well qualified, are employed as senior physicians, surgeons, &c.

The eastern and northern departments are filled with gentlemen of the first characters in those countries; and the publick may depend on it, that the greatest exertions of skill and industry shall be constantly made, and no cost spared, to make the sick and wounded soldiery comfortable and happy. As a consequence of the above liberal arrangement of the Honourable Congress, we do, with great pleasure, and equal truth, assure the publick (notwithstanding, many false and wicked reports propagated by the enemies of American liberty, and only calculated to retard the recruiting service) that all the military hospitals of the United States are in excellent order, and that the army enjoy a degree of health seldom to be seen or read of.

W. SHIPPEN, jun., *director general of the American hospitals.*

JOHN COCHRAN, *physician and surgeon general of the army in the middle department.*

Recreated from Purdie's Virginia Gazette, June 27, 1777.

THREE HUNDRED TORIES DESERT.

PHILADELPHIA, *June* 12, 1777.

WE hear that upwards of 300 Tories, belonging to general Delancey's brigade at Fort Independence, have deserted, and joined general Putnam's army, near Peekskill. Their leader was the reverend mr. Sayre, an Episcopal minister, well known formerly for his attachment to the English government. Severity of duty, scarcity of provisions, and ill treatment in other respects, they say, were the reasons for their deserting; and from their miserable appearance, being greatly emaciated, and almost destitute of clothing, there is no room to doubt the veracity of what the poor devils now assert, and that they have, in some measure, done penance for their misconduct and credulity.

We learn from good authority, that the governour of New Orleans, on the Mississippi, has seized 14 or 15 sail of vessels belonging to Great Britain, by way of reprisal for seizing a sloop on Lake Ponchartrain, and for several other insults offered to the Spanish government, particularly seizing a number of American vessels in the Mississippi last year, The governour also ordered all the subjects of George of Britain (or, as they are termed by the Spaniards, the royalists) to depart his government immediately.

By letters from the southward we learn, that col. Elbert has marched at the head of a small brigade against the enemy in East Florida; and that, from the well known abilities of this gentleman, great expectations are formed. The reduction of St. Augustine seems to be very properly considered by the southern states as an object of great importance. At present, it is the enemy's key to the Indians. It would be an excellent one in the hands of the continent, to the Spanish settlements.

We are told, that out of 60 sail of vessels with provisions for the West Indies, under convoy of the Druid, 40 of them were missing, out of which 26 are known to be taken by American privateers.

THE DRUM SOUNDS TO ARMS.

ENEMY AT BRUNSWICK.

Extract of a letter from general WEEDON, *dated camp at* MIDDLE BROOK, *June* 13, 1777.

THE enemy have assembled all their troops at Brunswick, and a formidable appearance they make. New York, Long Island, Staten Island, Amboy, and the communication from thence to Brunswick, are drained in a great measure of troops. Howe has come over himself, and seems determined to put his much talked of plan in execution.

However, if we can but give him a rap over his fingers, the campaign will be pretty well settled; and I have great hopes this may be done, as our army are in the highest spirits, and well founded with every necessary implement for the purpose. It is now as well arranged as any army in the universe, and it is a pleasure and honour to belong to it. Every thing goes on with the greatest regularity. The troops are well clothed, well armed, and there is great abundance of good provisions; the hospitals are furnished with every accommodation necessary for the sick (of which, thank God, we have but few), the ablest surgeons on the continent are employed to attend them, and, in short, so differently circumstanced than what we have been accustomed to, that the continental army is visited and admired by thousands from all parts of the world. Business in the fighting way accumulates; the drum sounds to arms. Adieu. God bless you.

Recreated from Purdie's Virginia Gazette, June 27, 1777.

To be SOLD cheap, A COACH, the body of which is out of repair, the carriage and wheels very good. For terms apply to the subscriber, about a mile from *Sewell's* ordinary, in *Gloucester* county.

JOHN WHITING.

Recreated from Purdie's Virginia Gazette, June 6, 1777.

In CONGRESS, June 14, 1777.
Resolved, That the FLAG of the United States be THIRTEEN STRIPES alternate red and white; that the Union be THIRTEEN STARS white in a blue field, representing a new constellation.

Recreated from The Pennsylvania Packet, September 2, 1777.

BRITISH DESIGNS TO NO EFFECT.

CORELL'S FERRY, *June* 15.—11 *o'clock p.m.*
To Major General MIFFLIN.

I have received no intelligence from General Washington since four o'clock last evening, at which time the enemy were encamped at Somerset Court House, supposed to be seven thousand in number, under the command of Generals Howe and Cornwallis. This is doubtless their main body. Their first design seems to have been to have cut off General Sullivan's retreat, and possessed themselves of this place; finding General Sullivan had frustrated their intentions by a forced march, they appeared to have given over their first design, and now wish to draw General Washington from his strong hold; which, if they can effect, probably a body from Brunswick will take possession of it. General Washington will doubtless disappoint them, as he remains quiet in his encampment.

The Militia turn out in great numbers in the Jersies. General Sullivan has gone to Fleming Town (twelve miles from this); the troops who arrive here are immediately sent after him. I am very fearful the enemy will retire to Brunswick before you arrive with your reinforcements, and oblige us to attack them at a disadvantage; for fight them we must; when all our reinforcements are in we cannot avoid it with honour. Our men are in high spirits, and in four days we shall have upwards of 20,000 men. General Putnam has 8000 men with him. General Washington has wrote three days since for 4000 to be sent immediately to him. I expect every minute to hear from our army and the enemy. Every intelligence of consequence shall be forwarded to you directly.   I am &c.
            B. ARNOLD.

Recreated from The Pennsylvania Packet, June 17, 1777.

BRITISH FANTASIES.

The following is a copy of an intercepted letter from a person at RHODE ISLAND, *to* Ned Winslow, *at* PLYMOUTH; *and is here inserted by way of specimen of the lying abilities of the Tories, never more necessary than at this time to cheer up each other's desponding spirits.*

RHODE ISLAND, *June* 17, 1777.

Dear SIR,

I CANNOT omit this opportunity of returning you, and *the rest of my friends*, my many thanks for your civilities to mrs. Esdaile during the time we were at Plymouth. There is no expressing the joys of our little party, on being safely landed among our own people. We found your amiable daughter here well, and in high spirits. I don't know how many colonels, majors, &c. &c. &c. the *white wench's* black eyes (according to Shakespear) have smote.

The rebel game, I take it, will be up this summer, when I fancy they will lose at a d___d rate. *Poor Ticonderoga*, we are credibly informed, was taken by general Carleton the 27th of last month! Philadelphia will soon follow the same fate.

Lord Howe is gone, or going very soon, up the Delaware, with a large force; and I suppose the general *beats his march* by land about the same time, with a considerable army. He has at least 30,000, with continentals, which are at least 10,000, the last return being 7800. Your son, I hear is well at New York, whom I hope soon to see; but, at present, we have no opportunity. I suppose you have heard of the boasted exploits of the Yankies in an attempt on the picket guard last Wednesday night, and two nights after on this island; and I make no doubt but they have, according to custom, killed 2 or 300 of the enemy; three they have killed, and wounded one, but in a *rascally* manner. I should write more but the bearer of this is going directly. My respects and compliments to all *friends*. I am, dear sir, *your much obliged* humble servant,   SAMUEL ESDAILE.

Recreated from Purdie's Virginia Gazette, July 25, 1777.

ENEMY RETIRE TO BRUNSWICK.

MILITIA ASSEMBLED.

Extract of a letter from General WASHINGTON *to* CONGRESS, *dated* MIDDLE BROOK, *June* 20, 1777.

"When I had the honour of addressing you last, I informed you that the main body of the enemy had marched from Brunswick and extended their van as far as Somerset Court house. I am now to acquaint you, that after encamping between these two points and beginning a line of redoubts, they changed their ground yesterday morning and in the course of the preceding night, and returned to Brunswick again, burning as they went several valuable dwelling houses.

"I must observe, and with peculiar satisfaction I do it, that on the first notice of the enemy's movements, the Militia assembled in the most spirited manner, firmly determined to give them every annoyance in their power and to afford us every possible aid. This I thought it my duty to mention, in justice to their conduct, and I am inclined to believe that General Howe's return, thus suddenly made, must have been in consequence of the information he received that the people were in and flying to arms in every quarter to oppose him."

Published by order of CONGRESS,
CHARLES THOMPSON, Secretary.

T I C K E T S
IN THE
AMERICAN STATES LOTTERY
TO BE SOLD BY
WALLACE AND DAVIDSON
IN
A N N A P O L I S.

Recreated from The Pennsylvania Packet, June 24, 1777.

ENEMY EVACUATE BRUNSWICK.

Extract of a letter from General WASHINGTON *to* CONGRESS, *dated Head Quarters*, MIDDLE BROOK, *June* 22, 1777. 11 *o'clock*, P.M.

I HAVE the honour and pleasure to inform you that the enemy evacuated Brunswick this morning, and retired to Amboy, burning many houses as they went along. Some of them, from the appearance of the flames, were considerable buildings.

From several pieces of information, and from a variety of circumstances, it was evident that a move was in agitation, and it was the general opinion that it was intended this morning. I therefore detached three brigades, under the command of Major General Green, to fall upon their rear, and kept the main body of the army paraded upon the heights, to support them if there should be occasion.

A party of Col. Morgan's regiment of light infantry attacked and drove the Hessian picket about sun-rise, and upon the appearance of General Wayne's brigade, and Morgan's regiment (who got first to the ground) opposite Brunswick, the enemy immediately crossed the bridge to the east side of the river, and threw themselves into redoubts, which they had before constructed. Our troops advanced briskly upon them, upon which they quitted the redoubts without making any opposition, and retired to the Amboy road.

As all our troops, from the difference of their stations in camp, had not come up when the enemy began to move off, it was impossible to check them, and as their numbers were far greater than we had any reason to expect, being, as we were informed afterwards, between four and five thousand men. Our people persued them as far as Piscataway, but finding it impossible to overtake them, and fearing they might be led on too far from the main body, they returned to Brunswick. By information of the inhabitants, General Howe, Lord Cornwallis, and General Grant, were in the town when the alarm was first given, but they quitted it very soon after.

In the pursuit, Colonel Morgan's rifle-men exchanged several sharp fires with the enemy, which, it is imagined, did considerable execution. I am in hopes that they afterwards fell in with General Maxwell, who was detached last night with a strong party to lie between Brunswick and Amboy, in order to interrupt any convoys or parties that might be passing; but I have yet heard nothing from him.

General Green desires me to make mention of the conduct and bravery of General Wayne and Colonel Morgan, and of their officers and men upon this occasion, as they constantly advanced upon an enemy far superior to them in numbers, and well secured behind strong redoubts.

General Sullivan advanced from Rocky Hill to Brunswick with his division, but as he did not receive his orders of march till very late at night, he did not arrive until the enemy had been gone some time.

Published by order of CONGRESS,
  CHARLES THOMPSON, *Secretary.*

THE ROAD TO AMBOY.

Extract of a letter from MOUNT PROSPECT, *June 22, 1777.*

"Here we have been some hours viewing the retreat of the enemy. They have left Brunswick, and all the road from thence to Amboy is covered with smoke, which we have the best reason to believe are the houses they have set fire to as they go. General Green was below the landing near Brunswick, on this side of the river. Two thousand of the enemy within half a mile. General Varnum advancing along the Rariton, and General Sullivan pushing direct to Brunswick. General Maxwell is on our left, towards Woodbridge, to intercept them on their way. We can, from this noble situation, trace many of their routs.

"Anxious for the event, and eagerly watching for return of messengers, I defer adding more than that every thing appears favourable to us."

THEIR USUAL BARBARITY.

PHILADELPHIA, *June* 24.—By an express arrived yesterday afternoon from New Jersey, we have the important intelligence of the enemy's having retreated from Somerset Court house to Brunswick, and were on their march from that place towards Amboy, burning and destroying many valuable houses on their way and exercising their usual barbarity to the inhabitants in their power:—That a part of our army had taken possession of Brunswick, while a large number were in pursuit of the enemy and had engaged some of their rear guards.—No particular accounts are yet come to hand, but the following letter, (received by the above express) tho' imperfect, will serve to convey some idea of the manner of their retreat—

"Camp *at* MIDDLEBROOK, *evening of* 22d *June.*

"Our troops were within a mile or less of the bridge at Brunswick when General Howe with the party passed from that place. Gen. Wayne with his brigade pushed the enemy so close, that they retired from redoubt to redoubt, without having time to form. All their troops that came up pushed forward with vigour, and had those on the West of Rariton been so lucky as to have come up at the same instant, the stroke must have been capital. The enemy seem to retire to Amboy in haste. They were pushed to Piscataway by Col. Morgan's Riflemen (a fine corps) and the troops under Gen. Green, and must have suffered considerably. Our loss is three or four killed, and as many wounded. They have burnt numbers of houses, and their whole possessions show what they must have suffered last winter; indeed their waste exceeds all I could fancy, tho' often described to me. They have left their reputation; their troops dispirited; their plans subverted; a new scene of action to commence; and of course one half of the campaign lost to them.

"Our troops are in good health, high spirits, and ready to pursue the blow."

ALL IN GREAT CONFUSION.

Extract of a letter from FREEHOLD, *June* 24.

"I laid a bait last Saturday to break up the plundering Col. George Taylor; it so far succeeded that I was within an ace of taking the whole; we took one white man and one negro. While the rest were swimming towards a boat that was coming to take them off, we fired upon them, and killed one, and wounded another, who were both hauled into the boat.

"Last Sunday we discovered the enemy ferrying over from Amboy to Staten Island, and this morning we took four Tories, who were coming over to throw themselves upon the mercy of their countrymen. They relate that they went as waggoners with the British army from Brunswick to Somerset, and expected they were coming to Philadelphia; that they retreated with them to Brunswick, from thence to Amboy, and thence to Staten Island; that so far as they could learn, General Howe retreated because he did not think proper to attack General Washington, or to leave him in his rear while he should attempt a march towards Philadelphia; that some said in the army, that they were going to England; others, that they were going up the North river; others, up the East river; but that they were all in great confusion. They have pitched their tents upon Staten Island."

Recreated from The Virginia Gazette, July 11, 1777.

Extract of a letter from PHILADELPHIA, *June* 24, 1777.

"We have certain accounts of the enemy's main body getting to Amboy, and throwing the bridge they intended last winter for the Delaware across the Sound, in order, it is thought, to get over to Staten Island, if they can. A number of our army is surrounding their advance guard, which is about four miles out. I think we should give them a severe check this time. I give you joy on having possession of Brunswick once more, and in hopes we should do very well yet."

ARMY MOVES TO QUIBBLETOWN.

To CONGRESS,
QUIBBLETOWN, *June* 25, 1777.

"When I had the honour to address you last, it was on the subject of the enemy's retreat from Brunswick to Amboy, and of the measures pursued to annoy them. At the time of writing, the information I had received respecting their loss was rather vague and uncertain; but we have reason to believe, from intelligence through various channels since, that it was pretty considerable and fell chiefly on the grenadiers and light infantry, who formed their covering party. The enclosed copy of a letter corresponds with other accounts on this head, and with the declarations of some deserters. Some of the accounts are, that officers were heard to say they had not suffered so severely since the affair at Princeton.

"After the evacuation of Brunswick, I determined, with the advice of my General officers, to move the whole army the next morning to this post, where they would be nearer the enemy, and might act according to circumstances. In this I was prevented by rain, and they only moved yesterday morning.

"It is much to be regretted, that an express sent off to General Maxwell on Saturday night, to inform him of General Green's movements towards Brunswick, that he might conduct himself accordingly, did not reach him. Whether the express went designedly to the enemy, or was taken, is not known, but there is reason to believe he fell into their hands. If General Maxwell had received the order, there is no doubt but their whole rear guard would have been cut off. This the enemy confessed themselves, as we are well informed by persons in Bonam Town.

"By a reconnoitering party just returned, it is reported as a matter of doubt whether any of the enemy have removed from Amboy; though it is almost certain they have transported a great deal of their baggage. I have the honour to be, &c."

G. WASHINGTON.

"May it please your Excellency,

"I have thought proper to trouble your Excellency with the following intelligence, received by three different ways, that the greatest part of the fleet, from New York harbour, has removed to the Watering Place and Prince's Bay, where the baggage and troops, passing from the Jerseys, are constantly embarking; that the transport at New York, cut down for a floating battery, has 26, 24, and 18 pounders, and lies off the ground battery in the river; another which they have been fitting for the same purpose, is neglected and unfinished. General Howe arrived at New York on Sunday afternoon, the whole of which day they were employed in removing the wounded soldiers from the docks to the hospitals there, said to amount to five hundred men."

Published by order of CONGRESS.
CHARLES THOMPSON, Secretary.

Recreated from The Virginia Gazette, July 11, 1777.

COUNTERFEIT THIRTY DOLLAR BILLS.

They are done in imitation of those dated May 10, 1775; the words in the face of the bill are pretty well imitated, but not so uniform as in the true bills; in the first line the top of the *y* in the word *thirty* appears deficient, and the words *Continental Currency* in the borders, are cut finer than the genuine bills. The back of the bill is not so well imitated; the flowers more open, the rays of the sun in the right hand device much smaller, and the ship appears plainer than in the true ones. The paper of the counterfeits, not so thick as the true bills, is smoother, and appears of a bluish dingy colour. On the least inspection they may be seen to be done from a copperplate, the letters of which do not make any impression in the paper like pointing types. We think, after this notice, the publick cannot be deceived by them.

By order of the Treasury Board,
JOHN GIBSON, Auditor General.

Recreated from The Virginia Gazette, June 13, 1777.

BURGOYNE IN CANADA.

Extract of a letter from PHILADELPHIA, *June* 26.

"By an express from general Schuyler, at Albany, we learn that Burgoyne was arrived in Canada, and that great preparations were making by him to attack Ticonderoga. It is expected Howe will now turn his attention that way."

ALBEMARLE, *June* 17, 1777.

BROUGHT by mistake from *Fredericksburg*, some time last fall, an old BLACK LEATHER TRUNK, much worn, marked W W on the outside, *John Merriman* the trunk maker's name. Supposing it to be the property of a lady just arrived from *Philadelphia*, it was broke open, and found to contain the 4th, 5th, and 6th volumes of *Shakespear's* works, a volume of plays with *R. Newsum* 1771 printed in red letters, the 3d volume of *Chrysal*, a small pocket and sundry letters directed to *James Haldane* coppersmith *Petersburg*, some wearing apparel, shirts and stocks marked W W, brass and iron wire, a bayonet, pair of pistols, buckle brushes, ivory sword handles, sword swivels, and sundry other articles. The owner of the said trunk, upon sending for it, will have it and the contents delivered by applying to

THOMAS WALKER, jun.

WANTED to purchase or hire immediately, a NEGRO GARDENER. Inquire of the Printer.

Recreated from Purdie's Virginia Gazette, July 4, 1777.

A SCALPING ACCIDENT.

Part of a letter from FORT STANWIX, *June* 27.

"There is not, at present, any appearance of our being attacked by the enemy. We are however making all the preparations for a defence, which the state of the garrison permits. The Six Nations are in general friendly, and seemed resolved not to take an active part against us. We are not therefore under any apprehensions from the body of Indians, though we have reasons to fear some mischief will be done by strolling individuals, who do not govern themselves by the sentiments of the nation to which they belong.

"A recent instance of barbarity shows that this fear is not groundless. I was but just come into the fort, when we received the disagreeable news of the cruel treatment of Captain Gregg, and the murder of one Matthison, an alert private. Two Indians, about three quarters of a mile from the fort, having fired upon them, killed Matthison on the spot, and wounded the captain in the back; after scalping them both, the savages ran off with precipitation.

"One of our dogs, lighting upon the spot where the unfortunate victims were lying, made the first discovery; running to some of the soldiers, hastening back to the tragical stage, and returning to the soldiers, with every appearance of uneasiness, he excited an anxiety in them to know what might be the cause of such extraordinary motions. This circumstance was the means of saving the life of Capt. Gregg; his wounds were immediately dressed, and he now lies under the care of Dr. Woodruff, who treats him with the greatest attention and tenderness; his recovery is possible.

"A number of sachems and warriors from the Oneida-Castle and Eriskie, soon waited upon Col. Gansevoort, and expressed their sorrow for the accident, asserting their innocence, throwing the blame upon the tory Indians, and declaring their readiness to use every means to discover the murderers and bring them to justice."

Recreated from The Maryland Gazette, August 7, 1777.

ESCAPE FROM A PRISON SHIP.

BOSTON, *June* 26, 1777.—Last Sunday arrived at Cape Ann, from Halifax in Nova Scotia, ten American sailors, in a whale boat, who made their escape from the Lord Stanley, a prison ship in that harbour, the 1st instant. They were part of seventy-five American prisoners, that were draughted from on board the said prison ship to help to man the Rainbow of 44 guns, the Milford of 28, and the Cabot of 16. We learn by the above men, that all the reinforcements coming to America from England consisted of about 4000 men; and that they had all sailed, in concert with a large fleet of victualers. We likewise learn, that two transports, laden with all kinds of brass cannon, ammunition, &c. arrived at Halifax, some time in May, from the enemy at New York.

The pirate ship of 64 guns (lately mentioned to have been chased by commodore Manly) with two transports under convoy, it is said, arrived safe at Pirate road, near Sandy Hook.

Two or Three transports, with recruits, arrived at Rhode Island last Wednesday, from Europe.

PORTSMOUTH, *June* 21.—Capt. Bartlet, in the brigantine Pinnet, arrived at a safe port the 11th instant, from Nantz, belonging to the state of Massachusetts, with a cargo of 400 barrels of powder, 400 chests of small arms, 4 casks of flints, 4 ditto files, 1000 bars of steel, 5 casks of leather shoes, 20 tuns of pig lead, 4 double fortified four-pounders, and 8 swivels.

Recreated from Purdie's Virginia Gazette, July 25, 1777.

August 1, 1777.

SALT-PANS, ten feet square, and fifteen inches deep, with screws ready to join and fit them up, made at Catoctin furnace, about ten miles from Frederick-Town, at fifty-five pounds per ton. If different fixes are desired, they will be attempted.—Carriage from the furnace to Baltimore is now at seven pounds a tun.

JAMES JOHNSON.

Recreated from The Maryland Gazette, August 7, 1777.

A HOWE FEINT?

To CONGRESS, MIDDLE BROOK, *June* 28.

On Thursday morning General Howe advanced with his whole army, in several columns, from Amboy as far as Westfield. We are certainly informed, that the troops sent to Staten Island returned the preceding evening, and it is said with an augmentation of marines; so that carrying them there was a feint, with intention to deceive us. His design, in this sudden movement, was either to bring on a general engagement upon disadvantageous terms, considering matters in any point of view, or to cut off our light parties, and Lord Stirling's division, which was sent down to support them, or to posses himself of the heights and passes in the mountains on our left. The two last seemed to be the first objects of his attention, as his march was rapid against these parties, and indicated a strong disposition to gain those passes.

In this situation of affairs, it was thought absolutely necessary that we should move our force from the low grounds to occupy the heights before them, which was effected. As they advanced they fell in with some of our light parties, and part of Lord Stirling's division, with which they had some smart skirmishing, with but very little loss, I believe, on our side, except in three field pieces, which unfortunately fell into the enemy's hands; but not having obtained returns yet, I cannot determine it with certainty, nor can we ascertain what the enemy's loss was.

As soon as we had gained the passes, I detached a body of light troops, under Brigadier General Scott, to hang on their flanks and to watch their motions, and ordered Morgan's corps of rifle men to join him since. The enemy remained at Westfield till yesterday afternoon, when about 9 o'clock they moved towards Spanktown, with our light troops in their rear, and pursuing. The enemy have plundered all before them, and it is said burnt some houses.

I have the honour to be, &c.
G. WASHINGTON.

Recreated from The Virginia Gazette, July 11, 1777.

BRITISH AT CROWN POINT.

By a letter from Albany, dated the 28th ult. we learn, that the enemy's fleet and army are arrived at Crown Point—that they have sent strong detachments, one to cut off Fort George, and the other either to surprise Skeensborough, or throw themselves on the communication between that and Ticonderoga.

The advices by the Hartford post make the enemy very considerable at Crown Point.

Recreated from The Maryland Gazette, July 24, 1777.

ENEMY REMAIN AT AMBOY.

Part of a letter from MIDDLE BROOK, *June* 30.

"The enemy still remain at Amboy. From intelligence received this day, it is doubtful wether they intend retreating to New York, or not. The enemy within these few days have committed the most wanton barbarities, burning houses, cutting down fine orchards, plundering the inhabitants, and threatening to destroy the poor helpless women, by burning them in their houses; these wanton barbarities convince me they intend to embark for New York, or to some other part of the continent; a few days will determine their route. All their horses are carried over to Staten Island, and the greatest part of their baggage on board their shipping.

"Our army is healthy, and in high spirits, and this campaign, I doubt not, will settle the dispute to our satisfaction. No doubt Howe must be greatly dispirited, finding those, to whom he last year gave protections, tuning out to a man, to oppose him. Should they turn and push for Philadelphia, on the banks of the Delaware, they will certainly meet the fate they deserve. The militia are in high spirits, and in readiness to turn out at a moment's warning. Should they attempt Philadelphia, I make not the least doubt but an army of 12,000 men will oppose them in front, while ours will gall them in the rear. Every day declares victory on our side."

Recreated from The Virginia Gazette, July 18, 1777.

THE LADIES OF AMELIA COUNTY.

We hear the young ladies of Amelia county, considering the situation of our country in particular, and that of the United States in general, having entered into a resolution not to permit the addresses of any person (be his circumstances or situation in life what they will) unless he has served in the American armies long enough to prove, by his valour, that he is deserving of their love.

We have the pleasure to acquaint the publick, that the harvest has turned out remarkable well in most parts of the country, and that there is a fine prospect of corn and fruit. These blessings, added to our being in a fair way of establishing our freedom and independence, must afford the highest satisfaction to every true American.

Recreated from Purdie's Virginia Gazette, July 4, 1777.

FISH-KILL, *July* 3.—Yesterday was executed at Peek's-Kill, a soldier who had several times enlisted and received the bounty, and was deserting to the enemy. He had enlisted and deserted from the enemy also.

Recreated from The Virginia Gazette, July 25, 1777.

Continental Navy Board, Philadelphia, June 26, 1777.

WHEREAS an exchange of prisoners in the Naval Department is now in agitation, and likely to be accomplished, NOTICE is hereby given to all officers, seamen, marines, and others, in or near this city, belonging to British vessels of war, or merchantmen, who have been taken by American privateers, or Continental vessels of war; and to all officers, seamen, marines, and others belonging to the American navy, privateers, or merchantmen, who are prisoners on parole, that they apply to this office as speedily as possible, in the forenoon, between the hours of nine and one o'clock, and enter their names and stations, with the times of their capture, for the purpose of negotiating an exchange.

JOHN NIXON.
JOHN WHARTON.
F. HOPKINSON.

Recreated from The Pennsylvania Packet, July 1, 1777.

THE 4TH OF JULY.

PHILADELPHIA, *July* 5, 1777.

YESTERDAY the 4th of July, being the Anniversary of the Independence of the United States of America, was celebrated in this city with demonstrations of joy and festivity. About noon all the armed ships and gallies in the river were drawn up before the city, dressed in the gayest manner, with the colours of the United States and streamers displayed. At one o'clock, the yards being properly manned, they began the celebration of the day by a discharge of thirteen cannon from each of the ships, and one from each of the thirteen gallies, in honour of the Thirteen United States.

In the afternoon an elegant dinner was prepared for Congress, to which were invited the President and Supreme Executive Council, and Speaker of the Assembly of this State, the General Officers and Colonels of the army, and strangers of eminence, and members of the several Continental Boards in town.

The Hessian band of music taken in Trenton the 26th December last, attended and heightened the festivity with some fine performances suited to the joyous occasion, while a corps of British deserters, taken into the service of the continent by the State of Georgia, being drawn up before the door, filled up the intervals with feux de joie. After dinner a number of toasts were drank, all breaking independence, and a generous love of liberty, and commemorating the memories of those brave and worthy patriots who gallantly exposed their lives, and fell gloriously in defence of freedom and the righteous cause of their country. Each toast was followed by a discharge of artillery and small arms, and a suitable piece of music by the Hessian band.

The glorious fourth of July was reiterated three times, accompanied with triple discharges of cannon and small arms, and loud huzzas that resounded from street to street through the city.

Towards evening several troops of horse, a corps of artillery, and a brigade of North Carolina forces, which was in town on its way to join the grand army, were drawn up in Second street and reviewed by Congress and the General Officers. The evening was closed with the ringing of bells, and at night there was a grand exhibition of fireworks, which began and concluded with thirteen rockets on the commons, and the city was beautifully illuminated. Every thing was conducted with the greatest order and decorum, and the face of joy and gladness was universal.

Thus may the 4th of July, that glorious and ever memorable day, be celebrated through America, by the sons of freedom, from age to age till time shall be no more. Amen, and amen.

Recreated from The Virginia Gazette, July 18, 1777.

CHARLESTOWN, [S. CAROLINA] *July* 7, 1777.

FRIDAY last being the first anniversary of the glorious formation of the American Empire, when Thirteen Colonies, driven by necessity, threw off the yoke, and rejected the tyranny, of Great Britain, by declaring themselves Free, Independent, and Sovereign States, the same was commemorated by every demonstration of joy. Ringing of bells ushered in the day. At Sunrise American colours were displayed from all the forts and batteries and vessels in the harbour. The Charles Town Regiment of Militia, commanded by the Hon. Col. Charles Pinkney and the Charles Town Artillery Company commanded by Capt. Thomas Gimbrel, were assembled upon the parade, and reviewed by His Excellency the President, who was attended upon this occasional by His Honour the Vice President, and the Honourable the Members of the Privy Council. At one o'clock the several forts, beginning at Fort Moultrie on Sullivan's Island, discharged 76 pieces of cannon, alluding to the glorious year 1776, and the militia and artillery fired three general volleys.

His Excellency the President then gave a most elegant entertainment in the Council Chamber, at which were present all the members of the legislature then in town, all the public officers, civil and military, the Clergy, and many strangers of note, to the amount of more than double the number that ever observed the birth-day of the present misguided and unfortunate King of Great Britain.

After dinner the following toasts were drank, viz. 1, The Free Independent, and Sovereign States of America. 2, The Great Council of America—may wisdom preside in all its deliberations. 3, General Washington. 4, The American army and navy—may they be victorious and invincible. 5, The nations in friendship or alliance with America. 6, The American Ambassadors at foreign Courts. 7, The 4th of July, 1776. 8, The memory of the officers and soldiers who have bravely fallen in defence of America. 9, South Carolina. 10, May only those Americans enjoy freedom who are ready to die for its defence. 11, Liberty triumphant. 12, Confusion, shame and disgrace, to our enemies—may the foes to America (slaves to tyranny) humble and fall before her. 13, May the Rising States of America reach the summit of human power and grandeur, and enjoy every blessing.

Each toast being succeeded by a salute of 13 guns, which were fired by Capt. Gimbrel's Company from their two field pieces with admirable regularity. The day having been spent in festivity and the most conspicuous joy and harmony, the evening was concluded with illuminations, &c. far exceeding any that had ever been exhibited before.

Princeton, July 10, 1777.

NOTICE is hereby given to the Public, That the COLLEGE of New-Jersey was opened on Tuesday, the eighth instant. It is therefore requested that the Under Graduates would repair to Princeton immediately, taking care to provide themselves with books, as none are to be had there.

JOHN WITHERSPOON.

Recreated from The Pennsylvania Packet, July 29, 1777.

DANGER AT TICONDEROGA.

At a council of GENERAL OFFICERS *held at* TICONDEROGA, *July 5, 1777.*

GENERAL St. Claire presented to the council, that as there is every reason to believe that the batteries of the enemy are ready to open upon the Ticonderoga side, and that the camp is very much exposed to their fire, and to be enfiladed on all quarters; and as there is also reason to expect an attack upon Ticonderoga and Mount Independence at the same time, in which case neither could draw any support from the other; he desires their opinion, whether it would be most proper to remove the tents to the low ground where they would be less exposed, or whether the whole of the troops should be drawn over to Mount Independence, the more effectually to provide for the defence of that post.

At the same time the general begged leave to inform them, that the whole of our force consisted of two thousand and eighty-nine effective rank and file, including one hundred and twenty-four artificers unarmed, besides the corps of artillery, and about nine hundred militia that have joined us, and cannot stay but a few days.

The council were unanimously of opinion, that it is impossible with our force to defend Ticonderoga and Mount Independence, and that the troops, cannon and stores should be removed this night, if possible, to Mount Independence.

2d. Whether, after the division of the army at Ticonderoga have retreated to Mount Independence, we shall be in a situation to defend that post, or in case it cannot be defended, if a retreat into the country will be practicable.

The council are unanimously of opinion, that as the enemy have already nearly surrounded us, and there remains nothing more to invest us completely but their occupying the neck of land betwixt the lakes and the east creek, which is not more than a quarter of a mile over, and possessing themselves of the Narrows betwixt us and Skeensborough, and thereby cutting off all communication with the country; a retreat ought to be undertaken as soon as possible, and that we shall be very fortunate to effect it.

Signed,   A. St. Clair, Maj. Gen.
            De Roche Fermoy, B.G.
            Enoch Poor, B.G.
            John Patterson, B.G.
            Col. Commandant Long.
            Isaac Budd Dunn, A.D.C.

Published by order of CONGRESS.
CHARLES THOMPSON, Secretary.

Recreated from Purdie's Virginia Gazette, August 1, 1777.

INDIAN ATROCITIES.

TOMAHAWK STICKING IN HIS HEAD.

Extract of a letter from FORT STANWIX, *dated July 4, 1777.*

"Ensign Spoore, of Captain De Witt's company, was out with 16 men cutting sods at the Wood Creek Landing, where a party of Indians fired on them. This place is about a half mile from the fort. I took a party of men and went after them, but was a little too late. I found one of our men on the road half dead and scalped, another coming in, shot through both arms; and about two miles further I found a third dead and scalped, with a tomahawk sticking in his head. I still pursued on further, but it being towards evening, and having no provision, I thought best to return, and brought in the wounded and dead men. Four men and the Ensign they took off with them, two of whom were of my company. This is another specimen of the tender mercies of the King of Britain, in his hiring the Savages to murder us. By this also, you may read what unnatural animals the Tories are, who have an immediate hand in promoting these barbarities."

BURNT, STRIPPED AND DESTROYED.

Extract of a letter from MORRISTOWN, *July* 5.

"The British burnt, stripped, and destroyed all as they went along. Women and children were left without food to eat, or raiment to put on. Three hundred barrels of flour were sent down towards Westfield and Ash swamp, by order of his Excellency, to be distributed among the sufferers. The enemy even destroyed all the bibles, and books of divinity they came across; this I assert as a fact."

FISH-KILL, *July* 10, 1777.—We hear by express, and by the Albany post, that Ticonderoga is in the hands of the enemy. The account we have received is very imperfect, the post says he just came off as the express arrived at Albany, and informs that our people had retreated from the fort, being unable to defend it; they brought off their small arms, &c.

We learn that a man was hanged at Albany a few days ago, who had been recruiting for the enemy. Another was hanged the other day at Livingston's Manor, for a similar crime.

PHILADELPHIA, *July* 12, 1777.—By late advices from New York, we hear the Hessian and British troops are upon such bad terms that the former have positively refused to do duty with the latter. And that General Howe is gone or going to Europe, being himself greatly disgusted.

Recreated from The Virginia Gazette, July 25, 1777.

ANNAPOLIS, July 10. BY a letter from Philadelphia we are informed that Howe has evacuated the Jerseys, and it is supposed his destination is for the highlands, up the North river, in order to facilitate a junction with general Burgoyne.

Recreated from Purdie's Virginia Gazette, July 18, 1777.

RETREAT FROM TICONDEROGA.

A NEW POST UNCERTAIN.

Extract of a letter from major general SCHUYLER *to* general WASHINGTON.

SARATOGA, *July* 7, 1777.

"*Dear Sir*,

"Soon after I had dispatched the Letter which I did myself the Honor to address to your Excellency from Stillwater I met with Lieutenant Colonel Hay, deputy quarter master general, who was at Ticonderoga. He informs me that on Saturday it had been agreed upon to retreat from Ticonderoga and Mount Independence. That between two & three o'clock on Sunday morning, General St. Clair, with the rest of the general officers and the army, marched out of the lines at Mount Independence. That Colonel Long, with about six hundred men, embarked on board our few vessels, and in batteaus. That just before they arrived at Skenesborough they were overtaken by the enemy's vessels, in which we lost all our ammunition.

"The Troops under colonel Long are arrived at Fort Ann; where general St. Clair is with the main body I have not yet learnt—Colonel Hay imagined he would come by the way of Skenesborough, if so, he will fall in with the enemy, who have taken possession there—Capt. Dantignore, who is just arrived here, confirms Col. Hay's account, except as to general St. Clair, who he understood was to march to No. 4. This is not likely. I have dispatched an officer to meet General St. Clair, and requested that he should march by the shortest rout to Fort Edward. As I have related the above from memory, I may have omitted some, and misapprehended other circumstances. It is impossible to say what post we shall take; it depends on the rout the enemy mean to pursue."

Published by order of CONGRESS.

CHARLES THOMPSON, Secretary.

Recreated from The Maryland Gazette, July 24, 1777.

300 BRITISH SHIPS READY.

PHILADELPHIA, *July* 10.—We this morning learn from Staten Island, that there are at the Watering Place about 300 sail of transports, and other ships; that the enemy's light infantry, light horse, and Hessians, as well as their artillery, baggage waggons, &c. were embarked on board the transports; that the British troops and grenadiers remain on Staten Island; that the sick are sent to New York; that the bloody flux is spreading among the enemy's troops; that they complain of very severe duty; and that general Howe is in New York.

Yesterday arrived a person who escaped from one of the men of war at New York last Saturday night, who says, that the embarkation of the enemy's baggage, waggons, artillery, draught horses, light horse, Hessians, and light infantry, was compleated on Friday last; that the transport boats were ordered to be ready at a minute's warning, to put on board the vessels the grenadiers and infantry, who were chiefly at Staten Island, off which the ships lay. He farther adds, that on board the ship he was, Delaware river was said to be the place of destination.

The Assembly of this sate have represented a very elegant coach to the Hon. Mrs. WASHINGTON, the worthy lady of his excellency general Washington, as a small testimonial of the sense they have of his great and important services to the American states, which she very politely accepted.

May 27, 1777.

IF THOMAS PINDLE, a native of Maryland, who left Annapolis about two years ago (and entered on board, as I was informed, either the Columbus or Alfred vessels of war, at Philadelphia) be now living, and will apply to his brother-in-law, Samuel Watson, living near Annapolis, he will hear of something to his advantage; and if he be dead, thanks will be returned to any one that will inform me of the same, under qualification.

SAMUEL WATSON.

Recreated from Purdie's Virginia Gazette, July 25, 1777.

GENERAL PRESCOTT PRISONER.

Extract of a letter from General WASHINGTON *to* CONGRESS, *dated camp, at the* CLOVE, *July* 16, 1777.

"Sir, I beg leave to congratulate Congress on the captivity of Major General Prescott and one of his Aids. The particulars of the fortunate event, you will find in the enclosed extract of a letter this minute received from General Spencer, which, I presume, are at large in the packet Mr. Greenleaf will deliver. Lieutenant Colonel Barton and the small handful under his command, who conducted the enterprise, have great merit."

NO ALARM GIVEN TO ENEMY.

Extract of a letter from major general SPENCER, *dated* PROVIDENCE, *July* 11, 1777.

I HAVE the pleasure to congratulate your Honour, and the Hon. Continental Congress, on the late success of lieut. col. Barton, who with the number of 40, including captains Adams and Phillips, and a number of brave officers, last night went on Rhode Island, and brought off major general Prescott, and major William Barrington, one of his aides de camp, and the sentry at the general's door, all that were at the general's quarters. This was done with such prudence that no alarm was given to the enemy until our party had got near to the main, on their return. They are now in this town.

Col. Barton went with his party in four whale boats from Warwick neck, about ten miles by water, to the west side of the island, landed about half way from Newport to Bristol ferry, then marched one mile to the general's quarters, returned again to Warwick, and had the good fortune to escape the discovery of the enemy's guard boats, although several ships of war lay round in those parts. Several attempts of this nature have been made without any loss on our side, and with some small success.

The above named capt. Phillips, some time since, with a party of about 200, brought off one Ensign Clark of the 43d regiment, now a prisoner. Another party attacked one of the enemy's guards, dispersed them, killed three, and wounded one. We have had several deserters from the British regiments.

Published by order of CONGRESS.
CHARLES THOMPSON, Secretary.

For SALE *at the Subscriber's Store, in* Waller *Street,* Williamsburg,

SUPERFINE BROADCLOTHS,	GAUZE HANDKERCHIEFS,
COARSE CLOTHS,	SILK KNEE GARTERS,
BATH COATING,	HAND-SAWS,
PLAIN GAUZE,	IVORY COMBS,
CAMBRICKS,	HYSON TEA,
GAUZE APRONS,	Black FANS,
RIBANDS, TAPE,	NECKLACES,
An Assortment of SATINS and PERSIANS,	WRITING PAPER,
	Black PEPPER, ALLSPICE,
India TAFFETAS,	POCKET-BOOKS,
OSNABRUGS,	SILK and WORSTED BINDINGS,
Womens SILK HATS,	GILT BUTTONS,
SILK STOCKINGS,	MOHAIR ditto,
Mens SHOES.	HAT BUCKLES,
Coarse and fine THREAD,	GUNPOWDER, INDIGO,
SILK TWIST, CRUEL,	WINE and BEER GLASSES,
SEWING SILK,	Mens GLOVES,
BOMBAZEEN,	SNUFF BOXES,
BLACK POPLIN,	A neat INK STAND,
BLACK CRAPE,	CHINA DISHES,
SILVER STOMACHERS,	DUTCH OVENS,
TEA POTS,	AUGERS, GOUGES, SPADES,
BROWN SUGAR,	Narrow HOES, TRIVETS,
PAINT BRUSHES,	Sets of COOPERS TOOLS,
PENKNIVES,	HINGES of different Sorts,
Mens BOOTS,	HASPS and STAPLES,
CORKSCREWS, SUGAR TONGS,	WELL CHAINS, IRON BOLTS,

and many other Articles too tedious to enumerate   A. DAVENPORT.

⁎⁎⁎ I have a few Boxes of CANDLES *which I will sell either Wholesale or Retail.*

TO BE SOLD for Cash, at public Auction, on *Monday* the 11th of *August,* before Mr. *Gait's* Door in *Richmond* Town, about 500 Barrels of FLOUR, and 10,000 lb. of BACON. The Sale will begin at two o'Clock in the Evening.   JOHN MAYO.

Recreated from The Virginia Gazette, August 1, 1777.

PUBLIC UNEASINESS.

The public are not appalled, though extremely uneasy at the news of the evacuation of Ticonderoga and Mount Independence. The States have sufficient resources left, and the success of the enemy there may finally turn out to their disadvantage. This however can be no good reason for a council of General officers to determine to abandon it to the enemy with all its stores, and without resistance.

Nothing since the commencement of the war has created so general a dissatisfaction. We would, however, avoid any hasty and partial conclusions. Our accounts at present are not very particular. We shall soon have fuller ones, which will be given to the public. The candid will be glad to find sufficient reasons for such an unexpected event, and for every step that has led to it. There can be no doubt that particular and public inquiry will be made into this matter. The people, whose all is at stake, and who have been at such vast expense to fortify and maintain that post, have a right to expect it, and the eyes of the whole continent must be turned upon it. If there is blame, let it fall where it is due.

It is said that our men behaved with great spirit in several smaller actions previous to the abandoning of the forts and lines at Ticonderoga. Lieutenant Hewitt bravely repulsed a party of the enemy at Mount Hope with only 26 men. Our picket guard drove back another larger part of the enemy, and could hardly be prevented from pursuing them further than was thought prudent. Our army was in high spirits, and under no apprehension of retiring from the enemy, just before orders for that purpose were given out.

The lines lately abandoned to the enemy, it is said, were too extensive; they required a larger force to man than was on the spot. If this is true, it is much to be regretted; as it is well known that a few Canadians and Indians, the last war, without any very regular and extensive works, stopped a large British army at that natural strong pass, and gave them a memorable defeat.

Recreated from The Virginia Gazette, August 15, 1777.

BATTLE AT HUBBARDTON.

BOSTON, *July* 24.—By an express arrived here last night, from Manchester, in the state of Vermont, which he left on Tuesday the 11th instant, we learn, that the enemy were then in possession of and fortifying Castle Town, on the Hampshire grants, so called, and cutting a road through towards South Bay, in order to get to Fort Ann; that there had been a battle in Hubbardton, between a body of our troops under the command of colonel Ebenezer Francis, of the Massachusetts state, and colonel Hale, of the Hampshire state, and about 2000 of the enemy, when our people retreated, being overpowered by numbers; that the loss on our side was reported to be 150 killed and missing, among the former were the above-mentioned colonels Francis and Hale; that there had been a second engagement at or near Fort Ann, between another body of our troops under the command of colonel Warner and about 1500 of the enemy, when they were repulsed with considerable loss; that it was reported and believed that the enemy, in both actions, had between four and five hundred killed, and must have a greater number wounded; and that major Skeene had got to Skeensborough with a number of Tories and soldiers, was determined to fortify and defend that place to the last extremity, being offered what assistance he required from the *humane* Howe.

Recreated from The Maryland Gazette, August 14, 1777.

PHILADELPHIA, *July* 22, 1777.—We cannot learn that the enemy are yet certainly moved to New York, but by an officer from Amboy we are informed there remained only 3000 British troops on Staten island; and that between 80 and 90 sail of vessels left Sandy Hook last Friday, but whether any troops were on board we cannot find.

General WASHINGTON, with his whole army, are moving towards the North river, to watch the motions of mr. Howe.

Recreated from Purdie's Virginia Gazette, August 1, 1777.

PRESCOTT'S BAGGAGE DELIVERED.

PROVIDENCE, *July* 19.—Saturday evening last a flag of truce came up the river from Newport with baggage, &c. for Gen. Prescott. The officer, who came in the flag, strongly solicited for leave to come up, and to have an interview with the General, which was not granted. The baggage, &c. was received, and next day the flag returned to Newport.

By some deserters from Rhode Island we learn that the capture of Gen. Prescott threw the enemy into great confusion. After recovering a little from the panic, parties were dispatched to every quarter of the island in search of their General, but finding him gone, they were obliged to console themselves in bestowing curses and imprecations on the rebels. The command of the troops at Rhode Island devolved on Gen. Smith.

• • • •

Capt. Benjamin Pearce, in the privateer United States, belonging to Warren, in company with a New London privateer, has taken a ship from the West Indies bound to London, having on board 450 hogsheads of sugar, 100 deerskins, 200 raw hides, 6000 white oak staves, &c. The prize is arrived in a safe port.

20,000 AMERICANS at FORT EDWARD.

KINGSTON, (NEW YORK) *July* 21.—We hear that upon the news of the evacuation of Ticonderoga, our troops and militia came in from all quarters in such numbers, that there were soon after at Fort Edward, and the posts near it, an army of above 20,000 men, who, it is hoped, may in their turn drive Gen. Burgoyne out of the country faster than he came in, and may also properly check and chastise those Indians, and worse Savages the Tories that joined them, who on the news of our quitting Ticonderoga, began to discover a hostile disposition towards us, and that they were only restrained by fear from acting as open enemies.

Recreated from The Pennsylvania Packet, August 5, 1777.

BRITISH FLEET SETS SAIL.
STEER A S.E. COURSE.

Extract of a letter from SHREWSBURY, *dated July 23, 1777.*

"On Sunday the 20th instant I had the honour of informing you that 160 sail of the enemy's fleet had come from the Watering Place, and lay in Sandy Hook bay. On Monday morning fifteen transports and men of war joined them, and about 10 o'clock 80 small brigs, schooners, and sloops, came out of the Narrows, and joined the grand fleet. On Tuesday they lay still, but this morning, at half past 6, the signal gun for the sailing was fired, the wind N.W., and at 7 they began to get under way, and stood for sea.

"After they got clear of the Hook, they steered a S.E. course, under a very easy sail, in three divisions. I attended their motions until sun down, and perceived very little difference in their course, sometimes appearing to steer a little to the eastward, at other times somewhat to the southward.

"By a deserter from on board the transport ship America, I am this morning informed that some part of general Howe's army, which crossed from this state to Staten Island, have been sent to New York; he cannot say what number, but thinks not exceeding 500. He also informs, that the remainder, except two Hessian regiments, which were left as a guard upon the island, are embarked on board this fleet."

LOST some time in *April*, between *Suffolk* and *Williamsburg*, two TICKETS in the STATES LOTTERY, No. 33,953 and 33,954. I will give two dollars to the person who finds and delivers them to col. *John Wilson* of Norfolk county, or the subscriber on board the ship *Caswell.*   WILLIS WILSON.

Recreated from Purdie's Virginia Gazette, August 8, 1777.

AN EXCHANGE OF GENERALS?

Extract of a letter from General WASHINGTON *to* CONGRESS, *dated July 25, 1777.*

SIR,
I do myself the honour to transmit you a copy of my letter to General Howe, of the 16th inst. proposing an exchange between Generals Lee and Prescott. I dispatched it early the next morning, and presume it was to hand on the 18th. As yet I have not received his answer.

Copy of a letter from General WASHINGTON *to* General HOWE, *dated* NEW JERSEY, *July* 16, 1777.

Sir—The fortune of war having thrown Major General Prescott into our hands, I beg leave to propose his exchange for that of Major General Lee. This proposition being agreeable to the letter and spirit of the agreement subsisting between us, will, I hope, have your approbation. I am the more induced to expect it, as it will not only remove one ground of controversy between us, but in its consequences effect the exchange of Lieut. Col. Campbell, and the Hessian field officers, for a like number of ours of equal rank in your possession.

I shall be obliged by your answer on the subject, assuring you that Major General Prescott shall be sent in if the proposed exchange is acceded to, either on the previous releasement of General Lee, or your promise that the same shall immediately take place on General Prescott's return. I have the honour to be, &c.
    G. WASHINGTON.

To his Excellency Sir William Howe.
Published by order of CONGRESS.
    CHARLES THOMPSON, Sec.

A FEW COPIES of Doctor PRICE's OBSERVATIONS on CIVIL LIBERTY, to be sold by JOHN DUNLAP.

Recreated from The Pennsylvania Packet, July 29, 1777.

A YOUNG WOMAN MASSACRED.

Part of a letter from MOSES'S CREEK, *July* 26.

"We have just had a brush with the enemy at Fort Edward, in which Lieut. Van Veghten was most inhumanly butchered and scalped. Two Serjeants and two Privates were likewise killed and scalped, one of the latter had both his hands cut off. They took a young woman, Janey M'Crea by name, out of a house at Fort Edward, carried her about half a mile into the bushes, and there killed and scalped her in cold blood. They have killed and scalped another woman near the same place."

Last Tuesday two men were taken up and interrupted on their errand to Gen. Howe. They both being Germans, were recommended to one Freleigh, their countryman, a staunch tory, to direct them the road. They unluckily made a mistake by calling on a Whig of the same name, who heard their enquiries and found out their errand; thinking it rather unsafe to let them pass without a further examination into their *real business*, sent them for that purpose under convoy to the Commissioners at Poughkeepsie.

Last Monday was hanged, at Fort Montgomery, one of Lord Howe's recruiting officers.

Last week another of the same gentlemen was hanged at Peek's-Kill.

Recreated from The Pennsylvania Packet, August 5, 1777.

THE MARQUIS de la FAYETTE.

WILLIAMSBURG, *July* 25.—A few days ago the baron De Kalb, a brigadier general in the French service, and the marquis de la Fayette, a young nobleman, and colonel of a regiment, with six other French officers, passed through Petersburg, from Charlestown, on their way to join the grand continental army. By these gentlemen we learn, that France is in great readiness of war, and only wait for England to declare, when they will take an active part in favour of America, being determined, at all events, to support her independency.

Recreated from Purdie's Virginia Gazette, July 25, 1777.

THE CASE FOR GEN. SCHUYLER.

Mr. HOLT,   KINGSTON, 26th *July*, 1777.

Be pleased to give the inclosed letter, which I have just received from Brigadier General St. Clair, a place in your paper. With the candour and ingenuity becoming a man of honour, he acquits Major General Schuyler of having ordered or been privy to the evacuation of Ticonderoga—a charge, which it seems has gained credit without proof, and found zealous advocates though unsupported by truth.

I am, Sir, your humble servant,

JOHN JAY.

Sir,   MOSES'S CREEK, *July* 25th, 1777.

GENERAL SCHUYLER was good enough to read to me part of a letter he received last night from you. I cannot recollect that any of my officers ever asked my reasons for leaving Ticonderoga; but as I have found the measure much decried, I have often expressed myself in this manner, "that as to myself I was perfectly easy. I was conscious of the uprightness and propriety of my conduct, and despised the vague censure of an uninformed populace," but had no allusion to orders from General Schuyler for my justification, because such orders never existed.

The calumny that has been thrown upon General Schuyler, upon account of that matter, has given me great uneasiness. I assure you, Sir, there never was any thing more cruel and unjust, for he knew nothing of the matter until it was over, more than you did at Kingston. It was done in consequence of a consultation with the other general officers, without the possibility of General Schuyler's concurrence; and had the opinion of the council been contrary to what it was, it would nevertheless have taken place, as I knew it to be impossible to defend the posts with our numbers.

In my letter to Congress, from Fort Edward, in which I gave them an account of the retreat, is this paragraph: "It was my original design to retire to this place, that I might be betwixt General Burgoyne and the inhabitants, and that the militia might have something in this quarter to collect to. It is now effected, and the militia are coming in, so that I have the most sanguine hopes that the progress of the enemy will yet be checked, and I may have the satisfaction to experience, that in quitting a post, I have saved a State."

Whether my conjecture is right or not is uncertain; but had our army been made prisoners, which it certainly would have been, the State of New York would have been much more exposed at present.

I proposed to General Schuyler, on my arrival at Fort Edward, to have sent a little note to the printer, to assure the people he had no part in abandoning what they thought their strong holds. He thought it was not so proper at that time, but it is no more than what I owe to truth and him, that he was totally unacquainted with the matter; and I should be very glad that this letter, or any part of it you may think proper to communicate, may convince the unbelieving. Simple unbelief is easily and soon convinced, but where *malice or envy* occasions it, it is needless to attempt it. I am, Sir, your ob't serv't,

A. St. CLAIR.

Recreated from The Pennsylvania Packet, August 5, 1777.

SIR JOHNSON'S SAVAGES.

Part of a letter from FORT STANWIX, *July* 28.

"We have received frequent intelligence here that Sir John Johnson has ordered col. Butler to send about 200 Indians to visit the fort and parts adjoining, who were to set out the 3d of August from near Oswego. And that Sir John, with about 1000 troops, made up of British, tories, and vagabond Canadians, are with Butler, and all the Indians they can muster to follow as soon as possible."

Part of another letter from FORT STANWIX, *July* 28, 1777.

"Yesterday this garrison was alarmed by the firing of four guns, when a party were immediately sent out to the place, which was about 500 yards from the fort; but the villains were fled, leaving shot, scalped, and tomahawked two girls, and wounded a third. By the best discoveries we could make they appear to have been four Indians who perpetrated these murders. We had four men with arms who had just passed that place; but these mercenaries of Britain came not to fight, but to lie in wait to murder; and it is equally the same to them, if they can get a scalp, whether it be from a soldier or an innocent babe. These Indians, we are informed, are some of those sent out by Sir John Johnson, col. Close and Butler."

Recreated from The Pennsylvania Packet, September 9, 1777.

TROOPS HEADING TO DELAWARE.

Intelligence from JERSEY, *Sunday July* 28.

I saw on their full march seven miles from Morris Town, on the road to Delaware, General Washington, General Mulenburgh, General Weeden, with four thousand men, and General Knox with his train of artillery, consisting of fourteen field pieces, and one howitz, seventy-nine ammunition waggons, and one hundred and thirty baggage waggons; and then proceeding on the road from Hackett's Town to Easton, there saw on their full march to Delaware, Generals Stevens and Scott with four thousand men and light field pieces, and on the road met twenty-nine flat-bottomed boats; and proceeded down to Quibble Town, where I saw General Stirling and General Conway with three thousand men and no field pieces. I am informed that General Sullivan has crossed the North river, and is bringing up the rear. As to the truth of that, I hope I shall be able to inform you in two or three days.

Published by order of CONGRESS.

CHARLES THOMPSON, Sec.

Recreated from The Maryland Gazette, August 21, 1777.

PHILADELPHIA.

In CONGRESS, *July* 29, 1777.

Resolved, That an enquiry be made into the reasons of the evacuation of Ticonderoga and Mount Independence, and into the conduct of the General Officers who were in the Northern department at the time of the evacuation.

That a Committee be appointed to digest and report the mode of conducting the enquiry.

July 30.—*Resolved*, That Major General St. Clair, who commanded at Ticonderoga and Mount Independence, forthwith repair to Head Quarters.

August 1.—*Resolved*, That Major general Schuyler be directed to repair to Head Quarters.

That General Washington be directed to order such General Officer as he shall think proper, immediately to repair to the Northern department, to relieve Major General Schuyler in his command there.

That Brigadier Poor, Brigadier Patterson, and Brigadier Roche de Fermoy be directed to repair to Head Quarters.

August 3.—*Resolved*, That General Washington be directed to order the General whom he shall judge proper, to relieve General Schuyler in his command, to repair with all possible expedition to the Northern department, giving him direction what number of the militia to call in from the States of New Hampshire, Massachusetts-Bay, Connecticut, New York, New Jersey and Pennsylvania.

That notice be immediately sent to the executive powers of the said States, and that they be earnestly requested to get the militia in those parts of their respective States most contiguous to the Northern department, ready to march at a moment's warning, and to send, with all possible expedition, such parts of them as the General commanding in the Northern department shall require, to serve till the 15th of November, if not sooner relieved by the Continental troops, or dismissed by the Commanding Officer of the department, and be entitled to Continental pay and rations.

That the Commanding Officer of the Northern department have discretionary power to make requisitions on the States aforesaid, from time to time, for such additional numbers of the militia to serve in that department as he shall judge necessary for the public service.

WHEREAS it is represented to Congress that General Washington is of opinion that the immediate recall of all the Brigadiers from the Northern department may be productive of inconvenience to the public service:

Resolved, That the order of Congress of the first day of this month, respecting the said Brigadiers, be suspended, until General Washington shall judge it may be carried into effect with safety.

Extract from the minutes,
CHARLES THOMPSON, Sec.

PHILADELPHIA.

In CONGRESS, *July* 30, 1777.

WHEREAS the States of New Jersey, Pennsylvania, and Delaware, are in danger of an immediate invasion from the enemy's army, a powerful fleet being daily expected within the capes of Delaware; and there is the strongest reason to suppose that the enemy will endeavour to secure, without delay, all the cattle, horses and teams, which are exposed to the water, in order to subsist their army and facilitate their military operations; and whereas the preventing of this measure is not only highly conducive to the general weal, but will ultimately tend to secure the property of the good people of these States from cruel ravages.

Resolved, That it be recommended to the Executive Powers of the States of Pennsylvania, New Jersey, and Delaware, to cause the horses, waggons, carts, cattle, and other live stock, contiguous to the bay and river Delaware, to be removed to the interior parts of the country, whenever the arrival of the enemy's forces at the cape shall announce the necessity and propriety of such a measure.

Resolved, That all Continental officers, and officers of the militia in Continental pay, in the said States, do afford the said Executive Powers such aid and assistance, in performing this service, as they may require.

We hear that Major General GATES is appointed to command in the Northern department, with orders immediately to repair thither.

Recreated from The Pennsylvania Packet, August 5, 1777.

In COUNCIL of SAFETY.

State of NEW YORK, *July* 30, 1777.

WHEREAS his excellency GEORGE CLINTON, Esq., has been duly elected governor of this state of New York, and hath this day qualified himself for the execution of his office by taking in this council the oaths required by the constitution of this state, to enable him to exercise his said office: This council do therefore, herby, in the name and by the authority of the good people of this state, proclaim and declare the said GEORGE CLINTON, Esq., governor, general and commander in chief of all militia, and admiral of the navy of this state; to whom the good people of this state are to pay all due obedience, according to the laws and constitution thereof.

By order of the council of safety,
PIERRE VAN CORTLANDT, *president,*
GOD SAVE THE PEOPLE.

Baltimore-Town, June 18, 1777.

WANTED,

TWO or three good SAIL-MAKERS, who will meet with constant employment, and the best encouragement given by the subscriber, living on Fell's Point.　　WILLIAM JACOBS.

Recreated from The Maryland Gazette, August 21, 1777.

WATCHING THE ENEMY.

Part of a letter from PHILADELPHIA, *July* 29.

"The enemy's fleet sailed last week, one division of which was seen last Saturday off Egg harbour, about 50 miles to the northward of these capes. It is yet uncertain whether this is not a feint to draw general Washington to the south, and harass his troops with long marches. We are preparing to receive mr. Howe, should he really intend an attack upon this city; and the general is so posted as to be ready to meet him, wherever he may go. I hear it is supposed at camp, upon what foundation I know not, that the enemy's design is to form a line from some where about Newcastle to the Head of the Elk, and enclose all the country from thence to Cape Charles; for which purpose one division of the fleet is to go to Chesapeake, and land the troops at Elk. If they have really any such intention, they are induced to it by the number of Tories in that quarter. It is but a paltry scheme, well fitted, however, to Howe's genius."

Extract of another letter, of the same date, from PHILADELPHIA.

"Gen. Howe sailed last Thursday morning, with 260 sail, from the Sound, supposed to have 18,000 troops on board, standing S.E. Gen. Clinton, with 3000, remains at New York.

"Gen. Nash came down here on Sunday from Trenton, with his brigade. Gen. Washington is marching with his army, in four divisions, by different routes, to this city. He can ferry 4000 men across the Delaware in an hour, with the boats he carries in waggons, &c. Gen. Mifflin has just received a letter from the general with orders to view the ground and passes low down on the Delaware, and to employ guides, &c. as he is determined to keep Howe and his army at bay. Orders are gone to employ all the bakers in this city to bake biscuit for the army, who are in high spirits, and well found with all necessaries for a campaign."

Recreated from Purdie's Virginia Gazette, August 8, 1777.

WASHINGTON AT PHILADELPHIA.

WILLIAMSBURG.—By Col. Finnie and Mr. Duncan Rose, just returned from Philadelphia, who left it last Friday morning, the 1st instant, we learn that his excellency general Washington arrived in that city the evening before, and next day set out for Chester, about 15 miles from Philadelphia, accompanied by general Gates and other officers, to reconnoitre the grounds on the Delaware; that the main body of our army is now at Germantown, general Putnam with 8000 men opposite to Peck's Kill, and general Nash's brigade, and col. Proctor with his artillery, at Chester, composing a body of about 2000. Eighteen hundred militia are posted at different stations on the Delaware.

An express arrived to general Mifflin, in Philadelphia, on Friday morning, from the capes of Delaware, with advice that Howe's fleet had disappeared.

A DASTARDLY PLOT.

From FREDERICKSBURG, *August* 5, 1777.

"Two persons, it is said, are apprehended at head quarters, who confess that they were sent out by the enemy to assassinate general Washington." [Almighty God defend and protect our beloved general from the machinations of such vile miscreants, the once famed and generous Britons! May he live to accomplish the glorious work of our independence, and receive the grateful plaudits of his country.]

Recreated from Purdie's Virginia Gazette, August 8, 1777.

WILLIAMSBURG, *August* 1.—General LEE, we have the pleasure to inform the publick, is in good health and spirits, although a close prisoner on board the Centurion man of war; but the exploit of col. Barton, in seizing and bringing off, *with so much address and gallantry*, the British major general Prescott, will no doubt secure his enlargement in a very short time, and restore our brave old general to the bosom of his friends.

Recreated from Purdie's Virginia Gazette, August 1, 1777.

BURGOYNE'S DECEIT.

Extract of a letter from STILLWATER *(10 miles on this side of* SARATOGA, *and* 25 *miles above* ALBANY), *dated August 4, 1777.*

"Our army has retreated to this place. We are about 3800 regulars and 1000 or 1200 militia. General Burgoyne is at Fort Edward, and has about 6000 regulars, 3 or 400 Indians, and 200 Canadians. We brought off the grain and forage and destroyed what we could not remove; many families fled, those that would not come away, relying on General Burgoyne's proclamation, were killed, scalped, and inhumanly butchered by the Indians, without any discrimination of whigs or tories.

"A Miss M'Crea, who was to have been married to one Jones, a tory, who had joined the enemy, and who she daily expected to bring her away, was dragged by the savages out of her house, shot twice through her body, her cloaths tore off her back, and left scalped in the bushes. This brutal scene was transacted by 4 Indians, under cover of 300 British regulars drawn up at a small distance, and in sight of an advance party of ours, who could give her no assistance. Several families whom we know have been murdered and scalped by the Indians—man, wife and 5 or 6 children, and their negroes.

"Doubtless many families have fell a sacrifice to their credulity in Burgoyne's proclamation, which promised protection to all who remained peaceable and quiet at their homes, with their stock, &c. &c. If New England people will not turn out to our assistance, our wives and children must fall into the hands of bloody Burgoyne and his merciless savage allies, and this country will be lost to the United States. Will our southern brethren and allies remain idle spectators of our misery? One regiment of riflemen would beat the Indians. God alone and southern troops can save us."

Recreated from The Maryland Gazette, August 21, 1777.

MOTIONS OF THE FLEET.

PHILADELPHIA, *August* 5.—The enemy's fleet of men of war and transports, on board which all their troops (except some few at New York and Staten Island) are embarked, have been hovering about the Capes of the Delaware this week past, sometimes standing into the Bay, and out to sea again, but on Friday last they disappeared, and were not seen again when the last accounts came away. The following letter was on Sunday last received from Mr. Fisher, who is stationed near the Capes to watch the motions of the men of war which infest that quarter—

LEWIS TOWN, *Aug.* 2, 1777. 8 *o'clock A.M.*

When I wrote to you last, I acquainted you of a large fleet being near the Capes; they made for our bay till the evening, and I expected next morning to have seen them within the Cape, but when day light appeared they were several leagues further out than they were the night before, which I imagine was owing to their being but very little wind and a whole ebb tide in the night; however at 9 o'clock, A.M. of the 31st ult. the Commodore, which was one of the nearest ships to the Cape, fired a gun and hoisted a flag, and bore down on the fleet, the wind being to the Westward. About noon it fell calm, and about 2 o'clock, P.M. the wind came to the Southward, and the fleet stood off by the wind, except 4 frigates and 4 tenders, which are in and near our road. Just before sun set we were alarmed from the light house that the fleet was standing in again; however, on the 1st of August they were entirely out of sight. Whether they are gone to the Southward or Northward is not in my power to tell. When they disappeared the wind was about South. I should have sent off this express before, but delayed it from reports being often brought that they were standing in again. The Roebuck went off with the fleet, and has not been seen since.

HENRY FISHER.

Recreated from The Pennsylvania Packet, August 5, 1777.

THE GENERAL'S LADY FETED.

WILLIAMSBURG, *Aug.* 8.—Last Tuesday the Hon. Mrs. Washington arrived in this city, amidst the ringing of bells, several discharges of artillery and volleys of small arms from the troops stationed here, and the cordial good wishes to all the inhabitants, who have the greatest regard for her Ladyship's own personal merit, and a grateful sense of the eminent services rendered to the United American States by her illustrious consort.

At a meeting of the Common Hall of this city on Friday the 1st instant, to take into their consideration the arrival of General Washington's Lady they came to the following resolutions:

Resolved unanimously, That the most respectful testimony be presented to her on the occasion of the high sense this Hall entertains of General Washington's distinguished merit, as the illustrious defender and deliverer of his country.

Resolved unanimously, That a golden emblematical medal be prepared, to be presented to the General's Lady, as the most suitable method of carrying that design into execution; and that the Mayor be desired to form the device, and agree with some proper persons to execute the same.

Resolved unanimously, That the freedom of this city be presented to General Washington, through his Lady; and that the Mayor be desired to wait upon her with the same, and with a copy of the several resolutions.

WANTED,

A SMART active young NEGRO, to wait on a Gentleman. Any person having such a Negro to dispose of, may hear of a purchaser by applying to the Printer.

A YOUNG WOMAN with a good breast of milk would gladly serve as a wet nurse in a genteel family; none else need apply: Her character will bear the strictest enquiry. Enquire of the Printer.

Recreated from The Pennsylvania Packet, August 19, 1777.

BATTLE OF ORISKANY.

A SCARLET COAT WITH GOLD TRIM.

Extract of a letter from ALBANY, *August* 11.

"I have to communicate to you an agreeable piece of intelligence. Last Wednesday about nine o'clock an engagement ensued between a part of the militia of Tryon county, under the command of general Herkemer, and a party of savages, tories, and regulars, about half way between Eriskie and Fort Stanwix. It lasted till three o'clock in the afternoon, when the enemy thought proper to retire, leaving gen. Herkemer master of the field; unluckily, however, the general and some valuable officers got wounded and killed in the beginning. This, however, did in no way intimidate the ardour of the men, and the general, although he had two wounds, did not leave the field till the action was over; he seated himself down on a log, with his sword drawn, animating his men.

"The enemy lost on this occasion some of their chief men, such as Joseph Brandt, William Johnson, Peter Johnson, bastards of the late Sir William Johnson; Stephen Watts, Johannes Herkemer (a brother to the general) and a number of others, Indians and regulars.

"About one o'clock the same day, col. Gansevoort having received information of gen. Herkemer's march, sent lieut. col. Willet out with 200 men, to attack an encampment of the enemy, and thereby facilitate gen. Herkemer's march. In this the colonel succeeded, for after an engagement of an hour he had completely routed the enemy, took one captain and four privates prisoners. The baggage taken was very considerable; such as money, bear skins, officers baggage, and camp equipage; one of the soldiers had for his share a scarlet coat, trimmed with gold lace to the full, and three laced hats. The plunder, at the most moderate computation, exceeds £1000.

"When the colonel returned to the fort he discovered 200 regulars in full march to attack him; he immediately ordered his men to prepare for battle, and having a field piece with him, capt. Savage of the artillery so directed its fire as to play in conjunction with one out of the fort; these, with a brisk fire from his small arms, soon made these heroes scamper off with great loss. Col. Willet then marched with his booty into the fort, where he arrived at four the same day, having not a single man killed or wounded. This account we had from a man, who was in the engagement, and left the fort on Thursday night last. We expect daily to hear of another engagement at that place.

"We have at this moment received an account that the enemy have left Saratoga, but what route they have taken is unknown."

Recreated from The Maryland Gazette, August 28, 1777.

GENERAL ARNOLD ON HIS MARCH.

Extract of a letter from General SCHUYLER *to his* Excellency General WASHINGTON, *dated Forts, six miles below* STILLWATER, *August* 15.

"I am just informed that Lieut. Col. Willet is arrived at Albany. He advises that after the engagement which Gen. Herkemer had with the enemy, Col. Gansevoort ordered a sortie with 206 men, commanded by Lieut. Col. Willet; that he made a successful attack on part of the enemy's line, drove them across the river, and killed many. That Sir John Johnson, he is informed, was among the slain. That he took and brought off a considerable quantity of baggage. That on his return to the fort he was ambuscaded, and attacked by a body of regular troops, who, after a fire by which Willet did not lose one man, were charged with fixed bayonets, and drove. He farther informs that between 3 and 400 Indians were killed, wounded, and left the besiegers after the engagement. That the militia with Gen. Herkemer lost about 160 killed and wounded. That Gen. St. Ledyard, who commands the enemy's force in that quarter, sent in a flag to demand the delivery of the fort, offering that the garrison should march out with their baggage, and not be molested by the Savages. That if this was not complied with, he would not answer for the conduct of the Indians, if the garrison fell into their hands; and that they would certainly fall on the inhabitants. That Gen. Burgoyne was in possession of Albany.

[*The public are desired to take notice, that Lieut. Col. Willet did not inform "That Gen. Burgoyne was in possession of Albany," but that Gen. Ledyard sent that false information to Col. Gansevoort, in order to induce him to surrender.*]

"That Col. Gansevoort, after animadverting on the barbarity and disgraceful conduct of the British officers, in suffering women and children to be butchered as they had done, informed the flag that he was resolved to defend the fort to the last; that he would never give it up as long as there was a man left alive to defend it. That he was well supplied with provisions and ammunition.

"Col. Gansevoort being informed that the militia were dispirited, expecting that the fort would soon fall, sent Lieut. Col. Willet out to cheer up their spirits. That he found the militia of Tryon county collecting with great alacrity, and as Gen. Arnold, with the troops marched under his command, will probably reach the German flats on the 16th or 17th. I have great hopes that the siege will soon be raised."

Published by order of CONGRESS.
CHARLES THOMPSON, Secretary.

WILLIAMSBURG (Virginia), *Aug.* 15.—Last night an express arrived here from the Eastern Shore, with advice that a large fleet, consisting of upwards of 150 sail, were then in sight, within about thirty miles of our Capes, but whither they are going we have not learnt.

ANNAPOLIS (Maryland), *Aug.* 21.—Between two and three hundred sail of British ships of war, transports, &c. passed the mouth of this harbour about 9 o'clock, and are still standing up the Bay.

STATE of VERMONT.
IN COUNCIL OF SAFETY.

BENNINGTON, *Aug.* 16.

Brigadier General Stark, from the state of New Hampshire, with his brigade, together with the militia and companies of rangers raised by this state, with part of Col. Symmons's regiment of militia, are now in action with a number of the enemy's troops assembled near this place, which has been for some time very severe. We have now in possession (taken from them this day) four brass filed pieces, ordnance stores, &c. This minute 4 or 500 prisoners have arrived. We have taken the ground, although fortified by entrenchments, &c. but after being drove about one mile, and the enemy being reinforced, made a second stand, and still continue the action. The loss on each side is doubtless considerable, but the numbers not ascertained. You are therefor in the most pressing terms requested by general Stark and his council, to forward the whole of the militia under your several commands to this place, without one minute's loss of time. They will proceed on horseback, with all the ammunition that can be provided conveniently. On our present exertions depends the fate of thousands.

I am, your most obedient humble servant,
JONAS FAY, Vice President.

Recreated from The Pennsylvania Packet, August 26, 1777.

PHILADELPHIA, *Aug.* 23.—We hear from Princeton, in New Jersey, that the attention of the publick in that state is strongly drawn to the execution of a law for confiscating and selling the estates of Tories who had openly taken part with the enemy. These parricides had a day assigned to them, within which they had room for repentance; which being now past, all who persisted in their guilt are treated according to the tenour of the statute in the eastern counties. These sales are soon to be holden in the western part of the state.

Recreated from Purdie's Virginia Gazette, September 12, 1777.

BATTLE OF BENNINGTON.

PHILADELPHIA, *August* 22, 1777.

By an Express arrived last Evening from General SCHUYLER to CONGRESS, we have the following important Intelligence.

VAN SCHAICK'S ISLAND, *in the mouth of the* MOHAWK RIVER, *August* 18*th*, 1777.

SIR, I have the honor to congratulate Congress on a signal Victory obtained by General STARK; an account whereof is contained in the following Letter from General LINCOLN, which I have this moment had the happiness to receive, together with General BURGOYNE'S instructions to Lieutenant-Colonel BERN; Copy whereof is inclosed.

BENNINGTON, *August* 18*th*, 1777.

"THE late signal success of a body of about 2000 troops, mostly Militia, under the command of Brigadier-General STARK, in this part of the country, on the 16th inst. over a party of about 1500 of the enemy, who came out with a manifest design to possess themselves of this town, as will appear by the enclosed, is an event happy and important. Our troops behaved in a very brave and heroic manner; they pushed the enemy from one work to another thrown up on advantageous ground and from different posts, with spirit and fortitude until they gained a compleat victory over them.

"The following is the best list I have been able to obtain of the prisoners, their killed and wounded, viz. One Lieut. Colonel, 1 Major, 5 Captains, 12 Lieutenants, 4 Ensigns, 2 Cornets, 1 Judge Advocate, 1 Baron, 2 Canadian Officers, and 3 Surgeons, 37 British Soldiers, 398 Hessians, 38 Canadians, and 151 Tories taken. The number of wounded fallen into our hands, exclusive of the above, are about 80. The number of their slain has not yet been ascertained, as they fought on the retreat for several miles in a wood, but supposed to be about 200.

"Their artillery which consisted of 4 brass field pieces, with a considerable quantity of baggage likewise fell into our hands. We have heard nothing of Burgoyne or his army for these two days past. The prisoners are sent into the State of Massachusetts-Bay, except the Tories; shall wait your directions respecting them, as most of them belong to the State of New-York.

I am, dear General, your very humble Servant,
B. LINCOLN.

* * * *

Copy of Orders from Gen. BURGOYNE, *to* Lieut. Col. BERN. *near* SARATOGA, *August* 14.

The accounts you have given me are very satisfactory, and I doubt not every proceeding under your direction will be the same.

I beg the favour of you to report whether the route you have marched would be practicable for a large corps with cannon, without repair, or with what sort of repair.

The desirable circumstance at present for your corps is to possess Bennington, but should you find the enemy too strongly posted, and maintaining such a countenance as would make a coup-de-main too hazardous, I wish you to take such a post as you can maintain till you hear further from me, and upon your report, and other circumstances, I will either support you in force, or withdraw you.

Will you please to send to my camp, as soon as you can, waggons and draft cattle, and likewise such other cattle as are not necessary for your subsistence; let the waggons and carts bring off what flour and wheat they can, that you do not retain for the same purpose. I will write to you in full to-morrow, in regard to purchasing horses out of the hands of the savages; in the mean time let them be assured that whatever you select from them, fit to mount the dragoons, shall be paid for at a proper price.

J. BURGOYNE, Lieut. General.

* * * *

I am in hopes that Congress will very soon have the satisfaction to learn that General Arnold has raised the siege of Fort Schuyler [aka Fort Stanwix]. If that takes place, I believe it will be possible to engage two or three hundred Indians to join this army, and Congress may rest assured that my best endeavors shall not be wanting to accomplish it.

I am informed that General Gates arrived at Albany yesterday.

Major Livingston, one of my Aids, will have the honor to deliver you this despatch.

I am, Sir, Your most obedient humble servant,
PHILIP SCHUYLER.

Published by order of CONGRESS.
JOHN HANCOCK, President.

Recreated from The Maryland Gazette, August 28, 1777.

THE FATE OF TRAITORS.

A VERY singular instance happened to a number of people from the town of Hancock. Forty of them had been lately draughted from the said town to reinforce the Continental army at the northward, twenty of whom (after they had received their marching orders, &c.) deserted, set off, and actually joined that part of our cruel enemy they were drawn to go against. But the other twenty who had joined Gen. Stark, and approached with him to the breast works of the enemy, saw to their great surprise, their fellow townsmen within the intrenchment ready to receive them, and knowing what treatment they should receive from them, should they obtain the victory, attacked their fort with the greatest fortitude, and success ensued; for out of the twenty who took shelter in the fort, fourteen were killed, and the other six, with many other poor devils, made prisoners of.

Thus may be seen the shameful death of a number of traitors to their much injured country. Heaven grant that this may be the fate of every other traitor to the glorious cause of American freedom.

Recreated from The Pennsylvania Packet, September 9, 1777.

TROOPS TO THE EASTERN SHORE.

PHILADELPHIA, *August* 26, 1777.—Last Sunday morning part of the Continental army, amounting to about 10,000 men, with His Excellency George Washington at their head, marched through this city and immediately proceeded over the river Schuylkill, on their way it is said to the eastern shore of Maryland, where the enemy's fleet have lately been seen, and it is thought will make a descent upon that State. And yesterday morning General Nash's brigade of North Carolina forces, and General Proder's regiment of artillery, passed through this city, and we hear are to pursue the same route, in order to join our most illustrious General.

On the enemy's fleet appearing off Baltimore the disaffected inhabitants were all seized and sent under a strong guard to Frederick Town.

Capt. Thomas Johnson, in the sloop Ruttleton, belonging to Baltimore, is arrived at St. Croix.

Recreated from The Pennsylvania Packet, August 26, 1777.

GENERAL BURGOYNE'S ROUT.

THE following are the distances from the several posts in General Burgoyne's rout to New York, by which it appears, that when he is at Fort Edward, he has marched 373 miles from Quebec, a march of 67 miles more carries him to Albany, and he is then 146 miles off New York, has the river open to him all the way from Albany, where the King's frigates and vessels have a free communication:

From Quebec		*Ticonderoga*	19
to Three Rivers	80	*Lake George*	22
Lake St. Peter	30	*Fort Edward*	34
Montreal	60	*Fort Miller*	10
Fort Chamblee	22	*Fort Hardy*	7
Fort St. John	10	*Albany*	53
Lake Champlain	52	*Kingston*	50
Crown Point	44	*New York*	92
		Miles	585

Recreated from The Public Advertiser, London, August 30, 1777.

THE BRITISH RETREAT FROM FORT STANWIX.

Head Quarters, *August 25th*, 1777.
To His Excellency John Hancock, Esq.
Sir,

A MESSENGER is just arrived with the inclosed letters from General Arnold and Colonel Gansevoort; I am happy in communicating them to your Excellency. Great honour is due to Colonel Gansevoort, Lieut. Colonel Willet, and the officers and soldiers of the garrison under their command; I cannot too warmly recommend them to Congress. The gallant defence of Fort Stanwix, must convince all the western nations of Indians of the Superiority of the American arms.

I am, Sir, your most obedient humble Servant,
HORATIO GATES.

• • • •

Head Quarters, *August 28th*, 1777.
To His Excellency John Hancock, Esq.
Sir,

In the packet, I have the honour to transmit to your Excellency a copy of a letter I received last night from Major General Arnold. The defeat and disgrace with which the enemy have been obliged to retreat from Fort Schuyler [aka Fort Stanwix], added to the compleat and brilliant victory gained by General Stark and Col. Warner, at Bennington, give the brightest lustre to the American arms, and covers the enemies of the United States with infamy and shame. The horrid murders and scalpings paid for and encouraged by Lieut. General Burgoyne, previous to his defeat at Bennington, will forever stain the honour of the British arms. In one house, the parents, with six children, were most cruelly butchered; and the polite Macaroni paid Ten Dollars for each of their scalps. Heaven has I hope in store, some punishment for such unheard of crimes.

I am, Sir, your most obedient humble Servant,
HORATIO GATES.

Fort Schuyler, *August 22d*, 1777.
To the Hon. General Arnold, or officer commanding the army on their march to Fort Schuyler.
DEAR SIR,

THIS morning at 11 o'clock I began a heavy cannonade upon our enemy's works, which was immediately returned by a number of shells and cannon. About 3 o'clock several deserters came in, who informed me that General St. Ledger with his army was retreating with the utmost precipitation; soon after which, I sent out a party of about sixty men to enter their camps, who soon returned and confirmed the above account. About 7 o'clock this evening Hanjort Schuyler arrived here, and informed me that General Arnold with two thousand men were on their march for this post; in consequence of which I send you this information. *I am, dear Sir, yours, &c.*
PETER GANSEVOORT, Colonel.

• • • •

Mohawk River, *ten miles above* Fort Dayton, *August 22d*, 1777. *Five o'Clock P.M.*
To Hon. Major General Gates.
DEAR GENERAL,

I wrote to you the 21st instant from the German Flats, that from the best intelligence I could procure of the enemy's strength, it was much superior to ours, at the same time I inclosed you a copy of the resolution of a Council of War, and requested you to send me a reinforcement of one thousand light troops. As the enemy had made their approaches within two hundred yards of the fort, I was determined at all events to hazard a battle, rather than suffer the garrison to fall a sacrifice. This morning I marched off from the German Flats for this place; where I have met an express with the inclosed letter from Col. Gansevoort, acquainting me the enemy had yesterday retired from Fort Schuyler with great precipitation; I am at a loss to judge their real intentions, whether they have returned home, or retired with a view of engaging us on the road.

I am inclined to the former, from the account of the deserters, and from their leaving their tents, and considerable baggage which our people have secured. I shall immediately detach about nine hundred men, and make a forced march to the fort, in hopes of coming up with the rear, and securing their cannon and heavy baggage.

I am, dear General, your obedient humble servant,
B. ARNOLD.

• • • •

FORT SCHUYLER, *Aug. 24th, Ten o'Clock P.M.*
To Hon. Major General Gates.
DEAR GENERAL,

I wrote you yesterday that the enemy had retreated from this place; at 5 o'clock this evening, by a forced march of 22 miles, through a thick wood, I reached this place in expectation of harassing the enemy in their retreat; Colonel Gansevoort had anticipated my design, by sending out a small party, who brought in four royals, and a considerable quantity of baggage, with a number of prisoners and deserters; the enemy went off with the greatest precipitation, leaving their tents standing, their provisions, ammunition, &c. &c. which have fallen into our hands.

I am dear General, your affectionate,
B. ARNOLD.
Published by order of CONGRESS.
CHARLES THOMPSON, Sec.

Recreated from The Pennsylvania Packet, September 2, 1777.

AUGUST 21, 1777.
WANTED immediately, one or two SURGEONS MATES, for the Hospital at York. MATTHEW POPE.

RICHMOND, August 25, 1777.
I shall leave the Country in a few Weeks. JOHN RO. STRACHAN.

Recreated from The Virginia Gazette, September 5, 1777.

ENEMY LAND AT HEAD OF ELK.

Extract of a letter from WILMINGTON, *Aug. 26.*

"The enemy have landed about 2000 men and are within four miles of the Head of Elk, they act with great caution even to timidity.

"His Excellency is gone out to reconnoitre the country near them, with three regiments of horse. To-morrow we shall take our station, so as to act against them; their horses are dying fast, nine have floated on shore within the space of a mile.

"The militia are collecting, and in three days, we shall have 30,000 men round them, we are afraid they will not leave the river, but keep possession of a neck of land called Turkey Point."

Recreated from The Hartford Courant, September 8, 1777.

UNSPEAKABLE BARBARITY.

NEW CASTLE.—THIS day came Francis Alexander, a reputable resident in the county aforesaid, before me the subscriber, a justice of the peace, and made oath, that he was eye-witness to several brutal ravages committed by the merciless troops of the tyrant of Great Britain, on their late landing on the Head of Elk, that he particularly saw one of them, in the presence of divers others, ravish, or attempt violently to effect a rape on the person of a young woman of spotless character, living at his house, notwithstanding her cries and resistance to the contrary, at the same time making use of severe menaces, in case of refusal; and sundry other acts of barbarity he saw there perpetrated, shocking to humanity, and which cry aloud for vengeance.

FRANCIS ALEXANDER.
Sworn before me this 31st August, 1777.
GEO. LATIMER.

[The above deposition, taken in the presence of Brig. Wm. Maxwell, Col. Alexander Martin and Col. Theo. Bland, of a regiment of light dragoons.]

Recreated from The North Carolina Gazette, October 24, 1777.

EVENTS IN CANADA.

Extract of a letter from general Gates, *head quarters,* VAN SCHAIK'S ISLAND, *Aug. 26, 1777.*

"Since my last no material alterations have taken place in this department. By accounts of prisoners and deserters, their main body, which consists of about five thousand men, is at Fort Miller. They have advanced parties at Saratoga, but none yet reached Stillwater.

"At Fort Edward they have stationed a regiment, and posted another at Fort George. They have also detached two regiments to Skeensborough, upon suspicion of our having sent a body of men that way.

"We remain very still on the island. Burgoyne has no inclination to follow us. We shall, however, pay him a complaisant visit, when our reinforcements arrive.

"The enemy at Fort Stanwix have raised the siege. This important intelligence arrived the 24th, by express, from general Arnold—the circumstances briefly are these.

"On the 22d col. Gansevoort commenced a heavy cannonade upon the enemy's works—they answered it by shells and cannon—at length general St. Leger, who commanded, thought proper to *retreat*—This was done with so much precipitation, that they left a considerable quantity of baggage and *all* their tents.

"It is much to be lamented that general Arnold was not near enough to co-operate with the fort—had this been the case, we must, beyond question, have taken their artillery—He did, notwithstanding, upon the earliest notice, detach nine hundred men with orders to force their march, and, if possible, to attack their rear—but their great distance, added to their quick step, will, I fear, prevent our people from being further successful.

"It is the opinion of all general officers, that they will retire into Canada, and disturb us no more in that quarter.

"General Arnold will, in a few days, join the army, at this post, with his whole force."

Recreated from The Maryland Gazette, September 25, 1777.

A DECLARATION.

By His Excellency WILLIAM HOWE, &c.

To the Inhabitants of PENNSYLVANIA, *the Lower Counties on* DELAWARE, *and the Counties on the* EASTERN SHORE *of* MARYLAND.

SIR William Howe, regretting the calamities to which many of his Majesty's faithful subjects are still exposed, by the continuance of the rebellion, and no less desirous of protecting the innocent than determined to pursue with the rigours of war, all those whom his Majesty's forces, in the course of their progress may find in arms against the King, doth hereby assure the inhabitants of the Province of Pennsylvania, the Lower Counties of Delaware, and the Counties of Maryland, on the Eastern Shore of Chesapeak Bay, that in order to remove any groundless apprehensions which may have been raised of their sufferings by depredations of the army under his command, he hath issued the strictest orders to the troops, for the preservation of regularity and good discipline, and has signified that the most exemplary punishment shall be inflicted upon those who shall dare to plunder the property, or molest the persons of any of his Majesty's well disposed subjects.

OCTOBER 15, 1777.

To be SOLD at public vendue, at the late dwelling-house of Richard Blackledge, Esq; deceased, on Tuesday the 4th of November next.

THREE Negro Slaves, and sundry Horses, Cattle, Sheep, and Hogs (among which are a number of fat cattle and sheep fit for slaughter) a new Copper Distill and Lead Worm, and sundry other articles. And on the 7th day of the same inst. will be sold in Newbern, at Mr. John Green's store, a quantity of Bar Iron and Rods for Nails, a quantity of Soal Leather, Saddle and upper Leather, and part of a Stock of Cattle at Pecoson Point. Twelve months credit will be allowed, the purchasers giving bond and approved security, and to be at interest from the day of sale. At the same time will be hired out in Newbern, for one year, a valuable Negro man, who understands shaving and dressing hair, and is a good house servant.

JACOB BLOUNT.
CHRISTOPHER NEALE,
RICHARD BLACKLEDGE, } Executors.
SPYERS SINGLETON,

Security and protection are likewise extended to all persons, the inhabitants of the province and counties aforesaid, who not guilty of having assumed legislative or judicial authority, may have acted illegally in subordinate stations, and conscious of their misconduct have been induced to leave their dwellings: Provided such persons do forthwith return and remain peaceably in their usual places of abode.

Considering moreover, that many officers and private men, now actually in arms against his Majesty, may be willing to relinquish the part they have taken in this rebellion, and return to their allegiance.

Sir William Howe, doth therefore promise a free and general pardon, to all such officers and private men as shall voluntarily come and surrender themselves to any detachment of his Majesty's forces before the day on which it shall be notified, that the said indulgence shall be discontinued.

Given under my hand, at Head Quarters, the 27th August, 1777, by his Excellency's command,
ROBERT M'KENSIE.

Recreated from The North Carolina Gazette, October 24, 1777.

Extract of a letter from Philadelphia, dated the 1st instant.

"General Howe moves very slowly on, not having advanced above 8 or 10 miles in a week. His main body is now between the Head of Elk and their place of landing, and his advanced parties about two miles on this side, upon Gray's Hill. General Washington's head quarters are at Wilmington, and his main body about 8 miles advanced towards the enemy. If general Howe should insist on coming forward, I suppose a battle must ensue, and that shortly.

"The militia turn out with spirit, and in considerable numbers. We have already, in various and successful skirmishes, taken 84 prisoners; and 20 have deserted. Capt. Lee (son of our friend Col. Henry) of Bland's light horse, brought 24 of the enemy in prisoners the other day. I believe they rather exceed in number the whole of his troop."

Recreated from Purdie's Virginia Gazette, September 12, 1777.

REWARDS FOR SCALPS STOPPED.

BURGOYNE VALUES HIS OWN.

KINGSTON, *September* 1, 1777.

We are credibly informed that *Burgoyne*, the chief and director of the King of Great Britain's band of thieves, robbers, cut-throats, scalpers, and murderers of every denomination, now infesting the northern and western frontiers, of several of the American United States, has not only discontinued the reward he had offered and given to the savage *Tories, Indians, Britons, Hessians, Brunswickers, Haldeckers*, and other profligate scum of the human race, now in his service, for the scalps they brought him from the murdered, and half murdered inhabitants, but has also strictly prohibited, for the future, under a severe penalty, the practice of *scalping*.

It must not however be supposed, that this chief of the ruffian band, was so weak as to be in the least influenced to this prohibition by any motives of compassion or humanity. His inducements were purely political. He had found by experience, that his rewards lessened the number of his emissaries—who not only scalped some of his tory friends, concealed among the inhabitants, but also scalped one another; and that a scalping party of a Lieutenant, and about 30 men, he lately sent out, with a larger number of Indians, were by the latter, all killed and scalped, none of the party having been since seen or heard of, and the Lieutenant's hair, which was remarkably full, bushy and red, being known.

We had intelligence by several persons, that Burgoyne had laid aside his usual practice of scalping, and strictly forbid it for the future—but we did not before know his reason for the prohibition. It is not improbable he might be apprehensive, that some of the dexterous hands about him, might take an opportunity, one time or other, and slip off his own night-cap.

Recreated from The Hartford Courant, September 8, 1777.

COPIES *of the following letters from Lieutenant General Burgoyne to Major General Gates, with General Gates's answer, are just come to hand; but the copier has probably made a mistake in the date of General Burgoyne's letter; for General Gates certainly received it by a flag on the 1st instant addressed to Major General Gates, or other officer commanding in the American troops in Half-moon.*

Head Quarters of the King's army upon HUDSON'S RIVER, *August* 30, 1777.

TO M. GEN. GATES.
SIR,
MAJOR General Reidsel has requested me to transmit the inclosed to Lieut. Baum, whom the fortune of war, put into the hands of your troops at Bennington.

Having never failed in my attention towards prisoners, I cannot entertain a doubt of your taking this opportunity to show me a return of civility; and that you will permit the baggage and servants of such officers, your prisoners, as desire it, to pass to them unmolested.

It is with great concern I find myself obliged to add to this application, a complaint of bad treatment the Provincial soldiers in the King's service received after the affair at Bennington. I have reports upon oath, that some were refused quarters after having asked it. I am willing to believe this was against the order and inclination of your officers; but it is my part to require an explanation, and to warn you of the horrors of retaliation, if such a practice is not in the strongest terms discountenanced and reprehended.

Duty and principle, Sir, make me a public enemy to the Americans, who have taken up arms; but I seek to be a generous one; nor have I the shadow of resentment against any individual, who does not enduce it by acts derogatory to those maxims, upon which all men of honour think alike.

Persuaded that a Gentleman of the station to which this letter is addressed, will not be comprized in the exception I have made.

I am personally, sir your humble servant,
J. BURGOYNE, Lieut. General.

• • • •

Major-General Gates's answer.

Head Quarters of the army of the UNITED STATES, *Sept.* 2, 1777.

TO LIEUT. GEN. BURGOYNE.
SIR,
LAST night I had the honour to receive your Excellency's letter of the 1st instant. I am astonished you should mention inhumanity, or threaten retaliation. Nothing happened in the action at Bennington, but what is common when works are carried by assault.

That the savages of America should, in their warfare, mangle and scalp the unhappy prisoners who fall into their hands, is neither new or extraordinary; but that the famous Lieutenant General Burgoyne, in whom the fine Gentleman is united with the soldier and the scholar, should hire the Savages of America to scalp Europeans and descendants of Europeans. Nay more, that he should pay a price for each scalp so barbarously taken, is more than will be believed in Europe, until authenticated facts in every gazette confirm the truth of the horrid tale.

Miss McRea, a young lady lovely to the sight, of virtuous character and amiable disposition, engaged to be married to an officer in your army, was, with other women and children, taken out of a house near Fort Edward, carried into the woods, and there scalped and mangled in a most shocking manner. Two parents, with their six children, were all treated with the same inhumanity, while quietly residing in their once happy and peaceful dwelling.

The miserable fate of Miss McRea was particularly aggravated, by her being dressed to receive her promised husband, but met her murderer, employed by you. Upwards of one hundred men, women and children, have perished by the hands of the ruffians, to whom, it is asserted, you have paid the price of blood.

Inclosed are letters from your wounded officers, prisoners in my hands. By them you will be informed of the generosity of their conquerors.

Such money, clothing, attendants and necessaries, which your Excellency pleases to send to the prisoners, shall be faithfully delivered. The late Col. Baum's servant is at Bennington, would come to your Excellency's camp; but when I offered him a flag, he was afraid to run the risque of being scalped, and declined.

When I know what surgeons and attendants your Excellency is desirous of sending to Bennington, I shall dispatch an officer to your lines to conduct them to my camp.

I am Sir, your most humble servant,
        HORATIO GATES, Major General.

Recreated from The Hartford Courant, September 22, 1777.

BATTLE OF STATEN ISLAND.

PHILADELPHIA, *September* 2.

A gentleman arrived in town last week from New Jersey informs us, General Sullivan, with 1500 men, under Generals Smallwood and de Borre, went from Morristown last Thursday fe'nnight at noon, crossed at Elizabethtown Point, and was on Staten Island at day break the next morning. One party went towards New York till they got in sight of it, the other went towards Amboy, and in their course killed many of the new levies, and took Colonels Allen, Barton, and Dongan, 2 Majors, 4 Captains, 6 Lieutenants, 2 Surgeon's Mates, and 203 Privates, with which they crossed to Amboy about two o'clock.

About three o'clock the rear guard of our army, consisting of 126 men, was attacked, and twice repulsed the assailants, who suffered much killed; but our party having expended all their ammunition, were obliged to surrender; among which are Col. Antill, Major John Stewart of Maryland, a Major of Col. Hazen's regiment, and two other Majors, with 6 or 7 other officers. Four officers of ours are missing.

We hear that since the enemy landed at the Elk, the number of prisoners and deserters from them amount to sixty. Friday last several were brought to this city.

By accounts of deserters from the enemy, their situation must be very disagreeable and distressing, as the number of sick is considerable, having increased greatly since they landed, and they are so closely observed by the militia, that they dare not venture out far to procure fresh provisions. That numbers of seamen as well as soldiers are determined to desert at the first opportunity; the latter in particular are greatly dissatisfied, on account of their bad provisions, for which even the best part of their pay is stopped, as they do not receive more than twopence halfpenny a day, and when that happens to be paid them, it is not in their power to purchase any vegetables, which the poor fellows are now more desirous of than ever they were of liquor. And that soon after their landing they left near thirty horses, having turned them into a corn field, where the creatures eat to such excess that they expired before the English farriers could discover their disorder, and administer any thing to their relief.

IF JOHN NEILL, from Lurgan, in the County Armagh, in Ireland, will appear at Mr. ROBERT DURKEE's quarters, in Morris-Town, he will hear of something considerably to his advantage.

THE MILITIA of this State are desired to call on the Muster-Master General (at Mr. Robeson's in Chesnut-street, opposite the Fountain Inn) as soon as their companies are ready for mustering.

Recreated from The Pennsylvania Packet, September 2, 1777.

COOCH'S BRIDGE.

Extract of a letter from General WASHINGTON *to* CONGRESS, *dated* WILMINGTON, *Sept.* 3.

"This morning the enemy came out with a considerable force and three pieces of artillery, against our light advanced corps, and after some pretty smart skirmishes obliged them to retreat, being far inferior in number, and without cannon. The loss on either side is not yet ascertained. Ours, though not exactly known, is not very considerable; theirs we have reason to believe was much greater, as some of our parties, composed of expert marksmen, had opportunities of giving them several close, well directed fires; more particularly in one instance, when a body of riflemen formed a kind of ambuscade. They advanced about two miles this side of Iron Hill, and then withdrew to that place, leaving a picket at Cooch's mill, about a mile in front.

"The design of their movement this morning seems to have been to disperse our light troops, who had been troublesome to them, and to gain possession of Iron Hill, to establish a post, most probably, for covering their retreat in case of accidents."

Published by order of CONGRESS, CHARLES THOMPSON, Sec.

BURGOYNE ANXIOUS.

FISH KILL, *September* 4, 1777.—A deserter from Kingsbridge informs, that the enemy have employed a number of Tories, both by night and day, to guard every road in order to take up deserters from their camp, for whom they have four pounds a head; they are extremely vigilant, and have lately taken many. Some of them are condemned to die.

It is said, that Burgoyne begins to grow anxious for the safety of his main body, having retired with it to the east side of the river at Saratoga, and building on the west side a picket fort.

Recreated from The Pennsylvania Packet, September 9, 1777.

STATE of VERMONT.
IN COUNCIL OF SAFETY.

BENNINGTON, *September* 11.

WHEREAS several persons in this State, have been so lost to the sense of their duty they owe to the supreme arbiter of rights; to their country, friends and relatives, as to join the tyrant of Great Britain, together with his foreign mercenary troops, and cruel savages in arms; and have been flagrantly guilty of shedding the guiltless blood of their innocent friends and neighbours. And whereas several women, wives to those merciless and unprovoked murderers, have aided and assisted in bringing about such of their designs, by harbouring, secreting, feeding, and giving private intelligence to the enemy's camp and scouts, are found to be dangerous persons to society, and instruments of great mischief to this and the United States of America.

Resolved therefore, That all such persons as have joined (or may hereafter join) the British troops, and left (or may hereafter leave) their wives and families within this State; have their wives and families sent to General John Burgoyne's head quarters, or some other branch of the ministerial army, as soon as may be.

Extract from the minutes, JOSEPH FAY, Sec.

Recreated from The Hartford Courant, October 21, 1777.

Extract of a letter from ALBANY, *Sept.* 15.

"Last Monday, the 8th instant, at gun-firing, our army moved forward, and they are now four miles above Stillwater, in the greatest spirits and health. The enemy have called in their Posts, which were stationed a little below Gen. Schuyler's house. Burgoyne continues his Head Quarters at Fort Miller. Gen. Lincoln with his army is at Pawler, a place from whence he can easily move in the rear of the enemy.

"Yesterday between 2 and 300 Indians arrived here; they almost all brought their arms with them, and no doubt they will now be taken into our service."

Recreated from The Hartford Courant, September 22, 1777.

BATTLE AT THE BRANDYWINE.

FLEET LEAVING ELK RIVER.

Extract of a letter from CHAD'S FORD, *dated Sept.* 11, 1777, 3 *quarters past* 8 *o'clock A.M.*

"The enemy are now advancing, and their present appearance indicates a disposition to pursue this route. If they do, I trust they will meet with a suitable reception, and such as will establish our liberties. They are now advanced near the Brandywine, and have fired several pieces of artillery."

By a gentleman last night from camp, which he left yesterday at noon, we learn that the enemy, about two o'clock in the morning, made a push, as was expected, to try to pass our army on the right, and to cross the Brandywine at Chad's Ford. On their moving, general Washington suspected their design, moved soon after, and took possession of the high grounds on this side of Chad's Ford, where the army lay last night. It is said the enemy halted at a place called Nicholas's Hill, about 7 miles from our army.

By various accounts, we learn that all the enemy's fleet, except 12 or 14 ships, have left Elk river, and gone down Chesapeake bay; and it is conjectured they mean to come up Delaware bay.

Recreated from Purdie's Virginia Gazette, September 26, 1777.

A letter from CHAD'S FORD, *September* 11, 1777, 5 *o'clock, P.M.*

To the Honourable JOHN HANCOCK, Esquire.

SIR,

WHEN I had the honor of addressing you this morning, I mentioned that the enemy were advancing and had began a cannonade. I would now beg leave to inform you, that they have kept up a brisk fire from their artillery ever since. Their advanced party was attacked by our light troops under General Maxwell, who crossed the Brandywine for that purpose, and had posted his men on some high grounds on each side the road.

The fire from our people was not of long duration, as the enemy pressed on in force, but was very severe. What loss the enemy sustained cannot be ascertained with precision, but from our situation and the briskness of the attack, it is the general opinion, particularly of those who were engaged, that they had at least three hundred men killed and wounded. Our damage is not exactly known, but from the best accounts we have been able to obtain, it does not exceed fifty in the whole.

After this affair the enemy halted upon the heights, where they have remained ever since, except a detachment of them which filed off about eleven o'clock from their left, and which has since passed Brandywine at Jones's Ford, between five and six miles above Chad's; the amount of it is not known, accounts respecting it being various, some making it two or three thousand strong, and others more. Generals Sullivan, Stirling, and Stevens, with their divisions, are gone in pursuit and to attack it, if they can with any prospect of success.

There has been a scattering loose fire between our parties on each side the brook, since the action in the morning, which just now became warm, when General Maxwell pushed over with his corps, and drove them from their ground, with the loss of thirty men left dead on the spot, among them a Captain of the 49th, and a number of intrenching tools, with which they were throwing up a battery.

At half after Four o'clock the enemy attacked General Sullivan at the Ford and above this, and the action has been very violent ever since. It still continues. A very severe cannonade has began here too, and I suppose we shall have a very hot evening. I hope it will be a happy one.

I have the honor to be, in great haste,
Sir, your most obedient servant,
ROBERT H. HARRISON.

Published by order of CONGRESS,
CHARLES THOMPSON, Sec.

Recreated from The Pennsylvania Packet, September 9, 1777.

ENEMY ARE MASTERS OF THE FIELD.

CHESTER, *Sept. 11, 1777. 12 o'Clock at Night.*
SIR,

I AM sorry to inform you that in this day's engagement we have been obliged to leave the enemy masters of the field. Unfortunately the intelligence received of the enemy's advancing up the Brandywine, and crossing at a ford about six miles above us, was uncertain and contradictory, notwithstanding all my pains to get the best. This prevented my making a disposition adequate to the force with which the enemy attacked us on our right; in consequence of which the troops first engaged were obliged to retire before they could be reinforced. In the midst of the attack on the right, that body of the enemy which remained on the other side of Chad's Ford, crossed it, and attacked the division there under the command of General Wayne and the light troops under General Maxwell; who after a severe conflict also retired. The Militia under the command of General Armstrong, being posted at a Ford about two miles below Chad's, had no opportunity of engaging. But though we fought under many disadvantages, and were from the causes above mentioned, obliged to retire; yet our loss of men is not, I am persuaded, very considerable; I believe much less than the enemy's. We have also lost seven or eight pieces of cannon, according to the best information I can at present obtain. The baggage having been previously moved off is all secure; saving the men's blankets, which being at their backs, many of them doubtless were lost.

I have directed all the troops to assemble behind Chester, where they are now arranging for this night. Notwithstanding the misfortune of the day, I am happy to find the troops in good spirits; and I hope another time we shall compensate for the losses now sustained.

The Marquis La Fayette was wounded in the leg, and General Woodford in the hand. Divers other officers were wounded, and some slain, but the numbers of either cannot now be ascertained.

I have the honor to be, Sir,
your obedient humble servant,
G. WASHINGTON.

P.S. It has not been in my power to send you earlier intelligence; the present being the first leisure moment I have had since the action.

Published by order of CONGRESS,
CHARLES THOMPSON, Sec.

Recreated from The Pennsylvania Packet, September 9, 1777.

MORE PARTICULARS OF BRANDYWINE.

Copy of a letter from a volunteer at Chester to his friend in ANNAPOLIS, *Sept. 12, 11 A.M.*

"I HAVE just time to drop you a few particulars of the bloody transaction of yesterday. Our army was posted in the heights of Brandywine, about 12 miles above Wilmington, at and contiguous to Chad's Ford. The enemy lay nearly opposite to them, though at a distance of several miles, on the other side of the creek. About sunrise a small body of the enemy appeared opposite Chad's Ford, and began a heavy cannonade upon our lines, which was returned with equal vigour. They at the same time, being posted upon the hills around, made several efforts as if to attack us with small arms.

"General Maxwell's light troops fell in with them upon the meadows of the Brandywine, and a very hot fire ensued, and each party was alternately drove back. In this skirmish we lost but few men, and the

---

TO BE LET,

NEAR one hundred acres of excellent PASTURE, fit to fatten a *number of Cattle* or *Horses*, with water in every field, in a retired corner of the country, about eight miles from town, in Lower Merion, opposite Righter's Ferry, on Schuylkill, the plantation where Mr. Thomas Norris lately lived. Apply to WILLIAM HULBERT, on the premises.

enemy suffered very considerably, not less I am assured than 500; for our troops were advantageously posted, and kept up a constant and well directed fire, almost the whole day.

"Their efforts to force the pass at Chad's Ford were evidently calculated only to amuse; for in the interim they had filed off up the creek in a large body, and crossed the forks of Brandywine, and marched very rapidly down upon our right, where General Sullivan's and Lord Stirling's divisions were posted. General Sullivan's division, in filing off to take possession of their ground on the right, fell into some disorder, and before they had time to form regularly the enemy approached, and immediately a hot and incessant discharge of small arms began, which continued most obstinately for near an hour, without cessation, when our troops gave way.

"However, being reinforced, about half after five o'clock, the attack began again, and lasted near one hour longer, when orders were given to retreat, which was done. The enemy at the same time passed Chad's Ford, where they suffered much. We have not lost many."

Several gentlemen, who saw a great part of the action of Thursday, have passed through this place; their accounts agree with the above letter. They add, that the enemy's loss is generally supposed to be from 1500 to 2000. One gentleman who passed through town yesterday evening, and left Chester late on Friday, informs, that from intelligence received, the enemy acknowledge their loss to be from 15 to 1800 men, amongst them three general officers killed, and a fourth wounded, having his leg broken. Our whole loss, according to the last and best accounts, killed, wounded, and missing, does not exceed 800.

WILLIAMSBURG, *Sept.* 26.—Last Tuesday near two hundred sail of the enemy's fleet of men war and transports went down the bay, and next morning were seen to clear the capes, supposed to be bound for Delaware. Five or six ships of war still remain in our bay.

Recreated from Purdie's Virginia Gazette, September 26, 1777.

A LETTER FROM ENGLAND.

BOSTON, *September* 29, 1777.

Extract of a letter from a Customs-House Officer at BRIXHAM, *in England, to his Son in* NEW YORK, *taken in a Prize lately arrived, dated June* 15, 1777.

"I was glad to hear of your health and safe arrival at New York, and am very glad to hear that the English army have made such great conquests in the East River, but should be better satisfied if a speedy reconciliation between England and America took place, and put an end to the rebellion, that trade may flourish here as it did before it began. I wish it may not make a Rebellion in England before there is an end put to it.

"There is a great many American privateers in the English channel, and on the coast of Ireland; they take a great many of our Coasters and Merchant vessels that go up and down the Coast, & send them all to France. I suppose it will at last end in a French war, and believe it will be soon.

"The press keeps on as when you went away, although the grand fleet of observation at Spithead are fully mann'd, I suppose it is to man other ships that are daily putting in commission. Every thing in trade goes on very dull in England; never was such times as is now; the very fishermen here at Brixham are starving for want of employment; however, smuggling keeps on here pretty well yet; but if there comes a French war, I suppose there will be an end to that too. Thank God, I have made a tolerable good hand of it since you went away, I made a middling good seizure Yesterday in Tingmouth Bay, of a Sloop and Cargo."

LOST, a GOLD RING, a feal made by the Letters N S engraved on the Ring. Whoever finds and returns the fame to the Printer, fhall be handfomely rewarded.

Recreated from The Hartford Courant, October 7, 1777.

BATTLE AT STILL WATER.

In Council at Lebanon.

September 23, 1777.

By Mr. Brown, *this moment arrived from the* NORTHERN ARMY, *we have the following authentic intelligence.*

ON Friday the 19th instant, the American Army lay encamped four miles above Still Water, on Behmus's Heights, the west side of Hudson's river; the enemy at Van Veghten's Mills, seven miles north. At one o'clock P.M. the advanced guard of our army, composed of Morgan's Corps of Riflemen from Virginia, and detachments from the other corps, posted about one mile and a half in front of the army, were attacked by three regiments of British troops, and after an obstinate dispute obliged the enemy to give way, with considerable loss. At three o'clock, the enemy being reinforced, renewed the attack. Our troops, being at the same time supported by the left wing of the army, consisting of the whole of General Arnold's division, received them warmly, and though the enemy brought on their whole force, against not more than one half of ours, maintained their ground till night, when both parties retired.

The loss of the enemy, in killed, wounded, and prisoners, (who are about 50) amounts to near a thousand. The enemy had two pieces of artillery in the action, one of which was taken by us, and retaken four different times, the enemy finally keeping it.

A general engagement was expected the next day, but did not take place. Deserters say that General Burgoyne is wounded in the small of his back. They likewise say, that they were informed in General Orders, that General Lincoln had arrived at Fort Edward with 6000 men, by which, all hopes of retreat being cut off, it remained for them only to conquer or perish.

A detachment of 500 men, were sent the 13th, from General Lincoln's division, lying then at Pawlet, nigh Skeensborough, under the command of Colonel Brown, to attack the enemy at the landing of Lake George, three miles from Ticonderoga, with a view to retake our prisoners and destroy the enemy's stores. Another detachment of equal number, under the command of Colonel Johnston, marched the same day for Mount Independence, to direct the enemy's attention from Colonel Brown; these parties have orders, (if they find it practicable) to attack Ticonderoga and the Mount, and endeavour to possess themselves of them. Colonel Woodbridge with an equal detachment, marched at the same time for Skeensborough, Fort Ann and Fort Edward; all places the enemy had evacuated, and collected their whole force at the Grand Army.

The day after the action nigh Still Water, General Gates was joined by 200 Indians (Oneidas) who, with the riflemen were detached the evening of the 20th, to give information of the enemy's situation, and to attack their out posts. The whole army expected to follow them early the 21st.

Lieut. Cols. Adams and Colburn of our troops were killed, and several other officers of inferior rank. The militia from this state were in the action, and it is with pleasure, we are informed that they behaved on the occasion with a bravery becoming Freemen.

Recreated from The Hartford Courant, September 29, 1777.

WASHINGTON CROSSES SCHUYLKILL.

BALTIMORE, *Sept.* 23.—A gentleman just arrived from camp informs, that General Washington crossed over the Schuylkill on Friday night, the 19th instant, with four divisions of his army, and are now encamped near the Swede's ford, in front of the enemy, lying on this side of the Schuylkill; Generals Wayne, Maxwell, and the militia under General Potter, in the rear of the enemy, whose camp is at the Valley Forge, about five or six miles from the Swede's ford. General Smallwood, with 2500 of the Maryland militia, joined General Wayne on Sunday morning, all in high spirits.

Recreated from Purdie's Virginia Gazette, October 10, 1777.

BURGOYNE WOUNDED AT STILLWATER.

FISH-KILL, *Sept.* 25, 1777.

Yesterday arrived here an express with the following intelligence:

Camp, four miles above STILLWATER, *Sept.* 20, 1777.

Dear SIR,

Being yesterday morning informed by our reconnoitering parties, that the enemy had struck their camp, and were advancing towards our left, the General detached Col. Morgan's light corps to examine their direction, and harass their advance. This party, at half past 12, fell in with a picket of the enemy, which they immediately drove and after a brisk fire, were beat back by a strong reinforcement. This skirmish drew a regiment from our camp, and the main body of the enemy, to support the action, which, after a short cessation, renewed with redoubled ardour, and continued incessant till the close of the day, when our men retired to camp, and the enemy to a small distance in the rear of the field. The succour, which we occasionally detached, amounted to nine regiments. I have not yet obtained a return, but have reason to believe, that our killed do not exceed eighty, and that the missing and wounded do not amount to two hundred.

The concurrent testimony of the prisoners and deserters, of various characters, assures us, that General Burgoyne, who commanded in person, was wounded in his left shoulder, that the 62d regiment was cut to pieces, and that the enemy suffered extremely in every quarter where they were engaged. As General Burgoyne's situation will shortly constrain him to a decisive action, reinforcements should be immediately pushed forward to our assistance, as our numbers are far from being equal to an insurance of victory, and every bosom must anticipate the consequences of defeat. The enemy have quietly licked their sores this day.

JAMES WILKINSON.

ALBANY IS BURGOYNE'S TARGET.

Extract of a letter from the Honourable General GATES *Monday morning,* 6 *o'clock, Sept.* 22.

To Matthew VISSCHER, ESQ.

By a number of scouts who came in from reconnoitering, I am convinced the enemy mean very speedily to renew their attack, Albany and not Ticonderoga, is undoubtedly General Burgoyne's target. Therefore, provide for the worst, and suffer not the least delay, in marching the militia to this camp. Inclosed, I send you a copy of the good news, received yesterday from Col. Brown.

I am, Sir, your most obedient humble servant,

HORATIO GATES.

Recreated from The Hartford Courant, September 29, 1777.

By his Excellency Sir William HOWE, K.B., *General and Commander in Chief, &c. &c.*

PROCLAMATION.

WHEREAS by my declaration, dated 27th of August, 1777, security and protection were promised to all persons, inhabitants of Pennsylvania, &c. &c. &c. excepting only those who have assumed legislative or judicial authority, provided they did forthwith return, and remain peaceably at their usual places of abode, this is to make known to all persons, who, in consequence of the said declaration, have complied with the same, that they may rely upon a due consideration hereafter shown to them, provided they do not forfeit their pretensions by a future conduct; and farther to proclaim, that those only who have availed themselves, before this date, of the indulgencies set forth in my said declaration, shall be esteemed entitled to the benefits thereof.

Given under my hand, at Head Quarters near GERMANTOWN, *the* 28*th day of September,* 1777.

WILLIAM HOWE.

Recreated from Purdie's Virginia Gazette, October 24, 1777.

SUCCESS IN THE NORTH.

BRITISH GAIN PHILADELPHIA.

WILLIAMSBURG.—*Extract of a letter from some of our Delegates in* CONGRESS *to a Gentleman in this city, dated* YORK *town, in* Pennsylvania*, September 30, 1777.*

CONGRESS have determined, upon due consideration, to hold their session in this place, where they are now assembled. We have the pleasure to congratulate you, Sir, on the success of our affairs in the North, the following state of which came this day to Congress from General Gates, by his Aid Major Troup.

"The American army being strongly posted about four miles above Stillwater, and 20 above Albany, was attacked upon the 19th instant by General Burgoyne, with his whole army. The action was entirely on our left wing, which sustained the whole force of the enemy until the night parted the combatants, when each withdrew to their respective camps. The enemy were divers times repulsed in this action, and, by the concurring accounts of prisoners, deserters, and some of our people, who escaped from them, have lost, in killed and wounded, between 1000 and 1200 men; 70 of them are our prisoners.

"All the accounts agree that General Burgoyne was wounded in the shoulder and carried off by some of his men. Previous to this battle, General Lincoln, who was in the rear of the enemy's army, had detached a body of troops to attack Ticonderoga and the passes between that place and General Burgoyne; in the waters of Lake George they took 50 batteaus, in the north end of Lake Champlain they got 150, including 17 gun boats and 1 armed sloop, on their passage they made 293 of the enemy's troops prisoners, and discharged 100 of our people, who were prisoners with them.

"Our troops are in possession of the old French lines at Ticonderoga, and had sent a summons to the commanders of Ticonderoga and Mount Independence to surrender, which met a spirited refusal; upon the whole it appears, that by the destruction of the enemy's vessels on Lake George, and in the upper part of Lake Champlain, with the force now in their rear under General Lincoln, that the retreat of the British army is extremely precarious. Major Troup informs us that he met large reinforcements going up to General Gates, that the army were in high spirits,, and that every thing promised success in that quarter.

"We understand that part of General Howe's army is now in possession of Philadelphia, and that General Washington was on his march towards the enemy. General M'Dougal, with about 1400 continental troops have joined the General, and our militia, with our State battalion, are well advanced towards the army, so that we hope, e'er long, to have the pleasure of sending you good news from that quarter.

"Captain Biddle, in the continental frigate Randolph, has taken and carried into Charlestown South Carolina, 2 ships and 2 brigs loaded with rum, sugar, &c. &c. One of the ships carried 20 guns, 6 pounders, and the other had eight guns."

Recreated from The Virginia Gazette, October 10, 1777.

LONDON, *October 3.*—In the late war, it was thought necessary to raise some troops in Virginia. At the same time, the present General Washington, by his indefatigable zeal for the service, raised a regiment called the Virginia Volunteers, which he commanded. Their activity and success were so remarkable, that the Reverend Mr. Davis, who preached a sermon, or rather delivered a panegyrick on the occasion, in Virginia, on his speaking of Mr. Washington, who was their Colonel, made use of the following sentence: "As for that young man (WASHINGTON) his uncommon bravery, conduct, and knowledge in the art of war, at his age, is superior to what I have ever read of; and he seems as if appointed by Providence to be, hereafter, the *protector and deliverer of his country.*"

Recreated from The North Carolina Gazette, December 26, 1777.

AMERICANS ATTACK AT GERMANTOWN.

Extract of a letter from a General officer, dated PAWLIN'S MILL, *October* 4, 1777.

"On the 2d of this instant the plan laid for attacking the enemy, by surprise, was put in execution yesterday the 3d, upon the disposition following. We began our march at 6 o'clock the evening before, with an intention to begin the attack at 5 next morning. Generals Sullivan's and Wayne's divisions formed the right wing, in order to attack the enemy's left; Generals Green and Stephen's divisions to form the left wing, and attack the enemy's right; General Conway's brigade to march in front of the troops that composed the right wing, and file off to attack the enemy's left flank; General MacDougall to march in front of the troops that composed the left wing, and to file off to attack the enemy's right flank; Generals Nash and Maxwell's brigades to form a corps of reserve; Generals Smallwood and Fenner's, with the militia from Maryland and Jersey, to attack the enemy's right wing in flank and rear; General Armstrong's militia of Pennsylvanians to attack the enemy on their left flank, and rear.

"The proper measures, previous to this enterprise, being concerted, we marched at the time mentioned, but having 14 miles to march, did not arrive so soon as we expected, so that it was near six in the morning of the 3d before the attack became general.

"The enemy's whole force was collected. We drove them two miles with considerable loss on their side. Our loss cannot be ascertained as yet; they have made some of our men prisoners. The loss of the enemy is uncertain, but believe they have suffered much, as we passed great numbers of them slain in the field. Our army arrived here again last night, much fatigued, having marched all night and all day without halting or refreshing; and am happy to find they have no objections to another trial, which must take place soon.

"The enemy were posted at Germantown, and all their troops from Philadelphia were called up the evening before, which makes me think they got wind of our intentions, notwithstanding the precautions used to prevent it."

Recreated from The Virginia Gazette, October 17, 1777.

PRINCESS ANNE, *Sept.* 23, 1777.

I intend to leave the Country in soon.   (tf)   ALEXANDER WATSON.

RICHMOND, *September* 25, 1777.

I intend for *Great Britain* by the first Opportunity.   (§)   JOHN SKELTON.

PRINCESS ANNE County, *Sept.* 20, 1777.

THE Subscriber intends for the *West Indies* in a few Weeks.   (§)   JOHN BRUCE.

For Sale, by DIXON & HUNTER,
THE
OFFICE and AUTHORITY
OF A
JUSTICE of PEACE
EXPLAINED AND DIGESTED,
Under proper TITLES.
By RICHARD STARKE, *Esquire.*

FOR SALE,
At the RALEIGH, in *Williamsburg*,
At a reasonable Price, for ready Money,
A great Variety of blue, brown, and light coloured broad and other
C L O T H S.

I HEREBY give Notice, that *Abraham Leafman* is under the Age of 14 Years, and, as I am informed he has enlisted into the Artillery Service, being an Apprentice of mine, I shall desire that he may be allowed to come with his Company, without further Trouble.
tf   FRANCIS LOCKETT.

Recreated from The Virginia Gazette, October 3, 1777.

CONFUSION IN THE FOG.

A BEATEN ENEMY KEEPS THE FIELD.

Extract of a letter from a member of CONGRESS, *dated* YORK, *Oct.* 10, 1777.

"On the 4th instant, our army made a wise and well concerted attack upon the British force, encamped at and near Germantown; the enemy were surprised, forced, and actually beaten; we were in possession of their camp, tents, artillery, &c. but they rallying to make a last effort, and our right and left columns in that instant approaching each other in their victorious progress, were, by each, mistaken for a fresh reinforcement coming up to the enemy, and instantly began to retreat, without allowing a possibility of being stopped. This was occasioned by a thick fog, and such a state of air as kept down the smoke of cannon, &c. so as to prevent the distinguishing of objects above 50 yards. Thus the enemy, though beaten, kept the field, and accident deprived us of a brilliant victory that was absolutely in our possession. Our troops however retired in order, though with too much precipitation, and brought off their wounded, cannon, and every thing else.

"Our loss in this affair is about 700 killed, wounded, and missing; that of the enemy very considerable no doubt, as they were pushed before our army two miles; but this is rendered more certain by an account brought from Philadelphia by a person who can be relied on, that left the city since the battle. He says that the enemy lost General Agnew, Colonels Abercrombie, Walcott, Byrd of Virginia, and General De Heister's son killed, General Kniphausen wounded in the hand, and that between 2 and 300 waggons load of wounded were brought into the city before he left it; this is confirmed by many Quakers who were at the yearly meeting, and who add, that Howe had actually sent 2000 Hessians over Schuylkill, probably to secure a retreat. He refused to let any of the inhabitants of Philadelphia see the field of battle.

"On our part, General Nash is dead of his wounds, Colonel Hendricks and Lieutenant Colonel Parker from Virginia, wounded, but not mortally; two of General Sullivan's aids mortally wounded, Colonel Stone of Maryland wounded, not mortally. We have not yet a particular list of the killed and wounded from the General.

"Last evening came an account to town that Captain Barry had attacked the frigate Delaware (lately taken from us at Philadelphia) with the brig Andrew Doria of 14 guns and two gallies, and had retaken the frigate. It is fine news if it proves true. Our army is in excellent spirits, satisfied they can beat the enemy, and keen for another opportunity of trying; they will probably be indulged in a few days, as our Virginia reinforcements of 17 or 1800 have got up since the engagement."

Recreated from Purdie's Virginia Gazette, November 7, 1777.

Extract of a letter, dated YORK *town, Oct.* 10.

"On Saturday morning, about day break, our troops attacked the enemy in Biggar's town and Germantown, two miles below it, nearly at the same time. We continued to drive them from every post we assaulted for three hours; they at last took shelter in the stone houses and churches, from whence they annoyed us much.

"While our men were endeavouring to dislodge them from Mr. Chew's house, they had time to bring up a reinforcement of fresh troops. In the mean while, two of our divisions, falling in from different quarters, mistook each other for reinforcements of the enemy; a mistake occasioned by the thick fog, which prevented our seeing the distance of thirty yards. This accident threw our troops in some confusion, and contributed to being on a retreat; however, the enemy did not dare to pursue.

"From pretty good authority, we are assured they had between 2 and 300 waggons employed in carrying their wounded to Philadelphia, and Howe would not permit the citizens to see the field of battle."

Recreated from Purdie's Virginia Gazette, October 24, 1777.

BATTLE OF FORT MONTGOMERY.

Fish-Kill, *October* 9, 1777.

LAST Friday a few of the enemy's vessels appeared standing up the North River, and the next morning about 30 sail, great and small, with a number of flat bottomed boats, came up as far as Tarry Town, where they landed some of their men, with a view, no doubt, to draw our forces at Peek's Kill that way; the next morning they re-shipped them, and, with a fresh southerly breeze, proceeded up the river, till nearly opposite Peek's Kill, where they again landed a few of their troops, but their main body they landed on the opposite shore; and on Monday those at Peek's Kill crossed likewise.

The enemy then, to the amount of 4000 men, marched towards forts Montgomery and Clinton, which were garrisoned by about 600 men, and between the hours of one and two P.M. attacked them. Our fire, which was very hot, put them into confusion several times; but about the dusk of the evening, through the superiority of their numbers, they got our breast-works, and possessed themselves of the forts. Many of the garrison, taking advantage of the night, made their escape, even after the enemy had been some time master of the posts.

It is said the enemy refused to give quarter, and continued firing on our people after they had scaled the ramparts, but being favoured by the night, our men received little damage from their fire. Our men fought with surprising bravery, made a gallant defence, and nothing was wanting but more men. His Excellency General Clinton narrowly made his escape, as did the general his brother, who is wounded. Colonels Dubois and Lamb, and several other officers, got safe off. The enemy knowing but too well our weakness, and the tardy march of our militia, availed themselves of their advantage by a most sudden attack; for had the forts been able to hold out but two or three hours longer, they would have been supplied with a reinforcement fully sufficient to defend them.

Our loss at these forts is considerable; and we were under the disagreeable necessity of destroying Fort Constitution, after removing part of the stores, and of burning the frigates Congress and Montgomery, to prevent their falling into the enemy's hands, the wind and tide being unfavourable to their moving farther up the river.

The enemy sent in a flag of truce to demand the fort, which the governor refused in the most peremptory terms; at the same time they were most dishonourably surrounding it.

Recreated from The Maryland Gazette, October 30, 1777.

A SEVERE TARTAR EMETICK.

New Windsor, *October* 11, 1777.

To General Putnam.

Dear General,

IN consequence of a severe tartar emetick, which I ordered to be given the spy I have in my possession, a small silver bullet came up, from which I have taken a letter from Clinton to Burgoyne, of which the enclosed is an exact copy.

With esteem, I am, dear general,
your obedient servant,
Gen. George Clinton.

• • • •

Fort Montgomery, *October* 8, 1777.

To General Burgoyne.

NOUS y voici, and nothing now between us but Gates. I sincerely hope this little success of ours may facilitate your operations. In answer to your letter of the 28th Sept. by C.C. I shall only say, I cannot presume to order, or even advise, for reasons obvious, I heartily wish you success.

Faithfully yours,
H. CLINTON.

Recreated from The Virginia Gazette, October 17, 1777.

THE BATTLE OF SARATOGA.

Extract of a letter from a Gentleman in ALBANY *to his friend in* BALTIMORE, *dated October 10, 1777.*

"Heaven has smiled upon us here most benignly. You doubtless have heard of our action with the enemy on the 19th ult. The particulars may nevertheless be agreeable. About 12 o'clock they attacked and drove in our piquet on the quarter where the riflemen were stationed, who were immediately ordered out, and presently engaged the enemy. They being in force, we were obliged to order out eight more regiments, who fought them until night parted them, when the enemy retired to the rear of the field, and our troops to their quarters. Our loss on the occasion was, killed, wounded, and missing, 319; the enemy's, by the best accounts, 744. This action was but a prelude to one of the most important events that has happened during the war.

"On the 7th instant they appeared in force, on the same ground where the last action was fought, about one mile from our camp. We turned out and met them at about one o'clock, when a pretty general and very severe engagement ensued, which lasted till night. The behaviour of our troops on the occasion is beyond description. General Arnold, with his usual bravery, led them on. They pushed the enemy with fixed bayonets from breastwork to breastwork, and mounted an intrenchment before the very mouths of their cannon.

"We finally drove them from eight different redoubts, in assaulting one of which poor General Arnold received a shot, which broke his leg, and killed his horse, and I am afraid he must either lose his leg or his life. The loss on either side we have not been able to ascertain. I rode over the field, and saw a number of the enemy's dead, and but few of ours. If I may judge from what I saw, I do not believe we have lost fifty; nor can I learn of any officer, excepting one captain and two lieutenants, being killed.

"We took from them in this affair eight pieces of cannon, a number of carriages, more ammunition than we expended in the action, and about 200 prisoners, besides wounded, who fell into our hands. Among the prisoners are Sir Francis Clarke, aid de camp to General Burgoyne, wounded through the body; Major Ackland, member of the House of Commons, who commanded the grenadiers, wounded through both legs; Major Williams, commanding their regiment of artillery; their quarter master general, and some other officers of distinction, whose names I do not recollect. But, to crown the whole, *General Fraser lost his life.*

"The next day, the eighth, we pushed the enemy so hard, that, about eleven at night the whole body retreated six miles to Saratoga, where our general has posted a strong party to dispute their passage over Hudson's river, which in all probability will retard them till we come up with them. They left behind them three hundred of their sick and wounded, about seventy batteaus, and fifty barrels of provisions and some other matters of no great consequence.

"On the eighth we met with a very severe misfortune. General Lincoln, a man universally respected, a well for his amiable character as his military abilities, received a shot which broke his leg, as he was reconnoitering the enemy. This loss is universally regretted, and with the greatest reason.

"The gentlemen who are prisoners with us have done us the honour of saying they never saw such attention paid to people in their station in their lives; the generous treatment they receive nearly compensates the painful ideas of being prisoners. I could wish we might with justice say as much for them."

Prince-George's county, Oct. 16, 1777.

COMMITTED to my custody, as a runaway, a NEGRO lad, by the name of Scipio, who says he belongs to Dr. Leper, of Anne-Arundel county. His master is desired to take him away, and pay charges.

THO. DUCKETT, Sheriff.

Recreated from The Maryland Gazette, October 23, 1777.

ARNOLD AND LINCOLN WOUNDED.

A letter from TRUMBULL, *Esq., Paymaster General of the northern department, to* Col. DYER, *member of* CONGRESS.

ALBANY, *October* 9, 1777.

DEAR SIR,

THE last two or three days have produced very important events in this department. On the afternoon of the seventh an action commenced, about three o'clock, between the pickets of the two armies, which, being reinforced on each side, continued till it drew out the whole of Major General Arnold's division. The contest was warm, and continued with obstinacy on both sides until the evening, when our troops gained the advanced lines of the enemy on their right, these lines and works forming an extent of about half a mile.

Our people entered, and kept encamping on the ground all night; they found themselves possessed of about three hundred and thirty tents with kettles boiling with corn, nine brass cannon from six to twelve pounders, two hundred prisoners, the dead a great number, with baggage and plunder of the flying camp. Among the prisoners are Sir Francis Carr Clark, aid to General Burgoyne, a Quarter Master General (said to be Carleton), Major Williams of artillery, and several others of distinction.

It was expected the action would be renewed this morning; an cannonade indeed began, but produced nothing material. On the action of the seventh we have to regret that Major General Arnold received a dangerous wound in the leg, a compound fracture, that endangers the limb.

The next morning Major General Lincoln was also wounded in near the same place and manner, and it is feared they must both lose a leg each. Besides these misfortunes, our troops suffered but little. They behaved with great bravery and intrepidity, and have a second time triumphed over the valour of veteran troops.

The cannonade yesterday proves now to have been kept up by way of cover to their preparations for retreating, which was begun last night about eleven o'clock, having improved the day in loading their baggage waggons, &c. and sending off what they could. General Gates, however, was not deceived by appearances; but, suspecting their designs, despatched yesterday two parties to go round on their rear, and this day two brigades are in pursuit of the flying army. It is said a body of men from the Eastward is already at Fort Edward. I have great hopes their retreat will be greatly impeded and harassed, if not totally cut off. They left us it is said, about three hundred sick and wounded in their hospital houses. Our army are on the enemy's late camp.

Recreated from Purdie's Virginia Gazette, October 24, 1777.

To be SOLD at *Westover*, the seat of the late Hon. *William Byrd*, Esq; in *Charles City* county, on *Thursday* the 6th of *November* next, if fair, otherwise next fair day, for ready money,

PART of the estate of the said deceased, consisting of forty likely Virginia born SLAVES, among whom are several very valuable tradesmen, particularly a fine blacksmith, a forgeman, colliers, carpenters, and very valuable miners; also the whole of his elegant and valuable household and kitchen furniture, five hundred ounces of fashionable plate, the plantation utensils, the whole of the stocks of horses, cattle, and sheep, the set of coach horses, together with the coach and chariot, several breeding mares, and some high-blooded colts, about 100 tuns of hay of last year's crop, in good order, and greatly improved by keeping, and many other articles too tedious to mention.

The EXECUTRIX.

☞ *The negroes will be well clothed.*

Recreated from Purdie's Virginia Gazette, October 17, 1777.

BURGOYNE'S CAPITULATION.

KINGSTON, *October* 15, 1777, 10 *o'clock*, P.M.

To General PUTNAM.

DEAR GENERAL,

WHAT follows is a copy of a letter from the chairman of the committee of safety of the city of Albany to the President of the Council of Safety. I congratulate you on the importance contained therein.

GEORGE CLINTON.

ALBANY, *October* 15, 1777.

"Last night, at 8 o'clock, the capitulation whereby General Burgoyne, and the whole army, surrendered themselves prisoners of war, was signed; and this morning they are to march out towards the river, about Fish creek, with the honours of war, and then to ground their arms, from thence they are to be marched to Massachusetts government. Glorious God be praised for his mercies. I cannot write more."

HUGH SMITH.

A CHEERFUL EVENING.

WILLIAMSBURG, *Oct.* 31.—By the Northern post yesterday are received a solid confirmation of the success of our arms to the North, in the surrender of General Burgoyne, with his whole army, to the victorious immortal GATES. Upon receiving this great and glorious news a general joy diffused itself amongst all the ranks, the regular troops and militia of the city were instantly paraded, and both from artillery and small arms resounded the glad tidings, the inhabitants illuminated their houses, and, with the gentlemen of the General Assembly, spent a cheerful and agreeable evening, wherein the names of WASHINGTON, GATES, ARNOLD, LINCOLN, &c. &c. &c. were often bumpered, with huzzas to the independence of America. Burgoyne's total overthrow was a very fortunate event to America, as general Clinton, at the head of 3000 men from New York, was forcing his way up the North river to relieve him, and had actually possessed himself of fort Montgomery in the highlands, but not without a severe conflict, and great loss.

Governour Clinton of the state of New York bravely defended the fort, with only 400 men, and thrice repulsed the enemy; but it was at length carried by assault. Our loss, killed, wounded, and missing, was about 200. Governour Clinton, with the remainder of the garrison, retreated above Windsor, where General Gates has reinforced him; and as General Putnam, with a stout body of men, is also pushing after the enemy, we hope soon to have the pleasure of congratulating our readers on the surrender of this *forlorn hope* of the British tyrant.

General Washington's army by the last accounts, was very strong, in high spirits, and advancing upon the enemy, who, on their part, seem apprehensive, by intrenching themselves, and breaking up and stopping all the roads leading to their camp.

During General Burgoyne's retreat before the conquering Gates his army marked their flight with every species of cruelty, and burnt and plundered all the gentlemen and farmers houses, amongst them the extensive buildings and mills belonging to General Schuyler, thereby endeavouring (to borrow General Gates's own words to Burgoyne) to ruin those whom they could not conquer, a conduct which he tells him betrays more of the vindictive malice of a monk than the generosity of a soldier. Our general's return for such base and unworthy treatment was the utmost tenderness and attention to the enemy's hospital of about three hundred sick and wounded, whom they were obliged, in the action before their surrender, to leave to our mercy.

Poor Old England, O how art thou fallen! Late so great among the nations! The ocean's stately queen!

Your spirit is gone, you coffers are empty, they fly to the west, where soon will reign

PEACE and PLENTY.

Recreated from Purdie's Virginia Gazette, October 31, 1777.

THE CONVENTION OF SARATOGA.

Copy of a letter from General Gates *to* CONGRESS, *dated camp at* SARATOGA, *Oct.* 18.

To His Excellency John HANCOCK, esq.

I HAVE the satisfaction to present your Excellency with the convention of Saratoga, by which his Excellency Lieutenant General Burgoyne has surrendered himself and his whole army into my hands; and they are now upon their march to Boston. This signal and important event is the more glorious, as it was effected with so little loss to the army of the United States. This letter will be presented to your Excellency by my Adjutant General, Col. Wilkinson, to whom I must beg leave to refer your Excellency for the particulars that brought this great business to so happy and fortunate a conclusion, and desire to be permitted to recommend this gallant officer in the warmest manner to Congress, and entreat that he may be continued in his present place, with the rank of Brigadier General. The Hon. Congress will believe me when I assure them, that from the beginning of this war I have not met with a more promising military genius than Col. Wilkinson, and whose services have been of the greatest benefit to this army.

I am, Sir, your Excellency's most obedient, humble servant,

HORATIO GATES.

To be SOLD for ready money,

THE sloop SWALLOW, now lying at Scar[ ] Quay, lately from sea, commanded by Captain Richard Idms. She is about three years old, sails fast, and is very completely fitted with sails, rigging, &c. The purchaser may have with her two four pounders, two swivel guns, and four muskets, also powder and ball sufficient for a voyage. The terms may be known of Robert F. Hoor, at Suffolk.

(2)   JENIFFER & HOOE.

ALEXANDRIA, October, 25. 1777.

Recreated from Purdie's Virginia Gazette, November 14, 1777.

GENERAL ORDERS.

Saturday, 18*th October,* 1777.

The general has his happiness completed relating to the success of our northern army; on the 14th instant gen. Burgoyne and his whole army surrendered themselves prisoners of war. Let every face brighten, and every heart expand with grateful joy, to the supreme disposer of all events, who has granted us this signal success.

All the chaplains of the army, are to prepare, suited to this joyful occasion, short disclosures to deliver to their several corps and brigades at 5 o'clock this afternoon; immediately after which 13 pieces of cannon are to be discharged at the artillery park, to be followed by a feu de joy with blank cartridges or powder, by every brigade and corps in the army, beginning at the right of the front line and running on to the left of it, and instantly beginning at the left of the second line and running to the right of it, where it will end.

ARMY AT CHESTNUT HILL.

Extract of a letter from BALTIMORE, *Oct.* 21.

"Jesse Hollingsworth came home, last evening, from Elk. He brings an account that the enemy have certainly abandoned Wilmington and gone on board their transports. A heavy cannonade at Fort Mifflin on Thursday and Friday; we beat off two ships, tore them to pieces, and dismasted the Phoenix; that our army on Friday were at Chestnut Hill."

PROVIDENCE, *Sept.* 13.—Last week a small privateer belonging to Bristol, prized a sloop at Nantucket, and conveyed her to a safe port. She was from New York and had taken on board, at Nantucket, a large quantity of valuable household furniture, &c. the property of Frederick William Geyer, a Boston tory, who fled from that place to Halifax with the British fleet, and has since taken up residence at New York.

Recreated from The Maryland Gazette, October 23, 1777.

BURGOYNE REPORTS TO HOWE.

ALBANY, *October* 20, 1777.

In conformity to my orders "to proceed by the most vigorous exertions to Albany," I passed Hudson's river at Saratoga the 13th of September. No exertions have been left untried. The army under my command has fought twice against great superiority of numbers. The first action was on the 19th of September, when, after four hours sharp conflict, we remained masters of the field of battle; the second action, on the 7th of October, was not so successful, and ended with a storm upon two parts of our intrenchments; the one defended by Lieut. Col. Breyman, who was killed on the spot, and the post was lost; the other defended by Lord Balcarras at the head of the British light infantry, who repulsed the enemy with great loss. The army afterwards made good their retreat to the heights of Saratoga, unable to proceed farther, the enemy having the possession of all the forts and the passes on the east side of Hudson's river.

The army there waited the chance of events, and offered themselves to the attack of the enemy till the 13th instant, when only three days provision at short allowance remained. At that time the last hope of timely assistance being exhausted, my numbers reduced by past actions to 3500 fighting men, of which about 1900 alone were British; invested by the enemy's troops to the amount of 16,000 men, I was induced by the general concurrence and advice of the generals, field officers, and captains commanding corps, to open a treaty with Major General Gates.

Your Excellency will observe by the papers transmitted herewith, the disagreeable prospect that attended the first overtures. The army determined to die to a man rather than submit to terms repugnant to national and personal honour. I trust you will think the treaty inclosed consistent with both.

I am, with the greatest respect and attachment,
J. BURGOYNE.

Recreated from The Hartford Courant, December 2, 1777.

NEWS REACHES BRITAIN.

LONDON, *December* 6.—On Wednesday morning early arrived in town express Capt. Moubray of the navy, who left Quebec about the end of October, having the homeward-bound fleet from that place under convoy; and by this gentleman, we are sorry to say, that Government have received the melancholy accounts, that Gen. Burgoyne and his army have been obliged to surrender themselves prisoners of war.

This disagreeable capitulation we learn, was effected on October the 16th, after two bloody actions between him and Gates's Rebel army, in which Gen. Burgoyne lost a great number of men. Early in the morning of the day, Mr. Gates (whose army consisting of 32,000 men, totally surrounded the shattered British troops) sent a Flag of Truce to Gen. Burgoyne, "requiring him to surrender himself and his army prisoners of war, to save the dreadful effusion of blood which must otherwise unavoidably ensue."

The gallant Burgoyne, without hesitation, returned for answer, "that he and his little army were determined never to be thus made prisoners in America, be the consequence what it might." Gates sent another Flag of Truce, "desiring him to re-consider the matter, in order for which, he gave him an hour to deliberate; for that nothing but a miracle could effect their escape, as he had environed him in such a manner, and with such a force, as rendered his retreat, or escape impossible." The British General now called a Council of War, who were unanimous, that further opposition could not avail, and therefor Gen. Burgoyne returned for answer to Mr. Gates, "that he would surrender, on the condition that he, and the remainder of his army, were permitted to return to England, either by the way of Boston, or Quebec;" at the same time passing his *parle d' bonneur*, that neither he nor any of his body should draw a sword against the Provisional forces, during the whole course of the war; which was acceded to on the part of the Rebel General.

We have it on good authority, that General Burgoyne, before he surrendered, sent a message to the Commander in Chief of the American Army, that he had consulted his officers and men, who were unanimously resolved, rather than submit without conditions, to sell their lives very dear, and to fall by the Sword. On which the terms he demanded were granted.

The Train of Artillery which fell into the hands of the Americans, in the late unfortunate affair, is said to be worth at least £500,000, besides three thousand guineas in the military chest.

Two thousand five hundred men were in garrison at Ticonderoga when Gen. Burgoyne capitulated, who were well provided both with provisions and military stores.

Letters from Quebec mention, that Lord Petersham had been wounded in the arm, and was conveyed, with several other disabled officers to Skeensborough, where they were attended by the surgeons in the British service, who were all set at liberty upon their parole.

HOUSE of COMMONS, *Dec.* 4.

Colonel Barre called on Lord George Germain to inform the House whether the report that General Burgoyne had surrendered to Arnold was true or false. Lord George Germaine said, that he had received dispatches from Quebec with this account, "that some deserters had arrived at Ticonderoga, who said that the remains of General Burgoyne's army had surrendered to the enemy on the 16th of October."

The event, he observed, was melancholy; nothing but the greatest distress, and superiority of strength could have forced General Burgoyne to submit. He knew himself to be responsible for the orders he had given. These he was ready to communicate to the House when called upon; as to the expedition, it was well planned; if on enquiry it should be found otherwise, he wished the Gentlemen would let their censure fall on the measure, not on the General, who, he was convinced, had done his duty, and who would, no doubt, be able at his return, to clear himself on any imputation that might be fastened on him; he repeated that the plan had been well concerted; and that it was only to be lamented that it had not been successful.

Colonel Barre exclaimed, with an averted look, great God! Who can refrain from rage and indignation, when the planner of so much misery, relates with the utmost composure the horrid tale of a British army destroyed through his measures? Who can look at him without contempt and scorn? We need not be told that superiority of numbers and the greatest distress were necessary to force Burgoyne to surrender. Who thought otherwise? We all know that General's bravery and skill. He is a Briton; his troops were British; he therefore could not surrender whilst there was a possibility of defence. But at the same time that justice commands us to give these just eulogiums where they are so deservedly due; what must we say of the man who reduced so gallant an Officer to the sad alternative of dying without the smallest advantage to his country, or disgracefully submitting to the Law of a Conqueror?

Mr. Burke observed, the Americans had been always represented as cowards. This was far from being true; and he appealed to the conduct of Arnold towards Gen. Burgoyne as a striking proof of this bravery. Our army was totally at their mercy. We had engaged the Indians to butcher them, their wives and children; yet, generous to the last degree, they give our men leave to depart on their parole, never more to bear arms against North America. Bravery and cowardice could never be inhabitants of the same bosom; generosity, valour, and humanity are ever inseparable. Poor, indeed, they are; but in that consists their great strength; 60,000 men have fallen at the feet of their magnanimous, because voluntary, poverty. They had not yet lost all regard for the country from whence they sprung; anxious still for our home defence, they have sent us back our troops, and left their hands free to fight against every enemy of Great Britain but themselves.

Recreated from The Leeds Intelligencer, England, December 9, 1777.

A JUST REVENGE?

Extract of a letter from General GATES, *to* CONGRESS, *dated October* 20, 1777.

Inclosed is the copy of a letter I have this day sent to Major Gen. Vaughn, who, I am told commands the burning party, on Hudson's river. It goes by the boat that carries Gen. Burgoyne's officer to Sir William Howe; such answer as I receive, shall be sent to your Excellency.

• • • •

ALBANY, 19th *October*, 1777.

To Hon. John VAUGHN, Maj. Gen.

With unexampled cruelty you have reduced the fine village of Kingston to ashes, and most of the wretched inhabitants to ruin. I am informed you also continue to ravage and burn all before you, on both sides of the river

It is thus your King's Generals think to make converts to the royal cause? It is no less surprising than true, that the measures they adopt to serve their master, have quite the contrary effect. Their cruelty establishes the glorious act of Independency, upon the broad basis of the general resentment of the people.

Abler Generals and much older officers, than you can pretend to be, are now by the fortune of war, in my hands; their fortune may one day, be yours, when, Sir, it may not be in the power of any thing human to save you from the just revenge of an injured people.

I am, Sir, your most obedient humble servant,

HORATIO GATES.

Published by order of CONGRESS,
CHARLES THOMPSON, Secretary.

Recreated from The Hartford Courant, December 9, 1777.

FOR SALE, a likely young Negro Wench with her fucking Child. She can wash, iron, and wait in the House equal to any in *Virginia*. Inquire of the Printers.

Recreated from The Virginia Gazette, October 3, 1777.

ENEMY LOSES 64 GUN SHIP.

Camp, WHITPAIN, 15 *miles from* PHILADELPHIA, *October* 24, 1777.

The night before last the Hessians with near 3000 men, attempted to storm the fort at Red Bank, were repulsed, about 400 or 500 killed and wounded; Count Donop, his Brigade Major, and upwards of 100 prisoners, and their cannon supposed to be left in the woods.

Yesterday a most severe cannonade all the morning; their ships came up to the Cheveaux de Frize, but were drove back with the loss of the Augusta, of 64 guns, and a frigate, some say the Apollo, but certainly two, of which the Augusta is one. I heard the explosion and saw the smoke from Germantown. They seem determined to carry those forts, but such another repulse must drive them off. We move a few miles to-morrow. *In haste, &c.*

C. BIDDLE.

Recreated from The Hartford Courant, November 4, 1777.

ATTEMPT ON FORT MIFFLIN.

Extract of a letter, dated Head Quarters, GERMANTOWN, *Oct.* 25, 1777.

I WAS a spectator to a most glorious sight yesterday. Placed on the top of a high house in Germantown, I beheld the destruction of two of the British ships attempting to bombard Fort Mifflin, on the Jersey shore, in order to facilitate their siege against Mud Fort; the most violent and awful cannonade ensued that perhaps ever happened in this quarter of the world.

The gondolas distinguished themselves; and so well concerted was the opposition to the attack, in the midst of confusion of smoke and fire, two ships were sent down and set fire to a 64 gun ship, said to be the Eagle, and a 32 gun frigate, by some said to be the Apollo; in an instant they were in flames, even up to the top gallant yards.

They must have had a valuable store of ammunition on board, for when their magazines were blown up, they surpassed the most horrid conception of noise. If all nature had been crushing to atoms, the sound could not have been more tremendous. During the time of this great cannonade the Hessians, in number about 3000, made an attack upon Fort Mifflin, and in a little time were defeated with the loss of 500 killed, wounded, and prisoners; among the prisoners we have Count Donop and his Aid de Camp, both wounded.

The destruction of the two ships, and defeat of the Hessians, is looked upon as one of the most capital strokes that has happened during the war. I hope a coup de main will be Mr. Howe's fate before long. And then for peace, freedom, and happiness.

Recreated from The North Carolina Gazette, November 21, 1777.

Extract of a letter from our Delegates in CONGRESS, YORK town, *October* 31, 1777.

SIR,

WE have the honour and the pleasure to enclose you a copy of the capitulation, by which General Burgoyne and his army surrendered themselves prisoners of war. This great affair might have been still greater, if the near approach of Sir Henry Clinton to Albany (where our military and provision stores were lodged) had not rendered despatch necessary with General Burgoyne''s army.

Two thousand brave men, under General Stark, are gone to Ticonderoga, and General Gates, with the main body of his army, is moving down the North river, to meet General Vaughn, who yet remains about 50 miles below Albany. Two brigades, with the light corps under Col. Morgan, are on their way to join General Washington. Nothing that we know of hath happened near Philadelphia since the enemy's unsuccessful attack on Red Bank and Fort Mifflin, in which two of their ships of war were lost, and Count Donop, with some inferior officers and 70 privates, made prisoners.

Recreated from The North Carolina Gazette, November 28, 1777.

ANOTHER BRITISH SCHEME.

A LETTER from a gentleman in New England, to his friend in Baltimore, mentions, that the valuable prize lately sent into Newbury Port proves to be a French brigantine, with a French Captain and crew, loaded at Yarmouth for Genoa and Leghorn, and had on board 250 bales of dry goods, and 30 tuns of lead, and supposed to be the richest prize brought into America since the commencement of the war. The Captain of her declares, that many other French vessels have been loaded in England by the British merchants, in hopes thereby of cloaking their property from American cruisers. This scheme has hitherto succeeded well for them, as it appears that many of the New England privateers have lately boarded such French vessels, which they did not conceive themselves at liberty to make prize of, having French crews and papers.

The same letter mentions another prize from London being brought into New England, on board of which was found concealed a letter to a house in Ireland, which confirms the report of the French Captain, advising that the merchants had adopted the scheme of shipping their goods in foreign bottoms to elude the Americans, being determined to haul up their own vessels.

It is well known how the British men of war and privateers served the Dutch in the late war, when employed as carriers for the French and with how little ceremony they condemned both vessels and cargoes, as legal prizes, upon scarcely any other evidence than their being loaded in French ports. To what wretched shifts are the haughty lords of the ocean already reduced, if necessitated to dispense with the boasted act of navigation, the great palladium of their commerce, and to copy after examples they so loudly condemned in others. It is hoped American cruisers will attend to this important discovery, and trace an insidious enemy through all their doublings.

Recreated from Purdie's Virginia Gazette, October 24, 1777.

ENEMY SHIPPING BLOCKED.

CITIZENS STARVING.

Extract of a letter dated WHITE MARSH, *November 6, 1777.*

SINCE my last, from Whippen camp, we have advanced the army to this place, about 12 miles from Philadelphia. Nothing, however, of any importance, has taken place in consequence. The enemy keep themselves close within their lines, which now extend from the Delaware to Schuylkill, and crosses about one mile above the town.

Their principal object at present seems to be our forts below the city, on which they have made several unsuccessful attempts. Whilst they are in our possession, it separates them from their shipping, which must distress them greatly for want of provisions and other necessaries.

We have daily accounts from town of a most distressing nature; the inhabitants are near starving. The head of an ox sold last Saturday in a market for twenty shillings, and beef shins at one shilling sixpence per pound.

The resolve of Congress declaring military law to all who shall be found aiding and assisting them with provisions has had a valuable effect. Some few individuals, indeed, are still so radically inclined as to risk their necks in support of them, and have at times found means to furnish them with small supplies of beef, &c. They have been at half allowance for some days, and till they do get their shipping up, their situation in that respect cannot be much better. This makes me think they will try every effort to open the communication of the river. Our little garrisons have for these six weeks held out with uncommon bravery; and if the enemy cannot reduce them, they must give up the city.

A heavy cannonade has just opened upon our forts. My mind is entirely engaged on the success of these important posts.

Recreated from The North Carolina Gazette, December 5, 1777.

BURGOYNE AT CAMBRIDGE.

BOSTON, *November 8.*—"Gen. Burgoyne, and the first division of his disarmed troops, are arrived at Cambridge, and the rest are expected next Saturday. To-morrow the Colonel of the Queen's dragoons is to dine with General Heath, in this town."

• • • •

The following is part of a resolve passed by the general Assembly of Massachusetts Bay, by which the publick will observe that the Bostonians mean to keep at a commendable distance from their British neighbours.

RESOLVED, that the troops under General burgoyne be quartered in the barracks on Prospect and Winter hills, and such other as a committee of both Houses hereafter to be appointed shall judge most safe, retired, and easily guarded, and that they obtain suitable houses for the General officers and proper rooms for other officers of rank; the foreign troops to be kept separate from the British, as far as practicable; both officers and soldiers to be prevented coming into the town of Boston, or on this side of Charlestown neck; and the committee aforesaid are directed to fix such limits for the restraint of officers and soldiers as may secure the publick from any ill consequences, so far as may be consistent with a strict fulfillment of the convention.

And it is farther resolved, that no inhabitant of the United States, or any other person whatever, shall at any time enter the limits assigned for preventing their communication with the prisoners, without a written license obtained for that purpose from the Council or Gen. Heath, under pain of military discipline, which Gen. Heath is hereby impowered and required to inflict. That the Hon. Council be requested to order 1000 men, including officers, and as many more as they shall find necessary, from such parts of the militia of this state as they shall judge equitable, to serve as guards, and be under the command of Gen. Heath.

Recreated from The North Carolina Gazette, January 2, 1778.

ENEMY EVACUATE TICONDEROGA.

Extract of a letter from ALBANY, *dated Nov.* 15, 1777.

"Ticonderoga is certainly evacuated; the works demolished, barracks burnt, and the post in general as bare as a bone."

The Hon. HENRY LAURENS, a member from South Carolina, is appointed President of the Hon. CONTINENTAL CONGRESS, in the Room of the Hon. JOHN HANCOCK, Esq.

By Order of CONGRESS; Thursday, the eighteenth Day of December next, is appointed to be observed as a Day of public Thanksgiving, throughout the United American States.

Recreated from The Hartford Courant, November 25, 1777.

NEW LONDON, *Nov.* 14.—Last Thursday morning a fleet of about 20 sail of shipping left Newport, bound to Gardiner's Island for wood, under convoy of the Syren frigate, Capt. Griffith, of 28 guns, which ship, together with two others of the fleet, (a ship and a schooner) soon after, in a gale of wind, ran ashore on the east side of Point Judith; when, by the vigilance of the troops on the shore, who had sundry pieces of artillery, the three vessels were taken possession of, together with near 200 prisoners; one or two were killed on board the vessels and several wounded. The guns, stores, &c. of the frigate were secured, but it being impracticable to save the vessel, she was on Sunday morning set on fire. The remainder of the fleet proceeded on their voyage, and are now in Gardiner's Bay.

HARTFORD, *November* 18, 1777.

On Friday last passed through this town, escorted by a party of Light Dragoons, the Hon. JOHN HANCOCK, Esq., President of the American Congress, with his Lady, on his way to Boston, after an absence, on publick business, of more than two and a half years.

Recreated from The Hartford Courant, November 18, 1777.

FORT MIFFLIN LOST.

Extract of a letter from a member of CONGRESS, *dated* YORK town, *November* 18.

"We were a few minutes ago informed, that we have lost Fort Mifflin. The enemy erected several batteries of very heavy cannon, with which they were able to knock the forts down. Our brave fellows behaved like men; they fought until all our cannon were dismounted. However, it gives me great pleasure to hear several gentlemen say that they do not believe Lord Howe will be able to raise the chevaux de frise, as we shall still annoy their ships, when they attempt it, by our gallies."

BRITISH RETREAT TO NEW YORK.

Extract of a letter from YORK town, *Nov.* 17.

"The Enemy have certainly blown up the forts Montgomery and Clinton, in the north river, and are retreated to New York, from whence they have sent a reinforcement to join Howe. Morgan's corps have joined our army at 6 mile stone; and three brigades from General Gates are on their way to join the same; what may be the consequence of these aids to both parties I cannot say. If Howe continues much longer in Philadelphia, by all accounts, there will be a dreadful famine in that city.

"The confederation is passed Congress, is now at press, and will be sent to the different states immediately."

Recreated from The North Carolina Gazette, December 12, 1777.

WILLIAMSBURG, *Nov.* 14, 1777.

Mann Page, Esq., junior, is elected a member of Congress, in the room of BENJAMIN HARRISON, Esq., whose ill state of health has prevented him serving his country any longer in that station.

JAMES MADISON, Esq., the younger, of Orange, is elected a member of the Privy Council of this State.

Recreated from The Virginia Gazette, November 14, 1777.

LOSS OF FORTS MIFFLIN & MERCER.

Extract of a letter from a Gentleman at EASTON, *November 23, 1777.*

An express has this morning arrived from camp, the accounts of him are, that 3000 of the enemy under the command of Gen. Cornwallis, crossed the Delaware to act in concert with 2000 men commanded by Gen. Wilson from New York.

On Thursday a very severe cannonade began, and continued all that day, supposed against the fort at Red Bank; which was renewed on Friday. In consequence of this Gen. Green, with his divisions and Col. Huntington's brigade, had marched into the Jersies. The event must be important, which we are waiting for with anxious expectation. Our fleet is above the city.

On Saturday evening the 15th inst. our people evacuated fort Mifflin; the attack was very severe, we lost about sixty men killed and wounded; our troops stood out until the fort was almost demolished; the stores were brought off, the barracks burnt, and the bank cut down to let in the water, which overflows the island. The enemy cut down an Indiaman for a floating battery, which greatly annoyed our people. Further particulars we have not been able to learn.

Thirty infamous tories, traitors, and deserters, are condemned to the gallows at Morris Town.

We are informed from good Authority, that Gen. Gates's command is enlarged to Peek's Kill, and that Gen. Putnam goes to the Southward.

By a gentleman who left Head Quarters at WHITE MARSH, 12 *miles from* Philadelphia, *the 20th of November, we have the following intelligence, viz.*

That Fort Mifflin was evacuated by our people Saturday the 15th, after they had defended it four days; in which time they lost 3 Captains, 1 Lieutenant, and about 40 men killed and wounded, and had all their cannon dismounted.

On the 19th about 5000 of the enemy landed at Billings fort, 7 miles below Red Bank, (a fort formerly in our possession) upon which our people retreated from fort Mercer 9 miles back to Haddonfield. Same day General M'Dougall's division crossed the Delaware about 17 miles above the city of Philadelphia. The 20th General Green's division crossed the same way, both divisions consisting of about 6000 men, in high spirits. Another division with Col. Proctor's regiment of artillery crossed Schuylkill, supposed to take possession of Province Island, which if executed, will cut off the enemy's supply of provisions.

Lord Cornwallis left the city of Philadelphia at one o'clock A.M. the 19th, supposed for Billings fort via Chester. At 9 o'clock, the 20th, Lord Stirling's division struck their tents. General Patterson's, Learned and Poor's brigades about 9 o'clock the 21st were within 14 miles of Head Quarters. General Glover's brigade at 12 o'clock were within 20 miles of Delaware, on their way to Trenton.

Recreated from The Hartford Courant, December 2, 1777.

NEW YORK, *November* 20.—Yesterday morning Mr. Brush, upwards of 19 months a prisoner in Boston goal, arrived here from that place, from whence he escaped on Wednesday evening the 5th instant.

Recreated from The North Carolina Gazette, January 30, 1778.

On Tuesday the 25th Instant will be sold at public Vendue, in the Town of Suffolk, sundry Merchandises, viz.

FIFTY one Pieces of coarse Woollen Cloth, fit for Negroes, &c. 130 ready made Shirts, 6 Pieces of Checks, 12 ditto of Cloth, 4 Bales of coarse Blankets, 218 Dozen of Sewing Thread. 1 lb. of Sewing Silk, 14 Bags of Coffee, 12 Hhds. of Molosses, 30 Casks of Rum. 2‖ JOHN & JOSEPH HARPER.

NOVEMBER 10, 1777.

Recreated from The Virginia Gazette, November 14, 1777.

ENEMY'S GALLANT RETREAT.

Extract of a letter from general GATES, *dated* ALBANY, *November* 16, 1777.

"I have the pleasure to acquaint the Congress, that the enemy have confirmed my opinion of their intentions, by burning and destroying all their works and buildings upon Mount Independence and Ticonderoga, and precipitately retiring to Isle aux Noix and St. John's. The heavy stores, &c. they threw into the lake, and it is believed carried off only the brass artillery, the powder, the provisions and the garrison.

"I take it for granted, that general Putnam and gen. George Clinton acquainted your excellency that the enemy abandoned all the forts and posts upon the North river the 28th ult. and retreated to New York; and that Fort Independence, near Kings-Bridge, is also evacuated and destroyed."

Recreated from The Maryland Gazette, December 18, 1777.

SHIP OF WAR GROUNDED.

PROVIDENCE, *Nov.* 15.—The British Ship of War SYREN, of 28 guns, Tobias Furneaux late commander, mentioned in our last to have ran on Point Judith, was compelled to strike her colours after receiving a few shot from an 18 pounder on the shore. The prisoners, including those taken out of the transport ship and schooner which ran ashore at the same time, amount to 166, and have been safely conducted here. The transport ship mounted carriage guns.

As it was judged impracticable to get off the Syren, a number of men were employed in stripping her, who got on shore her sails, the principal part of her rigging and stores, 17 puncheons of rum, &c. On Sunday night the enemy sent in some boats to set fire to the hull, which they effected; part of it however is only consumed, as her lower deck was under the water; the guns and many other valuable articles will still be saved. The transport ship is bilged, but the schooner we are told may be got off.

Recreated from The Hartford Courant, November 25, 1777.

THE CHARM OF LA FAYETTE.

Part of a letter from gen. WASHINGTON, *Nov.* 26.

"The marquis de la Fayette went to Jersey with gen. Green, and I find that he has not been inactive there; this you will perceive by the following extract from a letter just received from gen. Green, 'The marquis, with about 400 militia, and the rifle corps, attacked the enemy's piquet last evening; killed about twenty, wounded many more, and took about 20 prisoners. The marquis is charmed with the spirited behaviour of the militia and rifle corps. They drove the enemy about half a mile, and kept the ground until dark. The enemy's piquet consisted of about 500, and were reinforced during the skirmish. The marquis is determined to be in the way of danger'."

Recreated from The Maryland Gazette, December 18, 1777.

A DEADLIER RIFLE.

WILLIAMSBURG.—Captain Thomas Rowland, of Botetourt, last week, in this city, made an experiment of his new method of loading and firing rifles, which shows that rifles may be easily loaded and discharged in as short a time as muskets generally are, with their usual certainty as to aim, and with triple execution in time of action. He shot twelve balls into the compass of a large handkerchief, at the distance of sixty yards, in four discharges of his piece, in the space of 52 seconds. Several of the balls were within six inches of the center, and but three of the twelve would have missed a man's body.

In another experiment, after firing thirty balls in ten discharges, his rifle appeared as clean and cool in the barrel, though she was not wiped during the experiment, as if she had not been fired more than once. Capt. Rowland's method is looked upon as a valuable discovery; having rendered that instrument of death, which is already so much dreaded by our enemies, capable of being infinitely more destructive and terrible, and that by a simple and easy operation.

Recreated from The Virginia Gazette, October 3, 1777.

A PROCLAMATION.

By his Excellency GEORGE WASHINGTON, *Esq., General and Commander in Chief of the Forces of the* United States of America.

WHEREAS sundry soldiers,. belonging to the armies of the said States, have deserted from the same: These are to make known to all those, who have so offended, and who shall return to their respective corps, or surrender themselves to the officers appointed to receive recruits and deserters in their several states, or to any continental commissioned officer, before the first day of January next, that they shall obtain a full and free pardon. And do I further declare to all such obstinate offenders, as do not avail themselves of the indulgence hereby offered, that they may depend, when apprehended, on being prosecuted with the utmost vigour, and suffering the punishment justly due to crimes of such enormity.

Lest the hope of escaping punishment by remaining undiscovered, should tempt any to reject the terms now held out to them, they may be assured, that the most effectual measures will be pursued, in every State, for apprehending, and bringing them to a speedy trial.

GIVEN under my hand, at Head Quarters, this 24th day of *October*, Anno Domini 1777.

G. WASHINGTON.

NEWBERN, *Dec.* 1st, 1777.

TO the extent that deserters may have an opportunity of availing themselves of the pardon offered by the above proclamation, and for the more speedy and effectual apprehending and bringing to condign punishment, all those who are lost to every sene of honour, I have been ordered into this State for the express purpose of apprehending and receiving all deserted soldiers, and that none may hereafter plead ignorance, I hereby give notice that every deserted soldier from the continental troops, who shall surrender himself to me at Kingston, in Dobbs County, or to any officer under my command, before the first day of January next, will be entitled to pardon. And I do promise a reward of ten dollars for each deserter who shall be delivered to me at Kingston aforesaid, or to any officer under my command, after that time.

WILLIAM CASWELL
Capt. 5th N.C. battalion.

GENERAL WAYNE ACQUITTED.

WHITE MARSH, *Nov.* 1.—A General Court Martial, of which Gen. Sullivan was President, was held the 25th, 26th, 27th and 30th of October last, for the trial of Gen. Wayne, on the following charge, viz.

"That he had timely notice of the enemy's intention to attack the troops under his command, on the night of the 20th September last, and notwithstanding that intelligence neglected making a disposition until it was too late, either to annoy the enemy, or make a retreat without the utmost danger and confusion;" upon which the court pronounced the following sentence."

The court having fully considered the charge against Brigadier Gen. Wayne, and evidence produced to them; are unanimously of opinion, that Gen. Wayne is not guilty of the charge exhibited against him; but that he on the night of the 20th ultimo did every thing that could be expected from an *active, brave* and *vigilant officer*, under the orders he then had. The court do acquit him with the *highest honour*.

The Commander in Chief approves the sentence.

The action of that night has caused much speculation, the tongue of slander has not been idle. However sanguine some gentlemen were in their attempt to detract from the merits of the General, and his faithful officers and soldiers (who with unparalleled bravery stood the bayonet of the enemy, saved all the artillery, and in the face of every difficulty and danger, effected an honourable retreat with the loss of no more than 160 men killed wounded and taken) yet they find themselves egregiously disappointed.

INTELLIGENCE FROM LONDON.

Russia's Largesse.

Aug. 7. It is confidently reported, that on a late solicitation from our Ministry to the Empress of Russia, for hiring a certain number of troops to fight against our rebellious subjects in America, the Empress made the following reply to the negociator:

"That if Government would make over the Island of Minorca to her, she would send 30,000 men to subdue the Americans, and at her sole expence maintain and recruit them for two years." This proposal, if accepted of, by adding Minorca to her possessions in the Black sea, and her free navigation of the Archipelago, would throw the whole Mediterranean and Levant trade into her hands, and make her the first maritime power in Europe.

It is reported that a Great Personage has declared that the body guards, both horse and foot, shall be sent to America, rather than the service there shall want men.

Aug. 11. Fifty thousand blankets are ordered to be immediately got ready for the troops in America against the ensuing winter.

A COW TO CATCH A HARE.

Extract of a letter from Galloway, July 24.

"Every day the American streamers are shining on our coast. There is not a ship dare stir out of a harbour, as the ministry only ordered a large man of war into the channel, which is of no manner of service, either to distress the American privateers, or protect our trade, for Lord Sandwich might as well send a cow to catch a hare. This day we were alarmed with near eight hours cannonading, owing to the engagement of an American privateer, only of 20 guns, with two of the King's cutters, and a large letter of marque from Liverpool, when the privateer sunk the King's ships, but the letter of marque escaped, tho' much damaged."

Recreated from The North Carolina Gazette, December 5, 1777.

PHILADELPHIA LAID WASTE.

THE ROYAL PROTECTION.

LETTERS *of the 1st instant are received from* York Town. *We have the following summary, viz.*

"The enemy have at length got possession of the Delaware as far as Philadelphia, after a month's operation of the united naval and military British forces, at an expense of 1000 men, by the most moderate computation; the loss of a 64 gun ship, a frigate, 2 capital ships greatly shattered, and the rest of the fleet in their turn repulsed.

"General Howe has showed the royal protection in the environs of Philadelphia, by utterly laying the whole of it waste. All the elegant and other houses in the vicinity are burnt; not a garden pale is left standing; even fields of new sewn grain are destroyed.

"The inhabitants of the city are hard pressed with famine; great numbers of them have come out, and thrown themselves upon the mercy of General Washington, in order to procure bread; and many others would do so, but that their guilty consciences make them dread meeting with deserved punishment.

"The greatest part of the American naval force in the Delaware have escaped the enemy, by retreating above Philadelphia. In short, the American defence of the Delaware, when particularized to the publick, will astonish Europe. On the other hand, General Gates informs Congress, that the greatest part of the foreign, and a great part of the British troops, under the Captive-led General Burgoyne, deserted on their march to Boston. Ticonderoga and Mount Independence are abandoned by the enemy. Those in whom the greatest confidence is placed declare, that New York or Philadelphia, or both, will be taken by the Americans by the end of January. In a word, the American army are numerous, and in the highest spirits.

"Mr. Deane is recalled, and Mr. John Adams elected to succeed him at the court of France."

Recreated from The North Carolina Gazette, January 30, 1778.

Extract of a letter from ALBANY, *Dec.* 1, 1777.

"Our news is not very material, the enemy left Ticonderoga and its appendages with great precipitation indeed; burnt all the houses, barracks, hospital, and every thing burnable; left 40 pieces of iron ordnance broke and spiked. A party of ours followed their boats as far as Gillelands, took 49 prisoners, more than 100 horses, 14 yoke of oxen, 4 cows and 3 boats, also some wine, rum, brandy, &c. Several boats were found near Mount Independence sunken, in which were some provisions."

BOSTON, *Dec.* 4.—Arrived at Portsmouth since our last a French ship of 28 guns and 90 men, from Marseille, in France, with 5000 stand of arms, 50 brass field pieces, mortars, bombs, and all kinds of war-like stores.

Recreated from The Hartford Courant, December 9, 1777.

Extract of a letter from YORK-*town, Dec.* 9.

"We expect soon to hear of warm work. Mr. Howe has come out of Philadelphia with his whole army, and was last Saturday in sight of our army, which is at least as strong as it has ever been, and in pretty good spirits. A person out of Philadelphia says, a packet was received there last week, with advice that hostilities were commenced, or about to commence, between France and England.

"It is certain they are building forts to defend New York towards the sea; still I am afraid England will make them concessions. I saw a letter this morning from St. Eustatia, which says, it was agreed to restore all effects taken in French bottoms, without the limits."

Just published and to be sold at the Printing Office in Newbern, price half a dollar:

ARTICLES of CONFEDERATION and PERPETUAL UNION between the thirteen united colonies, lately published by order of Congress, and absolutely necessary to be had by every person who wishes well to this union, and wants to know how the glorious Fabrick of this new world is to be regulated.

Recreated from The North Carolina Gazette, January 2, 1778.

BATTLE OF WHITE MARSH.

IMPRUDENT USE OF RUM.

Extract of a letter from an officer at camp, dated Dec. 10, 1777.

"It is probable that by this time you expected to have been informed of a third general battle between the royal army and that of the United States. The former marched from its lines of Thursday the 5th, leaving only its sick, and a small necessary guard; passed through Germantown, driving before it our patrols of horse, and exchanging fire with our pickets and advanced parties of infantry. The British soldiers, as they advanced through the village, forced the doors of the inhabitants with the butts of their muskets, uttering execrations against the rebels and all their abettors.

"On the morning of the 6th we received intelligence that the enemy had encamped on Chestnut Hill, and from the enormous smoke, too large for the purpose of a camp, which appeared at different times and in different directions, we suspected that they were venting their spleen in wanton conflagrations; but we found afterwards that there was no house of consequence destroyed in this quarter. The barns, and a square tower, which had been built as a look-out, were the only sacrifices they offered to tyranny in this neighbourhood. Webb's regiment, and the Pennsylvania militia, which in our order of battle were destined to act in small detachments for the purpose of galling the enemy's flank, were ordered to advance and skirmish with their light troops; the militia behaved as usual, and Brigadier General Irvine was wounded and taken prisoner while he was making fruitless attempts to rally them.

"In the morning of the 7th, at 5 o'clock, the enemy filed off by their right; a party of them halted near Jenkin's town; by their movements it appeared they were endeavouring to turn our left; we changed our disposition in consequence, and upon hearing that they were advancing in two columns, Morgan's corps and the Maryland militia were ordered to harass their right flank; there was some very smart firing in consequence, between Morgan's and the British light infantry; the latter having made an imprudent use of their extraordinary allowance of rum, suffered, and every man that appeared would have been killed or taken if the rifle-men had been armed with bayonets. We had great reason to fear a general attack, but there was nothing more than a little bickering between our pickets.

"On the 8th the enemy remained in position, and under cover of their usual stratagem, leaving great fires on their ground, decamped in the evening. It was doubted at first whether they meant to retreat, or whether they were only filing off in order to prepare for an attack on our right. Count Pulaski with a party of horse, and a few infantry which he had collected, followed them, watching their motions. As soon as the real design of the enemy was ascertained, light parties were ordered to pursue, and a larger body to support them; but the enemy's march was too rapid to allow of their being overtaken by any other than Count Pulaski's party, who, with his handful of men, made an attack upon their rear guard.

HANOVER, December 1, 1777.

TO discharge my Sister's Fortunes, I will sell at private Sale 15 or 20 valuable Slaves (in Families) among them is a good Blacksmith, an excellent Laundry Servant, several good Spinners, Boys and Girls of different Ages. Those who incline to purchase are desired to apply in Person. (5)   NELSON BERKELEY.

ON Thursday the 8th of January 1778, will be sold, at the Plantation of Col. *Theodorick Bland*, Junior, the Stocks of Cattle, Crop of Corn, Wheat, and Fodder, with the Utensils of Husbandry, and on the 18th following will be offered for Sale, between 30 and 40 *Virginia* born Negroes, at Mr. *Bradley's* in *Petersburg*, the Whole for ready Money.

To be sold for ready Money, on Wednesday the 31st *Instant* (December) on the Plantation of William Ruffin, deceased, in Surry County,

ALL the Stock of Horses, Cattle, Sheep, and Hogs, about 400 Barrels of Corn and Flour, or 500 Bushels of Oats.--- At the same Time will be hired 8 or 9 fine Negro Fellows and 4 House Wenches.
2|| JOHN H. COCKE, Executor.

"Very early yesterday morning, after burning a tavern called the Rising Sun, near Philadelphia, and stealing a few milch cows and horses, they harboured themselves. Thus an expedition, which raised the expectations of every body, and from whence it was thought some great decisive stroke would arise, terminated in degrading the whole British army to a foraging party.

"The loss of Morgan's rifle-men was 27 killed and wounded, among the latter is the brave Major Morris; what the enemy lost in the several skirmishes is not known. Col. Morgan, who has no need of boasting to establish the reputation of his corps, says the British light infantry lost a great many in their skirmish with him.

"While the armies were in presence we had several deserters and prisoners from them; those taken the first day by small parties of horse in Germantown, in the rear of the enemy, were for the most part drunk. These parties of ours had been posted at Frankford, and as the enemy did not extend themselves to the right of Germantown, they fell in upon the enemy's rear, and collected stragglers with impunity.

"You will now probably ask, what account of the enemy's conduct is to be given? My idea of the matter is simply this; Sir William Howe imagined that on the first appearance of the British army the shivering, half-naked defenders of liberty, would have decamped and left him master of the country; that finding his parade ineffectual, he had recourse to the most trying manoeuvre of encamping our flank, but seeing us still moveable, he judged it most prudent to retire to peaceful winter quarters, than to attack us in a position, the strength of which would probably have obliged him to retire with loss; and which, even if he had gained from us by the greatest exertions, must have him too great a sacrifice of his best troops; while our army, light and free of encumbrance, even in case of this improbable disaster, would have suffered more in honour than in any other point."

Recreated from The Virginia Gazette, December 26, 1777.

TO HONOUR GENERAL STARKS.

The following letter, to the Hon. Brigadier General STARKS, *and* RESOLVE, *passed the general Assembly of this State (New Hampshire) on Friday last.*

THE general Assembly of this State, take the earliest opportunity to acknowledge the receipt of your acceptable present. The tokens of victory gained at the memorable BATTLE at BENNINGTON.

The events of that day strongly mark the bravery of the men, who unskilled in war, forced from their entrenchments, a chosen number of veteran troops, of boasted Britons; as well as the address and valour of the General who directed their movements and led them on to conquest.

This signal exploit opened the way to a rapid succession of advantages most important to America.

These Trophies shall be safely deposited in the archives of the State and there remind posterity, of the *irresistible power of the God of armies, and the honour due to the memory of the brave.*

Still attended with *like* successes, may you *long* enjoy the just reward of your grateful country.

RESOLVED unanimously, that the board of war of this State, be, and hereby directed, in the name of this court, to present to the Hon. Brigadier General STARKS, a compleat suit of clothes, becoming his rank, together with a piece of linen, as a testimony of the high sense this court have of the great and important services rendered by that brave officer, to save the United States of *America.*

35 SENTENCED TO DEATH.

BOSTON, *Dec. 8.*—By a gentleman from the Southward, we have an account that 35 men were sentenced to death at Morristown, the 7th of November, for high treason against the States; that the time of their execution was to be on Tuesday last; and that four were to be branded on the hand for trading with the enemy.

The following gentlemen are chosen by the general; Assembly of this State, as delegates to serve in the continental Congress the ensuing year, viz. Hon. John Hancock, Esq., Samuel Adams, Esq., John Adams, Esq., Robert T. Paine, Esq., Elbridge Gerry, Esq., Francis Dana, Esq., and James Lovell, Esq.

Dec. 16.—At the late meeting of this town it was voted, that the thanks of the town be given to the Hon. John Hancock, Esq., for his generous donation of 150 cords of wood to the poor of the town in this time of distress.

Wednesday night last a plot was formed by some of the prisoners on board one of the guard ships in this harbour, to destroy the guard, which was discovered a little time before it was to have been put into execution. The ringleader was committed to goal next day for trial.

Wednesday night last the barracks on Cobble Hill were burnt down; it is said they were designedly set on fire by some British prisoners stationed there. We doubt not an enquiry will be made into this affair.

Yesterday a flag returned from New York, without one prisoner, though she carried about 100 from hence.

FLANKING ABILITIES.

A correspondent has favoured us with the following anecdote.

"A brave Hibernian, in the American light-horse, having surprised and taken five unarmed British soldiers, he was ordered to appear at Head Quarters to give an account of his enterprize. Being asked by his Excellency the General by what manoeuvre he effected so considerable a capture, he laconically replied, in a manner expressive of his country, '*In truth, Sir, I surrounded them.*' The gallantry and address of this *surrounding* hero hath since been suitably rewarded, and his *fame* hath excited great emulation amongst the American soldiery, who are individually determined not to be exceeded by the light-horsemen in *flanking abilities.*"

Recreated from The North Carolina Gazette, January 30, 1778.

CUTTING, HACKING AND STABBING.

MORE BRITISH MAGNANIMITY.

Extract of a letter written by a Captain of Light-Horse in the Southern Department to his friend in CONNECTICUT.

"On the night of the 14th of December by order of his Excellency General Washington, I took post with a detachment of my troop, consisting of about twenty men, officers included, near Vandeering's mills, on the ridge road running by the Schuylkill to Philadelphia, with a view of observing the motion of the enemy; the army having crossed the Schuylkill at Swedes-ford. Notwithstanding we changed quarters every night, at late hours, the enemy got intelligence of our strength and situation, and by the help of some infernal tory, were conducted in a bye road till they had marched near a mile in our rear, by this route avoiding our sentinels and patrols, which were posted on all the main roads leading to Philadelphia; to make my post secure, as guarded on all sides, I ordered a vidette near half a mile in our rear, who at about two o'clock in the morning came in with an account, that a large body of horse was moving fast down the road directly in our rear. I ordered the men immediately to mount, (the horses being kept constantly saddled, and the men accoutred) and before all could parade in the road they began to fire upon us. We exchanged a few shot, but finding it impossible with about ten men to oppose an hundred, (as I am informed by those who counted them as they passed, this is a moderate computation) we moved off as fast as possible.

They immediately surrounded the house and barn, pursuing us not far, and took five prisoners, while attempting to escape; whose names for the satisfaction of any concerned, are Quarter Master Samuel Mills, Isaac Brown, John Chauncy, Ephraim Kirby, and Naboth Lewis. After they were brought in, being taken in the field, they were first disarmed, and plundered of their spurs, watches, &c. &c. and then ordered by the officers to be killed; notwithstanding the entreaties and prayers of the unfortunate prisoners for mercy, the soldiers fell upon them, the officers setting the example, and after cutting, hacking and stabbing them till they supposed they were dead, they left them (Brown escaped whom after most cruelly mangling they shot) setting fire to the barn to consume any who might be in it. Mr. Mills, after being wounded in several places on the head, had his life spared, and is now a prisoner. Brown, and Chauncy, are dead; Kirby and Lewis have been properly taken care of and I trust will recover.

"Thus both the army and country have a striking example of what they have to expect from the savage cruelty and barbarity of the British troops."

Recreated from The Hartford Courant, January 20, 1778.

COL. MEIGS OVER THE BRUNX.

FISH-KILL, *Dec.* 18.—On the 27th ult. General Putnam with the troops under his command, marched down towards Kingsbridge, with a view to draw out the enemy to battle; and for this purpose he detached Col. Meigs over the Brunx, near the fort, with orders to retreat in such a manner, as would most probably draw the enemy out to the main body, posted advantageously about one mile distant. This was attempted by Col. Meigs, but the enemy cautiously avoided the danger, only sending a small party of rangers, who could not be drawn over the river; a skirmish ensued between this party of the enemy and Col. Meigs, in which they lost three men killed, and about the same number wounded, and one or two made prisoners; Meigs had two men slightly wounded. The following night several small parties were sent down to alarm the enemy's camp, which they did, and turned them out in the severe storm and left them, bringing off Col. James Delancey, Mr. Ogilvie, a Lieutenant in Robinson's regiment, and four pother prisoners. The posts at the bridge, are strongly fortified, but with a suitable force and preparations may soon be reduced.

Recreated from The North Carolina Gazette, January 23, 1778.

BLOOD IN THEIR FOOTSTEPS.

From an American officer, Dec. 14, 1777.

"General Howe, 'tis believed, will winter in Philadelphia; for the country around are generally of the Quaker profession, who do not assist us in the force of arms, which renders the operation of this army very fatiguing. The enemy came out of their den yesterday week, it was imagined with a design to attack our lines; but to our sorrow they retreated, with the loss of about a hundred killed; both in their advance and retreating, they plundered the inhabitants of every individual thing, except such clothes as they had on. We are on our march the west side of Schuylkill, 'tis conjectured to go into winter quarters at Lancaster; if so then the fighting is over for this winter.

"A considerable quantity of clothing for the Continental troops has arrived; but not sufficient to clothe those that are barefooted and barelegged. It is amazing to see the spirit of the soldiery when destitute of shoes and stockings, marching cold nights and morning, leaving blood in their footsteps! Yet, notwithstanding, the fighting disposition of the soldiers is great. The troops are much better clothed than they were, and I believe will soon be very well supplied."

Recreated from The Hartford Courant, January 13, 1778.

FOOLING THE TORIES.

From an officer at WILMINGTON, *Dec. 25.*

ON the 17th inst. we left the main army, under the command of General Smallwood, in order to take up our winter quarters here. I expect Howe means to pay us a visit, as he has removed out as far as Chester, and there has extended his lines.

General Washington has removed down the Schuylkill, in order, should Howe advance farther, he may be in his rear. We took seven of their light horse the day before yesterday. Colonel Morgan is on the enemy's flank, and has lately taken a great many of their light horse and soldiers.

On our march to this place our regiment was in front, all clothed in red. As we advanced near the town, we met a number of tories, who, taking us for English troops, immediately came up and enquired for General Howe, when they were immediately conducted to General Smallwood, and they, taking him for Howe, said now we are safe. We took the hint, and asked them if they saw any of the rebels about or near that place. Ay, ay, we have seen too many of them, for they have not left us one fence rail; but we have kept a quantity of poultry, some good mutton, and fine fat hogs, which are at your service. Upon which we told them to come to town with us; they did, but soon found, to their great surprise, we were those they termed rebels.

Recreated from The Hartford Courant, January 20, 1778.

LONDON, *Dec.* 23.—Great jealousies and violent divisions have arisen both in civil as well as military branches of the rebel states; and a considerable number of the latter department had declared a resolution of having Mr. Washington removed from the command of their army, and requesting that Mr. Green, a native of Rhode Island, who is now become their favourite, should succeed Mr. Washington as Generalissimo.

• • • •

Dec. 25.—Yesterday, the Right Hon. Lord Petersham, eldest son of the Earl of Harrington, aid-de-camp to Gen. Burgoyne, arrived at his father's house in the Stable-yard St. James's, from gen. Burgoyne at Saratoga. His lordship brought the original articles of capitulation between Generals Burgoyne and Gates, with other dispatches and private letters for the King.

Yesterday a meeting was held at the King's Arms tavern, in Cornhill, to consider the most effectual mode of relieving the distresses of the American prisoners in the different gaols of Great Britain and Ireland. A committee were chosen, and a subscription opened, at which 800l. 11s. 6d. were subscribed in less than an hour.

Recreated from The Ipswich Journal, England, December 27, 1777.

GENERAL ORDERS.

HEAD QUARTERS ON SCHUYLKILL.
December 17, 1777.

THE Commander in Chief, with the highest satisfaction, expresses his thanks to the officers and soldiers, for the fortitude and patience with which they have withstood the fatigues of the campaign. Though, in some instances, we have unfortunately failed; yet, upon the whole, Heaven has smiled upon our arms, and crowned them with signal success; and we may, upon the best ground conclude, that by a spirited continuance of the measures necessary for our defence, we shall finally gain the end of our warfare; INDEPENDENCE, LIBERTY, and PEACE.—These are blessings worth contending for, at every *hazard*. But we hazard nothing; the power of America alone, duly exerted, would have nothing to dread from the force of Great Britain. Yet we stand not alone upon our own ground; France yields us every aid we ask; and there are reasons to believe, the period is not far distant, when she will take a more active part, by declaring war against the British Crown. Every motive therefore, irresistibly urges and commands us to a firm and manly perseverance, in our opposition to our cruel oppressors; to slight difficulties, endure hardships, and contemn every danger.

The General ardently wishes it were in his power to conduct the troops into the best winter quarters; but where are they to be found? Should we retire into the interior parts of the States, we should find them crowded with virtuous citizens, who sacrificed their ALL; have left Philadelphia, and fled from persecution. To their distress, humanity forbids us to add. This is not all; we should leave a vast extent of fertile country, to be despoiled and ravaged by the enemy, from which they would drain large supplies, and where many of our firm friends would be exposed to all the miseries of insulting and wanton depredations. A train of evils might be enumerated—but these will suffice.

These considerations make it indispensably necessary for the army to take such position, as will enable it, most effectually, to prevent distress, and to give the most extensive security; and in this position, we must make ourselves the best shelter in our power. With activity and diligence, huts may be erected that may be warm and dry; in those the troops will be more secure against surprise, than if in a divided State; and at hand to protect their country.

These cogent reasons has determined the General to take post in the neighbourhood of this camp; and influenced by them, he persuades himself, that the officers and soldiers, with one heart, and one mind, will resolve to surmount every difficulty, with a fortitude and patience becoming their profession, and the sacred cause in which they are engaged in. He himself will partake of the hardships, and partake of every inconvenience.

To-morrow being a day set apart by the hon. Congress for public thanksgiving and praise, and duty calling us devoutly to express our grateful acknowledgements to God for the manifold blessings he has granted us, the General directs that the army remain in its present quarters, and that the chaplains perform divine service with their several corps and brigades, and earnestly exhorts all officers and soldiers whose absence is not indispensably necessary, to attend with reverence the solemnities of the day.

Recreated from The North Carolina Gazette, January 23, 1778.

BURGOYNE REFUTED.

WORCESTER, *Dec.* 19.—We learn that Lieut. Gen. Burgoyne was so confident of having liberty to embark with his troops at Newport, Rhode Island, that the transports for the reception of him and his army had actually arrived there; but we are told it is no way likely that he will be permitted to take his departure from that port, notwithstanding it might be "*in conformity with*" his "*orders to proceed by the most vigorous exertions.*"

Recreated from The North Carolina Gazette, February 6, 1778.

A. LONDON, *Saturday, Dec.* 20.

YESTERDAY it was whispered thro' every public department at the West end of the town, that Lord Stormont had sent an express, desiring his immediate recall, and giving very convincing reasons to rouse the attention of government to the perfidy of France, who, his lordship is apprehensive, are upon the eve of declaring war against this kingdom. *Gen. Ev. Post.*

3. The Grand Signior has transmitted to London, by means of the British ambassador at the Ottoman Porte, some dispatches of a nature, which it will require some time to give a proper answer to.

4. Some English gentlemen of repute at Paris write as follows: "The French are irritating the Turks as much as possible to carry on a war with the Russians, with a view to employ Russia, that she may not give any assistance to Great Britain."

5. The last dispatches from Lord Viscount Stormont at the court of Versailles are said to contain very positive and direct assurances that the French ministry, through the mediation of Dr. Franklin, are entering into a treaty with the British Colonies in America.

6. It is remarkable that all the foreign Gazettes, at least 3 parts in 4, are taken up with the debates in the English parliament, and the accounts of the operations of our armies in America.

Recreated from The Ipswich Journal, England, December 27, 1777.

Extract of a letter from PARIS.

"When Dr. Franklin appears abroad it is more like a publick than a private gentleman, and the curiosity of the people to see him is so great, that he may be said to be followed by a genteel mob. A friend of mine paid something for a place at a two pair of stairs window to see him pass by in his coach, but the crowd was so great that he could but barely say he saw him."

Recreated from The North Carolina Gazette, December 26, 1777.

By His EXCELLENCY GEORGE WASHINGTON, Esq; General and Commander in Chief of the Forces of the UNITED STATES of AMERICA.

BY virtue of the power and direction to me especially given, I hereby enjoin and require all persons living within seventy miles of my Head Quarters to thresh one half of their grain by the first day of February, and the other half by the first day of March next ensuing, on pain, in case of failure, of having all that shall remain in sheaves after the period above-mentioned, seized by the Commissaries and Quarter-Masters of the Army, and paid for as Straw.

GIVEN under my hand, at Head Quarters, near the Valley Forge, in Philadelphia County, this 20th day of December, 1777.

G. WASHINGTON.

Recreated from The Pennsylvania Packet, December 31, 1777.

EVERY LITTLE HELPS.

December 31, 1777.—On Christmas day a brigade of militia marched down within musket shot of the enemy's lines near Philadelphia, and taking post between Third and Fourth streets, alarmed them by sending eight twelve pound balls among them. The enemy beat to arms and fired their artillery, but happily did no damage, although the shot raked both on the right and left of our people. The militia brought off one prisoner and several horses.

January 7, 1778.—We can assure the public, from the best authority, that by the assiduity and industry of Messrs. Otis and Andrews, of Boston, agents for the purchase of clothing for the continental troops, upwards of five thousand suits, with shoes, stockings, shirts, &c. have been procured, and are now on their way to camp. This, with the supplies which are expected from Virginia and other quarters, gives us the pleasing prospect of seeing our whole army completely clothed very soon. A very rich prize was lately taken by a continental brig, and carried into Boston. She is a large ship from Glasgow, loaded with dry goods, shoes, stockings, ticks, and a great variety of other necessary and useful articles. A brig has also arrived there from Holland, richly loaded with medicines, tea, linens, &c. &c. The Boston papers also mention the safe arrival of several other prizes of less value; but, as the old saying is, *every little helps*.

40 LADIES TAKEN WITH PRIZE.

On the 30th or 31st of December last, a most valuable prize fell into the hands of a body of Continental troops stationed at Wilmington on the river Delaware, commanded by General Smallwood.—a large brig from New York bound to Philadelphia was blown ashore about five miles below Wilmington, when a detachment with two field pieces was sent down to fire on her; and after a few shot she struck. Her cargo is chiefly as follows—350 chests of arms, with 25 stand in each, clothing for four regiments, the baggage belonging to the officers of four regiments, a quantity of wine and spirits, 4 Captains, 3 Subalterns, and 60 Privates, and—about 40 officers' Ladies, &c. &c.

Recreated from The North Carolina Gazette, February 6, 1778.

SUPPORTING OUR TROOPS.

Norwich, *January* 1, 1778.

Last Sabbath there was a Contribution in the several Parishes in this Town, for the Benefit of the non commissioned Officers and Soldiers in the Continental Army that belong here, when there was collected 386 Pairs of Stockings, 227 Pairs of Shoes, 118 Shirts, 78 Jackets, 48 Pair Breeches, 9 Coats, 22 Rifle Frocks, 19 Handkerchiefs, and £258 in Money; all which is forwarded on to the Army. Also a Quantity of Pork, Cheese, Wheat, Rye, Indian Corn, Sugar, Rice, Flax, Wood, &c. &c. engaged to be delivered by the Committee appointed to receive and distribute the Same to the needy Families of the Officers and Soldiers. The whole Value of this Donation, at a low Estimate, will exceed £1400.

WAS FOUND, The day after Christmas, on the Horse shoe road, about seven or eight miles from Lancaster, A NEW BOOT. The owner by applying to the Printer, proving his property and paying charges, may have it again.

Recreated from The Pennsylvania Packet, January 7, 1778.

Newbern, January 30, 1778. Extract of a letter from the delegates of this State, at York-Town, to his Excellency the Governor, dated Jan. 9. General Washington's army is about 23 miles from Philadelphia, in huts near the Schuylkill, as the most convenient place to prevent the enemy from plundering the country.

Recreated from The North Carolina Gazette, January 30, 1778.

Gerald Reilly is the editor of this anthology.

His previous books are:

*Things Change, a reflection on the 70's,
now and tomorrow thru images of Boston*

Irish Lives and Times, The Famine Years, 1845 to 1852

Irish Lives and Times, The Easter Rebellion and The Rise of Sinn Fein

Irish Lives and Times, The War of Independence - Part One

Irish Lives and Times, The War of Independence - Part Two

Mr. Reilly lives on Cape Cod, Massachusetts, near Buzzard's Bay.

www.ingramcontent.com/pod-product-compliance
Lightning Source LLC
Chambersburg PA
CBHW080917170426
43201CB00016B/2171